Charleston South Carolina Marriages

1877–1895

Susan L. King

HERITAGE BOOKS
2015

HERITAGE BOOKS

AN IMPRINT OF HERITAGE BOOKS, INC.

Books, CDs, and more—Worldwide

For our listing of thousands of titles see our website
at
www.HeritageBooks.com

Published 2015 by
HERITAGE BOOKS, INC.
Publishing Division
5810 Ruatan Street
Berwyn Heights, Md. 20740

International Standard Book Numbers
Paperbound: 978-0-7884-5668-8
Clothbound: 978-0-7884-6227-6

INTRODUCTION

Although many sacramental records predate them, the official marriage records of Charleston date from 1877. The state of South Carolina did not require marriage licenses to be issued until July 1, 1911. On October 12, 1877, City Council directed that "every Clergyman, Trial Justice, or other person who may perform a marriage ceremony, shall make and keep a registry of the marriage celebrated, and therein enter the full names of the parties married, the time and place of such marriage, and the color, age, residence and condition of each. That it shall be the duty of every person mentioned in the section to present to the City Registrar a copy of such register, signed by each person or a written statement by him or her signed, of all of the facts required to be entered in such registers within three days after the...marriage of any person to whom such registry relate...That the Board of Health are hereby authorized to enact all rules and regulation necessary to carry out effectually the provisions of the...preceding sections." (*Ordinances of the City of Charleston*, October 12, 1877). The official Marriage Registers are arranged chronologically and contain most of the information required by law.

What do these records tell us about the citizens of Charleston? Surprisingly, in a city founded by English Protestants, the majority of marriages were performed by a Lutheran clergyman, reflecting the large numbers of German immigrants in Charleston in the 1870s and 1880s. More than 25% of those married were natives of Germany, Prussia, Hanover and other German states; however, the majority, 57%, were natives of Charleston. The occupations of the bridegrooms indicate that Charleston was a hub for the railroads. More than 26% of the men worked in some capacity for the railroads. Others included clerks (16%), merchants (16%), planters or farmers (9%), laborers (8%) and mariners (8%). The rise of factories and mills in Charleston can be seen by 4% employed in cotton mills and 3% in the phosphate mines. Unfortunately, occupations are listed in only about 65% of the marriages. Although many of the marriages must have been the second or even the third for one or the other, only 10% of the woman are listed as widows and only two men are identified as widowers. The youngest bride, Emily Rose, was only 13 years old when she married. The oldest bridegroom, Theodore B. Lyman, was 78 years old when he married.

What follows is an alphabetical list of the 2,958 white marriages contained in the Marriage Registers of Charleston. The records are hand-written and as with all such records, sometime the writing is almost illegible. On November 30, 1896, the Registrar noted that he had transcribed the information from the clergyman "as near as I can make it out." I have followed his example.

Susan L. King
Charleston, South Carolina
June 24, 2002

1884 map courtesy of the South Caroliniana Library

ABBOT, F. V. aged 27 years married to DEHON, SARA JULIE aged 24 years October 15, 1885 by Rev. John Johnson at 50 South Bay Street. He was born "at sea" and she a native of South Carolina. He an army officer.

ABNEY, CORA aged 22 years married to PINCKNEY, ALFRED W. aged 34 years November 13, 1881 by Rev. J. V. Welsh at 5 Liberty Street.

ABNEY, MARY J. aged 21 years married to O'SHAUGHNESSY, JOSEPH J. aged 28 years October 16, 1894 by Rev. J. C. Yongue at 14 Hampstead Square. He a native of Charleston and she of Edgefield County, South Carolina. He a railroad watchman.

ABRAMS, ALEXANDER aged 31 years married to LOWE, REBECCA aged 19 years February 14, 1886 by Rev. J. V. Welch at 91 America Street. Both natives of Charleston. He a boilermaker.

ABRAMS, (Mrs.) CATHERINE FURSE aged 33 years married to McFAWN, JAMES R. aged 20 years February 15, 1888 by Rev. H. B. Browne at 30 Hanover Street. He a native of Massachusetts and she of Barnwell County, South Carolina. He a watchman.

ABRAMS, CORDELIA G. aged 17 years married to MELFI, LEONARD F. aged 24 years June 28, 1887 by Father P. J. McManus. Both natives of Charleston. He works for the railroad.

ABRAMS, J. P. aged 17 years married to HONOUR, J. C. aged 36 years August 21, 1882 by Father Daniel J. Quigley at 42 Spring Street. Both natives of Charleston. He a laborer.

ABRAMS, R. aged 20 years married to WEDE, J. T. aged 20 years February 21, 1882 by Rev. J. M. Green at 20 Amherst Street. He a native of Georgia and she of South Carolina. He a blacksmith.

ADAMS, ETTSEL aged 22 years married to GATEWOOD, LENORA aged 19 years December 31, 1877 by Rev. John Johnson in Tradd Street. He a native of Charleston and a planter.

ADAMS, LEWIS F. aged 18 years married to MITCHUM, IRENE aged 18 years September 17, 1893 by Rev. J. C. Yongue at 65 Drake Street. He a native of Colleton County, South Carolina and she of Greeleyville, South Carolina. He works in the cotton mills.

ADAMS, MAGGIE aged 24 years married to LAMB, JOHN JAMES aged 23 years December 6, 1893 by Rev. Edmund Wells at 82 Drake Street. Both natives of South Carolina. He works in the basket factory.

ADAMS, M. SUSAN aged 17 years married to SWEAT, BARNEY B. aged 23 years February 12, 1889 by Rev. H. B. Browne at 75 Columbus Street. Both natives of Colleton County, South Carolina. He works in the cotton mill.

ADAMS, WILLIAM HOOPER aged 40 years married to HOLMES, MARGARET EDWARDS aged 34 years March 20, 1878 by Rev. G. R. Brackett at 20 Charlotte Street. He a native of Boston, Massachusetts and she of Charleston. He a clergyman.

ADDICKS, ELIZABETH aged 40 years married to BLANCHE, JOHN aged 53 years April 28, 1895 by Father J. J. Monaghan at St. Patrick's Roman Catholic Church. He a native of Ireland and she of Beaufort County, South Carolina. He an engineer.

ADDISON, BEULAH R. aged 18 years married to VERDERY, GEORGE W. aged 27 years September 27, 1884 by Rev. Luther K. Probst. He a native of Augusta, Georgia and she of Charleston. He works for the railroad.

ADDISON, CHARLES E. aged 25 years married to GRAY, (Mrs.) ADA BUIST aged 22 years February 3, 1895 by Rev. John Johnson at 53 Church Street. He a native of Charleston and she of Albany, New York. He works for the railroad.

ADDISON, ELIZABETH CRAMER aged 20 years married to WRIGHT, JOHN WILSON aged 23 years November 28, 1883 by Rev. G. R. Brackett. He a native of Anderson, South Carolina and she of Sumter, South Carolina. He a telegraph operator in Manning, South Carolina.

ADDISON, FLORENCE aged 20 years married to BUTLER, T. WELSMAN aged 22 years February 14, 1878 by Rev. L. H. Shuck at 5 South Bay Street. Both natives of Charleston. He a weigher.

ADDISON, FRANCIS T. aged 30 years married to FLANAGAN, MARY J. aged 16 years March 17, 1887 by Rev. Robert Wilson at 44 Ann Street. Both natives of Charleston. He a watchmaker.

ADDISON, GERTRUDE FLORENCE aged 23 years married to KAUFFNER, ANDREW JOHN aged 42 years December 12, 1889 by Rev. G. R. Brackett at 164 Coming Street. Both natives of Charleston. He a machinist.

ADDISON, JANIE WARING aged 22 years married to LARSEN, CHRISTIAN J. aged 25 years June 2, 1886 by Rev. A. J. S. Thomas at 49 South Battery. He a native of Norway and she of Charleston. He a clerk.

ADDISON, JOSEPH C. aged 25 years married to LEE, LILLY ELIZABETH aged 19 years August 28, 1878 by Rev. W. S. Bowman at 79 Spring Street. He a native of Charleston and a farmer.

ADDISON, THOMAS M. aged 32 years married to HARVEY, AUGUSTA M. aged 26 years December 14, 1882 by Rev. J. H. Tillinghast at 170 Queen Street. He a native of Charleston and she of New York. He a farmer.

ADDISON, THOMAS M. aged 40 years married to BAIR, (Mrs.) LIZZIE A. KAISER aged 33 years December 28, 1893 by Rev. Edmund Wells at 7 Addison Court. He a native of Charleston and she of Orangeburg, South Carolina. He a laborer.

ADDISON, WALTER L. aged 21 years married to JEFFORDS, CATHERINE H. aged 17 years July 4, 1893 by Rev. J. C. Yongue at 9 Cooper Street. He a native of Charleston and she of Sumter, South Carolina. He works in the cotton mill.

AHNEJUN, MICHAEL H. aged 21 years married to LEY, AMALIA JOSEPHINE aged 17 years April 15, 1886 by Rev. Louis Muller at the residence of Capt. B. S. Aldret at Sullivans Island, South Carolina. He a native of New York and she of Charleston. He a merchant.

AHRENS, GEORGE FRANKLIN aged 35 years married to RAY, ALICE ELIZABETH aged 23 years December 29, 1886 by Rev. Charles S. Vedder at 97 Tradd Street. Both natives of Charleston. He a carpenter.

AHRENS, HENRIETTE MARGARETHE aged 23 years married to KENEER, JOHN CARTER aged 23 years May 10, 1888 by Rev. Louis Muller at the residence of the Bride's mother in Laurens Street.

AHRENS, JOHN J. aged 23 years married to DILLON, ALICE C. aged 21 years May 11, 1890 by Father F. J. Shadler at St. Joseph's Roman Catholic Church. Both natives of Charleston. He a baggage handler.

AHRENS, KATE LOUISE aged 20 years married to McDON, THOMAS BALLARD aged 26 years February 17, 1880 by Rev. Edward T. Horn at St. John's Lutheran Church. He a native of Liberty Hill, South Carolina and she of West Hoboken, New Jersey. He a physician in Memphis, Tennessee.

AIKEN, CARRIE married to ROBERTSON, McBRYDE C. December 12, 1889 by Rev. William H. Campbell at the residence of Dr. T. Grange Simmons - 18 Montagu Street. He resides in Columbia, South Carolina.

AIMAR, ANN MARIE MADELAINE aged 25 years married to DEVINEAU, PETER EMILE aged 25 years January 2, 1878 by Father Claudian B. Northrop at St. Mary of the Annunciation Roman Catholic Church. Both natives of Charleston. He a clerk.

AIMAR, ARTHUR P. aged 28 years married to COLLINS, PAMELA CECILE aged 26 years June 26, 1893 by Father Joseph D. Budds at St. Mary of the Annunciation Roman Catholic Church. He a native of South Carolina and she of Charleston. He a druggist.

AIMAR, CHARLES A. aged 25 years married to FISCHER, ELEANOR B. aged 22 years April 8, 1885 by Rev. E. C. L. Browne. Both natives of Charleston. He a bookkeeper.

ALBERS, CAROLINE ANNIE aged 21 years married to HORWIG, GEORGE aged 23 years June 25, 1895 by T. S. Rouse, Magistrate. Both natives of Oldenburg, Germany.

ALBERS, CAROLINE A. aged 21 years married to FISCHER, HEINRICH A. aged 27 years May 8, 1883 by Rev. Johannes Heckel at 8 Bogard Street. He a native of Germany and she of Charleston. He a grocer.

ALBERS, CATHARINE ELISE aged 24 years married to BUSCH, CARL FREDERICK aged 24 years April 8, 1883 by Rev. Louis Muller at 7 Bogard Street. He a native of Charleston and she of Walhalla, South Carolina. He a farmer.

ALBERS, DORETHA aged 23 years married to McDOUGAL, JOHN MACKEY aged 22 years April 12, 1883 by Rev. Edward T. Horn at the corner of Tradd and Council Streets. Both natives of Charleston. He an engineer.

ALBERS, FREDERICK aged 61 years married to HEISSENBUTTEL, CATHERINE aged 49 years January 16, 1878 by Rev. W. S. Bowman at 26 Woolfe Street. He a laborer.

ALMERS, MARGARET F. aged 21 years married to MEYNARDIE, JAMES H. aged 26 years February 11, 1883 by Rev. John H. Tellinghast at St. John's Lutheran Church. Both natives of Charleston. He works for the railroad.

ALBERTUS, M. aged 19 years married to BULKEN, (Mrs.) LULA FLOYD aged 23 years March 25, 1883 by Rev. Louis Muller at the St. Matthew's Lutheran Church. He a native of Georgia and she of Darlington County, South Carolina. He a grocer.

ALBRECHT, EMMA ADELAIDE aged 27 years married to TORCK, EIBE HEINRICH aged 27 years May 22, 1881 by Rev. Louis Muller in King Street above Spring Street. He a native of Charleston and she of New York. He a clerk.

ALBRECHT, JOHN H. aged 23 years married to POWERS, MAMIE aged 22 years December 3, 1878 by Father John P. Twigg at The Cathedral of St. John the Baptist. Both natives of Charleston. He a baker.

ALBRECHT, (Mrs.) JULIANE C. aged 19 years married to RICHTER, WILHELM F. aged 31 years April 7, 1892 by Rev. Louis Muller at the corner of Market and Meeting Streets. He a native of Prussia and she of Charleston. He an agent for the Palmetto Brewery.

ALBRECHT, M. aged 17 years married to MILLER, J. T. aged 31 years November 11, 1879 by Rev. W. S. Bowman. Both natives of New York City. He a woodworker.

ALBRECHT, PAULINE F. aged 22 years married to TOOMER, MAURICE S. aged 25 years January 31, 1886 by Rev. Luther K. Probst. Both natives of Charleston. He a painter.

ALBRECHT, S. P. aged 22 years married to ARMSTRIS (?), J. aged 24 years August 10, 1882 by Rev. Louis Muller at 329 King Street. Both natives of South Carolina. He a confectioner.

ALBRECT, WILLIAM aged 22 years married to RODGERS, A. E. aged 22 years June 17, 1879 by Rev. H. F. Chreitzberg at the Spring Street Methodist Church. He a native of Princeton, New Jersey and she of Charleston. He a farmer.

ALDERSON, ROBERT LEE aged 26 years married to VERONEE, WILLIE COLSON aged 18 years November 23, 1881 by Rev. E. J. Meynardie at Bethel Church. He a native of Charleston and she of South Carolina. He a mechanic.

ALDRET, BENJAMIN S. aged 21 years married to GOWAN, EVA F. aged 19 years March 22, 1887 by Rev. G. R. Brackett. Both natives of Charleston. He a clerk.

ALDRET, CORNELIA ESTELLE K. aged 17 years married to FINCKEN, EDWARD aged 22 years September 12, 1889 by Rev. Johannes Heckel at Moultrieville, South Carolina. He a native of Mt. Pleasant, South Carolina and she of Charleston. He a merchant in Mt. Pleasant.

ALDRET, JOSEPH S. aged 24 years married to BENNETT, LIZZIE aged 20 years October 23, 1883 by Father Daniel J. Quigley at The Cathedral of St. John the Baptist. Both natives of Charleston. He a pilot.

ALDRET, MARY CAROLINE aged 23 years married to HAYNES, OGDEN VINCENT aged 23 years December 6, 1883 by Rev. G. R. Brackett. He a native of Fairbluff, South Carolina and she of Charleston. He a clerk in Whiteville, North Carolina.

ALDRET, THOMAS JONES aged 21 years married to DAVIS, BEULAH LEE aged 18 years April 9, 1890 by Rev. R. D. Smart at 8 Laurens Street. Both natives of Charleston. He a policeman.

ALDRICH, W. C. aged 30 years married to THOMSON, MARY aged 25 years February 8, 1880 by Rev. John Johnson in Broad Street. Both natives of Charleston. He a machinist.

ALEXANDER, BLANCHE L. aged 21 years married to SIRES, OSCAR D. aged 25 years March 12, 1895 by Rev. J. L. Stokes at 145 St. Philip Street. She a native of England. He a baker.

ALEXANDER, FLORENCE aged 23 years married to LEVY, CHARLES aged 23 years March 3, 1884 by Rev. J. C. Pawley at 61 Anson Street. He a native of Charleston and she of Alabama. He a hostler.

ALEXANDER, VIOLA W. aged 16 years married to CORMIER, JOSIAH A. aged 26 years April 21, 1892 by Rev. J. L. Stokes at the Spring Street Methodist Episcopal Church.

ALFERO, VIRGINIA aged 21 years married to MEYER, CHARLES F. aged 29 years October 13, 1891 by Rev. R. C. Holland. He a native of Summerville, South Carolina and she of Charleston. He a merchant.

ALLAN, JESSIE aged 23 years married to McDERMID, GEORGE C. aged 35 years October 24, 1894 by Rev. G. R. Brackett at 84 Rutledge Avenue. Both natives of Charleston. He a salesman.

ALLAN, WILLIAM S. aged 28 years married to ROBINSON, SUSIE J. aged 20 years April 8, 1895 by Rev. G. R. Brackett at the 2nd Presbyterian Church. Both born Charleston. He a merchant.

ALLEMAN, FREDERICK O. aged 53 years married to RODGERS, FANNIE aged 36 years February 28, 1883 by Rev. J. V. Welsh at 192 Coming Street. He a native of Harrisburg, Pennsylvania and she of Charleston. He a physician.

ALLEN, FRANCIS M. aged 32 years married to McCANTS, IDA DWIGHT aged 28 years November 24, 1891 by Rev. R. C. Holland. He a native of Sumter County, South Carolina and she of Kingstree, South Carolina. He a farmer in Clarendon County, South Carolina.

ALLEN, GEORGE aged 23 years married to MARCHAL, GENETTA aged 22 years March 8, 1885 by Rev. John E. Beard. He a native of Sumter County, South Carolina and she of Kingstree, South Carolina. He a farmer in Clarendon County, South Carolina.

ALLEN, LOGAN M. aged 37 years married to OLDHAM, JENNIE A. aged 22 years April 6, 1893 by Rev. J. L. Stokes at 199 Spring Street. He a native of Richmond, Virginia and she of Augusta, Georgia. He works in the cotton mills.

ALLEN, ROBERT EMMETT aged 24 years married to SEYLE, CORNELIA BENNETT aged 23 years October 4, 1881 by Rev. A. Coke Smith at 100 St. Philip Street. He a native of Due West, South Carolina and she of Charleston. He a merchant.

ALLSTON, ESTHER S. aged 25 years married to WAYNE, WILLIAM O. aged 34 years July 1, 1891 by Rev. John Johnson at St. Philip's Church. He a native of Charleston and she of St. Stephen's Parish, South Carolina. He works in the phosphate mill.

ALMERS, AUGUSTINE aged 17 years married to STAKELEY, IDA F. aged 17 years March 17, 1884 by Rev. John E. Beard at 64 Nassau Street. Both natives of Charleston. He a laborer.

ALMERS, JOSEPH aged 22 years married to HAIR, AGGIE L. aged 16 years December 21, 1890 by Rev. Robert Wilson at 4 Wragg Square. He a native of Charleston and she of Branchville, South Carolina. He a laborer.

ALPHONSE, C. J. aged 22 years married to BOYLE, ELLEN aged 21 years June 10, 1883 by Father F. A. Schmetz at St. Patrick's Roman Catholic Church. He a native of Charleston and she of New York. He an engineer.

ALPHONSE, EMILY aged 19 years married to BROUGHTON, HENRY aged 22 years December 9, 1877 by Father Harry P. Northrop at St. Patrick's Roman Catholic Church. Both natives of Charleston. He works for the railroad.

ALSBROOK, J. DUPHRE aged 24 years married to NETTLES, ELLA C. aged 25 years June 25, 1884 by Rev. John Willson at the Pavilion Hotel. He a native of Clarendon County, South Carolina and she of South Carolina. He a lawyer in Manning, South Carolina.

ALSINA, IDA E. aged 19 years married to HAHN, WILLIE M. aged 19 years February 3, 1886 by Rev. H. B. Browne at 104 Nassau Street.

ALSINA, JOSEPHINE aged 24 years married to BISAR (?), M. aged 31 years May 2, 1887 by Father P. J. Wilson at St. Mary of the Annunciation Roman Catholic Church. He a native of Italy and she of Charleston. He a laborer.

ALSINA, MARY ANGELINA aged 18 years married to JONES, DANIEL EDWARD aged 22 years October 21, 1886 by Father F. J. Shadler at St. Joseph's Roman Catholic Church. Both natives of Charleston. He a boltmaker.

ALTMAN, (Mrs.) CAROLINE FRANCIS aged 36 years married to SIMMONS, JOHN W. aged 42 years December 23, 1888 by Rev. H. B. Browne at 78 Drake Street. Both natives of Colleton County, South Carolina. He a farmer on the King Street Road.

ALTMAN, ISAIAH married to SUMEN, SALIA October 11, 1881 by Jacob Mills. He a native of North Carolina and she of Adams Run, South Carolina. He a laborer.

AMAN, IDA VICTORIA aged 18 years married to HENDRICKS, FRANKLIN M. aged 28 years September 2, 1882 by Rev. A. H. Misseldine at the corner of Rutledge Avenue and Cannon Streets. He a native of Charleston and a clerk.

AMAU, LIZZIE W. aged 27 years married to HART, DAVID S. C. aged 37 years October 8, 1888 by Rev. H. B. Browne at the corner of America and Amherst Streets.

AMES, O. aged 35 years married to BURREN, J. G. M. aged 20 years January 18, 1882 by Rev. Louis Muller at 91 East Bay Street. He a native of Massachusetts and she of Charleston. He a sea captain.

AMME, DIETRICH A. aged 32 years married to ASHENBACH, ELISE C. H. aged 32 years January 31, 1892 by Rev. Louis Muller at King Street, opposite Radcliffe Street. He a native of Germany and a baker.

AMME, R. C. R. Aged 23 years married to SCHALLWIG, B. aged 28 years November 2, 1882 by Rev. Louis Muller in Magazine Street. He a native of Austria and a barkeeper.

ANATASH, ANDREW aged 28 years married to PUFF, E. B. aged 24 years November 12, 1895 by Father J. J. Monaghan at 371 Meeting Street. He a native of Constantinople and she of Charleston. He a merchant.

CHARLESTON SC MARRIAGES 1877-1895

ANDERSON, ALEXINA CAROLINE aged 22 years married to KENNEDY, WILLIAM T. J. aged 28 years April 25, 1888 by Rev. James Wallace Ford. He a native of Charleston and she of Summerville, South Carolina. He a bookkeeper.

ANDERSON, AUGUST W. aged 26 years married to ANDERSON, MARY L. McCLURE aged 39 years April 16, 1891 by Rev. R. D. Smart at 207 Calhoun Street. He a native of New Jersey and she of Charleston. He a photographer.

ANDERSON, C. Y. married to NEVILLE, M. L. October 11, 1880 by Father P. L. Duffy at the residence of the Bride -13 Logan Street. He a native of Charleston.

ANDERSON, DAVE H. aged 31 years married to HESTON, MARTHA J. aged 36 years November 24, 1884 by Rev. J. V. Welsh at 24 Bee Street. He a native of Charleston and she of South Carolina. He a tinner.

ANDERSON, DAVID THOMAS aged 28 years married to MARTIN, ANNIE FRANCES aged 19 years September 26, 1889 by Rev. R. D. Smart at 40 Spring Street. He a native of Giles County, Virginia and she of Richland County, South Carolina. He works for the railroad.

ANDERSON, GEORGE DURANT married to GREEN (GREER?), ELLEN C. October 17, 1884 by Rev. W. F. Junkin in Wentworth Street

ANDERSON, HANS aged 40 years married to DAVIDSON, HANNAH DONALDSON aged 43 years November 20, 1889 by Rev. C. E. Chichester at The Mariners Church. He a native of Norway and she of Ireland. He a mariner.

ANDERSON, IDA M. aged 22 years married to BETTISON, W. T. aged 46 February 27, 1894 by Rev. Lucius Cuthbert at the First Baptist Church. He a native of Barnwell County, South Carolina and she of Charleston. He in the "cotton business."

ANDERSON, I. aged 35 years married to HAGGARD, A. aged 32 years January 15, 1882 by Rev. E. J. Meynardie at 1 Mount Street. He a native of Norway and she of Georgia. He a laborer.

ANDERSON, (Mrs.) JANE WINDHAM aged 39 years married to REDMOND, DAVID aged 24 years August 3, 1885 by Rev. John E. Beard. He a native of Charleston and she of South Carolina.

ANDERSON, JOHN M. aged 27 years married to ROBINSON, SOPHIE N. aged 21 years November 18, 1895 by Rev. J. C. Yongue at 14 Hampstead Square. He a native of Bucksville, South Carolina and she of Charleston. He works in the cotton mill.

ANDERSON, JOSEPH HARVEY aged 40 years married to NEVILLE, KATE FRANCES aged 19 years July 14, 1881 by Rev. Charles S. Vedder at 13 Logan Street. He a native of New Jersey and she of Charleston. He a photographer.

ANDERSON, LAWRENCE W. aged 25 years married to MILLER, (Mrs.) HENRIETTA THOMPSON aged 28 years October 17, 1886 by Rev. H. B. Browne. He a native of Denmark and she of South Carolina. He a carpenter.

ANDERSON, MARY L. McCLURE aged 39 years married to ANDERSON, AUGUST W. aged 26 years April 16, 1891 by Rev. R. D. Smart at 207 Calhoun Street. He a native of New Jersey and she of Charleston. He a photographer.

ANDERSON, SUSAN E. aged 20 years married to GROOM, CLIFFORD W. aged 22 years July 18, 1893 by Rev. Edmund Wells at 579 King Street. He a native of Brooklyn, New York and she of Charleston. He a marine engineer.

ANDERSON, WILLIAM B. aged 21 years married to PASSAILAIGUE, MARY M. aged 16 years March 11, 1888 by Rev. H. B. Browne at 48 Aiken Street. He a native of Georgetown, South Carolina and she of Charleston. He works for the railroad.

ANGEL, ISAAC W. aged 51 years married to BLUME, (Mrs.) SUSANNA WESLEY COLLINS aged 27 years April 17, 1884 by Rev. J. Mercier Green at 4 Bay Street. He a native of Charleston and she of South Carolina. He a physician.

ANGERMANN, HENRY W. M. aged 25 years married to BURMESTER, LOUISA S. aged 19 years June 12, 1883 by Rev. Louis Muller at 283 East Bay Street.

ANGERMANN, MARIE M. BERTHA aged 27 years married to BUTT, HERMANN DIETRICH aged 32 years February 19, 1888 by Rev. Louis Muller. He a native of Prussia and she of Jacksonville, Florida. He a grocer.

ANHEUSER, C. J. F. aged 37 years married to McCOTTER, E. G. aged 19 years July 5, 1882 by Father P. J. Duffy at 20 Wentworth Street. Both natives of Germany. He a merchant.

ANSALDO, WALTER aged 23 years married to REID, WILHELMINA aged 19 years January 15, 1885 by Father Daniel J. Quigley at St. Patrick's Roman Catholic Church. Both natives of Charleston. He an engineer.

ANTONIO, MARY ANN aged 23 years married to THOMPSON, W. LOUIS aged 22 years June 3, 1889 by Rev. H. B. Browne at 78 Drake Street. He a native of New York and she of Winnsboro, South Carolina. He a plumber.

ANTORI, ACHILLE aged 35 years married to DECESARE, CLARA aged 29 years March 23, 1885 by Father John J. Wedenfeller at St. Patrick's Roman Catholic Church. He a fruitier.

APELER, JOHN H. aged 21 years married to DEVEREAUX AGATHA B. aged 18 years February 25, 1882 by Father J. J. Monaghan at St. Patrick's Roman Catholic Church. He a native of Germany and she of Charleston. He the superintendent of the phosphate mill.

ARCHER, ELIZABETH aged 34 years married to BRIGGS, CHRISTOPHER C. aged 34 years August 28, 1884 by Rev. James H. Hall. He a native of Canada and she of Ireland. He an expressman.

ARCHER, MARY E. aged 35 years married to HATCH, MELVIN S. aged 40 years July 28, 1881 by Rev. John Johnson in Judith Street. Both natives of Charleston. He a farmer.

ARMSTRIS, J. (?), aged 24 years married to ALBRECHT, S. P. aged 22 years August 10, 1882 by Rev. Louis Muller at 329 King Street. Both natives of Charleston. He a confectioner.

ARMSTRONG, D. G. aged 23 years married to TAYLOR, HARRIET aged 21 years July 8, 1891 by Rev. W. T. Thompson at 47 Rutledge Avenue.

ARMSTRONG, ALEXANDER C. aged 31 years married to MORRISON, THEDA MILDRED aged 18 years August 13, 1885 by Father J. J. Woolahan at St. Mary of the Annunciation Roman Catholic Church.

ARMSTRONG, JOHN A. aged 28 years married to O'NEILL, MARY E. aged 25 years May 2, 1881 by Father P. L. Duffy. He a native of Charleston and she of Florida. He an engineer.

ARMSTRONG, M. L. aged 18 years married to CORBETT, H. V. aged 22 years September 2, 1879 by Father P. L. Duffy at The Cathedral of St. John the Baptist. Both natives of Charleston. He an upholsterer.

ARNAU, D. A. aged 32 years married to ARNAU, (Mrs.) ELIZA C. N. ASHENBECK aged 32 years January 3, 1891 by Rev. Louis Muller. Both natives of Prussia.

ARNAU, (Mrs.) ELIZA C. N. ASHENBECK aged 32 years married to ARNAU, D. A. aged 32 years January 3, 1891 by Rev. Louis Muller. Both natives of Prussia.

ARNAU, LIZZIE W. G. aged 27 years married to NASH, DAVID C. aged 37 years October 8, 1888 by Rev. H. B. Browne. He a native of Orangeburg, South Carolina and she of Charleston. He a clerk.

ARNOLD, A. F. aged 19 years married to MOTTE, J. A. aged 27 years October 26, 1882 by Rev. C. C. Pinckney at Grace Church. He a native of South Carolina and a railroad worker.

ARNOLD, JANE aged 47 years married to STOUDEMIRE, MARTIN aged 55 years July 23, 1884 by Rev. W. P. Mouzon at 189 Coming Street. He a native of Goose Creek, South Carolina and she of Lexington County, South Carolina. He a carpenter.

ARNOLD, MARY CAROLINE aged 21 years married to GETTY, JAMES WHITE aged 27 years November 12, 1878 by Rev. W. S. Bowman at 12 Chapel Street. He a native of Charleston and a clerk.

ARRIAN, JULIA M. married to EDWARDS, JAMES B. June 4, 1890 by Rev. William A. Betts.

ARTHUR, FRANCES SUSAN married to WILKERSON, JAMES MORTON January 1, 1879 by Rev. William C. Power. He a native of St. James Parish, Goose Creek, South Carolina and she of Oglethorpe, Georgia. He an engineer.

ARTMAN, ANSLEY ROSALEE aged 25 years married to PRITCHARD, EUGENE P. aged 24 years October 6, 1886 by Rev. H. B. Brown at 83 Beaufain Street. He a native of Jacksonboro, South Carolina and she of Charleston. He works for the railroad.

ARTOPE, CAROLINE R. aged 22 years married to IKE, WILLIAM W. aged 34 years November 28, 1886 by Father Daniel J. Quigley at St. Patrick's Roman Catholic Church. Both natives of Charleston. He a clerk.

ASCHENBACH (?), IDA W. B. D. aged 21 years married to SCHROEDER, J. G. E. C. aged 31 years April 28, 1887 by Rev. Louis Muller. Both natives of Germany. He a druggist.

ASHBY, ESTHER M. aged 23 years married to ROUSE, CHARLES W. aged 23 years February 15, 1880 by Rev. R. N. Wells. Both natives of Charleston. He resides in Georgetown, South Carolina and she in Washington, D. C. He a printer.

ASHBY, LOUIS M. aged 26 years married to ROBERTS, MATTIE aged 21 years May 5, 1889 by Rev. Edwin C. Dargan at 7 Bull Street. He a native of Spartanburg, South Carolina and she of Georgia. He a clerk in Savannah, Georgia.

ASHE, F. M. aged 26 years married to LAROUSSELIERE, EUGENIA aged 24 years December 12, 1880 by Father P. L. Duffy at 9 Glebe Street. Both natives of Charleston. He an upholsterer.

ASHEN, MARY ELIZABETH aged 22 years married to McCAW, JOHN aged 50 years February 6, 1894 by Father J. J. Monaghan at 136 St. Philip Street. He a native of Scotland and she of York, South Carolina. He a watchman.

ASHENBACH, ELISE C. H. aged 32 years married to AMME, DIETRICH A. aged 32 years February 28, 1882 by Rev. Louis Muller at King Street, opposite Radcliffe Street. He a native of Germany and a baker.

ASTLE, FRANCIS M. aged 23 years married to McCRACKEN, NAOMI E. aged 32 years June 4, 1885 by Rev. John Johnson. Both natives of Charleston. He a mechanic.

ATKINSON, AZAILE V. aged 21 years married to BUCKHEISTER, WILLIAM H. aged 23 years September 26, 1894 by Rev. J. C. Yongue at 87 Columbus Street. Both natives of Charleston. He a car driver.

ATKINSON, FRANK aged 23 years married to BROWN, FANNIE aged 17 years October 5, 1884 by Rev. R. A. Lapsley at Bischoff's Square. Both natives of Charleston. He a carpenter.

ATKINSON, (Mrs.) MARY E. BECKER aged 32 years married to OTT, JOHN aged 43 years April 21, 1889 by Rev. J. V. Welsh at 40 Bee Street. He a native of Orangeburg, South Carolina and she of Charleston. He a blacksmith.

AUBINOE, ISABELLA aged 22 years married to WHEELER, JAMES HENRY aged 39 years August 29, 1878 by Rev. R. N. Wells. He a native of Washington, Texas and she of Alexandria, Virginia. He a clerk.

AULD, ISAAC aged 22 years married to MORRISSEY, EUGENIA J. March 20, 1884 by Rev. G. R. Brackett in McClellanville, South Carolina. He a native of Madison, Florida and she of South Carolina. He a planter in Summerville, South Carolina.

AUSTIN, HARRY aged 30 years married to DUFFIE, MARY CATHERINE aged 19 years December 26, 1894 by Rev. Edward T. Horn at 31 Pitt Street. He a native of Elkhart, Indiana and she of Charleston. He a showman in Marion, Indiana.

AUSTIN, JULIA aged 21 years married to MURRAY, JOHN H. aged 24 years September 9, 1888 by Rev. H. B. Browne at 31 Amherst Street. Both natives of Berkeley County, South Carolina. He a farmer.

AUSTIN, LOUISA ANNIE married to PETERMAN, JOHN W. February 25, 1886 by Rev. Richard S. Trapier in Tradd Street.

AUSTIN, MARY ELIZABETH married to HEISENBUTTEL, MARTIN F. April 25, 1889 by Rev. Richard S. Trapier.

AUSTIN, WILLIAM JAMES aged 29 years married to FULSE, (Mrs.) JULIA C. VALENTINE aged 30 years September 22, 1889 by Rev. T. P. Burgess at 100 Columbus Street. Both natives of Berkeley County, South Carolina. He a farmer.

AUTRY, S. M. aged 43 years married to CAVANAUGH, HUGH aged 45 years April 16, 1893 by Rev. D. F. Toppit at 3 Creamars Court.

AVERY, FRANCIS C. B. aged 30 years married to HANCKEL, CHARLOTTE H. aged 30 years December 16, 1890 by Rev. John Johnson at 20 Church Street. He a native of of New York and she of Charleston. He a merchant in New York.

AVILGAE (?), ESPENIZO aged 35 years married to DAVIS, MARY ANN aged 35 years January 30, 1891 by Father J. J. Monaghan at St. Patrick's Roman Catholic Church. He a native of Spain and she of Charleston. He a fisherman on the Boat Therese.

AXSON, EVA EVANGELINE aged 18 years married to VERONEE, JOHN S. aged 29 years May 19, 1887 by Rev. John O. Wilson at 114 Nassau Street. Both natives of Charleston. He a street car driver.

AXSON, LOUISE COURTNEY aged 26 years married to THAYER, JAMES HENRY aged 34 years July 12, 1889 by Rev. P. W. Lide at the residence of Mrs. J. W. Axson - 69 Cannon Street. He a native of Charleston and she of Greenville, South Carolina. He a bank teller.

AXSON, NANNIE OSWALD aged 22 years married to GELZER, JOHN aged 23 years December 6, 1883 by Rev. A. J. S. Thomas at 17 Meeting Street. He a native of Summerville, South Carolina and she of Charleston.

AXSON, SALLIE B. aged 25 years married to THAYER, JAMES H. aged 26 years June 23, 1881 by Rev. L. H. Shuck at 17 Meeting Street. He a native of Charleston. He a clerk in Augusta, Georgia.

AXSON, WILLIAM C. AXSON aged 37 years married to KLEMM, T. W. aged 29 years July 24, 1895 by Rev. Edmund Wells at 20 Bogard Street. He a native of Charleston and she of Mt. Pleasant, South Carolina. He works in the phosphate factory.

AXSON, W. C. aged 23 years married to BROWN, LAURA E. aged 19 years June 29, 1881 by Rev. L. H. Shuck at 32 Columbus Street. He a native of Charleston and a miner.

AYERS, M. J. aged 19 years married to DUREN, GEORGE W. aged 35 years March 12, 1895 by Rev. J. C. Yongue at 73 Line Street. He a native of Columbia, South Carolina and she of Berkeley County, South Carolina. He a street car condutor.

AZON, MARVIN married to WALLACE, GEORGIA October 29, 1886 by Rev. Richard S. Trapier.

BABCOCK, ALICE EVA aged 21 years married to CALDER, EVERETT EDWARD aged 22 years October 8, 1884 by Rev. John O. Wills at 82 Wentworth Street. He a native of Baltimore, Maryland and she of Charleston. He a machinist on Sullivans Island, South Carolina.

BACOT, DANIEL HUGER aged 41 years married to RHETT, JOSEPHINE H. aged 30 years January 19, 1888 by Rev. John Johnson at St. Philip's Church. He a native of Charleston and she of Alabama. He a merchant.

BACOT, LEWIS married to SELIGMAN, ELLA November 3, 1885 by Rev. William H. Campbell at the residence of Edward Locke. He a clerk.

BAGLEY, JOHN H. aged 23 years married to CHARLON, AMANDA B. aged 18 years November 19, 1893 by Rev. J. C. Yongue at 112 Nassau Street. He a native of Gerogia and she of Charleston. He works in a restaurant.

BAGNOLL, CARRIE J. aged 23 years married to SHULER, HENRY F. aged 24 years July 15, 1893 by Rev. J. L. Stokes at 603 King Street. He a native of South Carolina and she of North Carolina. He a bookkeeper.

BAHR, WILLIAM N. aged 23 years married to SHOKES, MARY ELIZABETH aged 18 years June 14, 1878 by Rev. W. S. Bowman. Both natives of Charleston. He a policeman.

BAHUTGE (?), ETTA aged 18 years married to JACOBSON, WILLIAM H. aged 20 years August 2, 1891 by Rev. R. C. Holland. Both natives of Charleston.

BAIL, ALICE LOUISA aged 19 years married to SANDERS, JAMES O'H. aged 33 years November 4, 1891 by Rev. Robert Wilson. Both natives of Charleston. He a clerk.

BAIL, E. F. aged 15 years married to CORKER, H. M. aged 35 years January 4, 1882 by Father J. M. Giessen. Both natives of Charleston. He a moulder.

BAIL (?), LAURA aged 25 years married to DARRELL, WILLIAM S. aged 43 years November 28, 1888 by Rev. John Johnson at 20 Washington Street. Both natives of Charleston. He a drayman.

BAILEY, CONSTANTIA C. aged 24 years married to THOMLINSON, ALVIN R. aged 32 years April 15, 1885 by Rev. C. C. Pinckney at Grace Church. Both natives of Charleston. He a merchant.

BAILEY, HERBERT L. aged 29 years married to MITCHELL, ELIZA B. aged 23 years April 20, 1893 by Rev. Henry M. Grant. He a native of South Carolina and she of Charleston. He a merchant on James Island, South Carolina.

BAILEY, JOSEPH E. aged 30 years married to MARSHALL, BELLE L. aged 21 years June 5, 1894 by Rev. Edward T. Horn at St. Johannes Lutheran Church. He a native of Orangeburg, South Carolina and a clerk.

BAILEY, JULIA aged 28 years married to BLOOD, EVERETT aged 29 years December 4, 1889 by Rev. Robert Wilson at 74 Drake Street. He a native of Massachusetts and she of Edisto Island, South Carolina. He a superintendent at the phosphate mill.

BAILEY, JULIA A. aged 21 years married to BENNETT, S. MURRAY aged 27 years October 29, 1881 by Rev. C. C. Pinckney at 15 Hasell Street. Both natives of Charleston. He a merchant.

BAILEY, LOTTIE MAY aged 24 years married to BATES, HAROLD E. aged 25 years May 24, 1895 by Rev. Robert Wilson at 79 Coming Street. He a native of New York and she of Massachusetts. He a physician in New York.

BAILEY, MARGARET aged 20 years married to BLOCKER, J. D. aged 22 years March 11, 1891 by Rev. J. Thomas Pate at 231 Coming Street. Both natives of Colleton County, South Carolina. He works for the railroad in Summerville, South Carolina.

BAILEY, SARAH LENORA aged 21 years married to FOSTER, JOHN ERNEST aged 23 years January 29, 1878 by Rev. C. C. Pinckney in Anson Street. Both natives of Charleston. He a clerk.

BAILEY, THOMAS aged 27 years married to BURDELL, ELIZABETH ST. JULIEN aged 20 years November 7, 1889 by Rev. Henry M. Grant at the Circular Congregational Church. He a native of South Carolina and she of Charleston. He an engineer in Mt. Pleasant, South Carolina.

BAIR, (Mrs.) LIZZIE A. KAISER aged 33 years married to ADDISON, THOMAS M. aged 40 years December 28, 1893 by Rev. Edmund Wells at 7 Addison Court. He a native of Charleston and she of Orangeburg, South Carolina. He a laborer.

BAKER, ANN married to VICEDOMINI, A. W. S. April 18, 1884 by Rev. W. T. Thompson at 161 King Street.

BAKER, ARTHUR W. aged 30 years married to CHOATE, SUSIE M. aged 25 years December 14, 1892 by Rev. W. T. Thompson at 43 Lynch Street. He a native of McClellanville, South Carolina and she of Charleston. He a merchant in Cordesville, South Carolina.

BAKER, ELLA E. married to BOLGER, WILLIAM W. July 8, 1885 by Father J. J. Woolahan at St. Mary of the Annunciation Roman Catholic Church. Both natives of Charleston. He a laborer.

BAKER, H. B. aged 19 years married to MAGRATH, NORA aged 17 years February 15, 1885 by Rev. R. A. Lapsley at 8 Drake Street. He a native of Camden, South Carolina and she of Charleston. He a drummer.

BAKER, JAMES C. aged 24 years married to LANGSTON, EDIE ONETA aged 18 years March 10, 1892 by Rev. Edward C. Wells at 42 H Street. He a native of Lancaster, South Carolina and she of Florence, South Carolina. He a farmer.

BAKER, JOHN A. aged 33 years married to EASTERBY, LILLIAN June 6, 1888 by Rev. R. W. Lide at First Baptist Church. He a native of Virginia and she of Charleston. He a clergyman in Louisville, Kentucky.

BAKER, JOHN RUSSELL aged 55 years married to BRANDFORD, SARAH JOHANNA aged 30 years April 3, 1878 by Rev. L. H. Shuck at the First Baptist Church. Both natives of Charleston. He a druggist/apothecary.

BAKER, JOHN C. aged 21 years married to McCARROLL, MARY C. aged 26 years June 9, 1895 by Rev. A. Ernest Cornish at the corner of Bee and President Streets. He a native of Lexington County, South Carolina and she of Charleston. He a laborer.

BAKER, LAURA A. aged 29 years married to FRIBBLE, WESTON A. aged 31 years February 8, 1887 by Rev. L. F. Beaty. Both natives of South Carolina. He a planter.

BAKER, LYDIA R. aged 17 years married to DOWNING, THADDEUS C. aged 20 years November 17, 1887 by Rev. G. R. Brackett. He a native of Charleston and she of Lexington, South Carolina. He works in the bagging factory.

BAKER, MOLLIE CECILE aged 19 years married to O'NEILL, HENRY JOHN aged 31 years August 8, 1878 by Father Daniel J. Quigley at The Cathedral of St. John the Baptist. Both natives of Charleston. He a merchant.

BAKER, WASHINGTON aged 38 years married to PRINCE, (Mrs.) EVA A. SEXTON aged 24 years February 8, 1887 by Rev. L. F. Beaty. Both natives of Charleston. He a clerk. Both natives of Charleston. He a clerk.

BALDWIN, STEPHEN aged 25 years married to PURSE, VIOLA aged 19 years March 11, 1891 by Rev. John Johnson at 1 Cooper's Court.

BALL, SAMUEL aged 39 years married to CAVANT, SUSAN aged 39 years May 13, 1884 by Rev. A. H. Misseldine at 7 Percy Street. He a native of Devonshire, England and she of Charleston. He an engineer.

BALL, WILLIAM CAISON aged 31 years married to FRASER, ISABEL aged 31 years April 10, 1889 by Rev. C. C. Pinckney at the residence of Gen. McCrady - 27 Montagu Street. He a native of New York and she of Charleston. He a clerk in New Jersey.

BALL, ELIAS aged 41 years married to WILSON, MARY HOWE aged 28 years April 2, 1891 by Rev. Robert Wilson at St. Luke's Church. He a native of Berkeley County, South Carolina and she of Columbia, South Carolina. He a planter in Berkeley County.

BALLANTINE, FANNY married to BANDUIL (?), WILLIAM March 25, 1878 by Rev. J. A. Chambliss at 7 Paines Court.

BALLANTINE, JESSIE aged 22 years married to JERVEY, J. E. B. aged 22 years June 4, 1892 by Rev. J. A. Clifton. Both natives of Charleston. He a mariner.

BALLANTINE, NELLIE E. aged 19 years married to BARRINEAU, WILLIAM R. aged 23 years November 29, 1891 by Rev. W. A. Betts at 24 Blake Street. He a native of Williamsburg County, South Carolina and she of St. Johns Parish, South Carolina. He works in a factory.

BALLANTINE, SUSAN B. aged 20 years married to JONES, MELVILLE aged 28 years March 24, 1881 by Rev. L. H. Shuck at the corner and Rutledge Avenue and Calhoun Street. He a native of Charleston and a mechanist.

BAMBERG, W. J. aged 29 years married to MAHONEY, J. J. aged 23 years November 11, 1879 by Rev. Edward T. Horn at 54 Tradd Street. He a native of Bamberg, South Carolina and she of Charleston. He a farmer in Bamberg.

BANCROFT, MATILDA aged 23 years married to STEADMAN, ARTHUR A. aged 27 years November 27, 1881 by Rev. C. C. Pinckney at 4 Thomas Street. Both natives of Charleston. He a clerk.

BANDUIL (?), WILLIAM married to BALLANTINE, FANNY March 25, 1878 by Rev. J. A. Chambliss in Paines Court.

BANONERO (?), MELVIN aged 22 years married to HYATT, EMMA C. aged 18 years February 18, 1894 by Rev. J. M. Knowles at 72 Drake Street.

BARBER, JESSEY aged 19 years married to THOMSON, ISABEL aged 17 years February 17, 1881 by Rev. J. V. Welsh at 5 Park Street. He a native of Summerville, South Carolina and a laborer.

BARBER, WILLIAM aged 29 years married to EADIE, ERNESTINE V. aged 18 years December 29, 1895 by Rev. A. Ernest Cornish. He a native of Summerville, South Carolina and she of Bonneau, South Carolina. He works in a factory.

BARBER, W. T. aged 27 years married to HOWARD, ELLA M. aged 14 years January 14, 1894 by Rev. John F. Mitchell at 31 Amherst Street.

BARBOT, CHARLES JULIUS aged 25 years married to ST. AMAND, FLORENCE E. aged 22 years October 13, 1890 by Father Claudian P. Northrop at The Cathedral of St. John the Baptist. Both natives of Charleston. He a clerk in Wilmington, North Carolina.

BARFIELD, EMMA C. aged 27 years married to LANNEAU, ALFRED E. aged 43 years February 5, 1886 by Rev. C. H. Chichester at the corner of Rutledge Avenue and Calhoun Streets.

BARFIELD, FLORENCE aged 23 years married to STURCKEN, WILLIAM HERMAN aged 44 years May 24, 1891 by Rev. G. R. Brackett at 2 Allway Street. He a native of Charleston and she of Richmond, Virginia. He a cigarmaker.

BARGMANN, META CATHARINE aged 22 years married to WIESSE, PAUL aged 25 years October 31, 1886 by Rev. Louis Muller at the corner of King and Calhoun Streets. Both natives of Germany. He a baker.

BARGAMANN, WILLIAM aged 24 years married to TIEDEMANN, KATHERINE aged 21 years November 23, 1881 by Rev. Johannes Heckel in King Street. He a native of Oldenburg, Germany and she of Hanover. He a baker.

BARINOE, SARAH aged 27 years married to RICH, MANUEL aged 35 years May 2, 1886 by Rev. C. E. Chichester at the Old Planters Hotel. He a native of Cadiz, Spain and she of Pee Dee, South Carolina. He a fisherman.

BARNES, EDWIN L. aged 30 years married to SANDERS, MARY H. aged 28 years August 29, 1889 by Rev. Robert Wilson at 77 Drake Street. He a native of Kershaw County, South Carolina and she of Beaufort County, South Carolina. He a teacher in Camden, South Carolina.

BARNETT, CHARLES D. aged 23 years married to WILLIAMS, RUBY aged 21 years November 12, 1890 by Father P. L. Duffy. He a native of Flat Rock, South Carolina and she of Augusta, Georgia. He a mechanic in Asheville, South Carolina.

BARNETT, JOHN B. married to BOLGER, ELLA EDITH April 27, 1881 by Rev. William H. Campbell at the residence of Mr. H. Bolger.

BARNETT, JOSEPH E. aged 28 years married to LORYEA, MINNIE R. aged 25 years June 8, 1881 by Rabbi David Levy at 369 King Street. He a native of Sumter, South Carolina and she of Charleston. He a merchant in Marysville, South Carolina.

BARNETT, J. aged 23 years married to REYELL, BESSIE aged 15 years November 2, 1890 by Rev. Charley Shevett at 7 Stone Court.

BARNWELL, GABRIELLA MANIGAULT married to FRANCISCAN, HARVEY CAMERON December 5, 1877 by Rev. Richard S. Trapier in Lamboll Street.

BARNWELL, JOSEPH WALKER aged 30 years married to CHEVES, HARRIET KINLOCH aged 25 years January 23, 1883 by Rev. John Johnson in South Bay Street. Both natives of Charleston. He a lawyer.

BARNWELL, M. GEORGINA aged 27 years married to GRIMBALL, JOHN aged 44 years March 24, 1885 by Rev. C. C. Pinckney. Both natives of Charleston. He a lawyer.

BARNWELL, WILLIAM H. aged 26 years married to McCRADY, LOUISA R. L. aged 24 years April 28, 1887 by Rev. John Johnson. Both natives of South Carolina. He an accountant.

BARR, JAMES aged 24 years married to TUCKER, MATILDA aged 20 years December 27, 1881 by Rev. H. F. Chreitzberg at 13 America Street. Both natives of Sumter, South Carolina. He a mechinist.

BARRAGAN, MELVIN aged 22 years married to MYATT, EMMA C. aged 18 years February 18, 1894 by Rev. J. C. Yongue. He a native of Williamsburg County, South Carolina and she of Charleston. He a fireman at the cotton mill.

BARRAGAN, WILLIAM FRANCIS aged 22 years married to TORCK, MARIE LILIA aged 21 years January 29, 1879 by Father Claudian B. Northrop at St. Mary of the Annunciation Roman Catholic Church. Both natives of Charleston. He a salesman.

BARRETT, PATRICK aged 30 years married to SPAIN, MARY aged 23 years September 2, 1888 by Father Daniel J. Quigley at St. Patrick's Roman Catholic Church. He a native of Ireland and she of Charleston.

BARRIDGE, THOMAS aged 33 years married to BROUGHTON, SARA ANN aged 31 years November 23, 1880 by Rev. J. V. Welsh at 11 Aiken Street. He a native of England and she of Charlotte, North Carolina. He a laborer.

BARRINEAU, JAMES F. aged 18 years married to ENTER, MOLLIE aged 15 years February 18, 1894 by Rev. J. C. Yongue at 75 Bay Street. He a native of Williamsburg County, South Carolina and she of Charleston. He works in the cotton mill.

BARRINEAU, JOHN A. aged 25 years married to SWEATMAN, ANNETTE aged 16 years July 28, 1889 by Rev. J. V. Welsh at 40 Bee Street. He a native of Williamsburg County, South Carolina and she of Summerville, South Carolina. He a farmer.

BARRINEAU, SARAH E. aged 17 years married to VANHORN, GEORGE M. aged 20 years December 23, 1894 by Rev. J. C. Yongue at 108 America Street. He a native of North Carolina and she of South Carolina. He works in a factory in Sumter, South Carolina.

BARRINEAU, WILLIAM R. aged 23 years married to BALLENTINE, NELLIE E. aged 19 years November 29, 1891 by Rev. W. A. Betts at 24 Blake Street. He a native of Williamsburg County, South Carolina and she of St. Johns Parish, South Carolina. He works in a factory.

BARRY, BRIDGET aged 21 years married to SCOTT, WILLIAM F. aged 21 years September 24, 1889 by Father Daniel J. Quigley at St. Patrick's Roman Catholic Church. Both natives of Charleston. He a boilermaker.

BARRY, EDMUND M. aged 24 years married to CORBETT, LIZZIE aged 21 years November 28, 1886 by Father Daniel J. Quigley at St. Patrick's Roman Catholic Church. He a native of Charleston and she of Georgia. He clerk.

BARRY, JAMES aged 43 years married to GIBSON, CARRIE aged 35 years May 3, 1885 by Father Daniel J. Quigley at St. Patrick's Roman Catholic Church. He a native of Ireland and she of South Carolina. He a machinist.

BARRY, JAMES aged 27 years married to PENDERS, M. A. aged 26 years April 9, 1882 by Father J. J. Monaghan at St. Patrick's Roman Catholic Church. He a native of Charleston and a laborer.

BARRY, KATIE aged 28 years married to MANSFIELD, JOHN June 24, 1886 by Father F. J. Shadler at St. Joseph's Roman Catholic Church. Both natives of Charleston. He a stevedore.

BARRY, MARGARET A. aged 21 years married to RIELLY, MICHAEL aged 23 years May 27, 1886 by Father Thomas E. McCormack at St. Patrick's Roman Catholic Church. Both natives of Charleston. He a clerk.

BARRY, MARY aged 24 years married to LIDDY, THOMAS J. aged 30 years October 27, 1895 by Father J. J. Monaghan at St. Patrick's Roman Catholic Church.

BARRY, MARY L. aged 22 years married to MURPHY, JOHN D. aged 23 years February 6, 1894 by Father J. J. Monaghan at 136 St. Philip Street.

BARRY, MICHAEL aged 25 years married to NAUGHTON, HONORA A. aged 25 years June 15, 1881 by Father F. J. Shadler at St. Joseph's Roman Catholic Church. He a native of Charleston and a carpenter.

BART, CHARLES E. aged 26 years married to O'BRIEN, MARGARET E. aged 17 years April 23, 1884 by Father P. L. Duffy at The Cathedral of St. John the Baptist. Both natives of Charleston. He a merchant.

BARTH, CATHERINE aged 20 years married to SIMKIN, ELSWORTH aged 21 years November 8, 1885 by Rev. J. V. Welsh at 24 Bee Street. He a native of Pennsylvania and she of South Carolina. He a machinist.

BARTH, EUGENE JAMES aged 20 years married to BURNS, LIZZIE AGNES aged 18 years June 18, 1890 by Father F. J. Shadler at St. Joseph's Roman Catholic Church. Both natives of Charleston. He a clerk.

BARTH, WILLIAM H. aged 35 years married to SIMS, (Mrs.) ALICE R. O'BRIEN aged 33 years July 8, 1893 by Rev. J. C. Yongue at 14 Hampstead Square.

BARTON, ESTELLE BERTHA aged 17 years married to DONALD, D. JOHNSTON aged 22 years October 7, 1884 by Rev. John O. Wilson at 315 East Bay Street. He a native of Charleston and she of Atlanta, Georgia. He an engineer.

BARTON, EMMA J. aged 18 years married to RICE, HORACE S. aged 32 years April 23, 1890 by Rev. John Johnson at 53 Church Street. She a native of Charleston.

BARWICK, EDWARD S. aged 23 years married to SCHARFF, REGINA aged 22 years December 11, 1890 by Rev. T. P. Burgess at 38 Percy Street. Both natives of Charleston. He a machinist.

BATCHELOR, FRANCES E. aged 30 years married to THOMPSON, CHARLES H. aged 25 years September 11, 1892 by Rev. John Johnson at 53 Church Street.

BATCHELDER, HIRAM M. aged 26 years married to JEFFORDS, MARY P. aged 35 years September 1, 1887 by Rev. Robert Wilson at 95 Broad Street. He a native of North Redding, Massachusetts and she of Charleston. He a decorator in Boston, Massachusetts.

BATEMAN, CHARLES D. married to KING, (Mrs.) SARAH QUINCY January 4, 1888 by Rev. William H. Campbell at the residence of John Paul.

BATEMAN, ELLA ROSA PELZER aged 25 years married to ROBB, JAMES J. aged 26 years January 8, 1884 by Rev. E. J. Meynardie in Vanderhorst Street. Both natives of Charleston. He a clerk.

BATES, HAROLD E. aged 25 years married to BAILEY, LOTTIE MAY aged 24 years May 24, 1895 by Rev. Robert Wilson at 79 Coming Street. He a native of New York and she of Massachusetts. He a physician in New York.

BATTERSON, ALICE W. aged 20 years married to DOUGLAS, GEORGE September 9, 1878 by William B. Yates.

BAUM, EMMA BROWN aged 23 years married to RASHBAUM, HENRY aged 27 years December 27, 1887 by Rabbi David Levy at the Hasell Street Synagogue.

BAUM, JACOB aged 27 years married to BROWN, EMMA aged 19 years Janaury 26, 1881 by Rabbi David Levy. He a native of Georgetown, South Carolina and she of New York. He a merchant in Georgetown.

BAUMIL, WILLIAM married to BALLENTINE, FANNIE March 25, 1878 by Rev. J. A. Chambliss at 7 Paine's Court.

BAXLEY, MARTHA E. MARTIN aged 39 years married to GRAHAM, JOHN C. aged 41 years July 25, 1891 by Rev. W. A. Betts at 21 Hanover Street. He a native of Scotland and she of Conway, South Carolina. He a cook.

BAXTER, CHARLES aged 22 years married to McELVEE, JANEY aged 17 years November 9, 1892 by Rev. A. M. Chreitzberg at Bishcoff's Square. Both natives of Charleston. He works in a factory.

BAYER, HENRY S. aged 26 years married to CROWELL, LILLIE L. aged 24 years November 28, 1878 by Rev. W. S. Bowman at 14 Bee Street. He a native of Alexandria, Virginia and she of New York. He a clerk.

BAYNARD, E. J. aged 24 years married to VARDELL, W. aged 24 years January 19, 1882 by Rev. C. C. Pinckney at Grace Church. He a native of Charleston and a clerk.

BAYNARD, S. LEE aged 42 years married to KING, (Mrs.) ANNA MARIA SWINTON aged 39 years November 24, 1891 by Rev. G. R. Brackett at 12 Wentworth Street. He a native of Edisto Island, South Carolina and she of St. Paul's Parish, South Carolina. He works at the phosphate mill.

BEAN, JAMES W. aged 23 years married to DOSCHER, MAGGIE aged 18 years November 15, 1892 by Father J. J. Monaghan at 143 St. Philip Street. He a native of Ireland and she of Athens, Georgia. He a laborer.

BEARD, BARNEY P. aged 22 years married to ELLIS, ANNA B. aged 16 years May 9, 1895 by Rev. J. C. Yongue at 24.5 Cooper Street. He a native of St. George, South Carolina and she of Charleston. He a tinner/plumber.

BEARD, JOHN C. aged 21 years married to POWERS, MARY aged 20 years October 12, 1884 by Rev. John E. Beard.

BEARDSLEY, ELBERT aged 44 years married to BENZ, (Mrs.) MARIE A. MAYER aged 40 years June 13, 1892 by Rev. J. A. Clifton at 207 Calhoun Street. He a native of Connecticut and she of Georgia. He a merchant in New York.

BEASLEY, CLARA O. aged 17 years married to MORSE, H. R. aged 23 years June 5, 1881 by Rev. T. H. Shuck at 27 Church Street. He a native of Charleston. He a farmer in Georgia.

BEASLEY, C. N. aged 21 years married to MELVIN, E. E. aged 21 years January 18, 1880 by Father Claudian B. Northrop in Wentworth Street. Both natives of Charleston. He a clerk.

BEATTIE, CLOELIA (?) E. aged 21 years married to HORSEY, FREDERICK W. aged 23 years November 10, 1885 by Father Daniel J. Quigley. He a native of South Carolina and she of Florida. He a patternmaker.

BEATTIE, EDWIN F. aged 24 years married to JARKES, GERALDINE ANNA aged 20 years April 20, 1879 by Father Claudian B. Northrop in Pitt Street. Both natives of Charleston. He a policeman.

BEATTIE, JULIUS B. aged 23 years married to SIGWALD, LILA M. aged 22 years December 7, 1884 by Father F. A. Schmetz at 269 Meeting Street. Both natives of Charleston. He works for the railroad.

BEATY, JAMES H. married to SINGLETARY, MARY J. October 5, 1890 by Rev. W. A. Betts.

BEATY, JAMES O'NEIL aged 30 years married to LANGAN, BESSIE aged 24 years February 8, 1891 by Father J. J. Monaghan at St. Patrick's Roman Catholic Church. He a native of Charleston and she of Ireland. He a blacksmith.

BEATY, L. G. aged 24 years married to HUGHES, V. E. aged 21 years February 26, 1882 by Rev. L. H. Shuck at 27 Church Street. Both natives of South Carolina. He a manufacturer.

BEAUDROT, EMMA AMELIA aged 25 years married to BRITTON, RICHARD B. aged 28 years January 20, 1886 by Rev. J. Walter Dickson at the Spring Street Lutheran Church. Both natives of Charleston. He a printer.

BEAUDROT, MAMIE A. aged 19 years married to HAGOOD, EDWARD A. aged 52 years July 1, 1892 by Rev. J. L. Stokes at 77 Line Street. He a native of Albany, Georgia and she of Charleston. He a broker in Toledo, Ohio.

BEAUFORT, CHARLES W. married to GILLILAND, KATE J. February 23, 1888 by Rev. William H. Campbell. He a machinist in Langley, South Carolina.

BEAUFORT, M. C. aged 20 years married to CANNON, T. M. aged 31 years January 24, 1882 by Rev. J. M. Green at 78 Smith Street. Both natives of Charleston. He a laborer.

BECHER, HARRY L. aged 28 years married to ROUMILLAT, MARY November 1, 1888 by Rev. J. E. Carlisle at 231 Coming Street. He a theatrical in New York City, New York.

BECK, HARRY L. aged 28 years married to ROMERILL, MARY November 1, 1888 by Rev. J. E. Carlisle at 231 Coming Street.

BECK, JOHN aged 22 years married to HELMEY, EMMA aged 18 years January 3, 1886 by Rev. H. B. Browne at 3 Lee Street. Both natives of Savannah, Georgia. He works for the railroad.

BECKAM, SIMON aged 28 years married to SANDERS, CLARA A. aged 22 years May 28, 1891 by Rev. Robert Wilson at 77 Drake Street. He a native of Lancaster County, South Carolina and she of Charleston. He a physician.

BECKER, ANNA META W. aged 22 years married to HOLLINGS, JURGEN D. aged 22 years June 21, 1891 by Rev. Louis Muller. Both natives of Prussia. He a grocer.

BECKER, F. W. aged 26 years married to BRESSELEAU, N. E. aged 18 years June 15, 1879 by Father John P. Twigg at The Cathedral of St. John the Baptist. He a clerk.

BECKER, GERTRUDE C. aged 18 years married to MILNER, HAMILTON S. aged 21 years April 7, 1894 by Rev. J. C. Stokes at 231 Coming Street. Both natives of Charleston. He a salesman.

BECKER, PAULINE aged 30 years married to LINDQUIST, JOHN E. aged 30 years April 7, 1892 by Rev. R. C. Holland at the Wentworth Street Lutheran Church. He a native of Sweden and she of Charleston. He a mariner.

BECKER, WILLIAM F. A. aged 27 years married to MORAN, (Mrs.) OCTAVIA WALES aged 35 years March 5, 1890 by Rev. C. E. Chichester at The Mariners Church. He a native of Charleston and she of Liverpool, England. He a baker.

BECKETT, ADELA M. aged 24 years married to SMITH, ALEXANDER aged 28 years August 3, 1892 by Rev. R. A. Webb at Westminster Presbyterian Church. He a native of England and she of Florida. He a civil engineer.

BECKETT, EMMA J. aged 43 years married to SEABROOK, CATO A. aged 52 years November 3, 1892 by Rev. G. R. Brackett at the Enston Homes. He a native of Edisto Island, South Carolina and she of Johns Island, South Carolina. He a teacher in Columbia, South Carolina.

BECKETT, JAMES L. aged 48 years married to BOGLE, ADELAIDE aged 37 years March 27, 1884 by Rev. C. C. Pinckney at St. Luke's Church. He a native of Charleston and she of Maryland. He a physician.

BECKMAN, A. S. aged 25 years married to ROBERTSON, E. aged 37 years November 11, 1879 by Rev. W. S. Bowman at the Wentworth Street Lutheran Church. Both natives of Charleston.

BECKMAN, E. C. aged 21 years married to HOURE (?), M. J. K. February 1, 1882 by Rev. Edward T. Horn at St. John's Lutheran Church. He a native of Darlington County, South Carolina and she of Charleston. He a merchant.

BECKMAN, JOHN WILLIAM aged 25 years married to LIVINGSTON, PAULINE A. aged 24 years June 26, 1895 by Father J. J. Monaghan at 10 Wragg Square. Both natives of Charleston. He a shipping clerk.

BECKMAN, J. F. aged 45 years married to WILLIAMS, ELLEN aged 35 years August 14, 1890 by Rev. J. Marion Boyce at 21 Montagu Street. He a native of Kentucky and she of Charleston. He a jeweller.

BECKROGE, JOHANN HEINRICH aged 24 years married to HILKEN, ANNA GESCHE aged 23 years January 12, 1888 by Rev. Louis Muller in King Street, opposite Marion Square.

BECKTEL, ROBERT married to BUTLER, SALLIE November 16, 1890 by Rev. W. A. Betts.

BECKWITH, LAWRENCE H. aged 26 years married to GLOVER, ELIZABETH A. aged 21 years December 7, 1893 by Rev. John Johnson at 25 Smith Street.

BEE, JOHN PRICE aged 39 years married to McCARREL, ANN E. CALDER aged 30 years February 22, 1891 by Rev. G. R. Brackett at 49 Tradd Street. Both natives of Charleston. He a mechanic.

BEE, JOHN S. aged 41 years married to COBURN, FRANCES A. ROBERTS aged 38 years April 11, 1893 by Rev. G. R. Brackett at 17 Smith Street. Both natives of Charleston. He a railroad clerk.

BEE, JOSEPH F. married to BICKLEY, JULIA R. June 17, 1891 by Rev. William H. Campbell.

BEE, MARY aged 27 years married to WELLING, ARTHUR aged 22 years September 24, 1880 by Rev. R. N. Wells in King Street near Morris Street. Both natives of Charleston. He a mechanic in Moultrieville, South Carolina.

BEE, M. E. aged 19 years married to WITHINGTON, H. P. aged 24 years September 2, 1879 by Rev. J. M. Greene in Cannon Street. Both natives of Charleston. He a mechanic.

BEE, SANDIFORD aged 26 years married to GREER (GREEN ?), EDITH aged 21 years February 2, 1892 by Rev. Edward T. Horn at 7 Logan Street. Both natives of Charleston. He a planter on James Island, South Carolina.

BEGEMANN, W. H. aged 26 years married to OLDENBERG, M. H. S. aged 25 years March 27, 1887 by Rev. Louis Muller. He a native of Germany and she of Charleston. He a saloon keeper.

BEGLEY, J. M. aged 21 years married to LANIGAN, C. J. aged 22 years March 20, 1882 by Father F. J. Shadler at St. Joseph's Roman Catholic Church. He a native of Charleston and a railroad worker.

BEHLING, HILMER aged 26 years married to SMITH, CHARLES K. aged 25 years September 9, 1894 by Rev. J. L. Stokes at 17 Laurel Street.

BEHLMAN, S. M. C. aged 27 years married to GROVENEUER (?), HENRY J. W. aged 22 years May 20, 1880 by Rev. Louis Muller at 637 King Street. He a native of Charleston and she of Hanover.

BEHLMER, G. H. G. aged 29 years married to BULWINKLE, C. M. aged 20 years April 27, 1887 by Rev. Louis Muller. Both natives of South Carolina. He a grocer.

BEHLMER, HEINRICH W. aged 30 years married to LANGE, MINNA ANNA aged 25 years December 12, 1886 by Rev. Louis Muller at the southeast corner of Columbus and Hanover Streets. He a native of Germany and she of Charleston. He a grocer.

BEHNLEN, EMMA aged 22 years married to NOTE, AUGUST aged 24 years February 15, 1887 by Father F. J. Shadler. Both natives of Germany. He a grocer.

BEHNSCHSEN (?), ANNA aged 25 years married to NOLTE, AUGUST aged 29 years December 4, 1892 by Rev. L. Boldt at 5 College Street.

BEHRENS, ADELINE A. aged 23 years married to PETIT, WILLIAM S. aged 23 years June 15, 1891 by Rev. Louis Muller at 526 King Street. Both natives of Charleston. He a mechanic.

BEHRE, ADOLPH G. aged 40 years married to ELLIS, JANIE TERESA aged 17 years August 5, 1891 by Rev. R. D. Smart at 422 Meeting Street. He a native of Germany and she of Charleston. He a machinist.

BEHRENS, ANNA aged 22 years married to MESSNER, WILLIAM aged 22 years May 1, 1878 by Rev. Johannes Heckel. He a native of Stein, Baden, Germany and she of Lehe near Bremenhaven, Germany. He a baker.

BEHRENS, H. C. E. aged 28 years married to METZ, M. R. aged 27 years September 1, 1887 by Rev. Johannes Heckel at the northwest corner of King and Line Streets. He a native of Germany and she of Charleston. He a storekeeper.

BEHRENS, JUSTINE W. F. aged 35 years married to SIEMSEN, CLAUS MATHIAS aged 21 years October 26, 1878 by Rev. Louis Muller at 31 Nassau Street. He a native of Schleswig-Holstein and she of Hanover. He a farmer.

BEHRMAN, SELIG aged 27 years married to SUDARSKY, SARA aged 22 years May 8, 1891 by Rabbi David Levy at the Hasell Street Synagogue.

BELDING, JASPER married to RELYEA, JANE B. March 22, 1879 by William B. Yates, Chaplain.

BELDING, J. C. aged 22 years married to SAWRASKEY, ANNIE aged 23 years May 1, 1881 by Rev. L. H. Shuck at 29 Nassau Street. He a native of St. Johns, New Brunswick and she of Charleston. He a porter.

BELITITZER, BLANCHE aged 25 years married to LEIDHOFF, HERMAN aged 41 years October 3, 1889 by Rabbi David Levy at 344 East Bay Street. He a native of Germany and she of Charleston. He a photographer.

BELITZER, FLORENCE A. aged 27 years married to ROSENSTEIN, JACOB aged 34 years June 30, 1892 by Rabbi David Levy at 344 East Bay Street. She a native of Kingstree, South Carolina. He a merchant.

BELL, A. W. aged 29 years married to SIGWALD, E. M. aged 28 years December 9, 1880 by Rev. W. S. Bowman at 55 Spring Street. He a native of Colleton County, South Carolina and she of Charleston. He a railroad conductor in Orangeburg, South Carolina.

BELL, CLARENCE EDWARD aged 26 years married to DeCOU, LIZZIE aged 22 years February 14, 1881 by Rev. Charles S. Vedder. He a native of Charleston and a clerk.

BELL, FANNIE aged 20 years married to PICKFORD, SAMUEL aged 24 years February 1, 1886 by Rev. C. E. Chichester at 46 Market Street.

BELL, STEPHEN R. aged 27 years married to TAVEL, ELIZABETH aged 25 years June 16, 1890 by Rev. Richard S. Trapier at St. Philip's Church. Both natives of Charleston. He a clerk.

BELLINGER, MARY R. married to TUPPER, HENRY February 3, 1891 by Rev. Richard S. Trapier at St. Michael's Church. Both natives of Charleston.

BELMAN, JESSIE married to CUMBEE, CLEMENT April 16, 1890 by Rev. R. N. Wells at Trinity Church.

BELTON, CARRIE aged 22 years married to DRUELLA, LEON aged 45 years September 29, 1884 by Rev. John Johnson. He a native of France and she of Charleston. He a tailor.

BELVIN, C. aged 17 years married to RODGERS, G. S. aged 23 years April 7, 1889 by Rev. H. B. Browne at 7 Stone Court. Both natives of Sumter, South Carolina. He a mill operator.

BENDICT, EMMA aged 20 years married to DENT, GEORGE aged 25 years February 2, 1886 by Rev. Louis Muller at 88 Society Street. Both natives of Savannah, Georgia. He a grocer in Savannah.

BENJAMIN, S. aged 29 years married to PINKUSSOHN (?), C. aged 20 years January 13, 1880 by Rabbi David Levy. He a native of Germany and she of Charleston. He a merchant.

BENKE, CLAUS R. aged 27 years married to SHRIVER, ALBERTINE aged 16 years August 10, 1893 by Rev. J. L. Shokes at 231 Coming Street. Both natives of Charleston. He a laborer.

BENKER, LOUISE GERTRUDE aged 25 years married to THOMPSON, GEORGE W. aged 55 years September 28, 1886 by Rev. H. B. Browne at 78 Drake Street. He a native of South Carolina and she of Charleston. He a farmer.

BENNETT, EMMA ISABELLE aged 21 years married to GODDARD, EDGAR M. aged 27 years December 23, 1886 by Father F. J. Shadler at 312 Meeting Street. He a native of Charleston and a physician.

BENNETT, JACKSON aged 21 years married to WHITE, MARY TERESA aged 18 years January 19, 1886 by Rev. H. B. Browne at 104 Nassau Street. Both natives of Charleston. He a mechanist.

BENNETT, JAMES aged 28 years married to MANSFIELD, ELLEN T. aged 23 years September 16, 1890 by Father J. J. Monaghan at St. Patrick's Roman Catholic Church. Both natives of Charleston. He a mariner.

BENNETT, JOSEPHINE GRIMBALL aged 42 years married to RIVERS, EDMUND BENNETT aged 36 years April 17, 1889 by Rev. Charles S. Vedder at 120 Beaufain Street. Both natives of Charleston. He works for the railroad.

BENNETT, JULIA married to SELDON, JOSEPH January 8, 1880 by Rev. A. Toomer Porter. She a native of Charleston. He a resident of Georgia.

BENNETT, J. R. married to BISSELL, MARY T. February 1, 1885 by Rev. William H. Campbell at St. Paul's Church.

BENNETT, LIZZIE aged 20 years married to ALDRET, JOSEPH S. aged 24 years October 23, 1883 by Father Daniel J. Quigley at The Cathedral of St. John the Baptist. Both natives of Charleston. He a pilot.

BENNETT, MARY M. aged 29 years married to KELLY, PATRICK C. aged 32 years May 2, 1888 by Father F. J. Shadler at St. Joseph's Roman Catholic Church. He a native of Dublin, Ireland and she of Charleston. He a bricklayer.

CHARLESTON SC MARRIAGES 1877-1895

BENNETT, MATTIE L. aged 23 years married to THOMPSON, CHARLES aged 27 years May 30, 1892 by Rev. John Johnson at 83 Church Street. He a native of New Jersey and she of Adams Run, South Carolina. He a ship carpenter.

BENNETT, M. E. aged 29 years married to CUTTER, H. F. aged 28 years August 3, 1882 by Rev. A. Coke Smith at 100 St. Philip Street. He a native of South Carolina and she of Bonneau, South Carolina. He an express agent.

BENNETT, S. MURRAY aged 27 years married to BAILEY, JULIA A. aged 21 years October 29, 1881 by Rev. C. C. Pinckney at 15 Hasell Street. Both natives of Charleston. He a merchant.

BENNETT, T. aged 21 years married to FASH, JESSIE aged 20 years February 15, 1886 by Father F. J. Shadler at St. Joseph's Roman Catholic Church. He a native of South Carolina and she of Charleston. He a laborer.

BENNETT, WILLIAM aged 22 years married to McGUINNES, ROSE E. aged 19 years September 25, 1891 by Rev. Robert Wilson at 4 Wragg Square. He a native of Charleston and she of Laurens County, South Carolina. He a wood turner.

BENSE, BERTHA aged 20 years married to DANIELS, G. R. aged 26 years December 12, 1880 by Rev. J. V. Welsh. Both natives of Charleston. Both reside in Columbia, South Carolina. He a carpenter.

BENSE, JOHN WILLIAM aged 24 years married to CARDO, MARY H. aged 18 years October 12, 1884 by Rev. R. A. Lapsley. Both natives of Charleston. He works for the railroad.

BENSE, M .A. aged 23 years married to BOLGER, A. Mc. aged 28 years November 9, 1880 by Rev. L. H. Shuck at 3 Cooper Street. Both natives of Charleston. He a sergeant of police.

BENSON, MAMIE aged 20 years married to THAMES, HENRY L. aged 22 years February 8, 1893 by Rev. G. L. Stokes at 476 Meeting Street. He a native of Columbus, Georgia and she of North Carolina. He a weaver in the cotton mill.

BENTLEY, WALTER aged 22 years married to CULP, ANNIE A. aged 19 years June 27, 1893 by Rev. Edmund Wells at 117 Drake Street.

BENTON, ANNE E. aged 19 years married to FLAGG, WILLIAM S. aged 19 years February 3, 1883 by Rev. J. V. Welsh at 24 Bee Street. Both natives of Charleston. He a laborer.

BENTSCHNER, SADIE A. aged 17 years married to ISRAEL, ISADORE aged 29 years April 3, 1894 by Rabbi David Levy. He a native of New York and she of Florence, South Carolina. He a merchant.

BENZ, (Mrs.) MARIE A. MAYER aged 40 years married to BEARDSLEY, ELBERT aged 44 years June 13, 1892 by Rev. J. A. Clifton at 207 Calhoun Street. He a native of Connecticut and she of Georgia. He a merchant in New York.

BEQUEST, JOHANN LUDWIG aged 35 years married to RIGBERS, CATHARINE MARGARETHE aged 25 years April 8, 1883 by Rev. Louis Muller at 8 Calhoun Street. Both natives of Germany. He a mariner.

BENTON, JOHN W. aged 21 years married to PULTZ, LAURA E. aged 18 years September 20, 1890 by Rev. J. Thomas Pate at 231 Coming Street. He a native of Laurens County, South Carolina and she of Charleston. He a clerk.

BERGEMANN, C. E. married to BOLGER, HENRY B. October 16, 1895 by Rev. William H. Campbell. He a clerk.

BERGEMAN, JUSTINE aged 22 years married to WALDEN, RUDOLPH aged 26 years January 30, 1878 by Father Harry P. Northrop at 94 St. Philip Street.

BERGMANN, MAGGIE aged 19 years married to BUTTS, ROBERT B. aged 21 years November 2, 1881 by Rev. L. H. Shuck at 27 Church Street. Both natives of Charleston. He an engineer.

BERRY, JAMES C. aged 23 years married to CARPENTER, MAGGIE E. aged 18 years June 4, 1895 by Rev. G. R. Brackett at 23 Mill Street. He a native of Marion County, South Carolina and she of Charleston. He a physician in Marion County, South Carolina.

BERRY, MARY ALICE aged 21 years married to JACKSON, ALFRED S. aged 19 years November 15, 1894 by Rev. Edmund Wells. He a native of Moncks Corner, South Carolina and she of Augusta, Georgia. He works in the cotton mill.

BESSINGER, HARRIET aged 21 years married to CRAFTS, JAMES D. aged 17 years August 3, 1884 by Rev. W. P. Mouzon. He a native of Orangeburg, South Carolina and she of Barnwell, South Carolina. He works in the cotton mill.

BESSINGER, HATTIE aged 24 years married to DUDLEY, JAMES aged 30 years July 24, 1887 by Rev. C. A. Stakeley. Both natives of South Carolina. He a laborer.

BESSINGER, HATTIE aged 20 years married to McCOY, JAMES aged 19 years April 15, 1884 by Rev. R. A. Lapsley at 22 Aiken Street.

BESSINGER, JANE aged 19 years married to SMITH, JABEZ aged 21 years July 22, 1883 by Rev. J. E. Beard at 14 Blake Street. He a native of Barnwell, South Carolina and she of Bamberg, South Carolina. He works in a factory.

BESSINGER, MARTHA aged 19 years married to DAVY, WILHELM aged 25 years July 12, 1883 by Rev. John E. Beard.

BETANCOURT, MARY aged 24 years married to ZOBEL, FREDERICK aged 26 years January 10, 1892 by Rev. Edward T. Horn in Smith Street. He a native of Helena, South Carolina and she of Columbia, South Carolina. He a clerk.

BETTISON, W. T. aged 46 years married to ANDERSON, IDA M. aged 22 years February 27, 1894 by Rev. Lucius Cuthbert at the First Baptist Church. He a native of Barnwell County, South Carolina and she of Charleston. He in the "cotton business."

BEVAN, DANIEL E. aged 24 years married to MAULL, IDA ISABELLA aged 19 years October 12, 1891 by Father J. J. Monaghan at 136 St. Philip Street. He a native of Ireland and she of Charleston. He a railroad brakeman.

BEVANS, A. J. married to GRUBER, A. C. November 25, 1879 by Rev. H. F. Chreitzberg at the residence of the Bride - 6 Blake Street. Both natives of Charleston. He an accountant.

BEVIN, LILA IDA aged 19 years married to SHACKLEFORD, HENRY DUBOIS aged 22 years June 10, 1879 by Rev. R. N. Wells. Both natives of Charleston. He a clerk.

BIBEL, ARTHUR W. married to HUGUELET, ROSALIE A. aged 24 years May 9, 1892 by Rev. Edward T. Horn. He a native of San Francisco, California and she of Charleston. He a watchmaker.

BICAISE, FLORENCE married to RIOLS, JOHN A. April 5, 1894 by Father Thomas F. Hopkins at St. Mary of the Annunciation Roman Catholic Church. He a clerk.

BICHLER, ELISE C. aged 16 years married to ELLIOTT, HENRY L. aged 30 years February 20, 1895 by Rev. Edward T. Horn at 31 Pitt Street. He a native of Winnsboro, South Carolina and she of Charleston. He an insurance agent.

BICKLEY, JOHN aged 27 years married to GETLEY, FANNIE MOORE aged 26 years April 9, 1890 by Bishop Harry P. Northrop at 48 Rutledge Avenue.

BICKLEY, JULIA R. married to BEE, JOSEPH F. June 17, 1891 by Rev. William H. Campbell.

BIEL, JOHN H. aged 19 years married to MEREE, IDA aged 16 years March 10, 1886 by Rev. H. B. Browne at 3 Lee Street. Both natives of Charleston. He a carpenter.

BIEL, MARY H. aged 19 years married to WOLFE, WILLIAM J. D. aged 23 years November 26, 1888 by Rev. T. P. Burgess at 7 Lee Street. Both natives of Charleston. He works for the railroad.

BIEMANN, HENRY D. aged 24 years married to RIEPPE, HELENE CATHARINA aged 19 years April 21, 1881 by Rev. Louis Muller at the northeast corner of George and St. Philip Streets. He a native of Walhalla, South Carolina and she of Charleston. He a merchant in Walhalla.

BIERFISCHER, HEINRICH E. aged 23 years married to FINCKENBERG, ANNA R. aged 24 years February 14, 1878 by Rev. William S. Bowman. He a native of Oldenburg, Germany and she of Hanover. He a grocer.

BILEY, SARAH LEONORA aged 21 years married to FOSTER, JOHN ERNEST aged 23 years January 29, 1878 by Rev. C. C. Pinckney at Grace Church. Both natives of Charleston. He a clerk.

BINGLY, A. Aged 24 years married to JONES, V. J. aged 24 years September 4, 1882 by Rev. J. M. Green at 27 Washington Street. He a native of Charleston and a carpenter.

BIRD, SALLIE M. aged 21 years married to MARSHALL, WILLIAM L. aged 22 years December 3, 1890 by Rev. G. R. Brackett at the 2nd Presbyterian Church. He a native of Charleston and she of Mountville, Laurens County, South Carolina. He a clerk.

BIRMINGHAM, W. aged 21 years married to PARDUE, MAGGIE aged 17 years December 11, 1894 by John Ahrens, Trial Justice. He a native of Wadesborough, South Carolina and she of Augusta, Georgia. He a weaver in the cotton mill.

BISAR (?), A. aged 31 years married to ALSINA, JOSEPHINE aged 24 years May 2, 1887 by Father P. J. Wilson at St. Mary of the Annunciation Roman Catholic Church.

BISCHOFF, A. M. S. aged 24 years married to HESSEMAN, JOHN H. aged 24 years June 16, 1887 by Rev. Johannes Heckel at the corner of Ann and Meeting Streets. Both natives of Charleston. He a merchant.

BISCHOFF, CATHERINE M. aged 21 years married to HEIDT, BEAUREGARD C. aged 30 years October 4, 1891 by Rev. Edward T. Horn. She a native of Charleston. He an engineer.

BISCHOFF, JULIE ANNA W. aged 26 years married to OETJEN, GUSTAV A. aged 28 years June 2, 1885 by Rev. Robert Wilson at the corner of Meeting and Ann Streets. Both natives of Charleston. He a druggist.

BISCHOFF, MARIE LOUISE aged 25 years married to BORNEMANN, WILLIAM G. aged 30 years November 10, 1881 by Rev. Louis Muller. He a native of Bremen, Germany and she of Charleston. He a cotton merchant.

BISCHOFF, W. B. aged 28 years married to MELCHERS, J. H. aged 20 years January 5, 1882 by Rev. Louis Muller. Both natives of Charleston. He a merchant.

BISSELL, CLAUDIA A. married to TRENHOLM, GEORGE M. November 17, 1881 by Rev. William H. Campbell. He a lawyer.

BISSELL, F. D. married to FASTIN, M. December 28, 1881 by Rev. L. H. Shuck at 27 Church Street. He a native of Maryland and she of Ireland. He a clerk.

BISSELL, LILLIE married to MARTIN, CLARK L. aged 42 years October 23, 1893 by Rev. David M. Ramsey at 2 Ashmead Place.

BISSELL, MARY T. married to BENNETT, J. R. February 1, 1885 by Rev. William H. Campbell at St. Paul's Church.

BISSELL, SALLIE H. married to KINLOCH, ROBERT H. November 22, 1893 by Rev. William H. Campbell. He resides in Montgomery, Alabama.

BISSELL, TITUS L. aged 30 years married to JENKINS, JUANITA H. aged 26 years June 14, 1892 by Rev. Edward T. Horn at St. Johannes Lutheran Church. Both natives of Charleston. He a merchant.

BIZE, JOHN D. aged 41 years married to CUBSTEDT, SARAH E. aged 23 years October 7, 1891 by Rev. Edwin C. Dargan at the Enston Homes. He a native of Charleston and a machinist.

BLACHS, JULIA aged 42 years married to MacALLEN, JAMES aged 54 years November 1, 1887 by Father P. J. McManus at St. Patrick's Roman Catholic Church. He a native of Ireland and she of Charleston. He a policeman.

BLACK, A. E. aged 24 years married to ORTIZ, ENRIQUE aged 26 years April 21, 1880 by Father Claudian B. Northrop at St. Mary of the Annunciation Roman Catholic Church. He a native of Madrid, Spain and she of Charleston. He the Vice-Consul for Spain.

BLACK, JAMES E. aged 21 years married to JONES, (Mrs.) GEORGIA A. TRAMMELL aged 22 years January 10, 1883 by Father F. A. Schmetz at St. Patrick's Roman Catholic Church. He a native of Ireland and she of Columbus, Georgia. He a railroad brakeman.

BLACK, MAMIE aged 20 years married to STAUBER, ADAM aged 29 years September 15, 1895 by Rev. Alfred Freyschmidt at 45 State Street. He a native of Germany and she of Savannah, Georgia. He a baker.

BLACK, MINNIE BELLE aged 22 years married to HYDE, TRISTAN T. aged 24 years April 28, 1886 by Rev. A. J. S. Toomer at the First Baptist Church. Both natives of Charleston. He a broker.

BLACK, PATRICK aged 29 years married to CAHILL, SARAH aged 22 years January 21, 1891 by Father J. J. Monaghan at St. Patrick's Roman Catholic Church. He a native of Ireland and she of Charleston. He a railroad conductor.

BLACK, PATRICK aged 29 years married to WEBB, MARY E. aged 24 years December 19, 1894 by Rev. G. R. Brackett at 12 Friend Street. He a native of New York and she of Charleston. He a clerk.

BLACK, P. aged 26 years married to WEST, JAMES H. aged 26 years July 6, 1880 by Rev. J. V. Welsh at 64 Radcliffe Street. He a native of Philadelphia, Pennsylvania and she of Charleston. He a clerk.

BLACKMAN, LIZZIE MOORE aged 21 years married to GALPHIN, GEORGE D. aged 23 years July 28, 1885 by Rev. G. R. Brackett. He a native of Florida and she of South Carolina. He works for the railroad.

BLACKWELL, SAMUEL aged 46 years married to STROHECKER, AMANDA December 15, 1881 by Rev. Edward T. Horn at St. Johannes Lutheran Church. He a native of Darlington County, South Carolina and she of Charleston. He a physician in Darlington.

BLAKE, MARGARET S. aged 19 years married to VAUGHN, JOHN J. aged 25 years January 26, 1887 by Father Daniel J. Quigley at St. Patrick's Roman Catholic Church. Both natives of Charleston. He a grocer.

BLAKE, MARY G. aged 26 years married to WILLIAMS, FREDERICK L. aged 28 years September 25, 1889 by Father W. J. Quigley at St. Patrick's Roman Catholic Church. He a native of Canada and she of Charleston. He an electrician.

BLAKE, WILLIAM aged 29 years married to PRENTISS, H. aged 38 years March 25, 1883 by Rev. J. V. Welsh at 24 Bee Street. He a native of London, England and she of Colleton County, South Carolina. He a laborer.

BLAKE, KATIE married to REDMOND, STEPHEN aged 32 years August 7, 1893 by Father J. J. Monaghan.

BLAKE, M. F. aged 18 years married to ORTMANN, T. M. aged 18 years June 25, 1882 by Rev. L. H. Shuck. She a native of New York. He a clerk.

BLAKE, WILLIAM aged 38 years married to PRENTISS, H. aged 29 years June 22, 1884 by Rev. John E. Beard at 3 Reid Street. He a native of London, England and she of Colleton County, South Carolina. He a laborer.

BLAKELY, ANNA aged 35 years married to KILGUS, FRIEDRICH aged 39 years August 10, 1884 by Rev. Louis Muller at St. Matthew's's Lutheran Church. He a native of Georgia and she of Charleston. He a laborer.

BLANCHARD, JEFFERSON aged 24 years married to BLANCHARD, M. R. aged 19 years January 13, 1881 by Rev. Sidi H. Browne in Meeting Street. He a native of Georgia and she of Charleston. He a railroad conductor.

BLANCHARD, M. R. aged 19 years married to BLANCHARD, JEFFERSON aged 24 years January 13, 1881 by Rev. Sidi H. Browne in Meeting Street. He a native of Georgia and she of Charleston. He a railroad conductor.

BLANCHARD, WILLIAM R. aged 30 years married to SEABROOK, H. H. aged 22 years November 3, 1880 by Rev. John Johnson at St. Philip's Church. Both natives of Columbus, Georgia. He a merchant.

BLANCHE, JOHN aged 53 years married to ADDICKS, ELIZABETH aged 40 years April 28, 1895 by Father J. J. Monaghan at St. Patrick's Roman Catholic Church. He a native of Ireland and she of Beaufort County, South Carolina. He an engineer.

BLANCHE, MATTHEW F. aged 20 years married to CULLINANE, JOHANNA B. aged 20 years May 21, 1894 by Father J. J. Monaghan at St. Patrick's Roman Catholic Church. He a native of York, South Carolina and she of Charleston. He laborer.

BLANCHE, W. JAMES aged 35 years married to KELLY, (Mrs.) A. GERTRUDE SMART October 6, 1889 by Rev. H. B. Browne at 25 Amherst Street. He a native of South Carolina and she of Charleston. He a millwright.

BLAND, ELVIRA aged 20 years married to SALVO, ANTONIO aged 25 years July 7, 1881 by Father Harry P. Northrop. He a native of Charleston and a railroad worker.

BLANK, ISADORE aged 23 years married to ELIAS, BELLE aged 23 years March 10, 1886 by Rabbi David Levy at the Hasell Street Synagogue. Both natives of Charleston. He a merchant.

BLASIACH, ELIZABETH aged 223 years married to FLUGG, SAMUEL aged 24 years December 4, 1890 by Rev. Robert O. Wilson at 4 Wragg Square. He a native of Charleston and she of Greenville, South Carolina. He works for the railroad.

BLISCH, T. aged 25 years married to CUMMINS, M. aged 22 years September 17, 1882 by Father Daniel J. Quigley at The Cathedral of St. John the Baptist. Both natives of South Carolina. He a merchant.

BLITCHINGTON, LOUIS BELLINGER aged 21 years married to BRICKMAN, SUSAN MARGARET aged 17 years April 25, 1883 by Rev. E. J. Meynardie in Hanover Street. Both natives of Charleston. He an engineer.

BLOCK, JOHANNA MARIA SOPHIA aged 24 years married to STELLO, KARL CHRISTIAN aged 26 years January 30, 1883 by Rev. Louis Muller at 76 Spring Street. He a native of Prussia and she of Charleston. He a grocer.

BLOCKER, J. D. aged 22 years married to BAILEY, MARGARET aged 20 years March 11, 1891 by Rev. J. Thomas Pate at 231 Coming Street. Both natives of Colleton County, South Carolina. He works for the railroad in Summerville, South Carolina.

BLOCKER, FRANKLIN O. aged 21 years married to LILLY, ELLA LENORA aged 22 years September 12, 1888 by Rev. T. P. Burgess at 91 Nassau Street. He a native of Newville, South Carolina and she of Grenada, Mississippi. He works for the railroad.

BLOCKER, WILLIAM R. T. aged 25 years married to O'BRIEN, ELLA A. aged 20 years May 29, 1895 by Rev. J. L. Stokes at 231 Coming Street. He a native of Savannah, Georgia and she of Charleston. He works for the railroad.

BLODGET, EBER aged 34 years married to LONGNICK (?), B. C. aged 20 years April 21, 1881 by Rev. Edward T. Horn at St. Johannes Church. He a native of Akron, Ohio and she of Charleston. He a merchant.

BLOHME, ANNA EMILY aged 21 years married to LILIENTHAL, JOHN FREDERICK November 15, 1877 by Rev. Louis Muller at the residence of the Bridegroom - Beaufain Street near Archdale Street. He a native of Germany and she of Charleston. He a carpenter.

BLOHM E, HENRIETTA D. aged 18 years married to KOSTER, JULIUS D. aged 24 years October 1, 1885 by Rev. Louis Muller at 4 Glebe Street. He a native of Brooklyn, New York and she of Charleston. He a clerk.

BLOOD, EVERETT aged 29 years married to BAILEY, JULIA aged 28 years December 4, 1889 by Rev. Robert Wilson at 74 Drake Street. He a native of Massachusetts and she of Edisto Island, South Carolina. He a superintendent at the phosphate mill.

BLOTH, EMMA E. aged 23 years married to BULWINKLE, H. aged 29 years January 13, 1887 by Rev. Louis Muller. Both natives of Charleston. He a farmer.

BLUME, C. DOWLING aged 29 years married to COLLINS, SUSANNA WESLEY aged 21 years July 7, 1878 by Rev. C. Power at 77 St. Philip Street. He a native of Barnwell, South Carolina and she of Beaufort, South Carolina. He a farmer in Orangeburg, South Carolina.

BLUME, (Mrs.) SUSANNA WESLEY COLLINS aged 27 years married to ANGEL, ISAAC W. aged 51 years April 17, 1884 by Rev. J. Mercier Green at 4 Bay Street. He a native of Charleston and she of South Carolina. He a physician.

BOATWRIGHT, LULA married to MERKHARDT (?), DAVID October 3, 1889 by N. L. P. Bolger, Trial Justice. He a native of Cambridge, New York and she of Augusta, Georgia. He a weaver in the cotton mill.

BOCH (Mrs.) DORETHA M. DURMANN aged 36 years married to PAUL, HEINRICH PETER aged 37 years March 9, 1879 by Rev. Johannes Heckel in East Bay Street. He a native of Sweden and she of Nordhobz. He a carpenter.

BODE, HENRIETTA aged 19 years married to SCHILLING, ALEXANDER M. aged 26 years June 17, 1886 by Rev. C. E. Chichester at 390 Meeting Street. Both natives of Charleston. He works for the railroad.

BODIE, HENRY D. aged 20 years married to CULLINANE, KATE L. aged 20 years September 22, 1889 by Father Daniel J. Quigley at 390 Meeting Street. Both natives of Charleston. He a railroad brakeman.

BOESCH, JOHN CASPAR aged 28 years married to ROHDE, ANNA HEDWIG aged 25 years January 22, 1878 by Rev. Louis Muller at M. C. Amme's bakery in King Street. He a native of Charleston and she of Germany. He a coppersmith.

BOETTE, CARL aged 24 years married to SCHUTTE, AUGUSTA W. H. aged 21 years October 2, 1891 by Rev. Louis Muller at the corner of Pitt and Montagu Streets. Both natives of Prussia. He a grocer.

BOFILE, MIGUEL aged 23 years married to LEVY, MARY B. aged 22 years April 17, 1895 by Charles W. Swinton, Circuit Court Judge. He a native of Puerto Rico and she of Charleston. He a clerk.

BOGART, IRENE married to DECKER, JOSEPH AUSTIN January 15, 1891 by Rev. Richard S. Trapier at 39 Meeting Street. He a native of Charleston and she of New York. He resides in Summerville, South Carolina.

BOGLE, ADELAIDE aged 37 years married to BECKETT, JAMES L. aged 48 years March 27, 1884 by Rev. C. C. Pinckney at St. Luke's Church. He a native of Charleston and she of Maryland. He a physician.

BOHLEN, FREDERICK C. aged 39 years married to SMITH, SARAH R. aged 31 years January 1, 1893 by Rev. J. C. Yongue at 44 Aiken Street. He a native of Bremen, Germany and she of Berkeley County, South Carolina. He a clerk.

BOHLEN, MATILDA CATHARINE MARGARET aged 18 years married to DOSCHER, AUGUST FREDERICK aged 25 years January 4, 1883 by Rev. Louis Muller at the corner of Beaufain and Coming Streets.

BOHLOCHS, J. H. C. married to MEYER, ANN M. January 28, 1879 by Rev. Louis Muller in Radcliffe Street. He a native of Hanover and she of Charleston. He a grocer.

BOINEST, CLARENCE L. aged 24 years married to BRANDT, EUGENIA F. aged 23 years September 1, 1891 by Rev. R. A. Webb at 15 Doughty Street. Both natives of Charleston. He a merchant in Florence, South Carolina.

BOKSEN, M. G. H. aged 32 years married to KOOPMAN, G. F. A. aged 27 years January 13, 1885 by Rev. Louis Muller in King Street near Broad Street. He a native of Charleston and she of Germany. He a farmer.

BOLCHOZ, ERNESTINE M. aged 16 years married to JOHNSON, THOMAS E. aged 19 years May 17, 1893 by Rev. Edwin C. Dargan at 475 Meeting Street. Both natives of Charleston. He a blacksmith.

BOLCHOZ, MAMIE L. aged 18 years married to SCHRAGE, JOHN F. aged 20 years December 18, 1895 by Father J. J. Monaghan at 497 Meeting Street. Both natives of Charleston. He a machinist.

BOLCHOZ, MARIE L. aged 17 years married to PRIESTER, JOHN B. aged 22 years November 5, 1894 by Father J. J. Monaghan at 499 Meeting Street. Both natives of Charleston. He a printer.

BOLDT, CARL L. J. aged 29 years married to OETJEN, JEANNETTE C. aged 23 years February 17, 1891 by Rev. Louis Muller at St. Johannes Lutheran Church. He a native of Prussia and she of Charleston. He a clergyman.

BOLDT, DORA E. aged 17 years married to HUNTER, FRANK JOSHUA aged 18 years September 23, 1883 by Rev. John O. Wilson at 82 Wentworth Street. Both natives of Charleston. He a bookkeeper.

BOLGER, A. Mc. aged 28 years married to BENSE, M. A. aged 23 years November 9, 1880 by Rev. L. H. Shuck at 3 Cooper Court. Both natives of Charleston. He a sergeant of police.

BOLGER, ELLA EDITH married to BARNETT, JOHN B. April 27, 1881 by Rev. William H. Campbell at the residence of Mr. H. Bolger.

BOLGER, HENRY B. married to BERGEMANN, C. E. October 16, 1895 by Rev. William H. Campbell.

BOLGER, JOHN aged 40 years married to SCOTT, MARY A. aged 28 years January 12, 1891 by Rev. M. S. Walkins at the 2nd Adventist Church. He a native of Edinborough, Scotland and she of Augusta, Georgia. He works in the cotton mill.

BOLGER, WILLIAM W. married to Baker, ELLA E. July 8, 1885 by Father J. J. Woolahan at St. Mary of the Annunciation Roman Catholic Church. Both natives of Charleston. He a laborer.

BOLLMANN, ANNIE aged 25 years married to PLENGE, EDWARD aged 25 years November 15, 1885 by Rev. Louis Muller at 33 Charlotte Street. Both natives of Charleston. He a merchant.

BOLLO, J. aged 23 years married to GALLEY, M. aged 17 years March 9, 1882 by Rev. L. H. Shuck at 27 Church Street. Both natives of Charleston. He a laborer.

BOLTON, L. aged 24 years married to DuBOSE, L. L. aged 22 years December 23, 1893 by Rev. J. C. Yongue. He a native of South Carolina and she of Charleston. He works in the cotton mill.

BOMBACH (?), (Mrs.) EMMA L. B. HERMANN aged 50 years married to OELRICH, JOHANN CARL aged 64 years August 4, 1886 by Rev. Louis Muller at 179 Meeting Street. Both natives of Germany. He an organ builder.

BOND, JAMES P. aged 22 years married to SHOMA, (Mrs.) EMMA C. BLAXMAN aged 23 years April 27, 1887 by Rev. John O. Wilson. He a native of South Carolina and she of Chicago, Illinois. He a physician.

BOND, STANLEY E. married to MYER, CAROLINE A. March 17, 1886 by Rev. J. V. Welch at 57 Cannon Street. He a native of Richmond, Virginia and she of Charleston. He a blacksmith.

BONDS, (Mrs.) JOHANNA ADELINE MARGARET LILIENTHAL aged 17 years married to SONNICHSEN, BOYD aged 26 years May 16, 1887 by Rev. Louis Muller at 96 Radcliffe Street. He a native of Germany and she of Charleston. He a farmer.

BONNEAU, CATHERINE J. aged 20 years married to HOLMES, FELIX WARLEY aged 25 years November 25, 1877 by Rev. Louis Muller at the South Carolina Hall. Both natives of Charleston.

BONNELL, ELIZABETH married to SCHIRMER, CHARLES C. October 2, 1884 by Rev. W. T. Thompson in Church Street.

BONSON, J. W. aged 25 years married to PRAUSE (?), F. S. aged 18 years September 7, 1882 by Rev. Luther K. Probst. Both natives of South Carolina. He a clerk.

BOOR, HELENA WILHELMINA DORETHA aged 23 years married to LUNDEN, JOHN WILLIAM aged 42 years November 25, 1877 by Rev. Louis Muller.

BOOZER, SIMON P. aged 24 years married to RICHMOND, LIZZIE B. aged 23 years February 17, 1886 by Rev. A. Hirschmeyer at 54 Society Street. He a native of South Carolina and she of Charleston. He works for the railroad.

BORINER, WILSON B. aged 49 years married to WILLIS, (Mrs.) SARAH E. MIDDLETON aged 44 years March 18, 1891 by Rev. R. C. Holland at 59 Tradd Street. Both natives of Charleston. He a builder.

BORNEMANN, JAMES SAMUEL aged 29 years married to MARTIN, MAGGIE aged 17 years December 2, 1894 by Rev. J. C. Yongue. He a native of Charleston and she of South Carolina. He a clerk.

BORNEMANN, J. HENRY aged 27 years married to OFFERMAN, DORA R. aged 24 years March 23, 1880 by Rev. Johannes Heckel at the residence of B. Webb - the corner of Church and Cumberland Streets. Both natives of Lindshedt, Hanover. He a merchant.

BORNEMANN, WILLIAM G. aged 30 years married to BISCHOFF, MARIE LOUSIE aged 25 years June 18, 1878 by Rev. Louis Muller. He a native of Bremen, Germany and she of Charleston. He a cotton merchant in Savannah, Georgia.

BORUER, JULIANNA F. aged 22 years married to HUNCHEN, GEORGE aged 26 years October 20, 1892 by Rev. Edward T. Horn at St. Johannes Lutheran Church. Both natives of Charleston. He a clerk.

BOSCH, JOHANNA C. M. aged 19 years married to DOSCHER, AUGUST aged 28 years June 15, 1892 by Rev. Louis Muller at the corner of Coming and Morris Streets. He a native of Prussia and she of Charleston. He a grocer.

BOSCH, J. A. aged 34 years married to CORDES, C. R. October 7, 1879 by Rev. Louis Muller at the corner of Marsh and Inspection Streets. Both natives of Charleston. He a merchant.

BOSWICK, C. O. aged 16 years married to SMITH, C. A. aged 16 years August 15, 1882 by Rev. J. V. Welsh at 12 Bogard Street. He a native of Charleston and a fireman.

BOTH (Mrs.), ANNA THERESE aged 34 years married to JAHNTZ (?), CARL GUSTAV aged 32 years July 12, 1889 by Rev. Louis Muller at St. Matthew's Lutheran Church.

BOTTYER (?), BECHA aged 27 years married to PUCKHABER, GEORGE aged 27 years October 22, 1893 by Rev. K. Boldt in Thomas Street. Both natives of Germany. He a merchant.

BOURU (?), ISAAC BROOKS aged 23 years married to FASH, AMY B. aged 20 years August 21, 1884 by Rev. J. O. Willson at 293 East Bay Street. He a native of Laurens County, South Carolina and she of Charleston. He works for the railroad.

BOWEN, ANNIE F. aged 22 years married to KENNEDY, JOHN D. aged 29 years May 18, 1883 by Father P. L. Duffy at The Cathedral of St. John the Baptist. Both natives of Charleston. He a printer.

BOWEN, BRIDGET E. married to O'CONNOR, THOMAS JOSEPH September 26, 1886 by Father P. J. Wilson at St. Mary of the Annunciation Roman Catholic Church. She a native of Charleston. He a blacksmith.

BOWEN, FRANCES E. aged 20 years married to WALLACE, EDWARD B. aged 20 years December 28, 1890 by Rev. G. R. Brackett at 40 Mary Street. He a native of Darlington County, South Carolina and she of Charleston. He a clerk in Savannah, Georgia.

BOWEN, (Mrs.) MARY RICHARDSON MOSES aged 23 years married to TAFT, WILLIAM NELSON aged 33 years August 2, 1881 by Rev. C. C. Pinckney at Grace Church. She a native of Sumter, South Carolina. He a postmaster.

BOWEN, M. aged 32 years married to MURTIN, ELIZA E. aged 22 years February 9, 1890 by Rev. R. D. Smart at Bethel Church. Both natives of Charleston. He a blacksmith.

BOWEY, ELIZABETH aged 21 years married to BUCKHEISTER, BENJAMIN A. aged 23 years November 30, 1892 by Rev. N. K. Smith at 544 Meeting Street. · He a native of Charleston and she of Plymouth, England. He a car driver.

BOWEY, FENWICK aged 20 years married to MEYERS, CHRISTINA aged 18 years October 11, 1895 by Rev. J. M. Steadman. He a native of England and she of Charleston. He an engineer.

BOWEY, MARGARET ANN aged 29 years married to SCADY, FREDERICK W. H. aged 26 years December 3, 1892 by Rev. N. K. Smith at 511 Meeting Street. He a native of Copenhagen, Denmark and she of New Castle on Tyne, England. He a steward on a boat.

BOWICK, EMMA S. aged 15 years married to SHAFER, ROBERT E. L. aged 23 years January 12, 1888 by Rev. H. B. Browne.

BOWICK, HENRY A. aged 21 years married to HASQUEDT (?), MARY aged 22 years November 22, 1894 by Rev. A. Freyschmidt at 2 Ashe street. He a native of Charleston and she of Germany. He a workman.

BOWICK, JAMES W. aged 22 years married to MEYERS, N. S. D. aged 18 years September 3, 1891 by Rev. T. P. Burgess at 38 Percy Street. He a native of Georgetown, South Carolina and she of Charleston. He a painter.

BOWICK, (Mrs.) M. B. WARNOCK aged 60 years married to SEXTON, A. M. aged 60 years July 23, 1879 by Rev. H. F. Chreitzberg at 63 America Street. He a native of Colleton County, South Carolina and she of Spartanburg, South Carolina. He a watchmaker.

BOWICK, OSCAR C. aged 19 years married to JACKSON, CARRIE J. aged 16 years July 29, 1894 by Rev. Edmund Wells at 84 America Street. Both natives of Charleston. He works in the cotton mill.

BOWICK, TRAVIS aged 18 years married to WALDEN, KATE aged 24 years May 23, 1886 by Rev. J. W. Dickson at 20 Blake Street. He a native of Charleston and she of South Carolina. He a laborer.

BOWMAN, KATIE aged 18 years married to ISEMAN, ISAAC aged 20 years September 7, 1892 by Rabbi David Levy. He a native of Charleston and she of Beaufort, South Carolina. He a clerk.

BOWMAN, SAUL aged 24 years married to ZELLER, (Mrs.) HANNAH SILVERSTEIN aged 22 years November 4, 1888 by Rabbi David Levy at 77 Wentworth Street. Both natives of Charleston. He a merchant.

BOYCE, ELIZABETH L. V. aged 20 years married to TURNER, LOUIS W. aged 22 years November 29, 1892 by Rev. J. L. Stokes at 22 Bogard Street. Both natives of Charleston. He a machinist.

BOYD, AMELIA aged 16 years married to WOTTON, CHARLES aged 20 years October 24, 1878 by Rev. I. S. Chambliss at the residence of the Bride's mother. Both natives of Charleston. He a farmer in Hamburg, South Carolina.

BOYD, ANNIE aged 16 years married to RICHON, A. C. aged 26 years May 17, 1883 by Rev. J. A. Clifton at 32 Columbus Street. Both natives of Charleston. He a clerk.

BOYD, JOHN married to O'BRIEN, M. February 20, 1889 by Father J. J. Wedenfeller at St. Joseph's Roman Catholic Church. He a native of Ireland and she of Augusta, Georgia. He a merchant.

BOYLE, ELLEN aged 21 years married to ALPHONSE, C. J. aged 22 years June 10, 1883 by Father F. A. Schmetz at St. Patrick's Roman Catholic Church. He a native of Charleston and she of New York. He an engineer.

BOYLE, ETTA L. aged 24 years married to HAWTHORNE, BENJAMIN M. aged 28 years November 13, 1893 by Rev. G. R. Brackett at 494 Meeting Street.

BOYLE, (BOYE) JEROME married to HURT, LIZZIE April 30, 1880 by William B. Yates, Chaplain.

BOYLE, MARTHA D. aged 21 years married to GALE, THOMAS J. C. aged 21 years December 28, 1893 by Rev. G. R. Brackett at 494 Meeting Street. He a native of London, England and she of Charleston. He an electrical engineer.

BOYLE, MARGARET JULIA aged 26 years married to VERONEE, EDWARD D. aged 26 years December 9, 1885 by Rev. G. R. Brackett. Both natives of Charleston. He a mechanic.

BRADLEY, IDA CLAYTON aged 22 years married to LEBBY, ROBERT CHARLTON aged 24 years April 9, 1890 by Rev. G. R. Brackett at 17 Smith Street. He a native of Gordonston, Virginia and she of Charleston. He a traveling salesman.

BRADLEY, WILLIAM A. aged 23 years married to SKIVINGTON, FANNIE R. aged 19 years April 3, 1883 by Rev. Luther K. Probst. He a native of Huntingdon County, Pennsylvania and she of Bloomfield, Tennessee. He a manufacturer.

BRADSHAW, M. E. aged 24 years married to DUBOSE, H. L. aged 29 years October 16, 1881 by Father J. E. Chapins at 51 Spring Street. He a native of Williamsburg County, South Carolina and she of Charleston. He an engineer.

BRADY, ELLEN R. aged 19 years married to DUUNE, PATRICK F. February 25, 1878 by Father C. J. Croghan. He a native of Augusta, Georgia and she of Charleston. He a telegraph worker in Augusta.

BRAID, ROBERT S. aged 36 years married to CANTY, SUSAN M. aged 31 years October 16, 1890 by Rev. R. C. Holland at Rickesville, Charleston County, South Carolina. He a native of Charleston and she of Colleton County, South Carolina. He an engineer.

BRAILSFORD, (Mrs.) JULIA SARAH WILSON aged 47 years married to KNOX, JOHN aged 53 years April 18, 1878 by Rev. G. R. Brackett. He a native of Ireland and she of Charleston. He a salesman.

BRANCH, E. A. married to HERBERT, C. D. October 8, 1879 by William B. Yates, Chaplain.

BRANDFORD, SARAH JANE aged 30 years married to Baker, JOHN RUSSELL aged 55 years April 3, 1878 by Rev. L. H. Shuck at the First Baptist Church. Both natives of Charleston. He a druggist/apothecary.

BRANDT, ADELINE C. aged 24 years married to PUCKHABER, WILLIAM H. aged 31 years October 29, 1891 by Rev. Louis Muller at 466 King Street. He a native of Charleston and she of Walhalla, South Carolina. He a baker.

BRANDT, ANN AMELIA aged 26 years married to BRANDT, EDWARD PIERRE aged 23 years April 18, 1878 by Rev. William Bower. Both natives of Charleston. He a mechanic.

BRANDT, ANNA PAULINE aged 20 years married to KULMINSKI, ALBERT JULIUS aged 24 years February 10, 1881 by Rev. Claudian B. Northrop. He a native of Washington, D. C. and she of Charleston. He a merchant.

BRANDT, EDWARD P. aged 30 years married to DUFFY, LIZZIE aged 19 years September 24, 1885 by Rev. John O. Wilson at 82 Wentworth Street.

BRANDT, EDWARD PIERRE aged 23 years married to BRANDT, ANN AMELIA aged 26 years April 18, 1878 by Rev. William Bower. Both natives of Charleston. He a mechanic.

BRANDT, EUGENIA F. aged 23 years married to BOINEST, CLARENCE L. aged 24 years September 1, 1891 by Rev. R. A. Webb at 15 Doughty Street. Both natives of Charleston. He a merchant in Florence, South Carolina.

BRANDT, JOHN HENRY CARL aged 25 years married to BULWINKLE, LENA MARIA WILHELMINA aged 21 years November 6, 1881 by Rev. Louis Muller at Brandt's Farm near the Race Course. Both natives of Charleston. He a farmer.

BRANDT, JULIAN V. aged 37 years married to MUSTARD, (Mrs.) ROSALIE SOUBEYROUX aged 28 years September 29, 1885 by Father J. J. Woolahan at St. Mary of the Annunciation Roman Catholic Church. Both natives of Charleston. He an accountant.

BRANFORD, EDWARDINA aged 51 years married to WATTS, JOHN N. aged 58 years August 21, 1890 by Rev. R. M. Lide at 62 Line Street. He a native of Manchester, Virginia and she of Charleston. He a blacksmith.

BRANFORD, SARAH JOHANNA aged 30 years married to Baker, JOHN RUSSELL aged 55 years April 3, 1878 by Rev. L. H. Shuck at 4 Water Street. He a native of Charleston and a clerk.

BRANFORD, SUSAN E. aged 30 years married to FREEMAN, RICHARD H. aged 35 years July 18, 1883 by Rev. J. A. Clifton at 26 Line Street. He a native of Charleston and a clerk.

BRANIGAN, EDWARD G. aged 30 years married to SELBY, (Mrs.) LILLIE ANN TAYLOR aged 23 years February 15, 1885 by Rev. John O. Wilson at 82 Wentworth Street. He a native of Pennsylvania and she of Zanesville, Ohio. He works at the cotton mill.

BRANNON, JOHN aged 25 years married to SUTTON, EMMA LEE aged 19 years July 17, 1884 by Rev. W. P. Mouzon. He a native of Ireland and she of Augusta, Georgia. He a painter.

BRASELL, JOHN aged 19 years married to SANDERS, JULIA aged 22 years July 16, 1886 by Rev. J. Walter Dickson at 203 Line Street. He a native of Charleston and she of Sullivans Island, South Carolina.

BRASELL, JOHN A. aged 28 years married to BURGESS, MAMIE EMMA aged 18 years August 27, 1894 by Rev. L. A. Groves at 14 Cramers Court. He a native of Berkeley County, South Carolina and she of Manning, South Carolina. He a laborer.

BRASSEN, HENRY aged 28 years married to MARRIE, ALICE aged 27 years December 26, 1880 by Rev. L. H. Shuck at 27 Church Street. Both natives of Charleston. He a carpenter.

BRAUER, MARY ANN aged 30 years married to LEWIS, THOMAS aged 41 years January 20, 1887 by Father Daniel J. Quigley at St. Patrick's Roman Catholic Church. He a native of Greece and she of Charleston. He a janitor.

BRAWLEY, LAURA aged 16 years married to KROSSE (KROOMSE), JOHN aged 26 years December 11, 1881 by Rev. L. H. Shuck. Both natives of Charleston. He a miner.

BRAZZEL, RICHARD aged 32 years married to SANDERS, (Mrs.) HARRIET HENRIETTA DANAMORE aged 36 years February 26, 1890 by Father F. J. Shadler at 7 Line Street. He a native of Fairfield County, South Carolina and she of Walterboro, South Carolina. He a laborer.

BRECKENRIDGE, M. JAMES aged 28 years married to STUART, EMMA aged 21 years February 26, 1890 by Rev. Edwin C. Dargan at 36 George Street. He a native of Walhalla, South Carolina and she of Kingstree, South Carolina. He a printer.

BREDEMAN, AUGUST W. aged 30 years married to SOHREN, VERONICA aged 32 years January 3, 1895 by Father Daniel J. Quigley at St. Patrick's Roman Catholic Church. He a native of Charleston and she of Germany. He a salesman.

BREDENBERG, JOHN H. aged 28 years married to KLENKE, JULIA D. aged 23 years January 6, 1887 by Rev. D. M. Martens at St. Johannes Lutheran Church. He a native of Augusta, Georgia and she of Charleston. He a merchant.

BREEDLOVE, WILLIAM R. aged 26 years married to RUDD, (Mrs.) ELIZABETH SEABROOK aged 29 years July 9, 1891 by Rev. W. A. Betts at 21 Allway Street. He a native of Richland County, South Carolina and she of st. Johns, Berkeley County, South Carolina. He a wharf builder.

BRELAND, MARY VICTORIA aged 19 years married to SHANAHAN, CHARLES F. aged 22 years October 7, 1888 by Rev. R. D. Smart at Bethel Church. He a native of Charleston and she of Berkeley County, South Carolina. He a railroad engineer.

BREMER, ANNA aged 28 years married to BRUNINGS, J. H. aged 34 years September 14, 1879 by Rev. Louis Muller at the corner of King and Tradd Streets. Both natives of Hanover. He a joiner.

BREMERMANN, SUSIE aged 24 years married to GREGG, WILLIAM aged 26 years April 5, 1893 by Father J. J. Monaghan. He a native of South Carolina and she of Germany. He works in the cotton mill.

BRESSELEAU, N. E. aged 18 years married to BECKER, F. W. aged 26 years June 15, 1879 by Father John P. Twigg at The Cathedral of St. John the Baptist. Both natives of Charleston. He a clerk.

BREWER, (Mrs.) M. AYER aged 31 years married to CADDIN, THOMAS E. aged 32 years July 9, 1879. Both natives of St. Paul, South Carolina. He a laborer.

BRICKMAN, BERNARD W. aged 23 years married to PATTERSON, BEULAH F. aged 18 years August 8, 1895 by Rev. Robert Wilson at 72 Drake Street. Both natives of Charleston. He works for the railroad.

BRICKMAN, HENRY C. aged 20 years married to PRIESTER, DORA HENRIETTA aged 16 years April 24, 1884 by Rev. John E. Beard. Both natives of Barnwell County, South Carolina. He works for the railroad.

BRICKMAN, MARY ELIZA aged 16 years married to SMITH, THEODORE aged 23 years June 10, 1884 by Rev. J. H. Tillinghast at 223 Meeting Street. He a native of Charleston and she of Augusta, Georgia. He a plumber.

BRICKMAN, (Mrs.) MARY Meynardie aged 46 years married to WESTENDORF, CHARLES H. aged 40 years August 4, 1887 by Rev. H. B. Browne. Both natives of Charleston. He a policeman.

BRICKMAN, SUSAN MARGARET aged 17 years married to BLITCHINGTON, LOUIS BELLINGER aged 21 years April 25, 1883 by Rev. E. J. Meynardie in Hanover Street. Both natives of Charleston. He an engineer.

BRIGGS, ABRAM J. aged 37 years married to WHILDEN, HATTIE J. aged 23 years November 30, 1887 by Rev. G. R. Brackett. He a native of Summerton, South Carolina and she of Sumter, South Carolina. He a physician in Summerton.

BRIGGS, CHRISTOPHER C. aged 34 years married to ARCHER, ELIZABETH aged 34 years August 28, 1884 by Rev. James H. Hall. He a native of Canada and she of Ireland. He an expressman.

BRIGMAN, MAGGIE M. aged 15 years married to RIGGS, CORNELIUS T. aged 17 years September 5, 1893 by Rev. J. O. Yongue at 22.5 Sheppard Street. He a native of Jedburg, South Carolina and she of Edgefield, South Carolina. He works in the cotton factory.

BRIGMON, MARGARET J. aged 16 years married to EDGAR, JOSEPH F. aged 20 years October 15, 1893 by Rev. J. C. Yongue at 121 Drake Street. He a native of Charleston and she of Camden, South Carolina. He works in the cotton mill.

BRILLANCEAU, (Mrs.) EUGENIA GUILLEMAN aged 41 years married to RUGIERO, RAPHAEL aged 48 years January 21, 1883 by Father P. L. Duffy at The Cathedral of St. John the Baptist. He a native of Naples, Italy and she of Charleston.

BRINGLOE, JULIA W. aged 17 years married to LEVIN, JULIAN C. aged 31 years April 23, 1879 by Rabbi David Levy at 106 Wentworth Street. Both natives of Charleston.

BRINGLOE, JULIA W. aged 22 years married to MOODY, JESSE G. aged 24 years October 5, 1887 by Rev. C. A. Stakely. He a native of Barnwell County, South Carolina and she of Charleston. He a bookbinder.

BRINGLOE, SALLIE H. aged 23 years married to FARRIER, MORRIS aged 27 years February 21, 1889 by Rev. R. W. Lide at the First Baptist Church. He a native of Illinois and she of Charleston. He a native of Illinois and she of Charleston. He a printer.

BRINSON, EDWARD aged 22 years married to PRATT, MARY S. aged 23 years February 21, 1889 by Rev. H. B. Browne at 3 Stone Court. Both natives of Berkeley County, South Carolina. He a mill hand.

BRINSON, FRANCES aged 19 years married to EDWARDS, JOHN C. aged 22 years December 23, 1894 by Rev. J. C. Yongue. Both natives of Berkeley County, South Carolina. He works in the cotton mill.

BRISSENDEN, EDWIN aged 28 years married to PRINCE, MARY CATHERINE aged 20 years June 26, 1883 by Rev. A. Coke Smith at 48 Rutledge Avenue. Both natives of Charleston. He a driver.

BRISTOL, FLORENCE MARY aged 20 years married to KENT, PHINEAS aged 26 years November 5, 1885 by Rev. W. T. Jenkins at Westminster Presbyterian Church. He a native of New Jersey and she of New York. He a bookkeeper.

BRISTOW, JOHN C. married to BURT, EMMA February 9, 1890 by Rev. W. A. Betts at the Cumberland Church.

BRITTAIN, M. BESSIE married to ORR, J. D. October 7, 1884 by Rev. William T. Thompson at the First Presbyterian Church. He a physician in Asbury, South Carolina.

BRITTLE, GEORGE married to MURRAY, KATIE December 18, 1889 by Rev. W. A. Betts at Cumberland Church.

BRITTON, JOHN R. aged 20 years married to MURRAY, LIZZIE aged 19 years June 7, 1888 by Father F. J. Shadler at St. Joseph's Roman Catholic Church. Both natives of Charleston. He a printer.

BRITTON, RICHARD B. aged 28 years married to BEAUDROT, EMMA AMELIA aged 25 years January 20, 1886 by Rev. J. Walter Dickson at the Spring Street Lutheran Church. Both natives of Charleston. He a printer.

BROADWATER, SARAH C. aged 19 years married to COOK, CEPHAS G. aged 21 years November 11, 1894. He a native of Horry County, South Carolina and she of Charleston. He a laborer.

BROCK, ANN FRANCIS aged 19 years married to McCLAIN, W. DAVID aged 24 years December 29, 1889 by Rev. C. E. Chichester at The Mariners Church, 44 Market Street.

BROCK, JAMES W. aged 24 years married to HENDRICKS, MARY E. aged 17 years March 24, 1886 by Rev. H. B. Browne at 104 Nassau Street. He a native of North Carolina and she of Charleston. He a mechanic.

BRODIE, ALEXANDER L. married to REVEL, LIZZIE A. February 26, 1879 by Father Daniel J. Quigley at The Cathedral of St. John the Baptist. He a native of Columbia, South Carolina and she of Charleston. He a clerk in Columbia, South Carolina.

BRODIE, WILLIAM M. aged 23 years married to WILDER, ELLEN L. aged 22 years November 6, 1887 by Rev. John O. Wilson at the corner of Rutledge Avenue and Beaufain Street. Both natives and residents of Augusta, Georgia. He a spring builder.

BROMIER, HELENA C. aged 25 years married to MEYER, AUGUST aged 26 years February 8, 1880 by Rev. Johannes Heckel at St. Johannes Lutheran Church. Both natives of Dorum, Hanover.

BROOKBANKS, ANNA E. aged 28 years married to CONNELLY, JESSE M. aged 28 years July 3, 1878 by Rev. L. H. Shuck at 369 King Street. He a native of Barnwell, South Carolina and she of Charleston. He a policeman.

BROOKBANKS, ELIZA A. aged 18 years married to JOHNSON, ALFRED H. aged 22 years March 3, 1892 by Rev. Edwin C. Dargan at Citadel Square Baptist Church. Both natives of Charleston. He a bookkeeper.

BROOKHEISTER, SARAH F. aged 19 years married to CAMERON, JOHN JAMES aged 23 years August 20, 1893 by Rev. J. C. Yongue at 546 Meeting Street. He a native of Charleston and a painter.

BROOKS, ARTHUR G. R. T. aged 26 years married to MERRITT, MARY ANNA aged 15 years August 22, 1886 by Rev. J. Walter Dickson at 37 Cooper Street. He a native of Germany and she of North Carolina. He a laborer.

BROOKS, WILLIAM J. aged 38 years married to CONWAY, MARY J. aged 21 years June 28, 1892 by Bishop Harry P. Northrop at The Cathedral of St. John the Baptist. He a native of New Haven, Connecticut and she of London, England. He a manufacturer in Columbia, South Carolina.

BROTHERS, ANNIE E. aged 15 years married to WEEKS, THOMAS J. aged 22 years June 28, 1893 by Rev. J. C. Yongue. He a native of Washington County, North Carolina and she of Georgia. He works for the railroad.

BROTHERS, FLORENCE VIRGINIA aged 17 years married to HANAHAN, EDWARD WALTER aged 25 years March 25, 1889 by Rev. G. R. Brackett at the Second Presbyterian Church. He a native of New York City and she of Charleston. He a printer in New York City.

BROTHERS, MARY JANE aged 17 years married to SAXTON, JAMES M. aged 24 years November 11, 1891 by Rev. W. A. Betts at 30 Shepherd Street. Both natives of Charleston. He a sashmaker.

BROUGHTON, HENRY aged 22 years married to ALPHONSE, EMILY aged 19 years December 9, 1877 by Father Harry P. Northrop at St. Patrick's Roman Catholic Church. Both natives of Charleston. He works for the railroad.

BROUGHTON, LAWRENCE aged 48 years married to HARRINGTON, (Mrs.) BRIDGET DUNN aged 45 years October 7, 1885 by Father F. J. Shadler at St. Joseph's Roman Catholic Church. Both natives of Ireland. He a laborer.

BROUGHTON, MAGGIE aged 21 years married to LIVINGSTON, WALTER F. aged 20 years January 30, 1895 by Father J. J. Monaghan at St. Patrick's Roman Catholic Church. Both natives of Charleston. He a clerk.

BROUGHTON, SARA ANN aged 31 years married to BARRIDGE, THOMAS aged 33 years November 23, 1880 by Rev. J. V. Welsh at 11 Aiken Street. He a native of Abbotsbury, England and she of Charlotte, North Carolina. He a laborer.

BROWN, ADDIE M. married to EVANS, ROBERT P. November 24, 1881 by Rev. William H. Campbell at St. Paul's Church. Both natives of Charleston. He a clerk.

BROWN, ANN ELIZA aged 20 years married to FULLER, MIDDLETON F. aged 26 years November 23, 1886 by Rev. A. H. Misseldine at 81 Wentworth Street. Both natives of South Carolina. He an engineer.

BROWN, CHARLES aged 48 years married to PARSELL, (Mrs.) HATTIE HIOTT aged 31 years August 18, 1895 by Rev. J. L. Stokes at 7 Payne Street. He a native of Europe and she of Charleston. He a laborer.

BROWN, ELIZA FISHBURNE aged 22 years married to LOCKWOOD, JOHN PALMER aged 27 years November 15, 1883 by Rev. A. H. Misseldine at 65 Wentworth Street. Both natives of Charleston. He a clerk.

BROWN, EMMA aged 19 years married to BAUM, JACOB aged 27 years January 26, 1881 by Rabbi David Levy. He a native of Georgetown, South Carolina and she of New York. He a merchant in Georgetown.

BROWN, EUGENE aged 24 years married to RYAN, NINA O. aged 19 years March 23, 1881 by Rev. A. S. Dobbs. Both natives of Charleston. He a livery proprietor.

BROWN, FANNIE aged 17 years married to ATKINSON, FRANK aged 23 years October 5, 1884 by Rev. R. A. Lapsley at Bischoff's Square. Both natives of Charleston. He a carpenter.

BROWN, FLORENCE A. married to FLINT, WILLIAM H. November 18, 1891 by Rev. William H. Campbell at 56 Lynch Street. Both natives of Charleston. He an insurance agent.

BROWN, FLORENCE E. aged 25 years married to WITHINGTON, WALTER T. aged 27 years October 7, 1886 by Rev. Robert Wilson at 26 Hanover Street. Both natives of Charleston. He a machinist.

BROWN, HENRY aged 30 years married to SAVERING, LAURA C. aged 17 years March 6, 1887 by Rev. Luther T. Beattie in King Street. He a native of Alabama and she of Virginia. He works for the railroad.

BROWN, HENRY aged 36 years married to ENRIGHT, MARY JANE aged 20 years August 8, 1878 by Father Harry P. Northrop at St. Patrick's Roman Catholic Church. He a native or Prussia and she of Charleston. He a machinist.

BROWN, HENRY aged 30 years married to SUTLET, EMILY aged 19 years July 16, 1884 by Rev. R. A. Lapsley at 1 Bischoff's Square. He a native of South Carolina and she of Georgia. He a carpenter.

BROWN, HENRY B. aged 25 years married to CAMERON, MINNIE aged 19 years June 28, 1889 by Rev. Robert O. Wilson at 14 Line Street. Both natives of Charleston. He an engineer.

BROWN, HENRY JAMES aged 38 years married to LaROCHE, (Mrs.) MARIE PATTERSON aged 37 years June 30, 1891 by Rev. W. A. Betts at 2 Hampstead Square. He a native of Portsmith, Virginia and she of Charleston. He a mechanic.

BROWN, JAMES P. married to MARTIN, JULIA July 15, 1886 by Rev. William H. Campbell at the residence of Joseph G. Martin. He a clerk.

BROWN, J. F. aged 29 years married to PARDEE, CATHERINE E. aged 47 years May 25, 1880 by Rev. G. R. Brackett at 21 Rutledge Avenue. He a native of Summerville, South Carolina and she of Charleston. He an engineer in Summerville.

BROWN, JULIA MARY aged 23 years married to LIEBENROOD, S. N. aged 23 years May 22, 1884 by Rev. A. J. D. Thomas at 27 Spring Street. He a native of New York.

BROWN, JULIA married to MARSHALL, E. K. November 10, 1887 by Rev. William H. Campbell. He a clerk.

BROWN, LAURA aged 19 years married to AXSON, W. C. aged 23 years June 29, 1881 by Rev. L. H. Suck at 32 Columbus Street. He a native of Charleston and a miner.

BROWN, MARGARET M. married to POYAS, SAMUEL H. November 12, 1891 by Rev. William H. Campbell. He a clerk.

BROWN, MARGARET MAGDALENA aged 26 years married to MAY, LAWRENCE JOSEPH aged 32 years November 7, 1881 by Father Claudian B. Northrop at St. Mary of the Annunciation Roman Catholic Church.

BROWN, MARY ELIZA aged 44 years married to HUGHES, THOMAS J. aged 35 years July 5, 1883 by Rev. J. H. Tillinghast at 1 Bischoff Square. Both natives of Charleston. He a painter.

BROWN, MARY J. aged 25 years married to MATSON, WALTER L. aged 26 years September 11, 1894 by Father J. J. Monaghan at St. Patrick's Roman Catholic Church. Both natives of Charleston. He an employee of the gas works.

BROWN, M. M. aged 21 years married to KELLY, M. aged 30 years January 25, 1882 by Father T. F. Kelly. He a native of Ireland and she of New Jersey. He a machinist.

BROWN, NELLIE P. aged 22 years married to HARRIS, WILLIAM J. aged 22 years October 7, 1888 by Father Daniel J. Quigley at St. Patrick's Roman Catholic Church. He a native of Georgia and a clerk in Savannah, Georgia.

BROWN, R. aged 20 years married to MAY, P. aged 31 years February 28, 1882 by Rev. R. D. Lide at 400 King Street. He a merchant.

BROWN, S. W. aged 27 years married to PITCHER, E. I. aged 25 years December 4, 1879 by Rev. W. S. Bowman at the residence of the Bride - 52 Hasell Street. He a native of Burke County, Georgia and she of Charleston. He a farmer in Georgia.

BROWN, WILLIAM JAMES aged 23 years married to MOUZON, ANNIE ELVIRA aged 22 years October 11, 1881 by Rev. A. Coke Smith at the corner of East Bay and Minority Streets. He a native of Darlington, South Carolina and she of Spartanburg, South Carolina. He a clerk in Edgefield, South Carolina.

BROWN, WILLIAM C. aged 26 years married to CLEARY, ELLEN L. M. aged 20 years August 1, 1887 by Father Daniel J. Quigley at St. Patrick's Roman Catholic Church. He a native of Maryland and she of Charleston. He a bridge builder.

BROWN, – aged 47 years married to FIELDS, PATRICK aged 58 years August 3, 1880 by Rev. Charles S. Vedder.

BROWNING, ALONSO aged 19 years married to MURRAY, JOSEPHINE H. aged 21 years October 1, 1887 by Rev. H. B. Browne at 22 Blake Street. He a native of Charleston and she of Berkeley County, South Carolina. He a railroad brakeman.

BROWNING, A. THOMAS aged 21 years married to SMITH, ROSA aged 16 years August 15, 1888 by Rev. H. B. Browne at 471 Meeting Street. Both natives of Charleston. He a railroad brakeman.

BRUGGERMAN, (Mrs.) ELIZABETH R. OTTGER aged 48 years married to ELBROOK, GEORGE aged 35 years October 24, 1886 by Rev. Johannes Heckel at St. Johannes German Lutheran Church. He a native of South Carolina and she of Georgia. He a farmer on Sullivans Island, South Carolina.

BRUGGERMAN, FRANTZ HEINE aged 21 years married to KLEE, ADELINE MARGARETHE aged 18 years November 28, 1881 by Rev. Louis Muller at the St. Matthew's Lutheran Church. He a native of Georgia and she of Charleston. He a baker.

BRUGGERMAN, FREDERICK H. G. aged 24 years married to BRUNING, ANNIE M. C. aged 23 years February 11, 1886 by Rev. Johannes Heckel at the residence of J. H. Patjens in Mt. Pleasant. He a native of Sullivans Island, South Carolina and she of Georgia. He a farmer on Sullivans Island.

BRUGGERMAN, G. W. aged 20 years married to ROBINSON, M. J. aged 20 years February 9, 1882 by Rev. A. Coke Smith at Trinity Church. He a native of Georgia and she of Charleston. He a machinist.

BRUNCKHORST, MARIA C. C. aged 24 years married to BUSCH, STEPHEN aged 28 years April 25, 1886 by Rev. Louis Muller at the northwest corner of Spring and Ashley Avenue. He a native of Germany and she of Charleston. He a merchant.

BRUNCKHOSS, ANNA N. aged 23 years married to MOHRING, HEINRICH aged 24 years July 14, 1889 by Rev. Louis Muller. Both natives of Prussia. He a grocer.

BRUNEMER, ADA aged 20 years married to MIMS, JAMES B. aged 23 years January 22, 1895 by father J. J. Monaghan at 87 Drake Street. He a native of Summerville, South Carolina.

BRUNES, MARY FLORENCE married to GAMEWELL, JOHN N. September 24, 1890 by Rev. John Gass at 41 Lynch Street.

BRUNINGS, ANNIE M. C. aged 23 years married to BRUGGERMAN, FREDERICK H. G. aged 24 years February 11, 1886 by Rev. Johannes Heckel at the residence of J. H. Patjens in Mt. Pleasant. He a native of Sullivans Island, South Carolina and she of Georgia. He a farmer on Sullivans Island.

BRUNINGS, J. H. aged 34 years married to s, ANNA aged 28 years September 14, 1879 by Rev. Louis Muller at the corner of King and Tradd Streets. Both natives of Hanover. He a joiner.

BRUNKHORST, MARGARETHE M. CATHERINE. aged 24 years married to KANGETER, JOHANN aged 24 years September 25, 1881 by Rev. Louis Muller. Both natives of Hanover. He a grocer.

BRUNNING, MARY aged 16 years married to STOPPELBEIN, JOSEPH aged 20 years February 14, 1884 by Father John P. Twigg.

BRUNS, ADELINE MARGARETHE aged 26 years married to STEINBRECKER, WILHELM aged 28 years February 11, 1886 by Rev. Louis Muller at the northwest corner of Calhoun and Alexander Streets. Both natives of Germany. He a saloon keeper.

BRUNSON, CLAUDIA H. aged 19 years married to DICK, WILLIAM E. aged 24 years November 27, 1885 by Rev. J. O. Wilson at the Charleston Hotel. Both natives of Sumter County, South Carolina. He a salesman.

BRUNSON, JOHN B. aged 56 years married to READ, ELLA W. aged 38 years December 12, 1893 by Rev. C. C. Pinckney at 10 Legare Street. He a native of Darlington, South Carolina and she of Charleston. He a mechanic in Orangeburg, South Carolina.

BRUNSON, MARIAN G. aged 20 years married to GRISER, JOHN J. aged 20 years April 11, 1893 by Father J. J. Monaghan at 136 St. Philip Street. Both natives of Charleston. He works for the railroad.

BRUSSEN, HENRY aged 28 years married to MARVIE (?), ALICE aged 27 years December 26, 1880 by Rev. L. H. Shuck. Both natives of Charleston. He a carpenter.

BRYAN, EDWARD B married to ROPER, GEORGIA July 9, 1878 by Rev. Richard S. Trapier.

BRYAN, ISAAC M. married to STONEY, ROSA M. April 30, 1878 by Rev. Ellison Capers at St. Michael's Church.

BRYAN, LAURA JOSEPHINE aged 20 years married to MANDERS, GEORGE aged 21 years November 22, 1891 by Rev. W. A. Betts at 14 Hampstead Square. He a native of Hendersonville, North Carolina and she of Colleton County, South Carolina. He a fireman.

BRYANT, FRANK E. aged 25 years married to SELBY, MARY ELIZABETH aged 22 years December 30, 1883 by Rev. John E. Beard at 2 Hampden Court. He a native of Chester County, South Carolina and she of Maryland.

BRYCE, JAMES E. aged 24 years married to CAULFIELD, MARY F. aged 23 years April 5, 1888 by Father F. J. Shadler at St. Joseph's Roman Catholic Church. He a native of Newark, New Jersey and she of Charleston. He resides in Newark.

BRYANT, LULA D. aged 22 years married to CHUBB, WILLIAM N. aged 24 years June 2, 1889 by Rev. H. B. Browne at Cumberland Church. He a native of Washington, D. C. and a farmer.

BUCH, AUGUST HENRY aged 28 years married to RODERMAN, JOHANNA aged 22 years October 29, 1885 by Rev. Johannes Heckel at the corner of Aiken and Blake Streets. Both natives of Charleston. He a grocer.

BUCK, (Mrs.) ANN L. E. BULL married to BUCK, JOHN W. March 24, 1878 by Rev. Louis Muller. Both natives of Germany. He a grocer.

BUCK, ANNA MARINA SOPHIA aged 23 years married to STEENCKEN, JOHANN H. aged 24 years March 4, 1886 by Rev. Louis Muller at 140 Calhoun Street. Both natives of Charleston. He a wheelwright.

BUCK, SOPHIE A. WILHELMINA aged 21 years married to WINTER, HEINRICH ALBERT FREDERICK aged 27 years November 6, 1884 by Rev. Louis Muller at 40 America Street. Both natives of Charleston. He a saloon keeper.

BUCK, CATHARINE MARY FREDERICKA aged 23 years married to SCHMIDT, WILHELM NICHOLAS aged 30 years September 20, 1888 by Rev. Louis Muller. He a widower.

BUCK, EMMA REBECCA aged 20 years married to CLAUSSEN, HERMANN aged 24 years April 25, 1881 by Rev. Johannes Heckel in Rafer's Alley. Both natives of Charleston. He a merchant.

BUCK, JOHN WILLIAM aged 32 years married to BUSE, ANNA LOUISE ELIZABETH aged 46 years March 24, 1878 by Rev. Louis Muller at the southeast corner of Coming and Spring Streets.

BUCK, M. A. aged 19 years married to MARINES (?) WILLIAM H. aged 23 years April 26, 1881 by Father Daniel J. Quigley at The Cathedral of St. John the Baptist. Both natives of Charleston. He a blacksmith.

BUCK, M. J. aged 19 years married to LANGER, THEODORE C. F. aged 21 years September 16, 1880 by Rev. Louis Muller in Market Street below Meeting Street. Both natives of Charleston. He a fruitier.

BUCKHEISTER, WILLIAM H. aged 23 years married to ATKINSON, AZAILE V. aged 21 years September 26, 1894 by Rev. J. C. Yongue at 87 Columbus Street. Both natives of Charleston. He a car driver.

BUCKHEISTER, BENJAMIN A. aged 23 years married to BOWEY, ELIZABETH aged 21 years November 30, 1892 by Rev. N. K. Smith at 544 Meeting Street. He a native of Charleston and she of Plymouth, England. He a car driver.

BUCKHEISTER, SARAH F. aged 19 years married to CAMMER, JOHN J. aged 23 years August 20, 1893 by Rev. J. C. Yongue at 546 Meeting Street.

BUCKLEY, JOHN married to CARR, HELEN December 1, 1878 by William B. Yates, Chaplain.

BUCKLEY, WILLIAM HENRY aged 22 years married to HARRISON, F. B. aged 21 years June 20, 1880 by Rev. L. H. Shuck. Both natives of Charleston. He a pilot.

BUDROW, MINNIE E. aged 16 years married to GARDNER, EDWARD aged 22 years December 26, 1888 by Rev. Robert Wilson at 41 Reid Street. Both natives of Charleston. He a ship carpenter.

BUERO, ANGELO aged 23 years married to TOBIN, MARGARET TERESA aged 17 years December 26, 1883 by Father J. J. Woolahan at St. Mary of the Annunciation Roman Catholic Church.

BUILDT, ANNIE T. aged 22 years married to STALEY, WELLINGTON A. aged 22 years December 12, 1886 by Rev. Luther K. Probst at the Wentworth Street Lutheran Church. Both natives of South Carolina. He works for the railroad.

BUIST, AGNES EWING aged 20 years married to PRINGLE, WALTER aged 29 years April 8, 1890 by Rev. C. C. Pinckney at Grace Church. Both natives of Charleston. He a merchant.

BUIST, ELIZA INGRAHAM married to RIVERS, M. RUTLEDGE February 2, 1893 by Rev. William H. Campbell at St. Paul's Church. He a lawyer.

BULKEN, E. aged 21 years married to PETERMAN, C. S. aged 20 years September 28, 1882 by Rev. Luther K. Probst. He a native of Charleston and a grocer.

BULKEN, (Mrs.) LULA FLOYD aged 23 years married to ALBERTUS, M. aged 19 years March 25, 1883 by Rev. Louis Muller at the St. Matthew's Lutheran Church. He a native of Georgia and she of Darlington County, South Carolina. He a grocer.

BULWINKLE, C. M. aged 20 years married to BEHLMER, G. H. G. aged 29 years April 27, 1887 by Rev. Louis Muller. Both natives of South Carolina. He a grocer.

BULWINKLE, ELIZA G. aged 21 years married to DOYLE, THOMAS A. aged 22 years August 17, 1884 by Rev. J. V. Welsh at 73 Spring Street. Both natives of Charleston. He a carpenter.

BULWINKLE, HENRIETTA aged 26 years married to WILBUR, HERBERT aged 26 years April 8, 1891 by Rev. Edwin C. Dargan at 23 Montagu Street. He a native of Columbia, South Carolina and she of Charleston. He a clerk.

BULWINKLE, H. aged 29 years married to BLOTH, EMMA E. aged 23 years January 13, 1887 by Rev. Louis Muller. Both natives of Charleston. He a farmer.

BULWINKLE, J. A. aged 25 years married to SAHLMAN, R. M. H. aged 20 years September 25, 1879 by Rev. Louis Muller at the corner of Meeting and Reid Streets. Both natives of Charleston. He a bookkeeper.

BULWINKLE, JOHANN H. aged 35 years married to PUCKHABER, GESCHE aged 29 years May 29, 1887 by Rev. Louis Muller at the southwest corner of Coming and Line Streets. Both natives of Germany. He a grocer.

BULWINKLE, LENA MARIA WILHELMINA aged 21 years married to BRANDT, JOHN HENRY CARL aged 25 years November 6, 1881 by Rev. Louis Muller at Brandt's Farm near the Race Course. Both natives of Charleston. He a farmer.

BUME, MARY LOUISE ISABEL aged 19 years married to LLOYD, JESSE WALTER aged 23 years April 26, 1883 by Rev. Edward T. Horn at 13 Charlotte Street.

BUMEMEYER, META aged 25 years married to MATHIES, AUGUST aged 24 years December 28, 1882 by Father F. J. Shadler at St. Joseph's Roman Catholic Church. He a native of Hanover and she of Oldenburg, Germany. He a machinist.

BUNCH, CAROLINE C. aged 23 years married to HERBERT, JAMES aged 21 years February 22, 1885 by Rev. John P. Wilson at 2 Dothage Court. Both natives of Charleston. He a clerk.

BUNCH, CATHARINE aged 17 years married to SADLER, ROBERT aged 31 years September 22, 1889 by Father J. J. Monaghan at St. Patrick's Roman Catholic Church. He a native of Ireland and she of South Carolina. He a laborer.

BUNCH, SILAS SYLVESTER aged 34 years married to SHOKES, HARRIET LENORA aged 28 years August 25, 1881 by Rev. A. Coke Smith at 217 Coming Street. Both natives of Charleston. He a painter.

BUNGER, HERMAN H. aged 21 years married to SCHLUTER, DORA H. aged 17 years January 18, 1886 by Rev. Luther K. Probst. He a native of Germany and she of Walhalla, South Carolina. He a merchant.

BURCH, WILLIAM P. aged 35 years married to CANNON, EMILY J. aged 25 years November 16, 1880 by Rev. John Johnson at the farmhouse of Mr. Cannon. He a native of Wadesboro, North Carolina and she of Charleston. He a horse racer in Cheraw, South Carolina.

BURDELL, CAROLINE aged 23 years married to FITZSIMONS, CHARLES M. aged 24 years April 7, 1887 by Rev. A. H. Misseldine. Both natives of South Carolina. He a carpenter.

BURDELL, ELIZABETH ST. JULIEN aged 20 years married to BAILEY, THOMAS aged 27 years November 7, 1889 by Rev. Henry M. Grant at the Circular Congregational Church. He a native of South Carolina and she of Charleston. He an engineer in Mt. Pleasant, South Carolina.

BURDEN, ISABELLA E. married to WALPOLE, JOHN B. December 12, 1895 by Rev. William H. Campbell. He a farmer on Johns Island, South Carolina.

BURDELL, EMMA MARIAN aged 24 years married to CART, RUEBEN ADAM aged 23 years April 17, 1890 by Rev. Henry M. Grant at the Circular Congregational Church. He a native of Indiana and she of Charleston. He works in an "agency" in Marionsville, Illinois.

BURDGES, MARY E. aged 19 years married to PATTERSON, WILLIAM J. aged 22 years January 28, 1885 by Rev. R. A. Lapsley at 7 Blake Street. He a native of Charleston and she of Mobile, Alabama. He works in a carriage factory.

BURGER, JOHANNA MARGARETHA ELISE aged 22 years married to SCHROEDER, WILHELM LUDWIG aged 24 years December 12, 1889 by Rev. Louis Muller at the home of the Bride's uncle in Summerville, South Carolina.

BURGESS, MAMIE E. aged 18 years married to BRASELL, JOHN A. aged 28 years August 27, 1894 by Rev. L. A. Groves at 14 Cramers Court.

BURK, MARY aged 20 years married to CONLON, EUGENE aged 35 years May 6, 1883 by Father John P. Twigg at St. Patrick's Roman Catholic Church. Both natives of Charleston. He a machinist.

BURK, WILLIAM H. aged 36 years married to WILLIFORD, LIZZIE M. aged 20 years January 23, 1894 by Rev. Lucius Cuthbert. He a native of Charleston and she of Sumter County, South Carolina. He a pilot.

BURK, ADDIE D. aged 24 years married to SHUCK, LEWIS aged 30 years November 15, 1887 by Rev. Charles Stackley at 12 Water Street. He a native of Warrenton, North Carolina and she of Charleston. He a clerk.

BURKE, ANNA A. aged 17 years married to JONES, JOHN J. aged 20 years July 17, 1881 by Father F. J. Shadler at St. Joseph's Roman Catholic Church. Both natives of Charleston. He a ship carpenter.

BURKE, CATHERINE married to SANDERS, GAINES H. February 8, 1879 by Father Daniel J. Quigley at The Cathedral of St. John the Baptist. He a native of Alabama and she of Charleston. He a longshoreman.

BURKE, JOHN aged 29 years married to WEINHOLTZ, ANNIE J. aged 25 years June 2, 1878 by Father Daniel J. Quigley at The Cathedral of St. John the Baptist. Both natives of Charleston. He a salesman.

BURKE, JOHN E. aged 25 years married to DINGATE, MARY A. aged 24 years November 28, 1881 by Father P. L. Duffy at The Cathedral of St. John the Baptist. Both natives of Charleston. He a plumber.

BURKE, M. H. D. aged 23 years married to WINTER, B. G. aged 22 years November 14, 1882 by Rev. Louis Muller at 24 America Street. He a native of Charleston and a clerk.

BURKE, MARY C. aged 35 years married to LYONS, THOMAS C. aged 44 years June 19, 1888 by Father Daniel J. Quigley at St. Patrick's Roman Catholic Church. He a native of Ireland and she of Charleston. He a carpenter.

BURKE, MARY E. aged 33 years married to CHICO, VINCENT aged 34 years August 16, 1885 by Father F. J. Shadler at St. Joseph's Roman Catholic Church. He a native of Italy and she of Charleston. He a policeman.

BURKHARDT, WILHELMINA aged 20 years married to LaVERGUE, JULES aged 25 years September 1, 1892 by Father J. J. Monaghan at St. Patrick's Roman Catholic Church. He a native of Augusta, Georgia and she of Baden, Germany. He a laborer.

BURLOW, DAISY married to GARDINER, JAMES J. January 7, 1890 by Rev. W. A. Betts.

BURMEISTER, JOHN W. aged 21 years married to DOYLE, MARY A. aged 21 years November 17, 1886 by Father F. J. Shadler at the residence of the Bride - 299 East Bay Street. Both natives of Charleston. He a grain dealer.

BURMEISTER, LOUISA S. aged 19 years married to ANGERMANN, HENRY W. M. aged 25 years June 12, 1883 by Rev. Louis Muller at 283 East Bay Street.

BURN, WILLIAM A. aged 23 years married to McDONALD, MARGARET aged 19 years July 16, 1890 by Father J. J. Monaghan at 136 St. Philip Street. Both natives of Charleston. He a railroad conductor.

BURNES, L. E. aged 24 years married to GOSS, JANEY aged 19 years July 6, 1885 by Rev. John E. Beard at 64 Nassau Street.

BURNHAM, SARAH ELLEN aged 28 years married to MOUZON, WILLIAM L. aged 32 years May 17, 1883 by Rev. W. P. Mouzon at 117 Coming Street.

BURNS, ALLAN McC. aged 23 years married to GIBSON, EMILY C. aged 21 years February 28, 1884 by Rev. W. P. Mouzon at the northeast corner of Meeting and Society Streets. Both natives of Charleston. He a merchant.

BURNS, ANNIE aged 27 years married to HARRIGAN, JOHN aged 34 years June 28, 1881 by Father F. J. Shadler at St. Joseph's Roman Catholic Church. He a native of Boston, Massachusetts and she of Charleston. He a boilermaker.

BURNS, GARRETT aged 40 years married to GARDINER, BRIDGET aged 35 years August 24, 1879 by Father C. J. Croghan at St. Joseph's Roman Catholic Church. Both natives of Ireland. He a politician.

BURNS, LIZZIE AGNES aged 18 years married to BARTH, EUGENE JAMES aged 20 years June 18, 1890 by Father F. J. Shadler at St. Joseph's Roman Catholic Church. Both natives of Charleston. He a clerk.

BURNS, MARY JOSEPHINE aged 23 years married to ClerkINS, EDWARD aged 25 years February 25, 1884 by Father F. J. Shadler at St. Joseph's Roman Catholic Church. Both natives of Charleston. He an employee at the gas works.

BURNS, SAMUEL aged 37 years married to O'MARA, MARY aged 20 years December 5, 1877 by Father John O. Schachte at St. Mary of the Annunciation Roman Catholic Church. He a native of Ireland and she of Charleston. He a liquor dealer.

BURNS, WILLIAM MELVILLE aged 21 years married to GIBSON, L. ADELAIDE aged 20 years May 6, 1880 by Rev. H. F. Chreitzberg at the southwest corner of Meeting and Spring Streets. Both natives of Charleston. He a salesman.

BURREN, J. G. M. aged 20 years married to AMES, O. aged 35 years January 18, 1882 by Rev. Louis Muller at 91 East Bay Street. He a native of Massachusetts and she of Charleston. He a sea captain.

BURRIDGE, THOMAS aged 33 years married to BROUGHTON, SARA ANN aged 31 years November 23, 1880 by Rev. J. V. Welsh at 11 Aiken Street. He a native of Abbotsbury, England and she of Charlotte, North Carolina. He a laborer.

BURSE, CAROLINE S. aged 18 years married to STEVENS, H. W. L. aged 21 years September 28, 1880 by Rev. John H. Honour at 14 John Street. He a native of Bluffton, South Carolina and a grocer. She a native of Walhalla, South Carolina.

BURT, EMMA married to BRISTOW, JOHN C. February 9, 1890 by Rev. W. A. Betts at the Cumberland Church.

BURTON, ELIZABETH aged 19 years married to COLEY, JOHN M. aged 33 years August 11, 1892 by Rev. A. N. Chreitzberg at the corner of Hanover and Columbus Streets. He a native of South Carolina and she of Moncks Corner, South Carolina. He in the mercantile business.

BURTON, E. J. aged 18 years married to RANTEN, J. aged 33 years December 25, 1882 by Rev. J. V. Welch in Paines Court. He a native of Charleston and a tinner.

BURTON, MARY aged 17 years married to RIGGS, JULIUS aged 22 years October 12, 1886 by Rev. H. B. Browne at 206 St. Philip Street. Both natives of Charleston. He a laborer.

BURTON, ROBERT A. aged 21 years married to ELLIS, CORNELIA aged 20 years November 16, 1880 by Father P. L. Duffy at 62 Church Street. He a native of Charleston and she of Williamsburg County, South Carolina. He works at the Adams Express Company.

BUSCH, CARL FREDERICK aged 24 years married to ALBERS, CATHARINE ELISE aged 24 years April 8, 1883 by Rev. Louis Muller at 7 Bogard Street. He a native of Charleston and she of Walhalla, South Carolina. He a farmer.

BUSCH, CATHERINE D. aged 19 years married to DUNNING, FRANCIS D. aged 22 years April 16, 1880 by Rev. J. V. Welsh. Both natives of Charleston. He a blacksmith.

BUSCH, HANNAH aged 18 years married to WITTSCHEN, ALBERT aged 22 years August 31, 1884 by Rev. John E. Beard. Both natives of Charleston. He a laborer.

BUSCH, HENRIETTA WILHELMINA aged 26 years married to THEILING, FRITZ CHRISTIAN aged 26 years August 8, 1886 by Rev. Louis Muller at the southwest corner of Ann and Elizabeth Streets. He a native of Charleston and she of Walhalla, South Carolina. He a baker.

BUSCH, HENRY M. aged 26 years married to JOYNER, ANNIE B. aged 18 years June 21, 1880 by Rev. J. V. Welsh at 68 Line Street. He a native of Charleston and she of St. Thomas Parish, South Carolina. He a baker.

BUSCH, (Mrs.) MARIE BRUNCKHORST aged 31 years married to CAPPELMANN, FREDERICK W. aged 43 years November 12, 1893 by Rev. K. Boldt at the corner of Spring Street and Ashley Avenue. He a native of Charleston and she of Germany.

BUSCH, STEPHEN aged 28 years married to BRUNCKHORST, MARIA C. C. aged 24 years April 25, 1886 by Rev. Louis Muller at the northwest corner of Spring and Ashley Avenue. He a native of Germany and she of Charleston. He a merchant.

BUSE, ANNA LOUISE aged 16 years married to JORDAN, FRIEDRICH WILHELM aged 26 years May 1, 1888 by Rev. Louis Muller.

BUSE, ANNA LOUISE ELIZABETH aged 46 years married to BUCK, JOHN WILLIAM aged 32 years March 24, 1878 by Rev. Louis Muller at the southeast corner of Coming and Spring Streets.

BUSE, DORA MARIA M. aged 31 years married to WALJEN, ERNST C. aged 45 years February 21, 1886 by Rev. Louis Muller at 526 King Street. Both natives of Germany. He a merchant.

BUSE, DORA ANN aged 28 years married to OSTENDORFF, HERMAN E. aged 31 years February 16, 1887 by Rev. Louis Muller. He a native of South Carolina and she of Charleston. He a grocer.

BUSE, DORETHA ADELAIDE married to ENTELMANN, JOHANN F. A. aged 24 years April 13, 1887 by Rev. Louis Muller at 520 King Street. He a native of Charleston and a merchant.

BUSE, ELIZA MARIA aged 25 years married to STELLO, KARL CHRISTIAN aged 30 years September 28, 1886 by Rev. Johannes Heckel at 520 King Street. He a native of Germany and she of Charleston. He a merchant.

BUTECHNER (?), SARAH F. aged 24 years married to VISANSKA (?), JULIUS M. aged 29 years March 12, 1895 by Rabbi I. P. Mender at 2 Bull Street. He a native of Richmond, Virginia and she of Charleston. He a merchant.

BUTLER, CECILIA aged 22 years married to OLSEN, ANDREW aged 24 years March 24, 1894 by Rev. John Johnson at 53 Church Street. He a native of Norway and she of South Carolina.

BUTLER, C. J. aged 32 years married to WALKER, HARRIET H. aged 21 years March 3, 1885 by Rev. C. C. Pinckney in Wentworth Street. Both natives of Charleston. He a turpentine manufacturer in Orangeburg, South Carolina.

BUTLER, ELLA aged 21 years married to PURCELL, JOHN aged 36 years May 29, 1884 by Father P. L. Duffy at The Cathedral of St. John the Baptist. He a native of Ireland and she of Union, South Carolina. He an engineer.

BUTLER, F. CARTER married to MISSROON, CLAUDIA H. July 31, 1886 by Rev. W. T. Thompson at the First Presbyterian Church.

BUTLER, GEORGE aged 29 years married to CANNON, FANNIE aged 36 years July 18, 1892 by Rev. J. L. Stokes at 231 Coming Street.

BUTLER, GEORGE FRANCIS aged 19 years married to KANAPAUX, MARY aged 16 years December 29, 1889 by Father J. J. Monaghan at 20 America Street. Both natives of Charleston. He a manufacturer in Charleston County.

BUTLER, HENRIETTA E. aged 17 years married to SANDERS, R. W. aged 30 years September 3, 1888 by P. E. Gleason, Trial Justice. Both natives of Charleston. He works in a factory.

BUTLER, JOSEPH aged 32 years married to WALKER, HARRIET HASELL aged 21 years March 3, 1885 by Rev. C. C. Pinckney in Wentworth Street.

BUTLER, MARIA IRVING aged 18 years married to GLOVER, MORTIMER M. aged 22 years March 9, 1892 by Rev. R. A. Webb in Westminster Presbyterian Church. He a native of Orangeburg, South Carolina and she of Charleston. He a clerk.

BUTLER, MARY A. aged 28 years married to SCHULLER, AUGUSTINE aged 31 years September 23, 1888 by Father F. J. Shadler at St. Joseph's Roman Catholic Church. He a native of Holland and she of Charleston. He a merchant.

BUTLER, SALLIE married to BECKTEL, ROBERT November 16, 1890 by Rev. W. A. Betts.

BUTLER, T. WELSMAN aged 22 years married to ADDISON, FLORENCE aged 20 years February 14, 1878 by Rev. L. H. Shuck at 55 Bay Street. Both natives of Charleston. He a weigher.

BUTT, GEORGE MILTON aged 27 years married to DOMINGO, MARY aged 18 years June 9, 1886 by Rev. J. Walter Dickson at 231 Coming Street. Both natives of Charleston. He a mechanic.

BUTT, HERMANN DIETRICH aged 32 years married to ANGERMANN, MARIE M. BERTHA aged 27 years February 19, 1888 by Rev. Louis Muller. He a native of Prussia and she of Jacksonville, Florida. He a grocer.

BUTT, JOHANN M. aged 35 years married to VON GLAHN, MINNA J. C. aged 25 years March 30, 1892 by Rev. Louis Muller at the corner of Warren and St. Philip Streets. He a native of Prussia and she of Charleston. He a grocer.

BUTTERFIELD, (Mrs.) FLORENCE SPEIN aged 21 years married to SCOTT, ALEXANDER C. aged 25 years February 8, 1888 by Rev. G. R. Brackett. He a native of Scotland and she of London, England. He a carpenter.

BUTTERFIELD, L. A. aged 25 years married to JACKSON, K. F. aged 22 years June 30, 1880 by Rev. William S. Bowman at the Wentworth Street Lutheran Church. He a native of Charleston and she of New York. He a telegraph operator.

BUTTS, ROBERT B. aged 21 years married to BERGMANN, MAGGIE aged 19 years November 2, 1881 by Rev. L. H. Shuck at 27 Church Street. Both natives of Charleston. He an engineer.

BYERS, WILLIAM J. married to SHIVER, NANNIE January 29, 1885 by Rev. C. E. Chichester at 55 Meeting Street. He a native of Charleston.

BYNUM, CLARENCE W. aged 38 years married to SIRES, (Mrs.) CLARA B FERGUSON aged 36 years December 20, 1894 by Rev. J. C. Yongue at the corner of Reid and Nassau Streets. He a native of Richland County, South Carolina and she of Charleston. He a planter in Richland County.

BYRNE, ELLEN aged 35 years married to O'SHAUGHNESSY, M. aged 52 years November 9, 1891 by Father J. J. Monaghan at St. Patrick's Roman Catholic Church. Both natives of Ireland. He a merchant.

BYRNE, JAMES F. aged 22 years married to McSWEENY, ELIZABETH aged 20 years September 29, 1878 by Father John P. Twigg at St. Patrick's Roman Catholic Church. He a native of Green Pond, South Carolina and she of Charleston. He a tinner.

CADDIN, THOMAS E. aged 32 years married to BREWER, (Mrs.) M. AYER aged 31 years July 9, 1879. Both natives of St. Paul, South Carolina. He a laborer.

CADE, JOHANN H. aged 23 years married to O'NEILL, MARGARET aged 21 years January 1, 1894 by Father J. J. Monaghan at St. Patrick's Roman Catholic Church. He a native of Brooklyn, New York and she of Charleston. He bricklayer and stonemason.

CADE, M. aged 20 years married to McGARY, F. F. aged 22 years August 16, 1882 by Father Daniel J. Quigley at The Cathedral of St. John the Baptist. He a native of Charleston and an inspector.

CADIZ, ELLEN J. WHITNEY married to LOWER, GEORGE E. July 20, 1887 by Rev. Richard S. Frazier in Smith Street. She a native of Charleston. She a native of Ireland. He a laborer.

CADIZ, FRANK A. married to WHITNEY, ELLA T. September 28, 1881 by Rev. Richard S. Trapier.

CAHILIN, CATHERINE aged 19 years married to DOWD, OWEN aged 32 years January 15, 1879 by Father John P. Twigg at The Cathedral of St. John the Baptist.

CAHILL, A. aged 26 years married to LOWREY, W. J. aged 34 years November 6, 1882 by Father Daniel J. Quigley at The Cathedral of St. John the Baptist. He a native of South Carolina and a merchant.

CAHILL, JOHN aged 45 years married to O'NEILL, MARGARET aged 35 years July 14, 1878 by Father John P. Twigg at The Cathedral of St. John the Baptist. Both natives of Ireland. He a laborer.

CAHILL, SARAH aged 22 years married to BLACK, PATRICK aged 29 years January 21, 1891 by Father J. J. Monaghan at St. Patrick's Roman Catholic Church. He a native of Ireland and she of Charleston. He a railroad conductor.

CAHILL, SUSAN C. aged 19 years married to KENNEDY, P. H. aged 32 years February 2, 1884 by Father Daniel J. Quigley at The Cathedral of St. John the Baptist. Both natives of Charleston. He a broker.

CAHILL, S. T. aged 20 years married to VAN DELKEN, H. aged 22 years January 17, 1882 by Father T. E. Chapins at St. Patrick's Roman Catholic Church. He a native of South Carolina and a railroad worker.

CAIN, ELIAS H. aged 25 years married to LOWNDES, HARRIET H. aged 24 years September 3, 1891 by Rev. Robert Wilson at 39 Legare Street. He a native of Berkeley County, South Carolina and she of Charleston. He a druggist in Columbia, South Carolina.

CALDER, ANNA ELIZA aged 19 years married to McCARROLL, JOHN REYNOLDS April 9, 1879 by Rev. W. S. Bowman at 14 Bee Street.

CALDER, CAROLINE VIRGINIA aged 20 years married to KING, CHARLES W. aged 22 years September 19, 1883 by Rev. A. Coke Smith at 134 St. Philip Street. He a native of Edisto Island, South Carolina and she of Charleston. He a sashmaker.

CALDER, EVERETT EDWARD aged 22 years married to BABCOCK, ALICE EVA aged 21 years October 8, 1884 by Rev. John O. Wills at 82 Wentworth Street. He a native of Baltimore, Maryland and she of Charleston. He a machinist on Sullivans Island, South Carolina.

CALDER, MARY married to SIMONS, WILLIAM W. April 16, 1895 by Rev. William H. Campbell at St. Paul's Church. He an insurance agent.

CALDER, (Mrs.) S. F. PRINCE aged 39 years married to WINGATE, T. E. aged 45 years September 28, 1879 by Rev. E. A. Wingard at 570 King Street. Both natives of Charleston. He a bootmaker.

CALDWELL, EMMA C. aged 30 years married to JAMISON, ARTHUR THOMAS aged 23 years October 3, 1889 by Rev. R. A. Webb at 54 Vanderhorst Street. He a native of Murfreesboro, Tennessee.

CALDWELL, RICHARD aged 50 years married to TRENHOLM, ELOISE aged 30 years April 16, 1895 by Bishop Ellison Capers in south Church Street. Both natives of Charleston. He a bookkeeper.

CALDWELL, RICHARD aged 28 years married to TUPPER, JEANIE DAVIS aged 25 years October 17, 1878 by Rev. L. H. Shuck at the corner of Meeting and Ann Streets. Both natives of Charleston. He a clerk.

CALVERT, WILLIAM L. aged 33 years married to MURRAY, L. ELIZABETH aged 25 years November 30, 1890 by Father Daniel J. Quigley at St. Patrick's Roman Catholic Church.

CAMERON, ARCHIBALD aged 28 years married to MURPHY, MARY FRANCES aged 18 years November 25, 1878 by Father Daniel J. Quigley at 72 East Bay Street. Both natives of Charleston. He a blacksmith.

CAMERON, CAROLINE T. aged 19 years married to DOAR, HENRY F. aged 24 years June 18, 1885 by Rev. Robert Wilson. Both natives of Charleston. He a mechanic.

CAMERON, ELIZABETH M. aged 22 years married to WATT, DANIEL aged 46 years May 20, 1891 by Rev. G. R. Brackett at 10 Mile Hill. He a native of Scotland and she of Walhalla, South Carolina.

CAMERON, FRANCES married to MAY, HENRY December 28, 1878 by William B. Yates, Chaplain.

CAMERON, JOHN JAMES aged 23 years married to BROOKEISTER, SARAH F. aged 19 years August 20, 1893 by Rev. J. C. Yongue at 546 Meeting Street. He a native of Charleston and a painter.

CAMERON, LULU aged 18 years married to MEYERS, EDWARD C. aged 24 years August 8, 1894 by Rev. A. Ernest Cornish at 71 Bay Street. He a native of St. Stephen's Parish, South Carolina and she of Charleston. He a fireman.

CAMERON, MARY aged 22 years married to LEE, CHARLES aged 44 years March 13, 1889 by Rev. Louis Muller at 10 Mile Hill. He a native of Charleston and she of Mt. Pleasant, South Carolina. He a grocer.

CAMERON, MINNIE aged 19 years married to BROWN, HENRY B. aged 25 years June 28, 1889 by Rev. Robert O. Wilson at 14 Line Street. Both natives of Charleston. He an engineer.

CAMERON, WILLIAM aged 22 years married to O'NEALE, ROSELLA aged 18 years September 23, 1885 by Rev. J. V. Welsh at 3.5 Blake Street. Both natives of Charleston. He a blacksmith.

CAMMER, EMILY aged 25 years married to KOLERA, ANTOINE aged 31 years August 17, 1888 by Rev. J. E. Carlisle at 55 Spring Street. He a native of Athens, Georgia and she of Charleston. He a carpenter.

CAMMER, JOHN J. aged 23 years married to BUCKHEISTER, SARAH F. aged 19 years August 20, 1893 by Rev. J. C. Yongue at 546 Meeting Street.

CAMMER, JULIAN F. aged 18 years married to TAVEL, MARY ANN aged 20 years March 10, 1892 by Rev. J. L. Stokes at 231 Coming Street. Both natives of Charleston. He works in the barrel factory.

CAMMER, MAMIE ELIZABETH aged 21 years married to STROBLE, HENRY aged 19 years May 6, 1892 by Rev. J. A. Clifton at 207 Calhoun Street. Both natives of Charleston. He a farmer.

CAMPBELL, ANNIE aged 25 years married to KELLY, JAMES aged 25 years July 28, 1880 by Father Daniel J. Quigley at The Cathedral of St. John the Baptist. He a native of Charleston and she of Ireland. He a street inspector.

CAMPBELL, ARTHUR M. married to ROACH, ANNIE T. December 29, 1887 by Rev. William H. Campbell at the residence of E. Roach. He a clerk.

CAMPBELL, CROSKEY S. O. aged 21 years married to PHILLIPS, LOUISA C. aged 18 years February 25, 1879 by Rev. John Johnson in George Street. Both natives of Charleston. He a factor.

CAMPBELL, JAMES A. aged 28 years married to SIMMS, ADDY E. aged 18 years April 12, 1887 by Rev. J. V. Welsh. Both natives of South Carolina. He a clerk.

CAMPBELL, JOHN J. J. aged 26 years married to McMAHON, MARY ANN aged 21 years December 26, 1886 by Rev. John Johnson at 53 Church Street. Both natives of Charleston. He works for the railroad.

CAMPBELL, JOHN G. married to FABIAN, E. L. November 3, 1878 by William B. Yates, Chaplain.

CAMPBELL, MOSES G. aged 28 years married to SMITH, MAUDE aged 27 years February 20, 1890 by Rev. Edwin C. Dargan at 36 Charlotte Street. He a native of Tuskegee, Alabama and she of Greenville, South Carolina. He a bookkeeper in Tuskegee.

CAMPBELL, NENA J. aged 17 years married to DEARBORN, GEORGE aged 22 years August 19, 1886 by Rev. Luther K. Probst. She a native of Charleston. He a Superintendent of Laundry.

CAMPBELL, WILLIAM T. married to DEIGHNAN (?), ISABEL May 18, 1880 by William B. Yates, Chaplain. He a gardener.

CAMPET, ANGELA aged 20 years married to HUCHTING (?), JOHN F. aged 40 years August 18, 1886 by Father Thomas E. McCORMACK at St. Patrick's Roman Catholic Church. He a merchant.

CAMPET, MARGARET MARTINA aged 21 years married to HAHN, WILLIAM MARTIN aged 23 years June 3, 1890 by Father J. J. Monaghan at St. Patrick's Roman Catholic Church. Both natives of Charleston. He a boilermaker.

CAMPSEN, ANNIE. A. aged 24 years married to RAVENEL, H. aged 24 years January 21, 1881 by Father Daniel J. Quigley at The Cathedral of St. John the Baptist. Both natives of Charleston. He a clerk.

CAMPSEN, FRANCES MARIE META aged 20 years married to WEBB, JOHN aged 23 years November 7, 1888 by Rev. Louis Muller at the residence of the Bride's mother in Hasell Street, 2 doors from Anson Street.

CANALE, ANGELO aged 46 years married to O'BRIEN, JULIA M. aged 76 years August 29, 1893 by Rev. Joseph D. Budds at 88 Beaufain Street. He a native of Genoa, Italy and she of Ireland. He a machinist.

CANALE, SUSIE M. aged 25 years married to WAY, WILLIAM B. aged 34 years October 5, 1887 by Rev. H. B. Browne at 35 Society Street. He a native of Colleton County, South Carolina and she of Charleston. He a physician in Ridgeville, South Carolina.

CANNON, CHARLIE aged 20 years married to DRIGGERS, BIRDY aged 16 years February 14, 1892 by Rev. J. O. Fludd at 23 Blake Street.

CANNON, DANIEL W. aged 24 years married to VERONEE, ALICE PAULINE aged 18 years April 15, 1881 by Rev. R. W. Memminger in Meeting Street. He a native of Charleston and she of Grahamville, South Carolina. He works for the railroad.

CANNON, DAISY ANNA LOCKWOOD aged 18 years married to EARLY, JAMES E. aged 23 years March 18, 1884 by Rev. J. H. Tellinghast. Both natives of Charleston. He a printer.

CANNON, EMILY J. aged 25 years married to BURCH, WILLIAM P. aged 35 years November 16, 1880 by Rev. John Johnson at the farmhouse of Mr. Cannon. He a native of Wadesboro, North Carolina and she of Charleston. He a horse racer in Cheraw, South Carolina.

CANNON, FANNIE aged 36 years married to BUTLER, GEORGE aged 29 years July 18, 1892 by Rev. J. L. Stokes at 231 Coming Street.

CANNON, FRANKLIN E. aged 27 years married to PURSE, MARY E. aged 27 years January 15, 1885 by Rev. Charles A. Stakely at 10 Hanover Street.

CANNON, HENRIETTA aged 24 years married to HEIDT, E. V. aged 31 years May 11, 1891 by Rev. Robert Wilson at 4 Wragg Square.

CANNON, JOHN J. aged 25 years married to CUMMINGS, WINIFRED F. aged 20 years October 14, 1883 by Father F. J. Shadler at St. Joseph's Roman Catholic Church.

CANNON, MARY ANNIE aged 23 years married to RIVERS, JAMES PHILIP aged 25 years July 26, 1881 by Rev. H. F. Chreitzberg at 43 Hanover Street.

CANNON, MELVILE aged 25 years married to DURR, H. C. aged 28 years March 6, 1889 by Rev. J. E. Carlisle. He a native of Berkeley County, South Carolina and she of Darlington County, South Carolina. He a farmer.

CANNON, OWEN aged 43 years married to DERICK, A. B. aged 45 years October 31, 1880 by Father Daniel J. Quigley at The Cathedral of St. John the Baptist. He a native of Ireland and she of Lexington, South Carolina. Both reside at the Waverly House. He a farmer.

CANNON, T. M. aged 31 years married to BEAUFORT, M. C. aged 20 years January 24, 1882 by Rev. J. M. Green at 78 Smith Street. Both natives of Charleston. He a laborer.

CANTWELL, JAMES C. aged 22 years married to KEENAN, JULIA aged 22 years December 29, 1886 by Father Daniel J. Quigley at St. Patrick's Roman Catholic Church. He a native of South Carolina and she of Charleston. He a clerk in Columbia, South Carolina.

CANTWELL, L. E. aged 29 years married to PRICE, ELIZABETH aged 23 years October 15, 1891 by Bishop Harry P. Northrop at The Cathedral of St. John the Baptist. Both natives of Charleston. He a clerk.

CANTWELL, RICHARD THOMAS aged 43 years married to McPHERSON, JOSEPHINE aged 23 years February 2, 1891 by Father J. J. Monaghan at St. Patrick's Roman Catholic Church. He a native of Graniteville, South Carolina and she of Columbia, South Carolina. He a railroad clerk.

CANTY, ELIZABETH aged 25 years married to DUANE, EDWARD aged 35 years July 16, 1883 by Father F. J. Shadler at St. Joseph's Roman Catholic Church. He a native of Ireland and she of Charleston. He a painter.

CANTY, MAGGIE aged 24 years married to SPEISSENGER (?), JOHN W. aged 21 years December 19, 1886 by Rev. J. V. Welsh at 40 Bee Street. Both natives of Charleston. He a mechanic.

CANTY, SUSAN M. aged 31 years married to BRAID, ROBERT S. aged 36 years October 16, 1890 by Rev. R. C. Holland at Rickesville, Charleston County, South Carolina. He a native of Charleston and she of Colleton County, South Carolina. He an engineer.

CAP, MARIE aged 19 years married to PERRIER, EUGENE aged 23 years July 21, 1883 by Father Harry P. Northrop at The Cathedral of St. John the Baptist. He a native of France and she of Germany. He a cabinetmaker.

CAPERS, CHARLES B. aged 24 years married to TUPPER, FLORENCE aged 22 years June 15, 1880 by Rev. L. H. Shuck. He a native of Beaufort, South Carolina and she of Charleston. He a clerk.

CAPERS, CLARA S. aged 29 years married to OWENS, LAWRENCE E. aged 31 years April 16, 1895 by Bishop Ellison Capers at 280 Calhoun Street. She a native of Marietta, Georgia. He a physician in Columbia, South Carolina.

CAPERS, JULIUS T. aged 28 years married to CATES, MARY J. aged 19 years August 3, 1881 by Rev. E. C. L. Browne. He a native of Beaufort, South Carolina and she of Charleston. He an engineer.

CAPERS, M. E. aged 24 years married to SMITH, R. A. aged 30 years December 19, 1882 by Rev. E. C. L. Browne. He a native of Charleston and a dentist.

CAPPEL, MATILDA LOUISE aged 21 years married to FISHER, AUGUST H. aged 25 years November 1, 1883 by Rev. Johannes Heckel at 36 Church Street. He a native of Charleston and she of Norfolk, Virginia. He a sashmaker.

CAPPELMANN, FREDERICK W. aged 43 years married to BUSCH, (Mrs.) MARIE BRUNCKHORST aged 31 years November 12, 1893 by Rev. K. Boldt at the corner of Spring Street and Ashley Avenue. He a native of Charleston and she of Germany.

CARD, ELIZABETH A. J. aged 24 years married to McEVOY, THOMAS J. aged 31 years July 7, 1895 by Father J. J. Monaghan at 136 St. Philip Street. He a native of Philadelphia, Pennsylvania and she of Charleston. He a marine engineer in Savannah, Georgia.

CARDO, MARY H. aged 18 years married to BENSE, JOHN WILLIAM aged 24 years October 12, 1884 by Rev. R. A. Lapsley. Both natives of Charleston. He works for the railroad.

CARDWELL, JOHN aged 28 years married to LANDRUM, IDA MARION aged 24 years January 16, 1881 by Rev. L. H. Shuck at 48 Church Street. He a native of England and she of Columbia, South Carolina. He a medical student.

CAREE, SAMUEL C. aged 50 years married to WYNNE, MARY A. aged 40 years February 14, 1893 by Father Daniel J. Quigley at 35 Mary Street. He a native of Wilmington, North Carolina and a railroad conductor.

CAREY, J. J. aged 26 years married to DEVINE, A. J. aged 22 years November 18, 1879 by Father D. F. Hurley at St. Joseph's Roman Catholic Church. Both natives of Charleston. He a plumber.

CAREY, LIZZIE M. aged 23 years married to MURPHY, CORNELIUS J. aged 24 years October 16, 1893 by Father J. J. Monaghan at St. Patrick's Roman Catholic Church. Both natives of Charleston. He a clerk.

CARHART, OSCAR D. aged 29 years married to RUGIERO, IRENE aged 19 years December 25, 1889 by Father F. J. Shadler at St. Joseph's Roman Catholic Church. He a native of New Jersey and she of Charleston. He the Superintendent of the Electric Light Company.

CARMODY, CATHERINE M. aged 22 years married to TURNER, CHRISTOPHER J. aged 24 years June 4, 1888 by Father Daniel J. Quigley at St. Patrick's Roman Catholic Church.

CARMODY, JEREMIAH J. aged 36 years married to COSTELLO, MARY ANN FRANCES aged 25 years April 30, 1884 by Father J. J. Wedenfeller at The Cathedral of St. John the Baptist. Both natives of Charleston. He an engineer in Brooklyn, New York.

CARNEY, MARGARET aged 23 years married to RAFFERTY, JOHN F. aged 29 years June 17, 1895 by Father Daniel J. Quigley at St. Patrick's Roman Catholic Church. Both natives of Charleston. He a machinist.

CARPENTER, EDITH F. aged 28 years married to FULLER, BUEL A. aged 45 years January 28, 1885 by Rev. E. C. L. Browne. Both natives of Illinois. He a lawyer.

CARPENTER, MAGGIE E. aged 18 years married to BERRY, JAMES C. aged 23 years June 4, 1895 by Rev. G. R. Brackett at 23 Mill Street. He a native of Marion County, South Carolina and she of Charleston. He a physician in Marion County.

CARPENTER, MARTHA ENSLOW aged 20 years married to HUTCHERSON, PHILIP HENRY aged 26 years June 13, 1888 by Rev. Charles S. Vedder at 23 Mill Street. He a native of Summerville, South Carolina and she of Charleston. He a machinist in Coosaw, South Carolina.

CARR, HELEN married to BUCKLEY, JOHN December 1, 1879 by William B. Yates, Chaplain.

CARRAGAN, MARY aged 18 years married to HUGHES, HOHN E. aged 20 years June 11, 1878 by Father Daniel J. Quigley at The Cathedral of St. John the Baptist. Both natives of Charleston.

CARRERE, FRANCES A. aged 20 years married to ROBERTSON, JAMES aged 23 years October 12, 1887 by Rev. G. R. Brackett. He a native of Chester, South Carolina and she of Charleston. He an insurance agent.

CARRIEGE, AGNES aged 20 years married to ROBERTSON, JOHN aged 32 years January 11, 1881 by Father Daniel J. Quigley at The Cathedral of St. John the Baptist. He a native of Scotland and she of Charleston. He a lighthouse keeper.

CARRIER, KITTY F. aged 19 years married to MERRIWEATHER, FRANK T. aged 21 years October 12, 1886 by Rev. G. R. Brackett. He a native of Louisville, Kentucky and she of Brookville, Pennsylvania. He a physician in Louisville.

CARROLL, ADELLA married to SPELLMAN, DANIEL June 9, 1889 by Rev. H. L. P. Boger at 63.5 Broad Street. He a merchant in Yemassee, South Carolina.

CARROLL, DELIA aged 23 years married to SULLIVAN, JERRIE aged 21 years September 4, 1881 by Rev. J. E. Chapins at the corner of St. Philip and Radcliffe Streets. He a native of Charleston and a farmer.

CARROLL, GEORGE aged 23 years married to WINKLER, LOUISE aged 20 years July 24, 1892 by Father A. Hirshmeyer at The Cathedral of St. John the Baptist. Both natives of Charleston. He a printer.

CARROLL, H. SARAH aged 21 years married to McCUE, H. WILLIAM aged 28 years January 29, 1890 by Father F. J. Shadler at St. Joseph's Roman Catholic Church. Both natives of Charleston. He a letter carrier.

CARROLL, JAMES H. aged 30 years married to DEASE, MARY L. aged 25 years September 18, 1887 by Rev. H. B. Browne at 114 Nassau Street. He a native of York County, South Carolina and she of Sumter County, South Carolina. He a porter.

CARROLL, JULIA A. married to DONEHEY (?), MICHAEL J. aged 25 years January 23, 1881 by Father Harry P. Northrop at St. Patrick's Roman Catholic Church. Both natives of Charleston. He a clerk.

CARROLL, MARGARET aged 25 yeears married to SANG, CHARLES CHIN aged 28 years January 12, 1879 by Father D. J. Quigley at The Cathedral of St. John the Baptist. He a native of China and she of Charleston. He a shopkeeper.

CARROLL, MARY aged 18 years married to SMITH, HENRY aged 28 years June 5, 1881 by Father F. J. Shadler at the residence of the Bride. He a native of Norwich, England and she of Charleston. He works in the gas house.

CARSON, RALPH R. aged 31 years married to JOHNSON, CATHERINE B. aged 23 years November 25, 1885 by Rev. John Johnson at 15 Franklin Street. Both natives of South Carolina. He a lawyer in Spartanburg, South Carolina.

CARSTEN, ADA PINCKNEY aged 24 years married to FOGLE, ALICE MARTHA aged 18 years January 9, 1883 by Rev. Luther K. Probst. He a native of Orangeburg, South Carolina and she of Charleston. He works in the phosphate factory.

CART, RUEBEN ADAM aged 23 years married to BURDELL, EMMA MARIAN aged 24 years April 17, 1890 by Rev. Henry M. Grant at the Circular Congregational Church. He a native of Indiana and she of Charleston. He works in an "agency" in Marionsville, Illinois.

CARTER, PATRICK aged 29 years married to CASEY, ELLA F. aged 24 years July 30, 1890 by Father J. J. Monaghan at St. Joseph's Roman Catholic Church. He a native of Ireland and she of Charleston. He a merchant.

CARTER, W. H. aged 23 years married to MILLER, (Mrs.) MARY E. VAUGHN aged 26 years April 14, 1892 by Rev. Edmund Wells at the Cannon Street Chapel. He a native of North Carolina and she of Wilmington, North Carolina. He works in the bagging factory.

CARTOMIL, JOHN aged 34 years married to STRONG, (Mrs.) MARGARET DARCEY aged 30 years November 3, 1878 by Father C. J. Croghan at St. Joseph's Roman Catholic Church. Both natives of Ireland. He a farmer.

CARTWRIGHT, ALEXANDER aged 26 years married to GUTHRIE, FANNIE E. aged 19 years August 2, 1883 by J. E. Hagood at the U. S. Custom House. Both natives of Georgia. He a clerk.

CARY, THOMAS F. aged 25 years married to CONNOR, JULIA M. aged 22 years February 5, 1888 by Father F. J. Shadler at St. Joseph's Roman Catholic Church. Both natives of Charleston. He a plumber.

CASEY, ELLA F. aged 24 years married to CARTER, PATRICK aged 29 years July 30, 1890 by Father J. J. Monaghan at St. Joseph's Roman Catholic Church. He a native of Ireland and she of Charleston. He a merchant.

CASHMAN, HESSIE aged 22 years married to GILLIGAN, CHARLES H. aged 30 years September 8, 1878 by Father John P. Twigg. He a native of Maine and she of Charleston. He a mariner.

CASHMAN, (Mrs.) MARY LALOR aged 40 years married to NEAGLE, JOHN aged 60 years November 6, 1883 by Father F. J. Shadler at St. Joseph's Roman Catholic Church. Both natives of Charleston.

CASEN, JOSEPHINE J. aged 22 years married to HENNEBERRY, JOHN J. aged 28 years September 15, 1886 by Father Daniel J. Quigley. Both natives of Charleston. He a butcher.

CASON, GEORGE W. aged 24 years married to MARKLEY, KATE H. aged 22 years March 9, 1880 by Rev. J. E. Jackson. Both natives of Charleston. He a clerk.

CASON, ROBERT J. aged 31 years married to EARLY, JULIA A. aged 21 years September 6, 1883 by Rev. J. V. Welsh at 44 Society Street. He a native of Exeter, England and she of Charleston. He an engineer.

CASPARY, JOSEPH aged 23 years married to SAMUELS, MARIE aged 27 years April 7, 1892 by Rabbi David Levy at 88 Wentworth Street. He a native of Laurens County, South Carolina and she of Eatonville, Georgia.

CASSIDY, DENNIS married to SEABROOK, J. October 25, 1880 by William B. Yates, Chaplain. He a native of Charleston.

CASSIDY, MARY ANN aged 25 years married to HUGHES, THOMAS aged 30 years October 4, 1888 by Father Daniel J. Quigley at St. Patrick's Roman Catholic Church. Both natives of Charleston. He a railroad dispatcher.

CASSIDY, M. A. married to HENRICKS, F. W. April 14, 1879 by William B. Yates, Chaplain.

CASSIMER, JOHN HENRY THEODORE aged 25 years married to HESS, WILHELMINA G. aged 20 years May 6, 1888 by Rev. Johannes Heckel at 123 Smith Street. He a native of Germany and she of Charleston. He a bookkeeper.

CASTON, JOHN W. married to JOYNER, ANNIE A. December 7, 1890 by Rev. W. A. Betts.

CATES, MARY J. aged 19 years married to CAPERS, JULIUS T. aged 28 years August 3, 1881 by Rev. E. C. L. Browne. He a native of Beaufort, South Carolina and she of Charleston. He an engineer.

CATHCART, W. RICHARD aged 35 years married to KELLY, CATHERINE S. aged 26 years July 18, 1878 by Rev. C. C. Pinckney in St. Philip Street. Both natives of Charleston. He a clerk.

CATHERWOOD, THOMAS B. married to MARTIN, SALLIE G. May 1, 1894 by Rev. William H. Campbell. He a bookkeeper in Savannah, Georgia.

CAULFIELD, GEORGE M. aged 31 years married to HOPPMAN, MARY aged 20 years August 3, 1892 by Father J. J. Monaghan at St. Patrick's Roman Catholic Church.

CAULFIELD, ANNA aged 19 years married to WALSH, JOHN aged 32 years August 21, 1879 by Father C. J. Croghan at St. Joseph's Roman Catholic Church. He a native of Ireland and she of Charleston. He a furniture dealer in Newark, New Jersey.

CAULFIELD, MARY F. aged 23 years married to BRYCE, JAMES E. aged 24 years April 5, 1888 by Father F. J. Shadler at St. Joseph's Roman Catholic Church. He a native of Newark, New Jersey and she of Charleston. He resides in Newark.

CAUTINE, A. aged 29 years married to MAKIN, S. aged 16 years October 12, 1879 by Father Daniel J. Quigley at The Cathedral of St. John the Baptist. He a native of Italy and she of Charleston. He a merchant.

CAVANAUGH, HUGH aged 45 years married to AUTRY, S. M. aged 43 years April 16, 1893 by Rev. D. F. Toppit at 3 Creamars Court.

CAVANAUGH, MARGARETHE aged 25 years married to JOHNSON, ARTHUR aged 40 years October 1, 1888 by Father Daniel J. Quigley at St. Patrick's Roman Catholic Church. She a native of Charleston. He a merchant.

CAVANT, SUSAN aged 39 years to BALL, SAMUEL aged 39 years May 13, 1884 by Rev. A. H. Misseldine at 7 Percy Street. He a native of Devonshire, England and she of Charleston. He an engineer.

CAVERT, D. aged 23 years married to SULLIVAN, T. aged 21 years September 4, 1881 by Father J. E. Chapins at the corner of St. Philip and Radcliffe Streets. He a native of Charleston.

CAY, JOHN EUGENE aged 24 years married to JENNINGS, MARY HENRIETTA aged 21 years June 19, 1879 by Father Claudian B. Northrop at 264 Calhoun Street. Both natives of Charleston. He a clerk.

CERCOPELY, JOSEPH W. aged 20 years married to FLEMING, FRANCES aged 20 years March 15, 1889 by Rev. H. B. Browne at 23 Line Street. He a native of Charleston.

CETCHOVEH, RAPHAEL aged 30 years married to MEYER, CATHERINE aged 29 years June 20, 1885 by Rev. Luther K. Probst. Both natives of Germany. He a mariner.

CETTE, FREDERICK R. aged 34 years married to DEVINE, MARY McI. aged 18 years August 8, 1878 by Father Joseph Redington at The Cathedral of St. John the Baptist. He a native of Italy and she of Charleston. He a fresco painter.

CHANSON, JOSEPH aged 23 years married to MALONE, GERTRUDE L. aged 16 years May 6, 1895 by Rev. A. Ernest Cornish at the corner of Bee and President Streets. Both natives of Charleston. He works for the railroad.

CHAPLAIN, EFFIE aged 20 years married to MEAGHER, JOHN F. aged 28 years November 26, 1894 by Father J. J. Monaghan at St. Patrick's Roman Catholic Church. Both natives of Charleston. He an engineer.

CHAPLIN, BENJAMIN aged 58 years married to HERREN, (Mrs.) MARGARET E. WITHERS aged 44 years July 20, 1887 by Rev. Leroy F. Beattie at 231 Coming Street. Both natives of South Carolina. He a machinist.

CHAPLIN, MARY H. married to NEVILS, ANDREW J. January 15, 1890 by Rev. William A. Betts.

CHAPLAIN, S. G. married to LAMB, SARAH ANN November 15, 1877 by William B. Yates, Chaplain.

CHAPMAN, JESSIE C. married to PICKRELL, PERCY A. aged 33 years June 7, 1892 by Rev. John Johnson at 37 Meeting Street. He a native of Richmond, Virginia and she of Camden, South Carolina. He a broker in New York.

CHARLON, AMANDA B. aged 18 years married to BAGLEY, JOHN H. aged 23 years November 19, 1893 by Rev. J. C. Yongue at 112 Nassau Street. He a native of Georgia and she of Charleston. He works in a restaurant.

CHARLON, JOHN T. aged 35 married to WARNER, EUDORA aged 18 years June 19, 1879 by Rev. J. Mercier Green at the corner of King Street Road and Lowndes Avenue. He a native of Charleston and she of Ridgeville, South Carolina. He a farmer.

CHARLON, WILLIAM aged 35 years married to ROUSELY, MAGGIE aged 35 years September 5, 1886 by Rev. H. B. Browne at 131 Sheppard Street. He a native of Charleston and she of Orangeburg, South Carolina. He a policeman.

CHAZAL, MARIE LOUISE aged 21 years married to PATRICK, CASIMIR CORNELIUS aged 29 years July 10, 1878 by Father Claudian B. Northrop at St. Mary of the Annunciation Roman Catholic Church. Both natives of Charleston. He a dentist.

CHEEK, CHARLES aged 27 years married to GROOM, BETTIE aged 16 years May 16, 1888 by Rev. H. B. Browne in America Street. He a native of Georgia and she of Darlington, South Carolina. He works in the cotton mill.

CHERRY, CATHERINE aged 22 years married to JERVEY, DANIEL D. aged 32 years February 26, 1884 by Father P. L. Duffy in Mt. Pleasant, South Carolina. Both natives of Charleston. He a farmer.

CHERRY, DOMINICK aged 25 years married to LARKIN, ELLEN VINCENT aged 26 years August 29, 1881 by Father P. L. Duffy at The Cathedral of St. John the Baptist. He a native of Charleston and she of New York City.

CHEVES, HARRIET KINLOCH aged 25 years married to BARNWELL, JOSEPH WALKER aged 30 years January 23, 1883 by Rev. John Johnson in South Bay Street. Both natives of Charleston. He a lawyer.

CHEVES, HENRY C. aged 34 years married to McCORD, L. CHEVES aged 23 years November 9, 1886 by Rev. Robert Wilson at St. Luke's Church. Both natives of Charleston. He a clerk.

CHICHESTER, JAMES G. aged 20 years married to TUCKER, R. aged 19 years May 4, 1882 by Rev. J. V. Welsh at 24 Bee Street. He a native of Charleston and a butcher.

CHICO, VINCENT aged 34 years married to BURKE, MARY E. aged 33 years August 16, 1885 by Father F. J. Shadler at St. Joseph's Roman Catholic Church. He a native of Italy and she of Charleston. He a policeman.

CHILDS, JESSIE aged 40 years married to GEHLKEN, HEINRICH E. aged 40 years January 11, 1892 by Rev. Louis Muller at 96 Radcliffe Street. He a native of Prussia and she of Charleston. He a cabinetmaker.

CLAFFY, MARY JANE aged 25 years married to HASSON, CECIL CALVERT aged 40 years December 25, 1887 by Rev. P. J. Wilson.

CHIN SANG, CHARLIE aged 28 years married to CARROLL, MARGARET aged 25 years January 12, 1879 by Father Daniel J. Quigley at The Cathedral of St. John the Baptist.

CHISOLM, HARRIET aged 18 years married to HORN, EDWARD TRIAL aged 30 years June 15, 1880 by Rev. W. S. Bowman at St. Johannes Lutheran Church. He a native of Eishorn, Pennsylvania and she of Charleston. He a clergyman.

CHISOLM, J. BUCKMAN married to DESSAUSSURE, OCTOAVIA October 5, 1882 by Rev. Richard S. Trapier.

CHISOLM, LOUISA H. married to WILLIAM SALLIE ROSE December 16, 1884 by Rev. Richard S. Trapier at St. Michael's Church.

CHISOLM, M. M. aged 37 years married to KENNEDY, J. W. aged 40 years July 23, 1882 by Rev. L. H. Shuck at the corner of Line Street and Rutledge Avenue.

CHISOLM, SUSAN EMMA aged 39 years married to PORCHER, PETER CORDES aged 39 years April 13, 1886 by Rev. LeGrand F. Guerry at 18 Meeting Street. Both natives of Charleston. He a phosphate worker in Colleton County, South Carolina.

CHISOLM, WILLIAM B. aged 19 years married to HALL, FELICIA O. aged 22 years November 28, 1877 by Rev. C. C. Pinckney at Grace Church.

CHOATE, SUSIE M. aged 25 years married to Baker, ARTHUR W. aged 30 years December 14, 1892 by Rev. W. T. Thompson at 43 Lynch Street. He a native of McClellanville, South Carolina and she of Charleston. He a merchant in Cordesville, South Carolina.

CHRISTIAN, FRANKIE FLANAGAN aged 28 years married to PENFIELD, MILTON R. aged 29 years July 19, 1885 by Rev. A. J. S. Thomas at First Baptist Church. He a native of Connecticut and she of Georgia. He a mariner.

CHRISTIAN, W. P. aged 18 years married to COLLINS, MAURICE J. aged 27 years May 18, 1880 by Father C. J. Gresin (?) at St. Joseph's Roman Catholic Church. Both natives of Charleston. He a baker.

CHRISTIAN, J. E. aged 34 years married to O'BRIEN, MARGARET aged 23 years June 28, 1882 by Father J. J. Monaghan at St. Patrick's Roman Catholic Church. He a native of Ireland and she of South Carolina. He a tailor.

CHRISTIE, WILLIAM McP. aged 29 years married to KNOX, LILLIAN L. aged 20 years May 28, 1885 by Rev. John Johnson at the Mills House Hotel. He a native of Nassau and she of Charleston. He works on a steamboat.

CHUBB, WILLIAM N. aged 24 years married to BRYANT, LULA D. aged 22 years June 2, 1889 by Rev. H. B. Browne at Cumberland Church. He a native of Washington, D. C. and a farmer.

CHUFF, ANDREW married to COLEMAN, E. September 4, 1879 by William B. Yates, Chaplain.

CHURCH, C. M. aged 23 years married to HORRES, C. E. aged 19 years September 9, 1879 by Rev. William C. Power at the corner of Nassau and Amherst Streets. Both natives of Charleston. He a barber.

CHURCH, J. E. aged 21 years married to MORIARITY (?), MARY aged 20 years March 29, 1891 by Rev. J. Thomas Pate at 231 Coming Street. He a native of Charleston and she of Worchester, Massachusetts. He a barber.

CHURCH, MARY S. aged 19 years married to MILLIGAN, G. H. aged 21 years July 12, 1881 by Rev. J. V. Welch in Spring Street. He a native of Charleston and a machinist.

CHURCHILL, F. aged 52 years married to HARTMAN, C. aged 43 years August 20, 1882 by Rev. Luther K. Probst. He a native of Germany and a laborer.

CHURCHILL, JOHN aged 34 years married to WILLIE, JOSEPHINE aged 26 years September 6, 1883 by Rev. Louis Muller at 80 America Street. He a native of Georgia and she of Charleston. He an engineer.

CHURCHILL, JULIA married to WATTS, JOHN W. May 13, 1890 by John Ahrens, Trial Justice, at 157 Nassau Street.

CHURCHILL, SUSAN E. aged 21 years married to DUC, HENRY C. aged 25 years February 24, 1886 by Rev. John O. Wilson at 85 East Bay Street. Both natives of Charleston. He a farmer.

CISA, BONAVENTUREA aged 27 years married to SCARPA, MARY J. aged 17 years December 19, 1883 by Father J. J. Woolahan at St. Mary of the Annunciation Roman Catholic Church. He a native of Spain and she of Charleston. He a stevedore.

CISSELL, FREDERICK S. aged 32 years married to FARLEY, MARY aged 35 years December 28, 1881 by Rev. L. H. Shuck.

CLAFFEY, JAMES H. aged 26 years married to CONLIN, MARY ELIZABETH aged 22 years October 27, 1884 by Father F. J. Shadler at St. Joseph's Roman Catholic Church. He a native of Columbia, South Carolina and she of Charleston. He a farmer.

CLAFFY, MARY JANE aged 25 years married to HASSON, CECIL CALVERT aged 40 years December 25, 1887 by Father P. J. Wilson at St. Patrick's Roman Catholic Church.

CLANCY, (Mrs.) SUSAN S. E. BERESFORD aged 53 years married to COIL, CLAYTON aged 57 years November 29, 1889 by Rev. Robert Wilson at 4 Wragg Street. She a native of Charleston. He a tanner in Philadelphia, Pennsylvania.

CLARENDON, (?) GRACE aged 22 years married to PINCKNEY, C. C. aged 25 years February 20, 1890 by Rev. E. W. Hughes at Grace Church. He a native of Berkeley County, South Carolina and she of Charleston. He a lawyer.

CLARK, DANIEL J. aged 30 years married to SHOKES, EMMA A. aged 24 years August 13, 1887 by Rev. T. P. Burgess. Both natives of Charleston. He works in the iron foundry.

CLARK, G. T. aged 22 years married to DORAN, E. M. aged 22 years June 8, 1882 by Father Daniel J. Quigley at The Cathedral of St. John the Baptist. He a native of Charleston and a boathand.

CLARK, HENRY aged 50 years married to REYNOLDS, ADELE aged 35 years April 28, 1880 by Father Claudian B. Northrop at St. Mary of the Annunciation Roman Catholic Church. He a native of Scotland and she of Washington, D. C. He a resident of Jacksonville, Florida and she of Buffalo, New York. He a merchant.

CLARK, IDA aged 25 years married to FRAIN, THOMAS J. aged 29 years November 21, 1888 by Father F. J. Shadler.

CLARK, MARY J. aged 26 years married to GERARD, E. aged 29 years October 23, 1887 by Rev. P. J. McManus. He a native of Alsace and she of Charleston. He a loom fitter.

CLARK, ROSIE E. aged 24 years married to WHEELER, JOHN W. aged 29 years October 30, 1893 by Rev. David M. Ramsey at 6 Court House Square.

CLARK, (Mrs.) SARAH COWLES RUSSELL aged 48 years married to WOLD, HELLE JUEL (?) aged 50 years November 5, 1880 by Rev. C. E. Chichester at the Sailors' Home in Market Street. He a native of Norway and she of Virginia. He a clerk.

CLARK, THOMAS A. aged 31 years married to CLAUSON, HENRIETTA L. aged 36 years March 18, 1887 by Rev. J. V. Welsh. He a native of Canada and she of Charleston. He a laborer.

CLARK, WILLIAM DUFF aged 28 years married to LAWRENCE, KATE aged 20 years September 21, 1891 by Rev. R. C. Holland at 145 Meeting Street. He a native of Perth, Scotland and she of Southampton, England. He a photographer.

CLARKE, M. F. aged 18 years married to McDONOUGH, JOHN E. aged 20 years November 21, 1890 by Rev. William P. Bolger, Trial Justice. Both natives of Savannah, Georgia. He an engineer in Savannah.

CLARKE, (Mrs.) VICTORIA E. HUNTER aged 29 years married to ILDERTON (?), FLYNN BROWNING aged 25 years March 1, 1880 by Rev. W. S. Bowman at the Wentworth Street Lutheran Church. He a native of Summerville, South Carolina and she of Charleston. He a medical student.

CLARKIN, P. R. aged 25 years married to KEENAN, MARY J. aged 25 years January 9, 1887 by Father F. J. Shadler at St. Joseph's Roman Catholic Church. He a native of Ireland and she of Charleston. He a laborer.

CLARKSON, CHARLES D. married to KERRISON, LOUISA HERIOT November 12, 1890 by Rev. William H. Campbell at St. Paul's Church. Both natives of Charleston. He a physician.

CLARKSON, JULIUS EUGENE aged 37 years married to PORCHER, MARY I'ON aged 30 years January 16, 1884 by Rev. John Johnson at 2 Franklin Street. He a native of Charleston and she of South Carolina. He a farmer.

CLARKSON, WILLIAM R. aged 23 years married to FINCKEN, MARY C. aged 27 years May 16, 1893 by Rev. J. L. Stokes at 56 Hanover Street. He a native of Kentucky and she of Walhalla, South Carolina. He an artist.

CLAUSS, ANDREW THEODORE aged 25 years married to STRAMM, AUGUSTA aged 21 years September 9, 1886 by Rev. Johannes Heckel at 16 Wentworth Street. He a native of Charleston and she of Georgia. He a clerk.

CLAUSS, LOUISA C. aged 26 years married to RIDGEWAY, L. MANNING aged 31 years March 4, 1886 by Rev. H. B. Browne at 192 Spring Street. He a native of South Carolina and she of Charleston. He a farmer in Berkeley County, South Carolina.

CLAUSSEN, CHRISTINA D. aged 23 years married to KERSTEN, EMIL aged 31 years May 7, 1886 by Rev. Oscar H. Kraft of Buffalo, New York. Both natives of Charleston. He a grocer.

CLAUSSEN, HERMANN aged 24 years married to BUCK, EMMA REBECCA aged 20 years April 25, 1881 by Rev. Johannes Heckel in Rafer's Alley. Both natives of Charleston. He a merchant.

CLAUSON, HENRIETTA L. aged 36 years married to CLARK, THOMAS A. aged 31 years March 18, 1887 by Rev. J. V. Welsh. He a native of Canada and she of Charleston. He a laborer.

CLEAPOR, ROSA aged 24 years married to PASSAS, NICOLAS aged 24 years January 2, 1881 by Rev. John Johnson at 104 Market Street. He a native of Greece and she of Charleston. He a fruitier.

CLEAPOR, WALTER G. aged 21 years married to HENDRIX, ANNIE LOUISA aged 18 years April 7, 1891 by Rev. W. A. Betts at 82 Bay Street.

CLEAR, MARIA aged 35 years married to DUFFY, FRANCIS aged 35 years October 12, 1884 by Father F. A. Schmetz at St. Patrick's Roman Catholic Church. He a native of Charleston and she of Ireland. He a merchant.

CLEAR, WILLIAM ROBERT aged 30 years married to McINERNEY, MAGGIE aged 25 years June 27, 1888 by Father Daniel J. Quigley at St. Patrick's Roman Catholic Church. Both natives of Charleston. He works for the railroad.

CLEARY, ANNIE E. aged 20 years married to DUGAN, JAMES J. aged 30 years November 29, 1880 by Father P. L. Duffy at The Cathedral of St. John the Baptist. Both natives of Charleston. He a carpenter.

CLEARY, ELLEN L. M. aged 20 years married to BROWN, WILLIAM C. aged 26 years August 1, 1887 by Father Daniel J. Quigley at St. Patrick's Roman Catholic Church. He a native of Maryland and she of Charleston. He a bridge builder.

CLEARY, MARIA aged 25 years married to LANIGAN, CORNELIUS aged 24 years October 15, 1890 by Father Harry P. Northrop at The Cathedral of St. John the Baptist. Both natives of Charleston. He a laborer.

CLEARY, MARY MAGDALEN aged 22 years married to HANLEY, MARTIN JOSEPH aged 26 years April 21, 1878 by Father John P. Twigg at The Cathedral of St. John the Baptist. He a native of Ireland and she of Charleston. He a laborer.

CLEMENT, MORTON W. aged 30 years married to ELFE, MARTHA ANN aged 27 years December 22, 1881 by Rev. John Johnson at 657 King Street. He a native of Adams Runs, South Carolina and she of Charleston. He a machinist.

CLERKINS, EDWARD aged 25 years married to BURNS, MARY JOSEPHINE aged 23 years February 25, 1884 by Father F. J. Shadler at St. Joseph's Roman Catholic Church. Both natives of Charleston. He an employee at the gas works.

CLIFFORD, ANNIE aged 18 years married to McINNERNEY, MICHAEL aged 23 years February 28, 1880 by Father Daniel J. Quigley at The Cathedral of St. John the Baptist. He a native of Charleston and she of England. He a stonecutter.

CLINTON, MARY CECILE aged 24 years married to JONES, WILLIAM G. aged 26 years April 21, 1890 by Father J. J. Woolahan at The Cathedral of St. John the Baptist. He a native of Baltimore, Maryland and she of Charleston. He an insurance agent in Baltimore.

CLOPTON, E. H. aged 23 years married to EASON, VIRGINIA aged 23 years November 3, 1887 by Rev. C. C. L. Browne at the Unitarian Church. He a native of Tuskegee, Alabama and she of Abbeville, South Carolina. He a manufacturer in Montgomery, Alabama.

COATES, EMILY ISABEL aged 16 years married to WALKER, HARRY CALEB aged 22 years September 1, 1884 by Rev. W. P. Mouzon at 6 President Street. Both natives of Charleston. He a blacksmith.

COATES, MARY G. aged 18 years married to HERON, WILLIAM I. aged 22 years June 24, 1890 by Rev. Robert Wilson at St. Luke's Church. Both natives of Charleston. He a clerk.

COATES, (Mrs.) MATTIE ELSWORTH aged 22 years married to PRESCOTT, JOHN F. aged 22 years April 16, 1889 by Rev. H. B. Browne at 78 Drake Street. Both natives of Charleston. He a merchant.

COATES, SAMUEL aged 23 years married to ELLSWORTH, MATTIE O. aged 21 years December 26, 1887 by Rev. A. H. Misseldine.

COBIA, MAGGIE aged 20 years married to PINKHAM, HORACE E. aged 30 years December 28, 1881 by Rev. J. V. Welsh at 24 Bee Street. He a native of Philadelphia, Pennsylvania and she of Charleston. He a mariner.

COBIA, S. WALTER aged 21 years married to LAFOURCADE, M. EVA aged 17 years September 29, 1889 by Rev. H. B. Browne at 78 Drake Street. Both natives of Charleston. He a printer.

COBIN, MARGARET married to JENTRY, J. T. September 18, 1878 by William B. Yates, Chaplain.

COBLE, ALICE C. aged 20 years married to VONDERLEITH, THEODORE R. aged 37 years December 21, 1893 by Rev. Edmund Wells at the Cannon Street Baptist Church. He a native of Athens, Georgia and she of Mecklenberg, North Carolina. He a clerk.

COBURN, FRANCES A. ROBERTS aged 38 years married to BEE, JOHN S. aged 41 years April 11, 1893 by Rev. G. R. Brackett at 17 Smith Street. Both natives of Charleston. He a railroad clerk.

COCHRAN, ANN aged 19 years married to MARSHALL, ANDREW A. aged 22 years February 26, 1880 by Rev. J. V. Welsh. He a native of Brownsville, Maine and she of Charleston. He a carpenter.

COCHRAN, A. M. aged 31 years married to GROTUS, LOUISA aged 23 years November 27, 1884 by Father F. J. Shadler at 56 Anson Street. He a native of Anderson, South Carolina and she of Charleston. He a segar dealer.

COCHRAN, ELEANOR L. aged 19 years married to MARSHALL, ANDREW A. aged 22 years February 26, 1880 by Rev. G. R. Brackett at the Second Presbyterian Church. Both natives of Charleston. He a hardware merchant.

COCHRAN, JEAN aged 20 years married to WITHAM (?), WILLIAM S. aged 31 years February 10, 1885 by Rev. John O. Wilson at 16 Ashley Avenue.

COCHRAN, KATE married to SIGWALD, PATRICK O. May 1, 1878 by William B. Yates, Chaplain.

COFFEY, THOMAS E. aged 38 years married to TIBBES, SARAH T. aged 27 years October 16, 1884 by Father Daniel J. Quigley.

COGSWELL, E. O. aged 23 years married to JOHNSON, S. J. aged 18 years August 13, 1882 by Rev. E. J. Meynardie in America Street. He a native of Charleston and a railroad conductor.

COGSWELL, JAMES L. aged 25 years married to CONDIT, AMELIA J. aged 26 years July 19, 1889 by Rev. R. D. Smart at Sullivans Island, South Carolina. She resides in Millsville, Wisconsin. He a journalist.

COGSWELL, WILLIAM HARVEY aged 30 years married to MUCKENFUSS, EDNA aged 19 years June 11, 1890 by Rev. R. D. Smart at Bethel Church.

COHEN, JACK W. aged 25 years married to GOLDSMITH, CARRIE aged 23 years April 3, 1895 by Rabbi Barnett A. Elzas.

COHEN, ISAAC S. married to ISRAEL, CARRIE aged 22 years January 18, 1894 by Rabbi David Levy at 54 Wentworth Street.

COHEN, JOSEPH aged 19 years married to TIMMONS, ELMIRA aged 18 years September 16, 1883 by Rev. E. J. Meynardie at 145 Calhoun Street. He a native of Columbia, South Carolina and she of Cincinnati, Ohio. He a weaver in the cotton mill.

COHEN, L. S. aged 26 years married to SOLOMON, H. aged 26 years May 26, 1882 by Rabbi David Levy at 3 Orange Street. He a native of Georgia and a merchant.

COHEN, MORRIS aged 32 years married to MEYER, DORA aged 22 years November 3, 1886 by S. E. Gleason, Trial Justice. He a native of Poland and she of Germany. He a merchant in Jacksonville, Florida.

COHEN, WILLIAM CECIL married to McKEE, AGNES May 7, 1889 by Rev. William H. Campbell at the residence of George McKee at 83 Cannon Street.

COIL, CLAYTON aged 57 years married to CLANCY, (Mrs.) SUSAN S. E. BERESFORD aged 53 years November 29, 1889 by Rev. Robert Wilson at 4 Wragg Street. She a native of Charleston. He a tanner in Philadelphia, Pennsylvania.

COLBERT, WILLIAM L. aged 33 years married to MURRAY, L. C. aged 25 years November 30, 1890 by Father Daniel J. Quigley at St. Patrick's Roman Catholic Church. Both natives of Charleston. He a stonecutter.

COLBURN, J. P. aged 26 years married to ROBERTS, T. A. aged 26 years February 9, 1882 by Rev. G. R. Brackett at the Second Presbyterian Church. He a native of Charleston and a broker.

COLCOCLOUGH, HENRY L. aged 25 years married to KENNEDY, MAMIE aged 22 years June 7, 1894 by Father Daniel J. Quigley at St. Patrick's Roman Catholic Church.

COLCOCLOUGH, MARY J. aged 23 years married to O'DONNELL, DANIEL P. aged 22 years May 18, 1884 by Father F. A. Schmetz at 25 Columbus Street. He a native of Wilmington, North Carolina and she of Charleston. He a clerk.

COLE, ANNA aged 28 years married to WHELAN, JAMES aged 29 years May 3, 1883 by Father J. J. Woolahan at St. Mary of the Annunciation Roman Catholic Church. Both natives of Ireland. He a laborer

COLE, HENRY THOMAS aged 23 years married to DOWNING, ROSA H. aged 17 years August 6, 1893 by Rev. Edmund Wells at 86 Mary Street. He a native of Effingham, South Carolina and she of Charleston. He works in the cotton mill.

COLE, RICHARD B. aged 26 years married to HERBERT, VIRGINIA S. aged 17 years July 3, 1885 by Rev. John O. Wilson at the corner of East Bay and Laurens Streets. He a native of Florida and she of Charleston. He a driver.

COLE, ROBERT aged 21 years married to DEHLS, A. ANNA aged 21 years April 16, 1885 by Father F. J. Shadler at the residence of the Bride.

COLEMAN, E. married to CHUFF, ANDREW September 4, 1879 by William B. Yates, Chaplain.

COLEMAN, JAMES E. aged 31 years married to CONROY, MAGGIE L. aged 27 years June 8, 1886 by Father F. J. Shadler at St. Joseph's Roman Catholic Church. Both natives of Charleston. He a jeweller.

COLEMAN, JOSEPH aged 28 years married to FOX, WINNIE F. aged 18 years May 1, 1895 by Rev. J. C. Yongue at 14 Inspection Street. Both natives of Charleston. He works on a dredge.

COLEMAN, WILEY M. aged 38 years married to DESPORTES, EMMELINE D. aged 27 years October 24, 1889 by Rev. Edwin C. Dargan at 89 Washington Street. He a native of Ridgeway, South Carolina and she of Charleston. He a farmer in Ridgeway.

COLEY, JOHN M. aged 33 years married to BURTON, ELIZABETH aged 19 years August 11, 1892 by Rev. A. N. Chreitzberg at the corner of Hanover and Columbus Streets. He a native of South Carolina and she of Moncks Corner, South Carolina. He in the mercantile business.

COLLINS, EMILY PALMER aged 27 years married to COLLINS, FRANCIS M. aged 24 years March 15, 1894 by Father J. S. Kelly at 119 Nassau Street. He a native of Columbia, South Carolina and she of Charleston. He works for the railroad.

COLLINS, FRANCIS M. aged 24 years married to COLLINS, EMILY PALMER aged 27 years March 15, 1894 by Father J. S. Kelly at 119 Nassau Street. He a native of Columbia, South Carolina and she of Charleston. He works for the railroad.

COLLINS, H. W. aged 19 years married to SIGWALD, A. L. aged 19 years October 21, 1880 by Rev. H. F. Chreitzberg at 22 Columbus Street. He a native of Summerville, South Carolina and she of Charleston. He works for the railroad.

COLLINS, JEREMIAH P. aged 24 years married to DUC, NOEMI M. aged 26 years April 13, 1879 by Father Harry P. Northrop at St. Patrick's Roman Catholic Church. Both natives of Charleston. He a clerk.

COLLINS, JONAH B. aged 21 years married to MATHIESSEN, E. E. aged 17 years September 13, 1887 by Rev. W. S. Bean at 439 Meeting Street. He a native of Summerville, South Carolina and she of Charleston. He a salesman.

COLLINS, MARY F. aged 22 years married to SLATTERY, JOHN P. aged 32 years January 16, 1889 by Father Daniel J. Quigley at St. Patrick's Roman Catholic Church. He a native of Hoboken, New Jersey and she of Charleston. He a planter in Colleton County, South Carolina.

COLLINS, MAURICE J. aged 27 years married to CHRISTIAN, W. P. aged 18 years May 18, 1880 by Father C. J. Giesin (?) at St. Joseph's Roman Catholic Church. Both natives of Charleston. He a baker.

COLLINS, PAMELA CECILE aged 26 years married to AIMAR, ARTHUR P. aged 28 years June 26, 1893 by Father Joseph D. Budds at St. Mary of the Annunciation Roman Catholic Church. He a native of South Carolina and she of Charleston. He a druggist.

COLLINS, SUSANNA WESLEY aged 21 years married to BLUME, C. DOWLING aged 29 years July 7, 1878 by Rev. William C. Power at 77 St. Philip Street. He a native of Barnwell, South Carolina and she of Beaufort, South Carolina. He a farmer in Orangeburg, South Carolina.

COLSON, C. BUNTING married to DAVIS, IDA B. April 14, 1887 by Rev. Richard S. Trapier at St. Luke's Church.

COLSON, EMELINE GEORGINA aged 29 years married to SANBURG, CHARLES C. aged 28 years May 10, 1881 by Rev. E. J. Meynardie at Bethel Church. He a native of Savannah, Georgia and she of Charleston. He a couchmaker.

COLSON, GEORGE aged 28 years married to HUTSON, ANNIE E. aged 18 years September 8, 1886 by Rev. H. B. Browne at 21 Blake Street. He a native of Maryland and she of Charleston. He a merchant.

COLSON, WILLIAM LEBBY aged 21 years married to MALIN (?), MARY aged 20 years November 4, 1891 by Bishop Harry P. Northrop at 79 Tradd Street. Both natives of Charleston. He a clerk at the West Point Mills.

COMAR, JAMES B. aged 20 years married to SIMMONS, GERTRUDE E. aged 20 years April 13, 1879 by Father Daniel J. Quigley at The Cathedral of St. John the Baptist.

COMAR, JOSEPH WILLIAM aged 24 years married to FURLONG, ELIZABETH aged 32 years February 8, 1890 by Father Daniel J. Quigley at The Cathedral of St. John the Baptist.

COMER, MARGARET aged 18 years married to McMANUS, MICHAEL aged 28 years February 8, 1880 by Father John P. Twigg at The Cathedral of St. John the Baptist. Both natives of Charleston. He a policeman.

COMAR, MARY E. aged 25 years married to PRICE, THOMAS J. aged 29 years June 11, 1889 by Father F. J. Shadler at St. Joseph's Roman Catholic Church. Both natives of Charleston. He a merchant.

COMAR, WILLIAM J. aged 26 years married to PENDER, ANARTASIS aged 24 years April 16, 1884 by Father F. A. Schmetz at St. Patrick's Roman Catholic Church. Both natives of Charleston. He a clerk.

CONANT, (Mrs.) COURNTEY E. WOLLING aged 27 years married to KENNEDY, JOSEPH aged 47 years July 6, 1886 by Rev. C. C. Pinckney at Grace Church. He a native of Charleston and she of South Carolina. He a butcher.

CONANT, E. I. aged 24 years married to WALLING, C. E. aged 20 years December 11, 1879 at residence of the Bride - the corner of Line Street and Sires Alley.

CONDIT, AMELIA J. aged 26 years married to COGSWELL, JAMES L. aged 25 years July 19, 1889 by Rev. R. C. Smart at Sullivans Island, South Carolina. She resides in Millsville, Wisconsin. He a journalist.

CONDON, J. T. aged 24 years married to McLAUGHLIN, M. A. aged 21 years May 27, 1882 by Father J. F. Shadler at St. Joseph's Roman Catholic Church. He a native of Charleston and a clerk.

CONKE, J. T. aged 24 years married to COOK. E. J. aged 22 years June 6, 1882 by Father J. J. Monaghan at St. Patrick's Roman Catholic Church. He a native of Charleston and a brickmason.

CONLEY, H. W. aged 20 years married to SCOTT, R. aged 15 years February 23, 1891 by Rev. W. S. Watkins at 24 Blake Street. He a native of Barnwell County, South Carolina and she of Williamsburg County, South Carolina. He works for the railroad.

CONLEY, MARY aged 26 years married to SQUIRES, (?) JOHN HENRY aged 25 years June 8, 1890 by Father J. J. Monaghan at 136 St. Philip Street. He a native of New York and she of Ireland. He a painter.

CONLEY, WILLIAM J. aged 23 years married to WARREN, KATIE aged 24 years February 20, 1884 by Father F. A. Schmetz at St. Patrick's Roman Catholic Church. He a native of Prince Edward Island, Canada and she of Charleston. He a barber.

CONLIN, MARY ELIZABETH aged 22 years married to CLAFFEY, JAMES H. aged 26 years October 27, 1884 by Father F. J. Shadler at St. Joseph's Roman Catholic Church. He a native of Columbia, South Carolina and she of Charleston. He a farmer.

CONLON, EUGENE aged 35 years married to BURK, MARY aged 20 years May 6, 1883 by Father John P. Twigg at St. Patrick's Roman Catholic Church. Both natives of Charleston. He a machinist.

CONLON, EUGENE aged 35 years married to O'BRIEN, ANNIE aged 32 years January 21, 1895 by Father J. J. Monaghan at St. Patrick's Roman Catholic Church. Both natives of Charleston. He an engineer.

CONLON, JOHN H. aged 24 years married to MURRAY, E. KATIE aged 20 years January 14, 1890 by Father Daniel J. Quigley at St. Patrick's Roman Catholic Church. Both natives of Charleston. He a blacksmith in Coosaw, South Carolina.

CONLON, M. P. aged 31 years married to LAVALLE, MARY F. aged 20 years June 3, 1888 by Father Daniel J. Quigley at The Cathedral of St. John the Baptist. Both natives of Charleston.

CONLON, THOMAS M. aged 24 years married to HYNES, M. L. aged 21 years November 10, 1886 by Father Daniel J. Quigley at St. Patrick's Roman Catholic Church. Both natives of Charleston. He a machinist.

CONNELLY, CARRIE E. aged 19 years married to McCORMACK, JOHN R. aged 24 years April 22, 1891 by Rev. Edwin C. Dargan at 143 Calhoun Street. He a native of Barnwell County, South Carolina and she of Graniteville, South Carolina. He a physician in Midway, South Carolina.

CONNELLY, JESSE M. aged 28 years married to BROOKBANKS, ANNA E. aged 28 years July 3, 1878 by Rev. L. H. Shuck at 369 King Street. He a native of Barnwell, South Carolina and she of Charleston. He a policeman.

CONNELLY, M. A. aged 24 years married to HASMAN, A. E. aged 43 years January 12, 1881 by Rev. L. H. Shuck at 27 Church Street. He a native of Germany and she of Charleston. He a tobacconist.

CONNELLY, M E. aged 23 years married to GRIMES, J. aged 22 years November 22, 1882 by Father John W. Twigg at St. Patrick's Roman Catholic Church. He a native of South Carolina and a bricklayer.

CONNOLLY, HENRY W. aged 21 years married to OSBORNE, (Mrs.) MARY TOOLE aged 27 years April 24, 1892 by Rev. A. W. Chreitzberg at 84 America Street. He a native of Barnwell, South Carolina and she of Aiken, South Carolina. He works for the railroad.

CONNOR, FRANCIS A. aged 65 years married to EVANS, (Mrs.) JULIA E. COGSWELL aged 53 years April 18, 1883 by Rev. W. P. Mouzon at 20 George Street. He a native of Abbeville, South Carolina and she of Charleston. He a merchant.

CONNOR, JESSIE aged 18 years married to HEATH, CHARLIE aged 26 years July 22, 1888 by Rev. T. P. Burgess at 47 Line Street. He a native of Milledgeville, Georgia and she of Charleston. He works for the railroad.

CONNOR, JOHN J. aged 25 years married to CUMMINGS, WINIFRED F. aged 20 years October 14, 1883 by Father F. J. Shadler at St. Joseph's Roman Catholic Church. Both natives of Charleston. He a machinist.

CONNOR, JULIA M. aged 22 years married to CARY, THOMAS F. aged 25 years February 5, 1888 by Father F. J. Shadler at St. Joseph's Roman Catholic Church.

CONNOR, MARY ANN aged 24 years married to MURRAY, WILLIAM JACOB aged 29 years October 7, 1884 by Rev. E. J. Meynardie at Summerville, South Carolina. He a native of St. George, South Carolina and she of Holly Hill, South Carolina. He a merchant.

CONNOR, MARY A. aged 26 years married to CONROY, JOHN aged 25 years January 27, 1887 by Father F. J. Shadler at St. Joseph's Roman Catholic Church. Both natives of Charleston. He a merchant.

CONNOR, MICHAEL N. aged 25 years married to CONROY, MARY ANNE aged 22 years May 7, 1879 by Father C. J. Croghan at St. Joseph's Roman Catholic Church. Both natives of Charleston. He an engineer.

CONNOR, WINNIE aged 19 years married to YOUNG, JOHN ALEX aged 19 years July 31, 1888 by Rev. John J. Wedenfeller at St. Joseph's Roman Catholic Church. Both natives of Charleston.

CONNOT, JULIA M. aged 22 years married to GARCY, THOMAS F. aged 25 years February 5, 1888 by Father F. J. Shadler at St. Joseph's Roman Catholic Church.

CONROY, MARY B. married to McGRANE, MARTIN January 22, 1890 by Father F. J. Shadler at St. Joseph's Roman Catholic Church. Both natives of Charleston. He a boilermaker.

CONROY, CATHARINE aged 33 years married to HOLST, JOHN aged 33 years August 18, 1887 by Father Daniel J. Quigley at St. Patrick's Roman Catholic Church. Both natives of Charleston. He a clerk.

CONROY, JOHN aged 56 years married to DARCEY, CATHARINE aged 30 years June 10, 1885 by Father F. J. Shadler at St. Joseph's Roman Catholic Church. He a native of Ireland and she of Charleston. He a coal merchant.

CONROY, JOHN aged 25 years married to CONNOR, MARY A. aged 26 years January 27, 1887 by Father F. J. Shadler at St. Joseph's Roman Catholic Church. Both natives of Charleston. He a merchant.

CONROY, MAGGIE L. aged 27 years married to COLEMAN, JAMES E. aged 31 years June 8, 1886 by Father F. J. Shadler at St. Joseph's Roman Catholic Church. Both natives of Charleston. He a jeweller.

CONROY, MARY ANNE aged 22 years married to CONNOR, MICHAEL N. aged 25 years May 7, 1879 by Father C. J. Croghan at St. Joseph's Roman Catholic Church. Both natives of Charleston. He an engineer.

CONROY, MARY MURRAY aged 33 years married to KILROY, JAMES aged 45 years July 28, 1885 by Father J. J. Woolahan at St. Mary of the Annunciation Roman Catholic Church. Both natives of Charleston. He a laborer.

CONWAY, MARY J. aged 21 years married to BROOKS, WILLIAM J. aged 38 years June 28, 1892 by Bishop Harry P. Northrop at The Cathedral of St. John the Baptist. He a native of New Haven, Connecticut and she of London, England. He a manufacturer in Columbia, South Carolin.

CONYERS, EDWARD CHARLES aged 20 years married to ROBERTS, JOSEPHINE aged 20 years February 10, 1879 by Rev. J. Mercier Green. Both natives of Charleston. He a painter.

CONYERS, JAMES aged 24 years married to PEMBERTON, ELVIRA aged 24 years November 3, 1878 by Father C. J. Croghan in Elizabeth Street. Both natives of Charleston. He a laborer.

COOK, ADDIE aged 20 years married to TAVAST, DANIEL aged 23 years March 13, 1884 by Rev. C. E. Chichester at 4 State Street. He a native of Finland and she of Charleston. He a mariner.

COOK, CEPHAS G. aged 21 years married to BROADWATER, SARAH C. aged 18 years November 11, 1894. He a native of Horry County, South Carolina and she of Charleston. He a laborer.

COOK, CHARLES aged 23 years married to O'ROURKE, ELIZABETH aged 17 years November 28, 1880 by Father Harry P. Northrop at St. Patrick's Roman Catholic Church. Both natives of Charleston. He works for the railroad.

COOK, FANNIE C. aged 17 years married to MOTES, JOHN T. aged 22 years October 3, 1893 by Rev. Edmund Wells in Cooper Street. He a native of Lowndes County, Alabama and she of Darlington County, South Carolina. He a weaver in the cotton mill.

COOK, GEORGE aged 36 years married to FELAHUSE (?), HARRIET aged 25 years May 19, 1889 by Rev. C. E. Chichester at the Mariners Church. He a native of England and she of South Carolina. He a mariner.

COOK, GEORGE LaGRANCE aged 29 years married to LaFAR, LYDIA SOPHIA October 22, 1878 by Rev. H. C. Dana. He a native of LaGrange, Georgia and she of Orangeburg, South Carolina. He a photographer.

COOK, HENRY A. aged 46 years married to WREDE, (Mrs.) MARY V. AHRENS aged 37 years Marcy 10, 1892. He a native of Germany and she of Charleston. He a baker.

COOK, ISADORA aged 21 years married to POSTON, ROBERT J. aged 33 years July 15, 1894 by Rev. Edmund Wells at 3 Melchers Court. He a native of Johnsonville, South Carolina and she of Horry County, South Carolina.

COOK, MARIE BEAURIE aged 22 years married to KOENNECKE, JOSEPH THEODORE aged 24 years August 10, 1884 by Rev. John H. Honour at 14 John Street.

COOKE, ANNE F. aged 22 years married to DOWELL, SAMUEL G. aged 31 years June 10, 1891 by Rev. W. T. Thompson at 6 Smith Street. Both natives of Charleston. He a bookkeeper.

COOKE, AUGUSTA O. aged 30 years married to KENNEDY, WILLIAM aged 39 years September 29, 1883 by Rev. John Johnson. He a native of Abbeville, South Carolina and she of New York. He a government employee.

COOKE, E. J. aged 22 years married to CONKE, J. T. aged 24 years June 6, 1882 by Father J. J. Monaghan at St. Patrick's Roman Catholic Church. He a native of Charleston and a brickmason.

COOMBS, ASHLEY B. aged 21 years married to PLANE, CHARLOTTE E. aged 20 years March 1, 1880 by Rev. Edward T. Horn. He a native of Pulaski County, Georgia and she of Charleston. He a farmer in Pulaski County.

COOPER, CHARLES W. aged 19 yeears married to WILLIAMS, EMMA aged 17 years November 15, 1886 by Rev. H. B. Browne at 16 Stone Court. Both natives of South Carolina. He a moulder.

COOPER, GEORGE E. aged 42 years married to GEHRELS, CAROLINE aged 18 years July 15, 1891 by Rev. Edwin C. Dargan. He a native of Dover, North Carolina and she of Orangeburg, South Carolina. He owns a marbleyard.

COPES, CHARLES aged 23 years married to FISHER, FLORENCE aged 20 years April 24, 1884 by Rev. Luther K. Probst. Both natives of Charleston. He a merchant.

CORBETT, H. V. aged 22 years married to ARMSTRONG, M. L. aged 18 years September 2, 1879 by Father P. L. Duffy at The Cathedral of St. John the Baptist. Both natives of Charleston. He an upholsterer.

CORBETT, LIZZIE aged 21 years married to BARRY, EDMUND M. aged 24 years November 28, 1886 by Father Daniel J. Quigley at St. Patrick's Roman Catholic Church. He a native of Charleston and she of Georgia. He a clerk.

CORBETT, MARGARET V. married to PRICE, JOSEPH ALBERT aged 40 years September 15, 1883 by Father F. J. Shadler. He a native of Ireland and she of Charleston. He a saloon keeper.

CORBY, JOHN T. aged 38 years married to TYRRELL, ADDIE L. aged 26 years June 12, 1889 by Rev. C. E. Chichester at 40 Spring Street. Both natives of Charleston. He a machinist.

CORCORAN, BRIDGET ANNE aged 31 years married to ROWAND, THOMAS Y. S. aged 40 years May 15, 1887 by Father P. J. Wilson at St. Mary of the Annunciation Roman Catholic Church. Both natives of Charleston. He a collector.

CORCORAN, JOHN P. aged 30 years married to KENNEDY, MARY C. aged 30 years December 4, 1884 by Father F. A. Schmetz at St. Patrick's Roman Catholic Church. Both natives of Charleston. He a fireman.

CORCORAN, JULIA A. married to KILEY, JOHN L. April 4, 1888 by Father P. J. Wilson at St. Patrick's Roman Catholic Church. She a native of Charleston. He a dealer in wood.

CORCORAN, M. J. aged 24 years married to MAY, JOHN aged 36 years November 1, 1880 by Father Harry P. Northrop at St .Patrick's Church. He a native of Ireland and she of Charleston. He an engineer.

CORDES, ALEX W. aged 23 years married to DENNIS, CYNTHIA E. aged 15 years April 9, 1893 by Rev. J. C. Yongue. He a native of Georgetown, South Carolina and she of Charleston. He works for the railroad.

CORDES, C. R. married to BOSCH, J. A. aged 34 years October 7, 1879 by Rev. Louis Muller at the corner of Marsh and Inspection Streets. Both natives of Charleston. He a merchant.

CORDES, HERMAN S. aged 40 years married to O'NEILL, MARY L. aged 33 years January 17, 1884 by Father Daniel J. Quigley at 76 America Street. She a native of Charleston. He a mariner.

CORDES, LAVINIA C. married to RICHARDSON, DAVISON M. December 28, 1881 by William H. Campbell. He a planter.

CORDES, MARGARETHE ADELINE aged 28 years married to KOSTER, JOHANN EMIL aged 32 years June 27, 1889 by Rev. Louis Muller at the residence of the Bride's father - 326 East Bay Street, north of Laurens Street. He a native of Brooklyn New York and she of Charleston. He a grocer and a widower.

CORDES, MARY R. married to SANDERS, JOHN P. June 4, 1885 by Rev. William H. Campbell at St. Paul's Church. Both natives of Charleston. He a clerk.

CORDES, SAMUEL aged 24 years marriedto COURTNEY, EMMA C. aged 21 years January 25, 1883 by Rev. C. C. Pinckney at the home of Mayor Courtney - Lynch Street. He a native of Charleston County, South Carolina and she of Charleston. He a railroad conductor.

CORKER, H. M. aged 35 years married to BAIL, E. F. aged 15 years January 4, 1882 by Father J. M. Giessen. Both natives of Charleston. He a moulder.

CORKLE, CHARLES aged 23 years married to TOBIN, MARY aged 15 years May 13, 1878 by Father John P. Twigg at The Cathedral of St. John the Baptist. Both natives of Charleston. He a stonecutter.

CORKLE, EDWARD T. aged 28 years married to VON HARTEN, ANNIE M. aged 32 years February 18, 1887 by Rev. Luther K. Probst. He a native of South Carolina and she of Georgia. He a merchant.

CORLEY, JACOB J. married to McKEE, CATHERINE N. February 8, 1893 by Rev. William H. Campbell at St. Paul's Church. He a machinist in Florence, South Carolina.

CORMIER, JOSIAH A. aged 26 years married to ALEXANDER, VIOLA W. aged 16 years April 21, 1892 by Rev. J. L. Stokes at the Spring Street Methodist Episcopal Church.

CORMIER, MARIAN ELIZABETH aged 18 years married to DAVENPORT, WILLIAM aged 21 years December 18, 1878 by Rev. J. Mercier Green at the residence of the Bride - 10 Woolfe Street.

CORMIER, VICTORIA ANGELIQUE AGATHA aged 18 years married to SOUBEYROUS, LOUIS L. aged 28 years January 11, 1881 by Father Claudian B. Northrop at St. Mary of the Annunciation Roman Catholic Church. Both natives of Charleston. He a clerk.

CORMIER, WILLIAM IRVIN aged 28 years married to DUFFIE, SARAH R. aged 25 years May 22, 1884 by Father Daniel J. Quigley at St. Patrick's Roman Catholic Church. Both natives of Charleston. He works for the railroad.

CORONES, ANDREW aged 30 years married to MEITZLER, MARGARET L. aged 21 years November 27, 1881 by Rev. Edward T. Horn in King Street. He a native of Athens, Georgia and she of Charleston. He a fruitier.

COSGROVE, BESSIE aged 25 years married to Dickson, JOHN aged 31 years November 8, 1891 by Father J. J. Monaghan at 136 St. Philip Street. He a native of Denmark and she of Ireland. He a laborer.

COSGROVE, ELLEN aged 20 years married to GALTEMAN (?), WILLIAM aged 23 years September 15, 1889 by Father Daniel J. Quigley. She a native of Ireland. He a bricklayer.

COSGROVE, ELLEN T. aged 26 years married to HANLY, JAMES F. aged 29 years June 18, 1891 by Father J. J. Monaghan at St. Patrick's Roman Catholic Church. Both natives of Charleston. He a railroad flagman.

COSGROVE, JAMES aged 46 years married to DALEY, M. A. aged 30 years February 12, 1882 by Father Daniel J. Quigley at The Cathedral of St. John the Baptist. He a native of Ireland and she of Charleston. He a merchant.

COSGROVE, THOMAS F. aged 26 years married to MORIARTY, LENORA aged 19 years September 15, 1885 by Father Thomas E. McCormack at St. Patrick's Roman Catholic Church. Both natives of Charleston. He a carpenter.

COSS, ALEXANDER aged 30 years married to FORD, ANNA aged 25 years June 7, 1887 by Rev. John Johnson. Both natives of Charleston.

COSTE, CHARLES aged 24 years married to HERON, AMANDA aged 20 years June 1, 1892 by Rev. Robert Wilson at 195 Smith Street. Both natives of Charleston.

COSTE, HANNAH P. aged 38 years married to MUNDELL, ROBERT D. aged 42 years May 11, 1893 by Rev. Robert Wilson at 4 Wragg Square. He a native of Winnsboro, South Carolina and she of Westbrook, North Carolina. He a mechanic.

COSTELLO, JAMES ERVIN aged 20 years married to SULLIVAN, CATHARINE aged 23 years March 20, 1884 by Rev. R. A. Lapsley at 76 America Street. He a native of Augusta, Georgia and she of Aiken, South Carolina.

COSTELLO, MARY ANN FRANCES aged 25 years married to CARMODY, JEREMIAH J. aged 36 years April 30, 1884 by Father J. J. Wedenfellen at The Cathedral of St. John the Baptist. Both natives of Charleston. He an engineer in Brooklyn, New York.

COSTNER, EMMA aged 20 years married to EPPS, HIRAM aged 21 years September 11, 1887 by Rev. H. B. Browne at 23 Cooper Street. He a native of Eatonton, Georgia and she of North Carolina. Both work in the cotton mill.

COTTEN, JOSEPH W. aged 27 years married to THEVEATT, MARTHA M. aged 25 years July 10, 1895 by Father J. J. Monaghan at 38 Mary Street. He a native of North Carolina and she of South Carolina. He a railroad conductor.

COUNTS, IRENE T. aged 18 years married to STODDARD, LAWRENCE E. aged 28 years October 2, 1889 by Rev. Edwin C. Dargan at Citadel Square Baptist Church. He a native of Charleston and she of Savannah, Georgia. He a baggegemaster.

COURIER, JOHN F. aged 22 years married to LEACH, MARY C. aged 19 years February 12, 1881 by Rev. C. C. Pinckney at Chisolm's Mill. He a native of Palatka, Florida and she of Charleston. He an engineer.

COURTNEY, AMELIA aged 26 years married to KIRK, ROBERT aged 30 years November 14, 1889 by Rev. C. C. Pinckney at Grace Church. He a native of Berkeley County, South Carolina and she of Savannah, Georgia. He a lawyer in Berkeley County.

COURTNEY, ANNA P. aged 20 years married to MEACHER, JOSEPH aged 21 years June 28, 1878 by Rev. J. V. Welsh. Both natives of Charleston. He a clerk.

COURTNEY, HENRY L. aged 21 years married to LOWE, ELIZA J. aged 18 years October 15, 1893 by Rev. A. Ernest Cornish at 6 Hampden Court. He a native of Washington, D. C. and she of Charleston. He works in the cotton mill.

COUTEWEIEN, JOHN E. H. married to MAZYCK, MARY R. B. February 22, 1880 by Rev. A. H. Misseldine.

COUTURIER, J. E. aged 40 years married to WHITE, W. E. aged 19 years July 11, 1882 by Rev. E. J. Meynardie at 145 Calhoun Street. He a native of Germany and she of South Carolina. He a merchant.

COWARD, MARY L. aged 26 years married to GLOVER, JOHN E. aged 30 years June 1, 1893 by Rev. C. C. Pinckney and Rev. E. N. Joyner at Grace Church. He a native of Orangeburg, South Carolina and she of Yorkville, South Carolina. He a bookkeeper in Orangeburg.

COWLEY, LUCINDA aged 24 years married to KREINSON (?), LUTHER H. aged 36 years August 9, 1885 by Rev. John O. Wilson at 82 Wentworth Street.

COX, JULIANNE aged 20 years married to MEYERS, FRED aged 20 years February 10, 1881 by Rev. J. V. Welsh at 40 Columbus Street. He a native of Charleston and a laborer.

COX, SAMUEL aged 27 years married to SMITH, MARY aged 23 years December 14, 1890 by Rev. W. S. Walkins at 47 Columbus Street. He a native of Charleston and she of Greenville, South Carolina. He a moulder.

COYNES, THOMAS aged 25 years married to O'NEILL, JOHANNA MURPHY aged 40 years June 15, 1892 by Father Daniel J. Quigley at St. Patrick's Roman Catholic Church. Both natives of Ireland. He a barkeeper.

CRADDOCK, LIZZIE M. aged 22 years married to HOGG, JACOB J. aged 21 years October 29, 1886 by Rev. J. Walter Dickson at the Spring Street Methodist Church. Both natives of South Carolina. He a farmer in Barnwell County, South Carolina.

CRAFT, JAMES D. aged 20 years married to TOYE, MARY aged 17 years August 3, 1884 by Rev. P. J. McManus. He a native of Charleston and she of South Carolina. He works in a factory.

CRAFTS, HARRIET M. married to ROSE, EDWARD P. April 10, 1890 by Rev. Richard S. Frazier at St. Michael's Church. Both natives of Charleston. He a physician in Colorado.

CRAFTS, WILLIAM H. aged 24 years married to GRANT, MARY D. aged 20 years May 3, 1881 by Rev. A. Coke Smith at 26 Vanderhorst Street. He a native of Charleston and she of Green County, Georgia. He a clerk.

CRAIG, JOHN E. aged 26 years married to REID, MARY A. aged 26 years February 23, 1887 by Father Daniel J. Quigley at St. Patrick's Roman Catholic Church. Both natives of Charleston. He a painter.

CRAMER, MARY J. aged 30 years married to SPENCE, LEON C. aged 25 years August 28, 1892 by John Ahrens, Trial Justice. He a native of Carol County, Georgia and she of Canada. He a doctor at the Waverly House.

CRAVEN, ELLA aged 22 years married to JEFFERSON, STEPHEN P. aged 31 years January 1, 1884 by Father F. J. Shadler at St. Joseph's Roman Catholic Church. Both natives of Charleston. He a stevedore.

CRAVEN, EMANUEL WILLIAM aged 22 years married to WALKER, EMILY aged 20 years December 27, 1877 by Father S. Redington at St. Patrick's Roman Catholic Church. He a native of Charleston

CRAWFORD, A. married to HALL, E. E. November 7, 1881 by Rev. C. C. Pinckney in Columbia, South Carolina. He a native of Columbia and she of Pendleton, South Carolina. He a sawyer in Columbia.

CRAWFORD, SUSAN aged 22 years married to GROTE, JACOB aged 27 years November 19, 1891 by Rev. W. A. Betts at 96 Columbus Street. He a native of Germany and she of St. Stephen's Parish, South Carolina. He a mariner.

CREIGHTON, J. P. aged 21 years married to KAYLEN, LENA aged 21 years August 24, 1891. He a native of Atlanta, Georgia and she of New York City. He a plumber in Savannah, Georgia.

CROCKER, MINNIE aged 19 years married to JEFFERS, GEORGE aged 19 years October 22, 1893 by Rev. Edward Wells. He a native of Sumter County, South Carolina and she of Spartanburg, South Carolina. He works in the cotton mill.

CROFFERT, S. E. aged 44 years married to LYONS, J. R. aged 37 years February 12, 1882 by Rev. J. V. Welch at Calvary Church. He a native of Charleston and a policeman.

CROFT, THOMAS H. aged 24 years married to JONES, IDA E. aged 21 years June 4, 1878 by Rev. C. C. Pinckney. Both natives of Charleston. He a bookkeeper.

CROGAN, FANNIE aged 23 years married to McGINNIS, WILLIAM FRANCIS aged 22 years January 21, 1878 by Rev. Claudian B. Northrop at St. Mary of the Annunciation Roman Catholic Church.

CROGHAN, A. aged 22 years married to PETERSON, N. aged 45 years January 19, 1882 by Father Daniel J. Quigley. He a native of Holstein, Germany and she of Charleston. He a professor of music.

CROGHAN, JOHN P. aged 30 years married to CUMMINGS, MARY A. aged 24 years October 28, 1885 by Father Daniel J. Quigley. Both natives of Charleston. He a farmer.

CROGHAN, PATRICK WASHINGTON aged 28 years married to WATSON, MARY J. aged 20 years January 23, 1881 by Father P. L. Duffy at The Cathedral of St. John the Baptist. Both natives of Charleston. He a stonecutter.

CRONHEIM, H. married to PINKHUSSON, S. January 13, 1880 by Rabbi David Levy at the Hasell Street Synagogue. He a native of Germany and she of Charleston. He a merchant.

CROSBY, IRVIN aged 30 years married to SPADY, MARION P. aged 30 years February 3, 1886 by Rev. C. C. Pinckney at 2 State Street. Both natives of Charleston. He a druggist.

CROSS, IRENE G. married to POTTER, BETTS A. December 11, 1890 by Rev. W. A. Betts.

CROSS, LILLA L. aged 18 years married to KRAUSE, WILLIAM E. aged 28 years March 27, 1879 by Rev. W. S. Bowman in Radcliffe Street. He a native of Bethlehem, Pennsylvania and she of Charleston. He a tailor.

CROSS, WILLIAM H. aged 27 years married to PORTER, MARY aged 22 years June 4, 1890 by Father Harry P. Northrop at St. Patrick's Roman Catholic Church. He a native of Charleston and she of New Orleans, Louisiana. He a pilot.

CROUCH, EDWARD P. aged 35 years married to WALKER, HARRIET A. aged 17 years April 12, 1889 by Rev. Charles A. Stakely. Both natives of South Carolina. He a contractor.

CROWELL, LILLIE S. aged 24 years married to BAYER, HENRY S. aged 26 years November 28, 1878 by Rev. W. S. Bowman at 14 Bee Street. He a native of Alexandria, Virginia and she of New York. He a clerk.

CUBSTEDT, (Mrs.) REBECCA SINGLETARY aged 35 years married to RIGGS, THOMAS L. aged 38 years December 27, 1893 by Rev. Edmund Wells at 23 Spring Street. He a native of Savannah, Georgia and she of Charleston. He a clergyman.

CUBSTEDT, SARAH E. aged 23 years married to BIZE, JOHN D. aged 41 years October 7, 1891 by Rev. Edwin C. Dargan at the Enston Homes. He a native of Charleston and a mechanist.

CULLEN, JAMES aged 22 years married to DUGGAN, JANE aged 22 years July 28, 1879 by Rev. Edward T. Horn. He a native of Savannah, Georgia and she of Charleston. He a clerk.

CULLEN, MARY aged 20 years married to SAMPSON, EDWARD aged 22 years May 7, 1879 by Father C. J. Croghan at St. Joseph's Roman Catholic Church. Both natives of Charleston. He an engineer.

CULLETON, EDWARD M. aged 31 years married to TIGHE, MARY ANN aged 30 years April 29, 1891 by Father J. J. Monaghan at St. Patrick's Roman Catholic Church. Both natives of Charleston. He a bricklayer.

CULLIMANE, MARY V. aged 20 years married to WILLIS, JACOB T. aged 26 years November 23, 1884 by Father F. A. Schmetz at St. Patrick's Roman Catholic Church. He a native of North Carolina and she of Charleston. He a blacksmith.

CULLINANE, JOHANNA B. aged 20 years married to BLANCHE, MATTHEW F. aged 20 years May 21, 1894 by Father J. J. Monaghan at St. Patrick's Roman Catholic Church. He a native of York, South Carolina and she of Charleston. He a laborer.

CULLINANE, KATE L. aged 20 years married to BODIE, HENRY D. aged 20 years September 22, 1889 by Father Daniel J. Quigley at 390 Meeting Street. Both natives of Charleston. He a railroad brakeman.

CULP, ANNIE A. aged 19 years married to BENTLEY, WALTER aged 22 years June 27, 1893 by Rev. Edmund Wells at 117 Drake Street.

CULP, WALTER married to JOYNER, ANNIE April 23, 1890 by Rev. William A. Betts.

CUMBEE, CLEMENT married to BELMAN, JESSIE April 16, 1890 by Rev. R. N. Wells at Trinity Church.

CUMBEE, BENJAMIN aged 33 years married to MEREE, (Mrs.) HARRIET ANN KENNEDY aged 34 years May 21, 1891 by Rev. William A. Beets at the Bone Factory in King Street. He a native of Berkeley County, South Carolina and she of Marion County, South Carolina. He a farmer in Accabee, Berkeley County.

CUMBEE, MILDRED L. aged 16 years married to WEBBER, ADAM aged 42 years January 20, 1895 by Rev. J. C. Yongue at 14 Hampstead Square. He a native of Wisconsin and she of Berkeley County, South Carolina. He a barber.

CUMBIE, SARAH aged 18 years married to THACKERY, ROBERT aged 27 years May 2, 1887 by Leroy F. Beaty, at 231 Coming Street. He a native of England and she of South Carolina. He a bricklayer.

CUMMINGS, GEORGE W. married to WAY, OLIVIA M. December 28, 1889 by Rev. W. A. Betts at the Cumberland Church.

CUMMINGS, MARGARET aged 23 years married to MELVIN, THOMAS aged 25 years August 11, 1878 by Father John Twigg at St. Mary of the Annunciation Roman Catholic Church. He a native of Ireland and she of Charleston. He a laborer.

CUMMINGS, MARGARET F. aged 22 years married to JERVEY, THOMAS K. aged 23 years October 30, 1895 by Father J. J. Monaghan at St. Patrick's Roman Catholic Church. Both natives of Charleston. He a plumber.

CUMMINGS, MARY A. aged 24 years married to CROGHAN, JOHN P. aged 30 years October 28, 1885 by Father Daniel J. Quigley. Both natives of Charleston. He a farmer.

CUMMINGS, PINCKNEY aged 27 years married to DENNIS, MARY CATHARINE aged 21 years May 8, 1892 by Rev. H. F. Chreitzberg. Both natives of Charleston. He a street car driver.

CUMMINGS, WINIFRED F. aged 20 years married to CONNOR, JOHN J. aged 25 years October 14, 1883 by Father F. J. Shadler at St. Joseph's Roman Catholic Church. Both natives of Charleston. He a machinist.

CUMMINS, M. aged 22 years married to BLISCH, T. aged 25 years October 17, 1882 by Father Daniel J. Quigley at The Cathedral of St. John the Baptist. Both natives of South Carolina. He a merchant.

CUNNINGHAM, GEORGE J. aged 46 years married to SMALL, ELLEN R. McINNES aged 40 years November 17, 1881 by Rev. Edward T. Horn at 3 George Street. He a native of Tennessee and she of Charleston. He a butcher.

CUNNINGHAM, J. aged 22 years married to MUSGROVE, JAMES aged 26 years August 31, 1879 by Father Daniel J. Quigley at The Cathedral of St. John the Baptist. Both natives of Charleston. He a sadler.

CUNNINGHAM, MARY A. aged 22 years married to DOTY, THOMAS W. aged 24 years May 1, 1881 by Father P. L. Duffy at 69 King Street. He a native of Charleston.
CUNNINGHAM, THOMAS H. aged 32 years married to STENHOUSE, JANET FULTON aged 25 years March 12, 1879 by Rev. W. F. Junkin. He a native of Anderson, South Carolina and she of Charleston.

CUNNINGHAM, WILLIAM aged 34 years married to FAULKNER, MARY aged 21 years December 9, 1881 by Rev. J. V. Welch at 100 St. Philip Street. He a native of Pike County, Georgia and she of Augusta, Georgia. He a printer.

CURRY, SALLIE J. aged 19 years married to HOOD, CHARLES aged 23 years April 7, 1889 by Rev. H. B. Browne at 93 America Street. He a native of Berkeley County, South Carolina and she of Colleton County, South Carolina. He works in the cotton mill.

CURTIS, ARTIMISHA EVELINE aged 17 years married to RANTIN, THOMAS BERNARD aged 22 years November 11, 1883 by Rev. J. H. Tellinghast at 23 Inspection Street. Both natives of Charleston. He a tinner.

CURTIS, LAWRENCE E. aged 23 years married to WHITE, ANNIE E. aged 20 years May 20, 1894 by Father J. J. Monaghan at St. Patrick's Roman Catholic Church. Both natives of Charleston. He a tinner.

CURTIS, M. A. aged 27 years married to MADDEN, J. aged 37 years November 14, 1882 by Rev. J. E. Curtis. He a native of Germany and a machinist.

CUTHBERT, FRANCIS P. married to YATES, CAROLINE S. April 20, 1893 by Rev. William H. Campbell at St. Paul's Church. He works in the phosphate mill.

CUTTER, H. F. aged 28 years married to BENNETT, M. E. aged 29 years August 3, 1882 by Rev. A. Coke Smith at 100 St. Philip Street. He a native of South Carolina and she of Bonneau, South Carolina. He an express agent.

CUTTS, JOHN A. aged 31 years married to EGAN, ELLA aged 25 years March 22, 1893 by Rev. John Johnson at 36 Hasell Street.

DADIN, ALEXANDER aged 35 years married to O'CONNOR, SUSAN J. aged 30 years April 23, 1883 by Rev. J. A. Clifton at 98 Cannon Street. Both natives of Charleston. He a painter.

DADIN, MARY L. aged 35 years married to MARTIN, HENRY R. aged 39 years February 11, 1883 by Rev. Luther K. Probst. Both natives of Charleston. He an engineer.

DAGGETT, MARY JANE aged 19 years married to FINNEGAN, GEORGE WASHINGTON aged 28 years August 30, 1878 by Father Claudian B. Northrop at St. Mary of the Annunciation Roman Catholic Church. Both natives of Charleston. He a mariner on Black Island, South Carolina.

DAGGETT, THOMAS aged 24 years married to FOLEY, MARGARET aged 20 years April 18, 1888 by Father F. J. Shadler at St. Joseph's Roman Catholic Church. Both natives of Charleston. He a railroad laborer.

DALEY, A. E. married to MYER, FERDINAND L. November 18, 1878 by William B. Yates, Chaplain.

DALEY, M. A. aged 30 years married to COSGROVE, JAMES aged 46 years February 12, 1882 by Father Daniel J. Quigley at The Cathedral of St. John the Baptist. He a native of Ireland and she of Charleston. He a merchant.

DALLAS, R. E. aged 29 years married to FIGARO, R. F. aged 20 years July 7, 1882 by Father Daniel J. Quigley at The Cathedral of St. John the Baptist. He a native of Charleston and a printer.

DAMON, EDWARD LORING aged 25 years married to FIELCHER, FANNIE aged 19 years June 24, 1888 by Rev. Johannes Heckel at 23 Smith Street.

DAN, AGNES aged 25 years married to MILNER, MAX aged 40 years February 5, 1884 by Robert Chisolm, Judicial Trial Justice.

DANEGA, SELINA aged 40 years married to LUDHOFF, HERMAN aged 36 years October 12, 1881 by Rabbi David Levy at the Hasell Street Synagogue. He a native of Berlin, Germany and she of Charleston. He a photographer.

DANEGHY (?), PATRICK J. aged 23 years married to HENRY, DORA aged 27 years November 24, 1888 by Father J. J. Monaghan at St. Patrick's Roman Catholic Church. Both natives of Charleston. He works for the railroad.

DANIELS, G. R. aged 26 years married to BENSE, BERTHA aged 20 years December 12, 1880 by Rev. J. V. Welsh at 64 Radcliffe Street. Both natives of Charleston. He a carpenter.

DANIELS, JOHN H. married to PHILIPS, EVA A. December 26, 1890 by Rev. W. A. Betts.

DANIELS, J. B. aged 30 years married to FINK, SUSAN E. aged 27 years November 7, 1880 by Rev. J. V. Welsh at Calvary Church. Both natives of Charleston. He a laborer.

DANIELS, MAGGIE F. aged 21 years married to FLAKE, JAMES aged 20 years December 24, 1895 by Rev. Griffin Holliman. He a native of Orangeburg, South Carolina and she of North Carolina. He works in a mill.

DARCEY, CATHARINE aged 30 years married to CONROY, JOHN aged 56 years June 10, 1885 by Father F. J. Shadler at St. Joseph's Roman Catholic Church. He a native of Ireland and she of Charleston. He a coal merchant.

DARRELL, WILLIAM S. aged 25 years married to BAIL (?), LAURA aged 43 years November 28, 1888 by Rev. John Johnson at 20 Washington Street. Both natives of Charleston. He a drayman.

DAUER, JAMES A. B. aged 25 years married to EYSENBACH, EMILY W. LOUISE aged 19 years February 8, 1881 by Rev. Louis Muller in St. Philip Street, north of the public school. He a native of Charleston and a professor of music.

DAVENPORT, JULIA MARCELLA aged 16 years married to SWAN, GEORGE N. aged 21 years January 7, 1878 by Rev. J. Mercier Green at 114 King Street. He a native of Jersey City, New Jersey and she of Charleston. He a pilot.

DAVENPORT, W. H. aged 24 years married to PARSELL, ELLA M. aged 22 years December 25, 1880 by Rev. L. H. Shuck. Both natives of Charleston. He a printer.

DAVENPORT, WILLIAM aged 21 years married to CORMIER, MARINA ELIZABETH aged 18 years December 18, 1878 by Rev. J. Mercier Green at the residence of the Bride - 10 Woolfe Street. Both natives of Charleston. He a printer.

DAVEY, EMMA J. aged 23 years married to HALL, SAMUEL ROBERTS aged 37 years June 10, 1894 by Rev. J. L. Stokes at 23 Bay Street.

DAVEY, WILLIAM ROBERT aged 23 years married to JOHNSON, MARTHA JANE aged 22 years June 29, 1892 by Rev. Edmund Wells at 13 Line Street. He a native of Charleston and she of St. Paul's Parish, South Carolina. He a railroad brakeman.

DAVID, BERTHA aged 24 years married to JACOBI, JACOB L. aged 24 years February 20, 1884 by Rabbi David Levy at 303 King Street. Both natives of Charleston. He a merchant.

DAVIDSON, HANNAH DONALDSON aged 43 years married to ANDERSON, HANS aged 40 years November 20, 1889 by Rev. C. E. Chichester at The Mariners Church. He a native of Norway and she of Ireland. He a mariner.

DAVIS, ALEXANDER aged 30 years married to RAY, LUCY E. aged 18 years March 17, 1884 by Rev. J. H. Tillinghast at the corner of Blake and America Streets. He a native of Smithfield, North Carolina and she of Aiken, South Carolina. He a baker.

DAVIS, ANNIE ELLEN aged 18 years married to SAWADSKI, JOHN HENRY aged 20 years May 3, 1881 by Rev. John H. Honour at 14 John Street.

DAVIS, ARTHUR L. aged 21 years married to THOMAS, MARY aged 18 years March 11, 1888 by Rev. H. B. Browne in America Street. Both natives of Columbia, South Carolina. He a railroad brakeman.

DAVIS, BEULAH LEE aged 18 years married to ALDRET, THOMAS JONES aged 21 years April 9, 1890 by Rev. R. D. Smart at 8 Laurens Street. Both natives of Charleston. He a policeman.

DAVIS, CALVIN aged 22 years married to DAVIS, SOPHRONIA aged 20 years March 11, 1883 by Rev. J. V. Welsh at 269 Meeting Street. Both natives of Charleston. He a laborer.

DAVIS, D. A. aged 22 years married to GRIFFIN, J. H. aged 23 years February 12, 1882 by Rev. A. S. Duffy at The Mills House Hotel. He a native of New Jersey and an oysterman. She a native of Charleston. He a resident of Edisto Island, South Carolina.

DAVIS, ELLA aged 22 years married to HAMMETT, LEWIS aged 20 years June 3, 1888 by Rev. H. B. Browne at 99 Drake Street. He a native of Jefferson County, Georgia and she of Milledgeville, Georgia. He works in the cotton mill.

DAVIS, EMMA E. aged 17 years married to McCULLOUGH, WILLIAM B. aged 20 years July 12, 1891 by Rev. G. R. Betts at 3 Blake Street.

DAVIS, (Mrs.) FLORENCE C. CAPP aged 32 years married to PERRY, WADE H. aged 39 years June 21, 1892 by Rev. W. T. Thompson at 10 Legare Street.

DAVIS, FLORENCE ERNESTINE aged 20 years married to OSWALD, GEORGE DOUGLAS aged 26 years April 30, 1889 by Rev. R. A. Webb at 12 Chinquapin Street. He a native of Georgia and she of Adams Run, South Carolina. He planter on James Island, South Carolina.

DAVIS, FLORENCE aged 18 years married to GOOLEY, JOHN aged 23 years January 2, 1881 by Father Daniel J. Quigley at The Cathedral of St. John the Baptist.

DAWSON, EDWARD L. aged 25 years married to FULCHER, FANNIE aged 19 years June 24, 1888 by Rev. Johannes Heckel. He a native of Aiken, South Carolina and she of Wilmington, North Carolina. He a clerk in Savannah, Georgia.

DAVIS, FRANCES IDA aged 22 years married to OLIVER, JOHN HENRY aged 34 years October 5, 1880 by Rev. John H. Honour at 14 John Street. He a native of Charleston. Both reside in Meeting Street. He a carpenter

DAVIS, HANNAH aged 25 years married to HOWELL, C. BASCOM aged 34 years December 4, 1889 by Rev. Edwin C. Dargan at Citadel Square Baptist Church. He a native of Virginia and she of Society Hill, South Carolina. He resides in Richmond, Virginia.

DAVIS, IDA B. married to COLSON, C. BUNTING April 14, 1887 by Rev. Richard S. Trapier at St. Luke's Church.

DAVIS, IDA aged 17 years married to McCULLEN, WILEY aged 20 years July 31, 1891 by Rev. J. Thomas Pate at 231 Coming Street. He a native of Atlanta, Georgia and she of Milledgeville, Georgia. He works in a factory.

DAVIS, JAMES M. aged 29 years married to BUTTS, MAMIE aged 25 years June 30, 1884 by Rev. John E. Beard at 18 Amherst Street. He a native of Augusta, Georgia and she of Charleston. He an engineer.

DAVIS, JOHN JAMES aged 30 years married to FAULLING, HENRIETTA DORA aged 27 years February 12, 1880 by Rev. W. S. Bowman. He a native of Charleston and she of Germany. He a farmer near Ridgeville, South Carolina.

DAVIS, J. A. aged 40 years married to JACKSON, M. J. aged 22 years April 3, 1881 by Rev. J. V. Welsh at Calvary Church. He a native of Providence, Rhode Island and she of Charleston. He a sailmaker.

DAVIS, JEREMIAH A. aged 53 years married to VALENTINE, CATHERINE E. HYOTT aged 35 years April 11, 1886 by Rev. C. E. Chichester at the Mariner's Chapel in Market Street. He a native of Providence, Rhode Island and she of South Carolina. He a sailmaker.

DAVIS, MAMIE married to SASSARD, A. D. March 13, 1890 by Rev. W. A. Betts.

DAVIS, MARY aged 22 years married to CHISOLM, WILLIAM B. aged 19 years November 28, 1878 by Rev. C. C. Pinckney at Grace Church. He a native of Charleston and she of Pendleton, South Carolina. He a phosphate manufacturer.

DAVIS, MARY ANN aged 35 years married to AVILGAE, ESPENIZO aged 35 years January 30, 1891 by Father J. J. Monaghan at St. Patrick's Roman Catholic Church. He a native of Spain and she of Charleston. He a fisherman on the Boat Therese.

DAVIS, MARY H. aged 19 years married to WILLIAMS, JOHN H. aged 29 years September 11, 1889 by Rev. R. D. Smart at 104 Rutledge Avenue. He a native of Richmond County, Georgia and she of Charleston. He works for the railroad.

DAVIS, MOSES aged 25 years married to MARTIN, SARAH VICTORIA aged 19 years November 21, 1886 by Rev. H. B. Browne at 78 Drake Street. Both natives of Charleston. He a painter.

DAVIS, SOPHRONIA aged 20 years married to DAVIS, CALVIN aged 22 years March 11, 1883 by Rev. J. V. Welsh at 269 Meeting Street. Both natives of Charleston. He a laborer.

DAVIS, WILHELM aged 19 years married to BESSINGER, MARTHA aged 25 years July 12, 1883 by Rev. John E. Beard at 3 Duc Road.

DAVIS, WILLIAM married to SMART, ELLA July 19, 1878 by William B. Yates, Chaplain.

DAWES, JOSEPHINE aged 22 years married to WHALEY, FRANK J. aged 33 years June 1, 1893 by Rev. N. Keff Smith at 15 Ann Street. He a native of Winnsboro, South Carolina and she of Charleston. He a machinist.

DAWSON, EMMA LUCIA aged 22 years married to WYLLY, FREDERICK COURTNEY aged 28 years October 12, 1881 by Rev. G. R. Brackett. Both natives of Georgia. He a merchant.

DAWSON, FLORENCE married to MURRAY, JOHN C. December 6, 1888 by Rev. William H. Campbell at St. Paul's Church. He a planter in Florida.

DAWSON, JAMES S. aged 35 years married to McSHERRY, CATHARINE ROWLAND aged 26 years October 16, 1892 by Father J. J. Monaghan at St. Patrick's Roman Catholic Church.

DAWSON, JULIA married to GRADY, JAMES October 31, 1883 by Rev. William H. Campbell in Church Street. Both natives of Charleston. He a clerk.

DAWSON, MARY A. aged 21 years married to WRAGG, WILLIAM WIGG aged 26 years January 3, 1894 by Rev. John Johnson at the residence of C. Dawson. Both natives of Charleston. He a stationer.

DAWSON, MARY aged 22 years married to PRATT, GEORGE WALKER aged 22 years June 28, 1883 by Rev. C. C. Pinckney at 17 Smith Street. Both natives of Charleston. He a clerk in Walhalla, South Carolina.

DAWSON, SUSAN L. married to JENKINS, JULIAN B. December 12, 1895 by Rev. William H. Campbell at St. Paul's Church. He a merchant.

DAWSON, WILLIAM T. aged 24 years married to LYONS, EMMA JULIA aged 17 years April 10, 1892 by Rev. J. L. Stokes at 231 Coming Street.

DAY, SELDON aged 41 years married to POLLARD, MARIE ELIZA aged 41 years March 11, 1880 by Rev. E. C. L. Browne at the Unitarian Church. He a native of Chilicothe, Ohio and she of Waltham, Massachusetts. He a soldier.

DEA, J. M. aged 24 years married to SIRES, M. J. aged 17 years May 26, 1882 by Rev. Luther K. Probst at 81 Queen Street. He a native of South Carolina and a pilot.

DeAGNESLARD married to VANASDALAW, L. October 16, 1879 by William B. Yates, Chaplain.

DEAL, JAMES married to IGOE, A. MARY September 22, 1885 by Father F. J. Shadler at the residence of the Bride. She a native of Charleston. He a pilot.

DEAN, JAMES F. aged 24 years married to MULLEN, ELLEN aged 30 years August 4, 1885 by Father J. J. Woolahan at St. Mary of the Annunciation Roman Catholic Church. He a native of Charleston and she of Ireland. He a blacksmith.

DeANTONIO, JOSEPH aged 29 years married to SCHULTZ, ADELINE M. aged 19 years April 23, 1889 by Rev. R. C. Holland at the Wentworth Street Lutheran Church. Both natives of Charleston. He a merchant.

DeANTONIO, PAUL J. aged 20 years married to QUINLIVAN, ELLEN T. aged 18 years January 15, 1893 by Father J. J. Monaghan at St. Patrick's Roman Catholic Church. Both natives of Charleston. He a merchant.

DEARBORN, GEORGE aged 22 years married to CAMPBELL, NENA J. aged 17 years August 19, 1886 by Rev. Luther K. Probst. She a native of Charleston. He a Superintendent of Laundry.

DEASE, MARY L. aged 25 years married to CARROLL, JAMES H. aged 30 years September 18, 1887 by Rev. H. B. Browne at 114 Nassau Street. He a native of York County, South Carolina and she of Sumter County, South Carolina. He a porter.

DeCAMPS, CLARA E. aged 22 years married to REILLY, EDWARD C. aged 27 years April 26, 1883 by Father John P. Twigg at St. Patrick's Roman Catholic Church. Both natives of Charleston. He a clerk.

DeCAMPS, HELENA CATHARINE aged 22 years married to STURCKEN, JOHN F. aged 27 years November 19, 1890 by Father J. J. Monaghan at St. Patrick's Roman Catholic Church. Both natives of Charleston. He a shipping clerk.

DeCARADENC, ST. JULIAN PAUL aged 25 years married to WARING, SARAH EMILY aged 20 years April 16, 1879 by Father Claudian B. Northrop in Radcliffe Street.

DECESARE, CLARA aged 29 years married to ANTORI, ACHILLE aged 35 years March 23, 1885 by Father John J. Wedenfeller at St. Patrick's Roman Catholic Church. He a fruitier.

DECKER, CLARENCE aged 32 years married to FELL, ROSA G. aged 25 years April 18, 1893. He a native of New York and she of Gillisonville, South Carolina. He a machinist.

DECKER, JOSEPH AUSTIN married to BOGART, IRENE January 15, 1891 by Rev. Richard S. Trapier at 39 Meeting Street. He a native of Charleston and she of New York. He resides in Summerville, South Carolina.

DeCOU, LIZZIE aged 22 years married to BELL, CLARENCE EDWARD aged 26 years February 14, 1881 by Rev. Charles S. Vedder. He a native of Charleston and a clerk.

DEERY, H. A. aged 22 years married to DEVEREAUX, MARIE U. aged 21 years November 25, 1887 by Father P. J. Wilson at St. Mary of the Annunciation Roman Catholic Church. He a native of New York and she of Charleston. He a pressman.

DEHLS, A. ANNA aged 21 years married to COLE, ROBERT aged 21 years April 16, 1885 by Father F. J. Shadler at the residence of the Bride.

DEHLS, CHARLES aged 40 years married to BLANCHARD, (Mrs.) MAXINE Baker aged 30 years June 25, 1879 by Rev. W. S. Bowman. He a native of Germany and she of Charleston. He a grocer.

DEHON, T. aged 22 years married to MIDDLETON, HELEN aged 20 years February 8, 1893 by Rev. John Johnson. He a native of Greenville, South Carolina and she of Mt. Pleasant, South Carolina. He a turner in Greenville.

DEIGHNAN (?), ISABEL married to CAMPBELL, WILLIAM T. May 18, 1880 by William B. Yates, Chaplain. He a gardener.

DEIGHNAN (?), MARY SARAH aged 20 years married to REMBERT, THOMAS F. A. aged 27 years April 23, 1878 by Rev. William S. Heckel at 115 Queen Street. He a native of Charleston and she of Havana, Cubs. He a tinsmith.

DEKSON, GENA A. C. aged 26 years married to WESTERLIND, OTTO aged 26 years July 18, 1884 by Rev. Luther K. Probst. He a native of Sweden and she of Denmark. He a carpenter.

DeLAND, AGNES married to WARD, L. V. L. October 16, 1879 by William B. Yates, Chaplain.

DELANEY, JULIA aged 17 years married to HEFFRON, JOHN aged 25 years July 8, 1888 by Father F. J. Shadler at St. Joseph's Roman Catholic Church. Both natives of Charleston. He an agent.

DELANEY, JOHN J. aged 25 years married to PONARD, MARY aged 23 years April 25, 1883 by Father F. J. Shadler at St. Joseph's Roman Catholic Church. Both natives of Charleston. He a mail carrier.

DELANY, KATE C. aged 20 years married to FRAIN, JAMES J. aged 26 years November 27, 1887 by Father F. J. Shadler at St. Joseph's Roman Catholic Church. Both natives of Charleston. He a stevedore.

DELANEY, MARY E. aged 28 years married to DREW, JOHN E. aged 28 years March 30, 1891 by Father F. J. Shadler at St. Joseph's Roman Catholic Church. Both natives of Charleston. He a machinist in Jacksonville, Florida.

DELANEY, TIMOTHY aged 25 years married to MAGRATH, MARY M. aged 22 years October 9, 1890 by Father F. J. Shadler at St. Joseph's Roman Catholic Church. Both natives of Charleston. He a collector.

DEHON, SARA JULIE aged 24 years married to ABBOT, F. V. aged 27 years October 15, 1885 by Rev. John Johnson at 50 South Bay Street. He born "at sea" and she a native of South Carolina. He an army officer.

DeLAWRENCIA, DOMINICK aged 26 years married to HEILER, W. aged 28 years July 10, 1880 by Rev. J. V. Welsh at Calvary Church. He a native of Naples, Italy and she of Charleston. He a fisherman.

DeLEON, JACQUELINE ELLEN aged 25 years married to KELLER, SAM aged 27 years June 12, 1889 by Rabbi David Levy at the Hasell Street Synagogue. He a native of New York City and she of Charleston. He a stockbroker in Sheffield, Alabama.

DELEPHINE, W. R. married to HARRINGTON, M. J. September 17, 1879 by William B. Yates, Chaplain.

DENAN, WILLIAM G. married to KIMMEY, MARY JESSIE aged 21 years August 29, 1888 by Rev. J. E. Carlisle at 27 Reid Street. She a native of Charleston.

DENHAMS, JOHN P. aged 21 years married to PETERMAN, LOUISE N. aged 22 years November 28, 1888 by Rev. R. C. Holleman at 15 New Street. He a native of Florida and she of Charleston. He works for the railroad.

DENIS, ANDREW J. aged 42 years married to HUTSON, MARY aged 34 years December 2, 1884 by Rev. John E. Beard at 6 Blake Street. He a native of South Carolina and she of Charleston.

DENIS, FRANCIS aged 38 years married to McGANNAGHAN, MARY aged 36 years February 14, 1885 by Rev. John E. Beard at 64 Nassau Street. He a native of England and she of Harrisburg, Pennsylvania. He works in a factory.

DENLE, LIZZIE M. aged 18 years married to THOMAS, JOSEPH M. aged 24 years June 17, 1880 by Rev. R. N. Wells at 72 Tradd Street. Both natives of Charleston. He a merchant.

DENNAL, JAMES aged 31 years married to MEYER, MARY aged 27 years May 14, 1878 by Father Harry P. Northrop at St. Patrick's Roman Catholic Church. Both natives of Ireland. He a soldier at The Citadel.

DENNIS, CAROLINE J. aged 17 years married to MILLS, LOUIS A. aged 21 years May 22, 1886 by Rev. C. A. Stakeley. Both natives of Charleston. He an engineer.

DENNIS, CATHARINE aged 17 years married to WIENGES, DANIEL M. aged 21 years September 25, 1888 by Rev. J. E. Carlisle at 19 Blake Street.

DENNIS, CORNELIA ELIZA aged 16 years married to HARRISON, MARION DRAYTON aged 21 years November 15, 1884 by Rev. Charles S. Vedder at the Huguenot Church.

DENNIS, CYNTHIA E. aged 15 years married to CORES, ALEX W. aged 23 years April 9, 1893 by Rev. J. C. Yongue. He a native of Georgetown, South Carolina and she of Charleston. He works for the railroad.

DENNIS, MARY CATHARINE aged 21 years married to CUMMINGS, PINCKNEY aged 27 years May 8, 1892 by Rev. H. F. Chreitzberg. Both natives of Charleston. He a street car driver.

DENNIS, M. C. aged 22 years married to NELSON, J. A. aged 24 years October 12, 1882 by Father P. L. Duffy at The Cathedral of St. John the Baptist. He a native of Florida and a telegraph worker.

DENNIS, WILLIAM J. aged 20 years married to DROSE, ANNA J. aged 20 years November 29, 1893 by Rev. J. C. Yongue at 2 Morris Street. He a native of Charleston and she of Moncks Corner, South Carolina.

DENT, GEORGE aged 25 years married to BENEDICT, EMMA aged 20 years February 2, 1886 by Rev. Louis Muller at 88 Society Street. Both natives of Savannah, Georgia. He a grocer in Savannah.

DENT, SIDNEY aged 39 years married to PRIOLEAU, ANNIE F. aged 28 years April 27, 1893 by Rev. John Johnson at St. Philip's Church. He a native of the United States and she of Charleston. He an insurance agent.

DERGEMAN, PAULINE E. married to MALONE, CLARENCE December 16, 1877 by William B. Yates, Chaplain.

DERICK, A. B. aged 45 years married to CANNON, OWEN aged 43 years October 31, 1880 by Father Daniel J. Quigley at The Cathedral of St. John the Baptist. He a native of Ireland and she of Lexington, South Carolina. Both reside at the Waverly House. He a farmer.

DERMS (?), MICHAEL J. B. aged 26 years married to MORRISSEY, BRIDGET L. aged 24 years January 6, 1884 by Father F. J. Shadler at St. Joseph's Roman Catholic Church. He a native of Charleston and she of Ireland. He a boilermaker.

DeSAUSSURE, MARY C. aged 26 years married to LaROCHE, CHRISTOPHER J. aged 26 years October 29, 1878 by Bishop W. B. W. Howe at St. Philip's Church. He a native of South Carolina and she of Charleston. He a clergyman.

DESAUSSURE, OCTAVIA married to CHISOLM, J. BUCKMAN October 5, 1882 by Rev. Richard S. Trapier.

DeSAUSSURE, WILLIAM P. aged 27 years married to LOGAN, SELENA GEORGINA aged 20 years October 29, 1878 by Rev. John Johnson at St. Philip's Church. Both natives of Charleston. He a lawyer.

DESEBROCK, A. H. aged 19 years married to MOHRMAN, H. aged 22 years February 27, 1883 by Rev. John H. Honour at St. John's Lutheran Church. He a native of Germany and she of Charleston. He a merchant in Augusta, Georgia.

DESPORTES, EMMELINE D. aged 27 years married to COLEMAN, WILEY M. aged 38 years October 24, 1889 by Rev. Edwin C. Dargan at 89 Washington Street. He a native of Ridgeway, South Carolina and she of Charleston. He a farmer in Ridgeway.

DETERS, HEINRICH W. aged 26 years married to JOHANNS, ADELINE F. M. aged 24 years June 10, 1886 by Rev. Johannes Heckel. He a native of Germany and she of Charleston. He a saloonkeeper.

DEVEAUX, JOHN P. aged 25 years married to GREEN, HARRIET H. aged 22 years October 20, 1886 by Rev. W. B. W. Howe at 23 Wentworth Street. Both natives of Charleston. He a government employee.

DEVEAUX, MARY E. aged 31 years married to RICE, CHARLES D. aged 31 years June 20, 1894 by Rev. C. C. Pinckney at 16 Limehouse Street. He a native of Walterboro, South Carolina and she of Charleston. He works for a newspaper in Walterboro.

DEVEAUX, WILLIAM B. aged 22 years married to FULLER, LUCY aged 21 years January 8, 1893 by Rev. C. E. Chichester at 119 King Street. He a native of Charleston and she of Georgia. He an upholsterer.

DEVEREAUX, AGATHA B. aged 18 years married to APELER, JOHN H. aged 21 years February 25, 1892 by Father J. J. Monaghan at St. Patrick's Roman Catholic Church. He a native of Germany and she of Charleston. He the superintendent of the phosphate mill.

DEVEREAUX, JAMES M. aged 22 years married to JEFFERSON, (Mrs.) MARY ANN BYRNES aged 27 years March 7, 1889 by Rev. J. E. Carlisle at 231 Coming Street. Both natives of Charleston. He a bookkeeper.

DEVEREAUX, JOHN E. aged 23 years married to MYER, ANNA S. aged 16 years September 15, 1881 by Rev. Louis Muller at 105 Wentworth Street. He a native of Connecticut and she of South Carolina. He an engineer.

DEVEREAUX, MARIE U. aged 21 years married to DEERY, H. A. aged 22 years November 25, 1887 by Father P. J. Wilson at St. Mary of the Annunciation Roman Catholic Church. He a native of New York and she of Charleston. He a pressman.

DeVILDRE, JANE CAMERON aged 40 years married to HEDRICKS, RICHARD F. aged 58 years December 9, 1883 by Rev. J. H. Tellinghast. He a native of Charleston and she of Glasgow, Scotland. He a clerk.

DEVINE, A. J. aged 22 years married to CAREY, J. J. aged 26 years November 18, 1879 by Father D. F. Hurley at St. Joseph's Roman Catholic Church. Both natives of Charleston. He a plumber.

DEVINE, MARY McI. aged 18 years married to CETTE, FREDERICK R. aged 34 years August 8, 1878 by Father Joseph Redington at The Cathedral of St. John the Baptist. He a native of Italy and she of Charleston. He a fresco painter.

DEVINEAU, PETER EMILE aged 25 years married to AIMAR, ANN MARIE MADELINE aged 25 years January 2, 1878 by Father Claudian B. Northrop at St. Mary of the Annunciation Church. Both natives of Charleston. He a clerk.

DIBBLE, T. O. SOMERS aged 25 years married to WHITEMAN, MARY P. aged 23 years January 23, 1884 by Rev. John Johnson in Queen Street. Both natives of Charleston. He a merchant in Orangeburg, South Carolina.

DICK, WILLIAM E. aged 24 years married to BRUNSON, CLAUDIA H. aged 19 years November 27, 1885 by Rev. J. O. Wilson at the Charleston Hotel. Both natives of Sumter County, South Carolina. He a salesman.

DICKENS, LOUIE LEE aged 17 years married to HOPPMAN, LEDWIG aged 22 years April 30, 1893 by Father J. J. Monaghan. He a native of Charleston and she of Sparta, Georgia. He a weaver in the cotton mill.

DICKINSON, ELLA married to WRIGHT, WILLIAM HENRY July 22, 1878 by William B. Yates, Chaplain.

DICKSON, CARRIE A. aged 19 years married to WRAGG, HENRY HARMON age 24 years December 25, 1881 by Rev. R. A. Mickle in America Street. He a native of Charleston and a carpenter.

DICKSON, D. J. U. aged 27 years married to GRAF, LOUISE aged 20 years November 30, 1887 by Rev. Johannes Heckel at 123 Smith Street. He a native of Sweden and she of Charleston. He a carpenter.

DICKSON, JOHN aged 31 years married to COSGROVE, BESSIE aged 25 years November 8, 1891 by Father J. J. Monaghan at 136 St. Philip Street. He a native of Denmark and she of Ireland. He a laborer.

DICKSON, MARY aged 23 years married to MOSELEY, THOMAS M. aged 24 years August 5, 1894 by Rev. J. C. Yongue at 14 Hampstead Square. He a native of Providence, Rhode Island and she of New York City. He works in the cotton factory.

DIERS, DORA aged 20 years married to KELLEY, P. T. aged 22 years January 10, 1881 by Rev. J. V. Welsh at Calvary Church. He a native of Walterboro, South Carolina and she of Charleston. He a printer.

DIERS, EMMA R. aged 20 years married to SERES, PETER A. aged 22 years December 9, 1883 by Rev. Luther K. Probst. Both natives of Charleston.

DIETZ, EDWARD F. aged 28 years married to HENKEN, ANNA CATHERINE aged 28 years November 25, 1886 by Rev. Louis Muller at the corner of Meeting and Jackson Streets. He a native of Ge

DILLINGHAM, JOSEPH C. aged 28 years married to MOFFETT, ANNA MORRIS aged 29 years January 7, 1890 by Rev. G. R. Brackett at 131 Coming Street. Both natives of Charleston. He a merchant.

DILLON, ALICE C. aged 21 years married to AHRENS, JOHN J. aged 23 years May 11, 1890 by Father F. J. Shadler at St. Joseph's Roman Catholic Church. Both natives of Charleston. He a baggage handler.

DILLON, M. C. Aged 30 years married to HAYDEN, JOHN F. aged 31 years May 28, 1882 by Rev. P. L. Duffy at The Cathedral of St. John the Baptist. She a native of Charleston. He a tinner in Virginia.

DINER, F. married to LAVAL, (Mrs.) A. S. DOBBS November 18, 1881. He a native of Pennsylvania and she of Ireland. He a laborer.

DINGATE, MARY A. aged 24 years married to BURKE, JOHN E. aged 25 years November 28, 1881 by Father P. L. Duffy at The Cathedral of St. John the Baptist. Both natives of Charleston. He a plumber.

DISHER, E. P. aged 19 years married to LITTLE, C. O. aged 35 years December 9, 1879 by Rev. W. S. Bowman at 17 Nassau Street. He a native of Georgia and she of Charleston. He works for the railroad.

DIVINE, KATE J. aged 25 years married to SPAIN, WILLIAM J. aged 25 years July 25, 1888 by Father John J. Wedenfeller at St .Joseph's Church. He a native of Augusta, Georgia and she of Charleston. He a clerk.

DIXON, JAMES A. aged 18 years married to MURPHY, SARAH JANE aged 16 years July 29, 1878 by Father Daniel J. Quigley. Both natives of Charleston. He a bookbinder.

DOAR, ARTHUR E. Aged 25 years married to O'BRIEN, MAGGIE R. aged 23 years January 16, 1894 by Father J. J. Monaghan at St. Patrick's Roman Catholic Church. Both natives of Charleston. He a machinist.

DOAR, (Mrs.) ELLA M. POOSER aged 27 years married to OPPEL, F. GEORGE aged 36 years September 30, 1890 by Rev. J. Thomas Pate at 21 Cooper Street. Both natives of Charleston. He a printer in Jacksonville, Florida.

DOAR, GEORGE P. aged 20 years married to POOSER, ELLA M. aged 20 years November 28, 1883 by Rev. J. A. Cliffton at the Spring Street Methodist Church. Both natives of Charleston. He a machinist.

DOAR, HENRY F. aged 24 years married to CAMERON, CAROLINE T. aged 19 years June 18, 1885 by Rev. Robert Wilson. Both natives of Charleston. He a mechanic.

DOAR, STEPHEN D married to TOOMER, HARRIET R. April 15, 1885. Both natives of South Carolina. He a physician.

DOBEREMAN, GOTTFRIED N. aged 33 years married to JOHANNS, ANN aged 26 years November 29, 1893 by Rev. Alfred Freyschmidt. He a native of Georgia and she of Charleston. He a contractor.

DODD, CECELIA aged 20 years married to HASSETT, JOHN J. aged 22 years May 2, 1887 by Father F. J. Shadler at St. Joseph's Roman Catholic Church. Both natives of Charleston. He a laborer.

DODDS, GEORGE aged 33 years married to GAYNOR, ANN aged 28 years July 16, 1878 by Father Harry P. Northrop at St. Patrick's Roman Catholic Church. He a native of Ireland and she of Charleston. He a laborer.

DOLAN, JOHN E. aged 30 years married to KENNY, ANNIE E. aged 27 years January 28, 1880 by Father Daniel J. Quigley in Tradd Street. He a native of Brooklyn New York and she of Charleston. He a painter.

DOLAN, JOHN married to KEEGAN, JANE June 2, 1878 by William B. Yates, Chaplain.

DOLAN, MARTIN aged 37 years married to HOLLOWAY, CHARLOTTE POOLE aged 29 years November 7, 1886 by Rev. H. B. Browne at 78 Drake Street. Both natives of New Jersey. He a carpenter.

DOMINGO, MARY aged 18 years married to BUTT, GEORGE MILTON aged 27 years June 9, 1886 by Rev. J. Walter Dickson at 231 Coming Street. Both natives of Charleston. He a mechanic.

DONAGHUE, PATRICK aged 30 years married to KELLY, KATE aged 20 years February 16, 1879 by Father Daniel J. Quigley at The Cathedral of St. John the Baptist. He a native of Ireland and she of Charleston. He a policeman.

DONAHUE, (Mrs.) MARY T. NOLAN aged 36 years married to VAUGHN, JAMES H. aged 36 years February 7, 1894 by Rev. J. Murray at St. Peter's Church. Both natives of Charleston. He a laborer.

DONALD, B. aged 21 years married to McDONALD, DAISY aged 17 years July 9, 1879 by Father Daniel J. Quigley. Both natives of Charleston. He a native of Charleston and she of Cold Spring, New York. He a pressman.

DONALD, D. JOHNSTON aged 22 years married to BARTON, ESTELLE BERTHA aged 17 years October 7, 1884 by Rev. John O. Wilson at 315 East Bay Street. He a native of Charleston and she of Atlanta, Georgia. He an engineer.

DONAN, GEORGE S. aged 21 years married to ROBINSON, ANN LAURA aged 15 years March 29, 1885 by Rev. John E. Beard at 51 America Street. He a native of Columbia, South Carolina and she of Charleston. He a laborer.

DONEHAN, WILLIAM P. J. aged 26 years married to FRANKLIN, HATTIE aged 16 years April 19, 1891 by Father J. J. Monaghan at St. Patrick's Roman Catholic Church. He a native of Charleston and she of South Carolina. He an iron moulder.

DONEHEY (?), MICHAEL J. aged 25 years married to CARROLL, JULIA A. January 23, 1881 by Father Harry P. Northrop at St. Patrick's Roman Catholic Church. Both natives of Charleston. He a clerk.

DONNELLY, LEON aged 22 years married to GREEN, ELLA F. aged 22 years January 6, 1884 by Father J. J. Woolahan at 74 Wentworth Street. He a native of Athens, Georgia and she of Charleston. He a tailor.

DONNELS, J. B. aged 30 years married to FINK, SUSAN G. aged 27 years November 7, 1880 by Rev. J. V. Welsh at the residence of J. B. Donnels - 64 Radcliffe Street. Both natives of Charleston. He a laborer.

DONOHUE, ANNE married to TIGHE, BERNARD J. March 12, 1879 by Father D. J. Croghan. He a native of Ireland and she of Charleston. He a clerk.

DONOHUE, JOHN T. aged 30 years married to WRIGHT, ROSA A. aged 28 years November 24, 1892 by Father J. J. Monaghan at St. Patrick's Roman Catholic Church. He a native of Wilmington, North Carolina and she of Charleston. He a moulder.

DOOD, BERNHARD JOHANN aged 24 years married to SCHARFER, ANNA MARY DOROTHEA aged 21 years March 28, 1889 by Rev. Louis Muller at the residence of the Bride's father - Spring Street at the corner of Rose Lane. He a native of Prussia and she of Charleston. He a grocer.

DOOGAN, MARTIN aged 22 years married to KEENAN, CATHARINE aged 20 years June 8, 1881 by Father F. J. Shadler at St. Joseph's Roman Catholic Church. He a native of Charleston and a mariner.

DORAN, E. M. aged 22 years married to CLARK, G. T. aged 22 years June 8, 1882 by Father Daniel J. Quigley at The Cathedral of St. John the Baptist. He a native of Charleston and a boathand.

DORAN, SARAH aged 20 years married to McKAY, JEFFERSON T. aged 23 years May 23, 1883 by Rev. P. L. Duffy at The Cathedral of St. John the Baptist. He a native of Bonneau, South Carolina and she of Charleston. He a bartender.

DORKEWITZ (?), A. C. aged 21 years married to YOUNGER, F. W. aged 34 years May 16, 1882 by Rev. Louis Muller in King Street. He a native of Germany and an engineer. She a native of Charleston.

DORN, JOHN L. aged 19 years married to WOOD, AMY C. aged 22 years April 16, 1895 by Rev. J. C. Yongue at 27 Blake Street. He a native of Edgefield County, South Carolina and she of Rhode Island. He works in the cotton mill.

DORRE (?), ANNIE M. aged 20 years married to SCHLUETER, HERMAN aged 27 years August 6, 1885 by Rev. Luther K. Probst. He a native of Germany and she of Charleston. He a baker.

DORSEY, PATRICK aged 35 years married to SANDERS, JANIE aged 19 years December 23, 1890 by Rev. Robert Wilson at 4 Wragg Street. Both natives of Charleston. He a laborer.

DOSCHER, AUGUST aged 28 years married to BOSCH, JOHANNA C. M. aged 19 years June 15, 1892 by Rev. Louis Muller at the corner of Coming and Morris Streets. He a native of Prussia and she of Charleston. He a grocer.

DOSCHER, AUGUST FREDERICK aged 25 years married to BOHLEN, MATILDA CATHARINE MARGARET aged 18 years January 4, 1883 by Rev. Louis Muller at the corner of Beaufain and Coming Streets. Both natives of Germany. He a grocer.

DOSCHER, ERNST H. aged 28 years married to STRECKFUSS, CATHARINE aged 18 years October 12, 1887 by Rev. Louis Muller at the corner of Line and King Streets. Both natives of Prussia. He a grocer.

DOSCHER, HENRY L. aged 30 years married to TORCK, MADELINE E. aged 25 years January 12, 1892 by Rev. R. C. Holland at the Wentworth Street Lutheran Church. He a native of Charleston and a packer.

DOSCHER, IDA aged 22 years married to SEIMERS, FREDERICK aged 28 years March 28, 1879 by Rev. Johannes Heckel at the residence of Mr. Oetjen. He a native of Hanover and she of Hamburg, Germany. He a merchant.

DOSCHER, MAGGIE aged 18 years married to BEAN, JAMES W. aged 23 years November 15, 1892 by Father J. J. Monaghan at 143 St. Philip Street. He a native of Ireland and she of Athens, Georgia. He a laborer.

DOSCHER, WILHELMINA G. aged 39 years married to HOLST, HEINRICH aged 29 years July 25, 1880 by Father Daniel J. Quigley at The Cathedral of St. John the Baptist. He a native of Charleston and she of Macon, Georgia. He a driver.

DOTEN, CORALIE married to OGLESBY, JOHN T. February 27, 1889 by Father John J. Wedenfeller at St. Joseph's Roman Catholic Church. He a native of Georgia and she of Charleston. He a railroad conductor.

DOTTERER, LOUIS P. aged 30 years married to GEDDINGS, ELIZABETH F. aged 22 years January 25, 1888 by Rev. John Johnson at St. Philip' Church. Both natives of Charleston. He a dentist.

DOTY, JOHN M. aged 25 years married to HODGES, CORENE aged 18 years May 25, 1885 by Rev. Herbert Jones at 189 Coming Street. He a native of Columbia, South Carolina and a car driver.

DOTY, THOMAS W. aged 24 years married to CUNNINGHAM, MARY A. aged 22 years May 1, 1881 by Father P. L. Duffy at 69 King Street. He a native of Charleston.

DOUGHERTY, CARRIE aged 25 years married to JOYNER, T. L. aged 29 years July 25, 1880 by Father Daniel J. Quigley at The Cathedral of St. John the Baptist. He a native of Charleston and she of Macon, Georgia. He a driver.

DOUGHERTY, JESSE E. aged 33 years married to McCOWAN, WILLIAM C. aged 37 years December 15, 1881 by Rev. Luther K. Probst at 18 Wentworth Street. He native of Abbeville, South Carolina and she of Charleston. He a printer.

DOUGHERTY, MARIA A. married to MYERS, EDWARD C. July 19, 1890 by Rev. W. A. Betts.

DOUGLAS, GEORGE married to BATTERSON, ALICE W. September 9, 1878 by William B. Yates, Chaplain.

DOWD, HELEN aged 20 years married to MEHRTENS, JOHN aged 26 years June 26, 1890 by Rev. Edwin C. Dargan at 61 Bull Street. He a native of Charleston and she of Lexington, Kentucky. He a salesman.

DOWD, OWEN aged 32 years married to CAHILIN, CATHERINE aged 19 years January 15, 1879 by Father John P. Twigg at The Cathedral of St. John the Baptist. He a native of Ireland and she of Charleston. He a laborer.

DOWELL, HARRIET MARY aged 27 years married to STRATTON, JOHN PAUL aged 25 years January 24, 1883 by Rev. P. L. Duffy at 1 Trumbo Court. Both natives of Charleston. He a clerk.

DOWELL, SAMUEL G. aged 31 years married to COOKE, ANNE F. aged 22 years June 10, 1891 by Rev. W. T. Thompson at 6 Smith Street. Both natives of Charleston. He a bookkeeper.

DOWIE, R. B. aged 38 years married to MURE, ELIZABETH aged 35 years August 7, 1879 by Rev. W. C. Dana. He a native of Scotland and she of Charleston. He a bank officer.

DOWLING, JENNIE aged 24 years married to POWERS, WILLIAM aged 25 years December 14, 1884 by Father F. A. Schmetz at St. Patrick's Roman Catholic Church. Both natives of Charleston. He works for the railroad.

DOWLING, JOHN JAMES aged 24 years married to FLYNN, ELLA MARY aged 22 years January 1, 1882 by Father Claudian B. Northrop at St. Mary of the Annunciation Roman Catholic Church. Both natives of Charleston. He a bookkeeper.

DOWLING, THOMAS J. aged 24 years married to HERMON, MARY CATHARINE aged 22 years December 8, 1889 by Father Daniel J. Quigley at St. Patrick's Roman Catholic Church. He a native of Charleston and she of Germany. He an engineer.

DOWNING, LENORA AGNES aged 21 years married to HAMILTON, RICHARD E. aged 22 years April 9, 1881 by Rev. L. H. Shuck at 27 Church Street. He a native of Charleston and a fireman.

DOWNING, ROSA H. aged 17 years married to COLE, HENRY THOMAS aged 23 years August 6, 1893 by Rev. Edmund Wells at 86 Mary Street. He a native of Effingham, South Carolina and she of Charleston. He works in the cotton mill.

DOWNING, SAMUEL aged 29 years married to HARRIGAN, SARAH aged 25 years May 1, 1889 by Father John J. Wedenfeller at The Cathedral of St. John the Baptist. He a native of Charleston and "in the cotton business."

DOWNING, THADDEUS C. aged 20 years married to Baker, LYDIA R. aged 17 years November 17, 1887 by Rev. G. R. Brackett. He a native of Charleston and she of Lexington, South Carolina. He works in the bagging factory.

DOYLE, ELIZABETH aged 25 years married to SCOWCROFT, JOHN COOPER aged 29 years December 25, 1878 by Father Claudian B. Northrop at 74 Wentworth Street. He a native of Bolton, England and she of Charleston. He a clerk.

DOYLE, JULIA aged 30 years married to DUGAN, JAMES J. aged 29 years May 26, 1880 by Father P. L. Duffy at St. Joseph's Roman Catholic Church. Both natives of Charleston. He a machinist.

DOYLE, MARY A. aged 21 years married to BURMEISTER, JOHN W. aged 21 years November 17, 1886 by Father F. J. Shadler at the residence of the Bride - 299 East Bay Street. Both natives of Charleston. He a grain dealer.

DOYLE, THERESA M. aged 26 years married to HUGHES, JOHN E. aged 29 years January 25, 1887 by Father F. J. Shadler at St. Joseph's Roman Catholic Church. Both natives of Charleston. He a clerk.

DOYLE, THOMAS C. aged 28 years married to LANIGAN, WINIFRED S. aged 26 years November 27, 1894 by Father J. J. Monaghan at St. Patrick's Roman Catholic Church. He a native of Orangeburg, South Carolina and she of New Jersey. He a physician in Orangeburg.

DOYLE, THOMAS aged 22 years married to BULWINKLE, ELIZA G. aged 21 years August 17, 1884 by Rev. J. V. Welsh at 73 Spring Street. Both natives of Charleston. He a carpenter.

DRAKE, E. A. aged 24 years married to SCHLEY, H. M. aged 33 years February 15, 1882 by Rev. Claudian B. Northrop at 176 Meeting Street. He a native of Germany and a planter.

DRAKE, JAMES A. aged 29 years married to PALMER, GABRIELLE J. aged 21 years May 18, 1881 by Rev. Edward T. Horn. He a native of Germany and she of Charleston. He a merchant.

DRAUGHTON, MATTHEW B. aged 24 years married to LANDER, GENEVA B. aged 17 years December 24, 1891 by Rev. Edwin C. Dargan at 29 Charlotte Street. He a native of North Carolina and she of Rocky Mount, North Carolina. He a clerk.

DREES, H. aged 22 years married to KUHNE, E. aged 23 years October 24, 1882 by Rev. Louis Muller at 90 Calhoun Street. He a native of Germany and a grocer.

DRESSEL, GEORGE F. PHILIP aged 27 years married to WERNER, ANNA MATHILDE aged 27 years November 10, 1886 by Rev. Louis Muller at 89 Smith Street. He a native of Georgia and she of Charleston. He a merchant.

DRESSEL, JOHANN GEORGE aged 24 years married to SMALL, MARY CAROLINE T. aged 22 years May 18, 1881 by Rev. Edward T. Horn at 4 Bull Street.

DRESSEL, J. G. aged 24 years married to SMALL, M. C. F. aged 22 years May 18, 1881 by Rev. Louis Muller at 4 Bull Street.

DREW, JOHN E. aged 28 years married to DELANEY, MARY E. aged 28 years March 30, 1891 by Father F. J. Shadler at St. Joseph's Roman Catholic Church. Both natives of Charleston. He a machinist in Jacksonville, Florida.

DREYER, BETA aged 28 years married to PLEIN, JOHANN aged 24 years April 15, 1883 by Rev. Louis Muller at the northwest corner of King and Line Streets. Both natives of Germany. He a grocer.

DREYER, HENRY aged 30 years married to KLOSS, AMANDA PAULINE FLORENTINE aged 30 years September 5, 1878 by Rev. Louis Muller at 3 Liberty Street.

DREYER, JOHN married to KRUER, MARY January 9, 1879 by Rev. Johannes Heckel. Both natives of Germany. He a merchant.

DRIGGERS, ALBERTA B. aged 15 years married to McDONALD, SAMUEL R. aged 20 years December 25, 1883 by Rev. J. C. Yongue at 14 Hampstead Square. He a native of Summerville, South Carolina and she of Sumter, South Carolina. He a farmer at Four Mile House.

DRIGGERS, BIRDY aged 16 years married to CANNON, CHARLIE aged 20 years February 14, 1892 by Rev. J. O. Fludd at 23 Blake Street.

DRIGGERS, DANIEL F. aged 18 years married to RUGIERO, TILLIE aged 16 years October 3, 1889 by Rev. H. B. Browne at 85 Columbus Street. He a native of Colleton County, South Carolina and she of Summerville, South Carolina. He a cotton mill operator in Adams Run, South Carolina.

DRIGGERS, M. married to FISHER, J. H. June 11, 1882 by Rev. J. V. Welch at 700 King Street. He a native of Charleston and a baker.

DRISCOLL, J. A. aged 18 years married to RICHARDSON, R. C. aged 23 years December 30, 1879 by Father Daniel J. Quigley in Wharf Street. He a native of Charleston and she of Coldspring, New York. He a pressman.

DRISCOLL, MAMIE aged 25 years married to FRIBERG, H. JOHN aged 40 years April 23, 1890 by Father Harry P. Northrop at The Cathedral of St. John the Baptist. He a native of Denmark and she of Charleston. He a ship builder.

DRISCOLL, WILLIAM J. aged 23 years married to FLYNN, FRANCES aged 21 years April 22, 1891 by Bishop Harry P. Northrop at The Cathedral of St. John the Baptist. Both natives of Charleston. He a postal clerk.

DROSE, ANNA J. aged 20 years married to DENNIS, WILLIAM J. aged 20 years November 29, 1893 by Rev. J. C. Yongue at 2 Morris Street. He a native of Charleston and she of Moncks Corner, South Carolina.

DROSE, JOHN HENRY aged 20 years married to HYATT, EVA A. aged 18 years May 17, 1891 by Rev. W. A. Betts at 2 Addison Court. He a native of St. John's Parish, South Carolina and she of St. James, Santee, South Carolina. He works in the bagging factory.

DROSE, SUSAN R. married to GEBE, HENRY W. October 14, 1890 by William B. Yates, Chaplain.

DROZE, EDWIN MARION aged 26 years married to STOLZE, ANNIE AMELIA aged 27 years September 11, 1884 by Rev. Luther K. Probst. Both natives of Charleston. He a tinsmith.

DRUELLA, LEON aged 45 years married to BELTON, CARRIE aged 22 years September 29, 1884 by Rev. John Johnson. He a native of France and she of Charleston. He a tailor.

DRYER, JOHN aged 25 years married to PRAUSE (?), LOUISE aged 23 years October 12, 1892 by Rev. Edward T. Horn at 29 State Street. He a native of Germany and she of Charleston. He a clerk.

DuBOIS, ELLA aged 22 years married to LEBBY, MONFORT aged 30 years November 26, 1884 by Rev. E. J. Meynardie. He a native of Savannah, Georgia and she of South Carolina. He a cotton weigher in Savannah.

DuBOSE, ANNIE aged 28 years married to SHOKES, ALEX W. aged 35 years December 14, 1884 by Rev. John E. Beard in Line Street. Both natives of Charleston. He a carpenter.

DuBOSE, EDWIN married to LUHN, LILLIE December 3, 1885 by Rev. William H. Campbell. He a clerk.

DuBOSE, HENRY S. aged 36 years married to KRESSEL, (Mrs.) ANNA BLANCHARD aged 33 years September 27, 1888 by Father Daniel J. Quigley at 313 King Street. He a native of Williamsburg County, South Carolina and she of South Carolina. He an engineer in Waycross, Georgia.

DuBOSE, H. L. aged 29 years married to BRADSHAW, M. E. aged 24 years October 16, 1881 by Father J. E. Chapins at 51 Spring Street. He a native of Williamsburg County, South Carolina and she of Charleston. He an engineer.

DuBOSE, JANE SCREVEN aged 19 years married to HEYWARD, EDWIN WILKINS aged 21 years November 13, 1884 by Rev. John Johnson in Wall Street. He a native of Grahamville, South Carolina and she of St. John's, Berkeley County, South Carolina. He a clerk.

DuBOSE, L. ISIDORE aged 71 years married to MILNE, E. C. S. aged 42 years May 20, 1884 by Father J. J. Woolahan at 2 Coming Street. He a native of France and she of Charleston. He a professor.

DuBOSE, L. L. aged 22 years married to BOLTON, L. aged 24 years December 23, 1893 by Rev. J. C. Yongue. He a native of South Carolina and she of Charleston. He works in the cotton mill.

DuBOSE, MARTHA A. aged 18 years married to WILLIFORD, LEON E. aged 21 years February 24, 1895 by Rev. Edmund Wells at 20 Cooper Street. He a native of Morrisville, North Carolina and she of Berkeley County, South Carolina. He a manufacturer.

DuBOSE, THEODOSIA A. aged 25 years married to WILSON, WILLIAM M. aged 25 years June 19, 1892 by Rev. A. M. Chreitzberg. He a native of Georgetown, South Carolina and she of Williamsburg County, South Carolina. He a printer in Augusta, Georgia.

98

DuBOSE, WILLIAM C. aged 28 years married to MAULL, PHILLIPINA E. aged 31 years December 13, 1884 by Rev. Robert Wilson at 4 Wragg Square. Both natives of Charleston. He a railroad brakeman.

DUC, CHARLES A. aged 33 years married to SMITH, MARY J. aged 16 years November 10, 1883 by Rev. J. A. Cliffton at 189 Coming Street. Both natives of Charleston. He a tinsmith.

DUC, HENRY C. aged 25 years married to CHURCHILL, SUSAN E. aged 21 years February 24, 1886 by Rev. John O. Wilson at 85 East Bay Street. Both natives of South Carolina. He a farmer.

DUANE, EDWARD aged 35 years married to CANTY, ELIZABETH aged 25 years July 16, 1883 by Father F. J. Shadler at St. Joseph's Roman catholic Church. He a native of Ireland and she of Charleston. He a painter.

DUC, CHARLES OTTO married to HARPER, CARRIE August 23, 1887 by Rev. William H. Campbell. He a clerk in New York.

DUC, HENRY ALEX aged 25 years married to MARTIN, AGNES M. aged 16 years June 17, 1889 by Rev. J. E. Carlisle. He a native of Columbia, South Carolina and she of Charleston. He a gunsmith.

DUC, NOEIMI M. aged 26 years married to COLLINS, JEREMIAH P. aged 24 years April 13, 1879 by Father Harry P. Northrop at St. Patrick's Roman Catholic Church.

DUDLEY, JAMES aged 30 years married to BESSINGER, HATTIE aged 24 years July 24, 1887 by Rev. C. A. Stakeley. Both natives of South Carolina. He a laborer.

DUDLEY, JESSIE McLEE aged 22 years married to VON HOLLAND, JOHN aged 22 years September 16, 1894 by Rev. Edmund Wells at 32 Line Street. Both natives of Charleston. He a stonecutter.

DUFF, AUGUST F. aged 25 years married to RAMBLEY, SALLIE E. aged 20 years January 6, 1892 by Rev. William A. Rogers at Trinity Church. He a steward at the Charleston Hotel.

DUFFIE, ANNIE MARIE aged 22 years married to McKIEVER, DANIEL J. aged 27 years February 11, 1885 by Father Daniel J. Quigley at St. Patrick's Roman Catholic Church. He a native of Charleston and a carpenter.

DUFFIE, MARY CATHERINE aged 19 years married to AUSTIN, HARRY aged 30 years December 26, 1894 by Rev. Edward T. Horn at 31 Pitt Street. He a native of Elkhart, Indiana and she of Charleston. He a showman in Marion, Indiana.

DUFFIE, SARAH R. aged 25 years married to CORMIER, WILLIAM IRVIN aged 28 years May 22, 1884 by Father Daniel J. Quigley at St. Patrick's Roman Catholic Church. Both natives of Charleston. He works for the railroad.

DUFFIE, WILLIAM P. aged 31 years married to WILLIE, ANNA S. aged 19 years September 8, 1885 by Rev. J. V. Welch at 47 Line Street. Both natives of Charleston. He a bookkeeper.

DUFFY, FRANCIS aged 35 years married to CLEAR, MARIA aged 35 years October 12, 1884 by Father F. A. Schmetz at St. Patrick's Roman Catholic Church. He a native of Charleston and she of Ireland. He a merchant.

DUFFY, LIZZIE aged 19 years married to BRANDT, EDWARD P. aged 30 years September 24, 1885 by Rev. John O. Wilson at 82 Wentworth Street.

DUFFY, MARY aged 28 years married to ROSE, JOSEPH aged 32 years February 16, 1887 by Father P. J. Wilson at St. Mary of the Annunciation Roman Catholic Church. He a native of Spain and she of Charleston. He a laborer.

DUFFY, MICHAEL aged 40 years married to FRAUTOWIG (?), (Mrs.) MARY FERM aged 35 years September 7, 1878 by Father John P. Twigg at The Cathedral of St. John the Baptist. Both natives of Ireland. He a laborer.

DUFFY, WILLIAM aged 30 years married to MABORE, (Mrs.) PAULINE E. DEIGHEN aged 30 years July 26, 1886 by Father Daniel J. Quigley at St. Patrick's Roman Catholic Church. Both natives of Charleston. He a blacksmith.

DuFORT, PAULINE C. aged 21 years married to SOUBEYROUX, HONORE T. aged 23 years October 15, 1885 by Father J. J. Woolahan at St. Mary of the Annunciation Roman Catholic Church. Both natives of Charleston. He an accountant.

DuFORT, T. E. aged 23 years married to GUILLEMIN, CLEMENCE E. aged 20 years April 17, 1884 by Rev. J. J. Woolahan at St. Patrick's Roman Catholic Church. Both natives of Charleston. He a clerk.

DUFORT, VIRGINIA aged 20 years married to RICHTER, G. E. aged 24 years December 14, 1890 by Bishop Harry P. Northrop at The Cathedral of St. John the Baptist. Both natives of Charleston. He a salesman.

DUGAN, JAMES J. aged 29 years married to DOYLE, JULIA W. aged 30 years May 26, 1880 by Father P. L. Duffy at St. Joseph's Roman Catholic Church. Both natives of Charleston. He a machinist.

DUGAN, JAMES J. aged 30 years married to CLEARY, ANNIE E. aged 20 years November 29, 1880 by Father P. L. Duffy at The Cathedral of St. John the Baptist. Both natives of Charleston. He a carpenter.

DUGAN, JANE aged 22 years married to CULLEN, JAMES aged 22 years July 28, 1879 by Rev. E. J. Horn. Both natives of Charleston. He a mechanic.

DUHRELS, META DORETHA aged 24 years married to STELLING, CLAUS aged 24 years October 11, 1891 by Rev. Louis Muller at 96 Radcliffe Street. Both natives of Prussia. He a clerk.

DUKES, (Mrs.) MARIE FURCHES aged 35 years married to HUGHES, GEORGE M. aged 26 years December 31, 1888 by Rev. H. B. Browne in Cumberland Street. He a native of Richmond County, Georgia and she of Orangeburg, South Carolina. He works in the cotton mill.

DUNBY, FRANCES married to WEBER, ADAM January 21, 1879 by Rev. Louis Muller. He a native of Nova Scotia and she of London, England.

DUNCAN, ANNA M. aged 17 years married to SCHROEDER, CHARLES H. aged 36 years April 14, 1887 by Rev. G. R. Brackett. Both natives of South Carolina. He a physician.

DUNCAN, CATHERINE A. aged 17 years married to WESTERLIND, JAMES C. aged 27 years February 10, 1881 by Rev. G. R. Brackett. He a native of Charleston and a railroad conductor.

DUNCAN, CHARLES married to FINCKEN, (Mrs.) MARY BOYLE September 28, 1894 by Rev. Edmund Wells at 579 King Street. He a native of Boston, Massachusetts and she of Highland City. He a merchant.

DUNCAN, D. aged 28 years married to LAROUSELIERE, M. aged 28 years November 11, 1882 by Father J. J. Woolahan at St. Patrick's Roman Catholic Church. Both natives of Charleston. He works for the railroad.

DUNCAN, J. E. aged 31 years married to MORROW, ARTHUR aged 48 years November 18, 1888 by Rev. G. R. Brackett. He a native of Ireland and she of England. He a drayman.

DUNCAN, MARY aged 22 years married to MASTERS, RAPHAEL M. aged 23 years November 10, 1881 by Rev. G. R. Brackett. He a native of Savannah, Georgia and she of Charleston. He a tinner.

DUNCAN, MARY married to TELMANOTEE, — May 9, 1878 by William B. Yates, Chaplain.

DUNKIN, WILLIAM H. married to MARTIN, EUNICE H. July 8, 1886 by Rev. William H. Campbell. He a native of Charleston and she of South Carolina. He a clerk in Martins Station, Barnwell, South Carolina.

DUNLAP, ALEX aged 20 years married to SPRAGUE, MARY E. aged 17 years April 5, 1893 by Rev. J. C. Yongue. Both natives of Charleston. He a blacksmith.

DUNLAP, LILLIAN LAURA aged 22 years married to HERNANDEZ, ARTHUR W. aged 25 years September 11, 1883 by Rev. E. J. Meynardie at 6 Percy Street. Both natives of Charleston. He a druggist.

DUNLEY, FRANCES aged 22 years married to WEBER, ADAM aged 25 years January 21, 1879 by Rev. Louis Muller at 1 Duncan Street.

DUNN, ELLEN aged 21 years married to GOOLEY, MICHAEL aged 22 years March 24, 1878 by Father Daniel J. Quigley. He a native of Ireland and she of Charleston. He a clerk.

DUNN, JOHN W. aged 22 years married to HARTNETT, CATHERINE aged 16 years June 17, 1892 by Father J. J. Monaghan. Both natives of Charleston. He a salesman.

DUNN, KATE aged 37 years married to PATRICK, JAMES B. aged 40 years September 2, 1883 by Father John P. Twigg at St. Patrick's Roman Catholic Church. He a native of Ireland and she of Charleston.

DUNN, MAGDALENA O. aged 24 years married to NABERS, GEORGE O. aged 24 years November 25, 1890 by Rev. Robert Wilson at 4 Wragg Square. Both natives of Charleston. He a drayman.

DUNNE, PATRICK F. aged 28 years married to BRADY, ELLEN R. aged 19 years February 25, 1878 by Father C. J. Croghan. He a native of Augusta, Georgia and she of Charleston. He a telegraph operator.

DUNNE, SARAH A. aged 25 years married to GUILT, JOHN W. aged 25 years November 9, 1892 by Father J. J. Monaghan at 203 St. Philip Street. He a native of Woodville, Georgia and she of Augusta, Georgia. He an engineer in Savannah, Georgia.

DUNNEMANN, EMILIE A. L. aged 25 years married to DUNNEMANN, HENRY L. aged 30 years March 10, 1892 by Rev. Louis Muller in Line Street. Both natives of Charleston. He a farmer on Ufferhardt's Farm.

DUNNEMANN, HENRY L. aged 30 years married to DUNNEMANN, EMILIE A. L. aged 25 years March 10, 1892 by Rev. Louis Muller in Line Street. Both natives of Charleston. He a farmer on Ufferhardt's Farm.

DUNNEMANN, JOHANNA DORETHA WILHELMINA aged 26 years married to SCHULTZ, HEINRICH aged 24 years July 13, 1884 by Rev. Louis Muller at the corner of Bull and Coming Streets. Both natives of Germany. He a grocer.

DUNNING, FRANCIS D. aged 22 years married to BUSCH, CATHERINE D. aged 19 years April 16, 1880 by Rev. J. V. Welsh. Both natives of Charleston. He a blacksmith.

DUNNING, FLORENCE E. aged 16 years married to LANGE, CHARLES L. aged 25 years May 16, 1893 by Rev. J. L. Stokes at 231 Coming Street. Both natives of Charleston. He a clerk in Summerville, South Carolina.

DUNNING, KATE C. WEBB aged 25 years married to FORTUNE, DANIEL E. aged 32 years March 17, 1892 by Father J. J. Monaghan at St. Patrick's Roman Catholic Church.

DUNNING, MELVINA C. aged 34 years married to SMITH, JOHN H. aged 32 years December 1, 1881 by Rev. Luther K. Probst in Mt. Pleasant, South Carolina. He a native of Albany, New York and she of Charleston. He a planter.

DUNNING, ROBERT OTTO aged 23 years married to FARRIS, ALICE aged 15 years April 14, 1890 by Rev. C. E. Chichester at the Mariners Church. He a native of Charleston and she of Ridgeland, South Carolina. He a hostler in Savannah, Georgia.

DUNNING, THOMAS F. aged 38 years married to FOXWORTH, ALICE aged 18 years March 2, 1886 by Rev. J. W. Dickson at 650 King Street. Both natives of Charleston. He a butcher.

DUNNING, WILLIAM HENRY aged 21 years married to WEBB, KATE CECELIA aged 17 years September 21, 1884 by Father Daniel J. Quigley. Both natives of Charleston. He an engineer.

DUNSETTER, WILLIAM L. aged 42 years married to PIERCE, (Mrs.) ELIZABETH MURRAY aged 38 years April 9, 1888 by Rev. J. E. Carlisle at the Spring Street Church. He a native of Germany and she of Charleston. He a painter.

DUPRE, JANE ELIZABETH aged 17 years married to HOWELL, THOMAS HENRY R. aged 24 years May 7, 1889 by Rev. T. P. Burgess at 10 Woolfe Street. Both natives of Charleston. He a laborer.

DURBEC, LOUIS S. aged 23 years married to WERNER, ISABEL G. aged 26 years November 9, 1885 by Rev. Luther K. Probst. He a native of South Carolina and she of Charleston. He a printer.

DUREN, GEORGE W. aged 35 years married to AYERS, M. J. aged 19 years March 12, 1895 by Rev. J. C. Yongue at 73 Line Street. He a native of Columbia, South Carolina and she of Berkeley County, South Carolina. He a street car conductor.

DURKIN, HONORA married to KEENAN, JOHN aged 25 years June 21, 1883 by Father F. J. Shadler at St. Joseph's Roman Catholic Church. Both natives of Charleston. He a clerk.

DURKIN, M. W. married to SIMONS, CHARLES L. August 6, 1885 by Rev. William H. Campbell. Both natives of Charleston. He a clerk.

DURKINS, ELISE G. aged 24 years married to SEIGLER, ALBERT aged 24 years April 27, 1884 by Rev. William Lonergan. He a native of Edgefield, South Carolina and she of Maryland. He a weaver.

DURMANN, (Mrs.) DORIS DORETHA BOCK married to PAUL, HEINRICH PETER March 9, 1879 by Rev. Johannes Heckel. He a native of Gothenburg and she of Hordholz. He a carpenter.

DURR, ANN ELIZA aged 30 years married to SIRES, EDMUND C. aged 34 years February 12, 1879 by Rev. J. E. Johnson at 308 Meeting Street. He a native of Charleston and a mechanic.

DURR, H. C. aged 28 years married to CANNON, MELVILLE aged 25 years March 6, 1889 by Rev. J. E. Carlisle. He a native of Berkeley County, South Carolina and she of Darlington County, South Carolina. He a farmer.

DURSE, VIOLA aged 20 years married to FARRELL, EUGENE ALEXANDER. aged 23 years October 9, 1878 by Rev. W. S. Bowman at 4 Mary Street. He a native of Marion County, South Carolina and she of Charleston. He a turpentine distributor.

DUVA, ESTELLE aged 23 years married to NIXON, DRURY M. aged 29 years May 15, 1890 by Rev. J. Thomas Pate at 497 Meeting Street. He a native of South Carolina and she of Conway, South Carolina. He works for the railroad.

DUVAL, GERTRUDE aged 24 years married to WOOD, NELSON aged 29 years January 9, 1895 by Father Daniel J. Quigley at 30 Pitt Street. He a native of Indiana and she of Charleston. He a horse dealer in Indiana.

DWYER, HENRY aged 30 years married to KLOSS, AMANDA PAULINE. aged 30 years September 5, 1878 by Rev. Louis Muller. He a native of Germany and she of Prussia. He a tailor.

DWYER, JOHN aged 27 years married to KREUER, MARY aged 30 years January 9, 1879 by Rev. Johannes Heckel in King Street. Both natives of Germany. He resides in Augusta, Georgia.

DYANLYNSKI, ROSALIE aged 22 years married to ISEMAN, SOLOMAN aged 24 years October 10, 1888 by Rabbi David Levy at the Hasell Street Synagogue. He a native of Charleston and she of Florida. He a merchant.

EADIE, ADOLPHUS aged 42 years married to ORVIN, (Mrs.) NELLIE ANN CRAWFORD aged 35 years by Rev. Edmund Wells. Both natives of St. Stephan's Parish, South Carolina. He railroad car counter.

EADIE, ERNESTINE B. aged 18 years married to BARBER, WILLIAM aged 29 years December 29, 1895 by Rev. A. Ernest Cornish. He a native of Summerville, South Carolina and she of Bonneau, South Carolina. He works in a factory.

EAGAN, EDWARD aged 25 yeears married to WEBB, EMMA C. aged 20 years July 20, 1884 by Rev. R. A. Lapsley at 8 Cooper Street. He a native of Charleston and she of Georgia. He a sashmaker.

EAGAN, LENORE married to McINNES, JOHN September 13, 1893 by Rev. D. A. Blackburn at 49 Gadsden Street. He a blacksmith.

EAGAN, MARIE ANTOINETTE aged 28 years married to THOMAS, JAMES WHITFIELD aged 25 years October 2, 1888 by Rev. R. J. Smart. He a native of Augusta, Georgia and she of Newport, Rhode Island. He works for the railroad.

EAGAN, SUSIE E. married to TILGHMAN (?), CHARLES C. July 12, 1894 by Rev. D. A. Blackburn. He works for the railroad.

EAGLE, J. E. aged 21 years married to RHODES, W. E. aged 23 years January 8, 1884 by Rev. R. A. Lapsley at 88 America Street. He a native of Augusta, Georgia and she of Baltimore, Maryland. He works in a factory.

EARL, THOMAS S. aged 30 years married to TURNER, KATIE ETHEL aged 18 years March 24, 1885 by Rev. John E. Beard at 64 Nassau Street. He a native of Canada and she of New York. He a newspaper correspondent in New York.

EARLE, THERON married to PRICE, MARY E. February 27, 1883 by Rev. William H. Campbell at the residence of James Price. He a native of Greenville, South Carolina and a farmer.

EARLEY, CORA B. aged 20 years married to EGGERS, ERNST HEINRICH aged 20 years December 8, 1887 by Rev. Luther K. Probst in King Street between Market Street and Horlbeck Alley.

EARLY, FREDERICK aged 21 years married to FRIEND, MARY ELLEN June 9, 1890 by Rev. Robert Wilson at 4 Wragg Square. Both natives of Charleston. He a boilermaker.

EARLY, JAMES E. aged 23 years married to CANNON, DAISY ANNA LOCKWOOD aged 18 years March 18, 1884 by Rev. J. H. Tellinghast. Both natives of Charleston. He a printer.

EARLY, JULIA A. aged 21 years married to CASON, ROBERT J. aged 31 years September 6, 1883 by Rev. J. V. Welch at 44 Society Street. He a native of Exeter, England and she of Charleston. He an engineer.

EASLEY, JOHN A. aged 30 years married to HYDE, NANNIE TUPPER aged 25 years October 15, 1880 by Rev. R. N. Wells. He a native of Greenville and she of Charleston. He a clerk in Greenville.

EASON, M. aged 25 years married to WHILDEN, F. F. aged 27 years March 30, 1882 by Rev. G. R. Brackett in Drake Street. He a native of Charleston and a clerk.

EASON, R. H. aged 32 years married to SPEISSINGER, ANNA J. aged 25 years October 15, 1880 by Rev. R. N. Wells. Both natives of Charleston. He a clerk.

EASON, VIRGINIA aged 23 years married to CLOPTON, E. H. aged 23 years November 3, 1887 by Rev. C. C. L. Browne at the Unitarian Church. He a native of Tuskegee, Alabama and she of Abbeville, South Carolina. He a manufacturer in Montgomery, Alabama.

EASON, WILHELMINA married to HUTCHINSON, WILLIAM January 16, 1889 by Rev. William H. Campbell at the residence of W. G. Eason. He a clerk.

EASON, WILLIAM A. aged 22 years married to KELLY, SARAH EDITH aged 20 years December 24, 1883 by Rev. Luther K. Probst. He a native of Charleston and she of Toronto, Canada. He an engineer.

EASTERBY, ADA aged 28 years married to LEGARE, EFFINGHAM W. aged 31 years November 28, 1883 by Rev. C. C. Pinckney at Grace Church. Both natives of Charleston. He a clerk.

EASTERBY, CHRISTOPHINE aged 27 years married to GAYNOR, WILLIAM J. aged 30 years December 17, 1885 by Rev. C. C. Pinckney in South Bay Street. Both natives of Charleston. He a clerk.

EASTERBY, E. F. aged 22 years married to PITCHER, C. L. aged 23 years November 9, 1882 by Rev. Luther K. Probst. He a native of Charleston and a merchant.

EASTERBY, F. C. married to THOMAS, M L. June 1, 1882 by Rev. Luther K. Probst at the Wentworth Street Lutheran Church. He a native of Charleston and a merchant.

EASTERBY, JOHN RUDOLPH married to McMILLAN, SARAH February 28, 1884 by Rev. William T. Thompson at 49 Morris Street. He a mechanic.

EASTERBY, LILLIAN married to Baker, JOHN A. aged 33 years June 6, 1888 by Rev. R. W. Lide at First Baptist Church. He a native of Virginia and she of Charleston. He a clergyman in Louisville, Kentucky.

EASTERBY, STEWART D. aged 23 years married to KORBER, ANNIE M. aged 20 years March 31, 1891 by Rev. R. C. Holland at the Wentworth Street Lutheran Church. Both natives of Charleston. He a salesman.

EASTERBY, V. F. aged 19 years married to MOORER, T. JOHN aged 24 years June 18, 1879 by Rev. H. F. Chreitzberg. He a native of Colleton County, South Carolina and she of New York. He a machinist.

EASTERLING, ELLA LEE aged 17 years married to SHIEDER, THOMAS B. aged 21 years August 5, 1888 by Rev. J. W. Ford.

ECKSTEIN, EMIL aged 28 years married to LIVINGSTON, FANNIE aged 17 years October 24, 1878 by Rabbi David Levy at 58 Wentworth Street. He a native of Munich, Bavaria, Germany and she of Charleston. He a merchant in Savannah, Georgia.

EDDINGS, JOSIE aged 24 years married to SOSNOSKI, JOSEPH S. aged 23 years September 1, 1894 by Rev. A. Ernest Cornish at 300 Meeting Street. Both natives of Edisto Island, South Carolina. He an engineering apprentice.

EDGAR, JOSEPH F. aged 20 years married to BRIGMON, MARGARET J. aged 16 years October 15, 1893 by Rev. J. C. Yongue at 121 Drake Street. He a native of Charleston and she of Camden, South Carolina. He works in the cotton mill.

EDWARDS, E. aged 17 years married to GATERO (?), F. aged 25 years December 22, 1882 by Rev. J. V. Welsh at 22 Bogard Street. He a native of Charleston and a mariner.

EDWARDS, ELIZA aged 17 years married to WILKINS, WILLIAM G. aged 24 years November 9, 1884 by Rev. Johannes Heckel at the corner of Anson and Market Street. He a native of Georgia and she of South Carolina. He a miller.

EDWARDS, JAMES A. aged 24 years married to SIMMONS, MARY E. aged 28 years November 22, 1891 by Rev. W. A. Betts at 20 Hampstead Square. He a native of Berkeley County, South Carolina and she of Colleton County, South Carolina. He works at the electric light company.

EDWARDS, JAMES B. married to ARRIAN, JULIA M. June 4, 1890 by Rev. W. A. Betts.

EDWARDS, JOHN C. aged 22 years married to BRINSON, FRANCES aged 19 years December 23, 1894 by Rev. J. C. Yongue. Both natives of Berkeley County, South Carolina. He works in the cotton mill.

EDWARDS, LONNIE aged 22 years married to LORETTE, JOSEPH CHARLES aged 22 years September 3, 1893 by Rev. J. C. Yongue at 14 Hampstead Square.

EDWARDS, L. aged 22 years married to LOVETTE, JAMES C. aged 22 years September 3, 1893 by Rev. J. C. Yongue at 14 Hampstead Square. He a native of Johnstown, Pennsylvania and she of Greenville, South Carolina. He works in the cotton mill.

EGAN, ELLA aged 25 years married to CUTTS, JOHN A. aged 31 years March 22, 1893 by Rev. John Johnson at 36 Hasell Street.

EGGERS, ERNST HEINRICH aged 20 years married to EARLEY, CORA B. aged 20 years December 8, 1887 by Rev. Luther K. Probst in King Street between Market Street and Horlbeck Alley.

EHLERS, ANNA aged 28 years married to TURNER, CARL W. aged 25 years June 19, 1894 by Rev. Alfred Freyschmidt. Both natives of Germany. He a butcher.

EHNEY, SUSAN aged 17 years married to JELLICO, M. THOMAS aged 21 years February 8, 1889 by Rev. Robert Wilson at 60 Drake Street. He a native of Charleston and she of Georgetown, South Carolina. He a railroad brakeman.

EHRHAUS, ELISE W. aged 38 years married to FORSTMEN, FREDERICK A. aged 48 years June 3, 1880 by Rev. Louis Muller at 59 Church Street.

EHRLICH, JULIA aged 29 years married to SMITH, JAMES M. aged 27 years February 14, 1894 by John Ahrens, Trial Justice. He a native of Pickens, South Carolina and she of Charleston. He a blacksmith.

EHRLICH, REBECCA aged 21 years married to SCREVEN, JOHN J. aged 21 years September 8, 1887 by Rev. Robert Wilson. Both natives of Charleston. He a driver.

EHRLICH, SARAH aged 39 years married to SMITH, J. HENRY aged 29 years January 23, 1887 by Rev. H. B. Browne at 98 America Street. He a native of South Carolina and she of Charleston. He a miller.

EHRMANS, ELISE W. aged 38 years married to FORSTMANN, FREDERICK A. aged 38 years June 3, 1880 by Rev. Louis Muller at 59 Church Street. He a native of Leipzig, Saxony and she of Prussia. He a tailor.

EILER, WILLIAM H. aged 29 years married to WILLE, MARY A. aged 17 years February 7, 1884 by Rev. Luther K. Probst. He a native of Reading, Pennsylvania and she of Charleston. He a moulder.

EISEMANN, VAN aged 24 years married to PUNDT, FLORENCE S. aged 18 years December 1, 1881 by Rev. R. W. Memminger at 43 Hanover Street. He a native of South Carolina and she of Charleston.

ELBROOK, GEORGE aged 35 years married to BRUGGERMAN, (Mrs.) ELIZABETH R. OTTGER aged 48 years October 24, 1886 by Rev. Johannes Heckel at St. Johannes German Lutheran Church. He a native of South Carolina and she of Georgia. He a farmer on Sullivans Island, South Carolina.

ELFE, BENJAMIN aged 24 years married to FOLLIN, ALICIA CLARA aged 23 years October 30, 1883 by Father J. J. Woolahan at the corner of College and Green Streets. Both natives of Charleston. He a clerk.

ELFE, GLOVER C. aged 22 years married to LOWREY, EMILY M. A. aged 19 years November 10, 1880 by Father Claudian B. Northrop at the residence of H. T. Lowrey. Both natives of Charleston. He a bookkeeper in Atlanta, Georgia.

ELFE, MARTHA ANN aged 27 years married to CLEMENT, MORTON W. aged 30 years December 22, 1881 by Rev. John Johnson at 657 King Street. He a native of Adams Run, South Carolina and she of Charleston. He a machinist.

ELFORD, GEORGIANA TAYLOR married to LAVAL, WILLIAM JACINTE February 19, 1879 by Rev. G. R. Brackett at 4 Orange Street. Both natives of Charleston. He a treasurer.

ELIAS, BELLE aged 23 years married to BLANK, ISADORE aged 23 years March 10, 1886 by Rabbi David Levy at the Hasell Street Synagogue. Both natives of Charleston. He a merchant.

ELIAS, RACHEL aged 21 years married to LEVY, ISAAC aged 29 years March 5, 1879 by Rev. G. R. Brackett at 4 Orange Street.

ELLINGTON, T. married to CALDER, S. F. September 28, 1879 by Rev. E. A. Wingard at 570 King Street. Both natives of Charleston.

ELLIOTT, HENRY L. aged 30 years married to BICHLER, ELISE C. aged 16 years February 20, 1895 by Rev. Edward T. Horn at 31 Pitt Street. He a native of Winnsboro, South Carolina and she of Charleston. He an insurance agent.

ELLIS, ANNA B. aged 16 years married to BEARD, BARNEY P. aged 22 years May 9, 1895 by Rev. J. C. Yongue at 24.5 Cooper Street. He a native of St. George, South Carolina and she of Charleston. He a tinner/plumber.

ELLIS, CARRIE S. aged 16 years married to SUGGS, W. CHARLES aged 20 years February 29, 1888 by Rev. H. B. Browne at 97 Drake Street. He a native of Darlington County, South Carolina and she of New York. He a mill operator.

ELLIS, CORNELIA aged 20 years married to BURTON, ROBERT A. aged 21 years November 16, 1880 by Father P. L. Duffy at 62 Church Street. He a native of Charleston and she of Williamsburg County, South Carolina. He works at the Adams Express Company.

ELLIS, JANIE TERESA aged 17 years married to BEHRE, ADOLPH G. aged 40 years August 5, 1891 by Rev. R. D. Smart at 422 Meeting Street. He a native of Germany and she of Charleston. He a machinist.

ELLIS, JEANNIE G. aged 22 years married to RAVENEL, WILLIAM B. aged 21 years November 9, 1880 by Rev. John Johnson at St. Philip's Church. He a native of Charleston and she of Leon County, Florida. He a merchant.

ELLIS, JOANNE G. aged 20 years married to RAVENEL, WILLIAM R. aged 21 years November 9, 1880 by William Yates, Chaplain. He a native of Charleston and she of Leon County, Florida.

ELLIS, JOSEPH F. aged 24 years married to WILLIAMS, ANNIE aged 23 years November 3, 1895 by Rev. A. Ernest Cornish at 104 America Street. He a native of Charleston and she of Barnwell County, South Carolina. He a laborer.

ELLIS, (Mrs.) R. B. DENNIS aged 59 years married to MORGAN, JOHN aged 60 years January 12, 1890 by Rev. T. P. Burgess at 7 Addison Court. He a native of England and he works in the phosphate mill.

ELLIS THOMAS J. aged 36 years married to MILLER, JOSEPHINE aged 34 years August 5, 1880 by Rev. R. N. Wells. Both natives of Charleston. He a bookkeeper.

ELLIS, WILLIAM aged 43 years married to McKENZIE, ELLEN L. aged 23 years May 9, 1888 by Rev. Robert Wilson at 4 Wragg Square. He a native of Charleston and she of Sumter, South Carolina. He a blacksmith.

ELLSWORTH, EUGENIA E. M. aged 22 years married to PICQUET, BENJAMIN McN. aged 27 years June 19, 1888 by Rev. Robert Wilson at 106 Reid Street. He a native of Augusta, Georgia and she of Charleston. He a confectioner.

ELLSWORTH, J. S. K. aged 22 years married to TIGHE, MARY ANN aged 20 years August 28, 1881 by Father Harry P. Northrop at St. Patrick's Roman Catholic Church.

ELLSWORTH, MATTIE O. aged 21 years married to COATES, SAMUEL aged 23 years December 26, 1887 by Rev. A. H. Misseldine.

EMANUEL, ADELINE W. aged 19 years married to HARBY, HENRY J. aged 23 years October 26, 1881 by Rabbi David Levy at the Hasell Street Synagogue. He a native of Sumter, South Carolina and she of Charleston. He a merchant.

EMANUEL, MARY M. aged 19 years married to HERNDEN, ARTHUR aged 30 years July 11, 1887 by Rev. J. V. Welch at 40 Bee Street. Both natives of Charleston.

EMERY, L. VICTOR aged 25 years married to JOHNSON, CAROLINE W. aged 20 years April 15, 1880 by Rev. John Johnson at St. Paul's Church, Summerville, South Carolina. He a native of Charleston and she of Georgetown, South Carolina. Both residents of Summerville, South Carolina. He works in the phosphate factory.

ENGELHARDT, LOUISA M. aged 30 years married to WEICKING, HERMANN R. aged 36 years January 13, 1878 by Rev. W. S. Bowman. He a native of Hanover and she of Strasbourg, Germany. He a merchant.

ENGELMANN, (Mrs.) ANNA RIGBERS aged 38 years married to JORGENSON, J. CHRISTIAN aged 34 years December 4, 1887 by Rev. Johannes Heckel at 123 Smith Street. He a native of Denmark and she of Germany. He a porter.

ENGLAND, MARY EMILY aged 45 years married to MATHIESSEN, WILLIAM aged 65 years July 24, 1878 by Father Daniel J. Quigley at The Cathedral of St. John the Baptist. She a native of Charleston. He a merchant.

ENRIGHT, ANNIE aged 14 years married to MOORE, ALEXANDER aged 24 years August 6, 1883 by Rev. J. A. Cliffton. He a native of Ireland and she of Charleston. He a miller.

ENRIGHT, JOHN aged 28 years married to LAROUSSELIERE, EMILIE aged 24 years May 26, 1885 by Rev. F. A. Schmetz at St. Patrick's Roman Catholic Church. Both natives of Charleston. He a miller.

ENRIGHT, MARY JANE aged 20 years married to BROWN, HENRY aged 36 years August, 1878 by Father Harry P. Northrop at St. Patrick's Roman Catholic Church. He a native of Prussia and she of Charleston. He a machinist.

ENRIGHT, THOMAS married to QUINAIN (?), JULIA ANN August 9, 1881 by Rev. R. W. Memminger at 23 Legare Street.

ENTELMANN, JOHANN F. A. aged 24 years married to BUSE, DORETHA ADELAIDE April 13, 1887 by Rev. Louis Muller at 520 King Street. He a native of Charleston and she a merchant.

ENTER, JACOB aged 24 years married to SCHWACKE, ANNIE aged 19 years January 2, 1893 by Rev. K. Boldt at the corner of Washington and Laurens Streets. He a native of Charleston and she of New York. He a contractor.

ENTER, MOLLIE aged 15 years married to BARRINEAU, JAMES F. aged 18 years February 18, 1894 by Rev. J. C. Yongue at 75 Bay Street. He a native of Williamsburg County, South Carolina and she of Charleston. He works in the cotton mill.

EPPS, HIRAM aged 21 years married to COSTNER, EMMA aged 20 years September 11, 1887 by Rev. H. B. Browne at 23 Cooper Street. He a native of Eatonton, Georgia and she of North Carolina. Both work in the cotton mill.

ERICKSON, VICTOR H. aged 23 years married to LINDSTROM, IDA aged 23 years April 30, 1881 by Rev. R. W. Memminger. Both natives of Stockholm, Sweden. He a News and Courier employee.

ERWIN, SALLIE M. aged 28 years married to RICH, ALBERT M. aged 38 years February 8, 1893 by Rev. Charles S. Vedder at 16 College Street. He a native of Blue City, Maine and she of South Carolina. He a mariner in New York.

ESCOFFIER, ELMER. F. aged 37 years married to HOOD, ROSINA M. aged 16 years June 3, 1880 by Rev. Claudian B. Northrop at St. Mary of the Annunciation Roman Catholic Church. He a native of St. Michel, France and she of Charleston.

ESTEE, CHARLES A. aged 22 years married to VON SANTEN, ANNE ISABELLA aged 21 years September 10, 1884 by Rev. Luther K. Probst. He a native of Washington, D. C. and she of Anderson, South Carolina. He a railroad clerk.

EVANS, ALICE C. aged 45 years married to STEINMEYER, JOHN H. aged 60 years by Rev. Edward T. Horn at 31 Pitt Street.

EVANS, BENJAMIN F. aged 30 years married to KINLOCH, IDA M. aged 23 years October 10, 1895 by Rev. W. T. Thompson. He a native of Columbia, South Carolina and she of Charleston. He a bank clerk.

EVANS, JOHN WILLIAM aged 30 years married to WINGATE, MARY aged 19 years November 14, 1886 by Rev. H. B. Browne. Both natives of Charleston. He works for the railroad.

EVANS, JOHN WILLIAM aged 25 years married to HAYS, ANNA JULIA aged 23 years September 23, 1883 by Rev. E. J. Meynardie at 156 Wentworth Street. He a native of Pendleton, South Carolina and she of Charleston. He a collector.

EVANS, (Mrs.) JULIA E. COGSWELL aged 52 years married to CONNOR, FRANCIS A. aged 65 years April 18, 1883 by Rev. W. P. Mouzon at 20 George Street. He a native of Abbeville, South Carolina and she of Charleston. He a merchant.

EVANS, LIZZIE ALLEN aged 24 years married to GRICE, ROBERT BLUM aged 22 years May 1, 1884 by Rev. John H. Honour at 165 st. Philip Street. Both natives of Charleston. He a clerk.

EVANS, ROBERT P. married to BROWN, ADDIE M. November 24, 1881 by Rev. William H. Campbell at St. Paul's Church. Both natives of Charleston. He a clerk.
EVANS, (Mrs.) SARAH REYNOLDS aged 41 years married to SHEPHARD, JOHN J. aged 36 years June 8, 1884 by Rev. John E. Beard. He a native of Onslow County, North Carolina and she of Brunswick, North Carolina. He an engineer.

EVANS, (Mrs.) SUSIE TIEDWELL aged 22 years married to JONES, WILLIAM E. aged 22 years August 2, 1887 by Rev. Robert Wilson at St. Luke's Chapel. He a native of Georgia and she of Charleston. He a cotton miller.

EVINGTON, JAMES aged 24 years married to MURRAY, SUSAN A. aged 18 years April 21, 1891 by Rev. J. Thomas Pate at 61 America Street. He a native of Yorkshire, England and she of Berkeley County, South Carolina. He a laborer.

EWERT, HOLDA WILHELMINA aged 28 years married to LEMWIG, FREDERICK L. aged 34 years April 14, 1884 by Rev. Johannes Heckel at 55 Smith Street. He a native of Denmark and she of Germany. He a steward.

EYE, THEODORE aged 29 years married to LOTZ, AUGUSTA ADELAIDE aged 21 years April 22, 1879 by Rev. Louis Muller at the corner of Beaufain and Mazyck Streets. He a native of New York and she of Charleston.

EYSENBACH, E. W. L. aged 19 years married to DAUER, JAMES A. B. aged 25 years February 8, 1881 by Rev. Louis Muller in St. Philip Street, north of the public school. He a native of Charleston and professor of music.

FABER, J. L. aged 26 years married to O'DONNELL, M. A. aged 21 years May 30, 1882 by Rev. P. L. Duffy at The Cathedral of St. John the Baptist. He a native of Massachusetts and a storekeeper.

FABIAN, ANDREW F. married to HOLST, GEORGIA D. March 16, 1879 by William B. Yates, Chaplain. Both natives of Charleston.

FABIAN, FRANCES E. aged 18 years married to HOLTZ, CHARLES E. aged 20 years June 10, 1880 by Rev. J. E. Jackson at 313 East Bay Street. He a native of New York and she of Charleston. He a locksmith.

FABIAN, JOHN G. married to FABIAN, E. L. November 3, 1878 by William B. Yates, Chaplain.

FABIAN, MARY E. aged 32 years married to GILBERT, JOHN D. aged 34 years June 11, 1893 by Rev. H. B. Browne. He a native of Wilmington, North Carolina and she of Charleston. He a clerk.

FAGAN, JOHN T. aged 21 years married to TIPPETT, MICKY aged 19 years June 7, 1885 by Rev. John E. Beard at 64 Nassau Street. He a native of South Carolina.

FAGAN, P. D. aged 21 years married to ROGERS, C. L. aged 18 years June 10, 1894 by Rev. D. F. Tippett at 9 Blake Street.

FAIRCHILD, WILLIAM HAMLIN aged 26 years married to PREGNALL, EMILY E. aged 19 years November 22, 1877 by Rev. E. C. L. Browne at 7 Cannon Street.

FALCONER, J. M. aged 25 years married to MARTIN, M.E. aged 21 years November 29, 1882 by Rev. G. R. Brackett at 11 Ann Street. He a native of Charleston and a machinist.

FALCONETTE, THOMAS aged 31 years married to SMALL, JOSEPHINE aged 19 years July 18, 1883 by Father Harry P. Northrop. He a native of Austria and she of Charleston. He a mariner.

FALK, CAROLINE B. aged 25 years married to VAUGHN, JAMES E. aged 35 years September 22, 1881 by Rev. L. H. Shuck at 27 Church Street. He a native of Dublin, Ireland and she of Orangeburg, South Carolina. Both reside in Orangeburg, South Carolina. He a mariner

FALK, J. M. aged 22 years married to SOLOMON, JANIE R. aged 22 years December 22, 1880 by Rabbi David Levy at the Hasell Street Synagogue. Both natives of Charleston. He a merchant.

FALLEN, ANNA aged 20 years married to O'CONNELL, JOHN JOSEPH aged 24 years June 4, 1878 by Father Daniel J. Quigley at The Cathedral of St. John the Baptist. He a native of Ireland and she of Charleston. He a merchant.

FALLS, ZORADA, aged 20 years married to WILKEN, HERMAN aged 23 years October 26, 1892 by Rev. William T. Thompson. He a native of Germany and she of South Carolina. He a bookkeeper.

FATMAN, WILLIAM aged 37 years married to MANTONE, FANNIE aged 21 years May 15, 1889 by Rabbi I. Mendelson at the Temple of Israel. He a native of New York and she of Charleston. He a merchant.

FARMER, ANNIE P. aged 20 years married to JONES, SYDNEY B. aged 26 years October 15, 1891 by Rev. T. R. Burgess at 532 Meeting Street. Both natives of Charleston. He a painter.

FARMER, A. R. aged 23 years married to OGIER, T. S. aged 21 years February 9, 1882 by Rev. J. V. Welsh at 27 Line Street. He a native of Charleston and a machinist.

FARR, RICHARD W. aged 25 years married to ULMO, MARY L. aged 20 years April 27, 1892 by Rev. Edwin C. Dargan at 128 Calhoun Street.

FARRELL, EUGENE ALEXANDER aged 23 years married to DURSE, VIOLA aged 20 years October 9, 1878 by Rev. W. S. Bowman at 4 Mary Street. He a native of Marion County, South Carolina and she of Charleston. He a turpentine distributor.

FARRIER, MORRIS J. aged 27 years married to BRINGLOE, SALLIE H. aged 23 years February 21, 1889 by Rev. R. W. Lide at the First Baptist Church. He a native of Illinois and she of Charleston. He a printer.

FARRIS, ALICE aged 15 years married to CUNNING, ROBERT OTTO aged 23 years April 14, 1890 by Rev. C. E. Chichester at the Mariners Church. He a native of Charleston and she of Ridgeland, South Carolina. He a hostler in Savannah, Georgia.

FASH, AMY B. aged 20 years married to BOURU, ISAAC BROOKS aged 23 years August 4, 1884 by Rev. J. O. Willson at Sullivans Island, South Carolina. Both natives of Charleston. He a merchant.

FASH, JESSIE aged 20 years married to BENNETT, T. aged 21 years February 15, 1886 by Father F. J. Shadler at St. Joseph's Roman Catholic Church. He a native of South Carolina and she of Charleston. He a laborer.

FASH, JULIA aged 18 years married to HOLST, HENRY E. aged 24 years January 28, 1880 by Rev. J. E. Jackson at 94 Calhoun Street.

FASH, JULIA aged 18 years married to SEYLE, WILLIAM E. aged 23 years August 15, 1886 by Rev. Robert Wilson at 44 Spring Street. Both natives of Charleston. He a mechanic.

FASS, MORRIS aged 25 years married to NACHMAN, ROSA aged 20 years October 10, 1894 by W. Aurbach, Cantor at the Mechanics Union Hall. Both natives of Austria. He a merchant.

FASTIN, M. married to BISSELL, F. D. December 28, 1881 by Rev. L. H. Shuck at 27 Church Street. He a native of Maryland and she of Ireland. He a clerk.

FAULBIER, HENRIETTA DORA aged 27 years married to DAVIS, JOHN JAMES aged 30 years February 12, 1880 by Rev. William S. Bowman at the Wentworth Street Lutheran Church. He a native of Charleston and she of Germany. He a farmer.

FAULKNER, H. J. aged 34 years married to WATSON, M.F. aged 23 years April 13, 1882 by Rev. John Johnson at 45 George Street. He a native of New York and a farmer. He a resident of Oak Hill, Florida.

FAULKNER, MARY aged 21 years married to CUNNINGHAM, WILLIAM aged 34 years December 9, 1881 by Rev. J. V. Welsh at 100 St. Philip Street. He a native of Pike County, Georgia and she of Augusta, Georgia. He a printer.

FAULLING, HENRIETTA DORA aged 27 years married to DAVIS, JOHN JAMES aged 30 years February 12, 1880 by Rev. W. S. Bowman. He a native of Charleston and she of Germany. He a farmer near Ridgeville, South Carolina.

FAULPIER, EVELINA aged 25 years married to NESTOR, JOSEPH HENRY aged 28 years May 9, 1889 by Father J. J. Monaghan at 75 America Street. Both natives of Charleston. He a sashmaker.

FEDDERWITZ, JOHN H. H. aged 22 years married to THOMPSON, JENNIE M. aged 22 years February 1, 1888 by Rev. John Johnson in Reid Street. He a native of Georgia and she of New York. He a clerk.

FEEHAN, ANNA A. aged 26 years married to MONAGHAN, RICHARD P. aged 29 years January 10, 1883 by Father J. J. Monaghan at St. Joseph's Roman Catholic Church. He a native of Sumter, South Carolina and she of Charleston. He a merchant in Sumter.

FELAHUSE (?), HARRIET aged 25 years married to COOK, GEORGE aged 36 years May 19, 1889 by Rev. C. E. Chichester at the Mariners Church. He a native of England and she of South Carolina. He a mariner.

FELDER, ANNA P. aged 19 years married to MITCHELL, JOHN S. aged 22 years April 26, 1892 by Rev. G. R. Brackett. Both natives of Parler, Orangeburg County, South Carolina. He a car driver.

FELDER, KATE aged 24 years married to LADSON, JAMES HENRY aged 31 years May 21, 1884 by Rev. E. J. Meynardie. He a native of Charleston and she of Orangeburg, South Carolina.

FELDKINS, L. J. married to JEFFORDS, HARRIET F. November 14, 1877 by William B. Yates, Chaplain.

FELGENTRAGER, GUSTAV aged 32 years married to VON EITZEN, MARIA aged 23 years December 15, 1887 by Rev. Johannes Heckel at 109 East Bay Street. He a native of Prussia and she of Charleston. He a carpenter.

FELL, ROSA G. aged 25 years married to DECKER, CLARENCE aged 32 years April 18, 1893 . He a native of New York and she of Gillisonville, South Carolina. He a machinist.

FENKEN, H. W. aged 50 years married to HEINRICH, A. M. M. aged 24 years December 31, 1882 by Rev. Louis Muller. He a native of Charleston and a restaurant worker.

FERGUSON, C. B. aged 23 years married to SIRES, A. aged 29 years December 28, 1880 by Rev. Luther K. Probst at 38 Reid Street. Both natives of Charleston. He an engineer.

FERGUSON, GEORGE MOUZON aged 24 years married to SMITH, WILHELMINA aged 19 years December 8, 1881 by Rev. A. Coke Smith. Both natives of Charleston. He a mechanic.

FERINA, GEORGE EDWARD aged 28 years married to INABINETT, ELLA F. G. aged 24 years May 9, 1883 by Rev. J. H. Tillinghast at 17 Woolfe Street. He a native of Charleston and she of Ridgeville, South Carolina. He a mechanic.

FERRARA, CATERIENA married to OLIVARA, MATTEO February 26, 1879 by Father Daniel J. Quigley at The Cathedral of St. John the Baptist. Both natives of Italy. He a mariner.

FERRARA, SARAH A. aged 21 years married to SARVIS, MARION C. aged 28 years June 7, 1885 by Rev. Robert Wilson at 16 Morris Street.

FERARRA, SETH JOSEPH aged 29 years married to PARSONS, WINIFRED aged 43 years October 1, 1882 by Rev. John C. Schachte. He a native of Charleston and a carpenter.

FERRELL, ALICE F. aged 21 years married to SHOKES, WILLIAM J. aged 25 years April 5, 1883 by Rev. J. V. Welsh at 24 Bee Street.

FERRELL, MELISSA aged 23 years married to SHULKEN JOHN aged 24 years January 25, 1880 by Rev. E. H. Horn in Savage Street. He a native of Germany and she of Ridgeville, South Carolina. He a merchant.

FERRIS, SARAH aged 23 years married to SIGALLES, NICHOLAS aged 27 years April 7, 1881 by Rev. L. H. Shuck in Meeting Street near Hibernian Hall. He a native of Greece and she of South Carolina. He a fruitier.

FICKLING, J. T. married to BROWN, C. December 5, 1879 by William B. Yates, Chaplain.

FICKLING, L. J. married to WILSON, CHARLES April 19, 1892 by Rev. John Gass. He a native of Barnwell, South Carolina and she of Charleston. He a railroad conductor.

FICKLING, PAULINE ROSA aged 22 years married to PRICE, GEORGE B. aged 24 years November 13, 1890 by Rev. Robert Wilson at 21 Alexander Street. He a native of Colleton County, South Carolina and she of Charleston. He an Editor in Walterboro, South Carolina.

FIEDLER, IDA aged 21 years married to JOHANNS, GUSTAV HENRY aged 28 years August 28, 1888 by Rev. Johannes Heckel. He a native of Hanover and she of Prussia. He a storekeeper on Wadmalaw Island, South Carolina.

FIELCHER, FANNIE aged 19 years married to DAMON, EDWARD LORING aged 25 years June 24, 1888 by Rev. Johannes Heckel at 23 Smith Street.

FIEDLER, JOSEPH J. aged 23 years married to LINDLEY, CORA D. aged 18 years November 19, 1890 by Rev. G. R. Brackett at 53 Line Street. He a native of South Carolina and she of Pennsylvania. He a fireman.

FIELDS, CORA L. aged 18 years married to GASKINS, JOHN F. aged 20 years May 31, 1891 by Rev. C. E. Chichester at 44 Market Street. He a native of Newborn, North Carolina and she of Sumter, South Carolina. He a mariner.

FIELDS, FANNIE R. aged 26 years married to FINA, WILLIAM M. aged 42 years April 27, 1886 by Rev. John O. Wilson at 33 Wentworth Street. He a native of New Jersey and she of Florida. He a dentist.

FIELDS, PATRICK aged 58 years married to BROWN, — aged 47 years August 3, 1880 by Rev. Charles S. Vedder.

FIELTZ, SARAH P. aged 21 years married to SCHERKE (?), S. HENRY aged 21 years May 9, 1895 by Rev. J. C. Yongue at 14 Hampstead Square. He a native of Charleston and she of Berkeley County, South Carolina. He a painter.

FIGARO, R. F. married to DALLAS, R. E. July 7, 1882 by Father Daniel J. Quigley at The Cathedral of St. John the Baptist. He a native of Charleston and a printer.

FILIBESTI, MICHAEL aged 20 years married to WILSON, MARY ANN aged 18 years December 7, 1891 by Rev. W. A. Betts at 21 Hanover Street. He a blacksmith.

FINA, WILLIAM M. aged 42 years married to FIELDS, FANNIE R. aged 26 years April 27, 1886 by Rev. John O. Wilson at 33 Wentworth Street. He a native of New Jersey and she of Florida. He a dentist.

FINKENBERG, M. aged 31 years married to HAAS, C. C. aged 30 years October 8, 1882 by Rev. Louis Muller at 66 Radcliffe Street. He a native of Germany and a laborer.

FINCKEN, ALBERT J. C. married to MEYER, IDA M. January 16, 1879 by Rev. W. S. Bowman. Both natives of Charleston. He a grocer.

FINCKEN, AUGUST W. aged 27 years married to SCHURFER, GESINE CATHERINE M. aged 20 years May 6, 1886 by Rev. Louis Muller in Mt. Pleasant, South Carolina.

FINCKEN, EDWARD aged 22 years married to ALDRET, CORNELIA ESTELLE K. aged 17 years September 12, 1889 by Rev. Johannes Heckel at Moultrieville, South Carolina. He a native of Mt. Pleasant, South Carolina and she of Charleston. He a merchant in Mt. Pleasant.

FINCKEN, EDWARD H. F. aged 20 years married to KWORE (?), EMMA JOHANNA aged 19 years February 12, 1880 by Rev. Louis Muller at St. Matthew's Lutheran Church. Both natives of Charleston. He a grocer in Walterboro, South Carolina.

FINCKEN, JOHN A. aged 26 years married to PETERSON, MARY J. aged 20 years January 5, 1885 by Rev. Luther K. Probst. He a native of South Carolina and she of Charleston. He a baker in Beaufort, South Carolina.

FINCKEN, LAVINIA ELISE aged 23 years married to SCHILLETTER, AUGUST aged 24 years April 25, 1889 by Rev. Louis Muller at St. Matthew's Lutheran Church. He a native of Prussia and she of Charleston. He a baker.

FINCKEN, (Mrs.) MARY BOYLE married to DUNCAN, CHARLES September 28, 1894 by Rev. Edmund Wells at 579 King Street. He a native of Boston, Massachusetts and she of Highland City. He a merchant.

FINCKEN, MARY C. aged 27 years married to CLARKSON, WILLIAM R. aged 23 years May 16, 1893 by Rev. J. L. Stokes at 56 Hanover Street. He a native of Kentucky and she of Walhalla, South Carolina. He an artist.

FINCKEN, META R. S. aged 19 years married to STELLJES, J. D. F. aged 29 years October 22, 1885 by Rev. Claudian B. Northrop at the corner of Smith and Vanderhorst Streets. Both natives of Charleston. He a grocer.

FINK, JOHN W. aged 30 years married to HARVEY, MARIA E. aged 32 years October 7, 1884 by Rev. E. C. Browne. He a native of Charleston and she of South Carolina. He a ship carpenter.

FINK, SUSAN G. aged 27 years married to DANIELS, J. B. aged 30 years November 7, 1880 by Rev. J. V. Welsh at the residence of J. B. Donnels - 64 Radcliffe Street. Both natives of Charleston. He a laborer.

FINKLEA, GEORGE W. aged 28 years married to MURRAY, SARAH ANN aged 29 years April 30, 1884 by Rev. Charles A. Stakely at 110 Anson Street. He a native of Georgia and she of South Carolina. He a clerk in Savannah, Georgia.

FINKENBERG, ANNA R. aged 24 years married to BIERFISCHER, HEINRICH E. aged 23 years February 14, 1878 by Rev. W. S. Bowman. He a native of Oldenburg, Germany and she of Hanover. He a grocer.

FINLEY, CAROLINE aged 24 years married to SINKLER, THOMAS S. aged 26 years October 20, 1887 by Rev. E. C. L. Browne at the Unitarian Church. Both natives of Charleston. He a clerk.

FINLEY, (Mrs.) LILLIE R. DOCK aged 32 years married to HASTINGS, HUGH aged 26 years April 5, 1883 by Rev. Charles S. Vedder. He a native of Albany, New York and she of Harrisburg, Pennsylvania. He a journalist.

FINN, PATRICK aged 24 years married to MAGUIRE, MARY aged 19 years January 12, 1881 by Father Daniel J. Quigley at The Cathedral of St. John the Baptist. He a native of Ireland. Witnessed by John Finn and Annie Finn.

FINNEGAN, GEORGE WASHINGTON aged 28 years married to DAGGETT, MARY JANE aged 19 years August 30, 1878 by Father Claudian B. Northrop at St. Mary of the Annunciation Roman Catholic Church. Both natives of Charleston. He a mariner on Black Island, South Carolina.

FINNEGAN, JAMES aged 25 years married to KANE, MARY ANN aged 23 years December 18, 1889 by Father F. J. Shadler at St. Joseph's Roman Catholic Church. Both natives of Charleston. He a plumber.

FISCHER, ELEANOR B. aged 22 years married to AIMAR, CHARLES A. aged 25 years April 8, 1885 by Rev. E. C. L. Browne. Both natives of Charleston. He a bookkeeper.

FISCHER, JAMES W. aged 20 years married to COBIA, ELLIE A. W. aged 20 years April 19, 1895 by Rev. J. C. Yongue at 530 Meeting Street.

FISCHER, DORIS aged 25 years married to KRUER, HANKE aged 40 years June 22, 1884 by Rev. Johannes Heckel at 3 Minority Street. Both natives of Germany. He a merchant.

FISCHER, E. V. aged 25 years married to TAVEL, W. KNOX aged 26 years December 21, 1880 by Rev. E. C. L. Brown. Both natives of Charleston. He in the mercantile business.

FISCHER, HEINRICH A. aged 27 years married to ALBERS, CAROLINE ANNIE aged 21 years May 8, 1883 by Rev. Johannes Heckel at 8 Bogard Street. He a native of Germany and she of Charleston. He a grocer.

FISHBURN, (Mrs.) JOHANNA BRUGGERMANN married to PINCKNEY, SAMUEL G. June 12, 1893 by Rev. William H. Campbell. at 25 Montagu Street.

FISCHER, E. V. married to TAVEL, W. KNOX December 21, 1880 by Rev. E. C. L. Brown.

FISHER, AUGUST H. aged 25 years married to CAPPEL, MATILDA LOUISE aged 21 years November 1, 1883 by Rev. Johannes Heckel at 36 Church Street. He a native of Charleston and she of Norfolk, Virginia. He a sashmaker.

FISHER, FLORENCE J. aged 20 years married to COPES, CHARLES aged 23 years April 24, 1884 by Rev. Luther K. Probst. Both natives of Charleston. He a merchant.

FISHER, JAMES aged 35 years married to McDERMOTT, ANNIE aged 35 years April 5, 1891 by Father J. J. Monaghan at St. Patrick's Roman Catholic Church. He a native of Belgium and she of Charleston. He a mariner.

FISHER, J. H. aged 22 years married to DRIGGERS, M. aged 21 years June 11, 1892 by Rev. J. V. Welch at 700 King Street. He a native of Charleston and a baker.

FITCH, WILLIAM M. aged 30 years married to VON KOLNITZ, MINNIE E. November 7, 1893 by Rev. Edward T. Horn at the corner of Smith and Vanderhorst Street. He a native of Columbia, South Carolina and she of Charleston.

FITZGERALD, ELLEN aged 35 years married to FITZPATRICK, TIMOTHY aged 35 years March 3, 1878 by Father C. J. Croghan at 4 Society Street. Both natives of Ireland. He a porter.

FITZGERALD, JOHN aged 22 years married to HOGAN, KATIE E. aged 21 years August 3, 1890 by Father J. J. Monaghan at St. Patrick's Roman Catholic Church. Both natives of Charleston. He a stonecutter.

FITZGERALD, JOSEPH aged 26 years married to JARRETT, MARY E. aged 19 years January 18, 1893 by Rev. John Johnson at 53 Church Street. She a native of Spartanburg, South Carolina. He an insurance agent.

FITZGERALD, MARY married to ROWAN, JOHN December 28, 1877 by William B. Yates, Chaplain.

FITZGERALD, WILLIAM T. aged 26 years married to WILSON, MARGARET E. aged 26 years June 6, 1886 by Father Daniel J. Quigley at St. Patrick's Roman Catholic Church. Both natives of Charleston. He works for the railroad.

FITZPATRICK, TIMOTHY aged 35 years married to FITZGERALD, ELLEN aged 35 years March 3, 1878 by Father C. J. Croghan at 4 Society Street. Both natives of Ireland. He a porter.

FITZSIMONS, CHARLES M. aged 24 years married to BURDELL, CAROLINE R. aged 23 years April 7, 1887 by Rev. A. H. Misseldine. Both natives of South Carolina. He a carpenter.

FITZSIMONS, CHRISTOPHER married to HUGER, FRANCES M. February 12, 1890 by Rev. Richard S. Frazier at St. Michael's Church. He a native of South Carolina and she of Charleston.

FITZSIMONS, THEODORE aged 28 years married to McCRADY, SABINA L. aged 25 years April 30, 1889 by Rev. John Johnson at St. Philip's Church. He a native of South Carolina and she of Clarendon County, South Carolina. He in the cotton business.

FLACKMAN, ISRAEL aged 22 years married to RIGGS, MINNIE M. aged 16 years February 13, 1887 by Rev. Robert O. Wilson at St. Luke's Chapel. He a native of South Carolina and she of Charleston. He works in a factory.

FLADYER (?), LUCIE married to NEWMAN, L. B. October 20, 1887 by Rev. William D. Kirkland at 14 Pitt Street. He a merchant in Jacksonville, Florida.

FLAGG, WILLIAM S. aged 19 years married to BENTON, ANNA E. aged 19 years February 3, 1883 by Rev. J. V. Welsh at 24 Bee Street. Both natives of Charleston. He a laborer.

FLAKE, JAMES aged 20 years married to DANIELS, MAGGIE F. MURRAY aged 21 years December 24, 1895 by Rev. Griffin Holliman. He a native of Orangeburg, South Carolina and she of North Carolina. He works in a mill.

FLANAGAN, MARY J. aged 16 years married to ADDISON, FRANCIS T. aged 30 years March 17, 1887 by Rev. Robert Wilson at 44 Ann Street. Both natives of Charleston. He a watchmaker.

FLATLEY, MARY FRANCES aged 18 years married to SIMONIN, GEORGE ANTHONY aged 30 years February 24, 1884 by Rev. P. L. Duffy at The Cathedral of St. John the Baptist. Both natives of Charleston. He a printer.

FLATMAN, CHARLES M. aged 20 years married to VALZEY, ANNIE aged 16 years January 10, 1892 by Rev. Edmund Wells at 28 Cooper Street. He a native of St. James Parish, South Carolina and she of Orangeburg, South Carolina. He a laborer.

FLATMANN, EDWARD S. aged 20 years married to HOLSENBACH, EMILY E. aged 18 years September 27, 1888 by Rev. J. E. Carlisle at the Spring Street Church. He a native of Richland County, South Carolina and she of New York. He a merchant.

FLEMING, EVELYN B. aged 24 years married to NIX, JAMES T. aged 31 years May 1, 1885 by Rev. Luther K. Probst. He a native of Nixville, South Carolina and she of Charleston. He a lawyer in Greenville, South Carolina.

FLEMING, FRANCES aged 20 years married to CERCOPELY, JOSEPH W. aged 20 years March 15, 1889 by Rev. H. B. Browne at 23 Line Street. He a native of Charleston.

FLEMING, MAGGIE V. aged 23 years married to TROUCHE, PAUL E. aged 27 years October 10, 1894 by Father J. J. Monaghan at St. Patrick's Roman Catholic Church. Both natives of Charleston. He a stationer.

FLEMING, MARY A. aged 25 years married to HAPPOLDT, T. C. aged 24 years October 11, 1887 by Father Daniel J. Quigley at 473 King Street. He a native of Ridgeville, South Carolina and she of Charleston. He a panter.

FLEMING, WILLIAM aged 40 years married to LYONS, SARAH aged 35 years January 17, 1878.

FLEMING, WILLIAM F. aged 23 years married to HARRINGTON, ELLA B. aged 23 years July 8, 1890 by Father F. J. Shadler at St. Joseph's Roman Catholic Church. Both natives of Charleston. He a clerk in Jacksonville, Florida.

FLINT, WILLIAM H. married to BROWN, FLORENCE A. November 18, 1891 by Rev. William H. Campbell at 56 Lynch Street. Both natives of Charleston. He an insurance agent.

FLOTMANN, JOSEPHINE aged 20 years married to KURNROW, CARL M. aged 28 years September 25, 1885 by Rev. Louis Muller at the residence of the Bride - 22 Pine Street. He a native of Georgia and she of Charleston. He a butcher.

FLUCK, ELI aged 28 years married WHETSTONE, (Mrs.) CELIA MORRELL aged 29 years July 11, 1886 by Rev. H. B. Browne at 78 Drake Street. He a native of Montgomery County, Pennsylvania and she of Savannah, Georgia. He a painter in Savannah.

FLUDD, JOHN OSCAR aged 24 years married to TIPPETT, CAROLINE aged 22 years February 10, 1889 by Rev. T. P. Burgess at 10 Amherst Street. He a native of Concord, North Carolina and she of Charleston. He a carpenter.

FLUDD, MARY JANE aged 21 years married to WEBB, R. aged 24 years April 10, 1879 by Rev. J. Mercier Green at the corner of Line and Meeting Streets.

FLUDGER, FLORENCE aged 33 years married to TREVAITHAM, JOHN D. aged 36 years December 17, 1890 by Rev. J. Thomas Pate at 116 Calhoun Street. He a native of North Carolina and she of South Carolina. He a baggage master in Florence, South Carolina.

FLUGG, SAMUEL aged 24 years married to BLASICH, ELIZABETH aged 23 years December 4, 1890 by Rev. Robert O. Wilson at 4 Wragg Square. He a native of Charleston and she of Greenville, South Carolina. He works for the railroad.

FLYNN, ELLA MARY aged 22 years married to DOWLING, JOHN JAMES aged 24 years January 1, 1882 by Father Claudian B. Northrop at St. Mary of the Annunciation Roman Catholic Church. Both natives of Charleston. He a bookkeeper.

FLYNN, FRANCES aged 21 years married to DRISCOLL, WILLIAM J. aged 23 years April 22, 1891 by Bishop Harry P. Northrop at The Cathedral of St. John the Baptist. Both natives of Charleston. He a postal clerk.

FLYNN, HATTIE aged 18 years married to KEE, JAMES aged 23 years December 29, 1895 by Rev. J. M. Steadman at 14 Hampstead Square. He a native of Graniteville, South Carolina and she of Augusta, Georgia. He works for the railroad.

FLYNN, J. aged 30 years married to KENNEDY, M. L. aged 25 years January 1, 1879 by Father P. L. Duffy at The Cathedral of St. John the Baptist. He a native of Ireland and she of Charleston. He a telegraph operator.

FLYNN, ROBERT E. aged 22 years married to MARTIN, LILLIE T. aged 23 years October 22, 1893 by Rev. J. L. Stokes at 231 Coming Street. Both natives of Charleston. He a telegraph operator.

FOGARTIE, ESTHER J. aged 46 years married to McKENZIE, SULTAN W. aged 48 years November 22, 1887 by Rev. G. R. Brackett. He a native of Fort Motte, South Carolina and she of Charleston. He a physician in Gadsden, South Carolina.

FOGEL, JOHN M. aged 24 years married to POLHEMUS (?), EMILY aged 19 years November 4, 1886 by Rev. John Johnson at 159 Tradd Street. He a native of South Carolina and she of Charleston. He an electrician.

FOGERTY, DANIEL aged 37 years married to WILKINSON, ELLEN M. 26 years August 11, 1893 by Rev. Joseph D. Budds at 134 Market Street. He a native of Charleston and she of New York.

FOGERTY, SIMON aged 37 years married to WALL, MARGARET aged 21 years November 29, 1878 by Father Harry P. Northrop at St. Patrick's Roman Catholic Church. He a native of Ireland and she of Charleston. He a merchant.

FOGLE, MARCUS N. aged 26 years married to CARSTEN, ADA PINCKNEY aged 24 years January 9, 1883 by Rev. Luther K. Probst. He a native of Orangeburg, South Carolina and she of Charleston. He works in the phosphate factory.

FOLEY, ALICE MARTHA aged 18 years married to MORGAN, DANIEL JOSEPH aged 23 years May 3, 1883 by Father J. J. Woolahan at St. Mary of the Annunciation Church. Both natives of Charleston. He works for the railroad.

FOLEY, MARGARET aged 20 years married to DAGGETT, THOMAS aged 24 years April 18, 1888 by Father F. J. Shadler at St. Joseph's Roman Catholic Church. Both natives of Charleston. He a railroad laborer.

FOLLIN, ALICIA CLARA aged 24 years married to ELFE, BENJAMIN aged 24 years October 30, 1883 by Father J. J. Woolahan at the corner of College and Green Streets. Both natives of Charleston. He a clerk.

FOLLIN, ANNIE L. aged 20 years married to SIMONS, ROBERT A. aged 23 years December 20, 1881 by Rev. C. C. Pinckney at Grace Church. He a native of Charleston and she of New Orleans, Louisiana. He a clerk.

FORBES, ANNIE E. aged 22 years married to MATTHEWS, SAMUEL aged 25 years October 25, 1887 by Father P. J. McManus at St. Patrick's Roman Catholic Church. Both natives of Charleston. He a merchant.

FORBES, (Mrs.) MARTHA EUGENIA RUSS married to SARVIS, JOSEPH January 2, 1879 by Rev. W. S. Bowman at 11 John Street. Both natives of Charleston. He a moulder.

FORD, ANNA aged 25 years married to COSS, ALEXANDER aged 30 years June 7, 1887 by Rev. John Johnson. Both natives of South Carolina. He a farmer.

FORD, GEORGE G. aged 22 years married to MIDDLETON, ALICE IZARD aged 22 years October 28, 1890 by Rev. John Johnson at 55 Church Street. Both natives of South Carolina. He a manufacturer in Greenville, South Carolina.

FORD, HELEN MAY aged 19 years married to LEWIS, JOHN R. aged 21 years October 15, 1891 by Rev. R. D. Smart at 182 Wentworth Street. Both natives of Charleston. He operates a press in the cotton mill.

FORD, MARIA C. married to JERVEY, LEWIS S. August 19, 1890 by Rev. William H. Trapier at St. Michael's Church.

FORD, T. ROBERT married to LUCUS, MYRA JANE December 20, 1889 by Rev. Richard S. Trapier at St. Michael's Church.

FORRESTER, CHARLOTTE aged 25 years married to MURRAY, GEORGE W. aged 25 years May 15, 1892 by Rev. J. L. Stokes at 66 Amherst Street. Both natives of South Carolina. He a laborer.

FORSTMANN, FREDERICK A. aged 38 years married to EHRHANS, ELISE W. aged 38 years June 3, 1880 by Rev. Louis Muller. He a native of Leipzig, Saxony and she of Prussia. He a tailor.

FORTUNE, DANIEL E. F. aged 22 years married to SMITH, MARY A. aged 23 years February 6, 1883 by Father P. L. Duffy at The Cathedral of St. John the Baptist. Both natives of Charleston. He a stevedore.

FOSBERRY, ISABELLA married to JENKINS, JAMES W. January 21, 1892 by Father Valerius D'Apreda in King Street below Broad Street. He a bartender.

FOSS, ALMON LEVI aged 21 years married to PECKMAN, THERESA CAROLINE aged 21 years August 14, 1883 by Rev. Louis Muller at 66 Radcliffe Street. He a native of Boston, Massachusetts and she of Liverpool, England. He an engineer.

FOSTER, DANIEL E. aged 32 years married to DUNNJING, KATE E. WEBB aged 25 years March 17, 1892 by Father J. J. Monaghan at St. Patrick's Roman Catholic Church.

FOSTER, JOHN ERNEST aged 23 years married to BAILEY, SARAH LENORA aged 21 years January 29, 1878 by Rev. C. C. Pinckney at Grace Church. Both natives of Charleston. He a clerk.

FOSTER, MARY LOUISE aged 18 years married to GUILES, SAMUEL D. aged 37 years December 9, 1880 by Rev. C. C. Pinckney at 37 Beaufain Street. He a native of London, England and she of Charleston. Both residents of St. James, Santee, South Carolina. He a mariner.

FOURES, MAGGIE A. aged 32 years married to WILSON, JOHN W. aged 39 years July 3, 1886 by Rev. Charles A. Stakely at 8 Wragg Square. He a native of Hartford, Connecticut and she of Orangeburg, South Carolina. He an engineer.

FOWLER, HENRY M. P. married to O'NEAL, ELLEN H. February 3, 1880 by Rev. Richard S. Trapier at St. Michael's Church.

FOX, ANDREW married to O'NEILL, MARY January 7, 1885 by Father Harry P. Northrop at The Cathedral of St. John the Baptist. Both natives of Charleston. He a clerk.

FOX, CATHARINE aged 24 years married to ROSE, HENRY P. aged 46 years May 19, 1883 by Rev. J. A. Clifton in Laurel Street. He a native of St. James Parish, South Carolina and she of Charleston. He a laborer.

FOX, JOSEPH M. married to READ, EMILY May 10, 1883 by Rev. Richard S. Trapier at 26 South Bay Street.

FOX, WINNIE F. aged 18 years married to COLEMAN, JOSEPH aged 28 years May 1, 1895 by Rev. J. C. Yongue at 14 Inspection Street. Both natives of Charleston. He works on a dredge.

FOXWORTH, ALICE aged 18 years married to DUNNING, THOMAS F. aged 38 years March 2, 1886 by Rev. J. W. Dickson at 650 King Street. Both natives of Charleston. He a butcher.

FOY, MARY aged 32 years married to JARRIS, WILLIAM aged 32 years June 5, 1883 by Rev. A. H. Misseldine. Both natives of South Carolina. He an employee of the bagging factory.

FOYE, LAURA J. aged 23 years married to MATTHEWS, THOMAS L. O. aged 23 years July 31, 1895 by Rev. J. C. Yongue at 14 Hampstead Square. He a native of Charleston and she of North Carolina. He a clerk.

FRAIN, THOMAS J. aged 29 years married to CLARK, IDA aged 25 years November 21, 1888 by Father F. J. Shadler.

FRAIN, JAMES J. aged 26 years married to DELANY, KATE C. aged 20 years November 27, 1887 by Father F. J. Shadler at St. Joseph's Roman Catholic Church. Both natives of Charleston. He a stevedore.

FRAMING, JOSEPHA aged 27 years married to KAILURUEIT (?), RHEINHOLD aged 26 years April 25, 1889 by Father F. J. Shadler at St. Joseph's Roman Catholic Church.

FRANCIS, DAVID ALEX aged 51 years married to GAISEA (?), CATHERINE aged 20 years October 12, 1885 by Rev. R. Herbert Jones at 269 Meeting Street. He a native of Vermont and she of South Carolina. He a machinist.

FRANCISCAN, HARVEY CAMERON married to BARNWELL, GABRIELLA MANIGAULT December 5, 1877 by Rev. Richard S. Trapier in Lamboll Street.

FRANK, HARRIS aged 26 years married to ISEAR (?), SARAH C. aged 21 years March 11, 1887 by Rev. B. Rubin at 207 King Street. He a native of Russia and she of Charleston. He a merchant.

FRANK, ROSA aged 22 years married to THORNLEY, M. N. aged 22 years August 4, 1895 by G. W. Rouse, Trial Justice. He a native of Berkeley County, South Carolina and she of Louisville, Kentucky.

FRANKLIN, HATTIE aged 16 years married to DONEHAN, WILLIAM P. J. aged 26 years April 19, 1891 by Father J. J. Monaghan at St. Patrick's Roman Catholic Church. He a native of Charleston and she of South Carolina. He an iron moulder.

FRANKLIN, WILLIAM M. aged 25 years married to GREGORY, (Mrs.) JOSEPHINE aged 19 years December 13, 1888 by Rev. H. B. Browne at 78 Drake Street. She a native of Richland County, South Carolina. He works in a mill.

FRASER, ISABEL aged 3 1 years married to BALL, WILLIAM CAISON aged 31 years April 10, 1889 by Rev. C. C. Pinckney at the residence of Gen. McCrady - 27 Montagu Street. He a native of New York and she of Charleston. He a clerk in New Jersey.

FRAUTOWIG, (?) (Mrs.) MARY FERM aged 35 years married to DUFFY, MICHAEL aged 40 years September 7, 1878 by Father John P. Twigg at The Cathedral of St. John the Baptist. Both natives of Ireland. He a laborer.

FREDERICK, FRITZ aged 24 years married to HOLSENBERG, CATHARINE December 18, 1889 by Rev. Johannes Heckel. He a native of Bremen, Germany and she of Hanover. He a clerk in Summerville, South Carolina.

FREDSBERG, JULIA C. aged 55 years married to LINDSTROM, ALEXANDER aged 58 years November 12, 1885 by Rev. Edward T. Horn at 239 Calhoun Street. He a native of Sweden and she of Germany. He a merchant.

FREEMAN, MARY C. aged 15 years married to MEYERS, JOHN M. aged 21 years April 28, 1892 by Rev. T. P. Burgess at 6 Aiken Row. Both natives of Charleston. He a carpenter.

FREEMAN, RICHARD H. aged 35 years married to BRANFORD, SUSAN E. aged 30 years July 18, 1883 by Rev. J. A. Clifton at 26 Line Street.

FREITAS, MARY EUGENIA aged 21 years married to STELLING, EIBE FREDERICK aged 20 years December 13, 1877 by Father Harry P. Northrop at St. Patrick's Roman Catholic Church. Both natives of Charleston. He a salesman.

FRIBBLE, WESTON A. aged 31 years married to Baker, LAURA A. aged 29 years February 8, 1887 by Rev. L. F. Beaty. Both natives of South Carolina. He a planter.

FRIBERG, H. JOHN aged 40 years married to DRISCOLL, MAMIE aged 25 years April 23, 1890 by Father Harry P. Northrop at The Cathedral of St. John the Baptist. He a native of Denmark and she of Charleston. He a ship builder.

FRICHS, HELENA aged 25 years married to LEOPOLD, BENJAMIN aged 28 years May 7, 1889 by Father J. Wendenfeller at 114 Tradd Street. He a native of Alsac Lorraine and she of Germany.

FRIDAY, ELMORE L. aged 27 years married to HANCOCK, MARY aged 22 years January 4, 1894 by Bishop Harry P. Northrop at The Cathedral of St. John the Baptist. He a native of Peterborough, Pennsylvania and she of Charleston. He an engineer.

FRIEDRICH, FRITZ M. aged 24 years married to HULDEBERG, KATHERINE aged 20 years December 18, 1889 by Rev. Johannes Heckel at 123 Smith Street.

FRIEND, GEORGE G. married to GARRISON, (Mrs.) ANNIE March 7, 1880 by William B. Yates, Chaplain.

FRIEND, JAMES W. aged 25 years married to HEUER, MARIE O. E. aged 19 years September 21, 1890 by Rev. John Johnson at 2 Chestnut Street. Both natives of Charleston. He a machinist in Florence, South Carolina.

FRIEND, JOHN married to WALLEN, C. September 6, 1879 by William B. Yates, Chaplain.

FRIEND, MARY ELLEN aged 18 years married to EARLY, FREDERICK aged 21 years June 9, 1890 by Rev. Robert O. Wilson at 4 Wragg Square. Both natives of Charleston. He a boilermaker.

FRIEND, ROBERT L. aged 20 years married to JONES, ELENORA aged 21 years February 15, 1892 by Rev. J. L. Stokes at 231 Coming Street. He a native of Charleston and she of Ridgeville, South Carolina. He a blacksmith.

FRIERSON, DICK P. aged 32 years married to HUTSON, CECELIA E. aged 19 years June 19, 1895 by Rev. Robert Wilson.

FRIERSON, THOMAS L. aged 26 years married to LEA, SARAH LIZZIE aged 18 years November 18, 1885 by Rev. L. K. Probst. Both natives of South Carolina. He a merchant.

FRIPP, MARY J. aged 21 years married to LUCAS, HENRY R. aged 27 years May 13, 1885 by Rev. Luther K. Probst. He a native of Charleston and she of Walterboro, South Carolina. He a merchant.

FROHOLM, J. S. aged 37 years married to SIMBERG, A. aged 45 years June 15, 1882 by Rev. Luther K. Probst at the Sailors Home. He a native of Sweden and a sailor.

FROHOLEN, M. aged 31 years married to KNUDSEN, INGRET aged 25 years April 3, 1882 by Rev. Luther K. Probst. He a native of Norway and she of Sweden. He a mariner.

FROMING, L. C. H. aged 25 years married to LUDWICK, JOSEPHINE aged 19 years February 15, 1891 by Rev. R. C. Holland. He a native of Charleston and she of Jersey City, New Jersey. He a baker.

FROST, EDWARD married to YATES, ANNIE December 4, 1888 by Rev. Richard S. Trapier.

FRUSER, EDITH aged 32 years married to MILLS, EDGAR aged 32 years December 28, 1893 by Rev. C. C. Pinckney at 137 Tradd Street. He a native of London, England and she of Charleston. He works for the railroad.

FULBIER (?), MAMIE H. married to HILTON, WASHINGTON, J. aged 25 years September 17, 1885 by Rev. John E. Beard at 20 Columbus Street. He a native of South Carolina and she of Charleston.

FULCHER, FANNIE aged 19 years married to DAWSON, EDWARD L. aged 25 years June 24, 1888 by Rev. Johannes Heckel. He a native of Aiken, South Carolina and she of Wilmington, North Carolina. He a clerk in Savannah, Georgia.

FULCHER, ROBERT B. aged 27 years married to WALSH, SARAH aged 26 years November 19, 1883 by Father J. J. Monaghan. He a native of North Carolina and she of Charleston. He a painter.

FULCHES, M. H. aged 24 years married to POTTER, MARY V. aged 21 years January 24, 1883 by Rev. L. H. Shuck at the Mariners Church. He a native of Beaufort, South Carolina and she of Brunswick, Georgia. He a mariner.

FULLER, BUEL A. aged 45 years married to Carpenter, EDITH F. aged 28 years January 28, 1885 by Rev. E. C. L. Browne. Both natives of Illinois. He a lawyer.

FULLER, LUCY aged 21 years married to DeVEAUX, WILLIAM V. aged 22 years January 8, 1893 by Rev. C. E. Chichester at 119 King Street. He a native of Charleston and she of Georgia. He an upholsterer.

FULLER, MIDDLETON G. aged 26 years married to BROWN, ANN ELIZA aged 20 years November 23, 1886 by Rev. A. H. Misseldine at 81 Wentworth Street. Both natives of Charleston. He an engineer.

FULLER, THOMAS aged 23 years married to PRIOLEAU, ISABELLA KINLOCH aged 24 years April 3, 1883 by Rev. Charles S. Vedder at the Huguenot Church. Both natives of Charleston. He an engineer.

FULSE, (Mrs.) JULIA C. VALENTINE aged 30 years married to AUSTIN, WILLIAM JAMES aged 29 years September 22, 1889 by Rev. T. P. Burgess at 100 Columbus Street. Both natives of Berkeley County, South Carolina. He a farmer.

FUNCHEN, LAURA ANN aged 27 years married to MILLER, ILLIARD aged 24 years June 19, 1884 by Rev. John E. Beard. He a native of St. Paul's Parish, South Carolina and she of Orangeburg, South Carolina. He a farmer.

FUNT, VINCENT aged 23 years married to THOMPSON, CAROLINE aged 17 years August 30, 1885 by Rev. John O. Wilson at 82 Wentworth Street. He a native of Spain and she of South Carolina. He a mariner.

FURLEY, MARY F. married to TOUHEY, DAVID J. January 1, 1879 by Father Claudian B. Northrop. Both natives of Charleston. He a bookkeeper.

FURLONG, ELIZABETH aged 28 years married to COMAR, JOSEPH WILLIAM aged 32 years February 8, 1890 by Father Daniel J. Quigley at St. Patrick's Roman Catholic Church.

FURLONG, MARGARET aged 25 years married to VAN DELKEN, HENRY aged 32 years February 7, 1893 by Father J. J. Monaghan at St. Patrick's Roman Catholic Church. Both natives of Charleston. He a railroad conductor.

FURLONG, MARY FRANCKS aged 23 years married to TOUHEY, DAVID JOSEPH aged 26 years January 1, 1879 by Father Claudian B. Northrop at St. Mary of the Annunciation Roman Catholic Church.

FURMAN, BOLIVAR B. aged 26 years married to HEYWARD, CAROLINE S. aged 27 years November 27, 1877 by Rev. John Johnson at 6 Legare Street.

GADSDEN, ALICE T. married to LYNAH, PAUL H. June 7, 1877 by Rev. Richard S. Trapier at St. Michael's Church.

GADSDEN, CATHERINE R. married to GUERARD, B. ELIOT August 14, 1877 by Rev. Richard S. Trapier.

GADSDEN, EDWARD H. aged 25 years married to LEGARE, JULIA T. aged 21 years April 26, 1887 by Rev. G. R. Brackett. Both natives of South Carolina. He a drayman.

GADSDEN, REBECCA H. married to VARDELL, JAMES C. May 11, 1892 by Rev. William H. Campbell at St. Paul's Church.

GAILLARD, ANNIE aged 21 years married to WHITEHEAD, AMOS P. aged 37 years December 5, 1888 by Rev. C. C. Pinckney at Grace Church. He a native of Atlanta, Georgia and she of Charleston County. He operates a cotton press.

GAILLARD, CHARLES R. married to GAILLARD, FANNIE November 7, 1888 by Rev. William H. Campbell at St. Paul's Church. He a railroad conductor.

GAILLARD, EDWARD T. aged 23 years married to STEPHENSON, JANE aged 17 years July 12, 1887 by Rev. C. C. Pinckney at Grace Church. He a native of South Carolina and she of Georgia. He a clerk.

GAILLARD, FANNIE married to GAILLARD, CHARLES R. November 7, 1888 by Rev. William H. Campbell at St. Paul's Church. He a railroad conductor.

GAILLARD, MARY J. married to SCHIRMER, WILLIAM August 5, 1891 by Rev. William H. Campbell at St. Paul's Church. He a mechanic.

GAILLARD, SAMUEL G. aged 38 years married to McCRADY, ESTHER L. B. aged 30 years June 13, 1892 by Rev. John Johnson. He a native of Eutawville, South Carolina and she of Charleston. He a civil and mining engineer.

GAILLARD, WILLIE aged 30 years married to GREEN, SELINA SNOWDEN aged 26 years April 12, 1887 by Rev. J. Mercier Green. Both natives of South Carolina. He works for the railroad.

GAINES, WYLIE aged 21 years married to HOLLEMAN, EDITH aged 17 years December 28, 1887 by Rev. H. B. Browne. He a native of Lenoir County, North Carolina and she of Darlington County, South Carolina. He works in the cotton mill.

GAISEA (?), CATHERINE aged 20 years married to FRANCIS, DAVID ALEX aged 51 years October 12, 1885 by Rev. R. Herbert Jones at 269 Meeting Street. He a native of Vermont and she of South Carolina. He a machinist.

GALE, CAROLINE BUDD aged 24 years married to OGILVIE, WILLIAM MATTHEW aged 22 years April 12, 1881 by Rev. L. H. Shuck at 78 America Street. He a native of Charleston and a clerk.

GALE, LILA L. aged 23 years married to HYDE, SIMEON aged 25 years November 15, 1881 by Rev. L. H. Shuck at First Baptist Church. Both natives of Charleston. He a lawyer.

GALE, THOMAS J. C. aged 21 years married to BOYLE, MARTHA D. aged 21 years December 28, 1893 by Rev. G. R. Brackett at 494 Meeting Street. He a native of London, England and she of Charleston. He an electrical engineer.

GALLAGHER, HENRY aged 46 years married to MATTHEWS, JULIA FRANCES aged 23 years September 4, 1886 by Rev. J. W. Dickson at 231 Coming Street. He a native of Philadelphia, Pennsylvania and she of Charleston. He a druggist in Savannah, Georgia.

GALLAGHAN, DAVID aged 26 years married to SYKES, G. C. M. aged 20 years May 6, 1886 by Rev. Louis Muller. Both natives of Charleston. He a grocer in Mt. Pleasant, South Carolina.

GALLNITZ (?), R. V. aged 31 years married to WINTERLEICH, E. W. aged 25 years November 16, 1880 by Rev. Louis Muller at 66 Radcliffe Street. Both natives of Saxony. He a watchmaker.

GALLOT, ROBERT B. aged 40 years married to SHOKES, MARIA aged 38 years December 10, 1884 by Rev. J. V. Welsh at 13 Aiken Street. He a native of Brooklyn, New York and Charleston. He a porter on a steamship.

GALLUCHAT, MINOR CLINTON aged 21 years married to THOMSON, THOMASINA WOODSON January 31, 1878 by Rev. Charles S. Vedder at the Huguenot Church. He resides in Manning, South Carolina.

GALPHIN, GEORGE D. aged 23 years married to BLACKMAN, LIZZIE MOORE aged 21 years July 28, 1885 by Rev. G. R. Brackett. He a native of Florida and she of South Carolina. He works for the railroad.

GALLEY, M. aged 17 years married to BOLLO, J. aged 23years March 9, 1882 by Rev. L. H. Shuck at 27 Church Street. Both natives of Charleston. He a laborer.

GALTEMAN, WILLIAM aged 23 years married to COSGROVE, ELLEN aged 20 years September 15, 1889 by Father Daniel J. Quigley. She a native of Ireland. He a bricklayer.

GAMBATTI, ALEXANDER aged 27 years married to WEAVER, LUCINDA aged 20 years February 18, 1879 by Father Harry P. Northrop. He a native of Charleston and she of Aiken, South Carolina. He a jeweler.

GAMBATTI, J. A. aged 23 years married to SCHLEPPEGRELL, F. W. aged 25 years August 28, 1882 by Rev. P. J. Wilson in King Street. He a native of Charleston and a clerk.

GAMBATTI, OLYMPIE FELIX aged 22 years married to HERTZ, MARY MARTHA aged 19 years November 29, 1877 by Father Harry P. Northrop at the residence of the Groom's mother - 667 King Street. He a native of Charleston and she of Palatka, Florida. He a dentist.

GAMEWELL, JOHN N. married to BRUNES, MARY FLORENCE September 24, 1890 by Rev. John Gass at 41 Lynch Street.

GANBY, FRANK N. aged 34 years married to ----aged 24 years February 26, 1880 by Rev. E. C. L. Browne at Caw Caw Plantation near Orangeburg, South Carolina. He a native of Somerset County, Maryland and she of Charleston. He a commission merchant.

GANNON, KATIE aged 16 years married to OSMUNDSEN, BERTHEL aged 25 years September 29, 1895 by Rev. C. E. Chichester at the Mariners Church. He a native of Norway and she of Columbia, South Carolina. He a clerk.

GANNON, M. J. aged 38 years married to SCHULTZ, FANNY aged 24 years September 4, 1886 by Rev. A. S. Thomas. He a native of New York and she of Atlanta, Georgia. He a mariner in New York.

GANTT, ELIZA B. aged 24 years married to LeMEINTUE (?), GEORGE A. aged 45 years October 19, 1887 by Rev. Charles A. Stakely. He a native of Dublin, Ireland and she of Charleston. He a phosphate manufacturer in Wilmington, Delaware.

GANTT, H. R. aged 24 years married to PHILIPS, H. S. aged 23 years November 29, 1882 by Father J. J. Woolahan at St. Mary of the Annunciation Roman Catholic Church. Both natives of Charleston. He a commercial traveler.

GANTT, J. LAWRENCE married to HAZAL, JOANNA DOUGLAS November 15, 1881 by Rev. W. H. Campbell at St. Paul's Church. Both natives of Charleston. He a clerk.

GANTT, M. H. aged 33 years married to JERVEY, JAMES L. aged 35 years August 3, 1880 by Rev. Charles S. Vedder. He a merchant

GARBIN, JOHN aged 26 years married to VAZY, DELIA aged 25 years September 8, 1878 by Father John P. Twigg at The Cathedral of St. John the Baptist. Both natives of Ireland. He works for the railroad.

GARCY, THOMAS F. aged 25 years married to CONNOR, JULIA M. aged 22 years February 5, 1888 by Father F. J. Shadler at St. Joseph's Roman Catholic Church.

GARDINER, BRIDGET aged 35 years married to BURNS, GARRETT aged 40 years August 24, 1879 by Father C. J. Croghan at St. Joseph's Roman Catholic Church. Both natives of Ireland. He a politician.

GARDNER, EDWARD aged 22 years married to BUDROW, MINNIE E. aged 16 years December 26, 1888 by Rev. Robert Wilson at 41 Reid Street. Both natives of Charleston. He a ship carpenter.

GARDNER, GEORGE D. aged 35 years married to GRIFFIN, MATTIE L. aged 35 years November 2, 1887 by Rev. G. R. Brackett. He a native of Philadelphia, Pennsylvania and she of Orangeburg, South Carolina. He works for the railroad.

GARDNER, JOHN F. married to MOULTON, MINNIE May 5, 1881 by Rev. William H. Campbell.

GARDNER, (Mrs.) MARTHA L. GRIFFITH aged 28 years married to McGINNIS, PETER McGREGOR aged 50 years May 21, 1890 by Rev. T. P. Burgess at 454 Meeting Street. He a native of Charleston and she of Orangeburg, South Carolina. He a horseshoer and farrier.

GARETY, A. R. aged 24 years married to PHILIPS, H. S. aged 23 years November 29, 1882 by Father J. J.Wedenfeller. He a native of Charleston and a "commercial traveler."

GARETY, CHRISTOPHER JOHN aged 30 years married to LAMBLE, JULIA CLEMENTINE aged 24 years June 9, 1881 by Rev. Claudian B. Northrop. He a native of Charleston and a clerk.

GARRETT, EMMA aged 27 years married to SCHMETZER, LOUIS aged 27 years June 6, 1885 by Rev. John E. Beard at 8 Aiken Street. Both natives of South Carolina.

GARRETT, HAMILTON aged 24 years married to MITCHELL, LOUISA aged 29 years February 9, 1885 by Rev. J. V. Welsh at 657 King Street. Both natives of Charleston. He a farmer.

GARRETT, HAMILTON aged 24 years married to MILLER, ELLA aged 29 years August 1, 1878 by Rev. William C. Power. Both natives of Charleston.

GARRISON, (Mrs.) ANNIE married to FRIEND, GEORGE G. March 7, 1880 by William B. Yates, Chaplain.

GARRISON, MAHALA married to LATTIMORE, HENRY W. January 30, 1879 by Rev. John Johnson at 45 George Street. Both natives of Pennsylvania.

GASKINS, JOHN F. aged 20 years married to FIELDS, CORA L. aged 18 years May 31, 1891 by Rev. C. E. Chichester at 44 Market Street. He a native of Newborn, North Carolina and she of Sumter, South Carolina. He a mariner.

GASQUE, FLORENCE aged 21 years married to GERROW (?), SEYMOUR aged 23 years September 22, 1888 by Rev. R. D. Smart at 49 Gadsden Street. He a native of Delaware County, New York and she of Marion County, South Carolina. He a carpenter.

GATCH, CHARLES B. aged 23 years married to HOFF, SELENA O. E. aged 24 years January 4, 1884 by Rev. Charles A. Stakely at 8 Bay Street. Both natives of South Carolina. He a farmer.

GATERO, (?), F. aged 25 years married to EDWARDS, E. aged 17 years December 22, 1882 by Rev. J. V. Welsh at 22 Bogard Street. He a native of Charleston and a mariner.

GATEWOOD, LENORA married to ADAMS, ETTSEL December 31, 1877 by Rev. John Johnson in Tradd Street. He a native of Charleston and a planter.

GATEWOOD, VIRGINIA A. aged 32 years married to TUPPER, FREDERICK aged 45 years June 9, 1881 by Rev. John Johnson at 24 South Bay Street. He a native of Charleston and an insurance salesman.

GAUSE, SALLY aged 22 years married to STROBLE, PRESTON aged 20 years February 9, 1890 by Rev. J. Thoms Pate at the residence of the Bride's mother. He a native of Charleston and she of Germany. He works for the railroad.

GAYNOR, ANN aged 28 years married to DODDS, GEORGE aged 33 years July 16, 1878 by Father Harry P. Northrop at St. Patrick's Roman Catholic Church.

GAYNOR, BRIDGET aged 25 years married to SCHNEPF, PHILIP aged 25 years February 7, 1878 by Father Harry P. Northrop at St. Patrick's Roman Catholic Church. He a native of Philadelphia, Pennsylvania and she of Ireland. He a painter.

GAYNOR, CORALIE C. aged 22 years married to GRIMKE, WILLIAM H. aged 23 years April 3, 1888 by Rev. John Johnson at 64 Meeting Street. Both natives of Charleston. He a clerk in New York.

GAYNOR, (Mrs.) SARAH STUART aged 26 years married to HICKMAN, JOHN H. aged 28 years May 14, 1889 by Father John J. Wedenfeller at 114 Tradd Street. He a painter.

GAYNOR, WILLIAM J. aged 30 years married to EASTERBY, CHRISTOPHINE aged 27 years December 17, 1885 by Rev. C. C. Pinckney in South Bay Street. Both natives of Charleston. He a clerk.

GEBE, HENRY W. married to DROSE, SUSAN R. October 14, 1890 by William B. Yates, Chaplain.

GEDDINGS, ANNA L. aged 25 years married to WITHERSPOON, JOHN aged 70 years October 2, 1888 by Rev. John Johnson in Broad Street. He a native of Society Hill, South Carolina and she of Charleston. He a planter in Society Hill.

GEDDINGS, D. F. aged 20 years married to TUPPER, SAMUEL Y. aged 25 years April 6, 1880 by Rev. John Johnson at St. Philip's Church. Both natives of Charleston. He an accountant.

GEDDINGS, ELIZABETH F. aged 22 years married to DOTTERER, LOUIS P. aged 30 years January 25, 1888 by Rev. John Johnson at St. Philips Church. Both natives of Charleston. He a dentist.

GEHLKEN, F. J. aged 22 years married to WEINKEN, C. H. aged 21 years February 26, 1882 by Rev. Luther K. Probst at 24 Montagu Street. He a native of Florida and she of South Carolina. He a grocer.

GEHLKEN, HEINRICH E. aged 40 years married to CHILDS, JESSIE aged 40 years January 11, 1892 by Rev. Louis Muller at 96 Radcliffe Street. He a native of Prussia and she of Charleston. He a cabinetmaker.

GEHRELS, CAROLINE aged 18 years married to COOPER, GEORGE E. aged 42 years July 15, 1891 by Rev. Edwin C. Dargan. He a native of Dober, North Carolina and she of Orangeburg, South Carolina. He own a marbleyard.

GEHRELS, EMMA aged 17 years married to JANTZONS, FRANK aged 33 years January 16, 1886 by Rev. Charles A. Stakely at 8 Wragg Street. He a native of Germany and she of Orangeburg County, South Carolina. He an artist.

GEHRELS, MARY THEODORA aged 19 years married to HIOTT, SAMUEL H. aged 50 years April 29, 1890 by Rev. Edwin S. Dargan at 269 King Street. He a native of North Carolina and she of Orangeburg, South Carolina.

GELDINGS, DEAS F. aged 20 years married to TUPPER, SAMUEL Y. aged 25 years April 6, 1880 by Rev. John Johnson at St. Philip's Church. Both natives of Charleston. He an accountant.

GELZER, JOHN aged 23 years married to AXSON, NANNIE OSWALD aged 22 years December 6, 1883 by Rev. A. J. S. Thomas at 17 Meeting Street. He a native of Summerville, South Carolina and she of Charleston.

GENTRY, AGNES BEATRICE aged 17 years married to LaPORTA, FRANCIS ALFRED aged 22 years July 30, 1894 by Father J. J. Monaghan at St. Patrick's Roman Catholic Church. He a native of New York and she of Charleston. He a confectioner.

GENTRY, (Mrs.) MARGARET COBIA aged 29 years married to O'HERREN, JOHN JAMES aged 38 years January 26, 1892 by Rev. H. B. Brown at 78 Drake Street. Both natives of Charleston. He a machinist.

GERAGHTY, M. E. aged 16 years married to WALSH, JAMES F. aged 29 years July 28, 1880 by Father Claudian B. Northrop at St. Mary of the Annunciation Roman Catholic Church. Both natives of Charleston. He a merchant.

GERARD, E. aged 29 years married to CLARK, MARY J. aged 26 years October 23, 1887 by Rev. P. J. McManus. He a native of Alsace and she of Charleston. He a loom fitter.

GERARD, FRIEDRICH GUSTAV aged 41 years married to WEINHEIMER, ANNA HELENE aged 33 years June 6, 1888 by Rev. Louis Muller at the corner of King and Tradd Streets. He a widower.

GERARD, GUSTAV F. aged 21 years married to NELSON, AMELIA aged 19 years February 19, 1890 by Rev. J. Thomas Pate at 47 Bogard Street. He a native of Summerville, South Carolina and she of New York City. He a clerk.

GERARD, WILLIE aged 30 years married to ROHDE, LENAH aged 22 years March 17, 1884 by Rev. J. V. Welsh at 187 St. Philip Street. He a native of Brooklyn, New York and she of Charleston. He a clerk.

GERDES, SOPHIE aged 36 years married to KIRK, SAMUEL G. aged 22 years March 12, 1891 by Rev. Louis Muller. He a native of Scotland and she of Hanover. He a printer.

GERKEN, ANNE aged 30 years married to SMITH, THOMAS aged 27 years September 11, 1892 by Rev. John Johnson at 53 Church Street. He a native of Liverpool, England and she of Germany. He a watchman.

GERKEN, ARTHUR J. H. aged 23 years married to OETJEN, ANNA G. C. S. aged 19 years April 4, 1886 by Rev. Johannes Heckel. He a native of Charleston and a bookkeeper.

GERROW (?), SEYMOUR aged 23 years married to GASQUE, FLORENCE aged 21 years September 22, 1888 by Rev. R. D. Smart at 49 Gadsden Street. He a native of Delaware County, New York and she of Marion County, South Carolina. He a carpenter.

GETLEY, FANNIE MOORE aged 26 years married to BICKLEY, JOHN aged 27 years April 9, 1890 by Bishop Harry P. Northrop at 48 Rutledge Avenue.

GETTY, JAMES WHITE aged 27 years married to ARNOLD, MARY CAROLINE aged 21 years November 12, 1878 by Rev. W. S. Bowman at 12 Chapel Street. Both natives of Charleston. He a clerk.

GIARETTI (?), STEFANO aged 53 years married to HAHN, (Mrs.) ELIZABETH ELLEN HODGES aged 44 years January 8, 1889 by Rev. C. E. Chichester. He a native of Italy and she of Charleston. He a hotel keeper.

130

GIBBON, GEORGE EDWARD aged 32 years married to WEBB, MARY WINTHROP aged 28 years August 25, 1885 by Rev. E. C. L. Brown. Both natives of Charleston. He works in the phosphate mill.

GIBBS, HENRY D. aged 24 years married to RANKIN, PHYLLIS aged 19 years March 8, 1894 by Rev. David M. Ramsey at 46 Rutledge Avenue. Both natives of New York. He an actor in Troy, New York.

GIBBS, W. HAMPTON aged 26 years married to HEYWARD, SUSAN K. aged 25 years November 30, 1887 by Rev. John Johnson at 10 Legare Street. Both natives of Columbia, South Carolina. He a merchant in Columbia.

GIBSON, L. ADELAIDE aged 20 years married to BURNS, WILLIAM MELVILLE aged 21 years May 6, 1880 by Rev. H. F. Chreitzberg at the southwest corner of Meeting and Spring Streets. Both natives of Charleston. He a salesman.

GIBSON, AGNES R. aged 21 years married to SKINNER, OLIN D. aged 24 years October 30, 1888 by Rev. J. E. Carlisle at 33 Radcliffe Street. He a native of Colleton County, South Carolina and she of Charleston. He a machinist in Cheraw, South Carolina.

GIBSON, CARRIE aged 35 years married to BARRY, JAMES aged 43 years May 3, 1885 by Father Daniel J. Quigley at St. Patrick's Roman Catholic Church. He a native of Ireland and she of South Carolina. He a machinist.

GIBSON, EMILY C. aged 21 years married to BURNS, ALLAN McC. aged 23 years February 28, 1884 by Rev. W. P. Mouzon at the northeast corner of Meeting and Society Streets. Both natives of Charleston. He a merchant.

GIBSON, LOUIS L. aged 31 years married to MORAN, EMMA C. aged 22 years March 26, 1894 by Father J. J. Monaghan at 591 King Street. He a native of Illinois and she of Charleston. He a salesman in Savannah, Georgia.

GIESEA (?), AMOS LEONARD aged 33 years married to STALVEY, CATHARINE MANSFIELD aged 19 years January 6, 1884 by Rev. John Willson at the corner of Church and Queen Streets, room 39, The Calder House. He a native of Germany and she of South Carolina. He an engineer.

GILBERT, (Mrs.) AMANDA EMERSON WIENGES aged 60 years married to HARPER, FURMAN MANLY aged 62 years July 24, 1888 by Rev. R. W. Lide at First Baptist Church. Both natives of Charleston. He a printer.

GILBERT, JOHN D. aged 34 years married to FABIAN, MARY E. aged 32 years June 11, 1893 by Rev. H. B. Browne. He a native of Wilmington, North Carolina and she of Charleston. He a clerk.

GILBERT, JOHN W. aged 27 years married to THOMPSON, GEORGIANA aged 29 years February 12, 1885 by Rev. John Johnson at 5 Franklin Street. Both natives of Charleston. He works in a factory.

GILBERT, LAMBERT C. aged 26 years married to VERONEE, ADDIE aged 20 years May 20, 1880 by Rev. G. R. Brackett. He a native of Charleston and she of Blackwell, South Carolina. He a painter.

GILL, MARY E. aged 23 years married to WYSONG, RUFUS C. aged 27 years June 29, 1887 by Rev. Robert Wilson. Both natives of Charleston. He an engineer.

GILLIGAN, CHARLES H. aged 30 years married to CASHMAN, HESSIE aged 22 years September 8, 1878 by Father John P. Twigg at The Cathedral of St. John the Baptist. He a native of Maine and she of Charleston. He a mariner.

GILLILAND, JAMES aged 26 years married to MEDLIN, DRUSCILLA aged 20 years June 24, 1893 by John Ahrens, Trial Justice at 1 New Street. He a native of Charleston and she of Columbia, South Carolina. He a printer.

GILLILAND, KATE J. married to BEAUFORT, CHARLES W. February 23, 1888 by Rev. William H. Campbell. He a machinist in Langley, South Carolina.

GILLILAND, SARAH AGNES married to GLOVER, JOHN M. M. December 26, 1887 by Rev. Richard S. Trapier at 30 Beaufain Street.

GIRARDEAU (?), THOMAS G. married to RIVERS, H. G. January 28, 1880 by William B. Yates, Chaplain.

GIRARDEAU, THOMAS aged 22 years married to RIVERS, HENRIETTA aged 23 years April 5, 1880 by Rev. A. Toomer Porter in King Street. He a native of Charleston and she of Johns Island, South Carolina.

GIRSCHMAN, JOHN H. married to HARLIN, MARY August 12, 1882 by Rev. Richard S. Frazier at 2 Lamboll Street.

GISSEL, SARAH G. aged 21 years married to HANSEN, HARVEY aged 29 years December 27, 1877 by Rev. W. S. Bowman. He a native of Denmark and she of Walhalla, South Carolina.

GIVEN, MINNIE aged 28 years married to ROWLAND, CHRISTOPHER J. aged 23 years December 27, 1883 by Rev. J. A. Clifton at 189 Coming Street. He a native of Charleston and she of Italy. He a machinist.

GLADDEN, GEORGE aged 35 years married to JACKSON, ELLEN aged 18 years March 7, 1886 by Rev. H. B. Browne at 6 Harris Street. He a native of Charleston and she of South Carolina. He a shoemaker.

GLADDEN, GEORGE aged 30 years married to ZWINGMANN, ANNIE AUGUSTA aged 18 years September 19, 1880 by Rev. R. N. Wells. Both natives of Charleston. He a shoemaker.

GLADDEN, MARY ELIZABETH married to THOMSON, SAMUEL February 12, 1878 by William B. Yates, Chaplain.

GLEASON, MATTHEW B. aged 25 years married to SELBY, ANNA LAURA aged 22 years September 22, 1889 by Rev. J. E. Carlisle at 231 Coming Street. He a native of Charleston and she of Ohio. He a lightman.

GLEASON, SARAH AGNES aged 21 years married to TOYE, JOHN H. aged 31 years January 25, 1881 by Father T. Edward Chapins at at 63 America Street. Both natives of Charleston. He a moulder.

GLEN, ALICE GERTRUDE aged 19 years married to JERVEY, JAMES MURRAY aged 26 years April 26, 1888 by Rev. G. R. Brackett. He a native of Mt. Pleasant, South Carolina and a clerk.

GLEN, MAMIE A. aged 18 years married to McKNIGHT, GEORGE M. aged 33 years February 20, 1893 by Rev. Edmund Wells at 82 Drake Street. He a native of Williamsburg County, South Carolina and she of Charleston. He a farmer in Gourdin, South Carolina.

GLENN, EMMA LAURA aged 25 years married to WILKINS, FREDERICK A. aged 41 years December 9, 1886 by Rev. A. H. Misseldine at 43 Anson Street. He a native of England and she of Charleston. He a baker.

GLENN, FRANK W. aged 23 years married to MOORE, E. IRENE aged 20 years April 19, 1892 by Rev. William A. Rogers at 21 Wentworth Street. Both natives of Charleston. He a bookkeeper.

GLOVER, A. M. aged 24 years married to HUGHES, S. aged 35 years October 18, 1882 by Rev. L. H. Shuck. He a native of Charleston and an ironworker.

GLOVER, ELIZABETH A. aged 21 years married to BECKWITH, LAWRENCE H. aged 26 years December 7, 1893 by Rev. John Johnson at 25 Smith Street.

GLOVER, JOHN E. aged 30 years married to COWARD, MARY L. aged 26 years June 1, 1893 by Rev. C. C. Pinckney and Rev. E. N. Joyner at Grace Church. He a native of Orangeburg, South Carolina and she of Yorkville, South Carolina. He a bookkeeper in Orangeburg.

GLOVER, JOHN M. M. married to GILLILAND, SARAH AGNES December 26, 1887 by Rev. Richard S. Trapier at 30 Beaufain Street.

GLOVER, JOSEPH aged 20 years married to NORTH, REBECCA B. aged 24 years January 24, 1884 by Rev. John Johnson at St. Philip's Church. He a native of South Carolina and she of Charleston. He a farmer in Grahamville, South Carolina.

GLOVER, LOUIS W. aged 20 years married to HILLS, ROSA L. A. aged 17 years March 20, 1893 by Rev. N. K. Smith at 25 Charlotte Street. He a native of Johns Island, South Carolina and she of James Island, South Carolina. He a planter in Stono, South Carolina.

GLOVER, MORTIMER M. aged 22 years married to BUTLER, MARIA IRVING aged 18 years March 9, 1892 by Rev. R. A. Webb in Westminster Presbyterian Church. He a native of Orangeburg, South Carolina and she of Charleston. He a clerk.

GLOVER, WILLIAM H. aged 34 years married to LADSON, (Mrs.) J. EUGENIA DAVIS aged 30 years July 1, 1888 by Rev. C. E. Chichester. She a native of Kingstree, South Carolina. He a painter.

GODDARD, EDGAR M. aged 27 years married to BENNETT, EMMA ISABELLE aged 21 years December 23, 1886 by Father F. J. Shadler at 312 King Street. He a native of Charleston and a physician.

GODFREY, MARY L. aged 18 years married to WHALEY, HENRY C. aged 22 years July 2, 1890 by Rev. T. P. Burgess at 18 Amherst Street.

GODFREY, R. S. aged 22 years married to HOHLMAN, W. H. aged 21 years January 29, 1882 by Rev. Louis Muller at 343 Meeting Street. He a native of Georgia and she of South Carolina. He works for the railroad.

GODSON, EDWARD aged 37 years married to WATSON, MARY aged 30 years December 10, 1883 by Rev. J. C. Butler at 96 Tradd Street.

GOETHE, JAMES E. aged 24 years married to LAMBERT, SUSAN WASHINGTON aged 17 years June 27, 1878 by Rev. R. N. Wells. He a native of Beaufort, South Carolina and she of Charleston. He a farmer.

GOLDSMITH, CARRIE aged 23 years married to COHEN, JACK W. aged 25 years April 3, 1895 by Rabbi Barnett A. Elzas.

GOLDSMITH, E. aged 25 years married to LOEB, J. H. aged 33 years January 7, 1880 by Rabbi David Levy. He a native of South Carolina and she of Charleston. He a merchant.

GOLDSMITH, FRANCES aged 36 years married to LEVY, EDWARD S. aged 29 years June 25, 1879 by Rabbi David Levy. He a native of Philadelphia, Pennsylvania and she of Charleston. He a clergyman in Augusta, Georgia.

GOLDSMITH, ISAAC A. aged 23 years married to TRIEST, FANNIE aged 20 years September 24, 1889 by Rabbi David Levy.

GOLDSMITH, KATE A. aged 21 years married to JACOBY, HENRY L. aged 39 years September 29, 1891 by Rabbi David Levy at the Hasell Street Synagogue. Both natives of Charleston. He a merchant.

GONZALEZ, ELIZABETH aged 21 years married to ZIEGLER, ROBERT A. aged 19 years January 16, 1889 by Father J. J. Monaghan at St. Patrick's Roman Catholic Church. Both natives of Charleston. He works for the railroad.

GOODIN, ELOISE aged 20 years married to SCOTT, F. G. aged 30 years September 21, 1880 by Rev. John Johnson in Eutawville, South Carolina. He a native of Virginia and she of St. Johannes, Berkeley County, South Carolina. He a clergyman. Both reside in Eutawville.

GOODWIN, (Mrs.) GENEVIEVE Baker aged 37 years married to REEVES, WILLIAM L. aged 43 years June 14, 1888 by Rev. C. C. Pinckney at Grace Church. Both natives of Charleston. He a woodworker.

GOODWIN, H. P. aged 30 years married to VACH, H. C. E. aged 22 years March 23, 1887 by Rev. Louis Muller. He a native of England and she of Germany. He a tailor.

GOODWIN, JESSE R. aged 21 years married to VALENTINE, (Mrs.) AGNES JACKSON aged 36 years March 27, 1889 by Rev. H. B. Browne at 22.5 Sheppard Street. He a native of Lexington, South Carolina and she of Berkeley County, South Carolina. He works in a mill.

GOODWIN, LAURA married to HUDSON, GEORGE S. May 18, 1892 by Rev. William A. Rogers. He a native of England and she of Bennettsville, South Carolina. He a clerk.

GOODWIN, MARY E. aged 26 years married to McNAMARA, J. B. aged 48 years August 18, 1887 by Rev. Robert Wilson. Both natives of South Carolina. He a carpenter.

GOOLEY, MICHAEL aged 22 years married to DUNN, ELLEN aged 21 years March 24, 1878 by Father Daniel J. Quigley. He a native of Ireland and she of Charleston. He a clerk.

GOOLEY, JOHN aged 23 years married to DAVIS, FLORENCE aged 18 years January 2, 1881 by Father Daniel J. Quigley at The Cathedral of St. John the Baptist. He a native of Ireland and she of Charleston. He a clerk.

GOOLEY, MARGARET aged 26 years married to QUINN, DAVIS aged 28 years September 22, 1878 by Father John P. Twigg at The Cathedral of St. John the Baptist. Both natives of Ireland. He a laborer.

GORDON, FLORENCE E. aged 22 years married to PREGNELL, ARTHUR H. aged 24 years May 1, 1889 by Rev. E. C. L. Browne. Both natives of Charleston. He a ship builder.

GORDON, MICHAEL MARTIN aged 27 years married to MITCHELL, (Mrs) MARGARET JULIA SMITH aged 26 years April 16, 1883 by Rev. J. A. Clifton at 32 Columbus Street. He a native of Ireland and she of Summerville, South Carolina. He a machinist.

GORMAN, JOHN A. aged 24 years married to MYERS, SUSAN aged 15 years July 4, 1880 by Rev. J. V. Welsh. Both natives of Charleston. He a laborer.

GORSE, PETER NICHOLAS aged 49 years married to OLDENBUTTLE, JOHANNA W. M. STEINBERG aged 40 years January 25, 1891 by Rev. Louis Muller at 388 Meeting Street. Both natives of Hanover. He a grocer.

GOSS, JANEY aged 19 years married to BURNES, L. E. aged 24 years July 6, 1885 by Rev. John E. Beard at 64 Nassau Street.

GOTGEN, CHATERINE aged 31 years married to RUMPEL, GEORGE W. aged 29 years May 15, 1884 by Rev. Luther K. Probst. He a native of Charleston and she of Germany. He a clerk.

GOULD, (Mrs.) MARY ANN LANAGHAN aged 32 years married to JADHU (?), NICHOLAS aged 33 years August 26, 1878 by Father John P. Twigg at The Cathedral of St. John the Baptist. He a native of Austria and she of Ireland. He a mariner.

GOWAN, EVA F. aged 19 years married to ALDRET, BENJAMIN S. aged 21 years March 22, 1887 by Rev. G. R. Brackett. Both natives of Charleston. He a clerk.

GOWERS, JANE F. aged 22 years married to WEST, EDWIN F. aged 28 years July 2, 1879 by Rev. Charles S. Vedder at the Huguenot Church. He a native of James Island, South Carolina and she of England. He a broker.

GRADICK, M. EMMA aged 17 years married to SIEBERT, THEODORE CONRAD aged 23 years November 24, 1880 by Rev. W. L. Bowman at the home of the Bride - 7 Aiken Street. She a native of Charleston. He a baker.

GRADY, JAMES married to DAWSON, JULIA October 31, 1883 by Rev. William H. Campbell in Church Street. Both natives of Charleston. He a clerk.

GRAF, (Mrs.) CHARLES BRUCKERMAN aged 50 years married to LEHRMAN, GEORGE aged 53 years October 20, 1884 by Rev. Johannes Heckel at 55 Smith Street. Both natives of Germany. He a mariner.

GRAF, LOUISE aged 20 years married to Dickson, C. J. U. aged 27 years November 30, 1887 by Rev. Johannes Heckel at 123 Smith Street. He a native of Sweden and she of Charleston. He a carpenter.

GRAFF, GEORGE W. aged 23 years married to MIRASKA, T. aged 19 years May 8, 1882 by Rev. P. L. Duffy at 30 Mazyck Street. He a native of Charleston and a baker.

GRAFFENREID, GEORGE T. aged 25 years married to McKAY, ISABELLA aged 21 years October 6, 1884 by Rev. A. J. S. Thomas at 94 Queen Street. Both natives of South Carolina. He a telegraph operator in Columbia, South Carolina.

GRAHAM, E. L. aged 18 years married to NELSON, A. aged 23 years October 18, 1882 by Rev. Luther K. Probst. He a native of Charleston and a mariner.

GRAHAM, H. ELLEN aged 42 years married to MUCKENFUSS, BENJAMIN A. aged 43 years June 16, 1881 by Rev. E. J. Meynardie at the corner of Rutledge Avenue and Spring Streets. He a native of Charleston and a dentist.

GRAHAM, JOHN C. aged 41 years married to BAXLEY, MARTHA E. MARTIN aged 39 years July 25, 1891 by Rev. W. A. Betts at 21 Hanover Street. He a native of Scotland and she of Conway, South Carolina. He a cook.

GRAHAM, JOSEPH aged 29 years married to MAY, ELIZA A. aged 27 years June 15, 1881 by Father F. J. Shadler. He a native of Whitehaven, England and she of Charleston. He a mariner.

GRANDY, JOHN H. aged 56 years married to MALONEY, ALICE M. aged 27 years November 23, 1892 by Rev. Edward T. Horn in Tradd Street.

GRANT, C. B. aged 24 years married to JOHNSON, M. I. aged 20 years December 31, 1882 by Rev. Luther K. Probst. Both natives of Charleston. He a painter.

GRANT, MARY D. aged 20 years married to CRAFTS, WILLIAM H. aged 24 years May 3, 1881 by Rev. A. Coke Smith at 26 Vanderhorst Street. He a native of Charleston and she of Green County, Georgia. He a clerk.

GRANT, M. H. aged 33 years married to JERVEY, JAMES L. aged 35 years August 3, 1880 by Rev. Charles S. Vedder at the Huguenot Church. Both natives of Charleston. He a merchant.

GRATZICK, FRANCES aged 31 years married to HANDKERVEN (?), JOHN aged 28 years August 6, 1894 by Father J. J. Monaghan at St. Patrick's Roman Catholic Church. Both natives of Poland. He a clerk.

GRAVER, (Mrs.) ANNA CATHERINE FUNKE aged 32 years married to WITT, HEINRICH aged 25 years December 28, 1882 by Rev. Louis Muller at the corner of King and Reid Streets. He a native of Germany and she of Charleston. He a grocer.

GRAY, (Mrs.) ADA BUIST aged 22 years married to ADDISON, CHARLES E. aged 25 years February 3, 1895 by Rev. John Johnson at 53 Church Street. He a native of Charleston and she of Albany, New York. He works for the railroad.

GRAY, ALICE aged 18 years married to LEVETT, JOHN HENRY aged 20 years September 16, 1883 by Rev. E. J. Meynardie at 145 King Street. He a native of Washington, Georgia and she of Alexandria, Virginia. He works in a factory.

GRAY, FLORENCE PAULINE aged 19 years married to GRIFFIN, ISAAC W. aged 28 years November 17, 1886 by Rev. P. J. Wilson at 19 Pinckney Street. He a native of Long Island, New York and she of Charleston. He an oysterman on Edisto Island, South Carolina.

GRAY, JOHN aged 49 years married to WEBB, MARY ANN aged 48 years September 24, 1890 by Rev. John Johnson at 46 King Street. He a native of Scotland and she of New York City. He an upholsterer.

GRAZICK, JULIE aged 25 years married to PECKMAN, RICHARD aged 27 years February 6, 1883 by Rev. Johannes Heckel at 125 Calhoun Street.

GREEN, CLARA E. aged 20 years married to WHITE, JOHN ALFRED aged 23 years November 27, 1886 by Father P. J. Wilson at St. Mary of the Annunciation Roman Catholic Church. Both natives of Charleston. He a bookkeeper.

GREEN, ELLA F. aged 22 years married to DONNELLY, LEON aged 22 years January 6, 1884 by Father J. J. Woolhan at 74 Wentworth Street. He a native of Athens, Georgia and she of Charleston. He a tailor.

GREEN (GREER?), ELLEN C. married to ANDERSON, GEORGE DURANT October 17, 1884 by Rev. W. F. Junkin in Wentworth Street.

GREEN, FRANCES G. aged 23 years married to JOHNSON, EUGENE W. aged 26 years November 25, 1885 by Rev. J. Mercier Green at Grace Church. He a native of Charleston and she of South Carolina. He a bookkeeper.

GREEN, FREDERICK L. aged 28 years married to WALTER, EUNICE aged 18 years July 8, 1884 by Rev. L. F. Guerry at St. Philip's Church. He a native of South Carolina and she of Charleston. He a bank officer.

GREEN, HARRIET H. aged 22 years married to DeVEAUX, JOHN P. aged 25 years October 20, 1886 by Rev. W. B. H. Howe at 23 Wentworth Street. Both natives of Charleston. He a government employee.

GREEN, HUGH LEON aged 28 years married to INGHAM, SARAH EUGENIA aged 19 years January 1, 1878 by Rev. Claudian B. Northrop at the residence of Mrs. Sarah Ingham. Both natives of Charleston. He a farmer in Orangeburg, South Carolina.

GREEN, MARY JANE aged 26 years married to WILSON, SAMUEL W. aged 27 years January 23, 1878 by Rev. W. C. Dana. He resides in Sumter County, South Carolina.

GREEN, REBECCA W. aged 27 years married to SMITH, HERBERT L. aged 27 years April 19, 1888 by Rev. G. R. Brackett. He a native of Georgetown, South Carolina.

GREEN, SELINA SNOWDEN aged 26 years married to GAILLARD, WILLIE aged 30 years April 12, 1887 by Rev. J. Mercier Green. Both natives of South Carolina. He works for the railroad.

GREEN, THOMAS DAVIDSON aged 26 years married to SHIER, ALICE M. M. aged 25 years July 8, 1878 by Rev. W. S. Bowman in Meeting Street, opposite Citadel Green. He a native of Baltimore, Maryland and she of Charleston. He a confectioner.

GREEN, THOMAS W. aged 25 years married to SALISBURY, AUGUSTA aged 17 years September 28, 1887 by Rev. H. B. Browne at 31 Blake Street. He a native of Wilmington, North Carolina and she of Berkeley County, South Carolina. He a railroad coupler.

GREER (GREEN ?), EDITH aged 21 years married to BEE, SANDIFORD aged 26 years February 2, 1892 by Rev. Edward T. Horn at 7 Logan Street. Both natives of Charleston. He a planter on James Island, South Carolina.

GREER, J. FORREST married to POOSER, MARY L. April 7, 1881 by Rev. William H. Campbell. He a clerk.

GREGG, WILLIAM aged 26 years married to BREMERMANN, SUSIE aged 24 years April 5, 1893 by Father J. J. Monaghan. He a native of South Carolina and she of Germany. He works in the cotton mill.

GREGORIE, EMMA aged 17 years married to WHITE, JAMES T. aged 23 years September 8, 1887 by Rev. H. B. Browne at 31 Columbus Street. He a native of Manning, South Carolina and she of Edgefield, South Carolina. He works in the cotton mill.

GREGORY, (Mrs.) JOSEPHINE aged 19 years married to FRANKLIN, WILLIAM M. aged 25 years December 13, 1888 by Rev. H. B. Browne at 78 Drake Street. She a native of Richland County, South Carolina. He works in a mill.

GREGORY, PHILO EDWIN aged 32 years married to McDOWELL, ELLEN F. aged 28 years April 13, 1887 by Rev. Robert Wilson. Both natives of South Carolina. He an lawyer.

GREMIN, JOHANN H. aged 24 years married to SCHMIDT, HENRIETTA D. aged 23 years February 18, 1880 by Rev. Louis Muller in King Street. Both natives of Hanvoer. He a grocer in Savannah, Georgia.

GRENVILLE, MARY AGNES aged 19 years married to MULLING, GEORGE MEACHER aged 25 years November 17, 1881 by Father F. A. Schmetz at 2 Smith Lane. Both natives of Atlanta, Georgia. He a bookkeeper.

GRESSETT, W. married to HALFORD, W. January 12, 1882 by Rev. A. Coke Smith. Both natives of Charleston. Both natives of Charleston. He a physician in Branchville, South Carolina.

GREYMAN (?), JOHN M. aged 56 years married to MAHONEY, ALICE M. aged 27 years November 23, 1892 by Rev. Edward T. Horn in Tradd Street. Both natives of Charleston. He a druggist.

GRICE, HELEN aged 24 years married to TRENHOLM, CHARLES L. aged 22 years April 5, 1893 by Rev. Edward T. Horn at the residence of George D. Grice.

GRICE, ROBERT BLUM aged 22 years married to EVANS, LIZZIE ALLEN aged 24 years May 1, 1884 by Rev. John H. Honour at 165 St. Philip Street. Both natives of Charleston. He a clerk.

GRIFFIN, BENJAMIN aged 22 years married to VARNER, LUCINA LONG aged 30 years June 26, 1894 by Rev. Thomas A. Grove. He a native of North Carolina and she of South Carolina. He works in the cotton mill.

GRIFFIN, E. MARY aged 27 years married to McINNERNEY, MICHAEL aged 34 years February 9, 1890 by Rev. J. Thomas Pate at the Spring Street Church. He a native of Charleston and she of Polk County, North Carolina. He works for the railroad.

GRIFFIN, ISAAC W. aged 28 years married to GRAY, FLORENCE PAULINE aged 19 years November 17, 1886 by Rev. P. J. Wilson at 19 Pinckney Street. He a native of Long Island, New York and she of Charleston. He an oysterman on Edisto Island, South Carolina.

GRIFFIN, J. H. aged 23 years married to DAVIS, D. A. aged 22 years February 12, 1882 by Rev. A. S. Duffy at The Mills House Hotel. He a native of New Jersey and an oysterman. She a native of Charleston. He a resident of Edisto Island, South Carolina.

GRIFFIN, MARY aged 47 years married to REYNOLDS, JOHN aged 60 years November 12, 1880 by Rev. J. V. Welsh at the corner of Rodgers Alley and St. Philip Street. He a native of Ireland and she of St. Paul's, South Carolina. He a laborer.

GRIFFIN, MATTIE L. aged 35 years married to GARDNER, GEORGE D. aged 35 years November 2, 1887 by Rev. G. R. Brackett. He a native of Philadelphia, Pennsylvania and she of Orangeburg, South Carolina. He works for the railroad.

GRIFFITH (Mrs.), MARY KEEGAN aged 34 years married to WHITTIG, JOHN aged 42 years April 2, 1884 by Father P. L. Duffy at The Cathedral of St. John the Baptist. He a native of Germany and she of Charleston. He a loom fixer at the cotton mill.

GRIEME (?), ELISE aged 20 years married to KLENTWORTH, PETER aged 27 years September 18, 1881 by Rev. Louis Muller. Both natives of Hanover. He a merchant.

GRIMBALL, JOHN aged 44 years married to BARNWELL, M. GEORGIA aged 27 years March 24, 1885 by Rev. C. C. Pinckney. Both natives of Charleston. He a lawyer.

GRIMBO, MARY ELIZABETH aged 27 years married to RIERHERS, M. F. N. aged 28 years December 2, 1880 by Rev. Louis Muller at 66 Radcliffe Street. He a native of Charleston and a mariner.

GRIMES, JAMES THOMAS aged 21 years married to WIGHTMAN, HARRIET CAROLINE aged 20 years April 18, 1883 by Rev. John Johnson in Queen Street. He a native of Branchville, South Carolina and she of Charleston. He works for the railroad.

GRIMES, J. aged 22 years married to CONNELLY, M. E. aged 23 years November 22, 1882 by Father John P. Twigg at St. Patrick's Roman Catholic Church. He a native of South Carolina and a bricklayer.

GRIMES, (Mrs.) ROSA ELLIS aged 33 years married to RIPKEN, ANTON H. F. aged 31 years June 23, 1895 by Rev. C. E. Chichester at 1 Atlantic Street. He a native of Georgia and she of Montiello, Florida. He a clerk in Savannah, Georgia.

GRIMKE, WILLIAM H. aged 23 years married to GAYNOR, CORALIE C. aged 22 years April 3, 1888 by Rev. John Johnson at 64 Meeting Street. Both natives of Charleston. He a clerk in New York.

GRIMM, C. M. aged 18 years married to PRESTON, THOMAS H. aged 27 years March 27, 1887 by Rev. C. A. Stakley. He native of England and she of New Jersey. He a painter.

GRIMM, E. aged 16 years married to RICHARDSON, CHARLES aged 25 years May 12, 1880 by Rev. R. N. Mills in Hasell Street. Both natives of New York. He a mariner.

GRIMM, JOHANN aged 24 years married to SCHMIDT, HENRIETTA D. aged 23 years February 18, 1880 by Rev. Louis Muller in King Street. Both natives of Hanover. He a grocer in Savannah, Georgia.

GRISER, JOHN J. aged 20 years married to BRUNSON, MARIAN G. aged 20 years April 11, 1893 by Father J. J. Monaghan at 136 St. Philip Street. Both natives of Charleston. He works for the railroad.

GRISSELL, FLORENCE ANNA married to HILBERT, THEODORE CARL June 24, 1884 by Rev. C. E. Chichester at the Mariners Church. She a native of Charleston. He a mariner.

GROOM, BETTIE aged 16 years married to CHEEK, CHARLES aged 27 years May 16, 1888 by Rev. H. B. Browne in America Street. He a native of Georgia and she of Darlington, South Carolina. He works in the cotton mill.

GROOM, CLIFFORD W. aged 22 years married to ANDERSON, SUSAN E. aged 20 years July 18, 1893 by Rev. Edmund Wells at 579 King Street. He a native of Brooklyn, New York and she of Charleston. He a marine engineer.

GROOMS, MADELINE aged 25 years married to HUSSEL, GEORGE J. aged 38 years May 7, 1893 by Rev. Edmund Wells at 65 Drake Street. He a native of Charleston and she of Summerville, South Carolina. He a clerk in Summerville.

GROSSMAN, JULIUS aged 27 years married to POMMERENKE, WILHELMINA aged 21 years May 10, 1883 by Rev. Louis Muller at the corner of Spring and President Streets. Both natives of Georgia. He a baker.

GROVERMAN (?) HENRY J. W. aged 22 years married to BEHLMAN, S. M. C. aged 27 years May 20, 1880 by Rev. Louis Muller at 637 King Street. He a native of Charleston. She a native of Hanover.

GROTE, JACOB aged 27 years married to CRAWFORD, SUSAN aged 22 years November 19, 1891 by Rev. W. A. Betts at 96 Columbus Street. He a native of Germany and she of St. Stephen's Parish, South Carolina. He a mariner.

GROTE, JOHN S. aged 24 years married to WELLS, ELLA R. aged 21 years October 22, 1895 by Rev. J. C. Yongue at 14 Hampstead Square. He a native of Germany and she of Charleston. He serves on a United States revenue cutter.

GROTUS, LOUISA aged 23 years married to COCHRAN, A. M. aged 31 years November 27, 1884 by Father F. J. Shadler at 56 Anson Street. He a native of Anderson, South Carolina and she of Charleston. He a segar dealer.

GROTUS (?), WILHELMINA aged 19 years married to McCARTHY, EUGENE aged 24 years July 8, 1884 by Father F. J. Shadler at St. Joseph's Roman Catholic Church. Both natives of Charleston. He a stonecutter.

GRUBER, A. J. married to BEVANS, W. J. November 25, 1879 by Rev. H. F. Chreitzberg at the residence of the Bride - 6 Blake Street. Both natives of Charleston. He an accountant.

GRUBER, BLANCHE W. aged 25 years married to RODGERS, ELMER O'G. aged 33 years February 15, 1894 by Rev. J. L. Stokes at the Spring Street Lutheran Church. He a native of South Carolina and she of Charleston. He a clerk in Florence, South Carolina.

GRUBER, CAROLINE A. married to MATTHEWS, ALEXANDER H. March 10, 1892 by Rev. William H. Campbell. He a railroad conductor.

GRUBER, NORMAN P. aged 37 years married to SMITH, EMILY aged 27 years March 16, 1890 by Rev. J. Thomas Pate in Spring Street. Both natives of Charleston. He a finisher and bookbinder.

GRUBER, SERENA P. aged 24 years married to KENNEDY, JAMES R. D. aged 25 years November 25, 1890 by Rev. John Johnson at 18 Blake Street. Both natives of Charleston. He a bookkeeper.

GRUBS, BENJAMIN aged 21 years married to ROGERS, PLACEDA aged 17 years April 13, 1895 by Rev. J. C. Yongue at 24 Cooper Street. He a native of South Florida and she of South Carolina. He works in the cotton mill.

GRUMMER, CHARLOTTE aged 21 years married to KRANZ, WILLIAM aged 24 years May 17, 1881 by Rev. Louis Muller at 8 Calhoun Street.

GUERARD, B. ELLIOT married to GADSDEN, CATHERINE R. August 14, 1877 by Rev. Richard S. Trapier.

GUILES, SAMUEL D. aged 37 years married to FOSTER, MARY LOUISE aged 18 years December 9, 1880 by Rev. C. C. Pinckney at 37 Beaufain Street. He a native of London, England and she of Charleston. Both residents of St. James Santee, South Carolina. He a mariner.

GUILT, JOHN W. aged 25 years married to DUNNE, SARAH A. aged 25 years November 9, 1892 by Father J. J. Monaghan at 203 St. Philip Street. He a native of Woodville, Georgia and she of Augusta, Georgia. He an engineer in Savannah, Georgia.

GUILLEMIN, CLEMENCE E. aged 20 years married to DuFORT, T. E. aged 23 years April 17, 1884 by Father J. J. Woolahan at St. Patrick's Roman Catholic Church. Both natives of Charleston. He a clerk.

GUILLEMIN, MARIE CATHERINE aged 22 years married to LeBUFFE, ADOLPH aged 25 years November 15, 1881 by Rev. Claudian B. Northrop at St. Mary of the Annunciation Roman Catholic Church. Both natives of Charleston. He a printer.

GUILLEMIN, PETER L. aged 50 years married to LARKIN, JANE aged 40 years June 29, 1885 by Father J. J. Wedenfeller at St. Mary of the Annunciation Catholic Church. Both natives of Charleston. He an employee of the gas works.

GUINAN, JOSEPHINE LENOR aged 34 years married to PARSONS, WILLIAM B. aged 33 years April 14, 1891 by Father F. J. Shadler at St. Joseph's Roman Catholic Church. Both natives of Charleston. He works for the railroad.

GUSTIN (?), GEORGE H. aged 29 years married to JOHNSON, ROSA W. aged 23 years June 28, 1892 by Rev. Charles S. Vedder at 110 Broad Street.

GUTEKUNST (?), GEORGE G. aged 23 years married to SONTAG, CAROLINE H. aged 25 years April 19, 1883 by Rev. Luther K. Probst. He a native of Georgia and she of Chicago, Illinois. He a brewer in Walhalla, South Carolina.

GUTHKE, EMILY ELIZABETH aged 16 years married to SALVO, VICTOR ROBERT aged 20 years February 15, 1891 by Rev. W. A. Betts at 1 Duc Court,

GUTHRIE, FANNIE E. aged 19 years married to CARTWRIGHT, ALEXANDER aged 26 years August 2, 1883 by J. E. Hagood at the U. S. Custom House. Both natives of Georgia. He a clerk.

HAAS, C. C. aged 30 years married to FINKENBERG, M. aged 31 years October 8, 1882 by Rev. Louis Muller at 66 Radcliffe Street. He a native of Germany and a laborer.

HAAS, THERESA aged 28 years married to ODENCRANTZ, CARL aged 34 years December 7, 1892 by Rev. Edward T. Horn at 31 Pitt Street. He a native of Sweden and she of Charleston. He an engineer.

HABENICHT (?), E. V. aged 21 years married to McMILLAN, M. G. aged 29 years October 27, 1890 by Rev. Charles S. Vedder at 167 Tradd Street. Both natives of Charleston. He a planter.

HACHE, SOPHIE DORETHA MANN aged 30 years married to SCHROEDER, DIETRICH aged 30 years February 8, 1891 by Rev. Louis Muller at 96 Radcliffe Street.

HACKER, ELLEN BUTLER aged 30 years married to JOHNSTON, JOHN WILLIAM aged 33 years April 13, 1887 by Rev. T. P. Burgess at Ebenezer Church. Both natives of South Carolina. He a machinist.

HADRE, MARIE B. aged 19 years married to WEINHOLTZ, RUDOLPH aged 27 years April 27, 1893 by Rev. Edward T. Horn. Both natives of Charleston. He a clerk.

HAGAN, JAMES aged 23 years married to WALSH, MARY J. aged 23 years February 17, 1885 by Father F. J. Shadler at St. Joseph's Roman Catholic Church. He a native of Charleston and a gas worker.

HAGGARD, A. aged 32 years married to ANDERSON, I. aged 35 years January 15, 1882 by Rev. E. J. Meynardie at 1 Mount Street. He a native of Norway and she of Georgia. He a laborer.

HAGOOD, EDWARD A. aged 52 years married to BEAUDROT, MAMIE A. aged 19 years July 1, 1892 by Rev. J. L. Stokes at 77 Line Street. He a native of Albany, Georgia and she of Charleston. He a broker in Toledo, Ohio.

HAGOOD, IRENE married to ROBINSON, WILLIAM December 12, 1878 by Rev. J. A. Chambliss in East Bay Street near Laurens Street.

HAHN, ANNIE C. aged 17 years married to STUCKE, CHARLES HENRY aged 20 years May 29, 1881 by Rev. Johannes Heckel. He a native of Walhalla, South Carolina and she of Charleston. He a baker.

HAHN, (Mrs.) ELIZABETH ELLEN HODGES aged 44 years married to GIARETTI (?), STEFANO aged 53 years January 8, 1889 by Rev. C. E. Chichester. He a native of Italy and she of Charleston. He a hotelkeeper.

HAHN, WILLIAM MARTIN aged 23 years married to CAMPET, MARGARET MARTINA aged 21 years June 3, 1890 by Father J. J. Monaghan at St. Patrick's Roman Catholic Church. Both natives of Charleston. He a boilermaker.

HAHN, WILLIE M. aged 19 years married to ALSINA, IDA E. aged 19 years February 3, 1886 by Rev. H. B. Browne at 104 Nassau Street.

HAINS, C. H. G. aged 23 years married to SCHARY, F. W. aged 23 years November 24, 1882 by Rev. Louis Muller at 169 Coming Street. He a native of Charleston and a mechanic.

HAIR, AGGIE L. aged 16 years married to ALMERS, JOSEPH aged 22 years December 21, 1890 by Rev. Robert Wilson at 4 Wragg Square. He a native of Charleston and she of Branchville, South Carolina. He a laborer.

HALBE, FREDERICK CHARLES aged 58 years married to LODERHOSE, (Mrs.) SOPHIE HENRIETTA G. aged 46 years June 28, 1888 by Rev. Johannes Heckel at 123 Smith Street. He a native of Hanover and she of Germany.

HALFORD, W. married to GRESSETT, W. January 12, 1882 by Rev. A. Coke Smith. Both natives of Charleston. Both natives of Charleston. He a physician in Branchville, South Carolina.

HALL, DORA C. aged 18 years married to STOLL, WILLIAM aged 24 years April 6, 1879 by Rev. J. V. Welsh in Radcliffe Street.

HALL, EDWARD OSCAR aged 25 years married to PINCKNEY, MARGARET aged 22 years November 27, 1889 by Rev. John Johnson at St. Philip's Church. He a native of South Carolina and she of Charleston. He a farmer in Mt. Pleasant, South Carolina.

HALL, FELICIA O. aged 22 years married to CHISOLM, WILLIAM B. aged 19 years November 28, 1877 by Rev. C. C. Pinckney at Grace Church. He a native of Charleston and a phosphate manufacturer.

HALL, GEORGE P. aged 39 years married to McGILL, DORA M. aged 22 years November 9, 1893 by Rev. J. C. Yongue at 29 Blake Street. He a native of Edgefield County, South Carolina and she of Timmonsville, South Carolina.

HALL, HARRY L. aged 30 years married to POULNOT, ROSA aged 35 years July 16, 1890 by Father J. J. Monaghan at St. Patrick's Roman Catholic Church. He a native of Massachusetts and she of Quebec. He a mariner.

HALL, JOHN W. aged 28 years married to HESTER, ELIZABETH P. aged 20 years April 8, 1891 by Rev. W. A. Betts at 83 America Street. He a native of Georgia and she of Greene County, Georgia. He works in the cotton mill.

HALL, LYMAN aged 24 years married to JENNINGS, ANN T. aged 21 years December 13, 1883 by Rev. C. C. Pinckney in Calhoun Street. He a native of Americus, Georgia and she of Pendleton, South Carolina.

HALL, SAMUEL J. aged 27 years married to McCUE, KATE aged 27 years January 7, 1885 by Father F. J. Shadler at St. Joseph's Roman Catholic Church. He a native of Ireland and she of Charleston. He a mariner.

HALL, SAMUEL ROBERTS aged 37 years married to DAVEY, EMMA J. aged 23 years June 10, 1894 by Rev. J. L. Stokes at 23 Bay Street.

HALL, THOMAS F. married to ZAERIUS (?), FANNY December 7, 1878 by William B. Yates, Chaplain.

HALL, WILLIAM HENRY aged 23 years married to RODGERS, VICTORIA AMANDA aged 18 years October 4, 1881 by Rev. H. F. Chreitzberg at 10 Aiken Street. He a native of Pennsylvania and she of Charleston. He an artist.

HALLENBECK, SARAH aged 20 years married to SENSENEY, HARVEY G. aged 27 years January 23, 1895 by Rev. J. L. Stokes at 201 Spring Street. He a native of Lexington County, South Carolina and she of New York. He an engineer.

HALPIN, A. J. aged 22 years married to STUCKENBROK, F. J. aged 25 years January 8, 1880 by Rev. Louis Muller at 66 Radcliffe Street. He a native of Hanover, and she of Prussia. Both residents of Summerville, South Carolina. He a grocer.

HALPIN, MARY E. aged 25 years married to PUCKHABER, JOHN F. aged 29 years April 16, 1893 by Father J. J. Monaghan at 199 Coming Street. Both natives of Charleston. He a baker.

HAM, ALICE R. aged 17 years married to SLANESON, W. M. aged 24 years June 27, 1880 by Rev. R. N. Wells at 15 Church Street. He a native of Clarendon County, South Carolina and she of Charleston

HAM, J. JOHN aged 28 years married to PONARD, TERESA A. aged 22 years February 10, 1890 by Father F. J. Shadler at St. Joseph's Roman Catholic Church. He a printer in Jacksonville, Florida.

HAMET, EMILY F. married to MINTZMEYER, HENRY February 10, 1880 by Rev. J. Mercier Green at the corner of Spring and St. Philip Streets. Both natives of Charleston. He a butcher.

HAMETT, A. C. aged 49 years married to WITHERS, ANNIE J. aged 42 years January 10, 1890 by Rev. R. A. Webb at 17 Ann Street. Both natives of Charleston. He a clerk.

HAMETT, GERTRUDE H. aged 23 years married to THOMPSON, WILLIAM R. aged 24 years December 5, 1888 by Rev. H. B. Browne at 95 Columbus Street. He a native of Pennsylvania and she of Charleston. He an insurance agent.

HAMILTON, E. LULA aged 19 years married to MILLER, JOHN aged 22 years January 27, 1892 by Rev. William A. Rogers. Both natives of Charleston. He a clerk.

HAMILTON, MILES B. married to PRINGLE, MARY R. April 10, 1883 by Rev. Richard S. Frazier in Legare Street. Both natives of Charleston. He a merchant.

HAMILTON, REBECCA M. married to RYAN, ARTHUR B. June 3, 1879 by Rev. Richard S. Trapier at St. Michael's Church.

HAMILTON, RICHARD E. aged 22 years married to DOWNING, LENORA AGNES aged 21 years April 9, 1881 by Rev. L. H. Shuck at 27 Church Street. He a native of Charleston and a fireman.

HAMLIN, WARREN D. married to HENDRICKS, SALLIE E. April 29, 1891 by Rev. William H. Campbell. He resides in Mt. Pleasant, South Carolina.

HAMMETT, LEWIS aged 20 years married to DAVIS, ELLA aged 22 years June 3, 1888 by Rev. H. B. Browne at 99 Drake Street. He a native of Jefferson County, Georgia and she of Milledgeville, Georgia. He works in the cotton mill.

HAMMETT, LIZZIE SINGLETON aged 21 years married to HATCH, MELVIN SPOFFORD aged 24 years July 19, 1888 by Rev. G. R. Brackett. He a native of Florence, South Carolina and she of Charleston. He raises stock in Asheville, North Carolina.

HAMPTON, PRESTON BROOKS aged 24 years married to CASON, DAISY FLORENCE aged 20 years October 18, 1881 by Rev. H. F. Chreitzberg at 246 Meeting Street. He a native of Charleston and a railroad conductor.

HANAHAN, EDWARD WALTER aged 25 years married to BROTHERS, FLORENCE VIRGINIA aged 17 years March 25, 1889 by Rev. G. R. Brackett at Second Presbyterian Church. He a native of New York City and she of Charleston. He a printer in New York City.

HANAHAN, JOSEPH aged 25 years married to OGIER, KATE L. aged 23 years April 6, 1893 by Rev. Robert O. Wilson at St. Luke's Chapel. Both natives of Charleston. He a clerk.

HANCKEL, CHARLOTTE H. aged 30 years married to AVERY, FRANCIS C. B. aged 30 years December 16, 1890 by Rev. John Johnson at 20 Church Street. He a native of New York and she of Charleston. He a merchant in New York.

HANCKEL, FRANCIS S. aged 28 years married to MILES, ANNE C. aged 25 years December 11, 1888 by Rev. John Johnson at St. Philip's Church. Both natives of Charleston. He a clerk.

HANCOCK, CARRIE F. aged 20 years married to MEYER, WILLIAM W. aged 21 years January 23, 1884 by Father P. L. Duffy at 17 Church Street. He a native of Aiken, South Carolina and she of Blackville, South Carolina. He a farmer in Augusta, Georgia.

HANCOCK, JULIA aged 18 years married to KELLY, JOHN aged 21 years May 16, 1892 by Rev. A. M. Chreitzberg. He a native of Columbia, South Carolina and she of Sumter, South Carolina. He works in the cotton mill.

HANCOCK, MAGGIE A. aged 16 years married to SINGLETARY, WILLIAM T. aged 22 years December 13, 1894 by Rev. J. C. Yongue at 24 Blake Street. Both natives of Berkeley County, South Carolina. He a farmer in Berkeley County.

HANCOCK, MARY aged 22 years married to FRIDAY, ELMORE L. aged 27 years January 4, 1894 by Bishop Harry P. Northrop at The Cathedral of St. John the Baptist. He a native of Peterborough, Pennsylvania and she of Charleston. He an engineer.

HANCOCK, SALLIE aged 16 years married to MONROE, DANIEL aged 20 years June 21, 1892 by Rev. W. A. Betts. He a native of Summerville, South Carolina and she of Sumter, South Carolina. He works in the cotton mill.

HANCOCK, SAMUEL S. married to LALOR, (Mrs.) SUSAN R. McKENZIE May 22, 1890 by Rev. William H. Campbell at 101 Broad Street. He a pilot.

HANEY, JOHN F. aged 38 years married to KINSMAN, (Mrs.) HATTIE S. HENRY aged 28 years December 19, 1894 by Rev. Edmund Wells at 369 Meeting Street. He a native of Darlington County, South Carolina and she of Colleton County, South Carolina. He a brickmason.

HANLEY, MARY AGNES aged 25 years married to O'GORMAN, HUGH D. aged 28 years April 29, 1891 by Father Daniel J. Quigley at St. Patrick's Roman Catholic Church. Both natives of Charleston. He a carpenter.

HANLY, JAMES F. aged 29 years married to COSGROVE, ELLEN T. aged 26 years June 18, 1892 by Father J. J. Monaghan at St. Patrick's Roman Catholic Church. Both natives of Charleston. He a railroad flagman.

HANLY, MARTIN JOSEPH aged 26 years married to CLEARY, MARY MAGDALEN aged 22 years April 21, 1878 by Father John P. Twigg at The Cathedral of St. John the Baptist. He a native of Ireland and she of Charleston. He a laborer.

HANLY, PATRICK J. aged 28 years married to O'MARA, MARY THERESA aged 25 years February 4, 1883 by Father John P. Twigg at St. Patrick's Roman Catholic Church. He a native of Ireland and she of Charleston. He a policeman.

HANSEN, HARVEY aged 29 years married to GISSEL, SARAH G. aged 21 years December 27, 1877 by Rev. W. S. Bowman. He a native of Denmark and she of Walhalla, South Carolina.

HAPPELL, HENRY H. aged 29 years married to JONES, ADELAIDE aged 22 years January 4, 1895 by Rev. A. Ernest Cornish. He a native of Castle, Georgia and she of Plainfield, New York. He a steward.

HAPPOLDT, (Mrs.) ADA M. BEATTIE aged 28 years married to PETTIS, WALKER JAMES aged 30 years January 23, 1890 by Father J. J. Monaghan at St. Patrick's Roman Catholic Church. She a native of Georgia. He a watchman.

HAPPOLDT, T. C. aged 24 years married to FLEMING, MARY A. aged 25 years October 11, 1887 by Father Daniel J. Quigley at 473 King Street. He a native of Ridgeville, South Carolina and she of Charleston. He a painter.

HARBISON, JOHN FRANCIS aged 28 years married to MAGRATH, MARY JANE aged 22 years December 29, 1886 by Father Daniel J. Quigley at St. Patrick's Roman Catholic Church. Both natives of Charleston. He a builder in New York.

HARBY, A. GERTRUDE aged 17 years married to RAFER, HENRY B. aged 35 years January 14, 1886 by Rev. C. C. Pinckney at 159 Wentworth Street. He a native of New Orleans, Louisiana and she of South Carolina. He a farmer in Fairfield, South Carolina.

HARBY, HENRY J. aged 23 years married to EMANUEL, ADELINE W. aged 19 years October 26, 1881 by Rabbi David Levy at the Hasell Street Synagogue. He a native of Sumter, South Carolina and she of Charleston. He a merchant.

HARD, P. MARY aged 29 years married to PRESSLEY, WILLIAM aged 42 years November 21, 1889 by Rev. Edwin C. Dargan at 88 Beaufain Street. He a native of Williamsburg County, South Carolina and she of Augusta, Georgia. He a farmer in Rio Vista, Georgia.

HARD, WILLIAM D. aged 37 years married to YOE, FANNIE K. aged 17 years June 16, 1887 by Rev. John O. Wilson at Trinity Church. Both natives of South Carolina. He a hospital superintendent.

HARDY, GASTON aged 26 years married to WALKER, SUE HOWARD aged 25 years April 16, 1884 by Rev. John Johnson at 5 Church Street. He a native of Virginia and she of Charleston. He works for the railroad.

HARKEN, JOHANN HEINRICH aged 24 years married to UFFERHAUS (?), ANNA MARIA aged 17 years October 23, 1887 by Rev. Louis Muller in Rutledge Avenue above Shephard Street. Both natives of Charleston. He a grocer.

HARLESTON, ELIZABETH married to LESESNE, WILLIAM aged 30 years November 25, 1880 by Rev. A. Toomer Porter at the Church of the Holy Communion. Both natives of Charleston. He a clerk.

HARLESTON, M. J. aged 30 years married to WARING, J. B. aged 29 years November 6, 1879 by Rev. J. E. Jackson in Columbus Street. He a stationer.

HARLESTON, TOOMER LAWRENCE aged 26 years married to JOHNSON, LOUISA MAGDALENA aged 31 years March 18, 1890 by Rev. Charles S. Vedder at the Huguenot Church. Both natives of Charleston. He the Superintendent of Palmers Manufacturing Company.

HARLESTON, R. M. aged 33 years married to VENNING, SOPHIA aged 21 years July 14, 1880 by Rev. A. Toomer Porter. Both natives of Charleston. He a planter in Ashepoo, South Carolina.

HARLESTON, ELIZABETH married to LESESNE, WILLIAM aged 30 years November 25, 1880 by Rev. A. Toomer Porter at Holy Communion Church. Both natives of Charleston. He a clerk.

HARLIN, MARY married to GIRSHMAN, JOHN H. August 12, 1882 by Rev Richard S. Frazier at 2 Lamboll Street.

HARLOW, (Mrs.) MARY CRONAN aged 32 years married to MURPHY, RICHARD aged 39 years December 15, 1878 by Father Daniel J. Quigley at The Cathedral of St. John the Baptist. Both natives of Ireland. He a saloon keeper.

HARLOW, MARY E. aged 24 years married to MURPHY, JOHN A. aged 27 years April 25, 1893 by Father J. J. Monaghan at St. Patrick's Roman Catholic Church.

HARMON, JULIA J. aged 16 years married to WADE, CLAUDIUS L. aged 21 years December 6, 1891 by Rev. T. P. Burgess at 25 Cooper Street. He a native of Jefferson County, Mississippi and she of Summerville, South Carolina. He a car driver.

HARMON, (Mrs.) MARGARETHA B. aged 30 years married to HODGES, WILLIAM PARKER aged 27 years July 4, 1889 by Father J. J. Monaghan at St. Patrick's Roman Catholic Church. Both natives of Charleston. He a barber.

HARPER, CARRIE married to DUC, CHARLES OTTO August 23, 1887 by Rev. William H. Campbell. He a clerk in New York.

HARPER, FURMAN MANLY aged 62 years married to GILBERT, (Mrs.) AMANDA EMERSON WIENGES aged 60 years July 24, 1888 by Rev. R. W. Lide at First Baptist Church. Both natives of Charleston. He a printer.

HARRENFRATZ, ROSA aged 20 years married to NIPSON, T. S. aged 23 years December 27, 1886 by A. F. Gleason, Trial Justice. He a native of Charleston and she of Nashville, Tennessee. He a clerk.

HARRIGAN, JOHN aged 34 years married to BURNS, ANNIE aged 27 years June 28, 1881 by Father F. J. Shadler at St. Joseph's Roman Catholic Church.

HARRIGAN, SARAH aged 25 years married to DOWNING, SAMUEL aged 29 years May 1, 1889 by Father John J. Wedenfeller at The Cathedral of St. John the Baptist. He a native of Charleston and "in the cotton business."

HARRINGTON, ANNA aged 26 years married to HARTNETT, JOHN P. aged 27 years April 13, 1883 by Father F. J. Shadler at St. Joseph's Roman Catholic Church. Both natives of Charleston. He operates a restaurant.

HARRINGTON, (Mrs.) BRIDGET DUNN aged 45 years married to BROUGHTON, LAWRENCE aged 48 years October 7, 1885 by Father F. J. Shadler at St. Joseph's Roman Catholic Church. Both natives of Ireland. He a laborer.

HARRINGTON, ELLA B. aged 23 years married to FLEMING, WILLIAM F. aged 23 years July 8, 1890 by Father F. J. Shadler at St. Joseph's Roman Catholic Church. Both natives of Charleston. He a clerk in Jacksonville, Florida.

HARRINGTON, M. J. married to DELEPHINE, W. R. September 17, 1879 by William B. Yates, Chaplain.

HARRIS, DAVID aged 30 years married to MARKS, KATIE H. aged 25 years June 11, 1895 by Rabbi Barnett A. Elzas at 372 King Street. He a native of New York City and she of Charleston. He a clerk at 245 Court Street in Brooklyn, New York.

HARRIS, JOHN B. aged 24 years married to O'NEIL, NELLIE E. aged 22 years October 16, 1884 by Father Daniel J. Quigley at St. Patrick's Roman Catholic Church. He a native of Georgia and she of South Carolina. He works for the railroad in Augusta, Georgia.

HARRIS, WILLIAM J. aged 22 years married to BROWN, NELLIE P. aged 22 years October 7, 1888 by Father Daniel J. Quigley at St. Patrick's Roman Catholic Church. He a native of Georgia and a clerk in Savannah, Georgia.

HARRIS, S. C. aged 19 years married to McCRACKEN, R. A. aged 26 years August 1, 1882 by Rev. L. H. Shuck at 27 Church Street. He a native of South Carolina and a railroad worker. She a native of England.

HARRISON, E. R. aged 24 years married to JURS (?), G. H. aged 23 years May 27, 1882 by Rev. Luther K. Probst at 60 Queen Street. He a native of Charleston and a tailor.

HARRISON, F. B. aged 21 years married to BURK, WILLIAM HENRY aged 22 years June 20, 1880 by Rev. L. H. Shuck. Both natives of Charleston. He a pilot.

HARRISON, H. MEACHER married to RICHARDSON, CHARLES E. April 27, 1879 by William B. Yates, Chaplain. Both natives of Charleston. He a bellsmith.

HARRISON, JOHN T. S. aged 45 years married to WILLIAMS, FLORENCE E. aged 35 years May 6, 1888 by Rev. G. R. Brackett. Both natives of Charleston. He a musician.

HARRISON, MARION DRAYTON aged 21 years married to DENNIS, CORNELIA ELIZA aged 16 years November 15, 1884 by Rev. Edwin C. Browne.

HART, BETA aged 19 years married to MEYER, WILLIE aged 22 years January 28, 1894 by Rev. Edmund Wells at 579 King Street. He a native of Charleston and works in the cotton mill.

HART, DAVID S. C. aged 37 years married to AMAU, LIZZIE W. aged 27 years October 8, 1888 by Rev. H. B. Browne at the corner of America and Amherst Streets.

HART, DAVID L. aged 23 years married to LEVY, LAURA L. aged 23 years June 4, 1890 by Rabbi David Levy at 80 Wentworth Street. Both natives of Charleston. He a clerk.

HART, HUGO G. aged 31 years married to MACKEY, EMMA G. aged 18 years April 27, 1886 by Rev. Charles A Stakely at 43 Nassau Street. He a native of Orangeburg, South Carolina and she of Charleston. He a farmer in Orangeburg.

HART, JOHN W. aged 22 years married to JOHNSON, LOUISA A. aged 16 years November 8, 1893 by Rev. J. C. Yongue at 532 Meeting Street. He a native of Berkeley County, South Carolina and she of Augusta, Georgia. He works for the railroad.

HART, RUPERT R. aged 23 years married to MOOD, GERTRUDE E. aged 21 years December 27, 1892 by Rev. Edward T. Horn at 26 Savage Street. He a native of Flat Rock, North Carolina and she of Charleston. He a merchant in Flat Rock.

HARTIGAN, THOMAS aged 41 years married to MURPHY, (Mrs.) SARAH O'MEARA aged 26 years July 9, 1894 by Father Daniel J. Quigley. He a native of Ireland and she of Charleston. He a taxidermist.

HARTMANN, E. FREDERICK aged 39 years married to KASSENS, SOPHIA CATHARINE MARGARETHE aged 26 years February 18, 1883 by Rev. Louis Muller at the corner of St. Philip and Cannon Streets.

HARTNETT, CATHERINE aged 16 years married to DUNN, JOHN W. aged 22 years June 17, 1892 by Father J. J. Monaghan. Both natives of Charleston. He a salesman.

HARTNETT, JOHN P. aged 27 years married to HARRINGTON, ANNA aged 26 years April 13, 1883 by Father F. J. Shadler at St. Joseph's Roman Catholic Church. Both natives of Charleston. He operates a restaurant.

HARTNETT, MARY RYAN aged 40 years married to JAHN, RICHARD aged 40 years February 17, 1889 by Father J. J. Monaghan 6 Paines Court. He a native of Germany and she of Ireland. He a laborer.

HARTZ, WILLIAM aged 43 years married to SCHWACKE, SARAH ELLA aged 29 years August 6, 1891 by Rev. R. C. Holland at 426 King Street. Both natives of Charleston. He a merchant.

HARVEN, G. C. aged 55 years married to TEXWARD (?), S. aged 24 years February 13, 1882 by Rev. J. V. Welsh at 56 Spring Street. He a native of South Carolina and a laborer.

HARVEY, AUGUSTA M. aged 26 years married to ADDISON, THOMAS M. aged 32 years December 14, 1882 by Rev. J. H. Tillinghast at 170 Queen Street. He a native of Charleston and she of New York. He a farmer.

HARVEY, C. F. aged 36 years married to JEFFORDS, JOSEPHINE aged 20 years November 23, 1882 by Father D. J. Simons at Sullivans Island, South Carolina. He a native of South Carolina and a carpenter.

HARVEY, JAMES aged 46 years married to RYAN, CATHERINE aged 40 years June 15, 1879 by Father John P. Twigg at The Cathedral of St. John the Baptist. Both natives of Ireland. He a policeman.

HARVEY, MARIA E. aged 32 years married to FINK, JOHN W. aged 30 years October 7, 1884 by Rev. E. C. L. Browne. He a native of Charleston and she of South Carolina. He a ship carpenter.

HARVEY, MARTHA E. aged 25 years married to ORTMANN, HENRY C. aged 25 years April 10, 1888 by Rev. Robert Wilson at 40 Mazyck Street. He a native of Charleston and a postal worker.

HASELDEN, MORTIMER V. aged 25 years married to HORLBECK, IRENE aged 21 years October 28, 1891 by Rev. Edward T. Horn at St. Johannes Lutheran Church. He a native of Marion, South Carolina and she of Charleston. He a bookkeeper.

HASELL, (Mrs.) ELISE E. EDWARDS aged 48 years married to HOLMES, WILMOT G. aged 57 years August 27, 1894 by Rev. John Johnson at Grace Church. Both natives of Charleston. He a bookkeeper.

HASELL, HARRY Z. aged 25 years married to SCHACHTE, NANNIE aged 23 years February 22, 1893 by Rev. Charles S. Vedder at 149 King Street. He a native of Edgefield County, South Carolina and she of Charleston. He an insurance agent.

HASQUEDT, MARY aged 22 years married to BOWICK, HENRY A. aged 21 years November 22, 1894 by Rev. A. Freyschmidt at 2 Ashe Street. He a native of Charleston and she of Germany. He a workman.

HAZAL, JOANNA DOUGLAS married to GANTT, J. LAWRENCE November 15, 1881 by Rev. William H. Campbell at St. Paul's Church. Both natives of Charleston. He a clerk.

HASELTON, EUGENIA E. aged 26 years married to WHITE, WILLIAM E. aged 38 years January 26, 1888 by Rev. J. E. Carlisle at 68 America Street. He a native of Grand Rapids, Michigan and she of Charleston. He a mechanic.

HASELTON, JULIA C. aged 26 years married to REEVES, WILLIAM L. aged 22 years July 31, 1879 by Rev. H. F. Chreitzberg at 56 America Street.

HASELTON, WALTER E. aged 24 years married to PULTING, THADIA O. aged 22 years April 22, 1891 by Rev. G. R. Brackett at 648 King Street. He a native of Charleston and she of Richmond, Virginia. He a machinist.

HASKELL, EVA aged 25 years married to PORCHER, JOHN T. aged 30 years December 24, 1877 by Rev. A. Toomer Porter at the Church of the Holy Communion. She a native of South Carolina. He a planter.

HASMAN, A. E. aged 43 years married to CONNELLY, M. A. aged 24 years January 12, 1881 by Rev. L. H. Shuck at 27 Church Street. He a native of Germany and a tobacconist. She a native of Charleston.

HASSETT, JOHN J. aged 22 years married to DODD, CECELIA aged 20 years May 2, 1887 by Father F. J. Shadler at St. Joseph's Roman Catholic Church. Both natives of Charleston. He a laborer.

HASSETT, NELLIE aged 22 years married to QUINN, PATRICK aged 33 years October 17, 1888 by Father F. J. Shadler at St. Joseph's Roman Catholic Church.

HASSON, CECIL CALVERT aged 40 years married to CLAFFY, MARY JANE aged 25 years December 25, 1887 by Rev. P. J. Wilson at St. Patrick's Roman Catholic Church.

HASTEDT, HERMAN H. aged 60 years married to MEYER, ANNA ROSALINA aged 22 years May 26, 1881 by Rev. Louis Muller in Rutledge Avenue, on the west side, near Spring Street. Both natives of Hanover.

HASTINGS, HUGH aged 26 years married to FINLEY, (Mrs) LILLIE R. DOCK aged 32 years April 5, 1883 by Rev. Charles S. Vedder. He a native of Albany, New York and she of Harrisburg, Pennsylvania. He a journalist.

HATCH, MELVIN SPOFFORD aged 24 years married to HAMMETT, LIZZIE SINGLETON aged 21 year July 19, 1888 by Rev. G. R. Brackett. He a native of Florence, South Carolina and she of Charleston. He raises stock in Asheville, North Carolina.

HATCH, MELVIN S. aged 40 years married to ARCHER, MARY E. aged 35 years July 28, 1881 by Rev. John Johnson in Judith Street. Both natives of Charleston. He a farmer.

HATCHELL, WILLIAM H. aged 20 years married to HOFFMANN, ANNA aged 21 years May 25, 1892 by Rev. William A. Rogers at 94 Wentworth Street.

HANDKERVEN (?), JOHN aged 28 years married to GRATZICK, FRANCES aged 31 years August 6, 1894 by Father J. J. Monaghan at St. Patrick's Roman Catholic Church. Both natives of Poland. He a clerk.

HAUSE, KATHERINE M. aged 19 years married to RIPLEY, CHARLES S. aged 28 years April 15, 1886 by Rev. G. R. Brackett. Both natives of New York. He a mariner.

HAWTHORNE, BENJAMIN M. aged 28 years married to BOYLE, ETTA L. aged 24 years November 13, 1893 by Rev. G. R. Brackett at 494 Meeting Street.

HAYDEN, JOHN F. aged 31 years married to DILLON, M. C. aged 30 years May 28, 1882 by Rev. P. L. Duffy at The Cathedral of St. John the Baptist. She a native of Charleston. He a tinner in Virginia.

HAYDEN, JULIA H. aged 30 years married to REESE, CHARLES M. aged 31 years February 14, 1893 by Rev. John Johnson. He a native of Statesboro, Georgia and she of Charleston. He a physician.

HAYES, NELLIE F. aged 21 years married to MURPHY, JOHN aged 24 years April 8, 1885 by Father F. J. Shadler at St. Joseph's Roman Catholic Church. He a native of Ireland and she of Charleston. He an employee of the gas works.

HAYNES, OGDEN VINCENT aged 23 years married to ALDRET, MARY CAROLINE aged 23 years December 6, 1883 by Rev. G. R. Brackett. He a native of Fairbluff, South Carolina and she of Charleston. He a clerk in Whiteville, North Carolina.

HAYS, ANNA JULIA aged 23 years married to EVANS, JOHN WILLIAM aged 25 years September 23, 1883 by Rev. E. J. Meynardie at 156 Wentworth Street. He a native of Pendleton, South Carolina and she of Charleston. He a collector.

HAZEL, HARRY Z. aged 25 years married to SCHACHTE, MAMIE aged 25 years February 22, 1893 by Rev. Charles S. Vedder at 149 King Street.

HAZELHURST, LOIS aged 17 years married to MIDDLETON, CHARLES F. aged 24 years August 4, 1884 by Rev. John Johnson at Sullivans Island, South Carolina. Both natives of Charleston. He a merchant.

HEACOX (?), EFFIE HUBBARD aged 35 years married to SEARLE, REGINALD F. aged 32 years by Rev. H. B. Browne at 78 Drake Street. He a native of Burke County, Georgia and she of Charleston. He a carpenter.

HEATH, CHARLIE aged 26 years married to CONNOR, JESSIE aged 18 years July 22, 1888 by Rev. T. P. Burgess at 47 Line Street. He a native of Millidgeville, Georgia and she of Charleston. He works for the railroad.

HECKEL, JOHANNES aged 43 years married to SCHARDT, (Mrs.) WILHELMINA ECKART aged 34 years April 30, 1878 by Rev. W. S. Bowman at the residence of J. C. H. Campsen. He a native of Bavaria and she of Germany.

HECKEL, PAUL G. aged 25 years married to REICH, MARIE L. aged 22 years August 8, 1892 by Rev. K. Boldt at 319 King Street. He a native of Illinois and she of Charleston. He a clergyman in Texas.

HEDERICH, GUSTAV FRANTZ aged 43 years married to MULLER, LOUISE C. F. aged 34 years October 25, 1881 by Rev. Louis Muller at the corner of King and Cannon Streets. He a native of Saxony and she of Prussia. He a druggist.

HEDLEY, EVELINE F. aged 20 years married to LOGAN, ALEXANDER R. aged 25 years March 31, 1884 by Rev. J. V. Welsh at 24 Bee Street. He a native of Scotland and she of Charleston. He a spinner in the cotton mill.

HEFFRON, JAMES aged 37 years married to TURNER, ALICE L. aged 34 years February 21, 1891 by Father F. J. Shadler. Both natives of Charleston. He a blacksmith.

HEFFRON, JOHN aged 25 years married to DELANEY, JULIA aged 17 years July 8, 1888 by Father F. J. Shadler at St. Joseph's Roman Catholic Church. Both natives of Charleston. He an agent.

HEGER, E. C. aged 19 years married to WIESER, J. H. aged 25 years October 14, 1879 by Rev. Louis Muller at 180 Coming Street. He a native of Austria and she of Charleston. He a photographer.

HEIDENREICH, (Mrs.) EMILIA DISHENDORG aged 45 years married to JACOBS, WILLIAM aged 54 years March 8, 1885 by Rev. Luther K. Probst at the Wentworth Street Lutheran Church. Both natives of Germany. He a sadler.

HEIDEWICH (?), BERNARD aged 26 years married to SONTAG, THERESA A. aged 20 years January 10, 1886 by Rev. Luther K. Probst. Both natives of Charleston. He a merchant.

HEIDT, BEAUREGARD C. aged 30 years married to BISCHOFF, CATHERINE M. aged 21 years October 4, 1891 by Rev. Edward T. Horn. She a native of Charleston. He an engineer.

HEIDT, E. V. aged 31 years married to CANNON, HENRIETTA aged 24 years May 11, 1891 by Rev. Robert Wilson at 4 Wragg Square.

HEIDT, GEORGE FRANCIS R. aged 22 years married to HEINS, JENNIE GERTRUDE aged 21 years October 16, 1889 by Rev. R. C. Holland at the residence of John Heins - 377 King Street. Both natives of Charleston. He an engineer.

HEIDT, WILLIAM JOSEPH aged 32 years married to HUTCHMACHER, CHRISTINE MAGDALENA aged 24 years January 19, 1881 by Rev. Claudian B. Northrop at St. Mary of the Annunciation Roman Catholic Church. He a native of Charleston and she of New Orleans, Louisiana. He a merchant.

HEILER, W. aged 28 years married to DeLAWRENCIA, DOMINICK aged 26 years July 10, 1880 by Rev. J. V. Welch in Line Street. He a native of Naples, Italy and she of Charleston. He a fisherman.

HEINRICH, A. M. M. aged 24 years married to FENKEN, H. W. aged 50 years December 31, 1882 by Rev. Louis Muller at 66 Radcliffe Street. He a native of Charleston and a restaurant worker.

HEINS, CARSTEN HEINRICH aged 26 years married to STURCKEN, HENRIETTA E. aged 18 years February 21, 1878 by Rev. Louis Muller at the corner of Meeting and Mary Streets. Both natives of Charleston. He a grocer.

HEINS, C. H. G. aged 23 years married to SCHARF, F. W. aged 23 years November 24, 1882 by Rev. Louis Muller at 169 Coming Street. He a native of Charleston and a mechanic.

HEINS, IDA B. aged 18 years married to KROEF, ANDREW A. aged 22 years December 7, 1880 by Rev. Luther K. Probst at 433 King Street. He a native of Charleston and a druggist.

HEINS, JOHN HENRY aged 33 years married to MAHONEY, MARGARET aged 28 years February 25, 1891 by Rev. Edward T. Horn. Both natives of Charleston. He a merchant.

HEINS, (Mrs.) LAURETTA BIRCH aged 25 years married to PRESCOTT, WILLIAM T. aged 28 years August 18, 1886 by Rev. J. Walter Dickson at 93 Queen Street. He a native of Charleston and she of Richmond, Virginia. He a plumber.

HEINS, JENNIE GERTRUDE aged 21 years married to HEIDT, GEORGE FRANCIS R. aged 22 years October 16, 1889 by Rev. R. C. Holland at the residence of John Heins - 377 King Street. Both natives of Charleston. He an engineer.

HEINSOHN, EGGERT aged 30 years married to MEYER, ANNA MARGARETHE aged 20 years April 15, 1886 by Rev. Louis Muller at the northwest corner and Church Street and Lightwood Alley. He a native of Germany and she of Charleston. He a grocer.

HEINSOHN, FRANTZ aged 22 years married to SAUER, JOHANNA LISETTE aged 20 years June 5, 1888 by Rev. Louis Muller at the residence of the Bride's father - east side of St. Philip Street.

HEINSOHN, JOHAN H. aged 24 years married to SAUER, EMMA MARY aged 19 years March 24, 1886 by Rev. Louis Muller at 64 St. Philip Street. He a native of Germany and she of Charleston. He a grocer.

HEINZ, FREDERICKE ELIZABETH HENRIETTA aged 20 years married to PAULS, CHARLES HENRY aged 24 years November 2, 1881 by Rev. Johannes Heckel at St. Johannes Lutheran Church. Both natives of Charleston. He a merchant.

HEINZ, J. E. H. aged 23 years married to MULLER, W. H. aged 23 years February 21, 1882 by Rev. Johannes Heckel in Rutledge Avenue. He a native of Germany and she of Charleston. He a grocer.

HEISSENBUTTEL, ANNA aged 22 years married to JACKSON, ALBERT aged 19 years November 24, 1884 by Rev. John E. Beard at 64 Nassau Street. He a native of South Carolina and she of Charleston. He a mechanic.

HEISSENBUTTEL, CATHERINE aged 49 years married to ALBERS, FREDERICK aged 61 years January 16, 1878 by Rev. W. S. Bowman at 26 Woolfe Street. He a laborer.

HEISSENBUTTEL, FREDRICH H. aged 21 years married to RATIGAN, MARY aged 20 years February 13, 1889 by Father P. L. Duffy at The Cathedral of St. John the Baptist.

HEISSENBUTTEL, MARTIN F. married to AUSTIN, MARY ELIZABETH April 25, 1889 by Rev. Richard S. Trapier in Church Street.

HEISENBUTTEL, R. C. aged 18 years married to RISTIG, A. W. aged 25 years December 21, 1879 by Rev. W. S. Bowman at 14 Bee Street. He a native of Germany and she of Charleston. He a grocer.

HEITERER, DANIEL aged 30 years married to LYONS, SARAH aged 25 years January 6, 1884 by Father F. A. Schmetz at St. Patrick's Roman Catholic Church. He a native of Germany and she of Charleston. He a miller.

HEITMAN, FREDRICH aged 24 years married to SEEL, LILLIE H. aged 17 years July 17, 1895 by Rev. Edward T. Horn at 587 King Street. Both natives of Charleston. He an engineer.

HELANDER, JOHN A. aged 32 years married to KRANTZ, AUGUSTA C. GROVER aged 29 years August 21, 1892 by Rev. Edward T. Horn at 31 Pitt Street.

HELEKIN, J. H. aged 21 years married to KUCK, A. F. aged 18 years January 16, 1882 by Rev. L. H. Shuck at 27 Church Street. Both natives of Savannah, Georgia. He a grocer.

HELLER, GUSTAV H. aged 32 years married to STURKIE, ROSE aged 1 5 years January 17, 1887 by Rev. Johannes Heckel at 524 King Street. He native of Germany and she of South Carolina. He a carpenter.

HELMEKEN, KATRINE married to MUSEGADES (?), JOHN HENRY aged 31 years January 2, 1889 by Rev. Charles S. Vedder. Both natives of Germany. He a master mariner.

HELMEY, EMMA aged 18 years married to BECK, JOHN aged 22 years January 3, 1886 by Rev. H. B. Browne at 3 Lee Street. Both natives of Savannah, Georgia. He works for the railroad.

HEMMERMAN, C. aged 22 years married to WALTER, M. aged 27 years April 16, 1882 by Rev. Louis Muller in King Street.

HEMMINGWAY, ARTHUR married to SPELL, ELLA January 20, 1891 by Rev. W. A. Betts.

HEMMINGWAY, ELIZA M. SEIGNIOUS aged 35 years married to PROCTOR, SAMUEL aged 35 years April 11, 1878 by Rev. J. T. Wightman at the residence of the Bride's father - in Cannon Street. Both natives of Charleston. He a bookkeeper.

HENDERSON, WILLIAM R. aged 27 years married to LUCAS, JULIA ELIZA aged 20 years November 1, 1883 by Rev. Edward T. Horn at 6 Bull Street. Both natives of Charleston. He a clerk.

HENDRICKS, CECILIA OCTAVIA married to MAN, JOHN C. October 18, 1881 by Rev. William H. Campbell.

HENDRICKS, EDGAR LEE aged 24 years married to VENNING, LILLIE BELLE aged 24 years January 9, 1884 by Rev. G. R. Brackett. He a native of Fayetteville, South Carolina and she of South Carolina. He a clerk.

HENDRICKS, FRANKIE V. married to HONOR, ARTHUR January 15, 1891 by Rev. William H. Campbell. He a clerk in Savannah, Georgia.

HENDRICKS, FRANKLIN M. aged 28 years married to AMAN, IDA VICTORIA aged 18 years September 2, 1881 by Rev. A. H. Misseldine at the corner of Rutledge Avenue and Cannon Streets. He a native of Charleston and a clerk.

HENDRICKS, GERALDINE aged 18 years married to MAULL, JAMES D. aged 30 years June 10, 1881 by Rev. J. V. Welch at the residence of the Bride's father. He a native of Charleston and a moulder.

HENDRICKS, JULIUS D. aged 22 years married to MATTHEWS, LULA aged 20 years April 16, 1889 by Rev. H. B. Browne at 21 Blake Street. He a native of Charleston and she of Williamsburg County, South Carolina. He an engineer.

HENDRICKS, MAGGIE A. CASSIDY aged 26 years married to TOLLISON, MARTIN aged 33 years March 29, 1892 by Rev. E. C. Chichester at 120 King Street.

HENDRICKS, MARY E. aged 17 years married to BROCK, JAMES W. aged 24 years March 24, 1886 by Rev. H. B. Browne at 104 Nassau Street. He a native of North Carolina and she of Charleston. He a mechanic.

HENDRICKS, RICHARD F. aged 58 years married to DeVILDRE, JANE CAMERON aged 40 years December 9, 1883 by Rev. J. H. Tellinghast. He a native of Charleston and she of Glasgow, Scotland. He a clerk.

HENDRICKS, SALLIE E. married to HAMLIN, WARREN D. April 29, 1891 by Rev. William H. Campbell. He resides in Mt. Pleasant, South Carolina.

HENDRICKSEN, MARY married to RYAN, MICHAEL B. April 7, 1880 by Rev. J. E. Jackson at St. Luke's Church. Both natives of Charleston. He a clerk at the Alms House.

HENDRICKSON, MARY married to RYAN, MICHEL BERRY April 7, 1880 by Rev. J. E. Jackson at the Alms House. Both natives of Charleston. He a clerk at the Alms House.

HENDRIX, ALICE M. aged 23 years married to LIVINGSTON, BENJAMIN aged 28 years December 25, 1895 by Rev. T. E. Morris at 231 Coming Street.

HENDRIX, ANNIE LOUISA aged 18 years married to CLEAPOR, WALTER G. aged 21 years April 7, 1891 by Rev. W. A. Betts at 82 Bay Street.

HENDRIX, CHARLES H. aged 22 years married to PIERCE, (Mrs.) ELIZABETH M. JOHNSON aged 28 years October 16, 1889 by Rev. J. C. Carlisle at the Spring Street Church. He a native of Georgia and she of Charleston. He a mechanic.

HENKEN, ANNA CATHERINE aged 28 years married to DIETZ, EDWARD F. aged 28 years November 25, 1886 by Rev. Louis Muller at the corner of Meeting and Jackson Streets. He a native of Georgia and she of South Carolina. He a saloonkeeper.

HENKIN, HENRY aged 28 years married to KOHLER, HENRIETTA aged 21 years March 6, 1881 by Rev. Johannes Heckel at 125 Calhoun Street. Both natives of Hanover. He a merchant.

HENNE, MAGGIE aged 16 years married to WILSON, JOHN J. aged 21 years April 9, 1890 by Rev. Edwin C. Dargan at the Citadel Square Baptist Church. Both natives of Charleston. He a laborer.

HENNEBERRY, PETER J. aged 29 years married to RYAN, MARGARET aged 26 years January 12, 1890 by Father Daniel J. Quigley at St. Patrick's Roman Catholic Church. Both natives of Charleston. He works for the railroad.

HENNEBERRY, JOHN J. aged 28 years married to CASEN, JOSEPHINE JOHANNA aged 22 years September 15, 1886 by Father Daniel J. Quigley at St. Patrick's Roman Catholic Church. Both natives of Charleston. He a butcher.

HENNESSY, JOHANNA aged 25 years married to MAGRATH, JOHN E. aged 24 years June 5, 1883 by Father J. J. Woolahan at St. Mary of the Annunciation Roman Catholic Church. He a native of Anderson, South Carolina and she of Charleston. He a merchant.

HENNESSY, THOMAS J. aged 26 years married to MORRIS, MARY A. aged 25 years August 11, 1893 by Father J. J. Monaghan at St. Patrick's Roman Catholic Church. Both natives of Charleston. He a bookkeeper.

HENRICKS, F. W. married to CASSIDY, M. A. April 14, 1879 by William B. Yates, Chaplain.

HENRICKS, JOHANN CHRISTOPHER aged 42 years married to WEDEMEYER, ANNA LOUISE aged 30 years May 12, 1889 by Rev. Louis Muller at the residence of the Groom - East Bay Street near Tradd Street.

HENRICKSEN, (Mrs.) BRIDGET JEREKING aged 28 years married to TANDER, HEINRICH aged 28 years December 16, 1885 by Rev. Edward T. Horn in State Street. He a native of Norway and she of Wales. He a ship builder.

HENRICKSEN, N, A, aged 25 years married to HOGAN, HONORA A. aged 22 years November 25, 1884 by Father F. A. Schmetz at St. Patrick's Roman Catholic Church. He a native of Denmark and she of Charleston. He a carpenter.

HENNS, W. MAGGIE aged 16 years married to WILLIS, J. JOHN aged 21 years April 9, 1890 by Rev. Edwin C. Dargan at Citadel Square Baptist Church.

HENRY, DORA aged 27 years married to DANEGHY (?), PATRICK J. aged 23 years November 24, 1888 by Rev. J. J. Monaghan at St. Patrick's Roman Catholic Church. Both natives of Charleston. He a railroad brakeman.

HERBERST, JAMES C. married to TUCKER, THEODORA June 17, 1879 by William B. Yates, Chaplain.

HERBERT, C. D. married to BRANCH, E. A. October 8, 1879 by William B. Yates, Chaplain.

HERBERT, JAMES aged 21 years married to BUNCH, CAROLINE C. aged 23 years February 22, 1885 by Rev. John O. Wilson. 2 Dothage Court. Both natives of Charleston. He a clerk.

HERBERT, VIRGINIA S. aged 17 years married to COLE, RICHARD B. aged 26 years July 3, 1885 by Rev. John O. Wilson at the corner of East Bay and Laurens Streets. He a native of Florida and she of Charleston. He a driver.

HERIOT, BENJAMIN GEORGE aged 35 years married to DOWELL, JOSEPHINE aged 25 years July 14, 1890 by Father Harry P. Northrop.

HERIOT, JULIAN W. aged 27 years married to SIMMONS, ELIZA aged 17 years June 11, 1889 by Rev. C. C. Pinckney at 344 East Bays Street. He a native of Richland County, South Carolina and she of Colleton County, South Carolina. He a clerk.

HERMON, MARY CATHARINE aged 22 years married to DOWLING, THOMAS J. aged 24 years December 8, 1889 by Father Daniel J. Quigley at St. Patrick's Roman Catholic Church. He a native of Charleston and she of Germany. He an engineer.

HERNHOLM, CATHERINE DORA aged 22 years married to WILSON, ARTHUR EDWIN aged 26 years February 6, 1881 by Rev. Louis Muller at the northeast corner of Spring and Norman Streets. He a native of Charleston and a cabinetmaker.

HERNANDEZ, ARTHUR W. aged 25 years married to DUNLAP, LILLIAN LAURA aged 22 years September 11, 1883 by Rev. E. J. Meynardie at 6 Percy Street. Both natives of Charleston. He a druggist.

HERNANDEZ, D. L. married to JORDAN, R. T. June 8, 1882 by Rev. B. J. Simons at 81 Cannon Street. He a native of Charleston and a railroad conductor.

HERNANDEZ, VIOLA aged 21 years married to WELBORN, H. EBIE aged 23 years April 24, 1890 by Rev. E. S. Dargan at 33 Nassau Street. He a native of Williamston, South Carolina and she of Charleston. He a farmer.

HERNDEN, ARTHUR aged 30 years married to EMANUEL, MARY M. aged 19 years July 11, 1887 by Rev. J. V. Welsh at 40 Bee Street. Both natives of Charleston. He a druggist.

HERON, AMANDA aged 20 years married to COSTE, CHARLES aged 24 years June 1, 1892 by Rev. Robert Wilson at 195 Smith Street.

HERON, WILLIAM I. aged 22 years married to COATES, MARY G. aged 18 years June 24, 1890 by Rev. Robert Wilson at St. Luke's Chapel. Both natives of Charleston. He a clerk.

HERREN, CECIL S. aged 20 years married to ROGERS, LUCIA A. aged 20 years September 7, 1885 by Rev. John O. Wilson.

HERREN, HARRIET A. aged 25 years married to SCARBOROUGH, HENRY aged 53 years January 11, 1887 by Rev. Leroy F. Beattie. He a native of South Carolina and she of Charleston. He a planter.

HERREN, (Mrs.) MARGARET E. WITHERS aged 44 years married to CHAPLIN, BENJAMIN aged 58 years by Rev. Leroy F. Beattie at 231 Coming Street. Both natives of South Carolina. He a machinist.

HERREN, SAMUEL J. aged 32 years married to VERONEE, KATE C. aged 24 years May 10, 1888 by Rev. J. E. Carlisle at the Spring Street Church. He a native of Lancaster County, South Carolina and she of Charleston. He works for the railroad in Marion, South Carolina.

HERRON, J. C. married to ABRAMS, J. P. August 21, 1882 by Rev. D. J. Simons. He a native of Charleston and a laborer.

HERTZ, MARY MARTHA aged 19 years married to GAMBATTI, OLYMPIE FELIX aged 22 years November 29, 1877 by Father Harry P. Northrop at the residence of the Groom's mother - 667 King Street. He a native of Charleston and she of Palatka, Florida.

HESLIN, WILLIAM F. aged 28 years married to WALSH, MARGARET M. aged 28 years July 29, 1891 by Father J. J. Monaghan at St. Patrick's Roman Catholic Church. He a native of Brooklyn, New York and she of Charleston.

HESS, PAUL GOTTFRIED aged 29 years married to OLDENBURG, MARIA MAGDALENA aged 23 years May 15, 1881 by Rev. Louis Muller.

HESS, WILHELMINA G. aged 20 years married to CASSIRER, JOHN HENRY THEODORE aged 25 years May 6, 1888 by Rev. Johannes Heckel at 123 Smith Street. He a native of Germany and she of Charleston. He a bookkeeper.

HESSE, C. H. married to JACOBSEN, J. September 1, 1879 by Rev. L. Heckel. He a native of Walhalla, South Carolina and she of Charleston. He a merchant.

HESSEMAN, JOHN H. aged 24 years married to BISCHOFF, A. M. S. aged 24 years June 16, 1887 by Rev. Johannes Heckel at the corner of Ann and Meeting Streets. Both natives of Charleston. He a merchant.

HESSENKAMP, WILLIAM aged 28 years married to MOMIER, LOUISE C. aged 33 years March 1, 1885 by Rev. Luther K. Probst. He a native of Germany and she of New York. He a merchant.

HESTER, ELIZABETH P. aged 20 years married to HALL, JOHN W. aged 28 years April 8, 1891 by Rev. W. A. Betts at 83 America Street. He a native of Georgia and she of Greene County, Georgia. He works in the cotton mill.

HESTON, MARTHA J. aged 36 years married to ANDERSON, DAVE H. aged 31 years November 24, 1884 by Rev. J. V. Welsh at 24 Bee Street. He a native of Charleston and she of South Carolina. He a tinner.

HEUER, ELISE A. aged 20 years married to VON GLAHN, HEINRICH aged 22 years April 12, 1888 by Rev. Louis Muller.

HEUER, MARIE O. E. aged 19 years married to FRIEND, JAMES W. aged 25 years September 21, 1890 by Rev. John Johnson at 2 Chestnut Street. Both natives of Charleston. He a machinist in Florence, South Carolina.

HEUSEN, HENRY F. aged 24 years married to SERES, (Mrs.) EMMA R. DIERS aged 24 years May 25, 1887 by Rev. Luther K. Probst at the Wentworth Street Lutheran Church. He a native of Germany and she of Charleston. He a laborer.

HEWETSON, NORA JANE aged 20 years married to McCALL, THOMAS HARLEY aged 27 years November 1, 1881 by Rev. A. Coke Smith at 14 Bull Street. He native of Florence, South Carolina and she of Bombay, India. He a planter.

HEYOTT, ANNIE J. aged 22 years married to TIMMONS, M. O. aged 29 years November 25, 1886 by Rev. H. B. Browne. Both natives of Charleston. He works in a factory.

HEYWARD, CAROLINE S. aged 27 years married to FURMAN, BOLIVAR B. aged 26 years November 27, 1877 by Rev. John Johnson at 6 Legare Street.

HEYWARD, EDWIN W. aged 21 years married to DuBOSE, JANE SCREVEN aged 19 years November 13, 1884 by Rev. John Johnson in Wall Street. He a native of Grahamville, South Carolina and she of St. John's, Berkeley County, South Carolina. He a clerk.

HEYWARD, GEORGIANA aged 22 years married to ROSE, WILLIAM H. aged 24 years October 20, 1892 by Rev. C. C. Pinckney at 99 Meeting Street. Both natives of Charleston. He works in the phosphate mill.

HEYWARD, JOHN BOYKIN married to PYATT, MARTHA HAYES April 15, 1886 by Rev. William H. Campbell. at St. Paul's Church.

HEYWARD, MARION married to CHISOLM, LOUISA ISABEL February 4, 1880 by Rev. Richard S. Trapier.

HEYWARD, SUSAN K. aged 25 years married to GIBBS, W. HAMPTON aged 26 years November 30, 1887 by Rev. John Johnson at 10 Legare Street. Both natives of Columbia, South Carolina. He a merchant in Columbia.

HEYWARD, WILLIAM M. married to WRAGG, MARY July 12, 1892 by Rev. William H. Campbell at Grace Church.

HEYWARD, WILLIAM NICHOLAS aged 34 years married to PIPKINS, ELIZABETH G. aged 23 years May 10, 1887 by Rev. C. E. Chichester, at 233 East Bay Street. He a native of Bermuda and she of South Carolina. He a mariner.

HEYWOOD, GERTRUDE married to TRAPIER, SHUBRICK September 4, 1879 by Rev. Richard S. Trapier at St. Michael's Church.

HEYWOOD, JAMES T. aged 39 years married to LUDWICK, MAMIE aged 22 years October 30, 1892 by Rev. C. E. Chichester at the Mariners Church. He a native of Charleston and she of New Jersey. He a baker.

HICKMAN, JOHN H. aged 28 years married to GAYNOR, (Mrs.) SARAH STUART aged 26 years May 14, 1889 by Father John J. Wedenfeller at 114 Tradd Street. He a painter.

HICKS, MARGARET MATILDA aged 25 years married to WINGARD, CHARLES N. aged 24 years September 23, 1883 by Rev. John E. Beard at 2 Cooper Street. He a native of Lexington, South Carolina and she of Sumter, South Carolina.

HIGGINS, ELIZABETH aged 25 years married to TEMPLE, CHARLES aged 36 years April 12, 1879 by Father John J. Wedenfeller at The Cathedral of St. John the Baptist.

HILBER, THEODORE CARL married to GRISSELL, FLORENCE ANNA June 24, 1884 by Rev. C. E. Chichester at the Mariners Church. She a native of Charleston. He a mariner.

HILDERBRANDT, JACOB aged 45 years married to PUCKHABER, LUCIE aged 36 years June 19, 1884 by Rev. Louis Muller. Both natives of Germany. He a grocer in Jacksonville, Florida.

HILKEN, ANNA GESCHE aged 23 years married to BECKROGE, JOHANN HEINRICH aged 24 years January 12, 1888 by Rev. Louis Muller in King Street, opposite Marion Square.

HILL, DRURY F. aged 22 years married to MARION, HANNAH B. aged 19 years June 9, 1889 by Father John J. Wedenfeller. He a stonecutter.

HILL, ELLA E. aged 22 years married to NEVILLE, THOMAS J. aged 26 years September 2, 1884 by Rev. Charles A. Stakely. He a native of Charleston and she of Augusta, Georgia. He a printer.

HILL, HERMAN aged 39 years married to WALSH, (Mrs.) ANNIE CATHARINE MAUDE JONES aged 35 years February 5, 1888 by Rev. H. B. Browne at 78 Drake Street. He a native of Darmstadt, Germany and she of Sumter County, South Carolina. He a stiller in Jacksonville, Florida.

HILL, JAMES THOMAS aged 21 years married to LABERGNE (?), MARY A. aged 20 years February 12, 1888 by Rev. J. J. McManus. He a native of Columbia, South Carolina and she of Charleston. He a granite cutter.

HILL, WILLIAM aged 42 years married to WEBB, MARY W. aged 44 years March 1, 1888 by Rev. E. C. L. Browne. He a native of James Island, South Carolina and she of Charleston. He a clerk.

HILL, W. C. married to MORGAN, A. December 24, 1879 by William B. Yates, Chaplain.

HILLS, ROSA L. A. aged 17 years married to GLOVER, LOUIS W. aged 20 years March 20, 1892 by Rev. N. K. Smith at 25 Charlotte Street. He a native of Johns Island, South Carolina and she of James Island, South Carolina. He a planter in Stono, South Carolina.

HILLS, WILLIAM S. aged 45 years married to BOYLE, SALLIE M. LEGARE aged 43 years November 2, 1888 by Rev. Hugh R. Muchuson.

HILSON, ARTHUR E. aged 26 years married to HERNHOLM, CATHARINE DORA aged 22 years February 6, 1881 by Rev. Louis Muller at St. Matthew's Lutheran Church. He a native of Charleston and a cabinetmaker.

HILSON, P. J. aged 18 years married to ROUNILLAT, L. J. aged 19 years March 17, 1881 by Father F. J. Shadler at St. Joseph's Roman Catholic Church. He a native of Charleston and a grocer.

HILTON, JESSE W. aged 32 years married to MUCKENFUSS, EMILY A. aged 24 years March 6, 1889 by Rev. H. B. Browne at 60 Tradd Street. He a native of Berkeley County, South Carolina and she of Charleston. He a turner.

HILTON, WASHINGTON J. aged 25 years married to FULBIER, MAMIE H. aged 25 years September 17, 1885 by Rev. John E. Beard at 20 Columbus Street. He a native of South Carolina and she of Charleston.

HINDLEY, WILLIAM E. aged 27 years married to MYERS, CHARLOTTE aged 18 years December 18, 1893 by Rev. J. C. Yongue. He a native of Savannah, Georgia and she of Charleston. He a clerk in Savannah.

HINE, LAURETTA J. aged 24 years married to PRESCOTT, WILLIAM T. aged 33 years May 26, 1892 by Rev. G. R. Brackett at 64 Rutledge Avenue.

HIOTT, H. SAMUEL aged 50 years married to GEHRELS, THEODORA MARY aged 19 years April 29, 1890 by Rev. Edwin S. Dargan at 269 King Street. He a native of North Carolina and she of Orangeburg, South Carolina.

HIRSCH, ANNA CAROLINE REBECCA aged 23 years married to NEWMAN, JOHN NICHOLAS aged 31 years May 1, 1879 by Rev. William S. Bowman at 1 Shepherd Street. Both natives of Charleston. He a driver.

HOATS, MARY ELLIS aged 26 years married to LOWRY, CAPERS DURANT aged 25 years February 11, 1886 by Rev. H. B. Browne at 178 Coming Street. Both natives of South Carolina. He works for the railroad.

160

HOCKADAY, JOHN B. married to RHOADES, JENNIE M. February 2, 1885 by Rev. William H. Campbell. He a clerk.

HODGE, ERNEST aged 21 years married to TISDEL, EMMA aged 21 years May 3, 1892 by Rev. A. F. Chreitzberg.

HODGE, SALLIE FERGUSON aged 16 years married to ROBINSON, WILLIAM T. aged 19 years December 14, 1886 by Rev. J. Walter Dickson at 475 Meeting Street. Both natives of South Carolina. He a mechanic.

HODGES, CORENE aged 18 years married to DOTY, JOHN M. aged 25 years May 25, 1885 by Rev. Herbert Jones at 189 Coming Street. He a native of Charleston and a car driver.

HODGES, ERNEST aged 21 years married to WATTS, KATIE aged 20 years January 5, 1891 by Rev. J. Thomas Pate. He a native of Charleston and she of Georgia. He a barrelmaker.

HODGES, JOHN T. aged 20 years married to WALKER, ANNA E. aged 17 years February 11, 1878 by Rev. J. V. Welsh at the residence of Mr. and Mrs. William. Both natives of Charleston. He a barber.

HODGES, J. S. aged 30 years married to MITCHELL, M. E. aged 26 years October 12, 1882 by Rev. E. J. Meynardie at 190 King Street. He a native of South Carolina.

HODGES, LOUISE aged 26 years married to PUGH, G. D. aged 31 years October 10, 1893 by Rev. David M. Ramsey at the Osceola Hotel.

HODGES, WILLIAM PARKER aged 27 years married to HARMON, (Mrs.) MARGARETHA B. aged 30 years July 4, 1889 by Father J. J. Monaghan at St. Patrick's Roman Catholic Church. Both natives of Charleston. He a barber.

HOFF, SELENA O. E. aged 24 years married to GATCH, CHARLES B. aged 23 years January 4, 1884 by Rev. Charles A. Stakely at 8 Bay Street. Both natives of South Carolina. He a farmer.

HOFFMANN, ANNA aged 21 years married to HATCHELL, WILLIAM H. aged 20 years May 25, 1892 by Rev. William A. Rogers at 94 Wentworth Street.

HOFFMAN, ISABEL aged 26 years married to LEVINSOHN, RUDOLPH aged 30 years June 21, 1893 by Rabbi David Levy. Both natives of Charleston. He a merchant in Mobile, Alabama.

HOFFMAN, JOHANNA aged 24 years married to JACOBSON, JULIUS aged 24 years January 16, 1884 by Rabbi David Levy at 210 King Street. He a native of Germany and she of Charleston. He a merchant.

HOFSTETTER, OTTILE ANGELICA CAROLINE aged 22 years married to WOHLTMANN, JOHN aged 22 years May 13, 1886 by Rev. Luther K. Probst. He a native of South Carolina and she of Charleston. He a merchant.

HOGAN, BRIDGET E. aged 24 years married to LLOYD, EDWARD A. aged 35 years July 30, 1891 by Father J. J. Monaghan at St. Patrick's Roman Catholic Church. He a native of New York City and she of Charleston. He a laborer.

HOGAN, HONORA A. aged 22 years married to HENRICKSON, M. A. aged 25 years November 25, 1884 by Father F. A. Schmetz at St. Patrick's Roman Catholic Church. He a native of Denmark and she of Charleston. He a carpenter.

HOGAN, JAMES aged 23 years married to WALSH, MARY J. aged 20 years February 12, 1885 by Father F. J. Shadler at St. Joseph's Roman Catholic Church.

HOGAN, JOHN FRANCIS aged 31 years married to MANNION, ELLEN CATHERINE aged 25 years January 1, 1891 by Father J. J. Monaghan at St. Patrick's Roman Catholic Church. Both natives of Charleston. He a painter.

HOGAN, KATIE E. aged 21 years married to FITZGERALD, JOHN aged 22 years August 3, 1890 by Father J. J. Monaghan at St. Patrick's Roman Catholic Church. Both natives of Charleston. He a stonecutter.

HOGAN, MARY BARRETT aged 22 years married to LINN, HUGH CAMPBELL aged 34 years April 25, 1886 by Rev. J. Walter Dickson at 231 Coming Street. He a native of Charleston and she of Ireland. He a mechanist.

HOGARTH, EDWARD HENRY aged 33 years married to JACKSON, ANNIE VICTORIA aged 24 years April 3, 1884 by Rev. W. P. Mouzon at 7 Blake Street. Both natives of Charleston. He a stenographer.

HOGARTH, FRANCES V. aged 40 years married to WATSON, THOMAS aged 42 years June 15, 1886 by Rev. John Johnson at St. Philip's Church. Both natives of Charleston. He a machinist.

HOGG, JACOB J. aged 21 years married to CRADDOCK, LIZZIE M. aged 22 years October 29, 1886 by Rev. J. Walter Dickson at the Spring Street Church. Both natives of South Carolina. He a farmer of Barnwell County, South Carolina.

HOHLMAN, W. H. aged 21 years married to GODFREY, R. S. aged 22 years January 29, 1882 by Rev. Louis Muller at 343 Meeting Street. He a native of Georgia and she of South Carolina. He works for the railroad.

HOLANDER, JOHN A. aged 32 years married to KRANTZ, (Mrs.) AUGUSTA C. GRAVER aged 29 years August 21, 1892 by Rev. Edward T. Horn at 31 Pitt Street. He a native of Finland and a merchant.

HOLLAND, SELINA married to ROBERTS, OSSIAN June 10, 1891 by Rev. William H. Campbell. He a merchant in Spartanburg, South Carolina.

HOLLEMAN, ALICE aged 20 years married to THORNHILL, JAMES aged 21 years December 28, 1887 by Rev. H. B. Browne. He a native of Sumter County, South Carolina and she of Darlington County, South Carolina. He works in the cotton mill.

HOLLEMAN, EDITH aged 17 years married to GAINES, WYLIE aged 21 years December 28, 1887 by Rev. H. B. Browne. He a native of Lenoir County, North Carolina and she of Darlington County, South Carolina. He works in the cotton mill.

HOLLEMAN, FANNIE aged 27 years married to MILLARD, THOMAS aged 21 years April 20, 1893 by Rev. Thomas B. Wright

HOLLER, LOUISE aged 14 years married to SIGWALD, BOWMAN aged 23 years December 25, 1889 by Rev. R. C. Holland at 47 Nassau Street. Both natives of Charleston. He a scroll driver.

HOLLWEY, (Mrs.) CHRISTINE OTTMER aged 30 years married to LUBECHE, MAX aged 36 years January 14, 1891 by Rev. R. C. Holland at 522 Meeting Street. He a native of Germany and she of Charleston. He a merchant.

HOLLINGS, EDWARD B. aged 20 years married to O'ROURKE, ANNIE MARIA aged 20 years April 17, 1886 by Father Daniel J. Quigley at St. Patrick's Roman Catholic Church. Both natives of Charleston. He a lawyer.

HOLLINGS, JURGEN D. aged 22 years married to BECKER, ANNA META W. aged 22 years June 21, 1891 by Rev. Louis Muller. Both natives of Prussia. He a grocer.

HOLLMAN, HENRY aged 28 years married to RHODES, ROSA aged 22 years June 7, 1891 by Rev. W. A. Betts at 4 Williams Court. He a native of Sumter County, South Carolina and she of Georgetown, South Carolina. He a clerk.

HOLLMAN, HIRAM aged 26 years married to WIDNER, MINNIE aged 22 years November 16, 1891 by Rev. J. H. Smith. He a native of Darlington County, South and she of North Carolina. He a car driver.

HOLLOWAY, CHARLOTTE POOLE aged 29 years married to DOLAN, MARTIN aged 37 years November 7, 1886 by Rev. H. B. Browne at 78 Drake Street. Both natives of New Jersey. He a carpenter.

HOLMES, FELIX WARLEY aged 25 years married to BONNEAU, CATHERINE J. aged 20 years November 20, 1884 by Rev. John Johnson at South Carolina Society Hall. Both natives of Charleston.

HOLMES, MARGARET EDWARDS aged 34 years married to ADAMS, WILLIAM HOOPER aged 40 years March 20, 1878 by Rev. G. R. Brackett at 20 Charlotte Street. He a native of Boston, Massachusetts and she of Charleston. He a clergyman.

HOLMES, MARY married to MARTIN, HENRY November 22, 1888 by Rev. William H. Campbell at St. Paul's Church. He a druggist in Summerville, South Carolina.

HOLMES, WILLIAM H. aged 31 years married to VON KOLNITZ, LENORA aged 19 years April 26, 1893 by Rev. Edward T. Horn at St. Johannes Lutheran Church. Both natives of Charleston. He a farmer in Georgetown, South Carolina.

HOLMES, WILMOT G. aged 57 years married to HASELL, (Mrs.) ELISE E. EDWARDS aged 48 years August 27, 1894 by Rev. John Johnson at Grace Church. Both natives of Charleston. He a bookkeeper.

HOLSENBACH, EMILY E. aged 18 years married toFLATMANN, EDWARD S. aged 20 years September 27, 1888 by Rev. J. E. Carlisle at the Spring Street Church. He a native of Richland County, South Carolina and she of New York. He a merchant.

HOLSENBERG, CATHARINE married to FREDERICK, GRITZ aged 24 years December 18, 1889 by Rev. Johannes Heckel. He a native of Bremen, Germany and she of Hanover. He a clerk in Summerville, South Carolina.

HOLST, GEORGIA D. married to FABIAN, ANDREW F. March 16, 1879 by William B. Yates, Chaplain.

HOLST, HEINRICH aged 29 years married to DOSCHER, WILHELMINA GEHLKEN aged 39 years January 1, 1888 by Rev. Louis Muller.

HOLST, JOHN aged 33 years married to CONROy, CATHERINE aged 33 years August 18, 1887 by Father Daniel J. Quigley at St. Patrick's Roman Catholic Church. Both natives of Charleston. He a clerk.

HOLSTEIN, MARY ELLEN aged 25 years married to McDERMID, THOMAS V. aged 27 years December 12, 1892 by Rev. G. R. Brackett at 64 Rutledge Avenue. He a native of Dublin, Ireland and she of Charleston. He a mariner.

HOLSTON, MARGARET A. aged 23 years married to KNIGHT, JOSEPH JAMES aged 27 years June 27, 1883 by Father P. L. Duffy at The Cathedral of St. John the Baptist. Both natives of Charleston. He a fireman.

HOLTZ, CHARLES E. aged 20 years married to FABIAN, FRANCES E. aged 18 years June 10, 1880 by Rev. J. E. Jackson at 313 East Bay Street. He a native of New York and she of Charleston. He a locksmith.

HOLWEG, JOHAN H. W. aged 28 years married to OTTMER, CHRISTINE HENRIETTA aged 23 years March 25, 1883 by Rev. Louis Muller. He a native of Germany and she of Charleston. He a grocer.

HONKLER, JOHN married to McGUIRE, ROSA April 28, 1888 by Rev. J. H. Wheeler. He a native of Charleston and she of Ireland. He a stonecutter.

HONOR, ARTHUR M. married to HENDRICKS, FRANKIE B. January 15, 1891 by Rev. William H. Campbell. He a clerk in Savannah, Georgia.

HONOUR, A. H. aged 22 years married to JOHNSTON, E. K. aged 22 years February 14, 1882 by Rev. J. H. Honour. He a native of Charleston and a clerk.

HONOUR, J. C. aged 36 years married to ABRAMS, J. P. aged 17 years August 21, 1882 by Father Daniel J. Quigley at 42 Spring Street. Both natives of Charleston. He a laborer.

HOOD, CHARLES aged 23 years married to CURRY, SALLIE J. aged 19 years April 7, 1889 by Rev. H. B. Browne at 93 America Street. He a native of Berkeley County, South Carolina and she of Colleton County, South Carolina. He works in the cotton mill.

HOOD, ROSINA M. aged 16 years married to ESCOFFIER, E. F. aged 37 years June 3, 1880 by Rev. Claudian B. Northrop. He a native of St. Michel, France and a workman. She a native of Charleston.

HOOKEY, CHARLES J. married to MALONEY, ANNIE January 7, 1879 by Father John P. Twigg at The Cathedral of St. John the Baptist. He a native of Augusta, Georgia and she of Charleston. He a merchant.

HOOTS, SARAH aged 20 years married to THOMAS, LEWIS aged 35 years February 28, 1880 by Rev. H. F. Chreitzberg in Cannon Street. Both natives of Colleton County, South Carolina. He a laborer.

HOPPMAN, LUDWIG aged 22 years married to DICKENS, LOUIE LEE aged 17 years April 30, 1893 by Father J. J. Monaghan. He a native of Charleston and she of Sparta, Georgia. He a weaver in the cotton mill.

HOPPMAN, MARY aged 20 years married to CAUFIELD, GEORGE M. aged 31 years August 3, 1892 by Father J. J. Monaghan at St. Patrick's Roman Catholic Church.

HOPPMAN, WILLIAM aged 21 years married to RICHBURG, MARY M. aged 21 years July 10, 1887 by Father F. J. Shadler at St. Joseph's Roman Catholic Church. Both natives of Charleston. He an ironworker.

HORENKUHE (?), ANNA M. E. aged 22 years married to KUNZE, JOHN HENRY aged 22 years June 27, 1886 by Rev. Johannes Heckel at 14 Inspection Street. Both natives of Germany. He a baker.

HORLBECK, HENRIETTA PORCHER married to LUCAS, ELLIOT M. December 16, 1886 by Rev. William H. Campbell. He a machinist.

HORLBECK, IRENE aged 21 years married to HASELDEN, MORTIMER V. aged 25 years October 28, 1891 by Rev. Edward T. Horn. He a native of Marion, South Carolina and she of Charleston. He a bookkeeper.

HORLBECK (?), VIRGINIA aged 19 years married to WILKERSON, EDWARD S. aged 25 years August 12, 1888 by Rev. H. B. Browne at 73 America Street. He a native of Charleston and she of Petersburg, Virginia. He an engineer.

HORN, EDWARD TRAIL aged 30 years married to CHISOLM, HARRIET aged 18 years June 15, 1880 by Rev. W. S. Bowman at St. Johannes Lutheran Church. He a native of Eishorn, Pennsylvania and she of Charleston. He a clergyman.

HORN, JOSEPH aged 25 years married to McGEE, OCTAVIA aged 18 years August 29, 1892 by Rev. K. Boldt. He a native of Germany and she of Camden, South Carolina. He a baker.

HORNE (Mrs.) MARY BRUCE aged 38 years married to McWHIRTER, ANDREW aged 40 years July 24, 1887 by Rev. Leroy F. Beattie at 231 Coming Street. He a native of Scotland and she of Georgia. He a laborer.

HORNEY, MAUD MARY aged 20 years married to MURPHY, WALTER aged 21 years September 19, 1892 by Rev. J. L. Stokes at 231 Coming Street. He a native of Salisbury, North Carolina and she of Jamestown, North Carolina. He a journalist in Salisbury.

HORRES, C. E. aged 19 years married to CHURCH, C. M. aged 23 years September 9, 1879 by Rev. William C. Power at the corner of Nassau and Amherst Streets. Both natives of Charleston. He a barber.

HORRES, THOMAS JESSIE aged 35 years married to TURNER, ALICE ESTELLE E. aged 22 years October 21, 1883 by Rev. John H. Tillinghast.

HORRIE, CHARLES F. aged 26 years married to ROBINSON, EUGENIA E. aged 19 years July 19, 1894 by Rev. S. E. Morris. Both natives of Charleston. He a mechanic.

HORSEY, FREDERICK W. aged 23 years married to BEATTIE, CLOELIA L. aged 21 years November 10, 1885 by Father Daniel J. Quigley. He a native of South Carolina and she of Florida. He a patternmaker.

HORTON, BENJAMIN F. aged 23 years married to STEVENS, ANNIE ELIZA aged 18 years October 12, 1890 by Rev. R. D. Smart at 81 Line Street. He a native of South Carolina and she of Charleston. He a fireman.

HORWIG, GEORGE aged 23 years married to ALEX, ROSA aged 19 years June 24, 1895 by G. H. Rouse, Magistrate. Both natives of Oldenburg, Germany.

HORWIG, GEORGE aged 23 years married to ALBERS, CAROLINE ANNIE aged 21 years June 25, 1895 by T. S. Rouse, Magistrate. Both natives of Oldenburg, Germany.

HOTTINGER, CHRISTOPHER aged 23 years married to RICHTER, ADELIA aged 19 years November 4, 1890 by Rev. K. Boldt at St. Johannes Lutheran Church. He a native of Germany and she of Charleston. He a merchant.

HOUGH, (Mrs) BELLE HUFFMAN aged 28 years married to JACKSON, ANDREW aged 22 years February 4, 1892 by Rev. Edmund Wells. He a native of Athens, Georgia and she of Orangeburg, South Carolina. He a mechanic.

HOURE (?), M. J. K. married to BECKMAN, E. C. aged 21 years February 1, 1882 by Rev. Edward T. Horn at St. John's Lutheran Church. He a native of Darlington County, South Carolina and she of Charleston. He a merchant.

HOWARD, ELLA M. aged 14 years married to BARBER, W. T. aged 27 years January 14, 1894 by Rev. John F. Mitchell at 31 Amherst Street.

HOWARD, H. aged 23 years married to McMAHAN, W. P. aged 24 years February 21, 1882 by Father J. J. Monaghan at St. Patrick's Roman Catholic Church. He a native of Charleston and a drayman.

HOWARD, JOHN J. aged 23 years married to QUINLIVAN, MARY E. aged 23 years March 3, 1889 by Father J. J. Monaghan at St. Patrick's Roman Catholic Church. Both natives of Charleston. He a carpenter.

HOWARD, THEODORA aged 20 years married to McINTYRE, GEORGE H. aged 27 years December 31, 1894 by Father Thomas F. Hopkins at St. Mary of the Annunciation Roman Catholic Church.

HOWARD, THOMAS J. aged 24 years married to INFINGER, JULIA L. aged 22 years May 12, 1892 by Father J. J. Monaghan.

HOWARD, WILLIAM H. aged 28 years married to TRUMBO, SALLIE HARVEY aged 40 years July 10, 1883 by Father P. L. Duffy at The Cathedral of St. John the Baptist. Both natives of Charleston.

HOWE, W. K. married to BECKMAN, E. C. February 1, 1882 by Rev. Edward T. Horn at St. John's Lutheran Church. He a native of Darlington County, South Carolina and she of Charleston. He a merchant.

HOWELL, A. W. aged 25 years married to MANN, HENRY H. aged 32 years September 21, 1887 by Rev. Robert Wilson. Both natives of Charleston. He a lawyer.

HOWELL, C. BASCOM aged 34 years married to DAVIS, HANNAH aged 25 years December 4, 1889 by Rev. Edwin C. Dargan at Citadel Square Baptist Church. He a native of Virginia and she of Society Hill, South Carolina. He resides in Richmond, Virginia.

HOWELL, EDWARD aged 24 years married to JONES, ELLA aged 20 years August 18, 1889 by Rev. H. B. Browne. He a native of Richmond County, Georgia and she of Washington County, Texas. He works in the cotton mill.

HOWELL, THOMAS HENRY R. aged 24 years married to DUPRE, JANE ELIZABETH aged 17 years May 7, 1889 by Rev. T. P. Burgess at 10 Woolfe Street. Both natives of Charleston. He a laborer.

HUCHET, CHARLES R. aged 43 years married to ROBERTS, (Mrs.) ADDIE R. BOZARD aged 29 years July 19, 1894 by Rev. Edmund Wells. He a native of Charleston and she of Orangeburg, South Carolina. He a clerk.

HUCHET, MARY THEODOSIA aged 23 years married to MELFI, DAVID aged 23 years August 29, 1878 by Father Claudian B. Northrop in Mew Street. Both natives of Charleston. He a clerk.

HUCHTING (?), JOHN F. aged 40 years married to CAMPETT, ANGELA aged 20 years August 18, 1886 by Father Thomas E. McCormick at St. Patrick's Roman Catholic Church. He a native of Germany and she of Charleston. He a merchant.

HUCKS, CHARLES married to LEGARE, FLORENCE December 8, 1878 by William B. Yates, Chaplain.

HUCKS, NEWTON J. aged 20 years married to MORRIS, MATILDA M. aged 20 years November 12, 1885 by Rev. John O. Wilson. He a native of South Carolina and she of Charleston. He a merchant in Yemassee, South Carolina.

HUDSON, ALBERT aged 36 years married to LYNES, FRANCES aged 19 years June 21, 1881 by Rev. L. H. Shuck. He a native of Colleton County, South Carolina and she of Charleston. He a farmer in Mt. Pleasant, South Carolina.

HUDSON, ANNIE aged 18 years married to THOMPSON, J. E. aged 26 years October 12, 1887 by Rev. H. B. Browne. He a native of Screven County, Georgia and she of Augusta, Georgia. He an engineer.

HUDSON, ELIZABETH O. aged 18 years married to LEA, STEPHEN T. aged 21 years April 4, 1877 by Rev. William H. Adams at the Circular Congregational Church. He a native of Charleston and she of Colleton County, South Carolina. He a physician.

HUDSON, ELLA J. aged 24 years married to HUDSON, RUSSELL S. aged 48 years January 23, 1887 by Rev. H. B. Browne at 340 Meeting Street. Both natives of South Carolina. He a collector.

HUDSON, F. M. aged 24 years married to MEYERS, J. W. A. aged 30 years August 24, 1882 by Father Daniel J. Quigley in Nunan Street. Both natives of Charleston. He a policeman.

HUDSON, GEORGE S. married to GODWIN, LAURA May 18, 1892 by Rev. William A. Rogers. He a native of England and she of Bennettsville, South Carolina. He a clerk.

HUDSON, LADSON M. aged 22 years married to WEST, JAMIE D. aged 26 years July 28, 1889 by Rev. J. E. Carlisle at 468 King Street. He a native of Colleton County, South Carolina and she of Berkeley County, South Carolina. He a collector.

HUDSON, (Mrs.) LYDIA MILLER aged 60 years married to NOLAN, WALTER aged 41 years January 12, 1890 by Rev. Edwin C. Dargan at 623 King Street. He a native of Portland, Maine and she of Colleton County, South Carolina. He a laborer.

HUDSON, MARY JANE aged 27 years married to SINGLETARY, GEORGE O. aged 24 years May 5, 1889 by Rev. R. W. Lide at the residence of A. Hudson - 623 King Street. He a native of Summerville, South Carolina and she of Colleton County, South Carolina. He a carpenter.

HUDSON, M. T. aged 18 years married to WILLIAMS, S. G. aged 22 years May 4, 1882 by Rev. L. H. Shucks at 27 Church. He a native of North Carolina and she of Georgia. He an engineer.

HUDSON, RUSSELL S. aged 48 years married to HUDSON, ELLA J. aged 24 years January 23, 1887 by Rev. H. B. Browne at 340 Meeting Street. Both natives of South Carolina. He a collector.

HUDSON, SUSAN ANN aged 29 years married to MEYER, JOHN EDWARD aged 53 years December 6, 1878 by Rev. T. E. Wannamaker. He a native of Charleston and she of Round O, Colleton County, South Carolina. He a clerk.

HUDSON, THOMAS aged 24 years married to MAXWELL, LIZZIE A. aged 24 years October 12, 1886 by Rev. J. Walter Dickson at 77 Bay Street. Both natives of Charleston. He a fireman.

HUDSON, THOMAS aged 31 years married to BAIL, OCTAVIA aged 27 years April 26, 1894 by Rev. John Johnson.

HUES, ROBERT R. aged 27 years married to ROBERTS, JOSEPHINE aged 25 years March 22, 1887 by Rev. J. V. Welsh at Calvary Church. Both natives of Charleston.

HUFFMAN, E. G. married to MATTHEWS, S. J. L. July 28, 1885 by Father P. L. Duffy.

HUGER, ANNE ISABELLE married to JERVEY, ARTHUR FREDERICK May 6, 1890 by Rev. J. S. Trapier.

HUGER, CAROLINE W. married to WILKINSON, WILLIAM M. April 30, 1877 by Rev. Richard S. Trapier at St. Michael's Church.

HUGER, FRANCES M. married to FITZSIMONS, CHRISTOPHER February 12, 1890 by Rev. Richard S. Frazier at St. Michael's Church. He a native of South Carolina and she of Charleston.

HUGER, W. EDWARD aged 25 years married to PINCKNEY, RANDOLPH VIRGINIA aged 22 years February 20, 1890 by Rev. C. C. Pinckney at Grace Church.

HUGGINS, STONEWALL JACKSON aged 20 years married to JONES, L. ADDIE aged 20 years November 7, 1883 by Rev. E. C. L. Brown. She a native of Williamston, South Carolina. He a planter in Johnsonville, South Carolina.

HUGHES, DWIGHT aged 29 years married to SHINGLER, LILLY aged 22 years February 15, 1882 by Rev. L. H. Shuck at the corner of Wentworth and St. Philip Streets. He a native of Summerville, South Carolina and a clerk.

HUGHES, GEORGE M. aged 26 years married to DUKES, (Mrs.) MARIE FURCHES aged 35 years December 31, 1888 by Rev. H. B. Brown at Cumberland Church. He a native of Richmond County, Georgia and she of Orangeburg, South Carolina. He works in the cotton mill.

HUGHES, HARRIET S. aged 28 years married to HUGHES, JOHN C. aged 28 years April 27, 1880 by Rev. G. R. Brackett at 34 South Battery. He a native of Beech Island, South Carolina and she of Summerville, South Carolina. He a clerk.

HUGHES, JOHN C. aged 28 years married to HUGHES, HARRIET S. aged 28 years April 27, 1880 by Rev. G. R. Brackett at 34 South Battery. He a native of Beech Island, South Carolina and she of Summerville, South Carolina. He a clerk.

HUGHES, JOHN E. aged 20 years married to DOYLE, TERESA M. aged 26 years January 25, 1887 by Father F. J. Shadler at St. Joseph's Roman Catholic Church. Both natives of Charleston. He a clerk.

HUGHES, J. aged 26 years married to WILSON, ELLA aged 22 years November 16, 1891 by Rev. J. H. Smith.

HUGHES, LILLA W. aged 22 years married to McCAFFER, WILLIAM JOHN aged 27 years December 13, 1877 by Rev. John H. Hanour. Both natives of Charleston. He a clerk.

HUGHES, ROBERT married to WALKER, JANE June 19, 1879 by William B. Yates, Chaplain.

HUGHES, S. married to GLOVER, A. M. October 18, 1882 by Rev. L. H. Shuck. He an ironworker.

HUGHES, THOMAS aged 30 years married to CASSIDY, MARY ANN aged 25 years October 4, 1888 by Father Daniel J. Quigley at St. Patrick's Roman Catholic Church. Both natives of Charleston. He a railroad dispatcher.

HUGHES, THOMAS J. aged 35 years married to BROWN, MARY ELIZA aged 44 years July 5, 1883 by Rev. J. H. Tillinghast at 1 Bischoff Square. Both natives of Charleston. He a painter.

HUGHES, V. E. aged 21 years married to BEATY, L. G. aged 24 years February 26, 1882 by Rev. L. H. Shuck at 27 Church Street. Both natives of South Carolina. He a manufacturer.

HUGUELET, GEORGE ARTHUR aged 28 years married to MELCHERS, MARIE KATE aged 19 years July 12, 1889 by Rev. William A. C. Muller at St. Matthew's Lutheran Church. Both natives of Charleston. He a watchmaker.

HUGUELET, HORTENSE L. H. aged 29 years married to LAWRENCE, RICHARD G. aged 23 years February 28, 1893 by Rev. Edward T. Horn. Both natives of Charleston. He a clerk.

HUGUELET, ROSALIE A. aged 24 years married to BIBEL, ARTHUR W. May 9, 1892 by Rev. Edward T. Horn. He a native of San Francisco, California and she of Charleston. He a watchmaker.

HUGUENIN, MARIA A. aged 24 years married to SMITH, J. EDWARD aged 27 years November 29, 1877 by Rev. C. C. Pinckney at Grace Church. He a native of Pendleton, South Carolina and she of Beaufort, South Carolina. He a railroad agent.

HULDEBERG, KATHERINE aged 20 years married to FRIEDRICH, FRITZ M. aged 24 years December 18, 1889 by Rev. Johannes Heckel at 123 Smith Street.

HUNCHEN, GEORGE aged 26 years married to BORUER, JULIANA F. aged 22 years October 20, 1892 by Rev. Edward T. Horn at St. Johannes Lutheran Church. Both natives of Charleston. He a clerk.

HUNT, ELLEN aged 30 years married to WILLIAMSON, WINFIELD aged 40 years April 21, 1892 by Rev. Robert Wilson at 4 Wragg Square. He a native of North Carolina and she of Columbia, South Carolina. He resides in Lincolnton County, North Carolina.

HUNTER, ELVIRA EUGENIA aged 17 years married to KENT, JOSEPH LEANDER aged 20 years April 10, 1879 by Rev. W. S. Bowman at the Wentworth Street Lutheran Church.

HUNTER, FRANK J. aged 18 years married to Boldt, DORA N. aged 17 years September 23, 1885 by Rev. J. O. Wilson. Both natives of Charleston. He a bookkeeper.

HUNTER, ROSA L. aged 22 years married to WESTCOTT, CHARLES B. aged 24 years November 1, 1881 by Rev. Luther K. Probst. He a native of Savannah, Georgia and she of Charleston. He a merchant.

HUNTER, SALVADOR BENJAMIN aged 24 years married to O'KIEFFE, ANNIE aged 19 years April 29, 1878 by Father C. J. Croghan at St. Joseph's Roman Catholic Church. Both natives of Charleston. He in the ship business.

HURT, LIZZIE married to BOYLE (BOYE), JEROME April 30, 1880 by William B. Yates, Chaplain.

HUSSEL, GEORGE J. aged 38 years married to GROOMS, MADALINA aged 25 years May 7, 1893 by Rev. Edmund Wells at 65 Drake Street. He a native of Charleston and she of Summerville, South Carolina. He a clerk in Summerville.

HUSTEDT, CATHARINE W. aged 20 years married to SUHRSTEDT, JOHANN F. C. aged 27 years October 14, 1891 by Rev. Louis Muller at King Street near Shephard Street. He a native of Charleston and she of Germany. He a fireman.

HUTCHERSON, PHILIP HENRY aged 26 years married to Carpenter, MARTHA ENSLOW aged 20 years June 13, 1888 by Rev. Charles S. Vedder at 23 Mill Street. He a native of Summerville, South Carolina and she of Charleston. He a machinist in Coosaw, South Carolina.

HUTCHINSON, WILLIAM married to EASON, WILHELMINA January 16, 1889 by Rev. W. S. Campbell at the residence of W. G. Eason. He a clerk.

HUTCHMACHER, CHRISTINE MAGDALENA aged 24 years married to HEIDT, WILLIAM JOSEPH aged 24 years January 19, 1881 by Rev. Claudian B. Northrop. He a native of Charleston and she of New Orleans, Louisiana. He a merchant.

HUTCHMACHER, C. married to JONES, FRANCES May 16, 1880 by William B. Yates, Chaplain.

HUTCHMACHER, LENA aged 29 years married to KNEBEL, ALBERT aged 33 years January 24, 1883 by Father J. J. Woolahan at the residence of the Bride's parents - 77 Meeting Street. He a native of Prussia and she of New Orleans, Louisiana. He a tailor.

HUTCHMACHER, MARGARET H. aged 20 years married to SASSARD, HERBERT W. aged 24 years July 4, 1883 by Father P. L. Duffy at 183 East Bay Street. He a native of Columbia, South Carolina and she of Charleston. He an engineer.

HUTCHMACHER, R. married to JONES, FRANCES May 16, 1880 by William B. Yates, Chaplain.

HUTCHMER, L. U. aged 21 years married to WICHMAN, A. aged 36 years February 15, 1882 by Father Harry P. Northrop at 74 Wentworth Street. He a native of Germany and she of South Carolina. He a tailor.

HUTSON, ANNIE E. aged 18 years married to COLSON, GEORGE aged 28 years September 8, 1886 by Rev. H. B. Browne at 21 Blake Street. He a native of Maryland and she of Charleston. He a merchant.

HUTSON, CECELIA E. aged 19 years married to FRIERSON, DICK P. aged 32 years June 19, 1895 by Rev. Robert Wilson. Both natives of Charleston. He a merchant.

HUTSON, IDA L. aged 19 years married to JEFFORDS, TAYLOR, P. aged 22 years June 7, 1886 by Rev. Charles A. Stakely at 3 Harris Street. He a native of Charleston and she of South Carolina. He a blacksmith.

HUTSON, JOSEPHINE R. aged 16 years married to WIENGES, FRANCIS M. aged 22 years May 3, 1892 by Rev. A. M. Chreitzberg. Both natives of Charleston. He works in the bagging factory.

HUTSON, KATIE aged 21 years married to RENNEDKER, WALTER E. aged 24 years October 8, 1895 by Rev. W. T. Thompson at the First Presbyterian Church. Both natives of Charleston. He works for the railroad.

HUTSON, MARY aged 34 years married to DENIS, ANDREW J. aged 42 years December 2, 1884 by Rev. John E. Beard at 6 Blake Street. He a native of South Carolina and she of Charleston.

HUTSON, OLIVER M. aged 21 years married to NIX, MARY ELIZABETH aged 21 years November 21, 1893 by Rev. Edmund Wells. Both natives of South Carolina. He a carpenter.

HUTTO, ELLENDER L. aged 22 years married to SMITH, JOHN D. aged 21 years December 3, 1893 by Rev. J. L. Stokes at 37 Cooper Street. He a native of Greenville, South Carolina and she of Augusta, Georgia. He a carriage trimmer.

HYAMS, M. D. aged 28 years married to WAY, EMMA A. aged 18 years April 7, 1887 by Rev. Leroy F. Beattie. Both natives of South Carolina. He a mechanic.

HYATT, EMMA C. aged 18 years married to BANONERO (?), MELVIN aged 22 years February 18, 1894 by Rev. J. M. Knowles at 72 Drake Street.

HYATT, EVA A. aged 18 years married to DROSE, JOHN HENRY aged 20 years May 17, 1891 by Rev. W. A. Betts at 2 Addison Court. He a native of St. John's Parish, South Carolina and she of St. James, Santee, South Carolina. He works in the bagging factory.

HYATT, HARRIOT aged 23 years married to PARSELL, EDWARD A. aged 21 years February 14, 1887 by Rev. H. B. Browne in Drake Street. He a native of Augusta, Georgia and she of Charleston. He a mill hand.

HYDE, ANNIE TUPPER aged 25 years married to EASLEY, JOHN A. aged 30 years March 17, 1884 by Rev. R. N. Wells. He a native of Greenville, South Carolina and she of Charleston. He a planter in Greenville.

HYDE, SIMEON aged 25 years married to GALE, LILA L. aged 23 years November 15, 1881 by Rev. L. H. Shuck at the First Baptist Church. Both natives of Charleston. He a lawyer.

HYDE, TRISTAN TUPPER aged 24 years married to BLACK, MINNIE BELLE aged 22 years April 28, 1886 by Rev. A. J. S. Toomer at the First Baptist Church. Both natives of Charleston. He a broker.

HYER, WIGHTMAN aged 25 years married to KENYON, SADIE R. aged 24 years June 12, 1895 by Rev. J. L. Stokes at 31 Rose Lane. Both natives of Charleston. He a farmer.

HYER, WILLIAM C. aged 25 years married to WAGENER, MATTIE E. aged 23 years October 6, 1891 by Rev. J. T. Pate at 418 Meeting Street. Both natives of Charleston. He a plumber in Greenville, South Carolina.

HYER, WRAGG K. aged 26 years married to MEW, MARY F. aged 20 years November 17, 1886 by Father Daniel J. Quigley at St. Patrick's Roman Catholic Church. Both natives of South Carolina. He a merchant.

HYNES, M. L. aged 21 years married to CONLON, THOMAS M. aged 24 years November 10, 1886 by Father Daniel J. Quigley. Both natives of Charleston. He a machinist.

ICARD, ELIZABETH W. aged 36 years married to STODDARD, FRANKLIN A. aged 38 years July 6, 1884 by Rev. Robert Wilson at 3 Marsh Street. He a native of Boston, Massachusetts and she of New York. He operates a steamboat.

IGOE, A. MARY married to DEAL, JAMES September 22, 1885 by Father F. J. Shadler at the residence of the Bride. She a native of Charleston. He a pilot.

IKE, WILLIAM W. aged 34 years married to ARTOPE, CAROLINE R. aged 22 years November 28, 1886 by Father Daniel J. Quigley at St. Patrick's Roman Catholic Church. Both natives of Charleston. He a clerk.

ILDERTON (?), FLYNN BROWNING aged 25 years married to CLARKE, (Mrs.) VICTORIA E. HUNTER aged 29 years March 11, 1880 by Rev. W. S. Bowman at the Wentworth Street Lutheran Church. He a native of Summerville, South Carolina and she of Charleston. He a medical student.

ILDERTON, WALTER aged 20 years married to LIMEHOUSE, ELLEN aged 16 years July 11, 1891 by Rev. Robert Wilson. Both natives of Summerville, South Carolina. He a stock raiser in Summerville.

INABINETT, DANIEL W. aged 20 years married to QUINLIN, MARGARET aged 19 years July 6, 1884 by Father F. A. Schmetz at St. Patrick's Roman Catholic Church. Both natives of Charleston. He works for the railroad.

INABINETT, ELLA F. G. aged 24 years married to FERINA, GEORGE EDWARD aged 28 years May 9, 1883 by Rev. J. H. Tellinghast at 17 Woolfe Street. He a native of Charleston and she of Ridgeville, South Carolina. He a mechanic.

INFINGER, JULIA L. aged 22 years married to HOWARD, THOMAS J. aged 24 years May 12, 1892 by Father J. J. Monaghan.

INGHAM, SARAH EUGENIA aged 19 years married to GREEN, HUGH LEON aged 28 years January 1, 1878 by Rev. Claudian B. Northrop at the residence of Mrs. Sarah Ingham. Both natives of Charleston. He a farmer in Orangeburg, South Carolina.

INGLAN, JAMES married to SPINK, KATE December 1, 1878 by William B. Yates, Chaplain.

INGLE, JAMES A. married to RHETT, CHARLOTTE August 2, 1894 by Rev. William H. Campbell at St. Paul's Church. He a missionary to China.

INGLESBY, CAROLINE aged 24 years married to SIMONS, ARTHUR ST. J. aged 33 years December 27, 1894 by Rev. C. C. Pinckney at Grace Church.

INGLESBY, J. aged 24 years married to WEBB, E. M. aged 19 years June 27, 1882 by Rev. Richard Webb at 25 Church Street. He a native of Charleston and she of Georgia. He a broker.

INGLESBY, J. married to WEBB, E. M. June 27, 1882 by Rev. Richard Webb. He a broker.

INNIS, ANNIE aged 21 years married to LaFOURCADE, AMADEE A. J. A. aged 39 years March 5, 1878 by Father Harry P. Northrop at St. Patrick's Roman Catholic Church. He a native of Bordeaux, France and she of Charleston. He a watchman.

IRBY, (Mrs.) MINERVA E. JACKSON aged 21 years married to LEVISTER, JAMES J. aged 38 years November 25, 1894 by Rev. Edmund Wells at 15 Chapel Street. He a native of Warrenton, North Carolina and she of east Tennessee. He works in the cotton mill.

IRVIN, (Mrs.) IDA CLARKE aged 29 years married to MELLARD, CHARLES E. aged 36 years June 1, 1892 by Rev. Edwin C. Dargan at 19 Alexander Street. He a native of Williamsburg County, South Carolina and she of Charleston. He a clerk.

ISEAR (?), CELIA aged 22 years married to SHOKES, WILLIAM H. aged 23 years June 30, 1890 by John Ahrens at 643 King Street.

ISEAR (?), SARAH C. aged 21 years married to FRANK, HARRIS aged 26 years March 11, 1887 by Rev. B. Rubin at 207 King Street. He a native of Russia and she of Charleston. He a merchant.

ISEMAN, AMELIA aged 22 years married to LEHMAN, ISIDORE aged 31 years April 15, 1885 by Rev. C. C. Pinckney at Grace Church. He a native of Georgia and she of South Carolina. He a merchant in Savannah, Georgia.

ISEMAN, G. EMANUEL aged 33 years married to LEWITH, HULDA aged 22 years July 14, 1886 by Rabbi David Levy at the Hasell Street Synagogue. Both natives of Charleston. He a merchant.

ISEMAN, ISAAC aged 20 years married to BOWMAN, KATIE aged 18 years September 7, 1892 by Rabbi David Levy at the Hasell Street Synagogue. He a native of Charleston and she of Beaufort, South Carolina. He a clerk.

ISEMAN, LIZETTE aged 19 years married to STRAUSS, LEOPOLD aged 30 years May 21, 1878 by Rabbi David Levy at 412 King Street. He a native of Germany and she of Darlington County, South Carolina. He a merchant in Bennettsville, South Carolina.

ISEMAN, SOLOMON aged 24 years married to DYANLYNSKI, ROSALIE aged 22 years October 10, 1888 by Rabbi David Levy at the Hasell Street Synagogue. He a native of Charleston and she of Florida. He a merchant.

ISRAEL, CARRIE aged 22 years married to COHEN, ISAAC S. January 18, 1894 by Rabbi David Levy.

ISRAEL, ISADORE aged 29 years married to BENTSCHNER, SADIE A. aged 17 years April 3, 1894 by Rabbi David Levy. He a native of New York and she of Florence, South Carolina. He a merchant.

IVERSON, ESSIE aged 16 years married to WOOD, CHARLES F. aged 22 years March 22, 1893 by Rev. N. K. Smith at 12 Drake Street. He a native of Rhode Island and she of Walhalla, South Carolina. He works in the cotton mill.

JACKSON, ALBERT aged 19 years married to HEISSENBUTTEL, ANNA aged 22 years November 24, 1884 by Rev. John E. Beard at 64 Nassau Street. He a native of South Carolina and she of Charleston. He a mechanic.

JACKSON, ALFRED S. aged 19 years married to BERRY, MARY ALICE aged 21 years November 15, 1894 by Rev. Edmund Wells. He a native of Moncks Corner, South Carolina and she of Augusta, Georgia. He works in the cotton mill.

JACKSON, ANDREW aged 22 years married to HOUGH, (Mrs.) BELLE HUFFMAN aged 28 years February 4, 1892 by Rev. Edmund Wells. He a native of Athens, Georgia and she of Orangeburg, South Carolina. He a mechanic.

JACKSON, ANNIE VICTORIA aged 24 years married to HOGARTH, EDWARD HENRY aged 33 years April 3, 1884 by Rev. W. P. Mouzon at 7 Blake Street. Both natives of Charleston. He a stenographer.

JACKSON, M. J. aged 16 years married to BOWICK, OSCAR C. aged 19 years July 29, 1894 by Rev. Edmund Wells at 84 America Street. Both natives of Charleston. He works in the cotton mill.

JACKSON, ELLEN aged 18 years married to GLADDEN, GEORGE aged 35 years March 7, 1886 by Rev. H. B. Browne at 6 Harris Street. He a native of Charleston and she of South Carolina. He a shoemaker.

JACKSON, G. S. aged 47 years married to LEPARD, (Mrs.) MARTHA THRIFT aged 40 years March 19, 1894 by Rev. Edmund Wells. He a native of Langley, South Carolina and she of Newberry, South Carolina. He works in the cotton mill.

JACKSON, K. F. aged 22 years married to BUTTERFIELD, L. A. aged 25 years June 30, 1880 by Rev. W. S. Bowman at the Wentworth Street Lutheran Church. He a native of Charleston and she of New York. He a telegraph worker.

JACKSON, LEWIS E. aged 24 years married to GRAY, ETTA aged 22 years April 3, 1881 by Rev. J. V. Welsh at Calvary Church.

JACKSON, M. J. aged 22 years married to DAVIS, J. A. aged 40 years April 4, 1881 by Rev. J. V. Welch at Calvary Church. He a native of Providence, Rhode island and she of Charleston. He a sailmaker.

JACKSON, MARTHA aged 19 years married to QUINN, SAMUEL aged 25 years June 17, 1885 by Rev. John E. Beard at 7 Harris Street. He a native of South Carolina and she of Georgia. He a laborer.

JACKSON, MARY JANE aged 22 years married to DAVIS, JEREMIAH A. aged 40 years April 3, 1881 by Rev. J. V. Welsh at Calvary Church. He a native of Providence, Rhode Island and she of South Carolina. He a sailmaker.

JACKSON, (Mrs.) ROSANNA NIXON aged 30 years married to TAYLOR, JOHN THOMAS aged 42 years June 17, 1891 by Rev. W. A. Betts at 14 Hampstead Square. He a native of Charleston and she of Berkeley County, South Carolina.

JACKSON, WILLIAM WARD aged 33 years married to MEYERS, SOPHIA aged 25 years September 18, 1894 by Rabbi Barnett A. Elzas. He a native of New York and she of Boston, Massachusetts. He a merchant.

JACOBY, HENRY L. aged 39 years married to GOLDSMITH, KATE A. aged 21 years September 29, 1891 by Rabbi David Levy at the Hasell Street Synagogue. Both natives of Charleston. He a merchant.

JACOBY, JACOB L. aged 24 years married to DAVID, BERTHA aged 24 years February 20, 1884 by Rabbi David Levy at 303 King Street. Both natives of Charleston. He a merchant.

JACOBS, LOUISA aged 19 years married to ROBINS, GEORGE D. aged 20 years October 6, 1889 by Rev. Johannes Heckel at 123 Smith Street. He a native of Savannah, Georgia and she of Charleston. He a printer in Brooklyn, New York.

JACOBS, OTTO aged 25 years married to RIVERS, MARY A. aged 22 years July 31, 1883 by Rev. A. Coke Smith. Both natives of Charleston. He a salesman.

JACOBS, WILLIAM aged 54 years married to HEIDENREICH, (Mrs.) EMILIA DISHENDORF aged 45 years March 8, 1885 by Rev. Luther K. Probst at the Wentworth Street Lutheran Church. Both natives of Germany. He a sadler.

JACOBSON, JOHANNA CHRISTINE aged 25 years married to SAHLMANN, JOHN CHRISTOPHER aged 35 years November 17, 1884 by Rev. Johannes Heckel at 55 Smith Street. He a native of Georgia and she of Charleston. He a clerk.

JACOBSON, JULIUS aged 24 years married to HOFFMAN, JOHANNA aged 24 years January 16, 1884 by Rabbi David Levy at 210 King Street. He a native of Germany and she of Charleston. He a merchant.

JACOBSON, J. married to HESSE, C. H. September 1, 1879 by Rev. Johannes Heckel. He a native of Walhalla, South Carolina and she of Charleston. He a merchant.

JACOBSON, WILLIAM H. aged 20 years married to BAHUTGE (?), ETTA A. aged 18 years August 2, 1891 by Rabbi David Levy. Both natives of Charleston.

JAEGER, CARL F. aged 24 years married to WREDE, KATHERINE M. aged 16 years September 30, 1894 by Rev. Edward T. Horn.

JADHU (?), NICHOLAS aged 33 years married to GOULD, (Mrs.) MAY ANN LANAGHAN aged 32 years August 26, 1878 by Father John P. Twigg at The Cathedral of St. John the Baptist. He a native of Austria and she of Ireland. He a mariner.

JAEGER, KATIE Z. aged 19 years married to ROACH, LUCIUS C. aged 31 years August 13, 1894 by Rev. Lucius Cuthbert at the First Baptist Church. He a native of Aiken, South Carolina and she of Charleston. He works for the railroad.

JAHN, RICHARD aged 40 years married to HARTNETT, MARY RYAN aged 40 years February 17, 1889 by Father J. J. Monaghan at 6 Paines Court. He a native of Germany and she of Ireland. He a laborer.

JAHNTZ, CARL GUSTAV aged 32 years married to BOTH, (Mrs.) ANNA THERESE aged 34 years July 12, 1889 by Rev. Louis Muller at St. Matthew's Lutheran Church. Both natives of South Carolina. He a merchant.

JAMES, A. CARRIE aged 21 years married to SHIVER, M. FRANK aged 23 years November 27, 1889 by Rev. J. E. Carlisle at 185 Spring Street.

JAMES, R. aged 31 years married to STEINMEYER, L. aged 25 years October 12, 1882 by Rev. Daniel J. Quigley in Spring Street. Both natives of Charleston. He a mechanic.

JAMISON, ARTHUR THOMAS aged 23 years married to CALDWELL, EMMA C. aged 30 years October 3, 1889 by Rev. R. A. Webb at 54 Vanderhorst Street. He a native of Murfreesboro, Tennessee.

JANTZEN, CARSTEN EIBE JOHN aged 27 years married to MULLER, ANNIE JOHANNA MARIA aged 24 years April 21, 1889 by Rev. Johannes Heckel. He a native of Hanover and she of Germany. He a merchant.

JANTZEN, META aged 24 years married to NOLTE, HENRY aged 22 years January 30, 1887 by Rev. Johannes Heckel at 123 Smith Street. Both natives of Germany. He a merchant.

JANTZONS, FRANK aged 33 years married to GEHRELS, EMMA aged 17 years January 16, 1886 by Rev. Charles A. Stakely at 8 Wragg Street.

JARCKES, MARGARET E. aged 20 years married to KIRKLAND, JOHN F. aged 27 years June 5, 1889 by Rev. Edwin C. Dargan at Citadel Square Baptist Church. He a native of Kershaw County, South Carolina and she of Charleston. He a railroad conductor.

JARKES, GERALDINE ANNA aged 20 years married to BEATTI, EDWIN FLORENCE aged 24 years April 20, 1879 by Father Claudian B. Northrop in Pitt Street. Both natives of Charleston. He a policeman.

JARRETT, JESSIE J. aged 20 years married to LENT, THEODORE L. aged 25 years September 30, 1895 by Rev. J. L. Stokes at 231 Coming Street. He a native of New York and she of Charleston. He works in the cotton mill.

JARRETT, MARY E. aged 19 years married to FITZGERALD, JOSEPH aged 26 years January 18, 1893 by Rev. John Johnson at 53 Church. He a native of Spartanburg, South Carolina. He an insurance agent.

JARRIS, WILLIAM aged 26 years married to FOY, MARY aged 32 years June 5, 1883 by Rev. A. H. Misseldine. Both natives of South Carolina. He an employee of the bagging factory.

JARROT, EUGENIA aged 19 years married to TAYLOR, JOSEPH aged 20 years March 11, 1891 by Rev. J. Thomas Pate. He a native of Charleston and she of Spartanburg, South Carolina. He a moulder.

JARVIS, WILLIAM NELSON aged 38 years married to STODDARD, LAURA B. aged 28 years July 9, 1888 by Rev. E. C. L. Browne at the Unitarian Church. He a native of Newark, New Jersey and she of Charleston. He a sea captain in Philadelphia, Pennsylvania.

JATHO, GEORGE WASHINGTON aged 24 years married to VON OWEN, ARNOLDE CORNELIA aged 24 years April 6, 1881 by Rev. Louis Muller. He a native of Charleston and she of Germany. He a merchant.

JATHO, W. G. married to MULLER, J. J. C. June 1, 1887 by Rev. Louis Muller at St. Matthew's Lutheran Church. Both natives of South Carolina. He a merchant.

JEFFERS, GEORGE aged 19 years married to CROCKER, MINNIE aged 19 years October 22, 1893 by Rev. Edmund Wells. He a native of Sumter County, South Carolina and she of Spartanburg, South Carolina. He works in the cotton mill.

JEFFERSON, (Mrs.) MARY ANN BYRNES aged 27 years married to DEVEREAUX, JAMES M. aged 22 years March 7, 1889 by Rev. J. E. Carlisle at 231 Coming Street. Both natives of Charleston. He a bookkeeper.

JEFFERSON, STEPHEN P. aged 31 years married to CRAVEN, ELLA A. aged 22 years January 1, 1884 by Father F. J. Shadler at St. Joseph's Roman Catholic Church. Both natives of Charleston. He a stevedore.

JEFFORDS, CATHERINE H. aged 17 years married to ADDISON, WALTER L. aged 21 years July 4, 1893 by Rev. J. C. Yongue at 9 Cooper Street. He a native of Charleston and she of Sumter, South Carolina. He works in the cotton mill.

JEFFORDS, FANNIE GEORGIANA aged 21 years married to STRECKFUSS, CHARLES F. aged 27 years November 10, 1878 by Rev. W. S. Bowman at 587 King Street. Both natives of Charleston. He a farmer in Athens, Georgia.

JEFFORDS, HARRIET F. married to FELDKINS, L. J. November 14, 1877 by William B. Yates, Chaplain.

JEFFORDS, JOSEPHINE aged 20 years married to HARVEY, C. F. aged 36 years November 23, 1882 by Father D. J. Simons at Sullivans Island, South Carolina. He a native of South Carolina and a carpenter.

JEFFORDS, LILLA A. aged 28 years married to THOMSON, CHARLES W. M. aged 28 years December 26, 1894 by Rev. C. C. Pinckney.

JEFFORDS, MARY P. aged 35 years married to BATCHELDER, HIRAM M. aged 26 September 1, 1887 by Rev. Robert Wilson at 95 Broad Street. He a native of North Redding, Massachusetts and she of Charleston. He a decorator in Boston, Massachusetts.

JEFFORDS, TAYLOR P. aged 22 years married to HUTSON, IDA L. aged 19 years June 7, 1886 by Rev. Charles A. Stakely at 3 Harris Street. He a native of Charleston and she of South Carolina. He a blacksmith.

JELLICO, M. THOMAS aged 21 years married to EHNEY, SUSAN aged 17 years December 8, 1889 by Rev. Robert Wilson at 60 Drake Street. He a native of Charleston and she of Georgetown, South Carolina. He a railroad brakeman.

JENKINS, D. F. aged 31 years married to RIVERS, BESSIE M. aged 18 years June 26, 1889 by Rev. John Johnson. Both natives of Wadmalaw Island, South Carolina. He a storekeeper on Wadmalaw Island.

JENKINS, EDWARD E. aged 48 years married to WELSMAN, CAROLINE aged 24 years June 13, 1878 by Rev. John Johnson. He a native of South Carolina and she of Charleston. He a physician.

JENKINS, EDWARD N. aged 24 years married to WILLIAMS, AMANDA T. aged 20 years February 12, 1885 by Father F. J. Shadler at St. Joseph's Roman Catholic Church. Both natives of Charleston. He a sashmaker.

JENKINS, (Mrs.) ELIZABETH WALTERS aged 38 years married to WEBB, RICHARD aged 37 years July 30, 1891 by Rev. Robert Wilson at 4 Wragg Square. He a native of Charleston and she of Orangeburg, South Carolina.

JENKINS, FAIRCHILD D. aged 31 years married to RIVERS, BESSIE M. aged 18 years June 26, 1889 by Rev. John Johnson at St. Philip's Church.

JENKINS, FRANCIS aged 23 years married to SPRAGUE, FRANK W. aged 35 years March 5, 1885 by Rev. Thomas A. Grove at 5 Nassau Street. He a native of New York and she of Sullivans Island, South Carolina. He a laborer.

JENKINS, G. A. aged 22 years married to WILLIAMS, THOMAS J. aged 24 years July 4, 1880 by Father P. L. Duffy at 1 Cedar Court. He a native of Sullivans Island, South Carolina and she of Charleston. He a tinner.

JENKINS, HAWKINS K. aged 30 years married to MANIGAULT, JOSEPHINE aged 25 years November 24, 1887 by Rev. John Johnson in Gibbes Street. Both natives of Charleston. He a lawyer.

JENKINS, JAMES W. married to FOSBERRY, ISABEL January 21, 1892 by Father Valerius D'Apreda in King Street below Broad Street. He a bartender.

JENKINS, JUANITA H. aged 26 years married to BISSELL, TITUS L. aged 30 years June 14, 1892 by Rev. Edward T. Horn at St. Johannes Church. Both natives of Charleston. He a merchant.

JENKINS, JULIA aged 24 years married to RAVENEL, LOUIS February 20, 1884 by Rev. J. M. Junkin at Westminster Church. He a native of Charleston and she of Virginia. He an agent in Atlanta, Georgia.

JENKINS, JULIAN B. married to DAWSON, SUSAN L. December 12, 1895 by Rev. William H. Campbell. He a merchant.

JENKINS, J. E. aged 38 years married to WARKEN, P. K. aged 34 years February 3, 1882 by Rev. T. A. Grove at 6 Nassau Street. He a native of South Carolina and a laborer.

JENKINS, LIZZIE B. aged 23 years married to ROBERTSON, CHARLES aged 24 years April 14, 1892 by Rev. Edward T. Horn at St. Johannes Lutheran Church. Both natives of Charleston. He a bookkeeper.

JENKINS, PHOEBE married to MINOT, WILLIAM April 2, 1884 by Rev. William H. Campbell. Both natives of South Carolina. He a clerk.

JENNINGS, ALFRED THOMAS aged 21 years married to PLAYER, HELEN ELIZABETH aged 18 years June 26, 1889 by Rev. John J. Hill. Both natives of Charleston. He a printer.

JENNINGS, ANN T. aged 21 years married to HALL, LYMAN aged 24 years December 13, 1883 by Rev. C. C. Pinckney in Calhoun Street. He a native of Americus, Georgia and she of Pendleton, South Carolina.

JENNINGS, MARY HENRIETTA aged 21 years married to CAY, JOHN EUGENE aged 24 years June 29, 1879 by Father Claudian B. Northrop at 264 Calhoun Street. Both natives of Charleston. He a clerk.

JOHNSON, S. E. aged 22 years married to MITCHELL, R. aged 23 years October 8, 1879 by Rev. William C. Power at 18 Montagu Street. He a native of York County, South Carolina and she of Union County, South Carolina. He a farmer.

JOHNSON, S. J. aged 18 years married to COGSWELL, E. O. aged 23 years August 13, 1882 by Rev. E. J. Meynardie in America Street. He a native of Charleston and a railroad conductor.

JOHNSON, THOMAS E. aged 19 years married to BOLCHOZ, ERNESTINE M. aged 16 years May 17, 1891 by Rev. Edwin C. Dargan at 475 Meeting Street. Both natives of Charleston. He a blacksmith.

JOHNSON, WILLIAM aged 26 years married to STEWART, SARAH ANNE aged 21 years July 7, 1885 by Father Thomas E. McCormick at St. Patrick's Roman Catholic Church. She a native of Charleston. He a laborer.

JOHNSON, WILLIAM H. aged 23 years married to MICHEL, A. B. aged 24 years October 26, 1882 by Rev. E. C. L. Browne. Both natives of South Carolina. He a telegraph worker.

JOHNSTON, JOHN WILLIAM aged 33 years married to HACKER, ELLEN BUTLER aged 30 years April 13, 1887 by Rev. T. P. Burgess at Ebenezer Church. Both natives of South Carolina. He a machinist.

JOHNSTON, WILLIAM married to WINTHROP, MARY R. April 18, 1883 by Rev. Richard S. Trapier at St. Michael's Church.

JONES, ADELAIDE aged 22 years married to HAPPELL, HENRY H. aged 29 years January 3, 1895 by Rev. A. Ernest Cornish. He a native of Castle, Georgia and she of Plainfield, New York. He a steward.

JONES, BEVERLIE C. aged 29 years married to THOMPSON, MINNIE S. aged 18 years April 14, 1895 by Rev. G. R. Brackett at 23 Cannon Street. Both natives of Charleston. He an engineer.

JONES, B. W. aged 22 years married to JONES, E. F. aged 21 years May 13, 1882 by Rev. E. C. L. Browne at the Unitarian Church. He a merchant.

JONES, DANIEL EDWARD aged 22 years married to ALSINA, MARY ANGELINA aged 18 years October 21, 1886 by Father F. J. Shadler at St. Joseph's Roman Catholic Church. Both natives of Charleston. He a boltmaker.

JONES, DAVID aged 30 years married to SOLTAIRE, AMELIA aged 19 years October 18, 1893 by Rev. Robert Wilson at 4 Wragg Square. He a native of Kershaw County, South Carolina and she of Charleston. He a carpenter.

JONES, EDWARD G. aged 56 years married to LADSON, LEILA A. aged 35 years November 6, 1890 by Rev. C. C. Pinckney at 4 Meeting Street. He a native of Connecticut and she of Charleston. He a manufacturer in New York.

JONES, ELLA aged 20 years married to HOWELL, EDWARD aged 24 years August 18, 1889 by Rev. H. B. Browne. He a native of Richmond County, Georgia and she of Washington County, Texas. He works in the cotton mill.

JONES, ELENORA aged 21 years married to FRIEND, ROBERT L. aged 20 years February 15, 1892 by Rev. J. L. Stokes at 231 Coming Street. He a native of Charleston and she of Ridgeville, South Carolina. He a blacksmith.

JONES, (Mrs.) ELMITA SMITH aged 32 years married to SMITH, JOHN aged 26 years January 23, 1887 by Rev. H. B. Browne at 98 America Street. He a native of England and she of Charleston. He a miller.

JONES, E. F. aged 21 years married to JONES, B. W. aged 24 years May 13, 1882 by Rev. E. C. L. Browne at the Unitarian Church. He a merchant.

JONES, FRANCES married to HUTCHMACHER, C. May 16, 1880 by William B. Yates, Chaplain.

JONES, WILLIAM G. aged 26 years married to CLINTON, MARY CECILE aged 24 years April 18, 1890 by Father John J. Wedenfeller at The Cathedral of St. John the Baptist. He a native of Baltimore, Maryland and she of Charleston. He an insurance agent in Baltimore.

JONES, (Mrs.) GEORGIA A. TRAMMELL aged 21 years married to BLACK, JAMES E. aged 22 years January 10, 1883 by Father F. A. Schmetz at St. Patrick's Roman Catholic Church. He a native of Ireland and she of Columbus, Georgia. He a railroad brakeman.

JONES, IDA E. aged 21 years married to CROFT, THOMAS H. aged 24 years June 4, 1878 by Rev. C. C. Pinckney. Both natives of Charleston. He a bookkeeper.

JONES, IRVING L. aged 32 years married to THOMPSON, IDA E. aged 18 years August 27, 1890 by Rev. John Johnson at 20 Laurens Street. She a native of Charleston. He a boilermaker.

JONES, ISAAC SEABORN aged 30 years married to PHILIPS, MAMIE BELLE aged 22 years June 26, 1890 by Rev. R. D. Smart at 77 George Street. He a native of Orangeburg, South Carolina and she of Augusta, Georgia. He a salesman.

JONES, JOHN aged 18 years married to THOMSON, ANNA S. aged 17 years February 14, 1884 by Rev. John E. Beard at 13 Columbus Street. He a native of Spartanburg, South Carolina and she of New York. He a weaver in the cotton mill.

JONES, JOHN J. aged 20 years married to BURKE, ANNA A. aged 17 years July 17, 1881 by Father F. J. Shadler at St. Joseph's Roman Catholic Church. Both natives of Charleston. He a ship carpenter.

JONES, JULIA J. aged 26 years married to PHILLIPS, DAVID A. aged 27 years April 10, 1890 by Rev. R. D. Smart at Bethel Church. He a native of Aiken, South Carolina and shoe of Charleston. He a clergyman.

JONES, J. S. married to BARNES, E. December 19, 1882 by Rev. J. V. Welch at 24 Bee Street. He a native of Charleston and a railroad worker.

JONES, LULA S. aged 19 years married to STORM, WALTON aged 23 years November 15, 1883 by Rev. C. C. Pinckney at Grace Church. He a native of New York and she of Charleston. He a lawyer.

JONES, L. ADDIE aged 20 years married to HUGGINS, STONEWALL JACKSON aged 20 years November 7, 1883 by Rev. E. C. L. Browne. She a native of Williamston, South Carolina. He a planter in Johnsonville, South Carolina.

JONES, MARY D. aged 18 years married to OWENS, ALLEN J. aged 20 years May 16, 1895 by Rev. Edmund Wells at 205 Spring Street. He a native of Blackville, South Carolina and she of Greenville, South Carolina. He a steer driver.

JONES, MELVILLE aged 28 years married to BALLENTINE, SUSAN B. aged 20 years March 24, 1881 by Rev. L. H. Shuck at the corner of Drake and Blake Streets. He a native of Charleston and a machinist.

JONES, (Mrs.) M. S. DAVIS aged 62 years married to WOODHALL, M. S. November 12, 1885 by Rev. W. T. Jenkins at the northwest corner of Wentworth Street and Rutledge Avenue. Both natives of New York. He a mariner on Long Island, New York.

JONES, RICHARD WILLIAM aged 29 years married to THOMASON, JANE ELIZABETH aged 20 years April 13, 1879 by Rev. Charles S. Vedder at 92 Church Street. Both natives of Charleston. He a machinist.

JONES, RICHARD WILLIAM aged 36 years married to McDONALD, EMILY VICTORIA aged 19 years February 28, 1886 by Rev. Charles S. Vedder at 116 Church Street.

JONES, ROSA LILLIAN aged 24 years married to YATES, CORNELIUS HARRINGTON aged 25 years November 8, 1888 by Rev. E. C. L. Browne at the Unitarian Church. He a native of Cheraw, South Carolina and she of Williamston, South Carolina. He a clerk.

JONES, SARAH JULIA aged 26 years married to PHILLIPS, ARTHUR DAVID aged 27 years April 10, 1890 by Rev. R. D. Smart at Bethel Church.

JONES, SYDNEY B. aged 26 years married to Farmer, ANNIE P. aged 20 years October 15, 1891 by Rev. T. P. Burgess at 532 Meeting Street. Both natives of Charleston. He a painter.

JONES, T. V. married to WATSON, L. November 30, 1879 by William B. Yates, Chaplain.

JONES, V. J. aged 24 years married to BINGLY, A. aged 24 years September 4, 1882 by Rev. J. M. Green at 27 Washington Street. He a native of Charleston and a carpenter.

JONES, WILLIAM E. aged 22 years married to EVANS, (Mrs.) SUSIE TIEDWELL aged 22 years August 2, 1887 by Rev. Robert Wilson at St. Luke's Chapel. He a native of Georgia and she of Charleston. He a cotton miller.

JORDAN, JAMES married to WESTERLY, CATHERINE April 13, 1880 by William B. Yates, Chaplain.

JORDAN, FREDRICH WILHELM aged 26 years married to BUSE, ANNA LOUISE aged 16 years May 1, 1888 by Rev. Louis Muller.

JORDAN, JAKE D. aged 22 years married to MITCHUM, AMANDA aged 17 years May 17, 1891 by Rev. J. O. Fludd at 76 America Street. He a native of Orangeburg, South Carolina and she of Berkeley County, South Carolina. He works in the cotton mill.

JORDAN, JAMES married to WESTERLY, CATHARINE April 13, 1880 by William B. Yates, Chaplain.

JORDAN, L. C. aged 25 years married to SMITH, W. S. aged 21 years April 11, 1882 by Rev. C. C. Pinckney in Queen Street. He a native of Charleston and a wharfinger.

JORGENSON, CHRISTIAN aged 25 years married to LEHRMANN, MARY aged 18 years May 21, 1878 by Rev. Johannes Heckel at 125 Calhoun Street. He a native of Denmark and she of Prussia. He a merchant.

JORGENSON, J. CHRISTIAN aged 34 years married to ENGELMANN, (Mrs.) ANNA RIGBERS aged 38 years December 4, 1887 by Rev. Johannes Heckel at 123 Smith Street. He a native of Denmark and she of Germany. He a porter.

JOSEPHS, CHARLES aged 22 years married to SOLTAIRE, LORENA aged 16 years May 10, 1885 by Rev. R. A. Rapsly at 2 Cooper Street. He a native of Augusta, Georgia and she of Charleston. He a carpenter.

JOWETT, MARIE R. married to KELLY, JOSEPH W. aged 22 years December 25, 1891 by Rev. William H. Rogers.

JOYNER, ANNIE married to CULP, WALTER April 23, 1890 by Rev. W. A. Betts.

JOYNER, ANNIE A. married to CASTON, JOHN W. December 7, 1890 by Rev. W. A. Betts.

JOYNER, ANNIE B. aged 18 years married to BUSCH, HENRY M. aged 26 years June 21, 1880 by Rev. J. V. Welsh at Calvary Church. He a native of Charleston and she of St. Thomas Parish, South Carolina. He a baker.

JOYNER, (Mrs.) MARGARET WELLING aged 43 years married to KIRK, JOHN P. aged 42 years October 28, 1894 by Rev. J. C. Yongue. Both natives of Charleston. He works for the municipal government.

JOYNER, T. L. aged 29 years married to DOUGHERTY, CARRIE aged 25 years July 25, 1880 by Father Daniel J. Quigley at The Cathedral of St. John the Baptist. He a native of Charleston and she of Macon, Georgia. He a driver.

JUDGE, MICHAEL aged 47 years married to SOUTHALL, (Mrs.) MARY MITCHELL aged 26 years November 16, 1881 by Rev. J. Mercier Green at St. Stephen's Church.

JURGESON, E. aged 30 years married to JOHNSON, J. aged 25 years July 3, 1882 by Rev. Johannes Heckel at 16 Market Street. He a native of Norway and she of Denmark. He a mariner.

JURS (?), G. H. aged 23 years married to HARRISON, E. R. aged 24 years May 27, 1882 by Rev. Luther K. Probst at 60 Queen Street. He a native of Charleston and a tailor.

JUST, ADAM married to McCRURY, NANNIE June 21, 1880 by William B. Yates, Chaplain.

JUTZELER, CHRISTINA F. aged 24 years married to SCHUMACHER, SOPHIA aged 20 years October 21, 1886 by Rev. Louis Muller at 128 Wentworth Street. Both natives of Germany. He a cooper.

KAHN, FANNIE F. aged 20 years married to LEVY, GABRIEL aged 22 years March 8, 1892 by Rabbi David Levy at 6 Liberty Street. He a native of France and she of Charleston.

KAILURUEIT (?), RHEINHOLD aged 26 years married to FRAMING, JOSEPHA aged 27 years April 25, 1889 by Father F. J. Shadler at St. Joseph's Roman Catholic Church.

KAISER, MARY aged 21 years married to TARKE (?), ANDREW aged 30 years July 1, 1888 by Father P. J. McManus at St. Patrick's Roman Catholic Church. He a native of Germany and a shoemaker.

KALES, GEORGIANA aged 18 years married to MURRAY, JAMES H. aged 21 years April 7, 1878 by Father Harry P. Northrop at St. Patrick's Roman Catholic Church. He a native of Macon, Georgia and she of St. Johns, Berkeley County, South Carolina. He a painter.

KALLOCH, PARKER C. aged 37 years married to LAWTON, FLORENCE aged 34 years October 25, 1893 by Rev. C. C. Pinckney at Grace Church. He a native of Maine and she of Beaufort County, South Carolina. He a physician in Cincinnati, Ohio.

KANAPAUX, ANNA C. aged 23 years married to MISSEL, CARL H. aged 25 years April 10, 1892 by Rev. Louis Muller in Poinsett Street. He a native of Prussia and she of Germany. He a bricklayer.

KANAPAUX, J. E. aged 24 years married to LePRINCE, J. S. aged 39 years June 8, 1882 by Father F. J. Shadler at St. Joseph's Roman Catholic Church. He a native of Charleston and a railroad worker.

KANAPAUX, MARY aged 16 years married to BUTLER, GEORGE FRANCIS aged 19 years December 29, 1889 by Father J. J. Monaghan at 20 America Street. Both natives of Charleston. He a manufacturer in Charleston County.

KANAPAUX, (Mrs.) SALLIE WEAVER aged 33 years married to LITSCHGI, CHARLES aged 45 years November 12, 1888 by Father Daniel J. Quigley at St. Patrick's Roman Catholic Church. He a native of Germany and she of South Carolina. He a bank officer.

KANE, MARY ANN aged 25 years married to FINNEGAN, JAMES aged 23 years December 18, 1889 by Father F. J. Shadler at St. Joseph's Roman Catholic Church. Both natives of Charleston. He a plumber.

KANGETER, HEINRICH aged 30 years married to WITTSCHEN, LINA CATHARINE aged 24 years November 25, 1883 by Rev. Louis Muller.

KANGETER, JOHANN aged 24 years married to BRUNKHORST, MARGARETHE M. CATHERINE aged 24 years September 25, 1881 by Rev. Louis Muller. Both natives of Hanover. He a grocer.

KARSEN, ANNIE E. married to THOMPSON, JACOB M. August 19, 1888 by Rev. William H. Campbell. He a machinist in Florence, South Carolina.

KASLAR, WILLIAM HENRY aged 23 years married to LEQUEUX, JULIA AMANDA aged 19 years June 16, 1878 by Rev. W. S. Bowman at 9 Paines Court. He a native of Edinborough, Scotland and she of St. Stephens, South Carolina. He a carpenter.

KASSENS, DIETRICH aged 23 years married to SPRECKEN, MARY ANN aged 24 years August 10, 1892 by Father J. J. Monaghan at St. Patrick's Roman Catholic Church. He a native of Charleston and she of Ireland. He a railroad conductor.

KASSENS, SOPHIA CATHARINE MARGARETHE aged 26 years married to HARTMANN, E. FREDERICK aged 39 years February 18, 1883 by Rev. Louis Muller at the corner of St. Philip and Cannon Streets.

KASTER, WILLIAM HENRY aged 23 years married to LEQUEUX, JULIA AMANDA aged 19 years June 16, 1875 by Rev. W. S. Bowman. He a native of Edinborough, Scotland and she of St. Stephen's Parish, South Carolina. He a carpenter.

KATHMANN, SUSAN ETTA married to WAULHAME (?), DIETRICH H. O. April 11, 1878 by William B. Yates, Chaplain.

KAUFFNER, ANDREW JOHN aged 42 years married to ADDISON, GERTRUDE FLORENCE aged 23 years December 12, 1889 by Rev. G. R. Brackett at 164 Coming Street. Both natives of Charleston. He a machinist.

KAYLAN, LENA aged 21 years married to CREIGHTON, J. P. aged 21 years August 24, 1891. He a native of Atlanta, Georgia and she of New York City. He a plumber in Savannah, Georgia.

KECKLEY, ANNA M. aged 24 years married to SPEAR, HORACE P. aged 38 years August 20, 1887 by Rev. John O. Wilson. Both natives of Georgia. He a broker.

KECKLEY, ARTHUR C. aged 23 years married to SEYLE, LORENA E. aged 20 years November 21, 1888 by Rev. J. E. Carlisle at the Spring Street Church. He a native of Charleston and a railroad worker.

KECKLEY, ETTA H. aged 20 years married to RUMPH, P. JOHN aged 30 years April 2, 1890 by Rev. J. Thomas Pate at the corner of Bogard and Percy Streets. He a native of Pregnale, South Carolina and she of Charleston. He operates a sawmill in Pregnale.

KECKLEY, HENRY H. aged 21 years married to WISE, JULIA EVELINE aged 21 years October 29, 1893 by Rev. Edmund Wells in Cramer Court. Both natives of Charleston. He a bricklayer.

KECKLEY, (Mrs.) MARY DAGGETT aged 38 years married to SIGWALD, HENRY W. aged 63 years October 23, 1887 by Rev. Robert Wilson at 311 East Bay Street. Both natives of Charleston. He an engineer.

KEE, JAMES E. aged 23 years married to FLYNN, HATTIE aged 18 years December 29, 1895 by Rev. J. M. Steadman at 14 Hampstead Square. He a native of Graniteville, South Carolina and she of Augusta, Georgia. He works for the railroad.

KEEGAN, JANE married to DOLAN, JOHN June 2, 1878 by William B. Yates, Chaplain.

KEEGAN, JOHN PATRICK aged 24 years married to McMAHON, SARAH aged 20 years November 25, 1883 by Father Daniel J. Quigley at The Cathedral of St. John the Baptist. Both natives of Charleston. He a machinist.

KEEGAN, MARY ELIZABETH aged 22 years married to REYNOLDS, EDWARD JAMES aged 22 years April 20, 1884 by Father F. J. Shadler at St. Joseph's Roman Catholic Church. He a native of New York and she of Charleston. He a stonecutter.

KEELAN, JOHN aged 21 years married to WHITE, ELLEN aged 21 years March 1, 1881 by Father Harry P. Northrop at St. Patrick's Roman Catholic Church.

KEELER, IGNATIUS aged 35 years married to PETER, AMALIA aged 26 years June 19, 1883 by Father F. J. Shadler at St. Joseph's Roman Catholic Church. Both natives of Germany. He a merchant.

KEELY, MARY aged 19 years married to LLOYD, EDWARD A. aged 25 years November 27, 1882 by Father F. J. Shadler at St. Joseph's Roman Catholic Church.

KEENAN, CATHARINE aged 20 years married to DOOGAN, MARTIN aged 22 years June 8, 1881 by Father F. J. Shadler at St. Joseph's Roman Catholic Church. He a native of Charleston and a mariner.

KEENAN, F. M. aged 24 years married to McCUE, A. E. aged 24 years November 27, 1882 by Rev. F. J. Shadler at St. Joseph's Roman Catholic Church. Both natives of Charleston. He a stevedore.

KEENAN, JOHN aged 25 years married to DURKIN, HONORA June 21, 1883 by Father F. J. Shadler at St. Joseph's Roman Catholic Church. Both natives of Charleston. He a clerk.

KEENAN, JULIA aged 22 years married to CANTWELL, JAMES C. aged 22 years December 29, 1886 by Father Daniel J. Quigley at St. Patrick's Roman Catholic Church. He a native of South Carolina and she of Charleston. He a clerk in Columbia, South Carolina.

KEENAN, WILLIAM B. aged 25 years married to KELLY, MARY A. aged 25 years November 27, 1890 by Father F. J. Shadler at St. Joseph's Roman Catholic Church. Both natives of Charleston. He a commercial traveler.

KEENER, JOHN CARTER aged 23 years married to AHRENS, HENRIETTE MARGARETHE aged 23 years May 10, 1888 by Rev. Louis Muller at the residence of the Bride's mother - in Laurens Street.

KEILAN, JOHN aged 26 years married to WHITE, ELLEN aged 25 years March 1, 1881 by Father Harry P. Northrop at St. Patrick's Roman Catholic Church. Both natives of Ireland. He a policeman.

KEILY, MARY aged 19 years married to LLOYD, EDWARD A. aged 25 years May 2, 1878 by Father Daniel J. Quigley. He a native of Philadelphia and she of Charleston. He a mariner.

KEIM, NANNIE aged 27 years married to LITSCHGI, ALBAN WILLIAM aged 25 years October 26, 1881 by Father Daniel J. Quigley at The Cathedral of St. John the Baptist. He a native of Beaufort, South Carolina and she of Georgia. He a clerk.

KEITH, P. S. married to TEAUX, M .J. February 21, 1882 by Father T. E. Chapins at The Cathedral of St. John the Baptist. Both natives of Charleston. He a bookkeeper.

KELLEHER, JOHN aged 42 years married to LAMB, (Mrs.) MARY JANE aged 34 years June 13, 1894 by Rev. Edmund Wells at 54 Washington Street. He a native of Fergus, Canada and she of South Carolina. He a weaver in the cotton mill.

KELLEN, THOMAS M. aged 26 years married to McGOWAN, JOHANNA aged 28 years November 2, 1892 by Father P. L. Duffy at The Cathedral of St. John the Baptist. He a native of Boston, Massachusetts and she of Augusta, Georgia. He a longshoreman.

KELLER, RUTH M. aged 20 years married to MITCHELL, J. WALTER aged 34 years May 30, 1888 by Rev. C. C. Pinckney. He a native of Edgefield County, South Carolina and she of Charleston. He a lawyer in Edgefield.

KELLER, SAM aged 27 years married to DeLEON, JACQUELINE ELLEN aged 25 years June 12, 1889 by Rabbi David Levy at the Hasell Street Synagogue. He a native of New York City and she of Charleston. He a stockbroker in Sheffield, Alabama.

KELLEY, PHILIP T. aged 22 years married to DIESS, DORA aged 20 years January 10, 1881 by Rev. J. V. Welsh.

KELLY, (Mrs.) A. GERTRUDE SMART married to BLANCHE, W. JAMES aged 35 years October 6, 1889 by Rev. H. B Browne at 25 Amherst Street. He a native of South Carolina and she of Charleston. He a millwright.

KELLY, B. D. aged 32 years married to LILIENTHAL, ANNIE JOSEPHINE aged 18 years March 20, 1881 by Rev. Luther K. Probst. He a native of Boston, Massachusetts and she of Charleston. He a mariner.

KELLY, CATHERINE S. aged 26 years married to CATHCART, W. RICHARD aged 35 years July 18, 1878 by Rev. C. C. Pinckney in St. Philip Street. Both natives of Charleston. He a merchant.

KELLY, C. D. aged 32 years married to LILIENTHAL, ANNIE JOSEPHINE aged 18 years March 30, 1881 by Rev. Luther K. Probst.

KELLY, FLORENCE aged 19 years married to RODGERS, FRANCIS S. J. aged 21 years January 24, 1889 by Rev. C. C. Pinckney at Grace Church. Both natives of Charleston. He a lawyer.

KELLY, JAMES aged 25 years married to CAMPBELL, ANNIE aged 25 years July 28, 1880 by Father Daniel J. Quigley at The Cathedral of St. John the Baptist. He a native of Charleston and she of Ireland. He a street inspector.

KELLY, JOHN aged 21 years married to HANCOCK, JULIA aged 18 years May 16, 1892 by Rev. A. M. Chreitzberg. He a native of Columbia, South Carolina and she of Sumter, South Carolina. He works in the cotton mill.

KELLY, JOSEPH W. aged 22 years married to JOWETT, MARIE T. December 25, 1891 by Rev. William H. Rogers.

KELLY, KATE aged 20 years married to DONAGHUE, PATRICK aged 30 years February 16, 1879 by Father Daniel J. Quigley at The Cathedral of St. John the Baptist. He a native of Ireland and she of Charleston. He a policeman.

KELLY, (Mrs.) MARGARET TOUGHEL married to McMAHON, JEREMIAH March 5, 1878 by Father John P. Twigg at The Cathedral of St. John the Baptist.

KELLY, MARY aged 24 years married to O'BRIEN, WILLIAM aged 23 years June 8, 1881 by Father T. Edward Chapins at St. Patrick's Roman Catholic Church. He a native of Charleston and she of Philadelphia, Pennsylvania. He a tinner.

KELLY, MARY A. aged 21 years married to KEENAN, WILLIAM B. aged 25 years November 27, 1890 by Father F. J. Shadler at St. Joseph's Roman Catholic Church. Both natives of Charleston. He a commercial traveler.

KELLY, M. aged 30 years married to BROWN, M. M. aged 21 years January 25, 1882 by Father T. F. Kelly. He a native of Ireland and she of New Jersey. He a machinist.

KELLY, PATRICK C. aged 32 years married to BENNETT, MARY M. aged 29 years May 2, 1888 by Father F. J. Shadler at St. Joseph's Roman Catholic Church. He a native of Dublin, Ireland and she of Charleston. He a bricklayer.

KELLY, P. T. aged 22 years married to DIERS, DORA aged 20 years January 10, 1881 by Rev. J. V. Welsh at Calvary Church. He a native of Walterboro, South Carolina and she of Charleston. He a printer.

KELLY, ROBERT aged 22 years married to SMART, ALICE aged 19 years June 4, 1878 by Rev. J. V. Welsh. He a native of St. Bartholomew's Parish, South Carolina and she of Charleston. He a laborer.

KELLY, SARAH EDITH aged 20 years married to EASON, WILLIAM A. aged 22 years December 24, 1883 by Rev. Luther K. Probst.

KELLY, THOMAS J. aged 27 years married to WILLIAMS, CATHARINE aged 24 years January 5, 1886 by Father F. J. Shadler at St. Joseph's Roman Catholic Church. Both natives of Charleston. He a postal worker.

KELLY, VICTORIA aged 19 years married to PETRINOVICH, FRANK A. aged 20 years February 3, 1889 by Rev. H. B. Browne at the corner of America and Blake Streets. He a native of Charleston and she of Graniteville, South Carolina. He works at the Custom House.

KENNEDY, ANDREW W. aged 26 years married to NEIL, (Mrs.) META A. BLACK aged 23 years December 3, 1878 by Rev. Charles S. Vedder. He a native Macon, Georgia and she of Charleston. He a commercial traveler.

KENNEDY, AUSTIN J. aged 26 years married to STOPFEL, PHISIPINA aged 29 years November 3, 1885 by Father F. J. Shadler at St. Joseph's Roman Catholic Church. Both natives of Charleston.

KENNEDY, ELIZA aged 26 years married to STALL, JOHN R. aged 35 years May 15, 1889 by Rev. H. B. Browne at 89 America Street.

KENNEDY, F. E. aged 25 years married to MALONY, E. T. aged 25 years January 10, 1882 by Father J. E. Chapins. Both natives of Charleston. He a tinner.

KENNEDY, HENRY aged 38 years married to KRAMER, LOUISA aged 36 years December 26, 1883 by Father F. J. Shadler at St. Joseph's Roman Catholic Church. She a native of Hamburg, Germany. He operates a restaurant.

KENNEDY, JAMES aged 34 years married to MORIARTY, ELIZABETH aged 23 years December 31, 1885 by Father Thomas E. McCormack. Both natives of Charleston. He a laborer.

KENNEDY, JAMES R. D. aged 25 years married to GRUBER, SERENA P. aged 24 years November 25, 1890 by Rev. J. Thomas Pate at 28 Blake Street. Both natives of Charleston. He a bookkeeper.

KENNEDY, JOHN married to WELSH, J. October 31, 1882 by Father John P. Twigg. He a native of Ireland and a farmer.

KENNEDY, JOHN aged 29 years married to POWER, ANNIE F. aged 22 years July 18, 1883 by Father P. L. Duffy at The Cathedral of St. John the Baptist.

KENNEDY, JOHN D. aged 29 years married to BOWEN, ANNIE F. aged 22 years May 18, 1883 by Father P. L. Duffy at The Cathedral of St. John the Baptist. Both natives of Charleston. He a printer.

KENNEDY, JOHN P. aged 21 years married to O'KEIFE, JULIA F. aged 18 years September 27, 1885 by Father F. A. Schmetz at 10 South Street.

KENNEDY, JOSEPH aged 47 years married to CONANT, (Mrs.) COURTNEY E. WOLLING aged 27 years July 6, 1886 by Rev. C. F. Chichester at the Mariners Church. He a native of Charleston and she of South Carolina. He a butcher.

KENNEDY, JOSEPH aged 24 years married to McCANTS, MARY J. aged 21 years August 15, 1889 by Rev. H. B. Browne at 94 America Street. He a native of Charleston and she of Berkeley County, South Carolina. He a carpenter.

KENNEDY, L. W. aged 40 years married to CHISOLM, M. M. aged 37 years July 23, 1882 by Rev. L. H. Shuck at the corner of Line Street and Rutledge Avenue. He a native of South Carolina and a planter.

KENNEDY, MAMIE aged 22 years married to COLCOCLOUGH, HENRY L. aged 25 years June 7, 1894 by Father Daniel J. Quigley at St. Patrick's Roman Catholic Church.

KENNEDY, MARY C. aged 30 years married to CORCORAN, JOHN P. aged 30 years December 4, 1884 by Father F. A. Schmetz at St. Patrick's Roman Catholic Church. Both natives of Charleston. He a fireman.

KENNEDY, MARY E. aged 24 years married to McSWEENEY, E. P. aged 26 years December 25, 1886 by Father Daniel J. Quigley at St. Patrick's Roman Catholic Church. Both natives of Charleston. He works for the railroad.

KENNEDY, MICHAEL J. aged 29 years married to MURRAY, LULA aged 24 years November 23, 1892 by Father P. L. Duffy at The Cathedral of St. John the Baptist. He a native of Quebec, Canada and she of Charleston. He a stevedore.

KENNEDY, MINNIE aged 20 years married to SEASE, GEORGE D. aged 37 years February 6, 1887 by Rev. H. B. Brown at 78 Drake Street. He a native of Burke County, Georgia and she of Charleston. He a carpenter.

KENNEDY, MINNIE ESTELLE aged 23 years married to ORTMAN, EDWIN PRIOLEAU aged 33 years March 12, 1890 by Rev. R. D. Smart at Bethel Church. Both natives of Charleston. He a painter.

KENNEDY, M. L. aged 25 years married to J. FLYNN aged 30 years January 1, 1880 by Father P. L. Duffy at The Cathedral of St. John the Baptist. He a native of Ireland and she of Charleston. He a telegraph employee.

KENNEDY, NOAH LANEY aged 28 years married to TURNER, ELIZABETH aged 29 years March 21, 1878 by Rev. John Johnson. Both natives of Charleston. He a streetcar conductor.

KENNEDY, P. H. aged 32 years married to CAHILL, SUSAN C. aged 19 years February 3, 1884 by Father Daniel J. Quigley at The Cathedral of St. John the Baptist. Both natives of Charleston. He a broker.

KENNEDY, RUBEN N married to HARRISON, JULIE M. SPENCER January 17, 1878 by Rev. Richard S. Trapier.

KENNEDY, (Mrs.) SARAH RIGGS aged 25 years married to RITTS, BENJAMIN H. aged 21 years September 9,1888 by Rev. H. B. Browne at 110 America Street. He a native of Rantowles, South Carolina and she of Charleston. He a moulder.

KENNEDY, ST. JOHN M. B. aged 23 years married to MEREE, ANNIE E. aged 19 years June 3, 1885 by Rev. Robert Wilson.

KENNEDY, WILLIAM aged 39 years married to COOKE, AUGUSTA O. aged 30 years September 29, 1883 by Rev. John Johnson. He a native of Abbeville, South Carolina and she of New York. He a government employee.

KENNEDY, WILLIAM T. J. aged 28 years married to ANDERSON, ALEXINA CAROLINE aged 22 years April 25, 1888 by Rev. James Wallace Ford. He a native of Charleston and she of Summerville, South Carolina. He a bookkeeper.

KENNERTY, SARAH JANE aged 20 years married to POWERS, JOHN aged 27 years March 12, 1878 by Father Harry P. Northrop at St. Patrick's Roman Catholic Church. He a native of County Kilkenny, Ireland and she of Charleston. He a farmer.

KENNERTY, THOMAS J. aged 30 years married to KOLDEWAY, ANNIE aged 17 years July 3, 1887 by Father Daniel J. Quigley at St. Patrick's Roman Catholic Church. He a native of Ireland and she of Charleston. He a farmer.

KENNY, ANNIE E. aged 27 years married to DOLAN, JOHN E. aged 30 years January 28, 1880 by Father Daniel J. Quigley in Tradd Street. He a native of Brooklyn, New York and she of Charleston. He a painter.

KENNY, CATHERINE aged 26 years married to McLAUGHLIN, JAMES J. aged 25 years June 11, 1883 by Rev. P. L. Duffy at The Cathedral of St. John the Baptist. Both natives of Charleston. He a policeman.

KENNY, JOHN H. aged 38 years married to WISE, CATHERINE aged 22 years November 17, 1887 by Father F. J. Shadler at St. Joseph's Roman Catholic Church. He a native of Charleston and she of Bennettsville, South Carolina. He a builder.

KENNY, M. aged 24 years married to TURLEY, A. aged 26 years September 24, 1882 by Father J. J. Monaghan at St. Patrick's Roman Catholic Church. He a native of Ireland and a laborer.

KENT, JONATHAN S. aged 28 years married to WISE, LILLIE aged 24 years February 6, 1881 by Rev. Luther K. Probst. He a native of Charleston and an engineer.

KENT, JOSEPH LEANDER aged 20 years married to HUNTER, ELVIRA EUGENIA aged 17 years April 10, 1879 by Rev. W. S. Bowman at the Wentworth Street Lutheran Church.

KENT, PHINEAS aged 26 years married to BRISTOL, FLORENCE MARY aged 20 years November 5, 1885 by Rev. W. T. Jenkins at Westminster Presbyterian Church. He a native of New Jersey and she of New York. He a bookkeeper.

KENYON, SADIE R. aged 24 years married to HYER, WIGHTMAN aged 25 years June 12, 1895 by Rev. J. L. Stokes at 31 Rose Lane. Both natives of Charleston. He a farmer.

KEOUGH, ANNE M. aged 30 years married to McGILL, JOHN aged 33 years May 11, 1879 by Bishop P. N. Lynch at The Cathedral of St. John the Baptist.

KEOGH, MARY F. aged 19 years married to MOULTON, CHARLES H. aged 27 years July 10, 1883 by Father F. J. Shadler at St. Joseph's Roman Catholic Church. He a native of Charleston and she of Savannah, Georgia. He works for the railroad.

KEPPARD, E. married to TAYLOR, GEORGE November 19, 1880 by William B. Yates, Chaplain.

KERR, FRANK BERNARD aged 25 years married to RAHALL, MARY LOUISE aged 23 years April 16, 1890 by Father J. J. Monaghan at St. Patrick's Roman Catholic Church. He a native of New York and she of Charleston. He a mechanic in Orangeburg, South Carolina.

KERRISON, E. L. aged 37 years married to WARD, E. H. aged 19 years July 15, 1882 by Rev. C. C. Pinckney at Grace Church. He a native of South Carolina and a planter.

KERRISON, LOUISA HERIOT married to CLARKSON, CHARLES D. November 12, 1890 by Rev. William H. Campbell at St. Paul's Church. Both natives of Charleston. He a physician.

KERSHAW, GEORGE TRENHOLM married to MIDDLETON, ALICE June 27, 1877 by Rev. Richard S. Trapier.

KERSTEN, EMIL aged 31 years married to CLAUSSEN, CHRISTINA D. aged 23 years May 7, 1886 by Rev. Oscar H. Kraft of the Buffalo, New York, Evangelical Lutheran Church. Both natives of Charleston. He a grocer.

KESELER, FRANK aged 22 years married to MITCHUM, WILHELMINA aged 21 years December 21, 1890 by Rev. M. S. Watkins at the Second Adventist Church. Both natives of South Carolina. He works in the cotton mill.

KIELBIN, MARIE A. aged 22 years married to RODE, OLIVER C. aged 35 years November 2, 1894 by Rev. C. E. Chichester at 1 Atlantic Street. Both natives of Norway. He a mariner.

KILEY, JOHN L. married to CORCORAN, JULIA A. April 4, 1888 by Father P. J. Wilson at St. Patrick's Roman Catholic Church. She a native of Charleston. He a dealer in wood.

KILEY, MICHAEL C. aged 26 years married to McSHERRY, CORINE G. aged 17 years December 1, 1892 by Father J. J. Monaghan at St. Patrick's Roman Catholic Church. Both natives of Charleston. He a policeman in Jacksonville, Florida.

KILGUS, FRIEDRICH aged 39 years married to BLAKELY, ANNA aged 35 years August 10, 1884 by Rev. Louis Muller at the St. Matthew's Lutheran Church. He a native of Georgia and she of Charleston. He a laborer.

KILGUS, LOUISE DORETHA aged 20 years married to ORTMANN, CARL HEINRICH aged 21 years October 2, 1887 by Rev. Louis Muller at 96 Radcliffe Street. He a native of Prussia and she of Germany. He a baker in Georgetown, South Carolina.

KILROY, JAMES aged 45 years married to CONROY, MARY MURRAY aged 33 years July 28, 1885 by Father J. J. Woolahan at St. Mary of the Annunciation Roman Catholic Church. Both natives of Charleston. He a laborer.

KIMBELL, SUSIE aged 33 years married to JERVEY, WALTER P. aged 38 years April 4, 1894 by Rev. Edmund Wells. He a native of Charleston and she of Chester, South Carolina. He a longshoreman.

KIMBELL, WILLIAM R. aged 28 years married to WEBB, AGNES MARY aged 27 years September 10, 1893 by Father J. J. Monaghan at St. Patrick's Roman Catholic Church. He a native of South Carolina and she of Charleston. He a fireman in Savannah, Georgia.

KIMMEY, MARGARET A. aged 20 years married to PUNDT, AUGUSTUS N. aged 21 years May 22, 1884 by Rev. J. H. Tillinghast at 22 Amherst Street. He a native of Charleston and she of Augusta, Georgia. He a merchant.

KIMMEY, MARY JESSIE aged 21 years married to DENAN, WILLIAM G. August 29, 1888 by Rev. J. E. Carlisle at 27 Reid Street. She a native of Charleston.

KING, ANDREW A. aged 22 years married to HEINS, IDA B. aged 18 years December 7, 1880 by Rev. Luther K. Probst. He a native of Charleston and a druggist.

KING, ANNA C. aged 21 years married to WINNINGHAM, HENRY H. aged 29 years February 5, 1879 by Rev. Charles S. Vedder at 92 Church Street. Both natives of Charleston. He a fireman.

KING, (Mrs.) ANNA MARIA SWINTON aged 39 years married to BAYNARD, S. LEE aged 42 years November 24, 1891 by Rev. G. R. Brackett at 12 Wentworth Street. He a native of Edisto Island, South Carolina and she of St. Paul's Parish, South Carolina. He works at the phosphate mill.

KING, CHARLES W. aged 22 years married to CALDER, CAROLINE VIRGINIA aged 20 years September 19, 1883 by Rev. A. Coke Smith at 134 St. Philip Street. He a native of Edisto Island, South Carolina and she of Charleston. He a sashmaker.

KING, CHRISTOPHER WALTER aged 22 years married to WARREN, ELIZA NORRIS aged 24 years February 21, 1884 by Rev. W. F. Junkin. He a native of Colleton County, South Carolina and she of Walterboro, South Carolina. He a merchant in Adams Run, South Carolina.

KING, FRANCIS married to THOMPSON, EMMA March 6, 1878 by William B. Yates, Chaplain.

KING, HENRY FROST aged 24 years married to McNEIL, SARAH JANE aged 18 years November 26, 1878 by Rev. G. R. Brackett. Both natives of Charleston. He a driver.

KING, JAMES PATRICK aged 23 years married to VERONEE, IDA MAY aged 16 years March 27, 1883 by Rev. J. H. Tellinghast. He a native of Augusta, Georgia and she of Charleston. He a mechanic.

KING, LOUISA HATTIE aged 19 years married to STALLINGS, S. ALFRED aged 23 years April 26, 1890 by Rev. T. P. Burgess at 6 Hampstead Court.

KING, MARY E. B. aged 20 years married to LLENORT (?), JOSEPH aged 22 years November 27, 1887 by Father John O. Schachte at The Cathedral of St. John the Baptist. He a native of Spain and she of Charleston.

KING, M. F. aged 26 years married to MAHON, P. aged 26 years January 1, 1880 by Father John P. Twigg at The Cathedral of St. John the Baptist. Both natives of Clarksburg, Virginia. He a ship carpenter.

KING, (Mrs.) SARAH QUINCY married to BATEMAN, CHARLES D. January 4, 1888 by Rev. William H. Campbell at the residence of John Paul. He a fireman.

KINGDON, GEORGE PORTER aged 22 years married to POOSER, SARAH REBECCA aged 20 years December 8, 1881 by Rev. H. F. Chreitzberg. Both natives of Charleston. He a railroad conductor.

KINLOCH, ROBERT H. married to BISSELL, SALLIE H. November 22, 1893 by Rev. William H. Campbell. He resides in Montgomery, Alabama.

KINLOCH, IDA M. aged 23 years married to EVANS, BENJAMIN F. aged 30 years October 10, 1895 by Rev. W. T. Thompson. He a native of Columbia, South Carolina and she of Charleston. He a bank clerk.

KINLOCH, JOHN M. married to SIMMS, MARY March 24, 1881 by Rev. William H. Campbell at St. Paul's Church. He a native of Charleston and a laborer.

KINLOCH, MATILDA aged 40 years married to WESTMORELAND, JESSE M. aged 60 years November 9, 1887 by Rev. John Johnson at St. Philip's Church. He a native of Greenwood, South Carolina and she of Charleston. He a wholesale druggist.

KINSMAN, (Mrs.) HATTIE S. HENRY aged 28 years married to HANEY, JOHN F. aged 38 years December 19, 1894 by Rev. Edmund Wells at 369 Meeting Street. He a native of Darlington County, South Carolina and she of Colleton County, South Carolina. He a brickmason.

KIRK, E. AUGUSTA married to SPARKMAN, EDWARD H. aged 33 years December 19, 1878 by Rev. Richard S. Trapier at St. Michael's Church.

KIRK, JOHN P. aged 42 years married to JOYNER, (Mrs.) MARGARET WELLING aged 43 years October 28, 1894 by Rev. J. C. Yongue. Both natives of Charleston. He works for the municipal government.

KIRK, ROBERT aged 30 years married to COURTNEY, AMELIA aged 26 years November 14, 1889 by Rev. C. C. Pinckney at Grace Church. He a native of Berkeley County, South Carolina and she of Savannah, Georgia. He a lawyer in Berkeley County.

KIRK, SAMUEL G. aged 22 years married to GERDES, SOPHIE H. aged 36 years March 12, 1891 by Rev. Louis Muller. He a native of Scotland and she of Hanover. He a printer.

KIRKLAND, JOHN F. aged 27 years married to JARCKES, MARGARET E. aged 20 years June 5, 1889 by Rev. Edwin C. Dargan at Citadel Square Baptist Church. He a native of Kershaw County, South Carolina and she of Charleston. He a railroad conductor.

KLATTE, DORETHA H. aged 24 years married to WULBURY, HENRY W. aged 24 years November 7, 1894 by Rev. Edward T. Horn.

KLATTE, JOHN aged 35 years married to SEEBER, CAROLINE aged 25 years February 5, 1884 by Rev. Luther K. Probst at Wentworth Street Lutheran Church.

KLEE, ADELINE MARGARETHE aged 18 years married to BRUGGERMAN, FRANTZ HEINE aged 21 years November 28, 1881 by Rev. Louis Muller at the St. Matthew's Lutheran Church. He a native of Georgia and she of Charleston. He a baker.

KLEIN, E. E. C. aged 45 years married to SEIGLING, FREDERICK C. aged 50 years December 9, 1880 by Rev. Louis Muller at the northeast corner of Wentworth and Lynch Streets. Both natives of Germany. He a grocer.

KLEINKE, H. L. aged 21 years married to WOHLERS, H. C. aged 24 years October 27, 1887 by Rev. Johannes Heckel. Both natives of Charleston. He a mechanic.

KLEINMANN, MAXIMILIANA aged 23 years married to LABOUSEUR, JOHANN LUDWIG aged 24 years April 17, 1881 by Rev. Johannes Heckel. He a native of Hanover and she of Wittenberg, Germany. He a laborer.

KLEMM, T. W. aged 29 years married to AXSON, WILLIAM C. aged 37 years July 24, 1895 by Rev. Edmund Wells at 20 Bogard Street. He a native of Charleston and she of Mt. Pleasant, South Carolina. He works in the phosphate factory.

KLENKE, CHARLES F. aged 22 years married to SEEDORF, GESINA aged 23 years December 15, 1895 by Rev. Alfred Freyschmidt.

KLENKE, JOHN aged 27 years married to TIEDEMANN, GERTRUDE aged 23 years December 7, 1886 by Rev. Johannes Heckel at St. Johannes Lutheran Church.

KLENKE, JULIA D. aged 23 years married to BREDENBERG, JOHN H. aged 28 years January 6, 1887 by Rev. D. M. Martens at St. Johannes Lutheran Church. He a native of Augusta, Georgia and she of Charleston. He a merchant.

KLENTWORTH, FRIEDRICH aged 41 years married to KOOPMANN, ALVINA MARIA ANNA aged 24 years February 26, 1879 by Rev. Louis Muller. He a native of Hanover and she of Charleston.

KLENTWORTH, PETER aged 27 years married to GRIEME (?), ELISE aged 20 years September 18, 1881 by Rev. Louis Muller. Both natives of Hanover. He a merchant.

KLINCK, MICHAEL S. aged 30 years married to MARTIN, G. J. aged 24 years May 25, 1880 by Rev. W. S. Bowman at the Wentworth Street Lutheran Church. Both natives of Charleston. He a merchant.

KLINGENBERG, LINA CAROLINE A. aged 22 years married to SELLMANN, HERMAN aged 27 years November 23, 1886 by Rev. Louis Muller at 14 Wentworth Street. Both natives of Germany. He a brewer.

KLOSS, AMANDA PAULINE FLORENTINE aged 30 years married to DWYER, HENRY aged 30 years September 5, 1878 by Rev. Louis Muller at 3 Liberty Street.

KNAPP, ELIZA J. aged 24 years married to SMITH, JOHN GRAY aged 29 years January 1, 1878 by Rev. John Johnson at 110 Tradd Street. Both natives of Charleston. He a mariner.

KNAUFF, THOMAS G. aged 31 years married to PETERS, META ELISE aged 26 years April 21, 1887 by Rev. Louis Muller at St. Matthew's Lutheran Church. Both natives of Charleston. He a carpenter.

KNEBEL, ALBERT aged 33 years married to HUTCHMACHER, LENA aged 29 years January 24, 1883 by Father J. J. Woolahan at the residence of the Bride's parents - 77 Meeting Street. He a native of Prussian and she of New Orleans, Louisiana. He a tailor.

KNIGHT, D. J. aged 25 years married to McINERNEY, A. H. aged 20 years August 6, 1882 by Rev. J. G. Guentzer at The Cathedral of St. John the Baptist. He a native of Charleston and a mariner.

KNIGHT, JOSEPH JAMES aged 27 years married to HOLSTON, MARGARET A. aged 23 years June 27, 1883 by Father P. L. Duffy at The Cathedral of St. John the Baptist. Both natives of Charleston. He a fireman.

KNIGHT, MARGARET aged 18 years married to O'SHAUGHNESSY, PATRICK aged 24 years January 26, 1878 by Father Harry P. Northrop at St. Patrick's Roman Catholic Church.

KNIGHT, MARGARET aged 18 years married to O'SHAUGHNESSY, PATRICK aged 24 years January 26, 1878 by Father Harry P. Northrop at St. Patrick's Roman Catholic Church.

KNIGHT, S. W. married to THOMPSON, CAROLINE E. January 9, 1878 by William B. Yates, Chaplain.

KNOPF, JOSEPH aged 21 years married to THOMPSON, U. CLAUDIA aged 25 years May 8, 1887 by Rev. Louis Muller at the St. Matthew's Lutheran Church. He a native of Blackville, South Carolina and she of Marion, South Carolina. He a clerk in Blackville.

KNOTT, JOHN W. married to POPE, SUSIE March 15, 1892 by Rev. John Gass. She a native of Alabama. He a clergyman in Norfolk, Virginia.

KNOWLES, SYNTHIA D. aged 18 years married to THOMPSON, J. D. aged 20 years September 13, 1891 by Rev. Edmund Wells at 22 Aiken Street. Both natives of Charleston. He the Superintendent at the spinning factory.

KNOX, C. aged 26 years married to PATTERSON, FRANK aged 28 years October 23, 1883 by Rev. J. V. Welsh at 61 Line Street. Both natives of Charleston. He an engineer.

KNOX, ELIZABETH married to SANDERS, HENRY March 26, 1880 by William B. Yates, Chaplain. Both natives of Charleston.

KNOX, JOHN aged 53 years married to BRAILSFORD, (Mrs.) JULIA SARAH WILSON aged 47 years April 18, 1878 by Rev. G. R. Brackett. He a native of Ireland and she of Charleston. He a salesman.

KNOX, LEWIS CHAFFEE aged 19 years married to SHOKES, MARTHA LOUISA aged 15 years March 5, 1883 by Rev. E. J. Meynardie at 12 Norman Street. Both natives of Charleston. He a laborer.

KNOX, LILLIAN L. aged 20 years married to CHRISTIE, WILLIAM McP. aged 29 years May 28, 1885 by Rev. John Johnson at the Mills House Hotel. He a native of Nassau and she of Charleston. He works on a steamboat.

KNOX, RIPLEY LEE aged 26 years married to RILEY, ANNIE ELIZABETH aged 19 years February 11, 1889 by Rev. R. G. Smart at Bethel Church. Both natives of Charleston. He a cardriver.

KNUDSON, INGRET aged 25 years married to FROHOLEN, M. aged 31 years April 3, 1882 by Rev. Luther H. Probst. He a native of Norway and she of Sweden. He a mariner.

KOENNECKE, JOSEPH THEODORE aged 24 years married to COOK, BEAURIE MARIE aged 22 years August 10, 1884 by Rev. John H. Honour at 14 John Street. Both natives of Charleston. He works for the railroad.

KOESTER, (Mrs.) C. W. C. H. SCHADE aged 38 years married to MERKHARDT(?), J. P. aged 64 years December 7, 1884 by Rev. Johannes Heckel at St. Johannes Lutheran Church. Both natives of Germany.

KOHLER, HENRIETTA aged 21 years married to HENKIN, HENRY aged 28 years March 6, 1881 by Rev. Johannes Heckel. Both natives of Hanover. He merchant.

KOLDEWAY, ANNIE aged 17 years married to KENNERTY, THOMAS J. aged 17 years July 3, 1887 by Father Daniel J. Quigley at St. Patrick's Roman Catholic Church. He a native of Ireland and she of Charleston. He a farmer.

KOLERA, ANTOINE aged 31 years married to CAMMER, EMILY aged 25 years August 17, 1888 by Rev. J. E. Carlisle at 55 Spring Street. He a native of Athens, Georgia and she of Charleston. He a carpenter.

KOLNDORFF, ERNST aged 28 years married to SCHELLETTER, CHARLOTTE aged 24 years September 19, 1878 by Rev. Johannes Heckel. He a native of Germany and she of Prussia. He a baker.

KOOPMAN, ALVINA MARIA ANN aged 24 years married to KLENTWORTH, FRIEDRICH aged 41 years February 26, 1879 by Rev. Louis Muller. He a native of Hanover and she of Charleston.

KOOPMANN, G. F. A. aged 27 years married to BOKSEN, M G. H. aged 32 years January 13, 1885 by Rev. Louis Muller in King Street near Broad Street. He a native of Charleston and she of Germany. He a farmer.

KOPER, ANNA HELENE aged 22 years married to SCHARFER, JOHANN HEINRICH aged 22 years January 24, 1889 by Rev. Louis Muller at the residence of the Bride's father in Mt. Pleasant, South Carolina. He a native of Charleston and she of Mt. Pleasant, South Carolina. He a grocer.

KOPER, CLAUS aged 21 years married to WITTSCHEN, E. C. ELIZABETH aged 24 years October 1, 1891 by Rev. R. C. Holland in Mt. Pleasant, South Carolina. He a native of Mt. Pleasant, South Carolina and she of Charleston. He a farmer in Mt. Pleasant.

KOPS, WILLIAM C. aged 23 years married to MALONE, ELIZABETH C. aged 22 years September 5, 1885 by Rev. John Johnson at The Pavilion Hotel. Both natives of Minnesota.

KORBER, ANNIE M. aged 20 years married to EASTERBY, STEWART D. aged 23 years March 31, 1891 by Rev. R. C. Holland at the Wentworth Street Lutheran Church. Both natives of Charleston. He a salesman.

KORNAHRENS, ANNA MARIA WILHELMINA aged 21 years married to STRAUSS, HENRY aged 25 years November 16, 1884 by Father Claudian B. Northrop at 56 Hasell Street. He a native of Walhalla, South Carolina and she of Charleston. He a merchant.

KORNAHRENS, HELENA aged 21 years married to WOLFE, WILLIAM J. aged 24 years September 14, 1890 by Rev. R. C. Holland at the Wentworth Street Lutheran Church. He a native of Orangeburg, South Carolina and she of Germany. He a merchant in Orangeburg.

KORNAHRENS, JOHN J. married to O'NEALE, SARAH ELIZABETH February 3, 1889 by Rev. William H. Campbell at the residence of William P. O'Neale. He a clerk.

KORNAHRENS, SOPHIE ENGEL aged 23 years married to SCHLUETER, WILLIAM HENRY aged 24 years October 14, 1884 by Rev. Claudian B. Northrop, at 53 Coming Street. He a native of Walhalla, South Carolina and she of Germany. He a saloon keeper in Washington, D. C.

KOSMINSKI, HANNAH aged 26 years married to ROSENTHAL, ISAAC P. aged 32 years July 14, 1886 by Rabbi David Levy at 154 King Street. Both natives of Germany. He a merchant.

KOSTER, JOHANN aged 37 years married to STEHMEYER, ANNA MARIA aged 21 years November 10, 1887 by Rev. Louis Muller at the corner of Meeting and Hasell Streets. He a native of Prussia and she of Bremen, Germany. He a grocer.

KOSTER, JOHANN EMIL aged 32 years married to CORDES, MARGARETHE ADELINE aged 28 years June 27, 1889 by Rev. Louis Muller at the residence of the Bride's father - 326 East Bay Street, north of Laurens Street. He a native of Brooklyn, New York and she of Charleston. He a grocer and a widower.

KOSTER, JULIUS D. aged 24 years married to BLOHME, HENRIETTE D. aged 18 years October 1, 1885 by Rev. Louis Muller at 4 Glebe Street. He a native of Brooklyn, South Carolina and she of Charleston. He a clerk.

KOSTER, LOUIS HENRY aged 28 years married to KOSTER, SOPHIE THEODORA aged 25 years April 8, 1891 by Rev. Louis Muller in Cumberland Street. He a native of Brooklyn, New York and she of Charleston. He a grocer.

KOSTER, M. A. aged 19 years married to LOSSE, P. aged 27 years November 22, 1882 by Rev. Louis Muller at the corner of Meeting and Radcliffe Streets. He a native of Germany and a tailor.

KOSTER, SOPHIE THEODORA aged 25 years married to KOSTER, LOUIS HENRY aged 28 years April 8, 1891 by Rev. Louis Muller in Cumberland Street. He a native of Brooklyn, New York and she of Charleston. He a grocer.

KOSTER, WILHELMINA SOPHIE HENRIETTA aged 23 years married to STELLJES, HERMAN DIETRICH aged 28 years March 26, 1878 by Rev. Louis Muller at the corner of Smith and Cannon Streets. He a native of Germany and she of Charleston. He a grocer.

KRACKE, FREDERICK D.C. aged 33 years married to WERNER, JULIANE W. M. aged 25 years October 2, 1883 by Rev. Louis Muller at 29 Rutledge Avenue. Both natives of Charleston. He a merchant.

KRAMER, IDA E. aged 16 years married to WEBBER, GEORGE aged 21 years April 13, 1880 by Rev. J. V. Welsh at 64 Radcliffe Street. Both natives of Charleston. He a moulder.

KRAMER, LOUIS aged 36 years married to KENNEDY, HENRY aged 38 years December 26, 1883 by Father F. J. Shadler at St. Joseph's Roman Catholic Church. She a native of Hamburg, Germany. He operates a restaurant.

KRANTZ, (Mrs.) AUGUSTA C. GRAVER aged 29 years married to HOLANDER, JOHN A. aged 32 years August 21, 1892 by Rev. Edward T. Horn at 31 Pitt Street. He a native of Finland and a merchant.

KRANZ, WILLIAM aged 24 years married to GRUMMER, CHARLOTTE aged 21 years May 17, 1881 by Rev. Louis Muller at 8 Calhoun Street.

KRAUSE, WILLIAM E. aged 28 years married to CROSS, LILLA L. aged 18 years March 27, 1879 by Rev. W. S. Bowman in Radcliffe Street. He a native of Bethlehem, Pennsylvania and she of Charleston. He a tailor.

KREINSON (?), LUTHER H. aged 36 years married to COWLEY, LUCINDA aged 24 years August 9, 1885 by Rev. John O. Wilson at 82 Wentworth Street.

KREMSON, (Mrs.) LUCINDA COWLEY aged 24 years married to KENSON, LUTHER H. aged 36 years August 9, 1885 by Rev. John O. Wilson. He a native of Philadelphia, Pennsylvania and she of South Carolina. He a policeman.

KREMSON, LUTHER H. aged 36 years married to KREMSON, (Mrs.) LUCINDA COWLEY aged 24 years August 9, 1885 by Rev. John O. Wilson. He a native of Philadelphia, Pennsylvania and she of South Carolina. He a policeman.

KRESSEL, (Mrs.) ANNA BLANCHARD aged 33 years married to DuBOSE, HENRY S. aged 36 years September 27, 1888 by Father Daniel J. Quigley at 313 King Street. He a native of Williamsburg County, South Carolina and she of South Carolina. He an engineer in Waycross, Georgia.

KREUER, MARY aged 30 years married to DWYER, JOHN aged 27 years January 9, 1879 by Rev. Johannes Heckel in King Street. Both natives of Germany. He a merchant in Augusta, Georgia.

KROEF, CHARLES W. aged 21 years married to MYERS, EDITH A. aged 24 years April 19, 1881 by Rev. Luther K. Probst in Gadsden Street.

KROEF, ANDREW A. aged 22 years married to HEINS, IDA B. aged 18 years December 7, 1880 by Rev. Luther K. Probst at 433 King Street. He a native of Charleston and a druggist.

KROEG, EMMA W. aged 19 years married to LUNZ, GEORGE aged 31 years May 31, 1881 by Rev. Luther K. Probst in Liberty Street.

KROEG, FLORENTINE B. aged 20 years married to PETERMAN, HENRY W. aged 29 years April 28, 1886 by Rev. Luther K. Probst. He a native of Gillisonville, South Carolina and she of Charleston. He a merchant in Gillisonville.

KROGUE, MAMIE aged 20 years married to McGORTY, JAMES aged 21 years March 4, 1883 by Rev. L. H. Shuck at 27 Church Street. He a native of Charleston and she of Augusta, Georgia. He a candymaker.

KROSSE (KROOMSE), JOHN aged 26 years married to BRAWLEY, LAURA aged 16 years December 11, 1881 by Rev. L. H. Shuck. Both natives of Charleston. He a miner.

KUCH, ADELAIDE ENTELMANN aged 35 years married to RENKEN, HEINRICH aged 33 years December 15, 1887 by Rev. Louis Muller at the southeast corner of Meeting and Columbus Streets.

KUCH, A. D. married to MESSERVY, F. December 25, 1881 by Rev. Edward T. Horn. Both natives of Charleston. He a druggist.

KUCH, A. F. aged 18 years married to HELEKIN, J. H. aged 21 years January 16, 1882 by Rev. L. H. Shuck at 27 Church Street. Both natives of Savannah, Georgia. He a grocer.

KRUER, HANKE aged 40 years married to FISCHER, DORIS aged 25 years June 22, 1884 by Rev. Johannes Heckel at 3 Minority Street. Both natives of Germany. He a merchant.

KUHL, CHARLES G. aged 25 years married to WALLACE, ELENORA aged 24 years May 15, 1887 by Rev. John Johnson at 53 Church Street. He a native of Virginia and she of Charleston. He a slater.

KUHLAND, WILHELM CHRISTOPHER aged 34 years married to TEAGUE, WILHELMINA DORIS aged 25 years December 1, 1889 by Rev. Louis Muller at the corner of Chapel and Alexander Streets.

KUHLEN, HENRIETTE aged 21 years married to HENKEN, HENRY aged 28 years March 6, 1881 by Rev. Johannes Heckel at 125 Calhoun Street.

KUHLEN, J. F. aged 30 years married to REHKOPF (?), L. A. aged 25 years November 27, 1879 by Rev. Louis Muller. He a native of Hanover and a grocer. She a native of Charleston.

KUHN, DAVID JACOB aged 21 years married to SCHARDT, BARBARA MAGDALENA aged 20 years January 3, 1889 by Rev. Johannes Heckel.

KUHNE, E. aged 23 years married to DREES, H. aged 22 years October 24, 1882 by Rev. Louis Muller at 90 Calhoun Street. He a native of Germany and a grocer.

KULING (?), DAVID J. aged 21 years married to SCHARDT, BARBARA MAGDALENA. aged 20 years January 3, 1889 by Rev. Johannes Heckel at St. Johannes Lutheran Church. Both natives of Nashville, Tennessee. He a druggist.

KULMINSKI, ALBERT JULIUS aged 24 years married to BRANDT, ANNA PAULINE aged 20 years February 10, 1881 by Rev. Claudian B. Northrop at St. Mary of the Annunciation Roman Catholic Church. He a native of Washington, D. C. and she of Charleston. He a merchant.

KUNZE, JOHN HENRY aged 22 years married to HORENKUHE (?), ANNA M. E. aged 22 years June 27, 1886 by Rev. Johannes Heckel at 14 Inspection Street. Both natives of Germany. He a baker.

KURNROW, CARL M. aged 28 years married to FLOTMANN, JOSEPHINE aged 20 years September 25, 1885 by Rev. Louis Muller at the residence of the Bride - 22 Pine Street. He a native of Germany and she of Charleston. He a butcher.

KURRE, W. C. aged 19 years married to MEYER, NICHOLAS A. M. aged 22 years March 26, 1885 by Rev. Louis Muller at St. Matthew's Lutheran Church. He a native of Savannah, Georgia and she of Charleston. He a restaurant worker.

KURNA (?), HAUS ANDERSON married to MOLLER, ELLEN NELSON January 1, 1879 by William B. Yates, Chaplain.

KUTCHER, CHARLES G. T. aged 29 years married to NAUGUCKS, LOUISA A. aged 24 years July 3, 1883 by Father Claudian B. Northrop at 125 Calhoun Street. Both natives of Germany. He a mariner.

KWORE (?), EMMA JOHANNA aged 19 years married to FINCKEN, EDWARD H. F. aged 20 years February 12, 1880 by Rev. Louis Muller at St. Matthew's Lutheran Church. Both natives of Charleston. He a grocer in Walterboro, South Carolina.

LABERGNE (?), MARY A. aged 20 years married to HILL, JAMES THOMAS aged 21 years February 12, 1888 by Father J. McManus. He a native of Columbia, South Carolina and she of Charleston. He a granite cutter.

LABOUSEUR, JOHANN LUDWIG aged 24 years married to KLEINMANN, MAXIMILIANA aged 23 years April 17, 1881 by Rev. Johannes Heckel. He a native of Hanover and she of Wittenberg, Germany. He a laborer.

LaCOSTE, J. C. married to ROBERTSON, HENRIETTA November 8, 1884 by Rev. W. T. Thompson at the First Presbyterian Church. He a bookkeeper.

LADSON, JAMES HENRY aged 31 years married to FELDER, KATE aged 24 years May 21, 1884 by Rev. E. J. Meynardie. He a native of Charleston and she of Orangeburg, South Carolina.

LADSON, (Mrs.) J. EUGENIA DAVIS aged 30 years married to GLOVER, WILLIAM H. aged 34 years July 1, 1888 by Rev. C. E. Chichester. She a native of Kingstee, South Carolina. He a painter.

LADSON, LEILA A. aged 35 years married to JONES, EDWARD G. aged 56 years November 6, 1890 by Rev. C. C. Pinckney at 4 Meeting Street. He a native of Connecticut and she of Charleston. He a manufacturer in New York.

LADSON, SARAH TILMAN aged 22 years married to ROBERTSON, EDWARD T. aged 26 years December 22, 1881 by Rev. C. C. Pinckney at Grace Church. Both natives of Charleston. He a clerk.

LADY, WILLIAM D. aged 30 years married to SCHLUETER, SOPHIE C. aged 28 years January 10, 1892 by Rev. R. C. Holland at 2 Montagu Street.

LaFAR, LOUISE aged 25 years married to MOLLENHAUER, ERNST aged 42 years April 19, 1883 by Rev. Luther K. Probst. He a native of Germany and she of Charleston. He a policeman.

LaFAR, LYDIA SOPHIA married to COOKE, GEORGE LaGRANGE aged 29 years October 22, 1878 by Rev. H. C. Dana. He a native of LaGrange, Georgia and she of Orangeburg, South Carolina. He a photographer.

LaFOURCADE, AMADEE J. A. aged 39 years married to INNIS, ANNIE aged 21 years March 5, 1878 by Father Harry P. Northrop at St. Patrick's Roman Catholic Church. He a native of Bordeaux, France and she of Charleston. He a watchman.

LaFOURCADE, ANNA aged 21 years married to LEE, HENRY aged 22 years September 26, 1886 by Rev. J. V. Welsh at 22 Spring Street. He a native of South Carolina and she of Charleston. He a laborer.

LAFOURCADE, M. EVA aged 17 years married to COBIA, S. WALTER aged 21 years September 29, 1889 by Rev. H. B. Browne at 78 Drake Street. Both natives of Charleston. He a printer.

LaFOURCADE, VICTOR aged 21 years married to MAVRY, ANNIE aged 18 years January 30, 1883 by Father John Twigg at St. Patrick's Roman Catholic Church. Both natives of Charleston.

LAIN, MARY ELLEN aged 16 years married to WILLIAMS, BENJAMIN M. aged 24 years May 14, 1894 by Rev. Edmund Wells at 579 King Street. He a native of Colleton County, South Carolina and she of Hampton County, South Carolina. He a weaver in the cotton mill.

LALOR, E. MARY married to WARREN, FREDERICK B. December 25, 1889 by Rev. William H. Campbell at 64 President Street. He a clerk in Jacksonville, Florida.

LALOR, (Mrs.) SUSAN R. McKENZIE married to HANCOCK, SAMUEL S. May 22, 1890 by Rev. William H. Campbell at 101 Broad Street. He a pilot.

LAMB, JAMES J. aged 30 years married to THOMPSON, ALMA G. aged 22 years December 25, 1895 by Rev. G. R. Brackett at 23 Cannon Street.

LAMB, JOHN JAMES aged 23 years married to ADAMS, MAGGIE aged 24 years December 6, 1893 by Rev. Edmund Wells at 82 Drake Street. Both natives of South Carolina. He works in the basket factory.

LAMB, MARY JANE aged 34 years married to KELLEHER, JOHN aged 42 years June 13, 1894 by Rev. Edmund Wells at 54 Washington Street. He a native of Fergus, Canada and she of South Carolina. He a weaver in the cotton mill.

LAMB, ROBERT L. aged 22 years married to PURSE, MARY ROBERTA aged 19 years March 2, 1884 by Rev. J. H. Tillinghast at 15 Nassau Street. He a native of Wilmington, North Carolina and she of Charleston. He a gardener.

LAMB, SARAH ANN married to CHAPLAIN, S.G. November 15, 1877 by William B. Yates, Chaplain.

LAMBERT, J. B. aged 29 years married to WATSON, F. D. aged 28 years December 28, 1880 by Rev. L. H. Shuck. He a native of Columbus, Georgia and she of Augusta, Georgia. He a merchant.

LAMBERT, SUSAN WASHINGTON aged 17 years married to GOETHE, JAMES E. aged 24 years June 27, 1878 by Rev. R. N. Wells. He a native of Beaufort, South Carolina and she of Charleston. He a farmer.

LAMBLE, JAMES W. married to McNAIL, MARGARET A. March 17, 1879 by Rev. G. R. Brackett. Both natives of Charleston. He an agent at the Gas Company.

LAMBLE, JULIA CLEMENTINE aged 24 years married to GARETY, CHRISTOPHER JOHN aged 30 years June 9, 1881 by Rev. Claudian B. Northrop. He a native of Charleston and a clerk.

LAMKIN, OCTAVIAN E. aged 22 years married to THORNAL, JULIA A. aged 17 years May 7, 1893 by Father J. J. Monaghan at 136 St. Philip Street. He a native of Charleston and she of St. Stephen's Parish, South Carolina. He a tinner in Savannah, Georgia.

LaMOTTE, HENRY JAMES aged 29 years married to REEVES, LIZZIE SUSAN aged 17 years November 29, 1883 by Rev. A. C. Smith in Drake Street. Both natives of Charleston. He a carpenter.

LANDER, GENEVA B. aged 17 years married to DRAUGHTON, MATTHEW aged 24 years December 24, 1891 by Rev. Edwin C. Dargan at 29 Charlotte Street. He a native of North Carolina and she of Rocky Mount, North Carolina. He a clerk.

LANDRUM, IDA MARION aged 24 years married to CARDWELL, JOHN aged 28 years January 16, 1881 by Rev. L. H. Shuck at 48 Church Street. He a native of Priston, England and she of Columbia, South Carolina. He a medical student.

LANG, LUKE aged 24 years married to OTT, MARY aged 22 years December 4, 1882 by Rev. John G. Guentzer at The Cathedral of St. John the Baptist. Both natives of Charleston. He a stonecutter.

LANGAN, BESSIE aged 24 years married to Beattie, JAMES O'NEIL aged 30 years February 8, 1891 by Father J. J. Monaghan at St. Patrick's Roman Catholic Church.

LANGAN, MARY aged 23 years married to TOBIN, Edmund J. aged 30 years October 23, 1890 by Bishop Harry P. Northrop at The Cathedral of St. John the Baptist. Both natives of Charleston. He a laborer.

LANGE, CHARLES L. aged 25 years married to DUNNING, FLORENCE E. aged 16 years May 16, 1893 by Rev. J. L. Stokes at 231 Coming Street. Both natives of Charleston. He a clerk in Summerville, South Carolina.

LANGE, GUSTAV L. aged 30 years married to TIEDEMANN, JOHANNA CATHERINE A. aged 24 years December 17, 1877 by Rev. Louis Muller at the St. Matthew's Lutheran Church. Both natives of Charleston. He a merchant.

LANGE, MINNA ANNA aged 25 years married to BEHLMER, HEINRICH W. aged 30 years December 12, 1886 by Rev. Louis Muller at the southeast corner of Columbus and Hanover Streets. He a native of Germany and she of Charleston. He a grocer.

LANGER, THEODORE C. F. aged 21 years married to BUCK, M. J. aged 19 years September 16, 1880 by Rev. Louis Muller at St. Matthew's Lutheran Church. Both natives of Charleston. He a fruitier.

LANGSTON, EDIE ONETA aged 18 years married to Baker, JAMES C. aged 24 years March 10, 1892 by Rev. Edward C. Wells at 42 H Street. He a native of Lancaster, South Carolina and she of Florence, South Carolina. He a farmer.

LANIER, ISOM F. aged 42 years married to LEGGETT, ADA G. aged 21 years July 25, 1895 by Rev. J. C. Yongue at 77 Hanover Street.

LANIER, JOHN FRANKLIN aged 35 years married to WRAGG, A. M. A aged 23 years April 5, 1887 by Rev. T. P. Burgess. He a native of North Carolina and she of South Carolina. He a mechanic.

LANIGAN, ANNIE E. aged 22 years married to WESTBERRY, JOHN W. aged 22 years December 11, 1892 by Father J. J. Monaghan at St. Patrick's Roman Catholic Church. He a native of South Carolina and she of Charleston. He a merchant.

LANIGAN, CORNELIUS aged 24 years married to CLEARY, MARIA aged 25 years October 15, 1890 by Father Harry P. Northrop at The Cathedral of St. John the Baptist. Both natives of Charleston. He a laborer.

LANIGAN, C. J. aged 22 years married to BEGLEY, J. M. aged 21 years March 20, 1882 by Father F. J. Shadler at St. Joseph's Roman Catholic Church. He a native of Charleston and a railroad worker.

LANIGAN, JAMES F. aged 28 years married to RILEY, THERESA F. aged 20 years January 3, 1895 by Father Thomas F. Hopkins at St. Mary of the Annunciation Roman Catholic Church. Both natives of Charleston. He works in the phosphate mill in Coosaw, South Carolina.

LANIGAN, T. MICHAEL aged 28 years married to RODDY, MAMIE aged 23 years April 15, 1890 by Father Harry P. Northrop at The Cathedral of St. John the Baptist. Both natives of Charleston. He a clerk.

LANIGAN, WINIFRED S. aged 26 years married to DOYLE, THOMAS C. aged 28 years November 27, 1894 by Father J. J. Monaghan at St. Patrick's Roman Catholic Church. He a native of Orangeburg, South Carolina and she of New Jersey. He a physician in Orangeburg.

LANNEAU, BASIL R. aged 22 years married to STANSELL, LIZZIE L. aged 24 years November 7, 1894 by Rev. David M. Ramsey at 53 Laurens Street.

LANNEAU, WILLIAM S. aged 22 years married to SEIGLING, MARY PATRICK aged 20 years June 30, 1892 by Rev. Edward T. Horn at St. Johannes Lutheran Church. Both natives of Charleston. He a clerk.

LANNEAU, ALFRED W. aged 43 years married to BARFIELD, EMMA C. aged 27 years February 5, 1890 by Rev. R. A. Webb at the corner of Rutledge Avenue and Calhoun Street.

LaPORTA, FRANCIS ALFRED aged 22 years married to GENTRY, AGNES BEATRICE aged 17 years July 30, 1894 by Father J. J. Monaghan at St. Patrick's Roman Catholic Church. He a native of New York and she of Charleston. He a confectioner.

LARISEY, H. M. aged 31 years married to THOMPSON, S. W. S. aged 32 years July 9, 1879 by Rev. G. R. Brackett. He a native of York County, South Carolina and she of Charleston. He an engineer.

LaROUCHE, CHRISTOPHER I. aged 26 years married to DESAUSSURE, MARY C. aged 26 years October 29, 1878 by Rev. Rev. W. B. Howe at St. Philip's Church.

LaROCHE, E. D. aged 28 years married to WILKINSON, CLAUDE H. aged 29 years June 30, 1891 by Rev. Charles S. Vedder. He a native of Edisto Island, South Carolina and she of Colleton County, South Carolina.

LAROYSSEIERE, EMILE aged 24 years married to OWYNS, BLANCHE aged 24 years December 20, 1877 by Father Harry P. Northrop at St. Patrick's Roman Catholic Church. Both natives of Charleston. He a painter.

LARKIN, ELLEN VINCENT aged 26 years married to CHERRY, DOMINICK aged 25 years August 29, 1881 by Father P. L. Duffy at The Cathedral of St. John the Baptist. He a native of Charleston and she of New York City.

LARKIN, JANE aged 40 years married to GUILLEMIN, PETER L. aged 50 years June 29, 1885 by Father J. J. Wedenfeller at St. Mary of the Annunciation Catholic Church. He an employee of the gas works.

LaROCHE, (Mrs.) MARIE PATTERSON aged 37 years married to BROWN, HENRY JAMES aged 38 years June 30, 1891 by Rev. W. A. Betts at 2 Hampstead Square. He a native of Portsmith, Virginia and she of Charleston. He a mechanic.

LAROUSSELIERE, EMILE aged 24 years married to OWENS, BLANCHE aged 26 years December 20, 1877 by Father Harry P. Northrop at St. Patrick's Roman Catholic Church. Both natives of Charleston. He a painter.

LAROUSSELIERE, EMILIE aged 24 years married to ENRIGHT, JOHN aged 28 years May 26, 1885 by Rev. F. A. Schmetz at St. Patrick's Roman Catholic Church. Both natives of Charleston. He a miller.

LAROUSSELIERE, EUGENIA aged 24 years married to ASHE, F. M. aged 25 years by Father P. L. Duffy. Both natives of Charleston. He an upholsterer.

LAROUSELIERE, M. aged 28 years married to DUNCAN, D. aged 28 years November 11, 1882 by Father J. J. Woolahan at St. Patrick's Roman Catholic Church. Both natives of Charleston. He works for the railroad.

LARSEN, ANDREW P. aged 27 years married to NEILSON, ANNA C. aged 19 years December 15, 1885 by Rev. John Johnson at 295 East Bay Street. Both natives of Denmark. He a farmer in Berkeley County, South Carolina.

LARSEN, CHRISTIAN J. aged 25 years married to ADDISON, JANIE WARING aged 22 years June 2, 1886 by Rev. A. J. S. Thomas at 49 South Battery. He a native of Norway and she of Charleston. He a clerk.

LARSEN, PETER aged 27 years married to JENSEN, TRINA aged 22 years June 21, 1881 by Rev. Johannes Heckel. He a native of Denmark and a rice planter.

LARSEN, PETER JOHN aged 23 years married to WOLD, AGNES CHRISTINA aged 23 years October 31, 1890 by Rev. C. E. Chichester at 23 Cumberland Street. He a native of Denmark and she of Arendal, Norway. He a driver.

LARSON, JOHN aged 28 years married to SPELL, VICTORIA aged 22 years May 18, 1884 by Rev. Luther K. Probst. He a native of Norway and she of South Carolina. He a carpenter.

LASSALLE, ADELA E. aged 17 years married to NORTON, JAMES E. aged 30 years August 22, 1886 by Rev. J. W. Dickson. He a native of North Carolina and she of South Carolina. He a laborer.

LASSITER, ROBERT B. aged 26 years married to TOWLES, MARTHA V. aged 26 years November 5, 1895 by Rev. David M. Ramsey.

LATTIMORE, HENRY W. married to HARRISON, MAHALA January 30, 1879 by Rev. John Johnson at 45 George Street. Both natives of Pennsylvania.

LAURENS, HENRY R. married to SIMONS, CHARLOTTE October 22, 1884 by Rev. William H. Campbell.

LAVAL, (Mrs.) A. S. DOBBS married to DINER, F. November 18, 1881. He a native of Pennsylvania and she of Ireland. He a laborer.

LAVAL, WILLIAM J. married to ELFORD, GEORGIANA T. February 19, 1879 by Rev. G. R. Brackett. Both natives of Charleston. He a treasurer.

LAVALLE, MARY F. aged 20 years married to CONLON, M. P. aged 31 years June 3, 1888 by Father Daniel J. Quigley at The Cathedral of St. John the Baptist. Both natives of Charleston. He a merchant.

LaVERGUE, JULES aged 25 years married to BURKHARDT, WILHELMINA aged 20 years September 1, 1892 by Father J. J. Monaghan at St. Patrick's Roman Catholic Church. He a native of Augusta, Georgia and she of Baden, Germany. He a laborer.

LAVES, HENRY D. F. aged 24 years married to MULLER, L. aged 21 years September 18, 1881 by Rev. Louis Muller at the southeast corner of Calhoun and Anson Streets. He a native of Hanover and she of Charleston. He a grocer.

LAW, ANNA CATHARINA aged 20 years married to REHKOPF, FREDERICK GEORGE aged 24 years June 28, 1888 by Rev. Louis Muller at the residence of the Bride's father - the southeast corner of St. Philip and Cannon Streets.

LAW, JOHANNA H. aged 20 years married to SEALEY, THOMAS J. aged 32 years September 17, 1891 by Rev. R. C. Holland at 186 St. Philip Street. He a native of Augusta, Georgia and she of Charleston. He a carpet layer.

LAW, OLIVER aged 29 years married to McCABE, PAULINE aged 30 years January 31, 1892 by Rev. J. O. Fludd. He a native of Beaufort County, South Carolina and she of Johnson County, North Carolina. He a watchman.

LAWES, LUCIE MILLER aged 31 years married to TRAUTWEIN, CARL A. aged 25 years July 15, 1891 by Rev. Louis Muller at 96 Radcliffe Street. He a native of Germany and she of Charleston. He a painter.

LAWRENCE, KATE aged 20 years married to CLARK, WILLIAM DUFF aged 28 years September 21, 1891 by Rev. R. C. Holland at 145 Meeting Street. He a native of Perth, Scotland and she of Southampton, England. He a photographer.

LAWRENCE, RICHARD G. aged 23 years married to HUGNELET, HORTENSE L. H. aged 23 years February 28, 1893 by Rev. Edward T. Horn. Both natives of Charleston. He a clerk.

LAWTON, FLORENCE aged 34 years married to KALLOCH, PARKER C. aged 37 years October 25, 1893 by Rev. C. C. Pinckney at Grace Church. He a native of Maine and she of Beaufort County, South Carolina. He a physician in Cincinnati, Ohio.

LAZARUS, MARK H. aged 34 years married to LEVY, MORDECAI aged 30 years January 12, 1881 by Rabbi David Levy. Both natives of Charleston. He a merchant.

LEA, J. W. aged 24 years married to SIRES, W. J. aged 17 years May 26, 1882 by Rev. Luther K. Probst at 81 Queen Street. Both natives of South Carolina. He a pilot.

LEA, SARAH LIZZIE aged 18 years married to FRIERSON, THOMAS L. aged 26 years November 18, 1885 by Rev. L. K. Probst.

LEA, STEPHEN T. aged 21 years married to HUDSON, ELIZABETH O. aged 18 years April 4, 1878 by Rev. William H. Adams at the Circular Congregational Church. He a native of Charleston and she of Colleton County, South Carolina. He a physician.

LEACH, MARY C. aged 19 years married to COURIER, JOHN F. aged 22 years February 12, 1881 by Rev. C. C. Pinckney at Chisolm's Mill. He a native of Palatka, Florida and she of Charleston. He an engineer.

LEBBY, BESSIE WILLIAMS aged 23 years married to WALSH, BARTON aged 25 years February 9, 1887 by Rev. G. R. Brackett. Both natives of South Carolina. He a bookkeeper.

LEBBY, MONFORT S. aged 30 years married to DuBOIS, ELLA aged 22 years November 26, 1884 by Rev. E. J. Meynardie. He a native of Savannah, Georgia and she of South Carolina. He a cotton weigher in Savannah.

LEBBY, ROBERT CHARLTON aged 24 years married to BRADLEY, IDA CLAYTON aged 22 years April 9, 1890 by rev. G. R. Bracket at 17 Smith Street. He a native of Gordonston, Virginia and she of Charleston. He a traveling salesman.

LeBUFFE, ADOLPH aged 25 years married to GUILLEMIN, MARIE CATHERINE aged 22 years November 15, 1881 by Rev. Claudian B. Northrop at St. Mary of the Annunciation Roman Catholic Church. Both natives of Charleston. He a printer.

LEE, ALLISON aged 25 years married to WRIGHT, E. M. aged 23 years June 28, 1887 by Rev. John Johnson. He a native of Alabama and she of South Carolina. He a salesman.

LEE, CHARLES aged 44 years married to CAMERON, MARY aged 22 years March 13, 1889 by Rev. Louis Muller at 10 Mile Hill. He a native of Charleston and she of Mt. Pleasant, South Carolina. He a grocer.

LEE, DELIA aged 39 years married to MOODIE, J .C. aged 41 years May 4, 1888 by P. E. Gleason, Trial Justice. Both natives of North Carolina. He a farmer in Florida.

LEE, ELIZA J. aged 42 years married to ONSAN, HENRICK aged 26 years October 25, 1885 by Rev. John E. Beard at 22 Aiken Street. He a native of Norway and she of North Carolina. He a blacksmith.

LEE, ETTA MILES aged 23 years married to TERRELL, ALBERT E. aged 25 years January 1, 1879 by Rev. William C. Power at Bethel Church. He a native of St. Thomas Parish, Virginia and she of Darlington County, South Carolina.

LEE, HENRY aged 22 years married to LaFOURCADE, ANNA aged 21 years September 26, 1886 by Rev. J. V. Welch at 22 Spring Street. He a native of South Carolina and she of Charleston. He a laborer.

LEE, LILLY ELIZABETH aged 19 years married to ADDISON, JOSEPH C. aged 25 years August 28, 1878 by Rev. W. S. Bowman at 79 Spring Street. He a native of Charleston and a farmer.

LEE, MARIE aged 33 years married to TAYLOR, WILLIAM aged 18 years January 7, 1885 by Father F. A. Schmetz at St. Patrick's Roman Catholic Church. He a native of New York and she of Charleston. He a mariner.

LEEKING, MARY aged 18 years married to MEMMINGER, C. G. aged 21 years January 6, 1886 by Rev. Robert Wilson at 4 Wragg Square. Both natives of Charleston. He a physician.

LEGARE, EFFINGHAM W. aged 31 years married to EASTERBY ADA aged 28 years November 28, 1883 by Rev. C. C. Pinckney at Grace Church. Both natives of Charleston. He a clerk.

LEGARE, EMILY W. aged 27 years married to STANTON, FRANKLIN L. aged 24 years August 12, 1881 by Rev. L. H. Shuck at 27 Church Street. He a native of Charleston and a printer.

LEGARE, FLORENCE married to HUCKS, CHARLES December 8, 1878 by William B. Yates, Chaplain.

LEGARE, JULIA aged 21 years married to GADSDEN, EDWARD H. aged 25 years April 26, 1887 by Rev. G. R. Brackett. Both natives of South Carolina. He a drayman.

LEGARE, THOMAS S. aged 23 years married to SEABROOK, ANNIE SARAH aged 19 years February 28, 1878 by Rev. George W. Stickney on Johns Island, South Carolina. He a native of Charleston and she of Beaufort, South Carolina. He a planter.

LEGGETT, ADA G. aged 21 years married to LANIER, ISOM F. aged 42 years July 25, 1895 by Rev. J. C. Yongue at 77 Hanover Street.

LEHMEYER (?), FREDERICK aged 23 years married to NEVA, DAISY D. aged 18 years April 10, 1892 by Rev. Robert Wilson at 4 Wragg Square. He a native of Germany and she of Charleston. He a clerk.

LEHRMAN, GEORGE aged 53 years married to GRAF, (Mrs.) CHARLES BUCKERMANN aged 50 years October 20, 1884 by Rev. Johannes Heckel at 55 Smith Street. Both natives of Germany. He a mariner.

LEHRMAN, ISIDORE aged 31 years married to ISEMAN, AMELIA aged 22 years April 15, 1885 by Rev. C. C. Pinckney at Grace Church. He a native of Georgia and she of South Carolina. He a merchant in Savannah, Georgia.

LEHRMAN, MARY aged 18 years married to JORGENSON, CHRISTIAN aged 25 years May 21, 1878 by Rev. Johannes Heckel at 125 Calhoun Street. He a native of Denmark and she of Prussia. He a merchant.

LEIDHOFF, HERMAN aged 41 years married to BELITZER, BLANCHE aged 25 years October 3, 1889 by Rabbi David Levy at 344 East Bay Street. He a native of Germany and she of Charleston. He a photographer.

LUDHOFF, HERMAN aged 36 years married to DANEGA, SELINA aged 40 years October 12, 1881 by Rabbi David Levy at the Hasell Street Synagogue. He a native of Berlin, Germany and she of Charleston. He a photographer.

LEITCH, MARY aged 25 years married to THOMPSON, CHARLES AUGUSTUS aged 26 years March 3, 1878 by Father Claudian B. Northrop in King Street near Liberty Street. He a native of Charleston and she of London, England. He a tinner.

LeMEINTUE (?), GEORGE A. aged 45 years married to GANTT, ELIZA B. aged 24 years October 19, 1887 by Rev. Charles A. Stakely. He a native of Dublin, Ireland and she of Charleston. He a phosphate manufacturer in Wilmington, North Carolina.

LEMKINS, CARRIE aged 22 years married to SUREN, PAUL aged 27 years September 10, 1884 by Rev. F. A. Stemitz at St. Patrick's Roman Catholic Church. He a native of Germany and she of Charleston. He a baker.

LEMWIG, FREDERICK L. aged 34 years married to EWERT, HOLDA WILHELMINA aged 28 years April 14, 1884 by Rev. Johannes Heckel at 55 Smith. He a native of Denmark and she of Germany. He a steward.

LENT, THEODORE L. aged 25 years married to JARRETT, JESSIE J. aged 20 years September 30, 1895 by Rev. J. L. Stokes at 231 Coming Street. He a native of New York and she of Charleston. He works in the cotton mill.

LENT, VALERIA aged 16 years married to McEVOY, MICHAEL aged 18 years August 2, 1893 by Rev. J. M. Knowles at 87 America Street. He a native of South Carolina and she of Charleston. He works in the cotton mill.

LENTE, VIRGINIA aged 20 years married to SABO, MARTIN aged 27 years June 24, 1895 by Father J. J. Monaghan at St. Patrick's Roman Catholic Church. He a native of Germany and she of Charleston. He a street car driver.

LEONARD, JOHN L. aged 22 years married to MOLONY, MARY ELLEN aged 19 years November 18, 1890 by Father J. J. Monaghan at St. Patrick's Roman Catholic Church. He a native of Charleston and an engineer.

LEONARD, KATE C. aged 21 years married to MANDEVILLE, JAMES C. aged 18 years January 31, 1883 by Father J. P. Tillinghast at St. Patrick's Roman Catholic Church. Both natives of Charleston. He a painter.

LEONARD, MARGARET E. aged 22 years married to POWER, JAMES HAYES aged 31 years February 11, 1885 by Father F. A. Schmetz at St. Patrick's Roman Catholic Church.

LEONARD, WILLIAM J. aged 28 years married to LYNCH, CATHARINE aged 24 years August 15, 1886 by Father F. J. Shadler at St. Joseph's Roman Catholic Church. He a native of Charleston and she of Ireland. He a boilermaker.

LEOPOLD, BENJAMIN aged 28 years married to FRICHS, HELENA aged 25 years May 7, 1889 by Father John J. Wedenfeller at 114 Tradd Street. He a native of Alsac Lorraine and she of Germany.

LEOPOLD, (Mrs.) EMILY GODFREY aged 35 years married to WITTSHIRE, TRUMAN G. aged 35 years June 25, 1891 by Rev. Robert Wilson at 47 Cannon Street. He a native of England and she of Berkeley County, South Carolina. He a weaver in the cotton mill.

LEOPOLD, R. L. aged 22 years married to MADRAY, R. W. aged 22 years November 13, 1879 by Rev. W. S. Bowman at 262 Meeting Street. He a native of Strawberry Station and a phosphate worker. She a native of Charleston. He a resident of Five Mile Curve.

LEPPARD, (Mrs.) MARTHA THRIFT aged 40 years married to JACKSON, G. S. aged 47 years March 19, 1894 by Rev. Edmund Wells. He a native of Langley, South Carolina and she of Newberry, South Carolina. He works in the cotton mill.

LePRINCE, J. S. aged 39 years married to KANAPAUX, J. E. aged 24 years June 8, 1882 by Father F. J. Shadler at St. Joseph's Roman Catholic Church. He a native of Charleston and a railroad worker.

LEQUEUX, JULIA AMANDA aged 19 years married to KASTER, WILLIAM HENRY aged 23 years June 16, 1878 by Rev. W. S. Bowman. He a native of Edinborough, Scotland and she of St. Stephen's Parish, South Carolina. He a carpenter.

LEQUEUX, O. aged 19 years married to WALTON, E. aged 20 years December 4, 1882 by Father Daniel J. Quigley. He a native of Charleston and a railroad worker.

LESEMANN, AUGUSTUS H. D. aged 25 years married to WERNER, ANNA WILHELMINA S. aged 23 years February 18, 1891 by Rev. Louis Muller in Smith Street near Calhoun Street.

LESENSE, AUGUST aged 25 years married to WERNER, ANNIE W. S. aged 23 years January 11, 1891 by Rev. L. R. Nichols at 24 South Battery. Both natives of Charleston. He a merchant.

LESENSE, HARRIET LOUISE aged 27 years married to SMITH, ROBERT PRINGLE aged 25 years November 30, 1882 by Rev. John Johnson in King Street. He a native of Charleston and she of Charleston. He a merchant in Savannah, Georgia.

LESESNE, WILLIAM aged 30 years married to HARLESTON, ELIZABETH November 25, 1880 by Rev. A. Toomer Porter at the Church of the Holy Communion. Both natives of Charleston. He a clerk.

LESSEMANN, EMILIE MARIE aged 25 years married to SCHROEDER, JULIUS NICHOLAS aged 27 years November 6, 1888 by Rev. Louis Muller at the residence of the Bride's mother - northwest corner of Laurens and Wall Streets.

LESLIE, GERTRUDE ANN aged 25 years married to LONG, HARRY L. aged 34 years April 29, 1884 by Rev. A. H. Misseldine at the Circular Congregational Church.

LETT, ANNA A. aged 20 years married to MEVAY, WILLIAM J. aged 32 years March 22, 1885 by Rev. J. V. Welch at 58 Line Street. Both natives of Charleston. He a laborer.

LETT, IDA aged 19 years married to MORGAN, JAMES aged 21 years March 1, 1891 by Rev. W. A. Betts at 19 Wescott Court. Both natives of Charleston. He works in the bagging factory.

LEVETT, JOHN HENRY aged 20 years married to GRAY, ALICE aged 18 years September 16, 1883 by Rev. E. J. Meynardie at 145 King Street. He a native of Washington, Georgia and she of Alexandria, Virginia. He works in a factory.

LEVETTE, ELIZABETH R. aged 19 years married to REED, JAMES M. aged 25 years April 26, 1891 by Father J. J. Monaghan at St. Patrick's Roman Catholic Church. He a native of Charleston and she of Georgia. He a woodworker.

LEVIN, CHARLES aged 30 years married to ROTHSTEIN, ESTELLE aged 20 years October 26, 1892 by Rabbi David Levy at 342 King Street. Both natives of New York. He a merchant.

LEVIN, JULIAN C. aged 31 years married to BRINGLOE, JULIA W. aged 17 years April 23, 1879 by Rabbi David Levy at 106 Wentworth Street. Both natives of Charleston.

LEVINSOHN, RUDOLPH A. aged 30 years married to HOFFMAN, ISABEL aged 26 years June 21, 1893 by Rabbi David Levy at 56 St. Philip Street. Both natives of Charleston. He a merchant in Mobile, Alabama.

LEVISTER, JAMES J. aged 38 years married to IRBY, (Mrs.) MINERVA E. JACKSON aged 21 years November 25, 1894 by Rev. Edmund Wells at 15 Chapel Street. He a native of Warrenton, North Carolina and she of east Tennessee. He works in the cotton mill.

LEVY, ALBERTINE aged 32 years married to LIDENBERGER, ADOLPH aged 29 years May 15, 1890 by Rabbi David Levy. He a native of Vienna, Austria and she of Charleston. He a fresco painter.

LEVY, A. aged 22 years married to WEISKOPF, S. aged 25 years December 6, 1882 by Rabbi David Levy at 7 Franklin Street. Both natives of Charleston and a merchant.

LEVY, CHARLES G. aged 23 years married to ALEXANDER, FLORENCE aged 23 years March 3, 1884 by Rev. J. C. Pawley at 61 Anson Street. He a native of Charleston and she of Alabama. He a hostler.

LEVY, CLARENCE aged 23 years married to PIERCE, MARY E. aged 21 years September 24, 1879 by Rev. John P. Twigg at The Cathedral of St. John the Baptist. Both natives of Charleston. He a policeman.

LEVY, EDWARD S. aged 29 years married to GOLDSMITH, FRANCES aged 36 years June 25, 1879 by Rabbi David Levy at the Hasell Street Synagogue. He a native of Philadelphia, Pennsylvania and she of Charleston. He a clergyman.

LEVY, GABRIEL aged 22 years married to KAHN, FANNIE F. aged 20 years March 8, 1892 by Rabbi David Levy at 6 Liberty Street. He a native of France and she of Charleston.

LEVY, ISAAC married to ELIAS, RACHEL March 5, 1879 by Rabbi David Levy. He a native of Germany and she of Columbia, South Carolina. He a merchant.

LEVY, LAURA L. aged 23 years married to HART, DAVID L. aged 23 years June 4, 1890 by Rabbi David Levy at 80 Wentworth Street. Both natives of Charleston. He a clerk.

LEVY, MARY B. aged 22 years married to BOFILE, MIGUEL aged 23 years April 17, 1895 by Charles W. Swinton, Circuit Judge. He a native of Puerto Rico and she of Charleston. He a clerk.

LEVY, MORDECAI aged 30 years married to LAZARUS, MARK H. aged 34 years January 12, 1881 by Rabbi David Levy.

LEWINTHAL, PHILIP aged 33 years married to WEINBERG, SARAH aged 24 years July 20, 1881 by Rabbi David Levy at 82 King Street. He a native of Georgia and she of Charleston. He a merchant in Darlington County, South Carolina.

LEWIS, JOHN R. aged 21 years married to FORD, HELEN MAY aged 19 years October 15, 1891 by Rev. R. D. Smart at 182 Wentworth Street. Both natives of Charleston. He operates a press in the cotton mill.

LEWIS, THOMAS aged 41 years married to BRAUER, MARY ANN aged 30 years January 20, 1887 by Father Daniel J. Quigley at St. Patrick's Roman Catholic Church. He a native of Greece and she of Charleston. He a janitor.

LEWITH, HULDA aged 22 years married to ISEMAN, G. EMANUEL aged 33 years July 14, 1886 by Rabbi David Levy at the Hasell Street Synagogue. Both natives of Charleston. He a merchant.

LEY, AMALIA JOSEPHINE aged 17 years married to AHNERJUN, MICHAEL H. aged 21 years April 15, 1886 by Rev. Louis Muller at the residence of Capt. B. S. Aldret at Sullivans Island, South Carolina. He a native of New York and she of Charleston. He a merchant.

LIBBY, CHARLTON ROBERT aged 24 years married to BRADLEY, C. IDA aged 22 years April 9, 1890 by Rev. G. R. Brackett at 17 Smith Street.

LEBBY, ROBERT BEE aged 23 years married to MIKELL, TESS WARING aged 21 years February 7, 1889 by Rev. John Johnson in Church Street. He a native of James Island, South Carolina and she of Charleston. He a merchant.

LIBBY, ROBERT C. aged 30 years married to ROBERTS, MARIAN C. aged 28 years November 24, 1893 by Rev. G. R. Brackett in Smith Street. He a native of Gordonsville, Virginia and she of Charleston. He a clerk.

LIDENBERGER, ADOLPH aged 29 years married to LEVY, ALBERTINE aged 32 years May 15, 1890 by Rabbi David Levy. He a native of Vienna, Austria and she of Charleston. He a fresco painter.

LIDDY, THOMAS J. aged 30 years married to BARRY, MARY aged 24 years October 27, 1895 by Father J. J. Monaghan at St. Patrick's Roman Catholic Church.

LIEBENROOD, G. W. aged 28 years married to MURRELL, WILHELMINA aged 21 years December 19, 1886 by Rev. T. P. Burgess at 99 Drake Street. He a native of Brooklyn, New York and she of Charleston. He works at the waterworks.

LIEBENROOD, S. N. aged 23 years married to BROWN, JULIA MARY aged 23 years May 22, 1884 by Rev. A. J. D. Thomas at 27 Spring Street.

LILIENTHAL, AMANDA N. aged 27 years married to PUCKHABER, HERMANN H. aged 29 years November 19, 1891 by Rev. Louis Muller at 466 King Street. Both natives of Charleston. He a baker.

LILIENTHAL, ANNIE JOSEPHINE aged 18 years married to KELLY, B. D. aged 32 years March 30, 1881 by Rev. L. K. Probst. He a native of Boston, Massachusetts and she of Charleston. He a mariner.

LILIENTHAL, JOHN A. aged 24 years married to THEILING, ANNA F. aged 19 years July 30, 1885 by Rev. Louis Muller at 66 Radcliffe Street. He a native of Germany and she of Charleston. He a carpenter.

LILIENTHAL, JOHN FREDERICK married to BLOHME, ANNA EMILY aged 21 years November 15, 1877 by Rev. Louis Muller at the residence of the Bridegroom - Beaufain Street near Archdale Street.

LILIENTHAL, MATILDA aged 18 years married to SEEBECH, JOHANN F. aged 20 years January 18, 1885 by Rev. Claudian B. Northrop at 24 Beaufain Street. Both natives of Germany. He a grocer.

LILLY, ELLA LENORA aged 22 years married to BLOCKER, FRANKLIN O. aged 21 years September 12, 1888 by Rev. T. P. Burgess at 91 Nassau Street. He a native of Newville, South Carolina and she of Grenada, Mississippi. He works for the railroad.

LILLY, LAURA ANNIE aged 24 years married to SCREVEN, CHARLES RUFUS aged 24 years December 2, 1883 by Rev. J. H. Tillinghast at 3 Cooper Street. Both natives of Charleston. He works for the railroad.

LIMEHOUSE, ELLEN aged 16 years married to ILDERTON, WALTER aged 20 years July 11, 1891 by Rev. Robert Wilson. Both natives of Summerville, South Carolina. He a stock raiser in Summerville.

LINDLEY, CORA BELLE aged 18 years married to FIEDLER, JOSEPH J aged 23 years November 19, 1890 by Rev. G. R. Brackett at 53 Line Street. He a native of South Carolina and she of Pennsylvania. He a fireman.

LINDQUIST, JOHN E. aged 30 years married to BECKER, PAULINE aged 30 years April 7, 1892 by Rev. R. C. Holland at the Wentworth Street Lutheran Church. He a native of Sweden and she of Charleston. He a mariner.

LINDSTROM, ALEXANDER aged 58 years married to FREDSBERG, JULIA C. aged 55 years November 12, 1885 by Rev. Edward T. Horn at 239 Calhoun Street. He a native of Sweden and she of Germany. He a merchant.

LINDSTROM, IDA aged 23 years married to ERICKSON, VICTOR H. aged 23 years April 30, 1881 by Rev. R. W. Memminger. Both natives of Stockholm, Sweden. He a News and Courier employee.

LINGE, HELENE HENRIETTE aged 20 years married to RHODES, WILLIAM aged 25 years October 7, 1886 by Rev. Louis Muller at the southeast corner of Meeting and Line Street. He a native of Augusta, Georgia and she of Charleston. He a mill hand.

LINING, CHARLES aged 56 years married to FOWLER, IDA M. aged 23 years August 26, 1879 by Rev. J. M. Green. Both natives of Charleston. He a warden.

LINK, SAMUEL aged 26 years married to WITHERHORN (?), HANNAH aged 20 years September 7, 1890 by Rabbi David Levy at the corner of Green and College Streets. He a native of Augusta, Georgia and she of Charleston. He a merchant in Orangeburg, South Carolina.

LINN, HUGH CAMPBELL aged 34 years married to HOGAN, MARY BARRETT aged 22 years April 25, 1886 by Rev. J. Walter Dickson at 231 Coming Street. He a native of Charleston and she of Ireland. He a mechanist.

LINN, MINNIE JULIA married to MOSELY, WILLIAM M. January 21, 1885 by Rev. William H. Campbell at 13 Ashley Avenue.

LINSIBRINK (?), E. N. H. aged 18 years married to SINDORT (?), C. H. F. W. aged 34 years July 20, 1880 by Rev. Louis Muller at the residence of the Bride's mother - King Street near Broad. He a native of Hanover and she of Charleston. He a merchant.

LINSKY, PATRICK aged 25 years married to STAUNTON, BRIDGET aged 22 years October 13, 1878 by Father Daniel J. Quigley at The Cathedral of St. John the Baptist. Both natives of Ireland. He a clerk.

LINSMAN, EVANGELINE REBECCA aged 30 years married to WIECKING, JOHN aged 45 years July 2, 1889 by Rev. Johannes Heckel at the residence of Mr. Jurgenson - 38 Calhoun Street. He a native of Hanover and she of Germany. He in the lighthouse service.

LIRMAN, JEAN NICOLAS aged 30 years married to STOHOFFER, MARIE aged 27 years July 19, 1888 by Father John O. Schachte at 3 New Street. Both natives of France. He an architect.

LITJEN (?), (Mrs.) ELISE B. aged 48 years married to WOHLERS, HEINRICH aged 62 years April 7, 1892 by Rev. Louis Muller at 3 Mile House. He a native of Prussia and she of Oldenburg, Germany.

LITSCHGI, ALBAN WILLIAM aged 27 years married to KIEM, NANNIE aged 25 years October 26, 1881 by Father Daniel J. Quigley at The Cathedral of St. John the Baptist. He a native of Beaufort, South Carolina and she of Georgia. He a clerk.

LITSCHGI, CHARLES aged 45 years married to KANAPAUX, SALLIE WEAVER aged 33 years November 12, 1888 by Father Daniel J. Quigley at St. Patrick's Roman Catholic Church. He a native of Germany and she of South Carolina. He a bank officer.

LITTLE, C. O. aged 35 years married to E. P. DISHER aged 19 years December 9, 1879 by Rev. G. S. Bowman at 17 Nassau Street. He a native of Georgia and she of Charleston. He works for the railroad.

LIVELY, THOMAS aged 22 years married to McELVAN, FANNIE aged 19 years December 26, 1892 by Rev. Edmund Wells at 29 Blake Street. He a native of Augusta, Georgia and she of Charleston. He works in the cotton mill.

LIVINGSTON, BENJAMIN aged 28 years married to HENDRIX, ALICE M. aged 23 years December 25, 1895 by Rev. T. E. Morris at 231 Coming Street.

LIVINGSTON, FANNIE aged 19 years married to ECKSTEIN, EMIL aged 28 years October 24, 1878 by Rabbi David Levy at 58 Wentworth Street. He a native of Munich, Bavaria, Germany and she of Charleston. He a merchant in Savannah, Georgia.

LIVINGSTON, FANNIE aged 19 years married to ECKSTEIN, EMIL aged 28 years October 24, 1878 by Rabbi David Levy. He a native Munich, Germany and she of Charleston. He merchant.

LIVINGSTON, PAULINE A. aged 24 years married to BECKMAN, JOHN WILLIAM aged 25 years June 26, 1895 by Father J. J. Monaghan at 10 Wragg Square. Both natives of Charleston. He a shipping clerk.

LIVINGSTON, THOMAS P. aged 24 years married to PHILLIPS, SARAH ODESSA aged 21 years June 9, 1891 by Father J. J. Monaghan at St. Patrick's Roman Catholic Church. He a native of Georgia and she of Washington, D. C.

LIVINGSTON, WALTER F. aged 20 years married to BROUGHTON, MAGGIE aged 20 years January 30, 1895 by Father J. J. Monaghan at St. Patrick's Roman Catholic Church. Both natives of Charleston. He a clerk.

LLENORT (?), JOSEPH aged 22 years married to KING, MARY E. B. aged 20 years November 27, 1887 by Father John O. Schachte at The Cathedral of St. John the Baptist. He a native of Spain and she of Charleston.

LLOYD, EDWARD A. aged 25 years married to KEILY, MARY aged 19 years May 2, 1878 by Father Daniel J. Quigley at The Cathedral of St. John the Baptist. He a native of Philadelphia, Pennsylvania and she of Charleston. He a mariner.

LLOYD, EDWARD A. aged 35 years married to HOGAN, BRIDGET E. aged 24 years July 30, 1891 by Father J. J. Monaghan at St. Patrick's Roman Catholic Church. He a native of New York City and she of Charleston. He a laborer.

LLOYD, (Mrs.) EMMA aged 26 years married to MILLER, JOHN H. aged 22 years October 21, 1891 by Rev. J. L. Fludd in Stone Court. He a native of Darlington County, South Carolina and she of Lexington County, South Carolina. He works in the cotton mill.

LLOYD, HATTIE aged 19 years married to PECKSEN, JOHN N. aged 23 years March 29, 1882 by Rev. Luther K. Probst. He a native of Georgia and she of Charleston. He a grocer.

LLOYD, JESSE WALTER aged 23 years married to BUME, MARY LOUSIE ISABEL aged 19 years April 26, 1883 by Rev. Edward T. Horn at 13 Charlotte Street.

LOCKWOOD, ANNA aged 22 years married to WEBB, THOMAS R. aged 32 years January 25, 1883 by Rev. C. C. Pinckney at the residence of Mrs. Webb in Wentworth Street. He a native of Colleton County, South Carolina and she of Charleston. He a clerk.

LOCKWOOD, CAROLINE LEE aged 27 years married to LOCKWOOD, HENRY T. aged 27 years July 22, 1891 by Rev. Henry M. Grant. He a native of Aiken, South Carolina and she of Charleston. He a merchant.

LOCKWOOD, HENRY T. aged 27 years married to LOCKWOOD, CAROLINE LEE aged 27 years July 22, 1891 by Rev. Henry M. Grant. He a native of Aiken, South Carolina and she of Charleston. He a merchant.

LOCKWOOD, JOHN PALMER aged 27 years married to BROWN, ELIZA FISHBURNE aged 22 years November 15, 1883 by Rev. A. H. Misseldine at 65 Wentworth Street. Both natives of Charleston. He a clerk.

LOCKWOOD, ROBERT H. aged 23 years married to WHILDEN, ELLA A aged 22 years November 26, 1885 by Rev. W. T. Junkin at the residence of W. W. Whilden in Rutledge Avenue. He a native of Charleston and she of South Carolina. He the captain of a tugboat.

LODERHOSE, (Mrs.) SOPHIE HENRIETTA G. aged 46 years married to HALBE, FREDERICK CHARLES aged 58 years June 28, 1888 by Rev. Johannes Heckel at 123 Smith Street. He a native of Hanover and she of Germany.

LOEB, J. H. aged 33 years married to GOLDSMITH, E. aged 25 years January 7, 1880 by Rabbi David Levy. He a native of South Carolina and she of Charleston. He a merchant.

LOEB, JACOB S. aged 36 years married to PINKUSSOHN, RACHEL aged 23 years September 22, 1885 by Rabbi David Levy at 47 Wentworth Street. He a native of Germany and she of Charleston. He a merchant.

LOGAN, ALEXANDER R. aged 20 years married to HEDLEY, EVELINE F. aged 20 years March 31, 1884 by Rev. J. V. Welsh at 24 Bee Street. He a native of Scotland and she of Charleston. He a spinner in the cotton mill.

LOGAN, ELIZABETH L. aged 18 years married to SORIA, MANUEL aged 28 years March 21, 1886 by Rev. Luther K. Probst at the Wentworth Street Lutheran Church. He a native of Cadiz, Spain and she of Charleston. He a laborer.

LOGAN, SELENA GEORGIANA aged 20 years married to DeSAUSSURE, WILLIAM P. aged 27 years October 29, 1878 by Rev. John Johnson at St. Philip's Church. Both natives of Charleston. He a lawyer.

LOMBARD, C. aged 44 years married to JOHNSON, P. aged 42 years October 24, 1882 by Rev. J. V. Welch at 24 Bee Street. He a native of England and a merchant.

LONEGAN, LIZZIE EMMELINE aged 20 years married to ULMO, HENRY WALTER aged 24 years April 7, 1881 by Rev. E. J. Meynardie. Both natives of Charleston. He a machinist in Savannah, Georgia.

LONG, HARRY L. aged 34 years married to LESLIE, GERTRUDE ANN aged 25 years April 29, 1884 by Rev. A. H. Misseldine at the Circular Congregational Church.

LONG, RICHARD F. aged 43 years married to SEYMOUR, MARY E. aged 32 years April 19, 1883 by Rev. C. C. Pinckney at Grace Church. He a native of Philadelphia, Pennsylvania and she of Charleston. He a merchant.

LONG, WALTER C. married to WILLIAMS, JANE E. March 11, 1894 by Rev. William H. Campbell at the residence of the bride's mother. He a painter.

LONGNICK (?), B. C. aged 20 years married to BLODGETT, EBER aged 34 years April 21, 1881 by Rev. Edward T. Horn at St. Johannes Church. He a native of Akron, Ohio and she of Charleston. He a merchant.

LOPEZ, EDWIN aged 28 years married to OTTOLENGUI (?), CECILE aged 28 years November 3, 1881 by Rabbi David Levy.

LOPEZ, JOSEPH P. aged 31 years married to PUNDT, JANIE A. aged 24 years November 14, 1884 by Rev. Luther K. Probst. He a native of Austria and she of Charleston. He a fruitier.

LORD, FRANCIS A. aged 28 years married to JOHNSON, FANNIE E. aged 22 years March 28, 1880 by Rev. W. S. Bowman at 19 Coming Street. Both natives of Charleston. He a hardware merchant.

LORETTE, JOSEPH CHARLES aged 22 years married to EDWARDS, LONNIE aged 22 years September 3, 1893 by Rev. J. C. Yongue at 14 Hampstead Square.

LORYEA, MINNIE R. aged 25 years married to BARNETT, JOSEPH E. aged 28 years June 8, 1881 by Rabbi David Levy at 369 King Street. He a native of Sumter, South Carolina and she of Charleston. He a merchant in Marysville, South Carolina.

LOSSE, P. aged 27 years married to KOSTER, M.A. aged 19 years November 22, 1882 by Rev. Louis Muller at the corner of Meeting and Radcliffe Streets. He a native of Germany and a tailor.

LOTTE, WILLIAM aged 22 years married to PLATT, E. EVELINE aged 18 years January 13, 1889 by Rev. H. B. Browne at 567 King Street.

LOTZ, AUGUSTA ADELAIDE aged 21 years married to EYE, THEODORE aged 29 years April 22, 1879 by Rev. Louis Muller at the corner of Beaufain and Mazyck Streets. He a native of New York and she of Charleston.

LOTZ, EDWARD aged 30 years married to RYAN, MAGGIE aged 20 years December8, 1878 by Father C. J. Croghan. He a native of Frankfort, Germany and she of Charleston. He a shopkeeper.

LOVETT, CHARLES HENRY aged 40 years married to THOMAS, CATHERINE aged 30 years March 3, 1884 by Father P. L. Duffy at The Cathedral of St. John the Baptist. Both natives of Charleston. He a machinist.

LOVETTE, JAMES C. aged 22 years married to EDWARDS, L. aged 22 years September 3, 1893 by Rev. J. C. Yongue at 14 Hampstead Square. He a native of Johnstown, Pennsylvania and she of Greenville, South Carolina. He works in the cotton mill.

LOWE, ELIZA J. aged 18 years married to COURTNEY, HENRY L. aged 21 years October 15, 1893 by Rev. A. Ernst Cornish at 6 Hampden Court. He a native of Washington, D. C. and she of Charleston. He works at the cotton mill.

LOWE, REBECCA aged 19 years married to ABRAMS, ALEXANDER aged 31 years February 14, 1886 by Rev. J. V. Welch at 91 America Street. Both natives of Charleston. He a boilermaker.

LOWER, GEORGE E. married to CADIZ, ELLEN J. WHITNEY July 20, 1887 by Rev. R. S. Frazier in Smith Street. She a native of Charleston.

LOWNDES, CAROLINE H. married to MULLALLY, LANE November 6, 1894 by Rev. J. Drayton Grimke in East Battery. "Both of legal age." He a physician.

LOWNDES, HARRIET H. aged 24 years married to CAIN, ELIAS H. aged 25 years September 3, 1891 by Rev. Robert Wilson at 39 Legare Street. He a native of Berkeley County, South Carolina and she of Charleston. He a druggist in Columbia, South Carolina.

LOWNDES, MARGARET W. aged 24 years married to WALKER, JULIUS aged 40 years November 3, 1892 by Rev. C. C. Pinckney at St. Philip's Church. He a native of Columbia, South Carolina and she of Charleston. He a barber in Columbia, South Carolina.

LOWREY, EMILY M. A. aged 19 years married to ELFE, GLOVER C. aged 22 years November 10, 1880 by Father Claudian B. Northrop at the residence of H. T. Lowrey. Both natives of Charleston. He a bookkeeper.

LOWREY, W. J. aged 34 years married to CAHILL, A. aged 26 years November 6, 1882 by Father Daniel J. Quigley at The Cathedral of St. John the Baptist. He a native of South Carolina and a merchant.

LOWRY, CAPERS DURANT aged 25 years married to HOATS, MARY ELLIS aged 26 years February 11, 1886 by Rev. H. B. Browne at 178 Coming Street. Both natives of South Carolina. He works for the railroad.

LOWRY, JULIA aged 22 years married to McCARROLL, W. aged 24 years November 19, 1879 by Father Daniel J. Quigley. Both natives of Charleston. He an engineer.

LOWRY, J. G. aged 29 years married to MIMS, HENRIETTA E. aged 19 years November 16, 1886 by Rev. H. B. Browne at 13 Line Street. He a native of South Carolina and she of Charleston. He a clerk.

LUBECHE, MAX aged 36 years married to HOLLWEY, CHRISTINE OTTMER aged 30 years January 14, 1891 by Rev. R. C. Holland at 522 Meeting Street. He a native of Germany and she of Charleston. He a merchant.

LUCAS, BENJAMIN L. aged 24 years married to LUCAS, SARAH B. aged 24 years October 17, 1893 by Rev. C. C. Pinckney at Grace Church. He a native of Darlington County, South Carolina and she of Charleston. He a farmer in Darlington.

LUCAS, ELLIOTT M. married to HORLBECK, HENRIETTA PORCHER December 16, 1886 by Rev. William H. Campbell. He a machinist.

LUCAS, HELEN T. married to TORBERT, JOHN E. January 8, 1890 by Rev. William H. Campbell at St. Paul's Church.

LUCAS, HENRY R. aged 27 years married to FRIPP, MARY J. aged 21 years May 13, 1885 by Rev. Luther K. Probst. He a native of Charleston and she of Walterboro, South Carolina. He a merchant.

LUCAS, JULIA ELIZA aged 20 years married to HENDERSON, WILLIAM R. aged 27 years November 1, 1883 by Rev. Edward T. Horn at 6 Bull Street. Both natives of Charleston. He a clerk.

LUCAS, MYRA JANE married to FORD, T. ROBERT December 20, 1889 by Rev. Richard S. Trapier at St. Michael's Church.

LUCAS, SARAH B. aged 24 years married to LUCAS, BENJAMIN L. aged 24 years October 17, 1893 by Rev. C. C. Pinckney at Grace Church. He a native of Darlington County, South Carolina and she of Charleston. He a farmer in Darlington.

LUCAS, WILLIAM H. aged 32 years married to WRIGHT, CAROLINE F. aged 22 years November 9, 1886 by Rev. John Johnson at St. Luke's Chapel. Both natives of Charleston. He a stationer.

LUDEN, MARTIN WILHELM aged 25 years married to WEBER, FREDERICKE JOHANNA aged 22 years February 26, 1885 by Rev. Louis Muller at the corner of King and Woolfe Streets. He a native of Germany and a grocer.

LUDER, ELVIRA ARMSTRONG aged 37 years married to YOUNGINER, GEORGE WASHINGTON aged 38 years December 20, 1877 by Rev. G. R. Brackett at 23 Cumberland Street.

LUDWICK, MAMIE aged 22 years married to HEYWOOD, JAMES T. aged 39 years October 30, 1892 by Rev. C. E. Chichester at the Mariners Church. He a native of Charleston and she of New Jersey. He a baker.

LUDWICK, JOSEPHINE aged 19 years married to FROMING, L. C. H. aged 25 years February 15, 1891 by Rev. R. C. Holland. He a native of Charleston and she of Jersey City, New Jersey. He a baker.

LUHN, GUSTAV JOHANN aged 41 years married to MASSOT, JOSEPHINE L. aged 28 years June 1, 1881 by Rev. Edward T. Horn at 8 Mary Street. He a native of Berlin, Germany and she of Charleston. He a druggist.

LUHN, LILLIE married to DuBOSE, EDWIN December 3, 1885 by Rev. William H. Campbell.

LUNDEN, JOHN WILLIAM aged 42 years married to BOOR, HELENA WILHELMINA DORETHA aged 23 years November 25, 1877 by Rev. Louis Muller.

LUNSING (?), C. N. aged 40 years married to SCHUMHOFF, H. H. aged 40 years married to SCHUMHOFF, H. H. aged 26 years June 25, 1882. He a native of South Carolina and she of Georgia. He a planter.

LUNZ, GEORGE aged 31 years married to KOEG, EMMA J. aged 19 years May 31, 1881 by Rev. Luther K. Probst in Liberty Street.

LUTJENS, ANNA aged 25 years married to ROHDE, G. F. aged 39 years December 3, 1880 by Rev. Johannes Heckel at 125 Calhoun Street. Both natives of Germany. He a laborer.

LUZE, LILLIE aged 19 years married to SUMMERALL, RICHARD A. aged 23 years February 12, 1893 at 13 Judith Street.

LYMAN, THEODORE B. aged 75 years married to ROBERTSON, SUSAN B. aged 49 years February 9, 1893 by Rev. C. C. Pinckney at Grace Church. She a native of Charleston. He a Bishop of the Protestant Episcopal Church in North Carolina.

LYNAH, PAUL H. married to GADSON, ALICE T. June 7, 1877 by Rev. Richard S. Trapier at St. Michael's Church.

LYNCH, CATHARINE aged 24 years married to LEONARD, WILLIAM J. aged 28 years August 15, 1886 by Father F. J. Shadler at St. Joseph's Roman Catholic Church. He a native of Charleston and she of Ireland. He a boilermaker.

LYNCH, JOHN R. aged 32 years married to MAY, BRIDGET aged 34 years January 12, 1885 by Father Daniel J. Quigley at St. Patrick's Roman Catholic Church. He a native of Charleston and she of Ireland. He a laborer.

LYNCH, MARGARET married to O'BRIEN, MICHAEL February 19, 1879 by Father John P. Twigg at The Cathedral of St. John the Baptist. He a native of Vermont and she of Charleston. He a laborer.

LYNCH, MARY ANN aged 28 years married to NELSON, NICHOLAS aged 45 years October 1, 1884 by Father P. L. Duffy at The Cathedral of St. John the Baptist. He a native of Sweden and she of Ireland. He a mariner in Cainhoy, South Carolina.

LYNCH, PETER F. aged 26 years married to ZWINGMAN (?), C. M. aged 23 years November 22, 1887 by Father John W. Schachte at The Cathedral of St. John the Baptist. Both natives of Charleston. He a storekeeper.

LYNCH, THOMAS P. aged 26 years married to SULLIVAN, JULIA A. aged 21 years October 26, 1885 by Rev. John E. Beard at 64 Nassau Street. Both natives of Charleston.

LYNES, FRANCES aged 19 years married to HUDSON, ALBERT aged 36 years June 21, 1881 by Rev. L. H. Shuck. He a native of Colleton County, South Carolina and she of Charleston. He a farmer in Mt. Pleasant, South Carolina.

LYONS, CATHERINE aged 22 years married to McCULLOUGH, ROBERT WILLIAM aged 25 years May 2, 1889 by Bishop Harry P. Northrop at 1 Tradd Street. He a native of Hendersonville, North Carolina and she of Charleston. He a gardener.

LYONS, J. R. aged 37 years married to CROFFERT, S. E. aged 44 years February 12, 1882 by Rev. J. V. Welch at Calvary Church at 24 Bee Street. He a native of Charleston and a policeman.

LYONS, EMMA JULIA aged 17 years married to DAWSON, WILLIAM T. aged 24 years April 10, 1892 by Rev. J. L. Stokes at 231 Coming Street.

LYONS, ROBERT B. aged 28 years marriedto SIMONS, ANNIE H. aged 25 years July 11, 1878 by Rev. C. C. Pinckney at Grace Church. He a native of Union County, South Carolina and she of Charleston. He a farmer.

LYONS, SARAH aged 35 years married to FLEMING, WILLIAM aged 40 years January 17, 1878 by Father Daniel J. Quigley at The Cathedral of St. John the Baptist.

LYONS, SARAH aged 25 years married to HEITERER, DAMIEN aged 30 years January 6, 1884 by Father F. A. Schmetz at St. Patrick's Roman Catholic Church. He a native of Germany and she of Charleston. He a miller.

LYONS, SARAH J. aged 21 years married to WHITE, WILLIAM J. aged 27 years July 14, 1880 by Father P. L. Duffy at The Cathedral of St. John the Baptist. He a native of New York and she of Charleston. He a plasterer.

LYONS, THOMAS C. aged 44 years married to BURKE, MARY C. aged 35 years June 19, 1888 by Father Daniel J. Quigley at St. Patrick's Roman Catholic Church. He a native of Ireland and she of Charleston. He a carpenter.

MacALLEN, JAMES aged 54 years married to BLACHS, JULIA aged 42 years November 1, 1887 by Father P. J. McManus at St. Patrick's Roman Catholic Church. He a native of Ireland and she of Charleston. He a policeman.

MABORE, (Mrs.) PAULINE E. DEIGHEN aged 30 years married to DUFFY, WILLIAM aged 30 years July 26, 1886 by Father Daniel J. Quigley at St. Patrick's Roman Catholic Church.

MACK, GEORGE aged 48 years married to MERRIERA, AMELIA aged 38 years April 4, 1893 by E. Milan, Trial Justice.

MacDONELL, LILLIAN aged 21 years married to McKAY, JAMES C. aged 27 years September 18, 1892 by John Ahrens, Trial Justice.

MACKEY (Mrs.) BEULAH MITCHELL aged 18 years married to NELSON, SAMUEL W. aged 19 years January 21, 1894 by Rev. Edmund Wells at 579 King Street. He a native of Bonneau, South Carolina and she of Augusta, Georgia. He a painter.

MACKEY, EMMA G. aged 18 years married to HART, HUGO G. aged 31 years April 27, 1886 by Rev. Charles A. Stakely, at 43 Nassau Street. He a native of Orangeburg, South Carolina and she of Charleston. He a farmer in Orangeburg.

MACKEY, JOHN RANDOLPH aged 25 years married to WARD, ANNA CATHARINE aged 22 years February 8, 1881 by Rev. H. F. Chreitzberg. He a native of New Orleans, Louisiana and she of Charleston. He a mechanic.

MACKIN, MARY ANN aged 19 years married to MOORE, EDWARD April 28, 1878 by Father Daniel J. Quigley. Both natives of Charleston. He a clerk.

MacMURPHY, WILLIAM C. married to CART, ELISE CRUGER June 10, 1891 by Rev. William H. Campbell.

MADDEN, JAMES E. aged 21 years married to WATSON, HANNAH B. aged 16 years October 19, 1890 by Father F. J. Shadler at St. Joseph's Roman Catholic Church. Both natives of Charleston. He a boilermaker.

MADDEN, J. aged 37 years married to CURTIS, M. A. aged 27 years November 14, 1882 by Rev. J. E. Curtis. He a native of Germany and a machinist.

MADRAY, R. W. aged 22 years married to LEOPOLD, R. L. aged 22 years November 13, 1879 by Rev. W. S. Bowman at 262 Meeting Street. He a native of Strawberry Station and a phosphate worker. She a native of Charleston. He a resident of Five Mile Curve.

MADRE, ELIZABETH aged 24 years married to MYERS, TRESPOLE aged 24 years October 5, 1880 by Rabbi David Levy at the Hasell Street Synagogue. He a native of London, England and a merchant. Both residents of Fernandina, Florida.

MAETZE, OSCAR aged 30 years married to MUCKENFUSS (?), ELISE M. aged 20 years November 10, 1886 by Rev. Johannes Heckel at the corner of East Bay and Pinckney Streets. Both natives of Germany. He a barkeeper.

MAGRATH, CHARLES H. aged 27 years married to McKIEVER, MARY T. aged 23 years May 20, 1885 by Father Daniel J. Quigley at St. Patrick's Roman Catholic Church. Both natives of Charleston. He a mechanist.

MAGRATH, CHARLES aged 29 years married to SULLIVAN, (Mrs.) ABBIE M. WEBBER aged 36 years May 24, 1890 by Rev. C. S. Vedder at 120 Meeting Street. He a native of Prussia and she of Walhalla, South Carolina. He a mariner.

MAGRATH, MARY JANE aged 22 years married to HARBISON, JOHN FRANCIS aged 28 years December 29, 1886 by Father Daniel J. Quigley at St. Patrick's Roman Catholic Church. Both natives of Charleston. He a builder in New York.

MAGRATH, MARY M. aged 22 years married to DELANEY, TIMOTHY aged 25 years October 9, 1890 by Father F. J. Shadler at St. Joseph's Roman Catholic Church. Both natives of Charleston. He a collector.

MAGRATH, NORA aged 17 years married to Baker, H. B. aged 19 years February 15, 1885 by Rev. R. A. Lapsley at 8 Drake Street. He a native of McClellanville, South Carolina and she of Charleston. He a merchant in Cordesville, South Carolina.

MAGUIRE, MARY aged 19 years married to FINN, PATRICK aged 24 years January 12, 1881 by Father Daniel J. Quigley at The Cathedral of St. John the Baptist. He a native of Ireland. Witnessed by John Finn and Annie Finn.

MAGUIRE, MORRIS aged 41 years married to WALSH, MARY ANN aged 33 years April 24, 1889 by Father Daniel J. Quigley at St. Patrick's Roman Catholic Church. He a native of Ireland and she of Charleston. He an engineer.

MAGUIRE, MORRIS DAVID aged 28 years married to McKIERNAN, MARY ANN aged 23 years February 4, 1880 by Rev. Claudian B. Northrop at St. Mary of the

Annunciation Roman Catholic Church. Both natives of Charleston. He a clerk. Witnessed by Margaret O'Brien and William F. Maguire.

MAHEN, JAMES J. aged 38 years married to PATTERSON, FANNIE J. aged 20 years February 5, 1894 by Father Daniel J. Quigley at St. Patrick's Roman Catholic Church. He a native of Charleston and she of Bridgeport, Connecticut. He a salesman.

MAHER, DANIEL aged 23 years married to NOLAN, CATHARINE aged 21 years June 19, 1894 by Father Thomas F. Hopkins. Both natives of Charleston. He a mechanic.

MAHON, P. aged 26 years married to KING, M. F. aged 26 years January 1, 1880 by Father John P. Twigg at The Cathedral of St. John the Baptist. Both natives of Clarksburg, Virginia. He a ship carpenter.

MAHONEY, ALICE M. aged 27 years married to GREYMAN (?), JOHN M. aged 56 years November 23, 1892 by Rev. Edward T. Horn in Tradd Street. Both natives of Charleston. He a druggist.

MAHONEY, E. aged 20 years married to NELSON, J. D. aged 22 years December 13, 1879 by Rev. R. N. Wells at the residence of the Bride - 74 Tradd Street. Both natives of Charleston. He a merchant.

MAHONEY, J. J. aged 23 years married to BAMBERG, W. J. aged 29 years November 11, 1879 by Rev. E. T. Horn at 54 Tradd Street. He a native of Bamberg, South Carolina and she of Charleston. He a farmer in Bamberg, South Carolina.

MAHONEY, MARGARET aged 28 years married to HEINS, JOHN HENRY aged 33 years February 25, 1891 by Rev. Edward T. Horn. Both natives of Charleston. He a merchant.

MAHONEY, MARY A. aged 37 years married to TILLISON, ANTONE aged 27 years January 30, 1887 by Rev. John Johnson at 53 Church Street. He a native of Norway and she of Ireland. He a mechanic.

MAHR, CHARLES married to SCHULTZ, ANNIE aged 19 years December 27, 1877 by Rev. W. S. Bowman. He a merchant.

MAHSTEDT, LOUIS D. aged 44 years married to SANTEELE (?), (Mrs.) FANNIE E. CLARK aged 46 years July 18, 1893 by Rev. Henry M. Grant at the Circular Congregational Church. He a native of Charleston and she of Paris, Maine.

MAJENSKI (?), ALBERT aged 42 years married to OLDHAM, MAMIE aged 21 years September 16, 1884 by Father F. J. Shadler. He a native of Germany and she of Augusta, Georgia. He a baker.

MAKIN, S. aged 16 years married to CAUTINE, A. aged 29 years October 12, 1879 by Father Daniel J. Quigley at The Cathedral of St. John the Baptist. He a native of Italy and she of Charleston. He a merchant.

MALIN (?), MARY aged 20 years married to COLSON, WILLIAM LEBBY aged 21 years November 4, 1891 by Bishop Harry P. Northrop at 79 Tradd Street. Both natives of Charleston. He a clerk at the West Point Rice Mills.

MALLOY, R. aged 22 years married to JOHNSON, EDITH aged 20 years April 5, 1893 by Father Harry P. Northrop at The Cathedral of St. John the Baptist. Both natives of Charleston. He a traveling salesman.

MALONE, CLARENCE M. married to DERGEMAN, PAULINE E. December 16, 1877 by William B. Yates, Chaplain.

MALONE, ELIZABETH C. aged 22 years married to KOPS, WILLIAM C. aged 23 years September 5, 1885 by Rev. John Johnson at The Pavilion Hotel. Both natives of Minnesota.

MALONE, GERTRUDE L. aged 16 years married to CHANSON, JOSEPH aged 23 years May 6, 1895 by Rev. A. Ernest Cornish at the corner of Bee and President Streets. Both natives of Charleston. He works for the railroad.

MALONEY, ALICE M. aged 27 years married to GRANDY, JOHN H. aged 56 years November 23, 1892 by Rev. Edward T. Horn in Tradd Street.

MALONEY, ANNIE aged 22 years married to HOOKEY, CHARLES aged 25 years January 7, 1879 by Father John P. Twigg. He a native of Augusta, Georgia and she of Charleston. He a merchant.

MALONEY, E. T. aged 25 years married to KENNEDY, F. V. aged 25 years January 10, 1882 by Father T. E. Chapins at St. Patrick's Roman Catholic Church.

MALONEY, MARIE married to HOOKEY, CHARLES J. January 7, 1879 by Father John P. Twigg at The Cathedral of St. John the Baptist. He a native of Augusta, Georgia and she of Charleston. He a merchant.

MAN, JOHN C. married to HENDRICKS, CECILIA OCTAVIA October 18, 1881 by Rev. William H. Campbell.

MAND, BARBERA E. aged 22 years married to WATSON, H. P. aged 36 years March 18, 1890 by Rev. Johannes Heckel at 123 Smith Street. He a native of Alabama and she of Germany. He the manager of a sewing machine company.

MAND, ELISE aged 23 years married to NELSON, WILLIAM H. aged 26 years August 26, 1885 by Rev. Louis Muller in St. Philip Street, near Line Street. He a native of Sweden and she of Germany. He a car driver.

MANDERS, GEORGE aged 21 years married to BRYAN, LAURA JOSEPHINE aged 20 years November 22, 1891 by Rev. W. A. Betts at 14 Hampstead Square. He a native of Hendersonville, North Carolina and she of Colleton County, South Carolina. He a fireman.

MANDEVILLE, JAMES C. aged 18 years married to LEONARD, KATE C. aged 21 years January 21, 1883 by Father John P. Tillinghast at St. Patrick's Roman Catholic Church. Both natives of Charleston. He a painter.

MANGELS, ANNA M. aged 23 years married to RADEMANN (?), G. F. aged 22 years February 5, 1880 by Rev. Louis Muller at the St. Matthew's Lutheran Church. Both natives of Hanover. He owns a restaurant.

MANGELS, E. A. aged 34 years married to RINCK, META aged 32 years May 28, 1891 by Rev. Louis Muller opposite the 3 Mile House. Both natives of Prussia. He a grocer.

MANIGAULT, ARTHUR married to SMITH, HARRIET KINLOCH March 30, 1891 by Rev. Richard S. Trapier in Meeting Street. He a native of South Carolina and she of Charleston. He a planter in Santee, South Carolina.

MANIGAULT, JOSEPHINE aged 25 years married to JENKINS, HAWKINS K. aged 30 years November 24, 1887 by Rev. John Johnson in Gibbes Street. Both natives of Charleston. He a lawyer.

MANN, HANNAH G. aged 33 years married to SWARTZBERG, MOSES aged 30 years March 30, 1886 by Rev. P. H. Diamondstein at 110 Coming Street. Both natives of Germany. He a merchant.

MANN, HENRY H. aged 32 years married to HOWELL, A. W. aged 25 years September 21, 1887 by Rev. Robert Wilson. Both natives of Charleston. He a lawyer.

MANN, THEODORE aged 25 years married to TODD, ALICE E. aged 17 years April 2, 1889 by Rev. H. B. Browne at 142 St. Philip Street. He a native of North Carolina and she of Charleston. He a farmer.

MANNING, JAMES E. aged 44 years married to McINTIRE, (Mrs.) MARY E. WALLACE aged 40 years January 10, 1878 by Rev. L. H. Shuck at 5 George Street. Both natives of Charleston. He a painter.

MANNING, MICHAEL L. aged 25 years married to O'CONNELL, JOANNA aged 26 years November 20, 1893 by Father Thomas F. Hopkins at St. Mary of the Annunciation Roman Catholic Church. Both natives of Ireland. He a laborer.

MANNION, ELLEN CATHERINE aged 25 years married to HOGAN, JOHN FRANCIS aged 31 years January 1, 1891 by Father J. J. Monaghan at St. Patrick's Roman Catholic Church. Both natives of Charleston. He a painter.

MANSFIELD, ELLEN T. aged 23 years married to BENNETT, JAMES aged 28 years September 16, 1890 by Father J. J. Monaghan at St. Patrick's Roman Catholic Church. Both natives of Charleston. He a mariner.

MANSFIELD, JOHN aged 28 years married to BARRY, KATIE aged 28 years June 24, 1886 by Father F. J. Shadler at St. Joseph's Roman Catholic Church. Both natives of Charleston. He a stevedore.

MANSFIELD, MARGARET AGNES aged 21 years married to McKENNA, JOHN JOSEPH aged 23 years April 21, 1889 by Father J. J. Monaghan at St. Patrick's Roman Catholic Church. Both natives of Charleston. He a clerk.

MANTONE, FANNIE aged 21 years married to FATMAN, WILLIAM aged 37 years May 15, 1889 by Rabbi Mendelson of the Temple of Israel at the Charleston Hotel. He a native of New York and she of Charleston. He a merchant.

MAPPUS, CHRISTIAN aged 24 years married to RICHTER, THERESA aged 22 years November 4, 1890 by Rev. K. Boldt at St. Johannes Lutheran Church. He a native of Germany and she of Charleston. He a machinist.

MAPPUS, HENRY aged 23 years married to WITZEL, CATHARINE LOUISA aged 19 years February 24, 1884 by Rev. Claudian B. Northrop at 4 Hampden Court. He a native of Germany and she of Charleston. He a grocer.

MARCHAL, GENETTA aged 22 years married to ALLEN, GEORGE aged 23 years March 8, 1885 by Rev. John E. Beard. He a native of Massachusetts and she of England. He a laborer.

MARE, AUGUSTA L. aged 18 years married to TURNER, RICHARD H. aged 27 years January 27, 1885 by Rev. G. R. Brackett in Aiken Row. He a native of Bryan County, Georgia and she of St. Mary's, Georgia. He a clerk in Savannah, Georgia.

MARINES, ROBERT A. aged 31 years married to O'BRIEN, MARY F. aged 26 years October 14. 1886 by Father F. J. Shadler. Both natives of Charleston. He a laborer.

MARINES, (?), WILLIAM H. aged 23 years married to BUCK, M. A. aged 19 years April 26, 1881 by Father Daniel J. Quigley at The Cathedral of St. John the Baptist. Both natives of Charleston. He a blacksmith.

MARION, J. FARRIER aged 27 years married to BRINGLOE, SALLIE H. aged 23 years February 21, 1889 by Rev. R. W. Line at the residence of J. H. Moody.

MARION, HANNAH B. aged 19 years married to HILL, DRURY F. aged 22 years June 9, 1889 by Father John J. Wedenfeller. He a stonecutter.

MARKENS, GEORGE aged 22 years married to WEISKOFF,— aged 18 years October 16, 1878 by Rabbi David Levy at 325 King Street. He a native of Richmond, Virginia and she of Charleston. He a merchant in Jacksonville, Florida.

MARKLEY, J. P. married to RAWORTH (?), T. S. aged 23 years November 13, 1878 by Rev. J. Mercier Green. He a native of Aiken, South Carolina and she of Charleston. He works for the railroad.

MARKLEY, KATE H. aged 22 years married to CASON, GEORGE W. aged 24 years March 9, 1880 by Rev. J. E. Jackson. Both natives of Charleston. He a clerk.

MARKLEY, LAURA ELIZABETH aged 28 years married to MAXWELL, JOHN ALEXANDER aged 29 years November 14, 1883 by Rev. J. H. Tillinghast in Meeting Street above Line Street.

MARKS, KATIE H. aged 25 years married to HARRIS, DAVID aged 30 years June 11, 1895 by Rabbi Barnett A. Elzas at 372 King Street. He a native of New York City and she of Charleston. He a clerk at 245 Court Street in Brooklyn, New York.

MARKS, THOMAS aged 28 years married to O'CONNOR, JENNIE aged 25 years September 13, 1893 by Rev. Joseph D. Budds.

MARLOW, ESSIE aged 18 years married to McGINN, JAMES H. aged 24 years July 6, 1895 by Rev. J. C. Yongue at 14 Hampstead Square. He a native of Newbern, North Carolina and she of New York City. He a machinist.

MARRIE, ALICE aged 27 years married to BRASSEN, HENRY aged 28 years December 26, 1880 by Rev. L. H. Shuck at 27 Church Street. Both natives of Charleston. He a carpenter.

MARSH, MARY HARRIET aged 18 years married to THORNLEY, JAMES WILLIAM aged 25 years September 27, 1883 by A. Coke Smith at 700 King Street. He a native of Moncks Corner, South Carolina and she of Charleston. He a merchant.

MARSHALL, ANDREW A. aged 22 years married to COCHRAN, ELEANOR L. aged 19 years February 26, 1880 by Rev. G. R. Brackett at the Second Presbyterian Church. Both natives of Charleston. He a hardware salesman.

CHARLESTON SC MARRIAGES 1877-1895

MARSHALL, BELLE L. aged 21 years married to BAILEY, JOSEPH E. aged 30 years June 5, 1894 by Rev. Edward T. Horn at St. Johannes Lutheran Church. He a native of Orangeburg, South Carolina and a clerk.

MARSHALL, E. K. married to BROWN, JULIA November 10, 1887 by Rev. William H. Campbell. He a clerk.

MARSHALL, FRANCIS H. aged 26 yeears married to STEVENS, ANN ELIZA aged 23 years April 8, 1886 by Rev. Luther K. Probst. He a native of Savannah, Georgia and she of Charleston. He a clerk in Savannah.

MARSHALL (Mrs.) MATTIE REYNOLDS LEITCH aged 33 years married to RIGGS, JOHN S. aged 44 years June 5, 1878 by Rev. Charles S. Vedder. He a native of Norfolk, Virginia and she of Charleston. He President of the City Railroad.

MARSHALL, WILLIAM F. aged 27 years married to SMITH, EDITH aged 21 years April 3, 1883 by Rev. C. C. Pinckney in Smith Street. He a native of South Carolina and she of Charleston. He a clerk.

MARSHALL, WILLIAM L. aged 22 years married to BIRD, SALLIE M. aged 21 years December 3, 1890 by Rev. G. R. Brackett at the 2nd Presbyterian Church. He a native of Charleston and she of Mountville, Laurens County, South Carolina. He a clerk.

MARSHER, MARTHA C. C. aged 23 years married to PARSONS, LUTHER TYLER aged 24 years February 24, 1886 by Rev. Louis Muller. He a native of Hartford, Connecticut and she of Charleston. He a machinist.

MARTIN, AGNES M. aged 16 years married to DUC, HENRY ALEX aged 25 years June 17, 1889 by Rev. J. E. Carlisle. He a native of Columbia, South Carolina and she of Charleston. He a gunsmith.

MARTIN, ANNIE FRANCES aged 19 years married to ANDERSON, DAVID THOMAS aged 28 years September 26, 1889 by Rev. R. D. Smart at 40 Spring Street. He a native of Giles County, Virginia and she of Richland County, South Carolina. He works for the railroad.

MARTIN, CATHARINE aged 40 years married to MURPHY, PATRICK aged 39 years March 7, 1886 by Father F. J. Shadler at St. Joseph's Roman Catholic Church. Both natives of Ireland. He a paver.

MARTIN, CHRISTINA LISETTE aged 19 years married to WATERMANN, RUDOLPH BERNHARDT aged 33 years February 20, 1881 by Rev. Luther K. Probst at 35 Market Street. He a native of Germany and she of Charleston. He a grocer.

MARTIN, CLARK L. aged 42 years married to BISSELL, LILLIE October 23, 1893 by Rev. David M. Ramsey at 2 Ashmead Place.

MARTIN, EUNICE H. married to DUNKIN, WILLIAM H. July 8, 1886 by Rev. William H. Campbell. He a native of Charleston and she of South Carolina. He a clerk in Martins Station, Barnwell County, South Carolina.

MARTIN, G. J. aged 24 years married to KLINCK, MICHAEL S. aged 30 years May 25, 1880 by Rev. W. S. Bowman at the Wentworth Street Lutheran Church. Both natives of Charleston. He a merchant.

MARTIN, HENRY married to HOLMES, MARY November 22, 1888 by Rev. William H. Campbell at St. Paul's Church. He a druggist in Summerville, South Carolina.

MARTIN, HENRY R. aged 39 years married to DADIN, MARY L. aged 35 years February 11, 1883 by Rev. Luther K. Probst. Both natives of Charleston. He an engineer.

MARTIN, JULIA married to BROWN, JAMES P. July 15, 1886 by Rev. William H. Campbell at the residence of Joseph G. Martin. He a clerk.

MARTIN, LILLIE T. aged 23 years married to FLYNN, ROBERT E. aged 22 years October 22, 1893 by Rev. J. L. Stokes at 231 Coming Street. Both natives of Charleston. He a telegraph operator.

MARTIN, MAGGIE aged 17 years married to BORNEMANN, JAMES SAMUEL aged 29 years December 2, 1894 by Rev. J. C. Yongue. He a native of Charleston and see of South Carolina. He a clerk.

MARTIN, M. E. aged 21 years married to FALCONER, J. M. aged 25 years November 29, 1882 by Rev. G. R. Brackett at 11 Ann Street. He a native of Charleston and a machinist.

MARTIN, OSCAR F. aged 30 years married to SIMKINS, KATIE aged 21 years January 18, 1887 by Rev. Johannes Heckel at 4 Short Street. He a native of Illinois and she of Charleston. He a gas fitter.

MARTIN, SALLIE G. married to CATHERWOOD, THOMAS B. May 1, 1894 by Rev. William H. Campbell. He a bookkeeper in Savannah, Georgia.

MARTIN, SARAH VICTORIA aged 19 years married to DAVIS, MOSES aged 25 years November 21, 1886 by Rev. H. B. Browne at 78 Drake Street. Both natives of South Carolina. He a painter.

MARTIN, THEODORE L. married to WHITE, ANN E. HOUCK April 15, 1881 by Rev. A. Misseldine. He a native of Charlotte, North Carolina and she of Charleston. He a physician.

MARTIN, WILLIAM F. aged 23 years married to MATTHEWS, KATIE A. aged 20 years April 24, 1892 by Rev. R. C. Holland at the Wentworth Street Lutheran Street. Both natives of Charleston. He a mechanic.

MARTIN, WILLIAM H. aged 28 years married to TERRELL, MALLIE aged 24 years February 24, 1887 by Rev. H. Browne. He a native of North Carolina and she of South Carolina. He a tinner.

MARTSCHINK, META D. aged 23 years married to WEBER, HEINRICH F. W. aged 24 years April 26, 1891 by Rev. Louis Muller at the corner of Tradd and Legare Streets. Both natives of Prussia. He a grocer.

MASCHE, E. J. D. aged 35 years married to SCHNEIDER, E. M. aged 23 years September 18, 1879 by Rev. Louis Muller. He a native of Prussia and she of Bavaria. He a shoemaker.

MASON, CHARLIE aged 20 years married to MOORE, FLORA aged 17 years February 6, 1894 by Rev. J. M. Knowles at 62 Drake Street.

MASON, MARY J. aged 19 years married to McKENNA, PETER aged 22 years November 28, 1880 by Father Daniel J. Quigley at The Cathedral of St. John the Baptist. Both natives of Charleston. He a pilot.

MASON, MOSES aged 24 years married to WHITESIDES, SARAH aged 20 years June 5, 1883 by Father Daniel J. Quigley at The Cathedral of St. John the Baptist. Both natives of Charleston. He a mariner.

MASORITY (?), MARY aged 20 years married to CHURCH, J. E. aged 21 years March 29, 1891 by Rev. J. Thomas Pate at 231 Coming Street. He a native of Charleston and she of Worchester, Massachusetts. He a barber.

MASSOT, JOSEPHINE L. aged 28 years married to LUHN, GUSTAV JOHANN aged 41 years June 1, 1881 by Rev. Edward T. Horn at 8 Mary Street. He a native of Berlin, Germany and she of Charleston. He a druggist.

MASTERS, RAPHAEL M. aged 23 years married to DUNCAN, MARY aged 22 years November 10, 1881 by Rev. G. R. Brackett. He a native of Savannah, Georgia and she of Charleston. He a tinner.

MATHERSON, FLORA McCRAE aged 30 years married to READ, WILLIAM BOND aged 30 years February 17, 1885 by Rev. John Johnson at the residence of Dr. William H. Huger. He a native of South Carolina and she of Charleston. He a planter on the Savannah River.

MATHIESSEN, E. E. aged 17 years married to COLLINS, JONAH B. aged 21 years September 13, 1887 by Rev. W. S. Bean at 439 Meeting Street. He a native of Summerville, South Carolina and she of Charleston. He a salesman.

MATHIESSEN, WILLIAM aged 65 years married to ENGLAND, MARY EMILY aged 45 years July 24, 1878 by Father Daniel J. Quigley at The Cathedral of St. John the Baptist. He a merchant.

MATHIES, AUGUST aged 24 years married to BUMEMEYER, META aged 25 years December 28, 1882 by Father F. J. Shadler at St. Joseph's Roman Catholic Church. He a native of Hanover and she of Oldenburg, Germany. He a machinist.

MATSON, WALTER L. aged 26 years married to BROWN, MARY J. aged 25 years September 11, 1894 by Father J. J. Monaghan at St. Patrick's Roman Catholic Church. Both natives of Charleston. He an employee of the gas works.

MATTHEWS, ALEXANDER H. married to GRUBER, CAROLINE A. March 10, 1892 by Rev. William H. Campbell. He a railroad conductor.

MATTHEWS, CLELIA P. aged 20 years married to McGOWAN, WILLIAM C. M. aged 27 years November 4, 1885 by Rev. John Gass at 9 Rutledge Avenue. He a native of Abbeville, South Carolina and she of South Carolina. He a lawyer.

MATTHEWS, ELIZABETH J. aged 22 years married to REYNOLDS, WILLIAM TOWNSEND aged 24 years December 16, 1881 by Rev. John Johnson at 16 Amherst Street. He a native of Alabama and she of Charleston. He a clerk.

MATTHEWS, JOHN R. aged 26 years married to POLLNITZ, JULIA A. aged 19 years December 15, 1892 by Rev. John Johnson. She a native of Alabama. He works for the railroad.

MATTHEWS, JULIA FRANCES aged 23 years married to GALLAGHER, HENRY aged 46 years September 4, 1886 by Rev. J. W. Dickson at 231 Coming Street. He a native of Philadelphia, Pennsylvania and she of Charleston. He a druggist in Savannah, Georgia.

MATTHEWS, J. E. aged 60 years married to SMITH, MARY HAMILTON aged 34 years September 18, 1890 by Rev. T. P. Burgess at 15 Limehouse Street. He a native of Charleston and she of Grahamville, South Carolina.

MATTHEWS, KATIE A. aged 20 years married to MARTIN, WILLIAM F. aged 23 years April 24, 1892 by Rev. R. C. Holland at the Wentworth Street Lutheran Church. Both natives of Charleston. He a mechanic.

MATTHEWS, LULA aged 20 years married to HENDRICKS, JULIUS D. aged 22 years April 16, 1889 by Rev. H. B. Browne at 21 Blake Street. He a native of Charleston and she of Williamsburg County, South Carolina. He an engineer.

MATTHEWS, SAMUEL aged 25 years married to FORBES, ANNIE E. aged 22 years October 25, 1887 by Rev. P. J. McManus at St. Patrick's Roman Catholic Church. Both natives of Charleston. He a merchant.

MATTHEWS, S. J. L. married to HUFFMANN, E. G. July 28, 1885 by Father P. L. Duffy.

MATTHEWS, THOMAS L. aged 23 years married to FOYE, LAURA J. aged 22 years July 31, 1895 by Rev. J. C. Yongue at 14 Hampstead Square. He a native of Charleston and she of North Carolina. He a clerk.

MAULL, IDA ISABELLA aged 19 years married to BEVAN, DANIEL E. aged 24 years October 12, 1891 by Father J. J. Monaghan at 136 St. Philip Street. He a native of Ireland and she of Charleston. He a railroad brakeman.

MAULL, JAMES D. aged 30 years married to HENDRICKS, GERALDINE aged 18 years June 10, 1881 by Rev. J. V. Welsh at the residence of the Bride's father. He a native of Charleston and a moulder.

MAULL, PHILLIPINA E. aged 31 years married to DuBOSE, WILLIAM C. aged 28 years December 13, 1884 by Rev. Robert Wilson at 4 Wragg Square. Both natives of Charleston. He a railroad brakeman.

MAURO, CHARLES aged 27 years married to VERDI, ROS aged 27 years December 30, 1895 by Father J. J. Monaghan at St. Patrick's Roman Catholic Church.

MAVRY, ANNIE aged 18 years married to LaFOURCADE, VICTOR aged 21 years January 30, 1883 by Father John P. Twigg at St. Patrick's Roman Catholic Church. Both natives of Charleston.

MAXEY, JULIA aged 42 years married to PATTERSON, EDMUND aged 47 years December 17, 1893 by Rev. N. Keff Smith at 72 Lee Street. Both natives of Charleston. He a laborer.

MAXWELL, JOHN ALEXANDER aged 29 years married to MARKLEY, LAURA ELIZABETH aged 28 years November 14, 1883 by Rev. J. H. Tillinghast in Meeting Street above Line Street.

MAXWELL, LIZZIE A. aged 24 years married to HUDSON, THOMAS aged 24 years October 12, 1886 by Rev. J. Walter Dickson at 77 Bay Street. Both natives of Charleston. He a fireman.

MAY, BRIDGET aged 34 years married to LYNCH, JOHN R. aged 34 years January 12, 1885 by Father Daniel J. Quigley at St. Patrick's Roman Catholic Church. He a native of Charleston and she of Ireland. He a laborer.

MAY, ELIZA A. aged 27 years married to GRAHAM, JOSEPH aged 29 years June 15, 1881 by Father F. J. Shadler. He a native of Whitehaven, England and she of Charleston. He a mariner.

MAY, HENRY married to CAMERON, FRANCES December 28, 1878 by William B. Yates.

MAY, JOHN aged 36 years married to CORCORAN, M. J. aged 24 years November 1, 1880 by Father Harry P. Northrop at St. Patrick's Roman Catholic Church. He a native of Ireland and she of Charleston. He an engineer.

MAY, LAWRENCE JOSEPH aged 32 years married to BROWN, MARGARET MAGDALENA aged 26 years November 7, 1881 by Father Claudian B. Northrop at St. Mary of the Annunciation Roman Catholic Church.

MAY, P. aged 31 years married to BROWN, R. aged 20 years February 28, 1882 by Rev. R. D. Lide at 400 King Street. Both natives of Germany. He a merchant.

MAYBANK, JOHN F. aged 25 years married to JOHNSON, ELEANOR S. aged 24 years August 31, 1893 by Rev. John Johnson at 107 Wentworth Street. Both natives of Charleston. He a cotton buyer.

MAYES, WILLIAM aged 25 years married to WESSEL, FREDERICKA J. H. aged 21 years February 14, 1891 by Rev. S. P. H. Elwell. He a native of Nashville, Tennessee and she of Germany.

MAYRANT, KATE D. aged 25 years married to SIMON, S. LEWIS aged 28 years November 16, 1887 by Rev. C. C. Pinckney at Grace Church. He a native of Charleston and she of Sumter County, South Carolina. He a civil engineer.

MAZIEL (?), THOMAS R. aged 22 years married to ROGERS, MARY E. aged 18 years March 18, 1894 by Rev. Griffin Holliman at the corner of Reid and Hanover Streets. He a native of Colleton County, South Carolina and she of Berkeley County, South Carolina. He works for the railroad.

MAZYCK, EDWARD K. married to TUCKER, MARTHA April 29, 1886 by Rev. William H. Campbell at the residence of William H. Tucker. He a clerk.

MAZYCK, MARY R. B. married to COUTOWRIEN (?), JOHN E. H. February 22, 1881 by Rev. A. H. Misseldine.

MAZYCK, ROSA F. aged 20 years married to WELCH, S. L. aged 22 years March 22, 1887 by Rev. L. F. Beattie. He a native of South Carolina and she of Charleston. He an electric worker.

McALISTER, ANDREW aged 40 years married to HOME, MARY BRUCE aged 38 years July 24, 1887 by Rev. Leroy T. Beattie at 231 Coming Street. He a native of Scotland and a laborer. She a native of Georgia.

McBALZER (?), A. aged 28 years married to BENSE, M. A. aged 23 years November 9, 1880 by Rev. L. H. Shuck at 3 Cooper Street. Both natives of Charleston. He a sergeant of police.

McBRIDE, ANDREW aged 50 years married to SIMS, ISABELLE aged 36 years September 6, 1881 by Rev. A. Coke Smith at 123 St. Philip Street. He a native of Charleston and a cotton manufacturer.

McBRIDE, ELIZABETH aged 23 years married to WATERS, FRANCIS aged 28 years April 19, 1883 by Rev. G. R. Brackett. Both natives of Charleston. He a painter.

McBRIDE, KATIE aged 22 years married to POWERS, MICHAEL aged 25 years January 29, 1884 by Father John P. Twigg at St. Patrick's Roman Catholic Church. Both natives of Charleston. He a policeman.

McBRIDE, LAWRENCE B. aged 19 years married to WELLS, OLIVET aged 17 years August 27, 1894 by Rev. J. L. Stokes at 231 Coming Street. He a native of Charleston and she of Winchester, Virginia. He a drug clerk.

McCABE, PAULINE aged 30 years married to LAW, OLIVER aged 29 years January 31, 1892 by Rev. J. O. Fludd. He a native of Beaufort County, South Carolina and she of Johnson County, North Carolina. He a watchman.

McCAFFER, CHARLES W. aged 28 years married to SCREVEN, LILLA W. aged 21 years January 28, 1885 by Rev. Robert Wilson at 17 Woolfe Street.

McCAFFER, JANE WALKER aged 33 years married to RAINIER, CHARLES E. aged 45 years May 9, 1885 by Rev. G. R. Brackett. He a native of New Jersey and she of Charleston. He an engineer.

McCAFFER, WILLIAM JOHN aged 27 years married to HUGHES, LILLA W. aged 22 years December 13, 1877 by Rev. John H. Honour. Both natives of Charleston. He a clerk.

McCALL, THOMAS HARLEY aged 27 years married to HEWETSON, NORA JANE aged 20 years November 1, 1881 by Rev. A. Coke Smith at 14 Bull Street. He a native of Florence, South Carolina and she of Bombay, India. He a planter.

McCANTS, IDA DWIGHT aged 28 years married to ALLEN, FRANCIS M. aged 32 years November 24, 1891 by Rev. R. C. Holland. He a native of Sumter County, South Carolina and she of Kingstree, South Carolina. He a farmer in Clarendon County, South Carolina.

McCANTS, HATTIE J. aged 20 years married to MUCKENFUSS, WILLIAM M. aged 24 years March 30, 1890 by Rev. J. Thomas Pate at 100 Columbus Street. He a native of Charleston and she of Berkeley County, South Carolina.

McCANTS, (Mrs.) MARY FOULTZ aged 41 years married to VERONEE, S. J. B. aged 56 years March 30, 1890 by Rev. J. Thomas Pate at 100 Columbus Street. He a native of Charleston and she of Berkeley County, South Carolina.

McCANTS, MARY J. aged 21 years married to KENNEDY, JOSEPH aged 24 years August 15, 1889 by Rev. H. B. Browne at 94 America Street. He a native of Charleston and she of Berkeley County, South Carolina. He a carpenter.

McCANTY, JOHANNA married to McCARLIFF, WILLIAM M. September 21, 1893 by Father T. P. Budds at St. Joseph's Roman Catholic Church. He a mechnic.

McCARLIFF, WILLIAM M. married to McCANTY, JOHANNA September 21, 1893 by Father T. P. Budds at St. Joseph's Roman Catholic Church. He a mechanic.

McCARREL, ANN E. CALDER aged 30 years married to BEE, JOHN PRICE aged 39 years February 22, 1891 by Rev. G. R. Brackett at 49 Tradd Street. Both natives of Charleston. He a mechanic.

McCARROLL, JOHN REYNOLDS aged 20 years married to CALDER, ANNA ELIZA aged 19 years April 9, 1879 by Rev. W. S. Bowman at 14 Bee Street.

McCARROLL, KATE aged 19 years married to ROBERTS, S. T. aged 20 years October 15, 1879 by Rev. J. V. Welsh at 64 Radcliffe Street. Both natives of Charleston. He a tinner.

McCARROLL, MARY C. aged 26 years married to Baker, JOHN C. aged 21 years June 9, 1895 by Rev. A. Ernest Cornish at the corner of Bee and President Streets. He a native of Lexington County, South Carolina and she of Charleston. He a laborer.

McCARROLL, W. aged 24 years married to LOWRY, JULIA aged 22 years November 19, 1879 by Father Daniel J. Quigley. Both natives of Charleston. He an engineer.

McCARTHY, EUGENE aged 24 years married to GROTUS (?), WILHELMINA aged 19 years July 8, 1884 by Father F. J. Shadler at St. Joseph's Roman Catholic Church. Both natives of Charleston. He a stonecutter.

McCARTHY, JOHANNA married to McCAULEY, WILLIAM H. September 21, 1883 by Rev. Joseph D. Budds.

McCAULEY, WILLIAM H. married to McCARTHY, JOHANNA September 21, 1893 by Rev. Joseph D. Budds.

McCAW, JOHN aged 50 years married to ASHEN, MARY E. aged 22 years February 6, 1894 by Father J. J. Monaghan at 136 St. Philip Street. He a native of Scotland and she of York, South Carolina. He a watchman.

McCLAIN, W, DAVID aged 24 years married to BROCK, ANN FRANCIS aged 19 years December 29, 1889 by Rev. C. E. Chichester at the Mariners Church.

McCLELLAN, J. P. aged 32 years married to MOORE, L. V. December 11, 1882 by Rev. A. Coke Smith at 21 Wentworth Street. Both natives of South Carolina He a farmer.

McCOOK, MARY ANN aged 29 years married to PATTON, GEORGE TAYLOR aged 66 years February 5, 1880 by Rev. C. C. Pinckney at 2 South Battery. He a native of New York and she of Richmond, Virginia. He a merchant.

McCORD, L. CHEVES aged 23 years married to CHEVES, HENRY C. aged 34 years November 9, 1886 by Rev. Robert Wilson at St. Luke's Church. Both natives of Charleston. He a clerk.

McCORMACK, JOHN R. aged 24 years married to CONNELLY, CARRIE E. aged 19 years April 22, 1891 by Rev. Edwin C. Dargan at 143 Calhoun Street. He a native of Barnwell County, South Carolina and she of Graniteville, South Carolina. He a physician in Midway, South Carolina.

McCOTTEN, C. D. aged 18 years married to POLLEN, J. D. aged 24 years May 30, 1882 by Father Claudian B. Northrop in Wentworth Street. He a native of Charleston and a clerk.

McCOTTEN, E. G. aged 19 years married to ANHEUSER, C. J. F. aged 37 years July 5, 1882 by Father P. J. Duffy at 20 Wentworth Street. Both natives of Germany. He a merchant.

McCOTTER, E. G. aged 19 years married to ANHEUSER, C. J. F. aged 37 years July 5, 1882 by Father P. L. Duffy at 20 Wentworth Street. Both natives of Germany. He a merchant.

McCOWAN, WILLIAM C. aged 37 years married to DOUGHERTY, JESSE E. aged 33 years December 15, 1881 by Rev. Luther K. Probst at 18 Wentworth Street. He a native of Abbeville, South Carolina and she of Charleston. He a printer.

McCOY, JAMES aged 19 years married to BESSINGER, HATTIE aged 20 years April 15, 1884 by Rev. R. A. Lapsley at 22 Aiken Street.

McCRACKEN, NAOMI E. aged 32 years married to ASTLE, FRANCIS M. aged 23 years June 4, 1885 by Rev. John Johnson. Both natives of Charleston. He a mechanic.

McCRACKEN, R. A. aged 26 years married to HARRIS, S. C. aged 19 years August 1, 1882 by Rev. L. H. Shuck at 27 Church Street. He a native of South Carolina and a railroad worker. She a native of England.

McCRADY, ESTHER L. B. aged 30 years married to GAILLARD, SAMUEL G. aged 38 years June 13, 1892 by Rev. John Johnson. He a native of Eutawville, South Carolina and she of Charleston. He a civil and mining engineer.

McCRADY, L. aged 30 years married to SHACKLEFORD, JANE aged 24 years October 24, 1882 by Rev. John Johnson at 16 Church Street. He a native of Charleston and a lawyer.

McCRADY, LOUISA R. L. aged 24 years married to BARNWELL, WILLIAM H. aged 26 years April 28, 1887 by Rev. John Johnson. Both natives of South Carolina. He an accountant.

McCRADY, SABINA L. aged 25 years married to FITZSIMONS, THEODORE aged 28 years April 30, 1889 by Rev. John Johnson at St. Philip's Church. He a native of South Carolina and she of Clarendon County, South Carolina. He in the cotton business.

McCRURY, NANNIE married to JUST, ADAM June 21, 1880 by William B. Yates, Chaplain.

McCUE, A. E. aged 24 years married to KEENAN, F. M. aged 24 years November 27, 1882 by Father F. J. Shadler at St. Joseph's Roman Catholic Church. Both natives of Charleston. He a stevedore.

McCUE, KATE aged 27 years married to HALL, SAMUEL J. aged 27 years January 7, 1885 by Father F. J. Shadler at St. Joseph's Roman Catholic Church. He a native of Ireland and she of Charleston. He a mariner.

McCUE, H. WILLIAM aged 28 years married to CARROLL, H. SARAH aged 21 years January 29, 1890 by Father F. J. Shadler at St. Joseph's Roman Catholic Church. Both natives of Charleston. He a letter carrier.

McCULLEN, WILEY aged 20 years married to DAVIS, IDA aged 17 years July 31, 1891 by Rev. J. Thomas Pate at 231 Coming Street. He a native of Atlanta, Georgia and she of Milledgeville, Georgia. He works in a factory.

McCULLOUGH, JOSEPHINE aged 20 years married to WALTON, SIMEON O. aged 26 years May 19, 1889 by Rev. H. B. Browne. He a native of Prussia and she of Charleston.

McCULLOUGH, ROBERT WILLIAM aged 25 years married to LYONS, CATHERINE aged 22 years May 2, 1889 by Bishop Harry P. Northrop at 1 Tradd Street. He a native of Hendersonville, North Carolina and she of Charleston. He a gardener.

McCULLOUGH, WILLIAM B. aged 20 years married to DAVIS, EMMA E. aged 17 years July 12, 1891 by Rev. G. R. Betts at 3 Blake Street.

McDERMID, GEORGE C. aged 35 years married to ALLAN, JESSIE aged 23 years October 24, 1894 by Rev. G. R. Brackett at 84 Rutledge Avenue. Both natives of Charleston. He a salesman.

McDERMID, THOMAS V. aged 27 years married to HOLSTEIN, MARY E. aged 25 years December 12, 1892 by Rev. G. R. Brackett at 64 Rutledge Avenue. He a native of Dublin, Ireland and she of Charleston. He a mariner.

McDERMID, NORMAN W. aged 36 years married to ROBSON, ANN ELIZA aged 26 years April 22, 1886 by Rev. G. R. Brackett.

McDERMOTT, ANNIE aged 35 years married to FISHER, JAMES aged 35 years April 5, 1891 by Father J. J Monaghan at St. Patrick's Roman Catholic Church. He a native of Belgium and she of Charleston. He a mariner.

McDON, THOMAS BALLARD aged 26 years married to AHRENS, KATE LOUISE aged 20 years February 17, 1880 by Rev. Edward T. Horn at St. John's Lutheran Church. He a native of Liberty Hill, South Carolina and she of West Hoboken, New Jersey. He a physician in Memphis, Tennessee.

McDONALD, ANNA E. aged 20 years married to O'BRIEN, JEREMIAH FRANCIS aged 25 years February 10, 1889 by Father J. J. Monaghan at St. Patrick's Roman Catholic Church. Both natives of Charleston. He a carpenter.

McDONALD, DAISY aged 17 years married to DONALD, B. aged 21 years July 9, 1879 by Rev. R. N. Wells. Both natives of Charleston. He a native of Charleston and she of Cold Spring, New York. He a pressman.

McDONALD, EMILY VICTORIA aged 19 years married to JONES, RICHARD WILLIAM aged 36 years February 28, 1886 by Rev. Charles S. Vedder at 116 Church Street. Both natives of Charleston. He a machinist.

McDONALD, GEORGE W. H. aged 42 years married to MORGANSTEIN, MARIE aged 22 years December 29, 1895 by Rev. J. M. Steadman at 74 Lee Street.

McDONALD, MARGARET aged 19 years married to BURN, WILLIAM A. aged 23 years July 16, 1890 by Father J. J. Monaghan at 136 St. Philip Street. Both natives of Charleston. He a railroad conductor.

McDONALD, MARY ELLEN aged 35 years married to SULLIVAN, WILLIAM PATRICK aged 23 years April 20, 1884 by Father Daniel J. Quigley.

McDONALD, SAMUEL R. aged 20 years married to DRIGGERS, ALBERTA B. aged 15 years December 25, 1893 by Rev. J. C. Yongue at 14 Hampstead Square. He a native of Summerville, South Carolina and she of Sumter, South Carolina. He a farmer at Four Mile House.

McDONALD, WILLIAM OGIER aged 23 years married to ST. CLAIR, KATIE aged 21 years July 1, 1891 by Rev. R. C. Holland. He a native of Charleston and she of Marion County, South Carolina. He a clerk.

McDONOUGH, JOHN E. aged 20 years married to CLARKE, M. F. aged 18 years November 21, 1890 by Rev. William P. Bolger, Trial Justice. Both natives of Savannah, Georgia. He an engineer in Savannah.

McDOUGAL, DAVID aged 25 years married to MENSING, BERTHA AUGUSTA aged 28 years April 24, 1883 by Rev. Louis Muller at the southeast corner of King and Broad Streets.

McDOUGAL, JOHN MACKEY aged 22 years married to ALBERS, DORETHA aged 23 years April 12, 1883 by Rev. Edward T. Horn at the corner of Tradd and Council Streets. Both natives of Charleston. He an engineer.

McDOWELL, ELLEN F. aged 28 years married to GREGORY, PHILO EDWIN aged 32 years April 13, 1887 by Rev. Robert Wilson. Both natives of South Carolina. He an lawyer.

McDUFF, MAMIE aged 23 years married to O'BRIEN, W. L. aged 23 years March 17, 1884 by Father F. A. Schmetz at 20 Line Street. Both natives of Charleston. He works for the railroad.

McELVEE, JANEY aged 17 years married to BAXTER, CHARLES aged 22 years November 9, 1892 by Rev. A. M. Chreitzberg at Bischoff's Square. Both natives of Charleston. He works in a factory.

McELVEN, FANNIE aged 19 years married to LIVELY, THOMAS aged 22 years December 26, 1892 by Rev. Edmund Wells at 29 Blake Street. He a native of Augusta, Georgia and she of Charleston. He works in the cotton mill.

McEVOY, MICHAEL aged 18 years married to LENT, VALERIA aged 16 years August 2, 1893 by Rev. J. M. Knowles at 87 America Street. He a native of South Carolina and she of Charleston. He works in the cotton mill.

McEVOY, THOMAS J. aged 31 years married to CARD, ELIZABETH A. J. aged 24 years July 7, 1895 by Father J. J. Monaghan at 136 St. Philip Street. He a native of Philadelphia, Pennsylvania and she of Charleston. He a marine engineer in Savannah, Georgia.

McFARLANE, BARBARA married to McFARLANE, JAMES September 12, 1894 by Rev. W. M. McPheeters at 421 Meeting Street. Both natives of Scotland. He a machinist.

McFARLANE, JAMES married to McFARLANE, BARBARA September 12, 1894 by Rev. W. M. McPheeters at 421 Meeting Street. Both natives of Scotland. He a machinist.

McFAWN, JAMES R. aged 20 years married to ABRAMS, (Mrs.) CATHERINE FURSE aged 33 years February 15, 1888 by Rev. H. B. Browne at 30 Hanover Street. He a native of Massachusetts and she of Barnwell County, South Carolina. He a watchman.

McGANNAGHAN, MARY aged 36 years married to DENIS, FRANCIS aged 38 years February 14, 1885 by Rev. John E. Beard at 64 Nassau Street. He a native of England and she of Harrisburg, Pennsylvania. He works in a factory.

McGARY, F. F. aged 22 years married to CADE, M. aged 20 years August 16, 1882 by Father Daniel J. Quigley at The Cathedral of St. John the Baptist. He a native of Charleston and an inspector.

McGEE, OCTAVIA aged 18 years married to HORN, JOSEPH aged 25 years August 29, 1892 by Rev. K. Boldt. He a native of Germany and she of Camden, South Carolina. He a baker.

McGEOUGH, ANNE aged 30 years married to McGILL, JOHN aged 33 years May 11, 1879 by Bishop Patrick N. Lynch at The Cathedral of St. John the Baptist. Both natives of Ireland. He a merchant.

McGILL, DORA M. aged 22 years married to HALL, GEORGE P. aged 39 years November 9, 1893 by Rev. J. C. Yongue at 29 Blake Street. He a native of Edgefield County, South Carolina and she of Timmonsville, South Carolina.

McGILL, JOHN aged 33 years married to KEOUGH, ANNE M. aged 30 years May 11, 1879 by Bishop P. N. Lynch at The Cathedral of St. John the Baptist. He a native of County Antrim, Ireland and she of Ireland. He a merchant.

McGILLIVRAY, Caroline aged 21 years married to STROMAN, JACOB P. aged 22 years December 15, 1885 by Rev. John Johnson at 10 Atlantic Street. He a native of South Carolina and she of Charleston. He a physician in Orangeburg, South Carolina.

McGILLIVRAY, SARAH W. aged 22 years married to MORRISON, HENRY T. aged 28 years January 6, 1892 by Rev. John Johnson at 10 Atlantic Street. He a native of McClellanville, South Carolina and she of Charleston. He works in a saw mill in Williamsburg, South Carolina.

McGINN, JAMES H. aged 24 years married to MARLOW, ESSIE aged 18 years July 6, 1895 by Rev. J. C. Yongue at 14 Hampstead Square. He a native of Newbern, North Carolina and she of New York City. He a machinist.

McGINNIS, PETER McGREGOR aged 50 years married to GARDNER, (Mrs.) MARTHA L. GRIFFITH aged 28 years May 21, 1890 by Rev. T. P. Burgess at 454 Meeting Street. He a native of Charleston and she of Orangeburg, South Carolina. He a horse shoer and farrier.

McGINNIS, WILLIAM FRANCIS aged 22 years married to CROGAN, FANNIE aged 23 years January 21, 1878 by Rev. Claudian B. Northrop at St. Mary of the Annunciation Roman Catholic Church.

McGORTY, JAMES aged 21 years married to KROGUE, MAMIE aged 20 years March 4, 1883 by Rev. L. H. Shuck at 27 Church Street. He a native of Charleston and she of Augusta, Georgia. He a candymaker.

McGOWAN, JOHANNA aged 26 years married to KELLEN, THOMAS M. aged 28 years November 2, 1892 by Father P. L. Duffy at The Cathedral of St. John the Baptist. He a native of Boston, Massachusetts and she of Augusta, Georgia. He a longshoreman.

McGOWAN, WILLIAM C. M. aged 27 years married to MATTHEWS, CLELIA P. aged 20 years November 4, 1885 by Rev. John Gass at 9 Rutledge Avenue. He a native of Abbeville, South Carolina and she of South Carolina. He a lawyer.

McGRANE, MARTIN married to CONROY, B. MARY January 22, 1890 by Father F. J. Shadler at St. Joseph's Roman Catholic Church. Both natives of Charleston. He a boilermaker.

McGRATH, JOHN E. aged 24 years married to HENNESSY, JOHANNA aged 25 years June 5, 1883 by Father J. J. Woolahan at St. Mary of the Annunciation Roman Catholic Church. He a native of Anderson, South Carolina and she of Charleston. He a merchant.

McGINNIS, ROSE E. aged 19 years married to BENNET, WILLIAM aged 22 years September 25, 1891 by Rev. Robert Wilson at 4 Wragg Square.

McGUINNES, ROSE E. aged 19 years married to BENNETT, WILLIAM aged 22 years September 25, 1891 by Rev. Robert Wilson at 4 Wragg Square. He a native of Charleston and she of Laurens County, South Carolina. He a wood turner.

McGUIRE, ROSA married to HONKLER, JOHN April 28, 1888 by Rev. J. H. Wheeler. He a native of Charleston and she of Ireland. He a stonecutter.

McGUIRE, WILLIAM H. aged 25 years married to WALTERS, MARY ANNA aged 26 years August 16, 1892 by Rev. Thomas B. Wright at Summerville, South Carolina.

McINDOE, BESSIE aged 20 years married to ROUMILLAT, WILLIAM H. aged 27 years April 19, 1888 by Rev. J. V. Welsh at 40 Bee Street. He a native of Aiken, South Carolina and she of Charleston. He a druggist in Gaffney, South Carolina.

McINERNEY, A. H. aged 20 years married to KNIGHT, D. J. aged 25 years August 6, 1882 by Rev. J. G. Guentzer. He a native of Charleston and a mariner. He a native of Charleston and a mariner.

McINERNEY, MAGGIE aged 25 years married to CLEAR, WILLIAM ROBERT aged 30 years June 27, 1888 by Father Daniel J. Quigley at St. Patrick's Roman Catholic Church. Both natives of Charleston. He works for the railroad.

McINNERNEY, LAWRENCE aged 26 years married to QUINN, HONORIA aged 23 years January 1, 1883 by Rev. F. A. Schmetz at St. Patrick's Roman Catholic Church. Both natives of Charleston. He a carpenter.

McINNERNEY, MICHAEL aged 34 years married to GRIFFIN, E. MARY aged 27 years February 9, 1890 by Rev. J. Thomas Pate at the Spring Street Church. He a native of Charleston and she of Polk County, North Carolina. He works for the railroad.

McINNERNEY, MICHAEL aged 23 years married to CLIFFORD, ANNIE aged 18 years February 28, 1880 by Father Daniel J. Quigley at The Cathedral of St. John the Baptist. He a native of Charleston and she of England. He a stonecutter.

McINNES, JOHN aged EAGAN, LENORE September 13, 1893 by Rev. D. A. Blackburn at 49 Gadsden Street. He a blacksmith.

McINNES, PETER McG. aged 44 years married to PETERS, MARY L. aged 25 years September 30, 1883 by Father F. J. Shadler. Both natives of Charleston. He a vet surgeon.

McINTIRE, (Mrs.) MARY E. WALLACE aged 40 years married to MANNING, JAMES E. aged 44 years January 10, 1878 by Rev. L. H. Shuck at 5 George Street. Both natives of Charleston. He a painter.

McINTOSH, BELLE aged 19 years married to WULBURN, JOHN H. aged 22 years November 5, 1891 by Rev. W. T. Thompson at 69 Wentworth Street. Both natives of Charleston. He a clerk.

McINTOSH, LIZZIE aged 25 years married to SIGWALD, LAWRENCE F aged 22 years April 5, 1892 by Rev. J. L. Stokes at 106 Columbus Street. Both natives of Charleston. He a horseshoer.

McINTYRE, GEORGE F. aged 33 years married to WIRTH, V. E. L. aged 20 years August 20, 1879 by Rev. E. A. Wingard at 14 Bee Street. Both natives of Charleston. He a merchant.

McINTYRE, GEORGE H. aged 27 years married to HOWARD, THEODORA aged 20 years December 31, 1894 by Rev. Thomas F. Hopkins at St. Mary of the Annunciation Roman Catholic Church.

McINTYRE, PATRICK aged 22 years married to MORGAN, JULIA aged 18 years October 9, 1878 by Father Daniel J. Quigley at The Cathedral of St. John the Baptist. He a native of Ireland and she of Charleston. He a mariner.

McINVAILLE, SARAH B. aged 23 years married to SHEPHARD, WILLIAM S. aged 36 years February 3, 1895 by Rev. Edmund Wells. He a native of Onslow, North Carolina and she of Darlington, South Carolina. He a clerk in Hartsville, South Carolina.

McKAY, ISABELLA M. aged 21 years married to GRAFFENREID, GEORGE T. aged 25 years October 6, 1884 by Rev. A. J. S. Thomas at 94 Queen Street. Both natives of South Carolina. He a telegraph operator in Columbia, South Carolina.

McKAY, JAMES C. aged 27 years married to MacDONELL, LILLIAN aged 21 years September 18, 1892 by John Ahrens, Trial Justice.

McKAY, JEFFERSON T. aged 23 years married to DORAN, SARAH aged 20 years May 23, 1883 by Rev. P. L. Duffy at The Cathedral of St. John the Baptist. He a native of Bonneau, South Carolina and she of Charleston. He a bartender.

McKEE, AGNES married to COHEN, WILLIAM CECIL May 7, 1889 by Rev. William H. Campbell at the residence of George McKee - 83 Cannon Street.

McKEE, CATHERINE N. married to CORLEY, JACOB J. February 8, 1893 by Rev. William H. Campbell at St. Paul's Church. He a machinist in Florence, South Carolina.

McKEE, WILLIAM EDWARD married to ROACH, C. C. December 29, 1887 by Rev. William H. Campbell at the residence of Edward Roach. He a clerk.

McKENNA, JOHN JOSEPH aged 23 years married to MANSFIELD, MARGARET AGNES aged 21 years April 21, 1889 by Father J. J. Monaghan at St. Patrick's Roman Catholic Church. Both natives of Charleston. He a clerk.

McKENNA, MARY aged 24 years married to SWEENEY, JOHN JAMES aged 24 years January 21, 1883 by Father John P. Twigg. Both natives of Charleston. He a policeman.

McKENNA, PETER aged 22 years married to MASON, MARY J. aged 19 years November 28, 1880 by Father Daniel J. Quigley at The Cathedral of St. John the Baptist. He a native of Charleston and a pilot.

McKENZIE, ELLEN L. aged 23 years married to ELLIS, WILLIAM aged 43 years May 9, 1888 by Rev. Robert Wilson at 4 Wragg Square. He a native of Charleston and she of Sumter, South Carolina. He a blacksmith.

McKENZIE, SULTAN W. aged 48 years married to FOGARTIE, ESTHER J. aged 46 years November 22, 1887 by Rev. G. R. Brackett. He a native of Fort Motte, South Carolina and she of Charleston. He a physician in Gadsden, South Carolina.

McKIERNAN, MARY ANN aged 23 years married to MAGUIRE, MORRIS D. aged 28 years February 4, 1880 by Rev. Claudian B. Northrop at St. Mary of the Annunciation Roman Catholic Church. Both natives of Charleston. He a clerk. Witnessed by Margaret O'Brien and William F. Maguire.

McKIEVER, MARY T. aged 23 years married to MAGRATH, CHARLES H. aged 27 years May 20, 1885 by Father Daniel J. Quigley at St. Patrick's Roman Catholic Church. Both natives of Charleston. He a mechanist.

McKIEVER, DANIEL J. aged 27 years married to DUFFIE, ANNIE MARIE aged 22 years February 11, 1885 by Father Daniel J. Quigley at St. Patrick's Roman Catholic Church. He a native of Charleston and a carpenter.

McKINNON, MARGARET E. aged 22 years married to RUFF, WALTER EDWARD aged 26 years June 17, 1891 by Rev. G. R. Brackett at 324 Meeting Street. He a native of Lexington County, South Carolina and she of Williamsburg County, South Carolina. He a builder and engineer.

McKINNON, NEILL C. aged 55 years married to WHITTAKER, CATHERINE S. aged 50 years February 27, 1878 by Rev. G. R. Brackett at 118 St. Philip Street. He a native of Richmond County, North Carolina and she of Charleston. He a farmer in Chesterfield County, South Carolina.

McKNIGHT, GEORGE M. aged 33 years married to GLEN, MAMIE A. aged 18 years February 20, 1893 by Rev. Edmund Wells at 82 Drake Street. He a native of Williamsburg County, South Carolina and she of Charleston. He a farmer in Gourdin, South Carolina.

McLAUGHLIN, JAMES J. aged 25 years married to KENNY, CATHERINE aged 26 years June 11, 1883 by Rev. P. L. Duffy at The Cathedral of St. John the Baptist. Both natives of Charleston. He a policeman.

McLAUGHLIN, M. A. aged 21 years married to CONDON, J. T. aged 24 years May 27, 1882 by Father J. F. Shadler at St. Joseph's Roman Catholic Church. He a native of Charleston and a clerk.

McLEISH, ARCHIBALD married to THARIN, VIRGINIA E. R. July 19, 1878 by William B. Yates, Chaplain, at 10 Church Street.

McMAHAN, (Mrs.) MARGARET aged 43 years married to MORRISSEY, TIMOTHY aged 53 years November 11, 1888 by Father J. J. Monaghan at St. Patrick's Roman Catholic Church. Both natives of Charleston. He a drayman.

McMAHON, JEREMIAH married to KELLY, (Mrs.) MARGARET TOUGHEL March 5, 1878 by Father John P. Twigg at The Cathedral of St. John the Baptist.

McMAHON, SARAH aged 20 years married to KEEGAN, JOHN PATRICK aged 24 years November 25, 1883 by Father Daniel J. Quigley at The Cathedral of St. John the Baptist. Both natives of Charleston. He a machinist.

McMAHAN, W. P. aged 24 years married to HOWARD, H. aged 23 years February 21, 1882 by Father J. J. Monaghan at St. Patrick's Roman Catholic Church. He a native of Charleston and a drayman.

McMAHON, MARY ANN aged 21 years married to CAMPBELL, JOHN J. J. aged 26 years December 26, 1886 by Rev. John Johnson at 53 Church Street. Both natives of Charleston. He works for the railroad.

McMANUS, (Mrs.) CATHERINE ANNA CORKLE aged 40 years married to VALDEZ, FRANCISCO A. aged 38 years December 12, 1887 by Rev. John O. Wilson at 58 Hasell Street. He a native of Havana, Cuba and she of Charleston. He a cigar packer.

McMANUS, MICHAEL W.aged 28 years married to COMER, MARGARET aged 18 years February 8, 1880 by Father John P. Twigg at The Cathedral of St. John the Baptist. Both natives of Charleston. He a policeman.

McMANUS, P. J. aged 28 years married to O'MEARA, M. A. aged 26 years June 8, 1887 by Rev. P. J. McManus. He a native of Ireland and she of Charleston. He a clerk.

McMILLAN, CHARLOTTE WOODWARD aged 21 years married to TERREL, THOMAS aged 22 years April 25, 1879 by Rev. R. N. Wells. Both natives of Charleston. He a mechanic. Both natives of Charleston. He a mechanic.

McMILLAN, CORNELIA E. aged 24 years married to RICHARDS, JOHN R. aged 25 years January 3, 1878 by Rev. T. E. Wannamaker at 127 St. Philip Street. Both natives of Charleston. He a planter in Orangeburg, South Carolina.

McMILLAN, JOHN CICERO aged 29 years married to ROBSON, MARTHA WILLIAMS aged 22 years April 11, 1888 by Rev. G. R. Brackett. He a native of Marion County, South Carolina and she of Spartanburg, South Carolina. He a physician in Marion County.

McMILLAN, M. G. aged 29 years married to HABENICHT (?), E. V. aged 21 years October 27, 1890 by Rev. Charles S. Vedder at 167 Tradd Street. Both natives of Charleston. He a planter.

McMILLAN, ROBERT BURNS aged 27 years married to MYERS, CATHERINE FRANCES aged 20 years December 23, 1886 by Rev. J. Walter Dickson. Both natives of Charleston. He a printer.

McMILLAN, SARAH married to EASTERBY, JOHN RUDOLPH February 28, 1884 by Rev. W. T. Thompson. He a mechanic.

McNAMARA, J. B. aged 48 years married to GOODWIN, MARY E. aged 26 years August 18, 1887 by Rev. Robert Wilson. Both natives of South Carolina. He a carpenter.

McNAMARA, CATHARINE aged 40 years married to REYNOLDS, FRANK aged 25 years May 23, 1895 by Rev. Charles S. Vedder. He a native of Italy and she of Charleston. He a mariner in Savannah, Georgia.

McNAMARA, LIZZIE aged 25 years married to NIELSON, ANTOINE aged 35 years November 8, 1877 by Father Daniel J. Quigley at 128 King Street.

McNEILL, GEORGE R. aged 24 years married to VON SPRECKELSEN (?), ANNA M. aged 22 years June 26, 1892 by Rev. G. R. Bracket at 113 St. Philip Street. He a native of Charleston and she of Augusta, Georgia. He a car driver.

McNEILL, MARGARET A. aged 19 years married to LAMBLE, JAMES W. aged 29 years March 17, 1879 by Rev. G. R. Brackett in Middle Street.

McNEILL, ROBERT aged 29 years married to RIECKE, D. AMALIE JOHANNA aged 20 years July 5, 1888 by Rev. Louis Muller at the residence of the Bride's mother - the corner of Aiken and Blake Streets.

McNEIL, SARAH JANE aged 18 years married to KING, HENRY FROST aged 24 years November 26, 1878 by Rev. G. S. Brackett. Both natives of Charleston. He a driver.

McPHERSON, JOSEPHINE aged 23 years married to CANTWELL, RICHARD THOMAS aged 43 years February 2, 1891 by Father J. J. Monaghan at St. Patrick's Roman Catholic Church. He a native of Graniteville, South Carolina and she of Columbia, South Carolina. He a railroad clerk.

McRAY, SARAH AGNES aged 22 years married to POSTON, ROBERT JEFFREY aged 26 years September 22, 1887 by Rev. T. P. Burgess at 98 America Street. He a native of Williamsburg, South Carolina and she of Charleston. He a bricklayer.

McROSE, EMILY aged 13 years married to RIGGS, JULIUS aged 20 years December 18, 1884 by Rev. John E. Beard at 64 Nassau Street. Both natives of Charleston. He a laborer.

McSHERRY, CATHARINE ROWLAND aged 35 years married to DAWSON, JAMES S. aged 26 years October 16, 1892 by Father J. J. Monaghan at St. Patrick's Roman Catholic Church.

McSHERRY, CORINE G. aged 17 years married to KILEY, MICHAEL C. aged 26 years December 1, 1892 by Father J. J. Monaghan at St. Patrick's Roman Catholic Church. Both natives of Charleston. He a policeman in Jacksonville, Florida.

McSWEENEY, DENNIS aged 23 years married to ROBERTS, V. aged 34 years May 4, 1882 by Father F. J. Shadler at St. Joseph's Roman Catholic Church. He a native of Ireland and a cooper.

McSWEENY, ELIZABETH aged 20 years married to BYRNE, JAMES F. aged 22 years September 29, 1878 by Father John P. Twigg at St. Patrick's Roman Catholic Church. He a native of Green Pond, South Carolina and she of Charleston. He a tinner.

McSWEENEY, E. P. aged 26 years married to KENNEDY, MARY E. aged 24 years December 25, 1886 by Father Daniel J. Quigley at St. Patrick's Roman Catholic Church. Both natives of Charleston. He works for the railroad.

McSWEENEY, HELENA aged 30 years married to O'DONNELL, DENNIS aged 40 years April 27, 1886 by Father Daniel J. Quigley at St. Patrick's Roman Catholic Church. Both natives of Ireland. He a merchant in Anderson, South Carolina.

McSWEENEY, W. aged 23 years married to SULLIVAN, M. A. aged 23 years October 3, 1882 by Father J. J. Monaghan at St. Patrick's Roman Catholic Church. He a native of Charleston and a laborer.

McWHIRTER, ANDREW aged 40 years married to HORNE, (Mrs.) MARY BRUCE aged 38 years July 24, 1887 by Rev. Leroy F. Beattie at 231 Coming Street. He a native of Scotland and she of Georgia. He a laborer.

MEACHER, EMILY DAVIS married to MEREE, EDWARD THOMAS October 19, 1884 by Rev. John Johnson at 285 Meeting Street. Both natives of Charleston. He a painter.

MEACHER, JOSEPH aged 21 years married to COURTNEY, ANNA P. aged 20 years June 28, 1878 by Rev. J. V. Welsh. Both natives of Charleston. He a clerk.

MEAGHER, JOHN F. aged 28 years married to CHAPLAIN, EFFIE aged 20 years November 26, 1894 by Father J. J. Monaghan at St. Patrick's Roman Catholic Church. Both natives of Charleston. He an engineer.

MEARS, R. M. aged 27 years married to PINCKNEY, M. B. aged 22 years December 28, 1880 by Rev. C. C. Pinckney at Grace Church. Both natives of Charleston. He a merchant.

MEDLIN, DRUSCILLA aged 20 years married to GILLILAND, JAMES aged 26 years June 24, 1893 by John Ahrens, Trial Justice at 1 New Street. He a native of Charleston and she of Columbia, South Carolina. He a printer.

MEGGETT, FLORENCE ESTELLE aged 22 years married to REID, HENRY B. aged 25 years February 18, 1891 by Rev. Edwin C. Dargan at 24 Rutledge Avenue. He a native of Rock Hill, South Carolina and she of Beaufort, South Carolina. He a clerk in Summerville, South Carolina.

MEGGETT, HELOISE M. aged 22 years married to RIVERS, LAURENCE WASHINGTON aged 22 years April 9, 1889 by Rev. Edwin C. Dargan. He a native of Charleston and she of Camden, South Carolina. He a tailor.

MEHRTENS, – aged 28 years married to ZERBST, J. aged 22 years December 21, 1879 by Rev. Louis Muller at the corner of Pitt and Duncan Streets. He a native of Charleston and a grocer. She a native of Hanover.

MEHRTENS, JOHN aged 26 years married to DOWD, HELEN aged 20 years June 26, 1890 by Rev. Edward C. Dargan at 61 Bull Street. He a salesman.

MEHRTENS, J. H. aged 26 years married to TIEPPE, W. C. A. aged 20 years October 19, 1880 by Rev. Louis Muller at St. Matthew's Lutheran Church. Both natives of Charleston. He a miller.

MEIBURG, (Mrs.) ANNA. M. S. aged 30 years married to SCHUMACHER, OTTO H. aged 27 years April 29, 1884 by Rev. Louis Muller at the corner of St. Philip and George Streets. He a native of Germany and she of Charleston. He a grocer.

MEITZLER, CAROLINE CATHARINE aged 20 years married to SAHLMAN, CARSTEN aged 22 years October 15, 1878 by Rev. Louis Muller in Broad Street. Both natives of Charleston. He a merchant in Bamberg, South Carolina.

MEITZLER, MARGARET L. aged 21 years married to CORONES, ANDREW aged 30 years November 27, 1881 by Rev. Edward T. Horn in King Street. He a native of Athens, Georgia and she of Charleston. He a fruitier.

MEITZLER, PHILIP aged 28 years married to DeYOUNG, JULIA C. aged 25 years May 8, 1880 by Rev. W. S. Bowman. Both natives of Charleston. He a shoemaker.

MELCHERS, AGNES WILHELMINA ADELA aged 19 years married to WELLING, LAWRENCE L. aged 21 years April 12, 1883 by Rev. Louis Muller in Drake Street near Blake Street. He a native of Charleston and she of Walhalla, South Carolina. He a merchant.

MELCHERS, ALEXANDER aged 52 years married to STOLL, LENA aged 29 years October 30, 1883 by Father F. J. Shadler at 381 King Street. Both natives of Charleston. He a baker.

MELCHERS, J. H. aged 20 years married to BISCHOFF, W. B. aged 28 years January 5, 1882 by Rev. Louis Muller. Both natives of Charleston. He a merchant.

MELCHERS, KATE JENNIE FREDERICKE aged 20 years married to PASSAILAIGUE, THEODORE W. aged 27 years December 10, 1888 by Rev. Louis Muller at St. Matthew's Lutheran Church.

MELCHERS, LOUIS A. aged 21 years married to REEVES, MINNIE E. aged 19 years August 16, 1887 by Rev. Louis Muller. Both natives of South Carolina. He a merchant.

MELCHERS, MARIE KATE aged 19 years married to HUGUELET, GEORGE ARTHUR aged 28 years July 12, 1889 by Rev. Louis Muller at St. Johannes Lutheran Church. Both natives of Charleston. He a watchmaker.

MELCHERS, SUSANNA C. J. H. aged 30 years married to MUNZEBROCK (?), FREDERICK A. aged 25 years February 11, 1892 by Rev. Louis Muller in Sheppard Street. Both natives of Germany. He a planter on Cattle Island, South Carolina.

MELFI, DAVID aged 23 years married to HUCHET, MARY THEODOSIA aged 23 years August 29, 1878 by Father Claudian B. Northrop in New Street. Both natives of Charleston. He a clerk.

MELFI, LEONARD F. aged 24 years married to ABRAMS, CORDELIA G. aged 17 years June 28, 1887 by Father P. J. McManus. Both natives of Charleston. He works for the railroad.

MELLARD, CHARLES E. aged 36 years married to IRVIN, (Mrs.) IDA CLARKE aged 29 years June 1, 1892 by Rev. Edwin C. Dargan at 19 Alexander Street. He a native of Williamsburg County, South Carolina and she of Charleston. He a clerk.

MELVIN, E. E. aged 21 years married to BEASLEY, C. N. aged 21 years January 18, 1880 by Father Claudian B. Northrop in Wentworth Street. Both natives of Charleston. He a clerk.

MELVIN, THOMAS aged 25 years married to CUMMINGS, MARGARET aged 23 years August 11, 1878 by Father John C. Twigg at St. Mary of the Annunciation Roman Catholic Church. He a native of Ireland and she of Charleston. He a laborer.

MEMMINGER, C. G. aged 21 years married to LEEKING, MARY aged 18 years January 6, 1886 by Rev. Robert Wilson at 4 Wragg Square. Both natives of Charleston. He a physician.

MENDERNIAN (?), J. H. aged 26 years married to STURCKEN, ELISE D. aged 20 years October 23, 1881 by Rev. Louis Muller at 8 Line Street. He a native of Hanover and she of Charleston. He a grocer.

MENSING, BERTHA AUGUSTA aged 28 years married to McDOUGAL, DAVID aged 25 years April 24, 1883 by Rev. Louis Muller at the southeast corner of King and Broad Streets.

MENSING, JENNIE N. aged 24 years married to WELBROCK, JOHANN H. aged 31 years February 25, 1892 by Rev. Louis Muller in Guignard Street. He a native of Hanover and she of Charleston. He a merchant.

MERBURG, F. aged 22 years married to MINTZMEYER, MATTIE aged 16 years March 1, 1881 by Rev. Luther K. Probst. He a native of Charleston and a clerk.

MEREE, ANNIE E. aged 19 years married to KENNEY, ST. JOHN M. B. aged 23 years June 3, 1885 by Rev. E. J. Meynardie.

MEREE, EDWARD THOM married to MEACHER, EMILY DAVIS October 19, 1884 by Rev. John Johnson at 285 Meeting Street. Both natives of Charleston. He a painter.

MEREE, (Mrs.) HARRIET ANN KENNEDY aged 34 years married to CUMBEE, BENJAMIN aged 33 years May 21, 1891 by Rev. W. A. Betts at the Bone Factory in King Street. He a native of Berkeley County, South Carolina and she of Marion County, South Carolina. He a farmer in Accabee, Berkeley County.

MEREE, IDA aged 16 years married to BIEL, JOHN H. aged 19 years March 10, 1886 by Rev. H. B. Browne at 3 Lee Street. Both natives of Charleston. He a carpenter.

MEREE, M. W. aged 52 years married to SAMSON, SARAH aged 48 years October 3, 1888. He a native of St. John's Parish, Berkeley County, South Carolina. She a native of Charleston. He a laborer.

MEREE, THOMAS D. aged 22 years married to SOUTHALL, ANNIE aged 14 years October 16, 1887 by Rev. S. S. Blanchard. He a native of Barnville, South Carolina and she of Charleston. He a bookbinder.

MERKHARDT (?), DAVID married to BOATWRIGHT, LULA October 3, 1889 by N. L. P. Bolger, Trial Justice. He a native of Cambridge, New York and she of Augusta, Georgia. He a weaver in the cotton mill.

MERKHARDT (?), J. P. aged 64 years married to KOESTER, (Mrs.) C. W. C. H SCHADE aged 38 years December 7, 1884 by Rev. Johannes Heckel at St. Johannes Lutheran Church. Both natives of Germany.

MERRES, W. aged 26 years married to MILLER, M. A. aged 29 years October 9, 1879 by Rev. J. V. Welch at 64 Radcliffe Street. He a native of Sumter, South Carolina and she of Charleston. He a laborer.

MERRIERA, AMELIA aged 38 years married to MACK, GEORGE aged 48 years April 4, 1893 by E. Milan, Trial Justice.

MERRILL, OSCAR M. aged 27 years married to COCHRAN, ANNA aged 19 years November 9, 1878 by Rev. J. V. Welsh. He a native of Brownsville, Maine and she of Charleston. He a carpenter.

MERRITT, HENRY married to LOWRIE, SUSIE February 25, 1880 by William B. Yates, Chaplain.

MERRITT, MARY ANNA aged 15 years married to BROOKS, ARTHUR G. R. T. aged 26 years August 22, 1886 by Rev. J. Walter Dickson at 37 Cooper Street. He a native of Germany and she of North Carolina. He a laborer.

MERRIWEATHER, FRANK T. aged 21 years married to CARRIER, KITTY G. aged 19 years October 12, 1886 by Rev. G. R. Brackett. He a native of Louisville, Kentucky and she of Brookville, Pennsylvania. He a physician in Louisville.

MESSERVY, F. married to KUCK, A. E. December 25, 1881 by Rev. Edward T. Horn. Both natives of Charleston. He a druggist.

MESSNER, WILLIAM aged 22 years married to BEHRENS, ANNA aged 22 years May 1, 1878 by Rev. Johannes Heckel. Both natives of Germany. He a baker.

METZ, M. R. aged 27 years married to BEHRENS, H. C. E. aged 28 years September 1, 1887 by Rev. Johannes Heckel at the northwest corner of King and Line Streets. He a native of Germany and she of Charleston. He a storekeeper.

MEVAY, JOHN ALLEN married to RONER, MARGARET O. September 10, 1878 by William B. Yates, Chaplain.

MEVAY, WILLIAM J. aged 32 years married to LETT, ANNA A. aged 20 years March 22, 1885 by Rev. J. V. Welch at 58 Line Street. Both natives of Charleston. He a laborer.

MEW, MARY F. aged 20 years married to HYER, WRAGG K. aged 26 years November 17, 1886 by Father Daniel J. Quigley at St. Patrick's Roman Catholic Church. Both natives of South Carolina. He a merchant.

MEYER, ANN M. married to BOHLOCKS, J. H. C. January 28, 1879 by Rev. Louis Muller. He a native of Hanover Germany and she of Charleston. He a grocer.

MEYER, ANNA LISETTE married to JESSEN, CARL ANDREAS aged 24 years November 17, 1881 by Rev. Louis Muller at St. Matthew's Lutheran Church. He a native of Hanover and she of Charleston. He a bookkeeper.

MEYER, ANNA MARGARETHA aged 21 years married to SCHUMACHER, JOHN D. aged 19 years January 26, 1879 by Rev. Louis Muller at the corner of King and Beresford Street. Both natives of Charleston. He a clerk at the express company.

MEYER, ANNA MARGARETHE aged 20 years married to HEINSOHN, EGGERT aged 30 years April 15, 1886 by Rev. Louis Muller at the northwest corner of Church Street and Lightwood Alley. He a native of Germany and she of Charleston. He a grocer.

MEYER, ANNA M. aged 18 years married to BOHLOCH, JOHN CONRAD HENRY aged 23 years January 28, 1879 by Rev. Louis Muller in Radcliffe Street. He a native of Hanover and she of Charleston. He a merchant.

MEYER, ANNA ROSALINE aged 22 years married to HASTEDT, HERMAN H. aged 60 years May 26, 1881 by Rev. Louis Muller in Rutledge Avenue, the west side near Spring Street. Both natives of Hanover.

MEYER, ANTOINETTE MAGDALENA aged 18 years married to SCHULTZE, JOHN WILLIAM GERHARDT aged 24 years April 29, 1884 by Rev. Louis Muller at the corner of King and Tradd Streets.

MEYER, AUGUST aged 26 years married to BROMIER, HELENA aged 25 years February 8, 1880 by Rev. Johannes Heckel at St. Johannes Lutheran Church. Both natives of Hanover.

MEYER, AUGUSTUS W. aged 34 years married to WOHLMER, MARIE ELLA A. aged 27 years March 25, 1883 by Rev. Luther K. Probst at the corner of Cooper and Aiken Streets. Both natives of Charleston. He a mechanic.

MEYER, CATHERINE aged 29 years married to CETCHOVEH, RAPHAEL aged 30 years June 20, 1885 by Rev. Luther K. Probst. Both natives of Germany. He a mariner.

MEYER, CHARLES F. aged 29 years married to ALFERO, VIRGINIA aged 21 years October 13, 1891 by Rev. R. C. Holland. He a native of Summerville, South Carolina and she of Charleston. He a merchant.

MEYER, DORA aged 22 years married to COHEN, MORRIS aged 32 years November 3, 1886 by S. E. Gleason, Trial Justice. He a native of Poland and she of Germany. He a merchant in Jacksonville, Florida.

MEYER, DORA LUCIA aged 17 years married to REHKOPF, WILHELM aged 24 years November 5, 1885 by Rev. Louis Muller at St. Matthew's Lutheran Church. Both natives of Charleston. He a cabinetmaker.

MEYER, EMMA F. aged 17 years married to OETJEN (?), WILLIAM H. aged 17 years April 28, 1891 by Rev. Edward T. Horn at 25 Church Street. He a native of Wilmington, North Carolina and she of Charleston. He a fish merchant.

MEYER, HENRY C. aged 34 years married to JOANELLI;, ELIZABETH aged 18 years December 4, 1884 by Rev. Luther K. Probst. He a native of Germany and she of Charleston. He a storekeeper.

MEYER, H. C. F. aged 26 years married to HAMMAN, MARIA aged 24 years March 13, 1887 by Rev. Louis Muller. Both natives of Germany. He a bricklayer.

MEYER, H. R. aged 29 years married to SCHUTTE, H. M. C. aged 24 years November 25, 1885 by Rev. Louis Muller at 66 Radcliffe Street. Both natives of Germany. He a grocer.

MEYER, IDA MARIE married to FINCKEN, ALBERT J. C. January 16, 1879 by Rev. W. S. Bowman. Both natives of Charleston. He a grocer.

MEYER, JOHANNA CAROL DORETHA aged 32 years married to OSTERHOLTZ, HENRY F. D. aged 31 years August 10, 1881 by Rev. Louis Muller at 121 East Bay Street. He a native of Charleston and she of Hanover. He a grocer.

MEYER, JOHAN F. aged 25 years married to REHKOPF, ANNA C. aged 21 years April 28, 1887 by Rev. Louis Muller. Both natives of South Carolina. He a grocer.

MEYER, JOHN EDWARD aged 53 years married to HUDSON, SUSAN ANN aged 29 years December 6, 1877 by Rev. T. E. Wannamaker. He a native of Charleston and she of Round O, Colleton County, South Carolina. He a clerk.

MEYER, J. D. E. aged 37 years married to REILS, M . S. R. aged 24 years January 14, 1886 by Rev. Louis Muller. He a native of Germany and she of Charleston. He a grocer.

MEYER, J. F. E. aged 32 years married to M. STENDER aged 18 years November 16, 1879 by Rev. G. R. Brackett at the residence of H. Stender - in King Street. He a native of York County, South Carolina and she of Charleston. He a farmer.

MEYER, MARY aged 27 years married to DENNAL, JAMES aged 31 years May 14, 1878 by Father Harry P. Northrop at St. Patrick's Roman Catholic Church. Both natives of Ireland. He a soldier at The Citadel.

MEYER, NICHOLAS A. M. aged 22 years married to KURRE, W. C. aged 19 years March 26, 1885 by Rev. Louis Muller at St. Matthew's Lutheran Church. He a native of Savannah, Georgia and she of Charleston. He a restaurant worker.

MEYER, REBECCA MARIA aged 26 years married to SOHL, HENRY aged 24 years May 15, 1881 by Rev. Louis Muller at the southwest corner of Coming and Bull Streets. He a native of Charleston and a butcher.

MEYER, ROBERT W. aged 29 years married to SCHWETMANN, SOPHIE H. C. aged 23 years October 28, 1891 by Rev. Louis Muller at 106 Broad Street. Both natives of Summerville, South Carolina. He a mechanist.

MEYER, WILLIAM H. aged 22 years married to WETZEL, ELOISE P. aged 23 years October 28, 1885 by Rev. Louis Muller at St. Matthew's Lutheran Church. Both natives of Charleston. He a bookkeeper.

MEYER, WILLIAM W. aged 21 years married to HANCOCK, CARRIE F. aged 20 years January 23, 1884 by Father P. L. Duffy at 17 Church Street. He a native of Aiken, South Carolina and she of Blackville, South Carolina. He a farmer in Augusta, Georgia.

MEYER, WILLIE aged 22 years married to HART, BETA aged 19 years January 28, 1894 by Rev. Edmund Wells at 579 King Street. He a native of Charleston and works in the cotton mill.

MEYERS, ANNIE C. married to WITHINGTON, EUGENE November 25, 1886 by Rev. Luther K. Probst. Both natives of Charleston. He a printer.

MEYERS, CHRISTINA aged 18 years married to BOWEY, FENWICK aged 20 years October 11, 1895 by Rev. J. M. Steadman. He a native of England and she of Charleston. He an engineer.

MEYERS, EDWARD C. aged 24 years married to CAMERON, LULU aged 18 years August 8, 1894 by Rev. A. Ernest Cornish at 71 Bay Street. He a native of St. Stephen's Parish, South Carolina and she of Charleston. He a fireman.

MEYERS, FRED aged 20 years married to COX, JULIANNE aged 20 years February 10, 1881 by Rev. J. V. Welsh at 40 Columbus Street. He a native of Charleston and a laborer.

MEYERS, JOHN M. aged 21 years married to FREEMAN, MARY C. aged 15 years April 28, 1892 by Rev. T. P. Burgess at 6 Aiken Row. Both natives of Charleston. He a carpenter.

MEYERS, JULIA ANNIE aged 22 years married to MORASKI, ALBERT aged 25 years March 31, 1891 by Father J. J. Monaghan at St. Patrick's Roman Catholic Church. He a native of Germany and she of Charleston. He a clerk.

MEYERS, J. aged 23 years married to O'KIEFFE, E. aged 21 years June 13, 1882 by Father F. J. Shadler at St. Joseph's Roman Catholic Church. Both natives of Charleston. He a machinist.

MEYERS, J. W. A. aged 30 years married to HUDSON, F. M. aged 24 years August 24, 1882 by Father Daniel J. Quigley in Nunan Street. Both natives of Charleston. He a policeman.

MEYERS, N. S. D. aged 18 years September 3, 1891 by Rev. T. P. Burgess at 38 Percy Street. He a native of Georgetown, South Carolina and she of Charleston. He a painter.

MEYERS, SOPHIA aged 25 years married to JACKSON, WILLIAM WARD aged 33 years September 18, 1894 by Rabbi Barnett A. Elzas. He a native of New York and she of Boston, Massachusetts. He a merchant.

MEYERS, STEDTMAN aged 28 years married to SIGWALD, CORNELID B. aged 16 years March 19, 1888 by Rev. J. W. Fuller at 11 Mount Street. Both natives of Charleston. He a grocer.

MEYERS, SUSAN aged 15 years married to TOURNES, JOHN A. aged 24 years July 4, 1880 by Rev. J. V. Welsh at 64 Radcliffe Street. Both natives of Charleston.

MEYNARDIE, JAMES H. aged 26 years married to ALMERS, MARGARET F. aged 21 years February 11, 1883 by Rev. John H. Tellinghast at St. John's Lutheran Church. Both natives of Charleston. He works for the railroad.

MICHEL, A. B. aged 24 years married to JOHNSON, WILLIAM H. aged 23 years October 26, 1882 by Rev. E. C. L. Browne. Both natives of South Carolina. He a telegraph worker.

MICHEL, LIZZIE L. aged 19 years married to WEIKERT, WILLIAM G. aged 27 years January 23, 1889 by Father Daniel J. Quigley at St. Patrick's Roman Catholic Church. He a native of Spartanburg, South Carolina and she of Charleston. He a railroad conductor.

MICHLKE, BERTHA HELENE CATHARINE aged 20 years married to THIEME, ALBERT aged 26 years April 16, 1888 by Rev. Louis Muller.

MIDDLETON, ALICE IZARD aged 22 years married to FORD, GEORGE G. aged 22 years October 28, 1890 by Rev. John Johnson at 55 Church Street. Both natives of Charleston. He a manufacturer in Greenville, South Carolina.

MIDDLETON, ALICE married to KERSHAW, GEORGE TRENHOLM June 27, 1877 by Rev. Richard S. Trapier.

MIDDLETON, CHARLES F. aged 24 years married to HAZELHURST, LOIS aged 17 years August 4, 1884 by Rev. John Johnson at Sullivans Island, South Carolina. Both natives of Charleston. He a merchant.

MIDDLETON, HELEN aged 20 years married to DEHON, T. aged 22 years February 8, 1893 by Rev. John Johnson. He a native of Greenville, South Carolina and she of Mt. Pleasant, South Carolina. He a turner in Greenville.

MIKELL, EPHRAIN aged 35 years married to RIVERS, REBECCA W. aged 22 years January 16, 1884 by Rev. J. V. Welch at Calvary Church. Both natives of Charleston. He a mariner.

MIKELL, TESS WARING aged 21 years married to LIBBY, ROBERT BEE aged 23 years February 7, 1889 by Rev. John Johnson in Church Street.

MILES, ANNE C. aged 25 years married to HANCKEL, FRANCIS S. aged 28 years December 11, 1888 by Rev. John Johnson at St. Philip's Church. Both natives of Charleston. He a clerk.

MILLARD, THOMAS aged 21 years married to HOLLIMAN, FANNIE aged 27 years April 20, 1893 by Rev. Thomas B. Wright.

MILLER, ELLA aged 17 years married to GARRETT, HAMILTON aged 19 years August 1, 1878 by Rev. William C. Power. Both natives of Charleston.

MILLER, HENRIETTA THOMPSON aged 28 years married to ANDERSON, LAWRENCE W. aged 25 years October 17, 1886 by Rev. H. B. Browne. He a native of Denmark and she of South Carolina. He a carpenter.

MILLER, ILLIARD aged 24 years married to FUNCHEN, LAURA ANN aged 27 years June 19, 1884 by Rev. John E. Beard. He a native of St. Paul's Parish, South Carolina and she of Orangeburg, South Carolina. He an engineer.

MILLER, JOHN aged 22 years married to HAMILTON, E. LULA aged 19 years January 27, 1892 by Rev. William A. Rogers. Both natives of Charleston. He a clerk.

MILLER, JOHN H. aged 22 years married to LLOYD, (Mrs.) EMMA aged 26 years October 21, 1891 by Rev. J. O. Fludd in Stone Court. He a native of Darlington County, South Carolina and she of Lexington County, South Carolina. He works in the cotton mill.

MILLER, JOSEPHINE aged 34 years married to ELLIS, THOMAS J. aged 36 years August 5, 1880 by Rev. R. N. Wells. Both natives of Charleston. He a bookkeeper.

MILLER, J. D. aged 36 years married to ROBERTS, ALICE R. aged 32 years July 1, 1895 by Rev. Edmund Wells in Percy Street. Both natives of Charleston. He a salesman.

MILLER, J. T. aged 31 years married to ALBRECHT, M. aged 17 years November 11, 1879 by Rev. W. S. Bowman. Both natives of New York City. He a woodworker.

MILLER, L. aged 29 years married to ROSE, C. aged 36 years September 20, 1882 by Rev. Edward F. Horn at 119 Queen Street. He a native of Charleston and a mate with the U. S. Revenue Service.

MILLER, (Mrs.) MARY E. VAUGHN aged 26 years married to CARTER, W. H. aged 23 years April 14, 1892 by Rev. Edmund Wells at the Cannon Street Chapel. He a native of North Carolina and she of Wilmington, North Carolina. He works in the bagging factory.

MILLER, M. A. aged 29 years married to MERRES, W. aged 26 years October 9, 1879 by Rev. J. Welch at 64 Radcliffe Street. He a native of Sumter, South Carolina and she of Charleston. He a laborer.

MILLER, M. F. aged 22 years married to SEYLE, W. J. aged 35 years December 16, 1879 by Rev. W. S. Bowman at 122 St. Philip Street. He a native of Charleston and she of Georgia. He works for the railroad.

MILLER, REBECCA V. married to STOPPELBEIN, MILTON S. October 3, 1878 by William B. Yates, Chaplain.

MILLER, SALLIE married to SCOTT, JAMES F. December 7, 1890 by Rev. W. A. Betts.

MILLER, WILLIAM T. aged 40 years married to WITTKE (?), CAROLINE aged 20 years May 22, 1894 by Rev. John Johnson. He a native of Charleston and she of Rock Hill, South Carolina. He a sailmaker.

MILLIGAN, G. H. aged 21 years married to CHURCH, MARY S. aged 19 years July 12, 1881 by Rev. J. V. Welch in Spring Street. He a native of Charleston and a machinist.

MILLINGS, C. J. aged 39 years married to WHILDEN (?), MARY L. aged 31 years April 27, 1892 by Rev. G. R. Brackett at 35 Bull Street. He a native of Darlington County, South Carolina and she of Charleston. He a turner in Darlington County.

MILLS, EDGAR aged 32 years married to FRUSER, EDITH aged 32 years December 28, 1893 by Rev. C. C. Pinckney at 137 Tradd Street. He a native of London, England and she of Charleston.

MILLS, LOUIS A. Aged 21 years married to DENNIS, CAROLINE J. aged 17 years May 22, 1886 by Rev. C. A. Stakeley. Both natives of Charleston. He an engineer.

MILLS, WILLIAM S. aged 24 years married to PINNER, FANNIE B. aged 23 years June 16, 1895 by Rev. J. C. Yongue at 64 Bay Street. Both natives of Charleston. He a railroad fireman.

MILNE, E. C. S. aged 42 years married to DUBOSE, L. ISIDORE aged 71 years May 20, 1884 by Father J. J. Woolahan. He a native of France and she of Charleston. He a professor.

MILNER, HAMILTON S. aged 21 years married to BECKER, GERTRUDE C. aged 18 years April 7, 1894 by Rev. J. C. Stokes at 231 Coming Street. Both natives of Charleston. He a salesman.

MILNER, MAX aged 40 years married to DAN, AGNES aged 25 years February 5, 1884 by Robert Chisolm, Judicial Trial Justice.

MIMS, HENRIETTA E. aged 19 years married to LOWRY, J. G. aged 29 years November 16, 1886 by Rev. H. B. Browne at 13 Line Street. He a native of South Carolina and she of Charleston. He a clerk.

MIMS, JAMES B. aged 23 years married to BRENEMER, ADA aged 20 years January 22, 1895 by Father J. J. Monaghan at 87 Drake Street. He a native of Sumter, South Carolina and she of Germany. He a street car driver.

MIMS, M. S. aged 18 years married to SEABROOK. R. aged 23 years August 19, 1882 by Rev. J. V. Welsh at 68 Line Street. He a native of South Carolina and a laborer.

MINCHAN (?), PATRICK J. aged 28 years married to PATRINOURTCH (?), F. A. aged 25 years October 27, 1881 by Father F. J. Shadler at St. Joseph's Roman Catholic Church. He a native of Ireland and she of Charleston. He a blacksmith.

MINOT, WILLIAM married to JENKINS, PHOEBE April 2, 1884 by Rev. William H. Campbell. Both natives of Charleston. He a clerk.

MINTZMEYER, HENRY married to HAMET, EMILY F. February 10, 1880 by Rev. J. Mercier Green at the corner of Spring and St. Philip Streets. Both natives of Charleston. He a butcher.

MINTZMEYER, MATTIE aged 16 years married to MERBURG, F. aged 22 years March 1, 1881 by Rev. Luther K. Probst. He a native of Charleston and a clerk.

MIOT, MARY E. aged 24 years married to OLD, GEORGE aged 25 years June 10, 1891 by Rev. Edwin C. Dargan at 51 Hasell Street. He a native of Elizabeth City, New Jersey and she of Palatka, Florida. He a bookkeeper in St. Augustine, Florida.

MIOT, MAUD aged 20 years married to O'GORMAN, WILLIAM aged 27 years November 16, 1892 by Rev. W. T. Thompson in Queen Street. He a native of St. Augustine, Florida and she of Columbia, South Carolina. He a merchant in St. Augustine.

MIRASKA, T. aged 19 years married to GRAFF, GEORGE W. aged 23 years May 8, 1882 by Rev. P. L. Duffy at 30 Mazyck Street. He a native of Charleston and a baker.

MISHAW, ADRIANNA V. aged 18 years married to SIMMONS, ARCHIBALD B. aged 22 years August 30, 1893 by Rev. J. C. Yongue at 43 Blake Street. He a native of Long Island, South Carolina and she of Georgetown, South Carolina. He works in the bagging factory.

MISSEL, CARL H. aged 25 years married to KANAPAUX, ANNA C. aged 23 years April 10, 1892 by Rev. Louis Muller in Poinsett Street. He a native of Prussia and she of Germany. He a bricklayer.

MISSROON, CLAUDIA H. married to BUTLER, F. CARTER July 31, 1886 by Rev. W. T. Thompson at the First Presbyterian Church. He a bookkeeper.

MITCHELL, ELIZA B. aged 23 years married to BAILEY, HERBERT L. aged 29 years April 20, 1893 by Rev. Henry M. Grant. He a native of South Carolina and she of Charleston. He a merchant on James Island, South Carolina.

MITCHELL, JOHN F. aged 37 years married to SCHIPMAN, A. C. aged 33 years February 16, 1891 by Rev. M. S. Watkins at 47 Columbus Street. He a native of Jacksonville, South Carolina and she of Berkeley County, South Carolina. He a painter.

MITCHELL, JOHN MAGILL aged 24 years married to VON KOLNITZ, ELLA JULIA aged 23 years November 1, 1877 by Rev. W. S. Bowman. Both natives of Charleston. He a farmer in Mt. Pleasant, South Carolina.

MITCHELL, JOHN S. aged 22 years married to FELDER, ANNA P. aged 19 years April 26, 1892 by Re. G. R. Brackett. Both natives of Parler, Orangeburg County, South Carolina. He a car driver.

MITCHELL, JULIAN married to WITT, BELLE May 14, 1895 by Rev. William H. Campbell at St. Paul's Church. He a lawyer.

MITCHELL, J. WALTER aged 34 years married to KELLER, RUTH M. aged 20 years May 30, 1888 by Rev. C .C. Pinckney. He a native of Edgefield County, South Carolina and she of Charleston. He a lawyer in Edgefield.

MITCHELL, LOUISA aged 24 years married to GARRETT, HAMILTON February 9, 1885 by Rev. J. V. Welsh at 657 King Street.

MITCHELL, (Mrs.) MAGGIE TAYLOR aged 34 years married to NECELLE, LOUIS aged 35 years November 27, 1892 by Rev. F. H. Smith in Blake Street. She a native of Columbia, South Carolina. He works in the cotton mill.

MITCHELL, (Mrs.) MARGARET JULIA SMITH aged 26 years married to GORDON, MICHAEL MARTIN aged 27 years April 16, 1883 by Rev. J. A. Clifton at 32 Columbus Street. He a native of Ireland and she of Summerville. He a machinist.

MITCHELL, M. E. married to HODGES, J. S. October 12, 1882 by Rev. E. J. Meynardie. He a native of South Carolina.

MITCHELL, R. aged 23 years married to JOHNSON, S. E. aged 22 years October 8, 1879 by Rev. William C. Power at 18 Montagu Street. He a native of York County, South Carolina and she of Union County, South Carolina. He a farmer.

MITCHELL, WILLIAM H. married to WEITZ, (Mrs.) SUSAN March 18, 1880 at 47 Spring Street.

MITCHUM, AMANDA aged 17 years married to JORDAN, JAKE D. aged 22 years May 17, 1891 by Rev. J. Fludd at 76 America Street. He a native of Orangeburg, South Carolina and she of Berkeley County, South Carolina. He works in the cotton mill.

MITCHUM, ALZIE STRICKLAND aged 24 years married to NEWBERRY, EDWARD aged 21 years November 13, 1892 by Rev. A. M. Chreitzberg in Blake Street. He a native of New York and she of Savannah, Georgia. He works in the cotton mill.

MITCHUM, IRENE aged 18 years married to ADAMS, LEWIS F. aged 18 years September 17, 1893 by Rev. J. C. Yongue at 65 Drake Street. He a native of Colleton County, South Carolina and she of Greeleyville, South Carolina. He works in the cotton mill.

MITCHUM, JOHN aged 22 years married to MIZELL, L. E. aged 18 years November 2, 1895 by Rev. J. C. Yongue at 110 America Street. He a native of Williamsburg County, South Carolina and she of Berkeley County, South Carolina. He works in the cotton mill.

MITCHUM, THOMAS aged 49 years married to ROBERTS, CORNELIA aged 26 years October 15, 1893 by Rev. J. C. Yongue at the Cumberland Church. He a native of Williamsburg County, South Carolina and she of Orangeburg, South Carolina. He a cooper.

MITCHUM, THOMAS B. aged 49 years married to SCOTT, MARY aged 27 years November 19, 1891 by Rev. W. A. Betts at 14 Hampstead Square. He a native of Williamsburg, South Carolina and she of Augusta, Georgia. He a cooper.

MITCHUM, WILHELMINA aged 21 years married to KESELER, FRANK aged 22 years December 21, 1890 by Rev. M. S. Watkins at the Second Adventist Church. Both natives of Charleston. He works in the cotton mill.

MIZELL, L. E. aged 18 years married to MITCHUM, JOHN aged 22 years November 28, 1895 by Rev. J. C. Yongue at 110 America Street. He a native of Williamsburg County, South Carolina and she of Berkeley County, South Carolina. He works in the cotton mill.

MOCHSING, META aged 26 years married to WITT, LOUIS aged 25 years October 13, 1881 by Rev. Johannes Heckel at the Freundschaftsbund Hall. Both natives of Hanover. He a grocer.

MODE, ELIZABETH aged 24 years married to MYERS, TRESPOLE aged 24 years October 5, 1880 by Rabbi David Levy at the Hasell Street Synagogue. He a native of London, England and a merchant.

MOFFETT, ANNA MORRIS aged 29 years married to DILLINGHAM, JOSEPH C. aged 28 years January 7, 1890 by Rev. G. R. Brackett at 131 Coming Street. Both natives of Charleston. He a merchant.

MOHRING, HEINRICH aged 24 years married to BRUNCKHUSS, ANNA N. aged 23 years July 14, 1889 by Rev. Louis Muller. Both natives of Prussia. He a grocer.

MOHRMAN, H. aged 22 years married to DESEBROCK, .A H. aged 19 years February 27, 1883 by Rev. John H. Honour at St. John's Lutheran Church. He a native of Germany and she of Charleston. He a merchant in Augusta, Georgia.

MOISSON, JULIA aged 28 years married to SCHULTZ, CHRISTIAN HENRY aged 27 years May 29, 1887 by Father F. J. Shadler at St. Joseph's Roman Catholic Church. Both natives of Charleston. He a grocer.

MOLLENHAUER, ERNST aged 42 years married to LaFAR, LOUISE aged 25 years April 19, 1883 by Rev. Luther K. Probst. He a native of Germany and she of Charleston. He a policeman.

MOLLER, ELLEN NELSON married to KUNA, HANS A. January 1, 1879 by William B. Yates, Chaplain.

MOLONY, E. T. aged 25 years married to KENNEDY, F. E. aged 25 years January 10, 1882 by Father J. E. Chapins. Both natives of Charleston. He a tinner.

MOLONY, MARY ELLEN aged 19 years married to LEONARD, JOHN L. aged 22 years November 18, 1890 by Father J. J. Monaghan at St. Patrick's Roman Catholic Church. He a native of Charleston and an engineer.

MOLYNEAUX, M. J. aged 20 years married to MORRISSEY, W. J. aged 22 years November 21, 1880 by Father Daniel J. Quigley at The Cathedral of St. John the Baptist. Both natives of Charleston.

MOMIER, LOUISE C. aged 33 years married to HESSENKAMP, WILLIAM aged 28 years March 1, 1885 by Rev. Luther K. Probst. He a native of Germany and she of New York. He a merchant.

MONAGHAN, RICHARD P. aged 29 years married to FEEHAN, ANNA A. aged 26 years January 1, 1883 by Rev. J. J. Monaghan at St. Joseph's Roman Catholic Church. He a native of Sumter, South Carolina and she of Charleston. He a merchant.

MONDELL, CAROLINE aged 19 years married to VON OLSEN, HENRY aged 19 years February 8, 1880 by Rev. W. S. Bowman at 14 Bee Street. He a native of Germany and she of Fairfield, South Carolina. He a baker.

MONGIN, KATIE aged 31 years married to SMITH, J. L. aged 21 years August 29, 1880 by Rev. R. N. Wells at 88 Church Street. Both natives of Charleston and residents of Savannah, Georgia. He a merchant.

MONROE, DANIEL aged 20 years married to HANCOCK, SALLIE aged 16 years June 21, 1892 by Rev. W. A. Betts. He a native of Summerville, South Carolina and she of Sumter, South Carolina. He works in the cotton mill.

MONROE, WILLIAM E. aged 21 years married to WHITEHEAD, (Mrs.) FRANCES GILL aged 22 years December 18, 1884 by Rev. John E. Beard at the corner of Aiken and Blake Streets. He a native of South Carolina and she of Maryland. He a cooper.

MONSERRAT, J. P. aged 27 years married to PRITCHARD, C. January 21, 1882 by Father J. J. Monaghan at St. Patrick's Roman Catholic Church. He a native of Spain and she of South Carolina. He a shoemaker.

MONTAGUE, RALPH R. married to YATES, FLORENCE October 8, 1894 at St. Michael's Church.

MOOD, GERTRUDE E. aged 21 years married to HART, RUPERT R. aged 23 years December 27, 1892 by Rev. Edward T. Horn at 26 Savage Street. He a native of Flat Rock, North Carolina and she of Charleston. He a merchant in Flat Rock.

MOOD, MARY KING aged 25 years married to SMITH, J. L. aged 21 years January 10, 1878 by Bishop W. M. Wightman. Both natives of Charleston. He a merchant.

MOOD, M. F. aged 28 years married to PLATT, M. F. January 29, 1879 by Rev. H. F. Chreitzberg at the Spring Street Methodist Church. He a native of Charleston and she of Adams Run, South Carolina. He an employee at the express company.

MOOD, SUSAN JANE married to O'CONNOR, PETER December 25, 1878 by Rev. William C. Power. Both natives of Charleston. He a resident of Adams Run, South Carolina.

MOOD, WILLIAM G. aged 37 years married to MOOD, MARY KING aged 25 years January 10, 1878 by Bishop W. M. Wightman. Both natives of Charleston. He a merchant.

MOODIE, J. C. aged 41 years married to LEE, DELIA aged 39 years May 4, 1888 by P. E. Gleason, Trial Justice. Both natives of North Carolina. He a farmer in Florida.

MOODY, JESSE G. aged 24 years married to BRINGLOE, JULIA W. aged 22 years October 5, 1887 by Rev. C. A. Stakeley. He a native of Barnwell County, South Carolina and she of Charleston. He a bookbinder.

MOORE, ALEXANDER aged 24 years married to ENRIGHT, ANNIE aged 14 years August 6, 1883 by Rev. J. A. Cliffton. He a native of Ireland and she of Charleston. He a miller.

MOORE, BRIDGET aged 50 years married to QUINLAN, MICHAEL aged 50 years February 21, 1879 by Father A. P. Northrop at St. Patrick's Roman Catholic Church. Both natives of Ireland. He a gardener.

MOORE, ELEANOR aged 16 years married to STROBONZE, JOHN aged 29 years December 18, 1890 by Rev. C. E. Chicester. He a native of Austria and she of England. He a longshoreman.

MOORE, EDWARD E. aged 22 years married to MACKIN, MARY ANN aged 19 years April 28, 1878 by Father Daniel J. Quigley. Both natives of Charleston. He a clerk.

MOORE, FLORA aged 17 years married to NIESON, CHARLES aged 20 years February 6, 1894 by Rev. L. M. Knowles at 62 Drake Street. He a native of Georgia and she of South Carolina. He works in the cotton mill.

MOORE, E. IRENE aged 20 years married to GLENN, FRANK W. aged 23 years April 19, 1892 by Rev. William A. Rogers at 21 Wentworth Street. Both natives of Charleston. He a bookkeeper.

MOORE, FLORA aged 17 years married to MASON, CHARLIE aged 20 years February 6, 1894 by Rev. J. M. Knowles at 62 Drake Street.

MOORE, HELENA OCTAVIA married to MORAN, WILLIAM April 29, 1879 by William B. Yates, Chaplain.

MOORE, L. V. married to MCCLELLAN, J. P. aged 32 years December 11, 1882 by Rev. A. Coke Smith at 21 Wentworth Street. Both natives of South Carolina. He a farmer.

MOORE, MARY M. aged 20 years married to FISCHER, CHRISTIAN aged 29 years April 17, 1895 by Rev. J. C. Yongue at 530 Meeting Street.

MOORE, SALLIE CHAPIN aged 25 years married to PARROTT, JOHNSTON aged 23 years December 4, 1884 by Rev. John O. Wilson at 3 George Street. He a native of South Carolina and she of Charleston. He a clerk.

MOORER, T. JOHN aged 24 years married to EASTERBY, V. F. aged 19 years June 18, 1879 by Rev. H. F. Chreitzberg. He a native of Colleton County, South Carolina and she of New York. He a machinist.

MORAN, EMMA C. aged 22 years married to GIBSON, LOUIS L. aged 31 years March 26, 1894 by Father J. J. Monaghan at 591 King Street. He a native of Illinois and she of Charleston. He a salesman in Savannah, Georgia.

MORAN, (Mrs.) OCTAVIA WALES aged 35 years married to BECKER, WILLIAM F. A. aged 27 years March 5, 1890 by Rev. C. E. Chichester at The Mariners Church. He a native of Charleston and she of Liverpool, England. He a baker.

MORAN, WILLIAM married to MOORE, HELENA OCTAVIA April 29, 1879 by William B. Yates, Chaplain.

MORASKA, MAGGIE aged 19 years married to STURGEON, CHARLES aged 21 years March 3, 1889 by Father Daniel J. Quigley at St. Patrick's Roman Catholic Church. He a native of Orangeburg, South Carolina and she of Poland. He a baker.

MORASKI, ALBERT aged 25 years married to MEYERS, JULIA ANNIE aged 22 years March 31, 1891 by Father J. J. Monaghan at St. Patrick's Roman Catholic Church. He a native of Germany and she of Charleston. He a clerk.

MORDECAI, THOMAS MOULTRIE aged 35 years married to MOSES, HANNAH aged 29 years April 29, 1890 by Rabbi David Levy at the Hasell Street Synagogue. He a native of Charleston and she of St. Louis, Missouri. He a lawyer.

MORELLI, SESTILIO aged 24 years married to TERRY, ADA aged 19 years March 8, 1893 by Rev. John Johnson at 49 King Street. He a native of Italy and she of Elberton County, Georgia. He a shoemaker.

MORGAN, DANIEL JOSEPH aged 23 years married to FOLEY, ALICE MARTHA aged 18 years May 3, 1883 by Father J. J. Woolahan at St. Mary of the Annunciation Church. Both natives of Charleston. He works for the railroad.

MORGAN, ELIZABETH aged 17 years married to SMITH, ANGUS aged 23 years November 15, 1885 by Rev. Luther K. Probst at Summerville, South Carolina. He a native of Charleston and she of Florida. He an engineer.

MORGAN, JAMES aged 21 years married to LETT, IDA aged 19 years March 1, 1891 by Rev. W. A. Betts at 19 Wescott Court. Both natives of Charleston. He works in the bagging factory.

MORGAN, JOHN aged 60 years married to ELLIS, (Mrs.) R. B. DENNIS aged 59 years January 12, 1890 by Rev. T. P. Burgess at 7 Addison Court. He a native of England and he works in the phosphate mill.

MORGAN, JULIA aged 18 years married to McINTYRE, PATRICK aged 22 years October 9, 1878 by Father Daniel J. Quigley at The Cathedral of St. John the Baptist. He a native of Ireland and she of Charleston. He a mariner.

MORGAN, MARGARET aged 18 years married to ROSE, JOSEPH aged 25 years December 2, 1890 by Rev. M. S. Walkins at 24 Cooper Street. He a native of Charleston and she of Darlington, South Carolina. He a fireman.

MORGANSTEIN, MARIE aged 22 years married to McDONALD, GEORGE W. H. aged 42 years December 29, 1895 by Rev. J. M. Steadman at 74 Lee Street.

MORIARTY, ELIZABETH aged 23 years married to KENNEDY, JAMES aged 34 years December 31, 1885 by Rev. John Johnson. Both natives of Charleston. He a laborer.

MORIARTY, LENORA aged 19 years married to COSGROVE, THOMAS F. aged 26 years September 15, 1885 by Father Thomas E. McCormack at St. Patrick's Roman Catholic Church. Both natives of Charleston. He a carpenter.

MORRIS, MARY A. aged 25 years married to HENNESSY, THOMAS J. aged 26 years August 11, 1893 by Father J. J. Monaghan at St. Patrick's Roman Catholic Church. Both natives of Charleston. He a bookkeeper.

MORRIS, MATILDA M. aged 20 years married to HUCKS, NEWTON J. aged 24 years November 12, 1885 by Rev. John O. Wilson. He a native of South Carolina and she of Charleston. He a merchant in Yemassee, South Carolina.

MORRIS, MICHAEL aged 28 years married to NOLAN, ALICE AGNES aged 16 years May 29, 1879 by Father John P. Twigg at The Cathedral of St. John the Baptist. Both natives of Charleston. He a tinsmith.

MORRISON, HENRY T. aged 28 years married to McGILLIVRAY, SARAH W. aged 22 years January 6, 1892 by Rev. John Johnson at 10 Atlantic Street. He a native of McClellanville, South Carolina and she of Charleston. He works in a saw mill in Williamsburg, South Carolina.

MORRISON, WILLIAM J. aged 22 years married to MOLYNEUX, MARY November 13, 1880 by William B. Yates, Chaplain. Both natives of Charleston.

MORRISON, RHODA MILDRED aged 18 years married to ARMSTRONG, ALEXANDER C. aged 31 years August 13, 1885 by Rev. J. J. Woolahan at St. Mary of the Annunciation Roman Catholic Church.

MORRISSEY, BRIDGET aged 40 years married to SPAIN, CORNELIUS aged 50 years November 17, 1878 by Father C. J. Croghan at St. Joseph's Roman Catholic Church. Both natives of Ireland. He a watchman.

MORRISEEY, BRIDGET aged 24 years married to DERMS (?), MICHAEL J. B. aged 26 years January 6, 1884 by Father F. J. Shadler at St. Joseph's Roman Catholic Church. He a native of Charleston and she of Ireland. He a boilermaker.

MORRISSEY, EUGENIA J. married to AULD, ISAAC aged 22 years March 20, 1884 by Rev. G. R. Brackett in McClellanville, South Carolina. He a native of Madison, Florida and she of South Carolina. He a planter in Summerville, South Carolina.

MORRISSEY, MARY aged 23 years married to WALSH, WILLIAM aged 24 years April 23, 1888 by Father F. J. Shadler at St. Joseph's Roman Catholic Church. He a native of Ireland and she of Charleston. He works at the gas house.

MORRISSEY, TIMOTHY aged 52 years married to McMAHAN, (Mrs.) MARGARET aged 43 years November 11, 1888 by Father J. J. Monaghan at St. Patrick's Roman Catholic Church. Both natives of Ireland. He a drayman.

MORRISSEY, W. J. aged 22 years married to MOLYNEAUX, M. J. aged 20 years November 21, 1880 by Father Daniel J. Quigley at The Cathedral of St. John the Baptist. Both natives of Charleston.

MORROW, ARTHUR aged 48 years married to DUNCAN, J. E. aged 31 years November 18, 1888 by Rev. G. R. Brackett. He a native of Ireland and she of England. He a drayman.

MORSE, H. R. aged 23 years married to BEASLEY, CLARA O. aged 17 years June 5, 1881 by Rev. T. H. Shuck at 27 Church Street. He a native of Charleston. He a farmer in Georgia.

MOSELEY, THOMAS M. aged 24 years married to Dickson, MARY aged 23 years August 5, 1894 by Rev. J. C. Yongue at 14 Hampstead Square. He a native of Providence, Rhode Island and she of New York City. He works in the cotton factory.

MOSELY, WILLIAM M. married to LINN, MINNIE JULIA January 21, 1885 by Rev. William H. Campbell at 13 Ashley Avenue.

MOSES, HANNAH aged 29 years married to MORDECAI, THOMAS MOULTRIE aged 35 years April 29, 1890 by Rabbi David Levy at the Hasell Street Synagogue. He a native of Charleston and she of St. Louis, Missouri. He a lawyer.

MOSIMANN, MARY F. aged 18 years married to WHITSON, MARTIN W. aged 23 years November 22, 1888 by Rev. J. E. Carlisle at 530 Meeting Street. He a native of Pittsburg County, North Carolina and she of Charleston. He a plasterer and brickmason in Chester County, South Carolina.

MOTES, JOHN T. aged 22 years married to COOK, FANNIE C. aged 17 years October 3, 1893 by Rev. Edmund Wells in Cooper Street. He a native of Lowndes County, Alabama, and she of Darlington County, South Carolina. He a weaver in the cotton mill.

MOTTE, J. A. aged 27 years married to ARNOLD, A. F. aged 19 years October 26, 1882 by Rev. C. C. Pinckney at Grace Church. He a native of South Carolina and a railroad worker.

MOULTON, CHARLES H. aged 27 years married to KEOGH, MARY F. aged 19 years July 10, 1883 by Father F. J. Shadler at St. Joseph's Roman Catholic Church. He a native of Charleston and she of Savannah, Georgia. He works for the railroad.

MOULTON, MINNIE married to GARDNER, JOHN F. May 5, 1881 by Rev. William H. Campbell.

MOUZON, ANNIE ELVIRA aged 22 years married to BROWN, WILLIAM JAMES aged 23 years October 11, 1881 by Rev. A. Coke Smith at the corner of East Bay and Minority Streets. He a native of Darlington, South Carolina and she of Spartanburg, South Carolina. He a clerk in Edgefield, South Carolina.

MUCKENFUSS, WILLIAM aged 24 years married to McCANTS, J. HATTIE aged 20 years March 30, 1890 by Rev. J. Thomas Pate at 100 Columbus Street. He a native of Charleston and she of Berkeley County, South Carolina.

MOUZON, WILLIAM aged 32 years married to BURNHAM, SARAH ELLEN aged 28 years May 17, 1883 by Rev. W. P. Mouzon at 117 Coming Street.

MUCKENFUSS, BENJAMIN A. aged 43 years married to GRAHAM, H. ELLEN aged 42 years June 16, 1881 by Rev. E. J. Meynardie at the corner of Rutledge Avenue and Spring Streets. He a native of Charleston and a dentist.

MUCKENFUSS, EDNA aged 19 years married to COGSWELL, WILLIAM HARVEY aged 30 years June 11, 1890 by Rev. R. D. Smart at Bethel Church.

MUCKENFUSS (?), ELISE M. aged 20 years married to MAETZE, OSCAR aged 30 years November 10, 1886 by Rev. Johannes Heckel at the corner of East Bay and Pinckney Streets. Both natives of Germany. He a barkeeper.

MUCKENFUSS, EMILY A. aged 24 years married to HILTON, JESSE W. aged 32 years March 6, 1889 by Rev. H. B. Browne at 60 Tradd Street. He a native of Berkeley County, South Carolina and she of Charleston. He a turner.

MUIRHEAD, J. MURRAY aged 37 years married to WAYNE, FLORENCE AMANDA aged 21 years November 10, 1880 by Rev. W. S. Bowman. He a native of Edisto Island, South Carolina and she of Charleston. He a planter.

MULLALLY, LANE married to LOWNDES, CAROLINE H. November 6, 1894 by Rev. J. Drayton Grimke in East Battery. "Both of legal age." He a physician.

MULLEN, ELLEN aged 30 years married to DEAN, JAMES F. aged 30 years August 4, 1885 by Father J. J. Woolahan at St. Mary of the Annunciation Roman Catholic Church. He a native of Charleston and she of Ireland. He a blacksmith.

MULLER, ANNE JOHANNA MARIA aged 24 years married to JANTZEN, CARSTEN EIBE JOHN aged 27 years April 21, 1889 by Rev. Johannes Heckel. He a native of Hanover and she of Germany. He a merchant.

MULLER, AUGUSTE aged 22 years married to REINCKE, RUDOLPH aged 27 years July 29, 1880 by Rev. Johannes Heckel at 125 Calhoun Street. He a native of Hanover and she of Prussia. He a merchant.

MULLER, HERMAN HEINRICH aged 28 years married to STELLJES, HENRIETTA ADELAIDE SOPHIE aged 19 years March 1, 1883 by Rev. Louis Muller at the northeast corner of King and Wentworth Streets. He a native of Georgia and she of Columbia, South Carolina. He a saloon keeper.

MULLER, J. J. C. married to JATHO, W. G. June 1, 1887 by Rev. Louis Muller at St. Matthew's Lutheran Church. Both natives of South Carolina. He a merchant.

MULLER LOUISE C. F. aged 34 years married to HEDERICH, GUSTAV FRANTZ aged 43 years October 25, 1881 by Rev. Louis Muller at the corner of King and Cannon Streets. He a native of Saxony and she of Prussia. He a druggist.

MULLER, L. aged 21 years married to LAVES, HENRY D. F. aged 24 years September 18, 1881 by Rev. Louis Muller at the corner of Calhoun and Anson Streets. He a native of Hanover and she of Charleston. He a grocer.

MULLER, M. F. aged 16 years married to O'SHAUGHNESSY, P. aged 28 years May 16, 1892 by Father P. L. Duffy at The Cathedral of St. John the Baptist. He a native of Ireland and a grocer.

MULLER, W. H. aged 23 years married to HEINZ, J. E. H. aged 23 years February 21, 1882 by Rev. Johannes Heckel in Rutledge Avenue. He a native of Germany and she of Charleston. He a grocer.

MULLING, GEORGE MEACHER aged 25 years married to GRENVILLE, MARY AGNES aged 19 years November 17, 1881 by Father F. A. Schmetz at 2 Smith Lane. Both natives of Atlanta, Georgia. He a bookkeeper.

MULVANEY, CATHARINE V. aged 31 years married to REGAN, JOHN J. aged 31 years June 22, 1892 by Father Joseph D. Budds at The Cathedral of St. John the Baptist.

MUNDELL, ROBERT D. aged 42 years married to COSTE, HANNAH aged 38 years May 11, 1893 by Rev. Robert Wilson at 4 Wragg Square. He a native of Winnsboro, South Carolina and she of Westbrook, North Carolina. He a mechanic.

MUNTER, F. E. R. A. aged 35 years married to STELLJES, (Mrs.) R. M. MOLLENHAUER aged 49 years February 7, 1884 by Rev. Louis Muller. Both natives of Germany. He a druggist.

MUNZEBROCK (?), FREDERICK A. aged 25 years married to MELCHERS, SUSANNA C. J. H. aged 30 years February 11, 1892 by Rev. Louis Muller in Sheppard Street. Both natives of Germany. He a planter on Cattle Island, South Carolina.

MUNZENMAIER (?), HENRIETTA L. aged 21 years married to NELSON, WALTER L. aged 23 years March 25, 1891 by Rev. J. Thomas Pate. Both natives of Charleston.

MURDOCH, JOHN H. aged 36 years married to OGIER, GRAYSON aged 22 years June 3, 1885 by Rev. John Johnson in Hasell Street. Both natives of Charleston. He a factor.

MURE, ELIZABETH aged 35 years married to DOWIE, R. B. aged 38 years August 7, 1879 by Rev. W. C. Dana. He a native of Scotland and she of Charleston. He a bank officer.

MURE (?), WILLIAM married to WRAGG, SEPTIMA July 8, 1884 by Rev. William H. Campbell at St. Paul's Church. Both natives of Charleston. He a clerk.

MURPHY, CORNELIUS J. aged 24 years married to CAREY, LIZZIE M. aged 23 years October 16, 1893 by Father J. J. Monaghan at St. Patrick's Roman Catholic Church. Both natives of Charleston. He a clerk.

MURPHY, ELLEN E. aged 20 years married to O'DONNEL, THOMAS F. aged 22 years February 12, 1880 by Father John P. Twigg at The Cathedral of St. John the Baptist. Both natives of Charleston. He a longshoreman.

MURPHY, E. T. aged 34 years married to SHAROGO (?), G. W. aged 34 years February 19, 1882 by Father J. J. Monaghan. He a native of Ohio and she of Ireland. He a painter.

MURPHY, FRANK J. aged 29 years married to COYNE, MARY A. aged 26 years April 28, 1891 by Father J. J. Monaghan at St. Patrick's Roman Catholic Church.

MURPHY, JOHN married to POWERS, HONORA EMILY July 25, 1886 by Rev. William H. Campbell at the residence of the minister.

MURPHY, JOHN aged 24 years married to HAYES, NELLIE F. aged 21 years April 8, 1885 by Father F. J. Shadler at St. Joseph's Roman Catholic Church. He a native of Ireland and she of Charleston. He an employee of the gas works.

MURPHY, JOHN A. aged 27 years married to HARLOW, MARY E. aged 24 years April 25, 1893 by Father J. Monaghan at St. Patrick's Roman Catholic Church.

MURPHY, JOHN D. aged 23 years married to BARRY, MARY L. aged 22 years February 6, 1894 by Father J. J. Monaghan at 136 St. Philip Street.

MURPHY, J. D. married to WELSH, E. JANIE November 6, 1877 by William B. Yates, Chaplain.

MURPHY, LAWRENCE aged 22 years married to QUINN, MARY E. aged 18 years February 3, 1884 by Father John P. Twigg at St. Patrick's Roman Catholic Church. Both natives of Charleston. He a clerk.

MURPHY, MARY aged 20 years married to REHKOPF, HENRY aged 22 years February 15, 1892 by Father J. J. Monaghan at St. Patrick's Roman Catholic Church. Both natives of Charleston. He an undertaker.

MURPHY, MARY FRANCES aged 18 years married to CAMERON, ARCHIBALD aged 28 years November 25, 1878 by Father Daniel J. Quigley at 72 East Bay Street. Both natives of Charleston. He a blacksmith.

MURPHY, MAURICE J. aged 25 years married to TOYE, ROSA aged 20 years June 19, 1895 by Father J. J. Monaghan at St. Patrick's Roman Catholic Church. Both natives of Charleston. He a railroad switchman.

MURPHY, PATRICK aged 39 years married to MARTIN, CATHARINE aged 40 years March 7, 1886 by Father F. J. Shadler at St. Joseph's Roman Catholic Church. Both natives of Ireland. He a paver.

MURPHY, RICHARD aged 39 years married to HARLOW, (Mrs.) MARY CRONAN aged 32 years December 15, 1878 by Father Daniel J. Quigley at The Cathedral of St. John the Baptist. Both natives of Ireland. He a saloon keeper.

MURPHY, SARAH JANE aged 16 years married to DIXON, JAMES A. aged 18 years July 29, 1878 by Father Daniel J. Quigley. Both natives of Charleston. He a bookbinder.

MURPHY, SARAH O'MEARA aged 26 years married to HARTIGAN, THOMAS aged 41 years July 9, 1894 by Father Daniel J. Quigley. He a native of Ireland and she of Charleston. He a taxidermist.

MURPHY, TERESA C. aged 15 years married to MYATT, FRANCIS R. aged 22 years November 12, 1883 by Rev. P. L. Duffy at 73 East Bay Street. Both natives of Charleston. He a pilot.

MURPHY, WALTER aged 21 years married to HORNEY, MAUD MARY aged 20 years September 19, 1892 by Rev. J. L. Stokes at 231 Coming Street. He a native of Salisbury, North Carolina and she of Jamestown, North Carolina. He a journalist in Salisbury.

MURPHY, WILLIAM J. aged 34 years married to O'MEARA, SARAH aged 27 years April 18, 1892. He a native of Ireland and she of Charleston. He a clerk.

MURRAY, E. KATIE aged 20 years married to CONLON, JOHN H. aged 20 years January 14, 1890 by Father Daniel J. Quigley at St. Patrick's Roman Catholic Church. Both natives of Charleston. He a blacksmith in Coosaw, South Carolina.

MURRAY, GEORGE W. aged 25 years married to FORRESTER, CHARLOTTE aged 25 years May 15, 1892 by Rev. J. L. Stokes at 66 Amherst Street. Both natives of South Carolina. He a laborer.

MURRAY, HESTER ANN aged 26 years married to O'NEILL, JOHN M. aged 25 years April 25, 1889 by Father J. J. Monaghan at St. Patrick's Roman Catholic Church. Both natives of Charleston. He a painter.

MURRAY, ISAAC married to ROSE, FLORENCE December 26, 1889 by Rev. W. A. Betts.

MURRAY, JAMES H. aged 21 years married to KALES, GEORGIANA aged 18 years April 7, 1878 by Father Harry P. Northrop at St. Patrick's Roman Catholic Church. He anative of Macon, Georgia and she of St. Johns, Berkeley County, South Carolina. He a planter.

MURRAY, JENNIE aged 18 years married to WILLIAMS, CAMPSON aged 21 years October 25, 1889 by Rev. T. P. Burgess at 2 Hampstead Square. Both natives of Colleton County, South Carolina. He a laborer.

MURRAY, JOHN C. married to DAWSON, FLORENCE December 6, 1888 by Rev. William H. Campbell at St. Paul's Church. He a planter in Florida.

MURRAY, JOHN H. aged 24 years married to AUSTIN, JULIA aged 21 years September 9, 1888 by Rev. H. B. Browne at 31 Amherst Street. Both natives of Berkeley County, South Carolina. He a farmer.

MURRAY, JOSEPHINE H. aged 21 years married to BROWNING, ALONSO aged 19 years October 1, 1887 by Rev. H. B. Browne at 22 Blake Street. He a native of Charleston and she of Berkeley County, South Carolina. He a railroad brakeman.

MURRAY, KATIE married to BRITTLE, GEORGE December 18, 1889 by Rev. W. A. Betts at Cumberland Church.

MURRAY, LIZZIE aged 19 years married to BRITTON, JOHN R. aged 20 years June 7, 1888 by Father F. J. Shadler at St. Joseph's Roman Catholic Church. Both natives of Charleston. He a printer.

MURRAY, LULA aged 24 years married to KENNEDY, MICHAEL J. aged 29 years November 23, 1892 by Father P. L. Duffy. He a native of Quebec, Canada and she of Charleston. He a stevedore.

MURRAY, L. C. aged 25 years married to COLBERT, WILLIAM L. aged 33 years November 30, 1890 by Father Daniel J. Quigley at St. Patrick's Roman Catholic Church. Both natives of Charleston. He a stonecutter.

MURRAY, L. ELIZABETH aged 25 years married to CALVERT, WILLIAM L. aged 33 years November 30, 1890 by Father Daniel J. Quigley at St. Patrick's Roman Catholic Church.

MURRAY, MARY F. aged 29 years married to PILS, HENRY A. aged 31 years October 13, 1891 by Father J. J. Monaghan at St. Patrick's Roman Catholic Church. Both natives of Charleston. He carpenter.

MURRAY, PETER aged 29 years married to SHARKEY, MAGGIE aged 20 years January 31, 1884 by Father J. J. Woolahan at St. Mary of the Annunciation Roman Catholic Church. Both natives of Charleston. He an engineer.

MURRAY, SARAH ANN aged 29 years married to FINKLEA, GEORGE W. aged 28 years April 30, 1884 by Rev. Charles A. Stakely at 110 Anson Street. He a native of Georgia and she of South Carolina. He a clerk in Savannah, Georgia.

MURRAY, SUSAN A. aged 18 years married to EVINGTON, JAMES aged 24 years April 21, 1891 by Rev. J. Thomas Pate at 61 America Street. He a native of Yorkshire, England and she of Berkeley County, South Carolina. He a laborer.

MURRAY, VANDERHORST aged 21 years married to SEIGNIOUS, EVA A. aged 21 years December 12, 1895 by Rev. John Kershaw at 155 Wentworth Street.

MURRAY, WILLIAM JACOB aged 29 years married to CONNOR, MARY ANN aged 24 years October 7, 1884 by Rev. E. J. Meynardie at Summerville, South Carolina. He a native of St. George, South Carolina and she of Holly Hill, South Carolina. He a merchant.

MURRELL, JAMES J. aged 21 years married to STURCKEN, ANNIE H. aged 20 years June 9, 1895 by Rev. J. L. Stokes at 32 Bogard Street. Both natives of Charleston. He a photographer.

MURRELL, JAMES J. aged 46 years married to THOMPSON, REBECCA aged 23 years October 12, 1890 by Rev. John Johnson at 53 Church Street. Both natives of Charleston. He railroad worker.

MURRELL, WILHELMINA aged 21 years married to LIEBENROOD, G. W. aged 28 years December 19, 1886 by Rev. J. B. Burgess at 99 Drake Street. He a native of Brooklyn, New York and she of Charleston. He works at the waterworks.

MURTIN, G. J. aged 24 years married to KLINCK, MICHAEL S. aged 30 years May 25, 1880 by Rev. W. S. Bowman at the Wentworth Street Lutheran Church. Both natives of Charleston. He a merchant.

MURTIN, ELIZA E. aged 22 years married to BOWEN, M. aged 32 years February 9, 1890 by Rev. R. D. Smart at Bethel Church. Both natives of Charleston. He a blacksmith.

MUSEGADES (?), JOHN HENRY aged 31 years married to HELMEKEN, KATRINA January 2, 1889 by Rev. Charles S. Vedder. Both natives of Germany. He a master mariner.

MUSGROVE, JAMES aged 26 years married to CUNNINGHAM, J. aged 22 years August 31, 1879 by Father Daniel J. Quigley at The Cathedral of St. John the Baptist. Both natives of Charleston. He a saddler.

MUSTARD, ALLEN CALVITT aged 28 years married to STOLL, MARY ELIZABETH aged 21 years October 19, 1881 by Rev. J. C. Stoll in King Street. He a dry goods salesman.

MUSTARD, (Mrs.) ROSALIE SOUBEYROUX aged 28 years married to BRANDT, JULIAN V. aged 37 years September 29, 1885 by Father J. J. Woolahan at St. Mary of the Annunciation Roman Catholic Church. Both natives of Charleston. He an accountant.

MYATT, EMMA C. aged 18 years married to BARRAGAN, MELVIN aged 22 years February 18, 1894 by Rev. J. L. Yongue. He a native of Williamsburg County, South Carolina and she of Charleston. He a fireman at the cotton mill.

MYATT, FRANCIS R. aged 22 years married to MURPHY, TERESA C. aged 15 years November 12, 1883 by Rev. P. L. Duffy at 73 East Bay Street. Both natives of Charleston. He a pilot.

MYATT, MARY CAROLINE aged 18 years married to JOHNSON, BENJAMIN FRANKLIN aged 22 years November 24, 1881 by Rev. H. F. Chreitzberg at the Spring Street Church. He a native of Charleston and she of South Carolina. He a mechanic.

MYER, ANNA aged 16 years married to DEVEREAUX, JOHN E. aged 23 years September 15, 1881 by Rev. Louis Muller at 105 Wentworth Street. He a native of Connecticut and she of South Carolina. He an engineer.

MYER, CAROLINE A. married to BOND, STANLEY E. March 17, 1886 by Rev. J. V. Welch at 57 Cannon Street. He a native of Richmond, Virginia and she of Charleston. He a blacksmith.

MYER, FERDINAND L. married to DALEY, A. E. November 18, 1878 by William B. Yates, Chaplain.

MYER, LOUISA T. married to RELYEA, BENJAMIN H. November 3, 1878 by William B. Yates, Chaplain. He a laborer.

MYERS, CATHERINE FRANCES aged 20 years married to McMILLAN, ROBERT BURNS aged 27 years December 23, 1886 by Rev. J. Walter Dickson. Both natives of Charleston. He a printer.

MYERS, CHARLOTTE aged 18 years married to HINDLEY, WILLIAM E. aged 27 years December 18, 1893 by Rev. J. C. Yongue. He a native of Savannah, Georgia and she of Charleston. He a clerk in Savannah.

MYERS, EDITH A. aged 24 years married to KROEF, CHARLES W. aged 21 years April 19, 1881 by Rev. Luther K. Probst in Gadsden Street.

MYERS, EDWARD C. married to DOUGHERTY, MARIA A. July 19, 1890 by Rev. W. A. Betts.

MYERS, JACOB S. married to PEIXOTTE (?), GRACE April 25, 1880 by William B. Yates, Chaplain.

MYERS, SUSAN aged 15 years married to GORMAN, JOHN A. aged 24 years July 4, 1880 by Rev. J. V. Welsh. Both natives of Charleston. He a laborer.

MYERS, TRESPOLE aged 24 years married to MADRE, ELIZABETH aged 24 years October 5, 1880 by Rabbi David Levy at the Hasell Street Synagogue. He a native of London, England and a merchant. Both residents of Fernandina, Florida.

MYERS, VIRGINIA A. aged 17 years married to PETIT, ARTHUR W. aged 22 years May 31, 1883 by Rev. J. V. Welsh at St. Johannes Chapel. Both natives of Charleston. He a clerk.

NABERS, GEORGE O. aged 24 years married to DUNN, MAGDALENA O. aged 24 years November 25, 1890 by Rev. Robert Wilson at 4 Wragg Square. Both natives of Charleston. He a drayman.

NACHMAN, ROSA aged 20 years married to FASS, MORRIS aged 25 years October 10, 1894 by W. Aurbach, Cantor and the Mechanic Union Hall. Both natives of Austria. He a merchant.

NASH, DAVID C. aged 37 years married to ARNAU, LIZZIE W. G. aged 27 years October 8, 1888 by Rev. H. B. Browne. He a native of Orangeburg, South Carolina and she of Charleston. He a clerk.

NASH, FRANCIS married to RYAN, CAROLINE February 15, 1887 by Rev. Richard S. Trapier at St. Luke's Church.

NAUGHTON, HONORA A. aged 25 years married to BARRY, MICHAEL aged 25 years June 15, 1881 by Father F. J. Shadler at St. Joseph's Roman Catholic Church. He a native of Charleston and a carpenter.

NAUGHTON, PATRICK aged 21 years married to WOODWARD, SARAH M. aged 22 years April 11, 1887 by Father F. J. Shadler at St. Joseph's Roman Catholic Church. He a native of South Carolina and she of Georgia. He a saloon keeper.

NAUGUCKS, LOUISA A. aged 24 years married to KUTCHER, CHARLES G. T. aged 29 years July 3, 1883 by Rev. Claudian B. Northrop, at 125 Calhoun Street. Both natives of Germany. He a mariner.

NEIL, META A. BLACK aged 23 years married to KENNEDY, ANDREW W. aged 26 years December 3, 1878 by Rev. Charles S. Vedder.

NEIMAN, ROSA SOPHIA ELIZABETH married to TERRY, OSCAR MORRIS January 10, 1878 by William B. Yates, Chaplain. Both natives of Charleston.

NEAGLE, JOHN aged 60 years married to CASHMAN, (Mrs.) MARY LALOR aged 40 years November 6, 1883 by Father F. J. Shadler at St. Joseph's Roman Catholic Church.

NECELLE, LOUIS aged 35 years married to MITCHELL, (Mrs.) MAGGIE TAYLOR aged 34 years November 27, 1892 by Rev. F. H. Smith in Blake Street. She a native of Columbia, South Carolina. He works in the cotton mill.

NEIL, (Mrs.) META A. BLACK aged 23 years married to KENNEDY, ANDREW aged 26 years December 3, 1878 by Rev. Charles S. Vedder. He a native of Macon, Georgia and she of Charleston. He a commercial traveler.

NELLIGAN, JAMES M. aged 28 years married to SEDRICK, MAGGIE aged 25 years June 23, 1884 by Father Daniel J. Quigley at 94 St. Philip Street. He a native of Green Brier, Virginia and she of Charleston.

NELSON, AMELIA aged 19 years married to GERARD, GUSTAV F. aged 21 years February 19, 1890 by Rev. J. Thomas Pate at 47 Bogard Street. He a native of Summerville, South Carolina and she of New York City. He a clerk.

NELSON, A. aged 23 years married to GRAHAM, E. L. aged 18 years October 18, 1882 by Rev. Luther K. Probst. He a native of Charleston and a mariner.

NELSON, CHRISTEN aged 32 years married to WESTERLIND, MARIA aged 40 years February 2, 1888 by Rev. C. E. Chichester at 119 King Street. He a native of Arendal, Norway and she of Lilla Edil, Sweden. He a carpenter.

NELSON, J. D. aged 22 years married to MAHONEY, E. aged 20 years December 13, 1879 by Rev. R. N. Wells at the residence of the Bride - 74 Tradd Street. Both natives of Charleston. He a merchant.

NELSON, J. A. aged 24 years married to DENNIS, M. C. aged 22 years October 12, 1882 by Father P. L. Duffy at The Cathedral of St. John the Baptist. He a native of Florida and a telegraph worker.

NELSON, NICHOLAS aged 45 years married to LYNCH, MARY ANN aged 28 years October 1, 1884 by Father P. L. Duffy at The Cathedral of St. John the Baptist. He a native of Sweden and she of Ireland. He a mariner in Cainhoy, South Carolina.

NELSON, SAMUEL W. aged 19 years married to MACKEY (Mrs.) BEULAH MITCHELL aged 18 years January 21, 1894 by Rev. Edmund Wells at 579 King Street. He a native of Bonneau, South Carolina and she of Augusta, Georgia. He a painter.

NELSON, SUSAN A. aged 20 years married to ROBESON, STEPHEN C. aged 31 years June 27, 1880 by Rev. J. V. Welsh at 64 Radcliffe Street. Both natives of Charleston. He a mechanic.

NELSON, SUSAN aged 49 years married to SCOFIELD, JAMES aged 41 years April 14, 1895 by Rev. J. C. Yongue at 9 Blake Street. He a native of New York and she of Union, South Carolina. He a painter.

NELSON, WALTER L. aged 23 years married to MUNZENMAIER (?), HENRIETTA L. aged 21 years March 25, 1891 by Rev. J. Thomas Pate. Both natives of Charleston.

NELSON, WILLIAM H. aged 26 years married to MAND, ELISE aged 23 years August 26, 1885 by Rev. Louis Muller in St. Philip Street, near Line Street. He a native of Sweden and she of Germany. He a car driver.

NELSON, WILLIAM DWIGHT aged 21 years married to JOHNSON, HARRIET URSULA aged 18 years December 16, 1883 by Rev. John H. Tillinghast at 11 Hampden Court. He a native of Charleston and a mechanic.

NESTOR, JOSEPH HENRY aged 28 years married to FAULPIER, EVELINA aged 25 years May 9, 1889 by Father J. J. Monaghan at 75 America Street. Both natives of Charleston. He a sashmaker.

NETTLES, ELLA C. aged 25 years married to ALSBROOK, J. DUPHRE aged 24 years June 25, 1884 by Rev. John Willson at the Pavilion Hotel. He a native of Clarendon County, South Carolina and she of South Carolina. He a lawyer in Manning, South Carolina.

NETTLES, SUSAN aged 29 years married to BLAKE, WILLIAM aged 30 years March 25, 1883 by Rev. J. V. Welsh at 24 Bee Street. He a native of London, England and she of Colleton County, South Carolina. He a laborer.

NEUFFER, AUGUST W. aged 30 years married to JOHNSON, LAURA aged 21 years April 11, 1889 by Rev. R. C. Holland at 233 Coming Street.

NEUMAN, J. F. aged 27 years married to SOHL, ANNA aged 40 years December 7, 1879 by Rev. Johannes Heckel at 125 Heckel at 125 Calhoun Street. He a native of Charleston and she of Hanover. He a baker.

NEVA, DAISY D. aged 18 years married to LEHMEYER, FREDERICK aged 23 years April 10, 1892 by Rev. Robert Wilson at 4 Wragg Square. He a native of Germany and she of Charleston. He a clerk.

NEVILLE, KATE FRANCES aged 19 years married to ANDERSON, JOSEPH HARVEY aged 40 years July 14, 1881 by Rev. Charles S. Vedder at 13 Logan Street. He a native of New Jersey and she of Charleston. He a photographer.

NEVILLE, M. L. married to ANDERSON, C. Y. October 11, 1880 by Father P. L. Duffy at 13 Logan Street. He a native of Charleston and a resident of Walterboro. He a planter.

NEVILLE, THOMAS J. aged 26 years married to HILL, ELLA E. aged 22 years September 2, 1884 by Rev. Charles A. Stakely. He a native of Charleston and she of Augusta, Georgia. He a printer.

NEVILS, ANDREW J. married to CHAPLIN, MARY H. January 15, 1890 by Rev. William A. Betts.

NEWBERRY, EDWARD aged 21 years married to HITCHINS, (?), ALZIE STRICKLAND aged 24 years November 13, 1892 by Rev. A. M. Chreitzberg in Blake Street. He a native of New York and she of Savannah, Georgia. He works in the cotton mill.

NEWMAN, JOHN NICHOLAS aged 31 years married to HIRSCH, ANNA CAROLINE REBECCA aged 23 years May 1, 1879 by Rev. William S. Bowman at 1 Shepherd Street. Both natives of Charleston. He a driver.

NEWMAN, L. B. married to FLADYER (?), LUCIE October 20, 1887 by Rev. William D. Kirkland at 14 Pitt Street. He a merchant in Jacksonville, Florida.

NEWMAN, (Mrs.) SARAH J. FORSYTH aged 53 years married to TENTON, W. J. aged 56 years September 4, 1892 by Rev. A. M. Chreitzberg at 75 Spring Street. He a native of North Carolina and she of South Carolina. He a carpenter in Denmark, South Carolina.

NIELSON, ANNA C. aged 19 years married to LARSEN, ANDREW P. aged 27 years December 15, 1885 by Rev. John Johnson at 295 East Bay Street. Both natives of Denmark. He a farmer in Berkeley County, South Carolina.

NIELSON, ANTOINE aged 35 years married to McNAMARA, LIZZIE aged 25 years November 8, 1877 by Father Daniel J. Quigley at 128 King Street.

NIESON, CHARLES aged 20 years married to MOORE, FLORA aged 17 years February 6, 1894 by Rev. L. M. Knowles at 62 Drake Street. He a native of Georgia and she of South Carolina. He works in the cotton mill.

NIPSON, T. S. aged 23 years married toHARRENFRATZ, ROSA aged 20 years December 27, 1886 by A. F. Gleason, Trial Justice. He a native of Charleston and she of Nashville, Tennessee. He a clerk.

NIX, JAMES T. aged 31 years married to FLEMING, EVELYN B. aged 24 years May 1, 1885 by Rev. Luther K. Probst. He native of Nixville, South Carolina and she of Charleston. He a lawyer in Greenville, South Carolina.

NIXON, DRURY M. aged 29 years married to DUVA, ESTELLE aged 23 years May 15, 1890 by Rev. J. Thomas Pate at 497 Meeting Street. He a native of South Carolina and she of Conway, South Carolina. He works for the railroad.

NIXON, MARY ELIZABETH aged 21 years married to HUTSON, OLIVER M. aged 21 years November 21, 1893 by Rev. Edmund Wells. Both natives of South Carolina. He a carpenter.

NOLAN, ALICE AGNES aged 16 years married to MORRIS, MICHAEL aged 28 years May 29, 1879 by Father John P. Twigg at The Cathedral of St. John the Baptist. He a native of Vermont and she of Charleston. He a laborer.

NOLAN, ARTHUR C. aged 25 years married to WITTINGTON, MAMIE E. aged 24 years December 25, 1891 by Rev. A. M. Chreitzberg at the corner of Meeting and Mary Streets. She a native of Macon, Georgia. He works in the cotton mill.

NOLAN, CATHARINE aged 21 years married to MAHER, DANIEL aged 23 years June 19, 1894 by Rev. Thomas F. Hopkins. Both natives of Charleston. He a mechanic.

NOLAN, MARY E. aged 23 years married to O'HAGAN, W. J. aged 24 years October 16, 1879 by Father Daniel J. Quigley at The Cathedral of St. John the Baptist. He a native of Brooklyn, New York and she of Charleston. He a grocer.

NOLAN, WALTER aged 41 years married to HUDSON, (Mrs.) LYDIA MILLER aged 60 years January 12, 1890 by Rev. Edwin C. Dargan at 623 King Street. He a native of Portland, Maine and she of Colleton County, South Carolina. He a laborer.

NOLIN, WILLIAM F. aged 26 years married to PALMER, MARGARET A. aged 21 years November 5, 18890 by Father J. J. Monaghan at St. Patrick's Roman Catholic Church. He a native of Kentucky and she of Charleston. He a bookkeeper.

NOLTE, AUGUST aged 29 years married to BEHNSCHSEN (?), ANNA aged 25 years December 4, 1892 by Rev. K. Boldt at 5 College Street.

NOLTE, AUGUST aged 24 years married to BEHNLEN (?), EMMA aged 22 years February 15, 1887 by Father F. J. Shadler. Both natives of Germany. He a grocer.

NOLTE, HENRY aged 22 years married to JANTZEN, META aged 24 years January 30, 1887 by Rev. Johannes Heckel at 123 Smith Street. Both natives of Germany. He a merchant.

NONTA, WILLIAM A. aged 49 years married to SCHUMACHER, MARGARETHE aged 28 years June 29, 1890 by Rev. Johannes Heckel at the residence of John H. Peate in King Street. Both natives of Hanover. He farmer on the King Street Road.

NORD, EDWARD aged 21 years married to WOHLERS, SOPHY aged 16 years July 3, 1889 by Rev. J. H. Wheeler at the residence of H. T. McGee - 20 Rutledge Avenue. He a native of Omaha, Nebraska and she of Charleston. He a watchmaker.

NORDEN, META ELIZA aged 25 years married to WILKIN, EDWARD H. aged 22 years March 26, 1887 by Rev. Charles S. Vedder at the Huguenot Church. He a native of England and she of Charleston. He a carpenter.

NORTH, REBECCA B. aged 24 years married to GLOVER, JOSEPH aged 20 years January 24, 1884 by Rev. John Johnson at St. Philip's Church. He a native of South Carolina and she of Charleston. He a farmer in Grahamville, South Carolina.

NORTON, JAMES E. aged 30 years married to LASSALLE, ADELA E. aged 17 years August 22, 1886 by Rev. J. W. Dickson. He a native of North Carolina and she of South Carolina. He a laborer.

NORTON, THOMAS P. aged 20 years married to PASSAILAIGUE, THERESA aged 18 years June 25, 1893 by Rev. J. C. Yongue at 14 Hampstead Square. He a native of Kingstree, South Carolina and she of Charleston. He works in the cotton mill.

O'BRIEN, ANNIE aged 32 years married to CONLON, EUGENE aged 35 years January 21, 1895 by Father J. J. Monaghan at St. Patrick's Roman Catholic Church. Both natives of Charleston. He an engineer.

O'BRIEN, ELLA A. aged 20 years married to BLOCKER, WILLIAM R. T. aged 25 years May 29, 1895 by Rev. J. L. Stokes at 231 Coming Street. He a native of Savannah, Georgia and she of Charleston. He works for the railroad.

O'BRIEN, ELLA F. aged 22 years married to WALLACE, JAMES W. aged 23 years May 5, 1885 by Father F. J. Shadler at St. Joseph's Roman Catholic Church. Both natives of Charleston. He a clerk.

O'BRIEN, JEREMIAH FRANCIS aged 25 years married to McDONALD, ANNA E. aged 20 years February 10, 1889 by Father J. J. Monaghan at St. Patrick's Roman Catholic Church. Both natives of Charleston. He a carpenter.

O'BRIEN, JOHN S. aged 24 years married to WHILDEN, SARAH aged 21 years September 3, 1891 by Rev. J. Thomas Pate at 231 Coming Street. Both natives of Charleston. He an engineer on board the USS Wistana.

O'BRIEN, JULIA M. aged 46 years married to CONALE, ANGELO aged 76 years August 29, 1893 by Father Joseph D. Budds at 86 Beaufain Street.

O'BRIEN, LIZZIE married to SWEENEY, JOHN November 29, 1881 by Father Daniel J. Quigley. She a native of Charleston. He a native of Ireland and a railroad conductor.

O'BRIEN, LULA T. aged 18 years married to SKINNER, WILLIAM J. aged 21 years October 10, 1888 by Rev. J. E. Carlisle at 50 Hanover Street. He a native of Colleton County, South Carolina and she of Charleston. He a clerk.

O'BRIEN, MAGGIE R. aged 23 years married to DOAR, ARTHUR E. aged 25 years January 16, 1894 by Father J. J. Monaghan at St. Patrick's Roman Catholic Church. Both natives of Charleston. He a machinist.

O'BRIEN, MARGARET E. aged 17 years married to BART, CHARLES E. aged 26 years April 23, 1884 by Father P. L. Duffy at The Cathedral of St. John the Baptist. Both natives of Charleston. He a merchant.

O'BRIEN, MARY F. aged 26 years married to MARINES, ROBERT A. aged 31 years October 14, 1886 by Father F. J. Shadler. Both natives of Charleston. He a laborer.

O'BRIEN, MICHAEL married to LYNCH, MARGARET February 19, 1879 by Father John P. Twigg at The Cathedral of St. John the Baptist. He a native of Vermont and she of Charleston. He a laborer.

O'BRIEN, M. married to BOYD, JOHN February 20, 1889 by Father J. J. Wedenfeller at St. Joseph's Roman Catholic Church. He a native of Ireland and she of Augusta, Georgia. He a merchant.

O'BRIEN, WILLIAM aged 23 years married to KELLY, MARY aged 24 years June 8, 1881 by Father T. Edward Chapins at St. Patrick's Roman Catholic Church. He a native of Charleston and she of Philadelphia, Pennsylvania. He a tinner.

O'BRIEN, W. L. aged 23 years married to McDUFF, MAMIE aged 23 years March 17, 1884 by Father F. A. Schmetz at 20 Line Street. Both natives of Charleston. He works for the railroad.

O'CONNELL, JANNA aged 26 years married to MANNING, MICHAEL L. aged 26 years November 20, 1893 by Father Thoms F. Hopkins at St. Mary of the Annunciation Roman Catholic Church. Both natives of Ireland. He a laborer.

O'CONNELL, JOHN JOSEPH aged 24 years married to FALLEN, ANN A. aged 20 years June 4, 1878 by Father Daniel J. Quigley at The Cathedral of St. John the Baptist. He a native of Ireland and she of Charleston. He a merchant.

O'CONNOR, JENNIE aged 25 years married to MARKS, THOMAS aged 28 years September 13, 1893 by Rev. Joseph D. Budds.

O'CONNOR, KATIE M. aged 22 years married to O'CONNOR, THOMAS J. aged 29 years June 17, 1890 by Father J. J. Monaghan at St. Patrick's Roman Catholic Church. Both natives of Charleston. He a clerk in Coosaw, South Carolina.

O'CONNOR, MARY A. aged 25 years married to RAY, WILLIAM aged 28 years June 10, 1891 by Father J. J. Monaghan. He a native of Louisville, Kentucky and she of Charleston. He a works in the phosphate mill.

O'CONNOR, PETER married to MOOD, SUSAN JANE December 25, 1878 by Rev. William C. Power. Both natives of Charleston.

O'CONNOR, SUSAN J. aged 30 years married to DADIN, ALEXANDER aged 35 years April 23, 1883 by Rev. J. A. Clifton at 98 Cannon Street. Both natives of Charleston. He a painter.

O'CONNOR, THOMAS JOSEPH married to BOWEN, BRIDGET E. September 26, 1886 by Father P. J. Wilson at St. Mary of the Annunciation Roman Catholic Church. She a native of Charleston. He a blacksmith.

O'CONNOR, THOMAS J. aged 29 years married to O'CONNOR, KATIE M. aged 22 years June 17, 1890 by Father J. J. Monaghan at St. Patrick's Roman Catholic Church. Both natives of Charleston. He a clerk in Coosaw, South Carolina.

O'DELL, KATIE BRONSON aged 25 years married to SIMMER, HARRY E. aged 27 years March 3, 1885 by Rev. John O. Wilson at 6 Montagu Street. He a native of England and she of New York. He the manager of the Singer Sewing Machine Company.

O'DONNEL, THOMAS F. aged 22 years married to MURPHY, ELLEN E. aged 20 years February 12, 1880 by Father John P. Twigg at The Cathedral of St. John the Baptist. Both natives of Charleston. He a longshoreman.

O'DONNELL, ALICE A. aged 24 years married to O'KEEFE, THOMAS C. aged 38 years September 25, 1888 by Father F. J. Shadler at St. Joseph's Roman Catholic Church. Both natives of Charleston. He a machinist.

O'DONNELL, DANIEL P. aged 22 years married to COLCOCLOUGH, MARY J. aged 23 years May 18, 1884 by Father F. A. Schmetz at 25 Columbus Street. He a native of Wilmington, North Carolina and she of Charleston. He a clerk.

O'DONNELL, DENNIS aged 40 years married to McSWEENEY, HELENA aged 30 years April 27, 1886 by Father Daniel J. Quigley at St. Patrick's Roman Catholic Church. Both natives of Ireland. He a merchant in Anderson, South Carolina.

O'DONNELL, M. A. aged 21 years married to FABER, J. L. aged 26 years May 30, 1882 by Rev. P. L. Duffy at The Cathedral of St. John the Baptist. He a native of Massachusetts and a storekeeper.

O'DONNELL, THOMAS F. aged 22 years married to MURPHY, ELLEN E. aged 20 years February 12, 1880 by Father John P. Twigg at The Cathedral of St. John the Baptist. Both natives of Charleston. He a longshoreman.

O'GORMAN, HUGH D. aged 28 years married to HANLEY, MARY AGNES aged 25 years April 29, 1891 by Father Daniel J. Quigley at St. Patrick's Roman Catholic Church. Both natives of Charleston. He a carpenter.

O'GORMAN, WILLIAM aged 27 years married to MIOT, MAUD aged 20 years November 16, 1892 by Rev. W. T. Thompson in Queen Street. He a native of St. Augustine, Florida and she of Columbia, South Carolina. He a merchant in St. Augustine.

O'GRADY, ANNIE aged 26 years married to RILEY, JOHN aged 40 years February 24, 1895 by Rev. Edmund Wells at 1 McSweeny Court. Both natives of Charleston. He works in the cotton mill.

O'HAGAN, W. J. aged 24 years married to NOLAN, MARY E. aged 23 years October 16, 1879 by Father Daniel J. Quigley at The Cathedral of St. John the Baptist. He a native of Brooklyn, New York and she of Charleston. He a grocer.

O'HERREN, JOHN JAMES aged 38 years married to GENTRY, (Mrs.) MARGARET COBIA aged 29 years January 26, 1892 by Father J. J. Monaghan at 136 St. Philip Street. Both natives of Charleston. He a machinist.

O'KEEFE, THOMAS C. aged 38 years married to O'DONNELL, ALICE A. aged 24 years September 25, 1888 by Father F. J. Shadler at St. Joseph's Roman Catholic Church. Both natives of Charleston. He a machinist.

O'KEIFE, ANNIE aged 19 years married to HUNTER, SALVADOR BENJAMIN aged 24 years April 29, 1878 by Father C. J. Croghan. Both natives of Charleston. He in the ship business.

O'KEIFE, JULIA F. aged 18 years married to KENNEDY, JOHN P. aged 21 years September 27, 1885 by Father F. A. Schmetz.

O'KIEFE, L. aged 22 years married to TOYE, E. aged 28 years May 16, 1882 by Rev. J. M. Green. He a native of Charleston and a boilermarker.

O'KIEFFE, ANNIE aged 19 years married to HUNTER, SALVADOR B. aged 24 years April 29, 1878 by Father C. J. Croghan at St. Joseph's Roman Catholic Church. Both natives of Charleston. He in the ship business.

O'KIEFFE, E. aged 21 years married to MEYERS, J. aged 23 years June 13, 1882 by Father F. J. Shadler at St. Joseph's Roman Catholic Church. Both natives of Charleston. He a machinist.

O'MARA, MARY aged 20 years married to BURNS, SAMUEL aged 37 years December 5, 1877 by Father John O. Schachte at St. Mary of the Annunciation Roman Catholic Church. He a native of Ireland and she of Charleston. He a liquor dealer.

O'MARA, MARY THERESE aged 25 years married to HANLY, PATRICK J. aged 28 years February 4, 1883 by Father John P. Twigg at St. Patrick's Roman Catholic Church. He a native of Ireland and she of Charleston. He a policeman.

O'MEARA, M. A. aged 26 years married to McMANUS, P. J. aged 28 years June 8, 1887 by Rev. P. J. McManus. He a native of Ireland and she of Charleston. He a clerk.

O'MEARA, SARAH aged 27 years married to MURPHY, WILLIAM J. aged 34 years April 18, 1892. He a native of Ireland and she of Charleston. He a clerk.

O'NEAL, ELLEN H. married to FOWLER, HENRY M. February 3, 1880 by Rev. Richard S. Trapier at St. Michael's Church.

O'NEALE, GEORGE E. aged 22 years married to STROBLE, ALICE U. aged 17 years October 25, 1883 by Rev. J. V. Welsh at the corner of Fishburne Street and Rutledge Avenue. Both natives of Charleston. He a carpenter.

O'NEALE, ROSELLA aged 18 years married to CAMERON, WILLIAM aged 22 years September 23, 1885 by Rev. J. V. Welsh at 3.5 Blake Street. Both natives of Charleston. He a blacksmith.

O'NEALE, SARAH ELIZABETH married to KORNAHRENS, JOHN J. February 3, 1889 by Rev. William H. Campbell at the residence of William P. O'Neale. He a clerk.

O'NEILL, E. L. aged 21 years married to PRENDERGAST, F. S. aged 23 years November 21, 1882 by Father Daniel J. Quigley at The Cathedral of St. John the Baptist. He a native of Georgia and a civil engineer.

O'NEILL, HENRY JOHN aged 31 years married to Baker, MOLLIE CECILE aged 19 years August 8, 1878 by Father Daniel J. Quigley at The Cathedral of St. John the Baptist. Both natives of Charleston. He a merchant.

O'NEILL, JOHANNA MURPHY aged 40 years married to COYNES, THOMAS aged 25 years June 15, 1892 by Father Daniel J. Quigley at St. Patrick's Roman Catholic Church. Both natives of Ireland. He a barkeeper.

O'NEILL, JOHN M. aged 25 years married to MURRAY, HESTER ANN aged 26 years April 25, 1889 by Father J. J. Monaghan at St. Patrick's Roman Catholic Church. Both natives of Charleston. He a painter.

O'NEILL, MARGARET aged 21 years married to CADE, JOHANN H. aged 23 years January 1, 1894 by Father J. J. Monaghan at St. Patrick's Roman Catholic Church. He a native of Brooklyn, New York and she of Charleston. He a bricklayer and stonemason.

O'NEILL, MARGARET aged 35 years married to CAHILL, JOHN aged 45 years July 14, 1878 by Father John P. Twigg at The Cathedral of St. John the Baptist. Both natives of Ireland. He a laborer.

O'NEIL, MARY L. aged 33 years married to CORDES, HERMAN S. aged 40 years January 17, 1884 by Father Daniel J. Quigley at 76 America Street. She a native of Charleston. He a mariner.

O'NEIL, MARY aged 23 years married to FOX, ANDREW aged 25 years January 7, 1885 by Father Harry P. Northrop at The Cathedral of St. John the Baptist at The Cathedral of St. John the Baptist. Both natives of Charleston. He a clerk.

O'NEIL, MARY E. aged 25 years married to ARMSTRONG, JOHN A. aged 28 years May 2, 1881 by Father P. L. Duffy. He a native of Charleston and she of Florida. He an engineer.

O'NEILL, NELLIE E. aged 22 years married to HARRIS, JOHN B. aged 24 years October 16, 1884 by Father Daniel J. Quigley at St. Patrick's Roman Catholic Church.
He a native of Georgia and she of South Carolina. He works for the railroad in Augusta, Georgia.

O'ROURKE, ANNIE MARIA aged 20 years married to HOLLINGS, EDWARD B. aged 24 years April 17, 1886 by Father Daniel J. Quigley at St. Patrick's Roman Catholic Church. Both natives of Charleston. He a lawyer.

O'ROURKE, ELIZABETH aged 17 years married to COOKE, CHARLES aged 23 years November 28, 1880 by Father Harry P. Northrop at St. Patrick's Roman Catholic Church. Both natives of Charleston. He works for the railroad.

O'ROURKE, JENNIE PHILOMENA aged 20 years married to TIERNEY, FRANCIS C. aged 20 years May 5, 1890 by Father J. J. Monaghan. He a native of Columbia, South Carolina and she of Charleston. He a laborer.

O'SHAUGHNESSY, JOSEPH J. aged 28 years married to ABNEY, MARY J. aged 21 years October 16, 1894 by Rev. J. C. Yongue at 14 Hampstead Square. He a native of Charleston and she of Edgefield County, South Carolina. He a railroad watchman.

O'SHAUGHNESSY, M. aged 52 years married to BYRNE, ELLEN aged 35 years November 9, 1891 by Father J. J. Monaghan at St. Patrick's Roman Catholic Church. Both natives of Ireland. He a merchant.

O'SHAUGHNESSY, PATRICK aged 24 years married to KNIGHT, MARGARET aged 18 years January 26, 1878 by Father Harry P. Northrop at St. Patrick's Roman Catholic Church.

O'SHAUGHNESSY, P. aged 28 years married to MULLER, M. F. aged 16 years May 16, 1892 by Father P. L. Duffy at The Cathedral of St. John the Baptist. He a native of Ireland and a grocer.

O'SULLIVAN, JOHN J. aged 31 years married to WALSH, NORAH C. aged 27 years November 29, 1883 by Father J. J. Woolahan at St. Mary of the Annunciation Roman

Catholic Church. He a native of Boston, Massachusetts and she of Charleston. He a bookkeeper.

ODENCRANTZ, CARL aged 34 years married to HAAS, THERESA aged 28 years December 7, 1892 by Rev. Edward T. Horn at 31 Pitt Street. He a native of Sweden and she of Charleston. He an engineer.

OELRICH, JOHANN CARL aged 64 years married to BOMBACH (?), (Mrs.) EMMA L. B. HERMANN aged 50 years August 4, 1886 by Rev. Louis Muller at 179 Meeting Street. Both natives of Germany. He an organ builder.

OETJEN, ANNA G. C. S. aged 19 years married to GERKEN, ARTHUR J. H. aged 23 years April 4, 1886 by Rev. Johannes Heckel. He a native of Charleston and a bookkeeper.

OETJEN, JEANETTE C. aged 23 years married to Boldt, CARL L. J. aged 29 years February 17, 1891 by Rev. Louis Muller at St. Johannes Lutheran Church. He a native of Prussia and she of Charleston. He a clergyman.

OETJEN, GUSTAV A. aged 28 years married to BISCHOFF, JULIE ANNA W. aged 26 years June 2, 1885 by Rev. Robert Wilson at the corner of Meeting and Ann Streets. Both natives of Charleston. He a druggist.

OETJEN, HENRY W. M. aged 23 years married to TOLLNER, HELENA M. aged 18 years February 17, 1885 by Rev. Johannes Heckel at 7 Wall Street. He a native of Charleston and she of Germany. He an oil salesman.

OETJEN (?), WILLIAM H. aged 17 years married to MEYER, EMMA F. aged 17 years April 28, 1891 by Rev. Edward T. Horn at 25 Church Street. He a native of Wilmington, North Carolina and she of Charleston. He a fish merchant.

OFFERMAN, DORA R. aged 24 years married to BORNEMANN, J. HENRY aged 27 years March 23, 1880 by Rev. Johannes Heckel at the residence of B. Webb - the corner of Church and Cumberland Streets. Both natives of Lindstedt, Hanover. He a merchant.

OGIER, GRAYSON aged 22 years married to MURDOCH, JOHN H. aged 36 years June 3, 1885 by Rev. John Johnson in Hasell Street. Both natives of Charleston. He a factor.

OGIER, HARRIET RUTLEDGE married to SIMONS, HARLESTON REID January 15, 1878 by Rev. Richard S. Trapier at the residence of Dr. Ogier.

OGIER, KATE L. aged 23 years married to HANAHAN, JOSEPH aged 25 years April 6, 1893 by Rev. Robert Wilson at 35 Bull Street. Both natives of Charleston. He a clerk.

OGIER, T. S. aged 21 years married to Farmer, A. R. aged 23 years February 9, 1882 by Rev. J. V. Welsh at 27 Line Street. He a native of Charleston and a machinist.

OGILVIE, WILLIAM MATTHEW aged 22 years married to GALE, CAROLINE BUDD aged 24 years April 12, 1881 by Rev. L. H. Shuck at 78 America Street. He a native of Charleston and a clerk.

OGLESBY, JOHN T. married to DOTEN, CORALIE February 27, 1889 by Father John J. Wedenfeller at St. Joseph's Roman Catholic Church. He a native of Georgia and she of Charleston. He a railroad conductor.

OGREW, JOHN A. aged 25 years married to TARRIS, ROWENA G. aged 27 years September 13, 1887 by Rev. Robert O. Wilson at 4 Wragg Square. Both natives of Charleston. He a mechanic.

OLD, GEORGE aged 25 years married to MIOT, MARY E. aged 24 years June 10, 1891 by Rev. Edwin C. Dargan at 51 Hasell Street. He a native of Elizabeth City, New Jersey and she of Palatka, Florida. He a bookkeeper in St. Augustine, Florida.

OLDENBERG, M. H. S. aged 25 years married to BEGEMANN, W. H. aged 26 years March 27, 1887 by Rev. Louis Muller. He a native of Germany and she of Charleston. He a saloon keeper.

OLDENBUTTEL, JOHANNA W. M. STEINBERG aged 40 years married to GORSE, PETER NICHOLAS aged 49 years January 25, 1891 by Rev. Louis Muller at 388 Meeting Street. Both natives of Hanover. He a grocer.

OLDHAM, JENNIE A. aged 22 years married to ALLEN, LOGAN M. aged 37 years April 6, 1893 by Rev. J. L. Stokes at 199 Spring Street. He a native of Richmond, Virginia and she of Augusta, Georgia. He works in the cotton mills.

OLDHAM, MAMIE aged 21 years married to MAJENSKI (?), ALBERT aged 42 years September 16, 1884 by Father F. J. Shadler. He a native of Germany and she of Augusta, Georgia. He a baker.

OLIVARA, MATTEO married to FERRARA, CATERIENA February 26, 1879 by Father Daniel J. Quigley at The Cathedral of St. John the Baptist. Both natives of Italy. He a mariner.

OLIVER, JOHN HENRY aged 34 years married to DAVIS, FRANCES IDA aged 22 years October 5, 1880 by Rev. John H. Honour at 14 John Street. He a native of Charleston. Both reside in Meeting Street. He a carpenter.

OLIVER, J. H. married to WISE, C. A. October 16, 1879 by William B. Yates, Chaplain.

OLIVER, LUCY B. aged 27 years married to STRONG, LOUIS CHARLES aged 23 years November 1, 1895 by Rev. Charles S. Vedder at 116 Church Street. He a native of Vermont and she of Boston, Massachusetts. He in the mercantile business in Boston.

OLSEN, ANDREW aged 24 years married to BUTLER, CECILIA aged 22 years March 24, 1894 by Rev. John Johnson at 53 Church Street. He a native of Norway and she of South Carolina.

ONSAN, HENRICK aged 26 years married to LEE, ELIZA J. aged 42 years October 25, 1885 by Rev. John E. Beard at 22 Aiken Street. He a native of Norway and she of North Carolina. He a blacksmith.

OPPEL, R. EVALINE aged 20 years married to POOSER, KEITH E. aged 25 years March 11, 1890 by Rev. J. Thomas Pate at 28 Vernon Street. He a native of Blackville, South Carolina and she of Charleston. He a car builder.

OPPEL, F. GEORGE aged 36 years married to DOAR, (Mrs.) ELLA M. POOSER aged 27 years September 30, 1890 by Rev. J. Thomas Pate at 21 Cooper Street. Both natives of Charleston. He a printer in Jacksonville, Florida.

ORR, J. D. married to BRITTAIN, M. BESSIE October 7, 1884 by Rev. William T. Thompson at the First Presbyterian Church. He a physician in Asbury, South Carolina.

ORTIZ, ENRIQUE aged 26 years married to BLACK. A. E. aged 24 years April 21, 1880 by Father Claudian B. Northrop at St. Mary of the Annunciation Roman Catholic Church. He a native of Madrid, Spain and she of Charleston. He the Vice-Consul for Spain.

ORTMANN, HENRY C. aged 25 years married to HARVEY, MARTHA E. aged 25 years April 10, 1888 by Rev. Robert Wilson at 40 Mazyck Street. He a native of Charleston and a postal worker.

ORTMANN, CARL HEINRICH F. aged 21 years married to KILGUS, LOUISE DORETHA aged 20 years October 2, 1887 by Rev. Louis Muller at 96 Radcliffe Street. He a native of Prussia and she of Germany. He a baker in Georgetown, South Carolina.

ORTMAN, EDWIN PRIOLEAU aged 33 years married to KENNEDY, MINNIE ESTELLE aged 23 years March 12, 1890 by Rev. R. D. Smart at Bethel Church. Both natives of Charleston. He a painter.

ORTMANN, R. J. aged 21 years married to STAWOVICH (?), MAMIE A. aged 19 years April 30, 1891 by Father Daniel J. Quigley at St. Patrick's Roman Catholic Church.

ORTMANN, T. M. aged 18 years married to BLAKE, M. F. aged 18 years June 25, 1882 by Rev. L. H. Shuck. She a native of New York. He a clerk.

ORTON, GERTRUDE married to SCHUTTE (?), HENRY November 8, 1877 by Rev. R. S. Trapier in King Street.

ORVIN, (Mrs.) NELLIE ANN CRAWFORD aged 35 years married to EADIE, ADOLPHUS aged 42 years March 4, 1894 by Rev. Edmund Wells. Both natives of St. Stephen's Parish, South Carolina. He a railroad car counter.

OSBORNE, (Mrs.) MARY TOOLE aged 27 years married to CONNOLLY, HENRY W. aged 21 years April 24, 1892 by Rev. A. W. Chreitzberg at 84 America Street. He a native of Barnwell, South Carolina and she of Aiken, South Carolina. He works for the railroad.

OSMUNDSEN, BERTHEL aged 25 years married to GANNON, KATIE aged 16 years September 29, 1895 by Rev. C. E. Chichester at the Mariners Church. He a native of Norway and she of Columbia, South Carolina. He a clerk.

OSTENBURG, A. married to ZEPRADEL, — September 21, 1879 by William B. Yates, Chaplain.

OSTENDORFF, HERMAN E. aged 31 years married to BUSE, DORA ANN aged 28 years February 16, 1887 by Rev. Louis Muller. He a native of South Carolina and she of Charleston. He a grocer.

OSTENDORFF, JOHN H. aged 23 years married to TIGHE, (Mrs.) ANNIE MURPHY aged 35 years November 15, 1891 by Father J. J. Monaghan at St. Patrick's Roman Catholic Church. He a native of Charleston and she of Ireland. He a merchant.

OSTERHOLTZ, HENRY F. D. aged 31 years married to MEYER, JOHANNA CAROL DORETHA aged 32 years August 10, 1881 by Rev. Louis Muller at 121 East Bay Street. He a native of Charleston and she of Hanover. He a grocer.

OSWALD, GEORGE DOUGLAS aged 26 years married to DAVIS, FLORENCE ERNESTINE aged 20 years April 30, 1889 by Rev. R. A. Webb at 12 Chinquapin Street. He a native of Georgia and she of Adams Run, South Carolina. He planter on James Island, South Carolina.

OSWALD, HENRY C. aged 25 years married to TOVEY, MARY aged 25 years November 18, 1885 by Rev. Edward T. Horn at St. Johannes Lutheran Church. He a native of Georgia and she of Charleston. He a bookkeeper.

OTT, JOHN aged 43 years married to ATKINSON, (Mrs.) MARY E. BECKER aged 32 years April 21, 1889 by Rev. J. V. Welsh at 40 Bee Street. He a native of Orangeburg, South Carolina and she of Charleston. He a blacksmith.

OTT, MARY aged 22 years married to LANG, LUKE aged 24 years December 4, 1882 by Father John G. Guentzer at The Cathedral of St. John the Baptist. Both natives of Charleston. He a stonecutter.

OTTMER, CHRISTINE HENRIETTA aged 23 years married to HOLWEG, JOHANN H. W. aged 28 years March 25, 1883 by Rev. Louis Muller. He a native of Germany and she of Charleston. He a grocer.

OTTOLENGUI (?), CECILE aged 23 years married to LOPEZ, EDWIN aged 28 years November 3, 1881 by Rabbi David Levy.

OWENS, ALLEN J. aged 20 years married to JONES, MARY D. aged 18 years May 16, 1895 by Rev. Edmund Wells at 205 Spring Street. He a native of Blackville, South Carolina and she of Greenville, South Carolina. He a steer driver.

OWEN, A. C. aged 24 years married to JATHO (?), G. W. aged 24 years April 6, 1881 by Rev. Louis Muller. He a native of Charleston and she of Germany. He a merchant.

OWENS, BLANCHE aged 24 years married to LAROUSSELIERE, EMILE aged 24 years December 20, 1877 by Father Harry P. Northrop at St. Patrick's Roman Catholic Church. Both natives of Charleston. He a painter.

OWENS, LAWRENCE E. aged 31 years married to CAPERS, CLARA S. aged 29 years April 16, 1895 by Bishop Ellison Capers at 280 Calhoun Street. She a native of Marietta, Georgia. He a physician in Columbia, South Carolina.

OWENS, MARIA aged 21 years married to TRISLEY (?), SAMUEL D. aged 30 years November 7, 1888 by Rev. J. E. Carlisle. He a native of Charleston and she of Berkeley County, South Carolina. He works for the railroad.

OWENS, ROSALIE aged 38 years married to SMITH, WILLIAM H. aged 55 years January 19, 1892 by Rev. Edward T. Horn at 108 Tradd Street. Both natives of Charleston. He the Assistant Chief in the Fire Department.

OWENS, WILLIAM H. aged 26 years married to WELLING, ELIZA R. aged 24 years January 16, 1894 by Rev. A. Ernest Cornish at 91 America Street. He a native of Lincolnville, North Carolina and she of Charleston. He works in a factory.

OWYNS, BLANCHE aged 24 years married to LAROUSSELIERE, EMILE aged 24 years December 20, 1877 by Father Harry P. Northrop at St. Patrick's Roman Catholic Church. Both natives of Charleston. He a painter.

PACETTY, ANDREW aged 49 years married to RUMLEY, MARY ANN aged 33 years October 21, 1885 by Father F. J. Shadler at St. Joseph's Roman Catholic Church. He a native of Georgia and she of Charleston. He an engineer.

PACORSKI, VERONICA JOSEPHINE aged 19 years married to SMITH, JULIUS EUGENIE A. November 17, 1889 by Father J. J. Monaghan at 66 Drake Street. He a native of Aiken, South Carolina and she of Charleston. He a plumber.

PACY, HAROLD aged 55 years married to WILKERSON, HELEN aged 36 years January 12, 1892 by Rev. T. P. Burgess at 6 Wragg Square. She a native of New York. He a clerk.

PALMER, BOLLER aged 21 years married to SPIKES, ORRIE aged 18 years July 28, 1889 by Rev. J. E. Carlisle at 603 King Street. He a native of Richmond County, Georgia and she of Graniteville, South Carolina. He a sashmaker in Savannah, Georgia.

PALMER, GABRIELLE aged 21 years married to DRAKE, JAMES A. aged 29 years May 18, 1881 by Rev. Edward T. Horn. He a native of Germany and she of Charleston. He a merchant.

PALMER, J. P. aged 28 years married to WOODWORTH, M. J. aged 29 years December 8, 1882 by Rev. Charles S. Vedder at the Planters Hotel. Both natives of South Carolina. He a plumber.

PALMER, LILLIE LUCY aged 18 years married to SEEL, FRANCIS J. aged 19 years April 18, 1895 by Rev. J. L. Stokes at 231 Coming Street. Both natives of Charleston. He a clerk.

PALMER, MARGARET A. aged 21 years married to NOLIN, WILLIAM F. aged 26 years November 5, 1890 by Father J. J. Monaghan at St. Patrick's Roman Catholic Church. He a native of Kentucky and she of Charleston. He a bookkeeper.

PALMER, MARY aged 22 years married to SULLIVAN, WILLIAM FRANCIS February 6, 1889 by Rev. John J. Wedenfuller at St. Joseph's Roman Catholic Church. Both natives of Charleston.

PARDEE, CATHERINE E. aged 47 years married to BROWN, J. F. aged 29 years May 25, 1880 by Rev. G. R. Brackett at 21 Rutledge Avenue. He a native of Summerville, South Carolina and she of Charleston. He an engineer in Summerville, South Carolina.

PARDUE, MAGGIE aged 17 years married to BIRMINGHAM, W. aged 21 years December 11, 1894 by John Ahrens, Trial Justice. He a native of Wadesborough, South Carolina and she of Augusta, Georgia. He a weaver in the cotton mill.

PARKER, LILLY aged 23 years married to STUBBS, RUSSELL A. aged 24 years October 15, 1895 by Rev. J. C. Yongue at 51 Wentworth Street. He a native of Alabama and she of Edisto Island, South Carolina. He a merchant.

PARROTT, JOHNSTON aged 23 years married to MOORE, SALLIE CHAPIN aged 25 years December 4, 1884 by Rev. John O. Wilson at 3 George Street. He a native of South Carolina and she of Charleston. He a clerk.

PARSELL, EDWARD A. aged 21 years married to HYATT, HARRIOT aged 23 years February 14, 1887 by Rev. H. B. Browne in Drake Street. He a native of Augusta, Georgia and she of Charleston. He a mill hand.

PARSELL, ELLA M. aged 22 years married to DAVENPORT, W. H. aged 24 years December 25, 1880 by Father Harry P. Northrop at St. Patrick's Roman Catholic Church. Both natives of Charleston. He a printer.

PARSELL, (Mrs.) HATTIE HIOTT aged 31 years married to BROWN, CHARLES aged 48 years August 18, 1895 by Rev. J. L. Stokes at 7 Payne Street. He a native of Europe and she of Charleston. He a laborer.

PARSELL, WILLIAM R. aged 21 years married to PASSAILAIGUE, PALMETTO E. aged 19 years September 1, 1881 by Rev. George W. Stickney in Radcliffe Street. He a native of Charleston and she of Columbia, South Carolina. He a clerk.

PARSONS, LUTHER TYLER aged 24 years married to MARSCHER, MARTHA C. C. aged 23 years February 24, 1886 by Rev. Louis Muller. He a native of Hartford, Connecticut and she of Charleston. He a machinist.

PARSONS, WILLIAM B. aged 33 years married to GUINAN, (Mrs.) JOSEPHINE LENOR aged 34 years April 14, 1891 by Father F. J. Shadler at St. Joseph's Roman Catholic Church. Both natives of Charleston. He works for the railroad.

PARSONS, WINIFRED aged 43 years married to FERRARA, S. J. aged 23 years October 1, 1882 by Rev. John C. Schachte. He a native of Charleston and a carpenter.

PASSAILAIGUE, JOHN C. aged 19 years married to WILLIAMS, MINNIE B. aged 16 years February 28, 1894 by Rev. J. L. Stokes at 231 Coming Street. Both natives of Charleston. He works for the railroad.

PASSAILAIGUE, MARY M. aged 16 years married to ANDERSON, WILLIAM B. aged 21 years March 11, 1888 by Rev. H. B. Browne at 48 Aiken Street. He a native of Georgetown, South Carolina and she of Charleston. He works for the railroad.

PASSAILAIGUE, PALMETTO E. aged 19 years married to PARSELL, WILLIAM R. aged 21 years September 1, 1881 by Rev. George W. Stickney in Radcliffe Street. He a native of Charleston and she of Columbia, South Carolina. He a clerk.

PASSAILAIGUE, THERESA aged 18 years married to NORTON, THOMAS P. aged 20 years June 25, 1893 by Rev. J. C. Yongue at 14 Hampstead Square. He a native of Kingstree, South Carolina and she of Charleston. He works in the cotton mill.

PASSAILAIGUE, THEODORE W. aged 27 years married to MELCHERS, KATE JENNIE FREDERICKE aged 20 years December 10, 1888 by Rev. Louis Muller at the St. Matthew's Lutheran Church.

PASSAS, NICOLAS aged 24 years married to CLEAPOR, ROSA aged 24 years January 2, 1881 by Rev. John Johnson at 104 Market Street. He a native of Ireland and she of Charleston. He a clerk.

PASSMORE, EMMA aged 23 years married to WEBER, WILLIAM aged 23 years February 25, 1885 by Rev. John O. Wilson at 82 Wentworth Street. He a native of Cincinnati, Ohio and she of Preston, Ohio. He a canvasser in Preston, Ohio.

PATORE, GEORGE T. aged 66 years married to McCOOK, MARY A. aged 29 years February 5, 1880 by Rev. C. C. Pinckney at 2 South Battery. He a native of New York and she of Richmond, Virginia. He a merchant.

PATRICK, ALICE SHEPHARD aged 29 years married to STEWART, AUGUSTINE C. aged 32 years November 6, 1892 by Rev. J. L. Stokes at 231 Coming Street. Both natives of Charleston. He a painter in Savannah, Georgia.

PATRICK, CASIMIR CORNELIUS aged 29 years married to CHAZAL, MARIE LOUISE aged 21 years July 10, 1878 by Father Claudian B. Northrop.

PATRICK, CHARLES SUMMERFIELD aged 22 years married to ROBERTS, JOSEPHINE GADSDEN aged 20 years December 4, 1878 by Rev. G. R. Brackett at 5 Smith Street. Both natives of Charleston. He a dentist.

PATRICK, JAMES B. aged 40 years married to DUNN, KATE aged 37 years September 2, 1883 by Father John P. Twigg at St. Patrick's Roman Catholic Church. He a native of Ireland and she of Charleston.

PATRICK, JULIA E. aged 21 years married to TYLEE, EDWIN A. aged 21 years January 22, 1893 by Rev. Edmund Wells at 95 Nassau Street. Both natives of Charleston. He a clerk in Summerville, South Carolina.

PATRICK, NINA aged 25 years married to STEVENS, WILLIAM S. aged 28 years November 16, 1892 by Rev. Edward T. Horn. He a native of Augusta, Georgia and she of Charleston. He a clerk.

PATRINOURTCH (?), F. A. aged 25 years married to MINCHAN, PATRICK J. aged 28 years October 27, 1881 by Father F. J. Shadler at St. Joseph's Roman Catholic Church. He a native of Ireland and she of Charleston. He a blacksmith.

PATTERSON, BEULAH F. aged 18 years married to BRICKMAN, BERNARD W. aged 23 years August 8, 1895 by Rev. Robert Wilson at 72 Drake Street. Both natives of Charleston. He works for the railroad.

PATTERSON, EDMUND aged 47 years married to MAXEY, JULIA aged 42 years December 17, 1893 by Rev. N. Keff Smith at 72 Lee Street. Both natives of Charleston. He a laborer.

PATTERSON, FANNIE J. aged 20 years married to MAHEN, JAMES J. aged 38 years February 5, 1894 by Father Daniel J. Quigley. at St. Patrick's Roman Catholic Church. He a native of Charleston and she of Bridgeport, Connecticut. He a salesman.

PATTERSON, FRANK aged 28 years married to KNOX, C. aged 26 years October 23, 1883 by Rev. J. V. Welsh at 61 Line Street. Both natives of Charleston. He an engineer.

PATTERSON, ULYSSES McP. aged 24 years married to WALTERS, ANNIE MARGARET aged 21 years November 12, 1883 by Rev. R. A. Lapsley at 94 Calhoun Street. He a native of Charleston and she of Bremen, Germany. He works in the phosphate factory.

PATTERSON, WILLIAM J. aged 22 years married to BURDGES, MARY C. aged 19 years January 28, 1885 by Rev. R. A. Lapsley at 7 Blake Street. He a native of Charleston and she of Mobile, Alabama. He works in a carriage factory.

PATTON, GEORGE TAYLOR aged 66 years married to McCOOK, MARY ANN aged 29 years February 5, 1880 by Rev. C. C. Pinckney at 2 South Battery. He a native of New York and she of Richmond, Virginia. He a resident of Georgia and she of Richmond, Virginia. He a merchant.

PATURZO, FRANCIS F. aged 27 years married to SWEENEY, MARY JANE aged 29 years November 28, 1883 by Father John P. Twigg at St. Patrick's Roman Catholic Church. Both natives of Charleston. He a clerk.

PATURZO, R. aged 19 years married to POWER, P. F. aged 33 years August 18, 1879 by Father C. J. Croghan at St. Joseph's Roman Catholic Church. He a native of Ireland and she of Charleston. He a ship carpenter.

PAUL, HEINRICH PETER married to DURMANN, (Mrs.) DORIS DORETHA BOCK March 9, 1879 by Rev. Johannes Heckel. He a native of Gothenburg and she of Nordhotlz. He a carpenter.

PAUL, HEINRICH PETER aged 37 years married to BOCH, (Mrs.) DORETHA M. DURMANN aged 36 years March 9, 1879 by Rev. Johannes Heckel in East Bay Street.

PAULS, CHARLES HENRY aged 24 years married to HEINZ, FREDERICKE ELIZABETH HENRIETTA aged 20 years November 2, 1881 by Rev. Johannes Heckel at St. Johannes Lutheran Church. Both natives of Charleston. He a merchant.

PEAKE, HENRY M. aged 27 years married to WIGHTMAN, MARTHA V. aged 20 years December 16, 1885 by Rev. John Johnson in Queen Street. He a native of Charleston and she of South Carolina. He works for the railroad.

PEAKE, MARY HARDEE married to WIGHTMAN, WILLIAM EDWARD July 30, 1889 by Rev. William H. Campbell at the residence of R. C. Barclay at 5 Rutledge Avenue. He an engineer.

PECK, BYANINA aged 24 years married to PORCHER, EDWARD P. aged 24 years December 15, 1885 by Rev. C. C. Pinckney at Grace Church. He a native of South Carolina and she of Georgia. He a farmer in Florida.

PECKMAN, RICHARD aged 27 years married to GRAZICK, JULIE aged 25 years February 6, 1883 by Rev. Johannes Heckel at 125 Calhoun Street.

PECKMAN, THERESA CAROLINE aged 21 years married to FOSS, ALMON LEVI aged 21 years August 14, 1883 by Rev. Louis Muller at 66 Radcliffe Street. He a native of Boston, Massachusetts and she of Liverpool, England. He an engineer.

PECKSEN, JOHN N. aged 23 years married to LLOYD, HATTIE aged 19 years March 29, 1882 by Rev. Luther K. Probst. He a native of Georgia and she of Charleston. He a grocer.

PEIXOTTE (?), GRACE married to MYERS, JACOB S. April 25, 1880 by William B. Yates, Chaplain.

PELZER, ARTHUR aged 21 years married to ROBERTSON, MARIAN S. aged 19 years May 26, 1886 by Rev. G. R. Brackett. Both natives of Charleston. He a merchant.

PEMBERTON, ELVIRA aged 24 years married to CONYERS, JAMES aged 24 years November 3, 1878 by Father C. J. Croghan in Elizabeth Street. Both natives of Charleston. He a laborer.

PENDER, ANARTASIS aged 24 years married to COMAR, WILLIAM J. aged 26 years April 16, 1884 by Father F. A. Schmetz at St. Patrick's Roman Catholic Church. Both natives of Charleston. He a clerk.

PENDERS, M. A. aged 26 years married to BARRY, JAMES aged 27 years April 9, 1882 by Father J. J. Monaghan at St. Patrick's Roman Catholic Church. He a native of Charleston and a laborer.

PENFIELD, MILTON R. aged 29 years married to CHASTAIN, FRANKIE FLANAGAN aged 28 years July 19, 1885 by Rev. A. J. S. Thomas at First Baptist Church. He a native of Connecticut and she of Georgia. He a mariner.

PERCY, HAROLD aged 55 years married to WICKHAM, HELENE aged 36 years January 12, 1892 by Rev. T. P. Burgess at 6 Wragg Square.

PERLESSEN, P. aged 23 years married to RAM, E. aged 32 years July 25, 1882 by Rev. Louis Muller at 3 Mile House. He a native of South Carolina and a mariner.

PERRIER, EUGENE aged 23 years married to CAP, MARIE aged 19 years July 21, 1883 by Father Harry P. Northrop at The Cathedral of St. John the Baptist. He a native of France and she of Germany. He a cabinetmaker.

PERRY, WADE H. aged 39 years married to DAVIS, (Mrs.) FLORENCE C. CAPP aged 32 years June 21, 1892 by Rev. W. T. Thompson at 10 Legare Street.

PETERMANN, CAROLINE MARGARET ADELLA aged 22 years married to ROESLER, LOUIS CONSTANTINE ALEXANDER aged 21 years May 1, 1883 by Rev. Louis Muller at the southeast corner of Amherst and America Streets. Both natives of Charleston. He a mechanic.

PETERMAN, C. S. aged 20 years married to BULKEN, E. aged 21 years September 28, 1882 by Rev. Luther K. Probst. He a native of Charleston and a grocer.

PETERMAN, HENRY W. aged 29 years married to KROEG, FLORENTINE B. aged 20 years April 28, 1886 by Rev. Luther K. Probst. He a native of Gillisonville, South Carolina and she of Charleston. He a merchant in Gillisonville.

PETERMAN, JOHN W. married to AUSTIN, LOUISA ANNIE February 25, 1886 by Rev. Richard S. Trapier in Tradd Street.

PETERMAN, LOUISE N. aged 22 years married to DENHAMS, JOHN P. aged 21 years November 28, 1888 by Rev. R. C. Holleman at 15 New Street. He a native of Florida and she of Charleston. He works for the railroad.

PETERMANN, JOHANNA aged 30 years married to SURAU, CHARLES E. aged 32 years February 13, 1881 by Rev. Luther K. Probst at 3 Ann Street. He a native of Charleston and a policeman.

PETERS, AMELIA aged 26 years married to KEELER, IGNATIUS aged 35 years June 19, 1893 by Father F. J. Shadler at St. Joseph's Roman Catholic Church. Both natives of Germany. He a merchant.

PETERS, MARY L. aged 25 years married to McINNES, PETER McG. aged 44 years September 30, 1883 by Father F. J. Shadler. Both natives of Charleston. He a vet surgeon.

PETERS, META ELISE aged 26 years married to KNAUFF, THOMAS G. aged 26 years April 21, 1887 by Rev. Louis Muller at the St. Matthew's Lutheran Church. Both natives of Charleston. He a carpenter.

PETERSON, EMMA CHARLOTTE aged 20 years married to SMITH, JULIUS E. aged 18 years February 3, 1884 by Rev. Luther K. Probst.

PETERSON, JOHN aged 52 years married to JOHNSON, HARRIET aged 31 years January 16, 1879 by Rev. F. Browne at 61 America Street. He a native of Sweden and she of Charleston. He a mariner.

PETERSON, MARY J. aged 20 years married to FINCKEN, JOHN A. aged 26 years January 5, 1885 by Rev. Luther K. Probst. He a native of South Carolina and she of Charleston. He a baker in Beaufort, South Carolina.

PETERSON, N. aged 45 years married to CROGHAN, A. aged 22 years January 19, 1882 by Father Daniel J. Quigley. He a native of Holstein, Germany and she of Charleston. He a professor of music.

PETIT, ARTHUR W. aged 22 years married to MYERS, VIRGINIA A. aged 17 years May 31, 1883 by Rev. J. V. Welsh at St. Johannes Chapel. Both natives of Charleston. He a clerk.

PETIT, WILLIAM S. aged 26 years married to BEHRENS, ADELINE A. aged 23 years June 15, 1891 by Rev. Louis Muller at 526 King Street. Both natives of Charleston. He a mechanic.

PETRINOVICH, FRANK A. aged 20 years married to KELLY, VICTORIA aged 19 years February 3, 1889 by Rev. H. B. Browne at the corner of America and Blake Streets. He a native of Charleston and she of Graniteville, South Carolina. He works at the Custom House.

PETSCH, ALEXANDER H. aged 27 years married to STROTHER, LOUISE A. aged 26 years January 3, 1883 by Rev. E. C. L. Browne at the Unitarian Church. Both natives of Charleston. He a clerk.

PETTIS, WALKER JAMES aged 30 years married to HAPPOLDT, (Mrs.) ADAM. BEATTIE aged 28 years January 23, 1890 by Father J. J. Monaghan at St. Patrick's Roman Catholic Church. She a native of Georgia. He a watchman.

PFABLER, OTTO ROBERT aged 26 years married to POMMERENKE, AUGUSTA O. aged 20 years March 9, 1884 by Rev. Louis Muller in Calhoun Street. He a native of Charleston and she of Germany. He a baker.

PHILIPS, EVA A. married to DANIELS, JOHN H. December 26, 1890 by Rev. W. A. Betts.

PHILIPS, H. S. aged 23 years married to GANTT, H. R. aged 24 years November 29, 1882 by Father J. J. Wedenfeller. He a native of Charleston and a "commercial traveler."

PHILIPS, MARNIE BELLE aged 22 years married to JONES, ISAAC SEABORN aged 30 years June 26, 1890 by Rev. R. D. Smart at 77 George Street. He a native of Orangeburg, South Carolina and she of Augusta, Georgia. He a salesman.

PHILIPS, MARY HESTER aged 19 years married to PLAGGEMYER (?), HERMANN FREDERICK aged 20 years August 7, 1884 by Rev. W. P. Mouzon at 47 Line Street. He a native of Germany and she of Charleston. He works in the bagging factory.

PHILLIPS, ARTHUR DAVID aged 27 years married to JONES, SARAH JULIA aged 26 years April 10, 1890 by Rev. R. D. Smart at Bethel Church.

PHILLIPS, DAVID A. aged 27 years married to JONES, JULIA J. aged 26 years April 10, 1890 by Rev. R. D. Smart at Bethel Church. He a native of Aiken, South Carolina and she of Charleston. He a clergyman.

PHILLIPS, LOUISA C. aged 18 years married to CAMPBELL, CROSKEY S. O. aged 21 years February 25, 1879 by Rev. John Johnson in George Street. Both natives of Charleston. He a factor.

PHILLIPS, SARAH ODESSA aged 21 years married to LIVINGSTON, THOMAS P. aged 24 years June 9, 1891 by Father J. J. Monaghan at St. Patrick's Roman Catholic Church. He a native of Georgia and she of Washington, D. C.

PHINN, MARY E. aged 26 years married to ROBERTSON, P. ALEXANDER aged 29 years December 27, 1888 by Rev. C. C. Pinckney at Grace Church. Both natives of Charleston. He a clerk in Brunswick, Georgia.

PICKENS, MARY R. aged 23 years married to SIMONS, JAMES S. aged 23 years October 27, 1892 by Rev. C. C. Pinckney at 34 Smith Street. Both natives of Charleston. He a weaver in the cotton mill.

PICKFORD, SAMUEL aged 24 years married to BELL, FANNIE aged 20 years February 1, 1886 by Rev. C. E. Chichester at 46 Market Street.

PICKRELL, PERCY A. aged 33 years married to CHAPMAN, JESSIE C. June 7, 1892 by Rev. John Johnson at 37 Meeting Street. He a native of Richmond, Virginia and she of Camden, South Carolina. He a broker in New York.

PICQUET, BENJAMIN McN. aged 27 years married to ELLSWORTH, EUGENIA E. M. aged 22 years June 19, 1888 by Rev. Robert Wilson at 106 Reid Street. He a native of Augusta, Georgia and she of Charleston. He a confectioner.

PIEPER, WILLIAM H. F. married to VERONEE, ALBERTINE August 6, 1890 by Rev. W. A. Betts.

PIERCE, (Mrs.) ELIZABETH M. JOHNSON aged 28 years married to HENDRIX, CHARLES H. aged 22 years October 16, 1889 by Rev. J. C. Carlisle at the Spring Street Church. He a native of Georgia and she of Charleston. He a mechanic.

PIERCE (Mrs.) ELIZABETH MURRAY aged 38 years married to DUNSETTER, WILLIAM L. aged 42 years April 9, 1888 by Rev. J. E. Carlisle at the Spring Street Church. He a native of Germany and she of Charleston. He a painter.

PIERCE, JOHN P. aged 33 years married to JOHNSON, E. M. M. aged 19 years September 4, 1880 by Rev. H. F. Chreitzberg at the residence of John Pierce - 566 King Street. She a native of Charleston. He a mariner in New Haven, Connecticut.

PIERCE, MARY E. aged 21 years married to LEVY, CLARENCE aged 23 years September 24, 1879 by Father John P. Twigg at The Cathedral of St. John the Baptist. Both natives of Charleston. He a policeman.

PIERSON, SUSANNA SPARKMAN aged 34 years married to SHIPE, MARTIN aged 32 years December 25, 1886 by Rev. H. B. Browne at 78 Drake Street.

PILS, HENRY A. aged 31 years married to MURRAY, MARY F. aged 29 years October 13, 1891 by Father J. J. Monaghan at St. Patrick's Roman Catholic Church. Both natives of Charleston. He carpenter.

PINCKNEY, ALFRED W. aged 34 years married to ABNEY, CORA aged 22 years November 13, 1881 by Rev. J. V. Welsh at 5 Liberty Street.

PINCKNEY, C. C. aged 25 years married to CLARENDON (?), GRACE aged 22 years February 20, 1890 by Rev. E. W. Hughes at Grace Church. He a native of Berkeley County, South Carolina and she of Charleston. He a lawyer.

PINCKNEY, LAWRENCE M. married to SMITH, ANNA May 9, 1893 by Rev. William H. Campbell at St. Paul's Church.

PINCKNEY, MARGARET aged 22 years married to HALL, EDWARD OSCAR aged 25 years November 27, 1889 by Rev. John Johnson. He a native of South Carolina and she of Charleston. He a farmer in Mt. Pleasant, South Carolina.

PINCKNEY, M. B. aged 22 years married to MEARS, R. M. aged 27 years December 28, 1880 by Rev. C. C. Pinckney at Grace Church. Both natives of Charleston. He a merchant.

PINCKNEY, RANDOLPH VIRGINIA aged 22 years married to HUGER, W. EDWARD aged 25 years February 20, 1890 by Rev. C. C. Pinckney at Grace Church.

PINCKNEY, SAMUEL G. married to FISHBURN, JOHANNA B. June 12, 1893 by Rev. William H. Campbell at 25 Montagu Street.

PINKHAM, HORACE aged 30 years married to COBIA, MAGGIE aged 20 years December 28, 1881 by Rev. J. V. Welsh at 24 Bee Street. He a native of Philadelphia, Pennsylvania and she of Charleston. He a mariner.

PINKHUSSON, C. aged 20 years married to BENJAMIN, S. aged 29 years January 13, 1880 by Rabbi David Levy. He a native of Germany and she of Charleston. He a merchant.

PINKHUSSON, RACHEL aged 23 years married to LOEB, JACOB S. aged 36 years September 22, 1885 by Rabbi David Levy at 47 Wentworth Street. He a native of Germany and she of Charleston. He a merchant.

PINKHUSSON, S. aged 21 years married to CRONHEIM, H. aged 29 years January 13, 1880 by Rabbi David Levy. He native of Germany and she of Charleston. He a merchant.

PINNER, FANNIE B. aged 23 years married to MILLS, WILLIAM S. aged 24 years June 16, 1895 by Rev. J. C. Yongue at 64 Bay Street. Both natives of Charleston. He a railroad fireman.

PIPKINS, ELIZABETH G. aged 23 years married to HEYWARD, WILLIAM NICHOLAS aged 34 years May 10, 1887 by Rev. C. E. Chichester at 233 East Bay Street. He a native of Bermuda and she of South Carolina. He a mariner.

PITCHER, C. L. aged 23 years married to EASTERBY, E. F. aged 22 years November 9, 1882 by Rev. Luther K. Probst. He a native of Charleston and a merchant.

PITCHER, E. I. aged 25 years married to BROWN, S. W. aged 27 years December 4, 1879 by Rev. W. S. Bowman at the residence of the Bride - 52 Hasell Street. He a native of Burke County, Georgia and she of Charleston. He a farmer in Geogia.

PITTMAN, JAMES B. aged 24 years married to WEBB, EMMA SLATER aged 22 years January 6, 1887 by Rev. John O. Wilson at 94 Wentworth Street. He a native of Columbia, South Carolina and she of Virginia. He a slater.

PITTS, JESSE W. aged 21 years married to SMITH, MARIAN aged 17 years August 6, 1893 by Rev. J. L. Stokes at 239 Coming Street.

PLAGGEMYER (?), HERMAN FREDERICK aged 20 years married to PHILIPS, MARY HESTER aged 19 years August 7, 1884 by Rev. W. P. Mouzon at 47 Line Street. He a native of Germany and she of Charleston. He works in the bagging factory.

PLANE, CHARLOTTE E. aged 20 years married to COOMBS, ASHLEY B. aged 21 years March 1, 1880 by Rev. Edward T. Horn. He a native of Pulaski County, Georgia and she of Charleston. He a farmer in Pulaski, County.

PLATT, EVELINE aged 18 years married to LOTTE, WILLIAM E. aged 22 years January 13, 1889 by Rev. H. B. Browne at 567 King Street.

PLATT, THOMAS D. aged 41 years married to THOMPSON, ELIZABETH aged 23 years April 30, 1893 by Rev. J. L. Stokes at 231 Coming Street. He a native of Summerville, South Carolina and she of Charleston. He a carpenter.

PLAYER, PETER aged 21 years married to STEWART, MAUD L. aged 15 years October 29, 1893 by Rev. J. C. Yongue. He a native of Berkeley County, South Carolina and he works in the cotton mill.

PLAYER, HELEN ELIZABETH aged 18 years married to JENNINGS, ALFRED THOMAS aged 21 years June 26, 1889 by Rev. John J. Hill. Both natives of Charleston. He a printer.

PLEIN, JOHANN aged 24 years married to DREYER, BETA aged 28 years April 15, 1883 by Rev. Louis Muller at the northwest corner of King and Line Streets. Both natives of Germany. He a grocer.

PLENGE, EDWARD aged 25 years married to BOLLMANN, ANNIE aged 25 years November 15, 1885 by Rev. Louis Muller at 33 Charlotte Street. Both natives of Charleston. He a merchant.

PLESSMAN, LOUISA FREDERICKA aged 32 years married to SORG, LUDWIG HUGO aged 30 years July 14, 1887 by Rev. Louis Muller at 96 Radcliffe Street. He a native of Germany and she of Charleston. He a butcher.

PLOWDEN, WALLACE McINNIS aged 28 years married to STENMEYER, MARY ELIZA aged 20 years April 19, 1881 by Rev. Charles S. Vedder. He a native of South Carolina and she of Charleston. He a farmer.

POLHEMUS (?), EMILY aged 19 years married to FOGEL, JOHN M. aged 24 years November 4, 1886 by Rev. John Johnson at 159 Tradd Street. He a native of South Carolina and she of Charleston. He an electrician.

POLLARD, MARIE ELIZA aged 41 years married to DAY, SELDEN A. aged 41 years March 11, 1880 by Rev. E. C. L. Browne at the Unitarian Church. He a native of Chilicothe, Ohio and she of Waltham, Massachusetts. He a soldier.

POLLEN, J. D. aged 24 years married to McCOTTEN, C. D. aged 18 years May 30, 1882 by Father Claudian B. Northrop in Wentworth Street. He a native of Charleston and a clerk.

POLLNITZ (?), JULIA R. aged 19 years married to MAATTHEWS, JOHN R. aged 26 years December 15, 1892 by Rev. John Johnson. She a native of Alabama. He works for the railroad.

POMMER, MAX L. aged 23 years married to SUHRSTEDT, CATHARINA A. aged 26 years May 23, 1892 by Rev. Louis Muller in King Street.

POMMERENKE, AUGUSTA O. aged 20 years married to PFABLER, OTTO ROBERT aged 26 years March 9, 1884 by Rev. Louis Muller in Calhoun Street. He a native of Charleston and she of Germany. He a baker.

POMMERENKE, A. married to BENCKEW, EGGERT February 18, 1879 by Rev. Johannes Heckel. He a native of Germany and she of Poland. He a policeman.

POMMERENKE, WILHELMINA aged 21 years married to GROSSMAN, JULIUS aged 27 years May 10, 1883 by Rev. Louis Muller at the corner of Spring and President Streets. Both natives of Georgia. He a baker.

PONARD, A. TERESA aged 22 years married to HAM, J. JOHN aged 28 years February 10, 1890 by Father F. J. Shadler at St. Joseph's Roman Catholic Church. He a printer in Jacksonville, Florida.

PONARD, JAMES M. aged 28 years married to RYAN, CATHERINE aged 24 years May 26, 1881 by Father F. J. Shadler at St. Joseph's Roman Catholic Church. He a native of Charleston and a carpenter.

PONARD, MARY aged 23 years married to DELANY, JOHN J. aged 25 years April 25, 1883 by Father F. J. Shadler at St. Joseph's Roman Catholic Church. Both natives of Charleston. He a mail carrier.

POOSER, ELLA M. aged 20 years married to DOAR, GEORGE P. aged 20 years November 28, 1883 by Rev. J. A. Cliffton at the Spring Street Methodist Church. Both natives of Charleston. He a machinist.

POOSER, KEITH E. aged 25 years married to OPPEL, EVALINE R. aged 20 years March 11, 1890 by Rev. J. Thomas Pate at 28 Vernon Street. He a native of Blackville, South Carolina and she of Charleston. He a car builder.

POOSER, MARY L. married to GREER, J. FORREST April 7, 1881 by Rev. William H. Campbell at St. Paul's Church. He a clerk.

POOSER, SARAH REBECCA aged 20 years married to KINGDON, GEORGE PORTER aged 22 years December 8, 1881 by Rev. H. F. CHREITZBERG. Both natives of Charleston. He a railroad conductor.

POPE, CLAUS JOHANN aged 22 years married to SPELL, ANNIE aged 22 years April 5, 1886 by Rev. Louis Muller at 93 Queen Street. He a native of Germany and she of Charleston. He a clerk in Coosaw, South Carolina.

POPE, DIETRICH aged 24 years married to STEINCKE, EMILIE FREIDA LOUISE aged 18 years February 5, 1878 by Rev. Louis Muller in Market Street between King and Meeting Streets. He a native of Hanover and she of Charleston. He a grocer.

POPE, SUSIE married to KNOTT, JOHN W. March 15, 1892 by Rev. John Gass. She a native of Alabama. He a clergyman in Norfolk, Virginia.

PORCHER, EDWARD P. aged 24 years married to PECK, BYANIANA aged 24 years December 15, 1885 by Rev. C. C. Pinckney at Grace Church. He a native of South Carolina and she of Georgia. He a farmer in Florida.

PORTER, HATTIE H. SIMONS married to SHACKLEFORD, LEE May 29, 1888 by Rev. Richard S. Trapier.

PORTER, JOSEPH J. aged 21 years married to SIGWALD, ALICE G. aged 23 years April 8, 1891 by Rev. J. Thomas Pate at 106 Columbus Street. He a native of Orangeburg, South Carolina. He a machinist.

PORCHER, JOHN T. aged 30 years married to HASKELL, EVA aged 25 years December 24, 1877 by Rev. A. Toomer Porter at the Church of the Holy Communion. Both natives of Charleston. He a lawyer.

PORCHER, MARY I'ON aged 30 years married to CLARKSON, JULIUS EUGENE aged 37 years January 16, 1884 by Rev. John Johnson at 2 Franklin Street. He a native of Charleston and she of South Carolina. He a farmer.

PORCHER, PETER CORDES aged 32 years married to CHISOLM, SUSAN EMMA aged 39 years April 13, 1886 by Rev. LeGrand F. Guerry at 18 Meeting Street. Both natives of Charleston. He a phosphate worker in Colleton County, South Carolina.

PORTER, JAMES aged 26 years married to SIMONS, HATTIE aged 21 years December 20, 1877 by Rev. A. Toomer Porter at St. Paul's Church. Both natives of Charleston. He a lawyer.

PORTER, MARY aged 22 years married to CROSS, WILLIAM H. aged 27 years June 4, 1890 by Father Harry P. Northrop at The Cathedral of St. John the Baptist. He a native of Charleston and she of New Orleans, Louisiana. He a pilot.

POSTON, ROBERT J. aged 33 years married to ISADORA COOK aged 21 years July 15, 1894 by Rev. Edmund Wells at 3 Melchers Court. He a native of Johnsonville, South Carolina and she of Horry County, South Carolina.

POSTON, ROBERT JEFFREY aged 26 years married to McRAY, SARAH AGNES aged 22 years September 22, 1887 by Rev. T. P. Burgess at 98 America Street. He a native of Williamsburg, South Carolina and she of Charleston. He a bricklayer.

POTTER, BETTS A. married to CROSS, IRENE G. December 11, 1890 by Rev. W. A. Betts.

POTTER, MARY V. aged 21 years married to FULCHER, M. H. aged 24 years January 24, 1883 by Rev. L. H. Shuck at the Mariners Church. He a native of Beaufort, South Carolina and she of Brunswick, Georgia. He a mariner.

POULNOT, ROSA de LIMA aged 35 years married to HALL, HARRY aged 30 years July 16, 1890 by Father J. J. Monaghan at St. Patrick's Roman Catholic Church. He a native of Massachusetts and she of Quebec. He a mariner.

POWELL, JAMES ABNEY aged 23 years married to WESTENDORFF, EMMA VIRGINIA aged 31 years December 27, 1887 by Rev. G. R. Brackett.

POWELL, JOHN A. aged 22 years married to THORNAL, ROSA B. aged 23 years September 30, 1894 by Rev. J. C. Yongue at 96 America Street. He a native of Massachusetts and she of Quebec. He a mariner.

POWER, ANNIE F. aged 22 years married to KENNEDY, JOHN aged 29 years July 18, 1883 by Rev. John Johnson.

POWER, JAMES HAYES aged 31 years married to LEONARD, MARGARET E. aged 22 years February 11, 1885 by Father F. A. Schmetz at St. Patrick's Roman Catholic Church.

POWER, P. F. aged 33 years married to PATURZO, R. aged 19 years August 18, 1879 by Father C. J. Croghan at St. Joseph's Roman Catholic Church. He a native of Ireland and she of Charleston. He a ship carpenter. Both reside in Marsh Street.

POWERS, HONORA EMILY married to MURPHY, JOHN July 25, 1886 by Rev. William H. Campbell at the residence of the minister.

POWERS, JOHN aged 27 years married to KENNERTY, SARAH JANE aged 20 years March 12, 1878 by Father Harry P. Northrop at St. Patrick's Roman Catholic Church. Both natives of Charleston. He a farmer.

POWERS, KATIE NOBLE aged 25 years married to WELSH, EDWARD ANDREW aged 33 years January 28, 1891 by Father J. J. Monaghan at St. Patrick's Roman Catholic Church. He a native of Mt. Pleasant, South Carolina and she of Ireland. He a sashmaker.

POWERS, MAMIE aged 22 years married to ALBRECHT, JOHN H. aged 23 years December 3, 1878 by Father John P. Twigg at The Cathedral of St. John the Baptist. Both natives of Charleston. He a baker.

POWERS, MARY aged 20 years married to BEARD, JOHN C. aged 21 years October 12, 1884 by Rev. John E. Beard.

POWERS, MICHAEL aged 25 years married to McBRIDE, KATIE aged 22 years January 29, 1884 by Father John P. Twigg at St. Patrick's Roman Catholic Church. Both natives of Charleston. He a policeman.

POWERS, M. J. aged 23 years married to RILEY, J. A. aged 21 years July 16, 1882 by Father P. L. Duffy at St. Mary of the Annunciation Roman Catholic Church. He a native of South Carolina and a clerk.

POWERS, WILLIAM aged 25 years married to DOWLING, JENNIE aged 24 years December 14, 1884 by Father F. A. Schmetz at St. Patrick's Roman Catholic Church. Both natives of Charleston. He works for the railroad.

POYAS, SAMUEL H. married to BROWN, MARGARET M. November 12, 1891 by Rev. William H. Campbell. He a clerk.

PRATT, GEORGE WALKER aged 22 years married to DAWSON, MARY aged 22 years June 28, 1883 by Rev. C. C. Pinckney at 17 Smith Street. Both natives of Charleston. He a clerk in Walhalla, South Carolina.

PRATT, MARY S. aged 23 years married to BRINSON, EDWARD aged 22 years February 21, 1889 by Rev. H. B. Browne at 3 Stone Court. Both natives of Berkeley County, South Carolina. He a mill hand.

PRAUSE (?), F. S. aged 18 years married to BONSON, J. W. aged 25 years September 7, 1882 by Rev. Luther K. Probst. Both natives of South Carolina. He a clerk.

PRAUSE (?), LOUISE aged 23 years married to DRYER, JOHN aged 25 years October 12, 1892 by Rev. Edward T. Horn at 29 State Street. He a native of Germany and she of Charleston. He a clerk.

PRAUSE (?), WILHELM C. D. aged 25 years married to STENKEN, HELEN aged 24 years February 26, 1892 by Rev. Louis Muller at 23 Aiken Street. Both natives of Charleston. He a clerk.

PREGNALL, EMILY E. aged 19 years married to FAIRCHILD, WILLIAM HAMLIN aged 26 years November 22, 1877 by Rev. E. C. L. Browne at 7 Cannon Street.

PREGNELL, ARTHUR H. aged 24 years married to GORDON, FLORENCE E. aged 21 years May 1, 1889 by Rev. E. C. L. Browne. Both natives of Charleston. He a ship builder.

PRENDERGAST, F. S. aged 23 years married to O'NEIL, E. L. aged 21 years November 21, 1882 by Father Daniel J. Quigley at The Cathedral of St. John the Baptist. He a native of Georgia and a civil engineer.

PRENTISS, H. aged 38 years married to BLAKE, WILLIAM aged 29 years June 22, 1884 by Rev. John E. Beard at 3 Reid Street.

PRESCOTT, JOHN F. aged 22 years married to COATES, (Mrs.) MATTIE ELSWORTH aged 22 years April 16, 1889 by Rev. H. B. Browne at 78 Drake Street. Both natives of Charleston. He a merchant.

PRESCOTT, JULIA ELIZABETH aged 20 years married to RIVERS, FRANK HOWARD aged 23 years October 7, 1886 by Rev. G. R. Brackett at 74 Coming Street. Both natives of Charleston. He a fireman.

PRESCOTT, WILLIAM T. aged 33 years married to HIND, LAURETTA J. aged 24 years May 26, 1892 by Rev. G. R. Brackett at 64 Rutledge Avenue.

PRESCOTT, WILLIAM T. aged 28 years married to HEINS, (Mrs.) LAURETTA BIRCH aged 25 years August 18, 1886 by Rev. J. Walter Dickson at 93 Queen Street. He a native of Charleston and she of Richmond, Virginia. He a plumber.

PRESSLEY, WILLIAM aged 42 years married to HARD, P. MARY aged 29 years November 21, 1889 by Rev. Edwin C. Dargan at 88 Beaufain Street. He a native of Williamsburg County, South Carolina and she of Augusta, Georgia. He a farmer in Rio Vista, Georgia.

PRESTON, HENRY K. aged 25 years married to RHETT, ANN B. aged 19 years December 27, 1888 by Rev. John Johnson at St. Philip's Church. Both natives of Charleston. He a clerk.

PRESTON, THOMAS H. aged 27 years married to GRIMM, C. M. aged 18 years March 27, 1887 by Rev. C. A. Stakley. He native of England and she of New Jersey. He a painter.

PRICE, ELIZABETH aged 23 years married to CANTWELL, L. E. aged 29 years October 15, 1891 by Bishop Harry P. Northrop at The Cathedral of St. John the Baptist. Both natives of Charleston. He a clerk.

PRICE, GEORGE B. aged 24 years married to FICKLING, PAULINE ROSA aged 22 years November 13, 1890 by Rev. Robert Wilson at 21 Alexander Street. He a native of Colleton County, South Carolina and she of Charleston. He an Editor in Walterboro, South Carolina.

PRICE, JOSEPH ALBERT aged 40 years married to CORBETT, MARGARET V. September 15, 1883 by Father F. J. Shadler. He a native of Ireland and she of Charleston. He a saloon keeper.

PRICE, MARY E. married to EARLE, THERON February 27, 1883 by Rev. William H. Campbell at the residence of James Price. He a native of Greenville, South Carolina and a farmer.

PRICE, THOMAS J. aged 29 years married to COMAR, MARY E. aged 25 years June 11, 1889 by Father F. J. Shadler at St. Joseph's Roman Catholic Church. Both natives of Charleston. He a merchant.

PRIESTER, DORA HENRIETTA aged 20 years married to BRICKMAN, HENRY C. aged 20 years April 24, 1884 by Rev. John E. Beard. Both natives of Barnwell County, South Carolina. He works for the railroad.

PRIESTER, JOHN B. aged 22 years married to BOLCHOZ, MARIE L. aged 17 years November 5, 1894 by Father J. J. Monaghan at 499 Meeting Street. Both natives of Charleston. He a printer.

PRIESTER, SALLIE A. aged 17 years married to WAY, GEORGE aged 22 years January 20, 1887 by Rev. H. B. Browne at 499 Meeting Street. Both natives of South Carolina. He a druggist in Ridgeville, South Carolina.

PRINCE, EUGENIA EVELINE aged 17 years married to WOLFE, JOHN FREDERICK aged 25 years April 29, 1879 by Rev. W. S. Bowman at 231 Meeting Street.

PRINCE, (Mrs.) EVA A. SEXTON aged 24 years married to Baker, WASHINGTON aged 38 years February 8, 1887 by Rev. L. F. Beaty. Both natives of Charleston. He a clerk. Both natives of Charleston. He a clerk.

PRINCE, L. H. aged 23 years married to SEXTON, EVA A. aged 17 years October 2, 1879 by Rev. J. V. Welsh at 64 Radcliffe Street. Both natives of Charleston. He a clerk

PRINCE, MARY CATHERINE aged 20 years married to BRISSENDEN, EDWIN aged 28 years June 26, 1883 by Rev. A. Coke Smith at 48 Rutledge Avenue. Both natives of Charleston. He a driver.

PRINCE, THOMAS L. aged 38 years married to SEY, ELIZA aged 22 years June 8, 1884 by Rev. John E. Beard. He a native of London, England and she of South Carolina. He a mechanic.

PRINGLE, MARY RAVENEL married to HAMILTON, MILES B. April 10, 1883 by Rev. Richard S. Frazier in Legare Street. Both natives of Charleston. He a merchant.

PRINGLE, ROBERT A. married to SIMONS, HARRIET November 10, 1886 by Rev. William H. Campbell at St. Paul's Church. He a merchant.

PRINGLE, WALTER aged 29 years married to BUIST, AGNES EWING aged 20 years April 8, 1890 by Rev. C. C. Pinckney at Grace Church. Both natives of Charleston. He a merchant.

PRIOLEAU, ANNIE G. aged 28 years married to DENT, SIDNEY aged 39 years April 29, 1893 by Rev. John Johnson at St. Philip's Church. He a native of the United States and she of Charleston. He an insurance agent.

PRIOLEAU, ELIAS aged 31 years married to SINKLER, CLARE L. aged 25 years June 1, 1893 by Rev. Charles S. Vedder at the Huguenot Church. He a native of Cordesville, South Carolina and she of Charleston. He a cotton shipper.

PRIOLEAU, ISABELLA KINLOCH aged 24 years married to FULLER, THOMAS aged 23 years April 3, 1883 by Rev. Charles S. Vedder at the Huguenot Church. Both natives of Charleston. He works for the railroad.

PRIOLEAU, THOMAS G. married to TUCKER, MARY POST January 31, 1885 by Rev. William H. Campbell at St. Paul's Church. Both natives of Charleston. He a clerk.

PRITCHARD, C. married to MONSERRAT, J. P. aged 27 years January 21, 1882 by Father J. J. Monaghan at St. Patrick's Roman Catholic Church. He a native of Spain and she of South Carolina. He a shoemaker.

PRITCHARD, EUGENE P. aged 24 years married to ARTMAN, ANSLEY ROSALEE aged 25 years October 6, 1886 by Rev. H. B. Brown at 83 Beaufain Street. He a native of Jacksonboro, South Carolina and she of Charleston. He works for the railroad.

PROCTOR, SAMUEL aged 35 years married to HEMMINGWAY, ELIZA M. SEIGNIOUS aged 35 years April 11, 1878 by Rev. J. T. Wightman at the residence of the bride's father - in Cannon Street. Both natives of Charleston. He a bookkeeper.

PRUNTY, MARY married to REILLY, WILLIAM April 3, 1888 by Father P. J. Wilson at St. Patrick's Roman Catholic Church. Both natives of Charleston. He a laborer.

PUCKHABER, GEORGE aged 27 years married to BOTTYER (?), BECHA aged 27 years October 22, 1893 by Rev. K. Boldt in Thomas Street. Both natives of Germany. He a merchant.

PUCKHABER, GEORGE LUDWIG aged 21 years married to STENDER, HENRIETTA JOHANNA aged 19 years November 19, 1889 by Rev. Louis Muller at the residence of the Groom's mother at 466 King Street above Ann Street. He a native of Charleston and she of Prussia. He a baker.

PUCKHABER, GESCHE aged 29 years married to BULWINKLE, JOHANN H. aged 35 years May 29, 1887 by Rev. Louis Muller at the southwest corner of Coming and Line Streets. Both natives of Germany. He a grocer.

PUCKHABER, HERMAN H. aged 29 years married to LILIENTHAL, AMANDA M. aged 27 years November 19,1891 by Rev. Louis Muller at 466 King Street. Both natives of Charleston. He a baker.

PUCKHABER, JOHANN HEINRICH aged 27 years married to STENDER, ANNA aged 17 years March 4, 1883 by Rev. Louis Muller at 490 King Street. He a native of Charleston and she of Germany. He a baker.

PUCKHABER, JOHN F. aged 29 years married to HALPIN, MARY E. aged 25 years April 16, 1893 by Father J. J. Monaghan at 199 Coming Street. Both natives of Charleston. He a baker.

PUCKHABER, LUCIE aged 36 years married to HILDERBRANDT, JACOB aged 45 years June 19, 1884 by Rev. Louis Muller. Both natives of Germany. He a grocer in Jacksonville, Florida.

PUCKHABER, WILLIAM H. aged 31 years married to BRANDT, ADELINE C. aged 24 years October 29, 1891 by Rev. Louis Muller at 466 King Street. He a native of Charleston and she of Walhalla, South Carolina. He a baker.

PUFF, E. B. aged 24 years married to ANATASH, ANDREW aged 28 years November 12, 1895 by Father J. J. Monaghan at 371 Meeting Street. He a native of Constantinople and she of Charleston. He a merchant.

PUGH, G. D. aged 31 years married to HODGES, LOUISE aged 26 years October 10, 1893 by Rev. David M. Ramsey at the Osceola Hotel.

PULTING, THADIA O. aged 22 years married to HASELTON, WALTER E. aged 24 years April 22, 1891 by Rev. G. R. Brackett at 648 King Street. He a native of Charleston and she of Richmond, Virginia. He a machinist.

PULTZ, LAURA E. aged 18 years married to BENTON, JOHN W. aged 21 years September 20, 1890 by Rev. J. Thomas Pate at 231 Coming Street. He a native of Laurens County, South Carolina and she of Charleston. He a clerk.

PUNDT, AUGUSTUS N. aged 21 years married to KIMMEY, MARGARET A. aged 20 years May 22, 1884 by Rev. J. H. Tillinghast at 22 Amherst Street. He a native of Charleston and she of Augusta, Georgia. He a merchant.

PUNDT, EDITH FLORA aged 18 years married to SCHELLING, AUGUST aged 28 years December 17, 1884 by Rev. Robert Wilson at 43 Hanover Street. Both natives of Charleston. He a mechanic.

PUNDT, FLORENCE S. aged 18 years married to EISEMAN, VAN aged 24 years December 1, 1881 by Rev. R. W. Memminger at 43 Hanover Street. He a native of South Carolina and she of Charleston.

PUNDT, JANIE A. aged 24 years married to LOPEZ, JOSEPH P. aged 31 years November 14, 1884 by Rev. Luther K. Probst. He a native of Austria and she of Charleston. He a fruitier.

PUNDT, MARIANNE aged 20 years married to SHARP, ALBERT A. aged 25 years November 30, 1895 by Rev. J. C. Yongue at 14 Hampstead Square. He a native of Orangeburg, South Carolina and she of Charleston. He works for the railroad in Jamison, South Carolina.

PURCELL, JOHN aged 36 years married to BUTLER, ELLA aged 21 years May 29, 1884 by Father P. L. Duffy at The Cathedral of St. John the Baptist. He a native of Ireland and she of Union, South Carolina. He an engineer.

PURCELL, LIZZIE A. aged 16 years married to TRAYNOR, CHARLES E. August 24, 1885 by Father F. J. Shadler at St .Joseph's Church. He a native of Ireland and she of Charleston. He a policeman.

PURSE, CARRIE W. aged 23 years married to WELCH, STEPHEN L. aged 27 years April 14, 1892 by Rev. Edwin C. Dargan at 29 Nassau Street. He a native of Orangeburg, South Carolina and she of Charleston. He an engineer.

PURSE, MARY E. aged 27 years married to CANNON, FRANKLIN E. aged 27 years January 15, 1885 by Rev. Charles A. Stakely at 10 Hanover Street.

PURSE, MARY ROBERTA aged 19 years married to LAMB, ROBERT L. aged 22 years March 2, 1884 by Rev. J. H. Tillinghast at 15 Nassau Street. He a native of Wilmington, North Carolina and she of Charleston. He a gardener.

PURSE, VIOLA aged 19 years married to BALDWIN, STEPHEN aged 25 years March 11, 1891 by Rev. John Johnson at 1 Cooper's Court.

PARSELL, ETTA M. aged 22 years married to DAVENPORT, W. H. aged 24 years December 25, 1880 by Rev. L. H. Shuck. Both natives of Charleston. He a printer.

PURTELL, MATTIE V. aged 22 years married to REEVES, EDWIN T. aged 26 years July 25, 1886 by Father F. A. Schmetz at St. Patrick's Roman Catholic Church. Both natives of Charleston. He works for the railroad.

PYATT, MARTHA HAYES married to HEYWARD, JOHN BOYKIN April 15, 1886 by Rev. William H. Campbell at St. Paul's Church.

QUICK, ELIZABETH aged 24 years LIZABETH married to WHALEY, JOSEPH B. aged 22 years March 31, 1884 by Rev. John E. Beard at 5 Johnson Court. Both natives of Charleston. He a laborer.

QUICK, MARY J. aged 16 years married to TOWELL, CHARLES W. aged 19 years March 19, 1885 by Rev. J. V. Welch at 6 Spring Street. Both natives of Charleston. He a laborer.

QUINAIN (?), JULIA ANN married to ENRIGHT, THOMAS August 9, 1881 by Rev. R. W. Memminger at 23 Legare Street.

QUINCY, WILLIAM F. married to SLAWSON, MARIAN November 25, 1891 by Rev. William H. Campbell. He an express company messenger.

QUINLAN, JAMES W. aged 24 years married to SHERIDAN, ELIZABETH aged 19 years May 2, 1893 by Father Joseph D. Budds at St. Mary of the Annunciation Roman Catholic Church. Both natives of Charleston. He a merchant.

QUINLAN, MICHAEL aged 50 years married to MOORE, BRIDGET aged 50 years February 21, 1879 by Father A. P. Northrop at St. Patrick's Roman Catholic Church. Both natives of Ireland. He a gardener.

QUINLIN, MARGARET aged 19 years married to INABINETT, DANIEL W. aged 20 years July 16, 1884 by Father F. A. Schmetz at St. Patrick's Roman Catholic Church. Both natives of Charleston. He works for the railroad.

QUINLIVAN, ELLEN T. aged 18 years married to DeANTONIO, PAUL J. aged 20 years January 15, 1893 by Father J. J. Monaghan at St. Patrick's Roman Catholic Church.

QUINLIVAN (?), JOHN EDWARD aged 29 years married to RAFTER, MARY aged 27 years October 13, 1891 by Father J. J. Monaghan at St. Patrick's Roman Catholic Church.

QUINLIVAN, MARY E. aged 23 years married to HOWARD, JOHN J. aged 23 years March 3, 1889 by Father J. J. Monaghan at St. Patrick's Roman Catholic Church. Both natives of Charleston. He a carpenter.

QUINN, DAVIS aged 28 years married to GOOLEY, MARGARET aged 26 years September 22, 1878 by Father John P. Twigg at The Cathedral of St. John the Baptist. Both natives of Ireland. He a laborer.

QUINN, HONORIA aged 23 years married to McINNERNEY, LAWRENCE aged 26 years January 1, 1883 by Rev. F. A. Schmetz at St. Patrick's Roman Catholic Church. Both natives of Charleston. He a carpenter.

QUINN, MARY E. aged 18 years married to MURPHY, LAWRENCE aged 22 years February 3, 1884 by Father John P. Twigg at St. Patrick's Roman Catholic Church. Both natives of Charleston. He a clerk.

QUINN, PATRICK aged 33 years married to HASSETT, NELLIE aged 22 years October 17, 1888 by Father F. J. Shadler at St. Joseph's Roman Catholic Church.

QUINN, SAMUEL aged 25 years married to JACKSON, MARTHA aged 19 years June 17, 1885 by Rev. John E. Beard at 7 Harris Street. He a native of South Carolina and she of Georgia. He a laborer.

RADEMANN, G. F. aged 22 years married to MANGELS, ANNA M. aged 23 years February 5, 1880 by Rev. Louis Muller at the St. Matthew's Lutheran Church. Both natives of Hanover. He owns a restaurant.

RADEMANN, META aged 20 years married to SCHWACKE, CARL L. aged 31 years February 21, 1886 by Rev. Louis Muller. Both natives of Germany. He a merchant.

RAFER, HENRY B. aged 35 years married to HARBY, A. GERTRUDE aged 17 years January 14, 1886 by Rev. C. C. Pinckney at 159 Wentworth Street. He a native of New Orleans, Louisiana and she of South Carolina. He a farmer in Fairfield, South Carolina.

RAFFERTY, JOHN F. aged 29 years married to CARNEY, MARGARET aged 23 years June 17, 1895 by Father Daniel J. Quigley at St. Patrick's Roman Catholic Church. Both natives of Charleston. He a machinist.

RAFTER, MARY aged 27 years married to QUINLIVAN (?), JOHN EDWARD aged 29 years October 13, 1891 by Father J. J. Monaghan at St. Patrick's Roman Catholic Church. Both natives of Charleston. He a clerk.

RAGON, HARVEY F. aged 22 years married to WISE, AGNES aged 17 years August 29, 1895 by Rev. J. L. Stokes. He a native of Chattanooga, Tennessee and she of Charleston. He a basketmaker.

RAHALL, MARY LOUISE aged 23 years married to KERR, FRANK BERNARD aged 25 years April 16, 1890 by Father J. J. Monaghan at St. Patrick's Roman Catholic Church. He a native of New York and she of Charleston. He a mechanic in Orangeburg, South Carolina.

RAINIER, CHARLES E. aged 45 years married to McCAFFER, JANE WALKER aged 33 years May 9, 1885 by Rev. G. R. Brackett. He a native of New Jersey and she of Charleston. He an engineer.

RAM, E. aged 32 years married to PERLESSEN, P. aged 23 years July 25, 1882 by Rev. Louis Muller at 3 Mile House. He a native of South Carolina and a mariner.

RAMBLEY, SALLIE E. aged 20 years married to DUFF, AUGUST F. aged 25 years January 6, 1892 by Rev. William A. Rogers at Trinity Church. He a steward at the Charleston Hotel.

RAMSEY, M. G. married to WILSON, E. M. aged 27 years December 30, 1879 by Rev. Edward T. Horn at St. Johannes Lutheran Church. He a native of Savannah, Georgia and she of Charleston. He a clerk.

RANDALL, MARY R. married to WRAGG, JOHN F. aged 33 years October 15, 1891 by Rev. Edwin C. Dargan at 20 Sheppard Street. He a native of Charleston and she of Columbus, Georgia. He a millwinger.

RANKIN, ISADORA aged 27 years married to STEWART, WILLIAM aged 33 years July 9, 1889 by Rev. J. E. Carlisle in Addison's Court. He a native of Philadelphia, Pennsylvania and she of Charleston. He works for the railroad.

RANKIN, PHYLLIS aged 19 years married to GIBBS, HENRY D. aged 24 years March 8, 1894 by Rev. David M. Ramsey at 46 Rutledge Avenue. Both natives of New York. He an actor in Troy, New York.

RANTEN, J. aged 33 years married to BURTON, E. J. aged 18 December 25, 1882 by Rev. J. V. Welch in Paines Court. He a native of Charleston and a tinner.

RANTIN, MAGGIE ELIZA aged 18 years married to WEATHERFORD, WILLIAM aged 21 years April 4, 1894 by Rev. J. C. Yongue at 14 Hampstead Square. He a native of South Carolina and she of Savannah, Georgia. He a wood turner and machinist.

RANTIN, THOMAS BERNARD aged 22 years married to CURTIS, ARTIMISHA EVELINE aged 17 years November 11, 1883 by Rev. J. H. Tellinghast at 23 Inspection Street. Both natives of Charleston. He a tinner.

RASHBAUM, HENRY aged 27 years married to BAUM, EMMA BROWN aged 23 years December 27, 1887 by Rabbi David Levy at the Hasell Street Synagogue.

RAUL, AUGUSTE HENRIETTA CAROLINE aged 25 years married to WESSEN, FREDERICK HEINRICH aged 33 years July 3, 1884 by Rev. Louis Muller in Nassau Street near Jackson Street. Both natives of Germany. He a carpenter.

RAVENEL, ANNA ELIZA aged 30 years married to SASS, GEO HERBERT aged 37 years December 20, 1883 by Rev. Charles S. Vedder at the Huguenot Church. Both natives of Charleston. He a lawyer.

RAVENEL, EMILY CHARDON aged 21 years married to WALKER, ROBERT MURDOCH aged 25 years February 18, 1890 by Rev. Charles S. Vedder at the Huguenot Church. He a native of Columbia, South Carolina and she of South Carolina.

RAVENEL, H. aged 24 years married to CAMPSEN, ANNIE A. aged 24 years January 21, 1881 by Father Daniel J. Quigley at The Cathedral of St. John the Baptist. Both natives of Charleston. He a clerk.

RAVENEL, H. aged 24 years married to CAMPSEN, ANNIE A. aged 24 years January 21, 1881 by Father D. J. Quigley at The Cathedral of St. John the Baptist.

RAVENEL, LOUIS married to JUNKINS, JULIA aged 24 years February 20, 1884 by Rev. W. F. Jenkins. He a native of Charleston and she of Virginia. He an agent in Atlanta, Georgia.

RAVENEL, WILLIAM B. aged 21 years married to ELLIS, JEANNIE G. aged 22 years November 9, 1880 by Rev. John Johnson at St. Philip's Church. He a native of Charleston and she of Leon County, Florida. He a merchant.

RAWORTH, T. S. aged 23 years married to MARKLEY, J. P. November 13, 1878 by Rev. J. Mercier Green. He a native of Aiken, South Carolina and she of Charleston. He works for the railroad.

RAY, ALICE ELIZABETH aged 23 years married to AHRENS, GEORGE FRANKLIN aged 35 years December 29, 1886 by Rev. Charles S. Vedder at 97 Tradd Street. Both natives of Charleston. He a carpenter.

RAY, LUCY E. aged 18 years married to DAVIS, ALEXANDER aged 30 years March 17, 1884 by Rev. J. H. Tillinghast at the corner of Blake and America Streets. He a native of Smithfield, North Carolina and she of Aiken, South Carolina. He a baker.

RAY, WILLIAM aged 28 years married to O'CONNOR, MARY A. aged 25 years June 10, 1891 by Father J. J. Monaghan. He a native of Louisville, Kentucky and she of Charleston. He a works in the phosphate mill.

RAYMOND, THOMAS married to WILEY, HENRIETTA August 13, 1879 by William B. Yates, Chaplain. Both natives of Charleston.

READ, BENJAMIN HUGER aged 27 years married to SMITH, ANNE CLELAND aged 27 years December 9, 1884 by Rev. John Johnson at 18 Meeting Street. Both natives of Charleston. He a cotton broker in Baltimore, Maryland.

READ, ELLA W. aged 38 years married to BRUNSON, JOHN B. aged 56 years December 12, 1893 by Rev. C. C. Pinckney at 10 Legare Street. He a native of Darlington, South Carolina and she of Charleston. He a mechanic in Orangeburg, South Carolina.

READ, EMILY married to FOZ, JOSEPH M. May 10, 1883 by Rev. Richard S. Trapier at 26 South Bay Street.

READ, WILLIAM BOND aged 30 years married to MATHERSON, FLORA McCRAE aged 30 years February 17, 1885 by Rev. John Johnson at the residence of Dr. William M. Huger. He a native of South Carolina and she of Charleston. He a planter on the Savannah River.

REDMUND, A. aged 17 years married to ROOKS, M. aged 22 years February 5, 1882 by Rev. L. H. Shuck. He a native of South Carolina and a carpenter.

REDMOND, DAVID aged 24 years married to ANDERSON, (Mrs.) JANE WINDHAM aged 39 years August 3, 1885 by Rev. John E. Beard. He a native of Charleston and she of South Carolina.

REDMOND, STEPHEN aged 32 years married to BLAKE, KATIE August 7, 1893 by Father J. J. Monaghan.

REED, JAMES M. aged 25 years married to LEVETTE, ELIZABETH R. aged 19 years April 26, 1891 by Father J. J. Monaghan at St. Patrick's Roman Catholic Church. He a native of Charleston and she of Georgia. He a woodworker.

REED, JAMES POWELL aged 37 years married to SIGWALD, LOUISE LOCKWOOD aged 23 years December 10, 1885 by Rev. Luther K. Probst at the Wentworth Street

Lutheran Church. He a native of Wilmington, Delaware and she of Charleston. He a car builder.

REEDER, ANNIE A. aged 29 years married to WHITE, GEORGE M. aged 32 years April 29, 1895 by Father J. J. Monaghan at 260 Coming Street. He a native of Oconee, County, Georgia and she of Montreal, Canada. He a farmer in Walhalla, South Carolina.

REEDER, OSWALD married to SIMMONS, JULIA June 26, 1883 by Rev. William H. Campbell.

REESE, CHARLES M. aged 31 years married to HAYDEN, JULIA H. aged 30 years February 14, 1893 by Rev. John Johnson. He a native of Statesboro, Georgia and she of Charleston. He a physician.

REEVES, EDWARD LEROY married to ZIEGLER, GEORGINA April 14, 1879 by William B. Yates.

REEVES, EDWIN T. aged 26 years married to PURTELL, MATTIE V. aged 22 years July 25, 1886 by Father F. A. Schmetz at St. Patrick's Roman Catholic Church. Both natives of Charleston. He works for the railroad.

REEVES, EDWIN T. aged 32 years married to WAGENER, ALETHA aged 21 years October 29, 1891 by Rev. Edward T. Horn at Sullivans Island, South Carolina. Both natives of Charleston. He works for the railroad.

REEVES, LIZZIE SUSAN aged 17 years married to LaMOTTE, HENRY JAMES aged 29 years November 29, 1883 by Rev. A. C. Smith in Drake Street. Both natives of Charleston. He a carpenter.

REEVES, NINNIE E. aged 19 years married to MELCHERS, LOUIS A. aged 21 years August 16, 1887 by Rev. Louis Muller. Both natives of South Carolina. He a merchant.

REEVES, WILLIAM L. aged 22 years married to HASELTON, JULIA C. aged 26 years July 31, 1879 by Rev. H. F. Chreitzberg at 56 America Street.

REEVES, WILLIAM L. aged 43 years married to GOODWIN, (Mrs.) GENEVIEVE Baker aged 37 years June 14, 1888 by Rev. C. C. Pinckney at Grace Church. Both natives of Charleston. He a woodworker.

REGAN, JOHN J. aged 31 years married to MULVANEY, CATHARINE V. aged 31 years June 22, 1892 by Father Joseph D. Budds at The Cathedral of St. John the Baptist.

REHKOPF, ANNA C. aged 21 years married to MEYER, JOHAN F. aged 25 years April 28, 1887 by Rev. Louis Muller. Both natives of Charleston. He a grocer.

REHKOPF, FREDERICK G. aged 55 years married to STRECKFUSS, (Mrs.) CHRISTINE MEYER aged 54 years February 7, 1884 by Rev. Louis Muller at 66 Radcliffe Street. Both natives of Germany. He an undertaker.

REHKOPF, FREDERICK GEORGE aged 24 years married to LAW, ANNA CATHARINA aged 20 years June 28, 1888 by Rev. Louis Muller at the residence of the Bride's father - the southeast corner of St. Philip and Cannon Streets.

REHKOPF, HENRY aged 22 years married to MURPHY, MARY aged 20 years February 15, 1892 by Father J. J. Monaghan at St. Patrick's Roman Catholic Church. Both natives of Charleston. He an undertaker.

REHKOPF (?), L. A. aged 25 years married to KUHLEN, J. F. aged 30 years November 27, 1879 by Rev. Louis Muller. He a native of Hanover and a grocer. She a native of Charleston.

REHKOPF, WILHELM G. aged 24 years married to MEYER, DORA LUCIA aged 17 years November 5, 1885 by Rev. Louis Muller at the St. Matthew's Lutheran Church. Both natives of Charleston. He a cabinetmaker.

REICH, MARIE L. aged 22 years married to HECKEL, PAUL G. aged 25 years August 8, 1892 by Rev. K. Boldt at 319 King Street. He a native of Illinois and she of Charleston. He a clergyman in Texas.

REID, ANNA CATHERINE aged 24 years married to STELLO, HERMANN aged 28 years September 12, 1878 by Rev. W. S. Bowman in Spring Street near King Street. He a native of Hanover and she of Charleston. He a laborer..

REID, HENRY B. aged 25 years married to MEGGETT, FLORENCE ESTELLE aged 22 years February 18, 1891 by Rev. Edwin C. Dargan at 24 Rutledge Avenue. He a native of Rock Hill, South Carolina and she of Beaufort, South Carolina. He a clerk in Summerville, South Carolina.

REID, MARY A. aged 26 years married to CRAIG, JOHN E. aged 26 years February 23, 1887 by Father Daniel J. Quigley at St. Patrick's Roman Catholic Church. Both natives of Charleston. He a painter.

REID, WILHELMINA aged 19 years married to ANSALDO, WALTER aged 23 years January 15, 1885 by Father Daniel J. Quigley at St. Patrick's Roman Catholic Church. Both natives of Charleston. He an engineer.

REILLY, EDWARD C. aged 27 years married to DeCAMPS, CLARA E. aged 22 years April 26, 1883 by Father John P. Twigg at St. Patrick's Roman Catholic Church. Both natives of Charleston. He a clerk.

REILLY, WILLIAM married to PRUNTY, MARY April 3, 1888 by Father P. J. Wilson at St. Patrick's Roman Catholic Church. Both natives of Charleston. He a laborer.

REILS, M. S. R. aged 24 years married to MEYER, J. D. E. aged 37 years January 14, 1886 by Rev. Louis Muller. He a native of Germany and she of Charleston. He a grocer.

REILS, W. F. aged 22 years married to SMITH, G. E. aged 20 years December 30, 1880 by Rev. Johannes Heckel at 125 Calhoun Street. Both natives of Charleston. He a blacksmith.

REINCKE, RUDOLPH aged 27 years married to MULLER, AUGUSTE aged 22 years July 29, 1880 by Rev. Johannes Heckel at 125 Calhoun Street. He a native of Hanover and she of Prussia. He a merchant.

REINHARDT, ALINE aged 23 years married to RUGHEIMER, JOHN aged 41 years February 23, 1879 by Rev. Louis Muller in King Street. Both natives of Bavaria. He a tailor.

REINDHARDT, MARIA M. F. aged 28 years married to WOHLERS, BERNARD aged 43 years February 23, 1891 by Rev. Louis Muller at the residence of Mr. Rugheimer at 154 King Street. Both natives of Germany. He a merchant.

REMBERT, THOMAS F. A. aged 27 years married to DEIGHEN, MARY SARAH aged 20 years April 23, 1878 by Rev. William H. Hanckel at 115 Queen Street. He a native of Charleston and she of Havana, Cuba. He a tinsmith.

REMION, LOUIS aged 47 years married to WILDREN, MATILDA aged 40 years July 27, 1885 by Father Daniel J. Quigley at St. Patrick's Roman Catholic Church. Both natives of France. He a merchant.

RENKEN, HEINRICH aged 33 years married to SCHULTZ, (Mrs.) DOROTHY DUNNEMANN aged 33 years April 26, 1891 by Rev. Louis Muller at the corner of Morris and Smith Streets. He a native of Hanover and she of Germany. He a grocer.

RENKEN, HEINRICH aged 33 years married to KUCK, ADELAIDE ENTELMANN aged 35 years December 15, 1887 by Rev. Louis Muller at the southeast corner of Meeting and Columbus Streets.

RENNEKER, WALTER E. aged 24 years married to HUTSON, KATIE aged 21 years October 8, 1895 by Rev. W. T. Thompson at the First Presbyterian Church. Both natives of Charleston. He works for the railroad.

REVEL, LIZZIE ANN married to BRODIE, ALEXANDER L. February 26, 1879 by Father Daniel J. Quigley at The Cathedral of St. John the Baptist. He a native of Columbia, South Carolina and she of Charleston. He a clerk in Columbia, South Carolina.

REYELL, BESSIE aged 15 years married to BARNEE, J. aged 23 years November 2, 1890 by Rev. Charley Shevett at 7 Stone Court.

REYLEA, BENJAMIN H. married to MYER, LOUISA T. November 3, 1878 by William B. Yates, Chaplain. He a laborer.

REYLEA, JANE B. married to BELDING, JASPER March 22, 1879 by William B. Yates, Chaplain.

REYLEA, M. A. aged 16 years married to STROBLE, R. aged 23 years December 26, 1882 by Rev. J. V. Welsh at 2 Fishburne Street. He a native of Charleston and a laborer.

REYNOLDS, ADELE aged 35 years married to CLARK, HENRY aged 50 years April 28, 1880 by Father Claudian B. Northrop at St. Mary of the Annunciation Roman Catholic Church. He a native of Scotland and she of Washington, D. C. He a resident of Jacksonville, Florida and she of Buffalo, New York. He a merchant.

REYNOLDS, EDWARD JAMES aged 33 years married to KEEGAN, MARY ELIZABETH aged 22 years April 20, 1884 by Father F. J. Shadler at St. Joseph's Roman Catholic Church. He a native of New York and she of Charleston. He a stonecutter.

REYNOLDS, FRANK aged 25 years married to McNAMARA, CATHARINE aged 40 years May 23, 1895 by Rev. Charles S. Vedder. He a native of Italy and she of Charleston. He a mariner in Savannah, Georgia.

REYNOLDS, JOHN aged 60 years married to GRIFFIN, MARY aged 47 years November 12, 1880 by Rev. J. V. Welsh at the corner of Rodgers Alley and St. Philip Street. He a native of Ireland and she of St. Paul's, South Carolina. He a laborer.

REYNOLDS, THOMAS H. aged 26 years married to SMYTHE, MARY F. aged 22 years April 29, 1880 by Father P. L. Duffy at The Cathedral of St. John the Baptist. He a native of New York and she of Charleston. He a stonemason.

301

REYNOLDS, WILLIAM TOWNSEND aged 24 years married to MATTHEWS, ELIZABETH J. aged 22 years December 16, 1881 by Rev. John Johnson at 16 Amherst Street. He a native of Alabama and she of Charleston. He a clerk.

RHETT, ANN B. aged 19 years married to PRESTON, HENRY K. aged 25 years December 27, 1888 by Rev. John Johnson at St. Philip's Church. Both natives of Charleston. He a clerk.

RHETT, CHARLOTTE married to INGLE, JAMES A. August 2, 1894 by Rev. William H. Campbell at St. Paul's Church. He a missionary to China.

RHETT, ELIZABETH G. aged 23 years married to TRENHOLM, EDWARD G. aged 23 years December 17, 1889 by Rev. John Johnson at St. Philip's Church. He a native of Buncombe County, North Carolina and she of South Carolina. He a merchant.

RHETT, JOSEPHINE H. aged 30 years married to BACOT, DANIEL HUGER aged 41 years January 19, 1888 by Rev. John Johnson at St. Philip's Church. He a native of Charleston and she of Alabama. He a merchant.

RHETT, MARIE ALICE aged 25 years married to STUART, WILLIAM C. aged 26 years October 15, 1892 by Rev. Albert R. Stuart. He a native of Richland County, South Carolina and she of Charleston. He a lawyer in Newport News, Virginia.

RHETT, MARY B. married to SIMONDS, LOUIS D. December 11, 1894 by Rev. William H. Campbell at St. Paul's Church. He a bank officer.

RHETT, R. GOODWYN aged 27 years married to WHALEY, HELEN SMITH aged 20 years November 15, 1888 by Rev. C. C. Pinckney at Grace Church. He a native of Columbia, South Carolina and she of Charleston. He a lawyer.

RHOADES, JENNIE M. married to HOCKADAY, JOHN B. February 2, 1885 by Rev. William H. Campbell. He a clerk.

RHOADES, LOTTIE married to TURNER, WILLIAM S. April 14, 1891 by Rev. William H. Campbell. He resides in Greenville, South Carolina.

RHODES, ROSA aged 22 years married to HOLLMAN, HENRY aged 28 years June 7, 1891 by Rev. W. A. Betts. at 4 Williams Court. He a native of Sumter County, South Carolina and she of Georgetown, South Carolina. He a clerk.

RHODES, WILLIAM E. aged 25 years married to LINGE, HELENE HENRIETTE aged 20 years October 7, 1886 by Rev. Louis Muller at the southeast corner of Meeting and Line Streets. He a native of Augusta, Georgia and she of Charleston. He a mill hand.

RHODES, W. E. aged 23 years married to EAGLE, J. E. aged 21 years January 8, 1884 by Rev. R. A. Lapsley at 88 America Street. He a native of Augusta, Georgia and she of Baltimore, Maryland. He works in a factory.

RICE, CHARLES D. aged 31 years married to DEVEAUX, MARY E. aged 31 years June 20, 1894 by Rev. C. C. Pinckney at 16 Limehouse Street. He a native of Walterboro, South Carolina and she of Charleston. He works for a newspaper in Walterboro.

RICE, HORACE S. aged 32 years married to BARTON, EMMA J. aged 18 years April 23, 1890 by Rev. John Johnson at 53 Church Street. She a native of Charleston.

RICH, ALBERT M. aged 38 years married to ERWIN, SALLIE M. aged 28 years February 8, 1893 by Rev. Charles S. Vedder at 16 College Street. He a native of Blue City, Maine and she of South Carolina. He a mariner in New York.

RICH, MANUEL aged 35 years married to BARINOE, SARAH aged 27 years May 2, 1886 by Rev. C. E. Chichester at the Old Planters Hotel. He a native of Cadiz, Spain and she of Pee Dee, South Carolina. He a fisherman.

RICHARDS, JOHN R. aged 25 years married to McMILLAN, CORNELIA E. aged 24 years January 3, 1878 by Rev. T. E. Wannamaker at 127 St. Philip Street. Both natives of Charleston. He a planter in Orangeburg, South Carolina.

RICHARDS, SUSAN VILLEPONTEAUX aged 32 years married to ROBERTS, THEOPHILUS N. aged 42 years December 1, 1881 by Rev. Charles S. Vedder. He a native of Savannah, Georgia and she of South Carolina. He a physician in Columbia, South Carolina.

RICHARDSON, CHARLES aged 25 years married to GRIMM, E. aged 16 years May 12, 1880 by Rev. R. N. Mills in Hasell Street. Both natives of New York. He a mariner.

RICHARDSON, CHARLES E. married to HARRISON, H. MEACHER April 27, 1879 by William B. Yates, Chaplain. Both natives of Charleston. He a bellsmith.
RICHARDSON, DAVISON M. married to CORDES, LAVINIA C. December 28, 1881 by Rev. William H. Campbell. He a planter.

RICHARDSON, DAVISON married to SIMONS, JEANNIE R. December 30, 1891 by Rev. William H. Campbell. He a planter in Sumter, South Carolina.

RICHARDSON, R. C. aged 23 years married to DRISCOLL, J. A. aged 18 years December 30, 1879 by Father Daniel J. Quigley in Wharf Street. He a native of Charleston and she of Coldspring, New York. He a pressman.

RICHBOURG, SARAH ELIZABETH married to SCARVEY (?), JAMES FRANCIS aged 25 years May 4, 1890 by Father F. J. Shadler at St. Joseph's Roman Catholic Church. Both natives of Charleston. He a policeman.

RICHBURG, MARY M. aged 19 years married to HOPPMAN, WILLIAM aged 19 years July 10, 1887 by Father F. J. Shadler at St. Joseph's Roman Catholic Church. Both natives of Charleston. He an ironworker.

RICHMOND, LIZZIE B. aged 23 years married to BOOZER, SIMON P. aged 24 years February 17, 1886 by Rev. A. Hirschmeyer at 54 Society Street. He a native of South Carolina and she of Charleston. He works for the railroad.

RICHON, A. C. aged 26 years married to BOYD, ANNIE aged 16 years May 17, 1883 by Rev. J. A. Clifton at 32 Columbus Street. Both natives of Charleston. He a clerk.

RICHTER, ADELIA aged 19 years married to HOTTINGER, CHRISTOPHER aged 23 years November 4, 1890 by Rev. K. Boldt at St. Johannes Lutheran Church. He a native of Germany and she of Charleston. He a merchant.

RICHTER, THERESA aged 22 years married to MAPPUS, CHRISTIAN aged 24 years November 4, 1890 by Rev. K. Boldt at St. Johannes Lutheran Church. He a native of Germany and she of Charleston. He a machinist.

RICHTER, WILHELM F. aged 31 years married to ALBRECHT, (Mrs.) JULIANE C. aged 19 years April 7, 1892 by Rev. Louis Muller at the corner of Market and Meeting Streets. He a native of Prussia and she of Charleston. He an agent for the Palmetto Brewery.

RICHTER, G. E. aged 24 years married to DUFORT, VIRGINIA aged 20 years December 14, 1890 by Bishop Harry P. Northrop at The Cathedral of St. John the Baptist. Both natives of Charleston. He a salesman.

RICHTER, HENRIETTA R. D. C. aged 25 years married to WEILE, FRANTZ L. aged 27 years March 24, 1885 by Rev. Louis Muller at 16 Archdale Street. Both natives of Charleston. He a baker.

RICKELS, DORIS REBECCA aged 17 years married to SMITH, AUGUST W. aged 22 years January 8, 1884 by Rev. Johannes Heckel at 55 Smith Street. He a native of Augusta, Georgia and she of South Carolina. He a blacksmith.

RICKLES, ELIZABETH M. aged 18 years married to SHERIDAN, MATTHEW P. aged 23 years April 27, 1884 by Rev. P. L. Duffy at The Cathedral of St. John the Baptist. Both natives of Charleston. He a bookbinder.

RIDGEWAY, L. MANNING aged 31 years married to CLAUSS, LOUISA C. aged 26 years March 4, 1886 by Rev. H. B. Browne at 192 Spring Street. He a native of South Carolina and she of Charleston. He a farmer in Berkeley County, South Carolina.

RIDGEWAY, L. M. aged 28 years married to SCHELLING, C. aged 20 years November 16, 1882 by Rev. E. J. Meynardie at 145 Calhoun Street. He a native of South Carolina and a merchant.

RIECKE, D. AMALIE JOHANNA aged 20 years married to McNEILL, ROBERT aged 29 years July 5, 1888 by Rev. Louis Muller at the residence of the Bride's mother - the corner of Aiken and Blake Streets.

RIELLY, MICHAEL aged 23 years married to BARRY, MARGARET A. aged 21 years May 27, 1886 by Father Thomas E. McCormack at St. Patrick's Roman Catholic Church. Both natives of Charleston. He a clerk.

RIEPER, NICHOLAS W. aged 28 years married to VACH, BARBARA ELIZABETH aged 27 years February 14, 1888 by Rev. Johannes Heckel at the residence of C. N. Doscher at the corner of Meeting and Hasell Streets. He a native of Hanover and she of Nassau. He a merchant.

RIEPPE, HELENE CATHARINE aged 19 years married to BIEMANN, HENRY D. aged 24 years April 21, 1881 by Rev. Louis Muller at the northeast corner of George and St. Philip Streets. He a native of Walhalla, South Carolina and she of Charleston. He a merchant in Walhalla.

RIEPPE, W. C. A. aged 20 years married to MEHRTENS, J. H. aged 26 years October 19, 1880 by Rev. Louis Muller at the St. Matthew's Lutheran Church. Both natives of Charleston. He a miller.

RIERHERS, M. F. N. aged 28 years married to GRIMBO, MARY ELIZABETH aged 27 years December 2, 1880 by Rev. Louis Muller at 66 Radcliffe Street. He a native of Charleston and a mariner. Both natives of Charleston. He a mariner.

RIGBERS, CATHARINE MARGARETHE aged 25 years married to BEQUEST, JOHANN LUDWIG aged 35 years April 8, 1883 by Rev. Louis Muller at 8 Calhoun Street. Both natives of Germany. He a mariner.

RIGGS, CORNELIUS T. aged 17 years married to BRIGMAN, MAGGIE M. aged 15 years September 5, 1893 by Rev. J. O. Yongue at 22.5 Sheppard Street. He a native of Jedburg, South Carolina and she of Edgefield, South Carolina. He works in the cotton factory.

RIGGS, JOHN S. aged 54 years married to MARSHALL, (Mrs.) M. REYNOLDS LEITCH aged 33 years June 5, 1878 by Rev. Charles S. Vedder at Sullivans Island, South Carolina. He a native of Norfolk, Virginia and she of Charleston. He the president of the City Railroad.

RIGGS, JULIUS aged 22 years married to BURTON, MARY aged 17 years October 12, 1886 by Rev. H. B. Browne at 206 St. Philip Street.

RIGGS, JULIUS aged 20 years married to McROSE, EMILY aged 13 years December 18, 1884 by Rev. John E. Beard at 64 Nassau Street. Both natives of Charleston. He a laborer.

RIGGS, MINNIE M. aged 16 years married to FLACKMAN ,ISRAEL aged 22 years February 13, 1887 by Rev. Robert Wilson at St. Luke's Chapel. He a native of South Carolina and she of Charleston. He works in a factory.

RIGGS, SUSAN MARY married to JERVEY, JAMES D. February 26, 1879 by Rev. William C. Power. He a native of Christ Church Parish, South Carolina and she of Charleston. He a clerk.

RIGGS, THOMAS L. aged 38 years married to CUBSTEDT (Mrs.) REBECCA SINGLETARY aged 35 years December 27, 1893 by Rev. Edmund Wells at 23 Spring Street. He a native of Savannah, Georgia and she of Charleston. He a clergyman.

RIGGS, WALTER aged 25 years married to SHINGLER, ELLA aged 22 years January 12, 1881 by Rev. L. H. Shuck at 5 South Bay Street. Both natives of Charleston. He a collector.

RIGHER, CATHARINE MARGARETHE aged 25 years married to BEQUEST, JOHANN LUDWIG aged 35 years April 8, 1883 by Rev. Louis Muller at 8 Calhoun Street.

RILEY, ALEX A. aged 26 years married to SULLIVAN, ELLA E. aged 26 years December 26, 1892 by Father J. J. Monaghan at St. Patrick's Roman Catholic Church. Both natives of Charleston. He a blacksmith.

RILEY, ANNIE ELIZABETH aged 19 years married to KNOX, RIPLEY LEE aged 26 years February 11, 1889 by Rev. R. D. Smart at Bethel Church. Both natives of Charleston. He a car driver.

RILEY, JOHN aged 40 years married to O'GRADY, ANNIE aged 26 years February 24, 1895 by Rev. Edmund Wells at 1 McSweeny Court. Both natives of Charleston. He works in the cotton mill.

RILEY, J. A. aged 21 years married to POWERS, M. J. aged 23 years July 16, 1882 by Father P. L. Duffy at St. Mary of the Annunciation Roman Catholic Church. He a native of South Carolina and a clerk.

RILEY, KATE M. aged 26 years married to SCOFIELD, WILLIAM R. aged 31 years March 22, 1887 by Rev. Luther T. Beattie at 231 Coming Street. He a native of New Jersey and she of Charleston. He a mechanic.

RILEY, MARY ANN aged 25 years married to ROCHE, JOHN PATRICK aged 35 years July 8, 1888 by Father Daniel J. Quigley at St. Patrick's Roman Catholic Church. Both natives of Charleston. He a railroad dispatcher.

RILEY, THERESA F. aged 20 years married to LANIGAN, JAMES F. aged 28 years January 3, 1895 by Father Thomas F. Hopkins at St. Mary of the Annunciation Roman Catholic Church. Both natives of Charleston. He works in the phosphate mill in Coosaw, South Carolina.

RIMOND, ANA C. aged 19 years married to ROBERTS, SAMUEL T. aged 25 years November 9, 1884 by Rev. J. V. Welsh at 24 Bee Street. Both natives of Charleston. He a tinner.

RINCK, META aged 32 years married to MANGELS, E. A. aged 34 years May 28, 1891 by Rev. Louis Muller opposite the 3 Mile House. Both natives of Prussia. He a grocer.

RIOLS, JOHN A. married to BICAISE, FLORENCE April 5, 1894 by Father Thomas F. Hopkins at St. Mary of the Annunciation Roman Catholic Church. He a clerk.

RIPKEN, ANTON H. F. aged 31 years married to GRIMES, ROSA ELLIS aged 33 years June 23, 1895 by Rev. C. E. Chichester at 1 Atlantic Street. He a native of Georgia and she of Montiello, Florida. He a clerk in Savannah, Georgia.

RIPLEY, CHARLES S. aged 28 years married to HAUSE (?), KATHERINE M. aged 19 years April 15, 1886 by Rev. G. R. Brackett. Both natives of New York. He a mariner.

RISTIG, A. W. aged 25 years married to HEISENBUTTEL, R. C. aged 18 years December 21, 1879 by Rev. W. S. Bowman at 14 Bee Street. He a native of Germany and she of Charleston. He a grocer.

RITTS, BENJAMIN H. aged 21 years married to KENNEDY, SARAH RIGGS aged 25 years September 9, 1888 by Rev. H. B. Browne at 110 America Street. He a native of Rantowles, South Carolina and she of Charleston. He a moulder.

RIVERS, BESSIE M. aged 18 years married to JENKINS, D. F. aged 31 years June 26, 1889 by Rev. John Johnson. Both natives of Wadmalaw Island, South Carolina. He a storekeeper on Wadmalaw Island.

RIVERS, EDMUND BENNETT aged 36 years married to BENNETT, JOSEPHINE GRIMBALL aged 42 years April 17, 1889 by Rev. Charles S. Vedder at 120 Beaufain Street. Both natives of Charleston. He works for the railroad.

RIVERS, FRANK HOWARD aged 23 years married to PRESCOTT, JULIA ELIZABETH aged 20 years October 7, 1886 by Rev. G. R. Brackett at 74 Coming Street. Both natives of Charleston. He a fireman.

RIVERS, F. LEBBY aged 30 years married to JOHNS, MARY E. L. aged 16 years November 17, 1887 by Rev. John Willson at 79 Washington Street. He a native of Mt. Pleasant, South Carolina and she of Charleston. He a driver.

RIVERS, HENRIETTA aged 23 years married to GIRARDEAU, THOMAS aged 22 years April 5, 1880 by Rev. A. Toomer Porter in King Street. He a native of Charleston and she of Johns Island, South Carolina. He a clerk.

RIVERS, H. G. married to GIRARDEAU, THOMAS G January 28, 1880 by William B. Yates, Chaplain.

RIVERS, JAMES PHILIP aged 25 years married to CANNON, MARY ANNIE aged 23 years July 26, 1881 by Rev. H. F. Chreitzberg at 43 Hanover Street.

RIVERS, LAURENCE WASHINGTON aged 22 years married to MEGGETT, HELOISE M. aged 22 years April 9, 1889 by Rev. Edwin C. Dargan. He a native of Charleston and she of Camden, South Carolina. He a tailor.

RIVERS, LELA aged 15 years married to STRANGHAN, HENRY aged 24 years September 29, 1890 by Rev. R. J. Smart at 207 Calhoun Street. He a native of Charleston and she of Bullock County, Georgia. He in the turpentine business.

RIVERS, LUCIA B. aged 24 years married to VERONEE, WILLIAM C. aged 51 years November 1, 1885 by Rev. J. V. Welsh at 24 Bee Street. He a native of Beaufort, South Carolina and she of Charleston. He a policeman.

RIVERS, MARY A. aged 22 years married to JACOBS, OTTO aged 25 years July 31, 1883 by Rev. A. Coke Smith. Both natives of Charleston. He a salesman.

RIVERS, M. RUTLEDGE married to BUIST, ELIZA INGRAHAM February 2, 1893 by Rev. William H. Campbell at St. Paul's Church. He a lawyer.

RIVERS, RECECCA W. aged 22 years married to MIKELL, EPHRAIN aged 35 years January 16, 1884 by Rev. J. V. Welch at Calvary Church.

RIVERS, WILLIAM McC. aged 31 years married to JOHNSON, ELLEN R. aged 24 years April 19, 1881 by Rev. John Johnson in Wentworth Street.

ROACH, ANNIE T. married to CAMPBELL, ARTHUR M. December 29, 1887 by Rev. William H. Campbell at the residence of E. Roach. He a clerk.

ROACH, C. C. married to McKEE, WILLIAM EDWARD December 29, 1887 by Rev. William H. Campbell at the residence of Edward Roach. He a clerk.

ROACH, LUCIUS C. aged 31 years married to JAEGER, KATIE Z. aged 19 years August 13, 1894 by Rev. Lucius Cuthbert at the First Baptist Church. He a native of Aiken, South Carolina and she of Charleston. He works for the railroad.

ROBB, JAMES J. aged 26 years married to BATEMAN, ELLA ROSA PELZER aged 25 years January 8, 1884 by Rev. E. J. Meynardie in Vanderhorst Street. Both natives of Charleston. He a clerk.

ROBERTS, ADDIE R. BOZARD aged 29 years married to HUCHET, CHARLES F. aged 43 years July 19, 1894 by Rev. Edmund Wells. He a native of Charleston and she of Orangeburg, South Carolina. He a clerk.

ROBERTS, (Mrs.) ANNIE TAYLOR aged 26 years married to ROBERTS, JOHN aged 29 years November 28, 1888 by Rev. Robert Wilson at 4 Wragg Square. Both natives of England. He a laborer.

ROBERTS, CORNELIA aged 26 years married to MITCHUM, THOMAS aged 49 years October 15, 1893 by Rev. J. C. Yongue at Cumberland Church. He a native of Williamsburg County, South Carolina and she of Orangeburg, South Carolina. He a cooper.

ROBERTS, DAVID married to YATES, BELLE SUMTER June 13, 1881 by Rev. Richard S. Trapier.

ROBERTS, JOHN aged 29 years married to ROBERTS, ANNIE TAYLOR aged 26 years November 28, 1888 by Rev. Robert Wilson at 4 Wragg Square. Both natives of England. He a laborer.

ROBERTS, JOSEPHINE married to CONYERS, EDWARD C. February 10, 1879 by Rev. J. Mercier Green. Both natives of Charleston. He a painter.

ROBERTS, JOSEPHINE aged 25 years married to HUES, ROBERT R. aged 27 years March 22, 1887 by Rev. J. V. Welsh at Calvary Episcopal Church. Both natives of Charleston.

ROBERTS, JOSEPHINE GADSDEN aged 20 years married to PATRICK, CHARLES SUMMERFIELD aged 22 years December 4, 1878 by Rev. G. R. Brackett at 5 Smith Street. He a dentist.

ROBERTS, MARIAN C. aged 28 years married to LIBBY, ROBERT C. aged 30 years November 24, 1893 by Rev. G. R. Brackett in Smith Street. He a native of Gordonsville, Virginia and she of Charleston. He a clerk.

ROBERTS, MATTIE aged 21 years married to ASHBY, LOUIS M. aged 26 years May 5, 1889 by Rev. Edwin C. Dargan at 7 Bull Street. He a native of Spartanburg, South Carolina, and she of Georgia. He a clerk in Savannah, Georgia.

ROBERTS, OSSIAN married to HOLLAND, SELINA June 10, 1891 by Rev. William H. Campbell. He a merchant in Spartanburg, South Carolina.

ROBERTS, SAMUEL T. aged 25 years married to RIMOND, ANA C. aged 19 years November 9, 1884 by Rev. J. V. Welsh at 24 Bee Street. Both natives of Charleston. He a tinner.

ROBERTS, S. T. aged 20 years married to McCARROLL, KATE aged 19 years October 15, 1879 by Rev. J. V. Welsh at 64 Radcliffe Street. Both natives of Charleston. He a tinner.

ROBERTS, THEOPHILUS N. aged 42 years married to RICHARDS, SUSAN VILLEPONTEAUX aged 32 years December 1, 1881 by Rev. Charles S. Vedder. He a native of Savannah, Georgia and she of Summerville, South Carolina. He a physician in Columbia, South Carolina.

ROBERTS, T. A. aged 26 years married to COLBURN, J. P. aged 26 years February 9, 1882 by Rev. G. R. Brackett at the Second Presbyterian Church. He a native of Charleston and a broker.

ROBERTS, V. aged 34 years married to McSWEENEY, DENNIS aged 23 years May 4, 1882 by Father F. J. Shadler at St. Joseph's Roman Catholic Church. He a native of Ireland and a cooper.

ROBERTSON, CHARLES aged 24 years married to JENKINS, LIZZIE B. aged 23 years April 14, 1892 by Rev. Edward T. Horn at St. Johannes Lutheran Church. Both natives of Charleston. He a bookkeeper.

ROBERTSON, EDWARD T. aged 26 years married to LADSON, SARAH TILMAN aged 22 years December 22, 1881 by Rev. C. C. Pinckney at Grace Church. Both natives of Charleston. He a clerk.

ROBERTSON, E. aged 37 years married to BECKMAN, A. S. aged 25 years November 11, 1879 by Rev. W. S. Bowman at the Wentworth Street Lutheran Church. Both natives of Charleston. He a grocer.

ROBERTSON, FRANCIS MARION aged 25 years married to RODGERS, MINNIE aged 21 years May 7, 1890 by Rev. R. A. Webb at 149 Wentworth Street. He a native of Summerville, South Carolina and she of Charleston. He an insurance agent.

ROBERTSON, HENRIETTA married to LaCOSTE, J. C. November 8, 1884 by Rev. W. T. Thompson at the First Presbyterian Church. He a bookkeeper.

ROBERTSON, HENRIETTA R. aged 24 years married to WHALEY, THOMAS P. aged 25 years November 7, 1895 by Rev. G. R. Brackett at 166 Broad Street. He a native of Pendleton, South Carolina and she of Charleston. He a physician.

ROBERTSON, JAMES aged 23 years married to CARRERE, FRANCES A. aged 20 years October 12, 1887 by Rev. G. R. Brackett. He a native of Chester, South Carolina and she of Charleston. He an insurance agent.

ROBERTSON, JOHN aged 32 years married to CARRIEGE, AGNES aged 20 years January 11, 1881 by Father Daniel J. Quigley at The Cathedral of St. John the Baptist. He a native of Scotland and she of Charleston. He a lighthouse keeper.

ROBERTSON, McBRYDE C. married to AIKEN, CARRIE December 12, 1889 by Rev. William H. Campbell at the residence of Dr. T. Grange Simmons - 18 Monatagu Street. He resides in Columbia, South Carolina.

ROBERTSON, MARIAN S. aged 19 years married to PELZER, ARTHUR aged 21 years May 26, 1886 by Rev. G. R. Brackett. Both natives of Charleston. He a merchant.

ROBERTSON, MARY ANN aged 22 years married to TEAGUE, WILLIAM FRANCIS April 1, 1883 by Father P. L. Duffy at The Cathedral of St. John the Baptist. Both natives of Charleston. He a lighthouse keeper.

ROBERTSON, P. ALEXANDER aged 29 years married to PHINN, MARY E. aged 26 years December 27, 1888 by Rev. C. C. Pinckney at Grace Church. Both natives of Charleston. He a clerk in Brunswick, Georgia.

ROBERTSON, SUSAN B. aged 49 years married to LYMAN, THEODORE B. aged 78 years February 9, 1893 by Rev. C. C. Pinckney at Grace Church. She a native of Charleston. He a Bishop of the Protestant Episcopal Church in North Carolina.

ROBESON, STEPHEN C. aged 31 years married to NELSON, SUSAN A. aged 20 years June 27, 1880 by Rev. J. V. Welsh at 64 Radcliffe Street. Both natives of Charleston. He a mechanic.

ROBINS, GEORGE D. aged 20 years married to JACOBS, LOUISA aged 19 years October 6, 1889 by Rev. Johannes Heckel at 123 Smith Street. He a native of Savannah, Georgia and she of Charleston. He a printer in Brooklyn, New York.

ROBINSON, ANN LAURA aged 15 years married to DONAN, GEORGE S. aged 21 years March 29, 1885 by Rev. John E. Beard at 51 America Street. He a native of Columbia, South Carolina and she of Charleston. He a laborer.

ROBINSON, EUGENIA E. aged 19 years married to HORRIE, CHARLES F. aged 26 years July 19, 1894 by Rev. S. E. Morris. Both natives of Charleston. He a mechanic.

ROBINSON, FANNIE aged 18 years married to SALISBURY, JOHN E. aged 45 years February 3, 1891 by Rev. T. P. Burgess at 34 Line Street. Both natives of Charleston. He a mechanic.

ROBINSON, MARY GERVAIS married to TUPPER, JAMES February 5, 1883 by Rev. Richard S. Trapier at St. Michael's Church.

ROBINSON, M. J. aged 20 years married to BRUGGERMAN, G. W. aged 20 years February 9, 1882 by Rev. A. Coke Smith at Trinity Church. He a native of Georgia and she of Charleston. He a machinist.

ROBINSON, SOPHIE M. aged 21 years married to ANDERSON, JOHN M. aged 27 years November 18, 1895 by Rev. J. C. Yongue at 14 Hampstead Square.

ROBINSON, SUSIE J. aged 20 years married to ALLAN, WILLIAM S. aged 28 years April 8, 1895 by Rev. G. R. Brackett at the 2nd Presbyterian Church. Both born Charleston. He a merchant.

ROBINSON, WILLIAM married to HAGOOD, IRENE December 12, 1878 by Rev. J. A. Chambliss in East Bay Street near Laurens Street.

ROBINSON, WILLIAM T. aged 19 years married to HODGE, SALLIE FERGUSON aged 16 years December 14, 1886 by Rev. J. Walter Dickson at 475 Meeting Street. Both natives of South Carolina. He a mechanic.

ROBLIBS, M. H. aged 21 years married to RUVIS, H. aged 36 years April 18, 1882 by Rev. Louis Muller at 309 East Bay Street. He a native of Charleston and a merchant.

ROBSON, ANN ELIZA aged 26 years married to McDERMID, NORMAN W. aged 36 years April 22, 1886 by Rev. G. R. Brackett.

ROBSON, JOHN W. aged 30 years married to TIEDEMAN, HELEN H. aged 20 years June 15, 1893 by Rev. Edward T. Horn at 152 Broad Street. He a native of Spartanburg, South Carolina and she of Charleston. He a merchant.

ROBSON, MARTHA WILLIAM aged 22 years married to McMILLAN, JOHN CICERO aged 29 years April 11, 1888 by Rev. G. R. Brackett. He a native of Marion County, South Carolina and she of Spartanburg, South Carolina. He a physician in Marion County.

ROCHE, JOHN PATRICK aged 35 years married to RILEY, MARY ANN aged 25 years July 8, 1888 by Father Daniel J. Quigley at St. Patrick's Roman Catholic Church. Both natives of Charleston. He a railroad dispatcher.

RODDY, MAMIE aged 23 years married to LANIGAN, T. MICHAEL aged 28 years April 15, 1890 by Father Harry P. Northrop at The Cathedral of St. John the Baptist. Both natives of Charleston. He a clerk.

RODE, OLIVER C. aged 35 years married to KIELBIN, MARIE A. aged 22 years November 2, 1894 by Rev. C. E. Chichester at 1 Atlantic Street. Both natives of Norway. He a mariner.

RODEMANN, ANNA CATHARINE aged 24 years married to STELLING, HEINRICH aged 23 years October 31, 1886 by Rev. Louis Muller at the corner of King Street and Rogers Alley. Both natives of Germany. He a grocer.

RODERMAN, JOHANNA aged 22 years married to BUCH, AUGUST HENRY aged 28 years October 29, 1885 by Rev. Johannes Heckel at the corner of Aiken and Blake Streets. Both natives of Charleston. He a grocer.

RODGERS, AMELIA ELIZABETH aged 22 years married to ALBRECHT, WILLIAM ANDERSON aged 24 years June 17, 1879 by Rev. H. F. Chreitzberg at the Spring Street Methodist Episcopal Church. He a native of Princeton, New Jersey and she of Charleston. He a farmer.

RODGERS, ELMER O'G. aged 33 years married to GRUBER, BLANCHE W. aged 25 years February 15, 1894 by Rev. J. L. Stokes at the Spring Street Lutheran Church. He a native of South Carolina and she of Charleston. He a clerk in Florence, South Carolina.

RODGERS, FANNIE aged 36 years married to ALLEMAN, FREDERICK O. aged 53 years February 28, 1883 by Rev. J. V. Welsh at 192 Coming Street. He a native of Harrisburg, Pennsylvania and she of Charleston. He a physician.

RODGERS, FRANCIS S. J. aged 21 years married to KELLY, FLORENCE aged 19 years January 24, 1889 by Rev. C. C. Pinckney at Grace Church. Both natives of Charleston. He a lawyer.

RODGERS, G. S. aged 23 years married to BELVIN, C. aged 17 years April 7, 1889 by Rev. H. B. Browne at 7 Stone Court. Both natives of Sumter, South Carolina. He a mill operator.

RODGERS, JENNIE LEGARE aged 18 years married to WIGGINS, WILLIAM T. aged 21 years November 19, 1893 by Rev. J. L. Stokes at 231 Coming Street. He a native of Beaufort, South Carolina and she of Charleston. He a stevedore in Berkeley County, South Carolina.

RODGERS, MINNIE aged 21 years married to ROBERTSON, FRANCIS MARION aged 25 years May 7, 1890 by Rev. R. A. Webb at 149 Wentworth Street. He a native of Summerville, South Carolina and she of Charleston. He an insurance agent.

RODGERS, VICTORIA AMANDA aged 18 years married to HALL, WILLIAM HENRY aged 23 years October 4, 1881 by Rev. H. F. Chreitzberg at 10 Aiken Street.

ROESLER, LOUIS CONSTANTINE ALEXANDER aged 21 years married to PETERMANN, CAROLINE MARGARET ADELLA aged 22 years May 1, 1883 by Rev. Louis Muller at the southeast corner of Amherst and America Streets. Both natives of Charleston. He a mechanic.

ROGANS, THOMAS J. aged 29 years married to WILLIAMS, FLORENCE E. aged 20 years November 29, 1891 by Rev. R. C. Holland. He a native of England and she of Charleston. He a traveling salesman.

ROGERS, C. L. aged 18 years married to FAGAN, P. D. aged 21 years June 10, 1894 by Rev. D. F. Tippett at 9 Blake Street.

ROGERS, JOHN E. aged 24 years married to SIMMONS, ANNA L. aged 23 years October 3, 1888 by Father J. J. Monaghan at 493 Meeting Street. He a native of New York and she of Charleston. He a paperhanger.

ROGERS, LUCIA A. aged 20 years married to HERREN, CECIL S. aged 20 years September 7, 1885 by Rev. John O. Wilson.

ROGERS, MARY E. aged 18 years married to MAZIEL (?), THOMAS R. aged 22 years March 18, 1894 by Rev. Griffin Holliman at the corner of Reid and Hanover Streets. He a native of Colleton County, South Carolina and she of Berkeley County, South Carolina. He works for the railroad.

ROGERS, PLACEDA aged 17 years married to GRUBS, BENJAMIN aged 21 years April 13, 1895 by Rev. J. C. Yongue at 24 Cooper Street. He a native of South Florida and she of South Carolina. He works in the cotton mill.

ROHDE, ANNA HEDWIG aged 25 years married to BOESCH, JOHN CASPAR aged 28 years January 22, 1878 by Rev. Louis Muller at M. C. Amme's bakery in King Street.

ROHDE, LENAH aged 22 years married to GERARD, WILLIE aged 30 years March 17, 1884 by Rev. J. V. Welsh at 187 St. Philip Street. He a native of Brooklyn, New York and she of Charleston. He a clerk.

ROHDE, G. F. aged 39 years married to LUTJEN, ANNA aged 25 years December 3, 1880 by Rev. Johannes Heckel at 125 Calhoun Street. Both natives of Germany. He a laborer.

ROMERILL, MARY married to BECK, HARRY L. aged 28 years November 1, 1888 by Rev. J. E. Carlisle at 231 Coming Street.

RONNER, ANNA REBECCA CATHERINE aged 22 years married to TWEITMANN (?), HEINRICH W. aged 23 years September 8, 1887 by Rev. Louis Muller in King Street near Line Street. He a native of Charleston and she of Prussia. He a merchant.

ROOKS, M. aged 22 years married to REDMOND, Edmund, A. aged 17 years February 5, 1882 by Rev. L. H. Shuck. He a native of South Carolina and a carpenter.

ROPER, GEORGIA married to BRYAN, EDWARD B. July 9, 1878 by Rev. Richard S. Trapier.

ROSE, C. aged 36 years married to MILLER, L. aged 29 years September 20, 1882 by Rev. Edward F. Horn at 119 Queen Street. He a native of Charleston and a mate with the U. S. Revenue Service.

ROSE, EDWARD P. married to CRAFTS, HARRIET M. April 10, 1890 by Rev. Richard S. Frazier at St. Michael's Church. Both natives of Charleston. He a physician in Colorado.

ROSE, FLORENCE married to MURRAY, ISAAC December 26, 1889 by Rev. W. A. Betts.

ROSE, HENRY P. aged 46 years married to FOX, CATHARINE aged 24 years May 19, 1883 by Rev. J. A. Clifton in Laurel Street. He a native of St. James Parish, South Carolina and she of Charleston. He a laborer.

ROSE, JOSEPH aged 32 years married to DUFFY, MARY aged 28 years February 16, 1887 by Father P. J. Wilson at St. Mary of the Annunciation Roman Catholic Church. He a native of Spain and she of Charleston. He a laborer.

ROSE, JOSEPH aged 25 years married to MORGAN, MARGARET aged 18 years December 2, 1890 by Rev. M. S. Walkins at 24 Cooper Street. He a native of Charleston and she of Darlington, South Carolina. He a fireman.

ROSE, WILLIAM H. aged 24 years married to HEYWARD, GEORGIANA aged 22 years October 20, 1892 by Rev. C. C. Pinckney at 99 Meeting Street. Both natives of Charleston. He works in the phosphate mill.

ROSENBERG, ABROM aged 24 years married to WINSTOCK, REBECCA aged 23 years May 27, 1885 by Rabbi David Levy in St. Philip Street near Wentworth Street.

ROSENBERGER, S. M. aged 30 years married to WILLIAMS, BERTHA V. aged 20 years June 16, 1885 by Rabbi David Levy at 95 St. Philip Street. He a native of New York and she of Charleston. He a merchant in Camden, South Carolina.

ROSENSTEIN, JACOB aged 34 years married to BELITZER, FLORENCE A. aged 27 years June 30, 1892 by Rabbi David Levy at 344 East Bay Street. She a native of Kingstree, South Carolina. He a merchant.

ROSENTHAL, ISAAC P. aged 32 years married to KOSMINSKI, HANNAH aged 26 years July 14, 1886 by Rabbi David Levy at 154 King Street. Both natives of Germany. He a merchant.

ROSIER, SUSAN aged 17 years married to RUGIERO, JULIUS aged 28 years September 9, 1894 by Rev. J. C. Yongue at 18 Cooper Street. He a native of Charleston and she of Athens, Georgia. He a ship builder.

ROSIS, ISIDORE aged 23 years married to STEPHENS, DELLA VICTORIA aged 19 years August 9, 1878 by Father J. J. Woolahan at St. Patrick's Roman Catholic Church. Both natives of Charleston. He a cigar maker.

ROTHSTEIN, ESTELLE aged 20 years married to LEVIN, CHARLES aged 30 years October 26, 1892 by Rabbi DAVID Levy at 342 King Street. Both natives of New York. He a merchant.

ROUMILLAT, LELA T. aged 19 years married to WILSON, PAUL J. aged 18 years March 17, 1881 by Father F. J. Shadler at St. Joseph's Roman Catholic Church.

ROUMILLAT, L. J. aged 19 years married to HILSON, P. J. aged 18 years March 17, 1881 by Father F. J. Shadler at St. Joseph's Roman Catholic Church. He a native of Charleston and a grocer.

ROUMILLAT, MARY married to BECHER, HARRY L. aged 28 years November 1, 1888 by Rev. J. E. Carlisle at 231 Coming Street. He a theatrical in New York City, New York.

ROUMILLAT, WILLIAM H. aged 27 years married to McINDOE, BESSIE aged 20 years April 19, 1888 by Rev. J. V. Welsh at 40 Bee Street. He a native of Aiken, South Carolina and she of Charleston. He a druggist in Gaffney, South Carolina.

ROUSE, CHARLES W. aged 23 years married to ASHBY, ESTHER M. aged 23 years February 15, 1880 by Rev. R. N. Wells. Both natives of Charleston. He resides in Georgetown, South Carolina and she in Washington, D. C. He a printer.

ROUSE, WILHELM C. D. aged 25 years married to SENEKEN, HELENE W. aged 24 years February 24, 1892 by Rev. Louis Muller at 23 Aiken Street.

ROUSELY, MAGGIE aged 35 years married to CHARLON, WILLIAM aged 35 years September 5, 1886 by Rev. H. B. Browne at 131 Sheppard Street. He a native of Charleston and she of Orangeburg, South Carolina. He a policeman.

ROUSELEY, SALLIE ELIZABETH aged 16 years married to THOMPSON, LOUIS NAPOLEON aged 21 years November 16, 1884 by Rev. Richard S. Lapsley at the corner of Nassau and Sheppard Streets. He a native of Augusta, Georgia and she of Charleston. He works in the cotton factory.

ROWAN, JOHN married to FITZGERALD, MARY December 28, 1877 by William B. Yates, Chaplain.

ROWAND, THOMAS Y. S. aged 40 years married to CORCORAN, BRIDGET ANNE aged 31 years May 15, 1887 by Father P. J. Wilson at St. Mary of the Annunciation Roman Catholic Church. Both natives of Charleston. He a collector.

ROWE, AUGUST married to SWARTZ, C. September 9, 1879 by William B. Yates, Chaplain.

ROWLAND, CHRISTOPHER J. aged 23 years married to GIVEN, MINNIE aged 28 years December 27, 1883 by Rev. J. A. Clifton at 189 Coming Street. He a native of Charleston and she of Italy. He a machinist.

ROYA, MARY L. aged 19 years married to TODD, EDWARD W. aged 23 years February 4, 1895 by Rev. J. C. Yongue at 23 America Street. Both natives of Charleston. He works for the railroad.

RUDD, CHRISTINA ANNIE aged 44 years married to SEABROOK, PETER G. aged 58 years March 25, 1891 by Rev. W. A. Betts at 14 Hampstead Square. He a native of St. John's Parish, South Carolina and she of Charleston. He a gardener on Enston's Farm.

RUDD, (Mrs.) ELIZABETH SEABROOK aged 29 years married to BREEDLOVE, WILLIAM R. aged 26 years July 9, 1891 by Rev. W. A. Betts at 21 Allway Street. He a native of Richland County, South Carolina and she of St. Johns, Berkeley County, South Carolina. He a wharf builder.

RUDD, J. MARGARET aged 18 years married to STEPHENS, JAMES aged 25 years December 27, 1889 by Rev. J. Thomas Pate at 231 Coming Street. Both natives of Colleton County, South Carolina. He a laborer in Summerville, South Carolina.

RUDD, T. H. aged 29 years married to SEABROOK. E. E. aged 29 years August 17, 1882 by Father Daniel J. Quigley in Meeting Street. He a mechanic.

RUFF, WALTER EDWARD aged 26 years married to McKINNON, MARGARET E. aged 22 years June 17, 1891 by Rev. G. R. Brackett at 324 Meeting Street. He a native of

Lexington County, South Carolina and she of Williamsburg County, South Carolina. He a builder and engineer.

RUGHEIMER, AUGUST RUDOLPH aged 23 years married to TITJEN, MARGARETHA ANNA aged 21 years April 3, 1889 by Rev. Louis Muller in King Street. Both natives of Charleston. He a tailor.

RUGHEIMER, JOHN aged 41 years married to REINHARDT, ALINE aged 23 years February 23, 1879 by Rev. Louis Muller in King Street. Both natives of Bavaria. He a tailor.

RUGHEIMER, AUGUST RUDOLPH aged 23 years married to TITJEN, MARGARETHA ANNA aged 21 years April 3, 1889 by Rev. Louis Muller in King Street. Both natives of Charleston. He a tailor.

RUGIERO, IRENE aged 19 years married to CARHART, OSCAR D. aged 29 years December 25, 1889 by Father F. J. Shadler at St. Joseph's Roman Catholic Church. He a native of New Jersey and she of Charleston. He the Superintendent of the Electric Light Company.

RUGIERO, JULIUS aged 28 years married to ROSIER, SUSAN aged 17 years September 9, 1894 by Rev. J. C. Yongue at 18 Cooper Street. He a native of Charleston and she of Athens, Georgia. He a ship builder.

RUGIERO, M. aged 28 years married to VICEDOMINI, E. aged 27 years November 26, 1882 by Father P. L. Duffy at The Cathedral of St. John the Baptist. He a native of Charleston and a mariner.

RUGIERO, RAPHAEL aged 48 years married to BRILLANCEAU, (Mrs.) EUGENIA GUILLEMAN aged 41 years January 21, 1883 by Father P. L. Duffy at The Cathedral of St. John the Baptist. He a native of Naples, Italy and she of Charleston.

RUGIERO, TILLIE aged 16 years married to DRIGGERS, DANIEL F. aged 18 years October 3, 1889 by Rev. H. B. Browne at 85 Columbus Street. He a native of Colleton County, South Carolina and she of Summerville, South Carolina. He a cotton mill operator in Adams Run, South Carolina.

RUMLEY, MARY ANN aged 33 years married to PACETTY, ANDREW aged 49 years October 21, 1885 by Father F. J. Shadler at St. Joseph's Roman Catholic Church. He a native of Georgia and she of Charleston. He an engineer.

RUMPEL, GEORGE W. aged 29 years married to GOTGEN, CATHERINE aged 31 years May 15, 1884 by Rev. Luther K. Probst. He a native of Charleston and she of Germany. He a clerk.

RUMPH, P. JOHN aged 30 years married to KECKLEY, ETTA H. aged 20 years April 2, 1890 by Rev. J. Thomas Pate at the corner of Bogard and Percy Streets. He a native of Pregnale, South Carolina and she of Charleston. He operates a sawmill in Pregnale.

RUNCKEN, BERTHA MARGARETHE aged 17 years married to SMITH, JOHN DILL aged 26 years May 10, 1885 by Rev. Louis Muller at the southwest corner of East Bay and Laurens Streets. He a native of Beaufort, North Carolina and she of Charleston. He a mariner.

RUNEY, JOHN aged 24 years married to ZWINGMANN, HENRIETTA aged 22 years January 16, 1889 by Father F. J. Shadler at St. Joseph's Roman Catholic Church. Both natives of Charleston. He a clerk.

RUTLEDGE, EMMA B. married to SMITH, HENRY A. M. June 24, 1879 by Rev. R. Trapier in Legare Street.

RUVIS, H. aged 36 years married to ROBLIBS, M. H. aged 21 years April 18, 1882 by Rev. Louis Muller at 309 East Bay Street. He a native of Charleston and a merchant.

RYAN, ARTHUR B. married to HAMILTON, REBECCA M. June 3, 1879 by Rev. Richard S. Trapier at St. Michael's Church.

RYAN, CAROLINE married to NASH, FRANCIS February 15, 1887 by Rev. Richard S. Trapier at St. Luke's Church.

RYAN, CATHERINE aged 40 years married to HARVEY, JAMES aged 46 years June 15, 1879 by Father John P. Twigg. Both natives of Ireland. He a policeman.

RYAN, CATHERINE aged 24 years married to PONARD, JAMES M. aged 28 years May 26, 1881 by Father F. J. Shadler at St. Joseph's Roman Catholic Church. He a native of Charleston and a carpenter.

RYAN, MAGGIE aged 20 years married to LOTZ, EDWARD aged 30 years December 8, 1878 by Father C. J. Croghan. He a native of Frankfort, Germany and she of Charleston. He a shopkeeper.

RYAN, MARGARET aged 26 years married to HENNEBERRY, PETER J. aged 29 years January 12, 1890 by Father Daniel J. Quigley at St. Patrick's Church. Both natives of Charleston. He works for the railroad.

RYAN, MARY ANN aged 27 years married to WALSH, ANDREW M. aged 28 years November 25, 1883 by Father P. L. Duffy at The Cathedral of St. John the Baptist. He a native of Charleston and she of Brooklyn, New York. He a drayman.

RYAN, MICHEL BERRY married to HENDRICKSON, MARY April 7, 1880 by Rev. J. E. Jackson at the Alms House. Both natives of Charleston. He a clerk at the Alms House.

RYAN, NINA aged 19 years married to BROWN, EUGENE aged 24 years March 23, 1881 by Rev. A. S. Dobbs. Both natives of Charleston. He a livery proprietor.

RYAN, NINA O. aged 19 years married to BROWN, EUGENE aged 24 years March 23, 1881 by Rev. A. S. Dobbs.

RYAN, WALTER BRAY aged 23 years married to WEBB, ANNIE VIRGINIA aged 23 years March 19, 1891 by Rev. G. R. Brackett at 12 Friend Street. Both natives of Charleston. He a shipping clerk.

RYAN, WILLIAM aged 23 years married to WINKLER, MAMIE aged 23 years October 10, 1889 by Father Daniel J. Quigley at St. Patrick's Roman Catholic Church. Both natives of Charleston. He a physician.

SABO, MARTIN aged 27 years married to LENTE, VIRGINIA aged 20 years June 24, 1895 by Father J. J. Monaghan at St. Patrick's Roman Catholic Church. He a native of Germany and she of Charleston. He a street car driver.

SACK, W. H. married to VARNIE, E. August 10, 1882 by Rev. J. V. Welch at 24 Bee Street. Both natives of South Carolina. He a laborer.

SADLER, ROBERT aged 31 years married to BUNCH, CATHARINE aged 17 years September 22, 1889 by Father J. J. Monaghan at St. Patrick's Roman Catholic Church. He a native of Ireland and she of South Carolina. He a laborer.

SAHLMANN, CARSTEN aged 22 years married to MEITZLER, CAROLINE C. aged 20 years October 15, 1878 by Rev. Louis Muller in Broad Street. Both natives of Charleston. He a merchant in Bamberg, South Carolina.

SAHLMANN, FRITZ aged 28 years married to TIEDEMANN, SOPHIA W. C. aged 23 years September 15, 1880 by Rev. Louis Muller at the residence of Mrs. Tiedemann - Judith Street. Both natives of Charleston. He a miller.

SAHLMANN, JOHN CHRISTOPHER aged 25 years married to JACOBSON, JOHANNA CHRISTINE aged 35 years November 17, 1884 by Rev. Johannes Heckel at 55 Smith Street. He a native of Georgia and she of Charleston. He a clerk.

SAHLMANN, JOHN C. aged 28 years married to SONNICHSEN, HELEN S. aged 23 years March 21, 1878 by Rev. Louis Muller. He a native of Charleston and she of Prussia. He a grocer.

SAHLMAN, R. M. H. aged 20 years married to BULWINKLE, J. A. aged 25 years September 25, 1879 by Rev. Louis Muller at the corner of Meeting and Reid Streets. Both natives of Charleston. He a bookkeeper.

SALISBURY, AUGUSTA aged 17 years married to GREEN, THOMAS W. aged 25 years September 28, 1887 by Rev. H. B. Browne at 31 Blake Street. He a native of Wilmington, North Carolina and a railroad coupler. She a native of Berkeley County, South Carolina.

SALISBURY, JOHN E. aged 45 years married to ROBINSON, FANNIE aged 18 years February 3, 1891 by Rev. T. P. Burgess at 34 Line Street. Both natives of Charleston. He a mechanic.

SALTERS, T. aged 23 years married to THOMPSON, M. J. aged 22 years November 29, 1882 by Father John P. Twigg at St. Patrick's Roman Catholic Church. He a native of Charleston and a laborer.

SALVO, ANTONIO aged 25 years married to BLAND, ELVINA aged 20 years July 7, 1881 by Father Harry P. Northrop in Spring Street. Both natives of Charleston. He works for the railroad.

SALVO, EMON C. aged 26 years married to WARD, ELIZA B. aged 25 years June 3, 1884 by Rev. W. P. Mouzon. He a native of Colleton County, South Carolina and she of Charleston. He a farmer in Colleton County.

SALVO, JAMES R. aged 21 years married to SIGWALD, JULIA aged 23 years October 26, 1886 by Rev. J. Walter Dickson at 106 Columbus Street. He a native of South Carolina and she of Charleston. He a salesman.

SALVO, JOSEPH H. aged 25 years married to SIGWALD, ADELE L. aged 20 years May 26, 1885 at 22 Columbus Street. Both natives of Charleston. He a carpenter.

SALVO, VICTOR ROBERT aged 20 years married to GUTHKE, EMILY ELIZABETH aged 16 years February 15, 1891 by Rev. W. A. Betts at 1 Duc Court.

SALVO, VINCENT Y. aged 22 years married to SHOKES, FLORENCE aged 20 years September 25, 1890 by Rev. John Johnson at 31 Hanover Street. Both natives of Charleston. He a carpenter.

SAMPSON, EDWARD aged 22 years married to CULLEN, MARY aged 20 years May 7, 1879 by Father C. J. Croghan at St. Joseph's Roman Catholic Church. Both natives of Charleston. He an engineer.

SAMS, STANHOPE aged 26 years married to JOHNSON, CAMILLA CANTEY aged 22 years November 22, 1888 by Rev. John Johnson at St. Philip's Church. He a native of Atlanta, Georgia and she of Charleston. He a journalist in Greenville, South Carolina.

SAMSON, SARAH aged 48 years married to MEREE, M. W. aged 52 years October 3, 1888. He a native of St. John's Parish, Berkeley County, South Carolina and she of Charleston. He a laborer.

SAMUELS, MARIE aged 27 years married to CASPARY, JOSEPH aged 23 years April 7, 1892 by Rabbi David Levy at 88 Wentworth Street. He a native of Laurens County, South Carolina and she of Eatonville, Georgia.

SANBURG, CHARLES C. aged 28 years married to COLSON, EMELINE GEORGINA aged 29 years May 10, 1881 by Rev. E. J. Meynardie at Bethel Church. He a native of Savannah, Georgia and she of Charleston. He a couchmaker.

SANDERS, CATHARINE MARY ELIZABETH aged 31 years married to WHITE, IVAN PATRICK aged 29 years January 15, 1888 by Father John O. Schachte at The Cathedral of St. John the Baptist. He a native of Oconee, County, Georgia and she of Montreal, Canada. He a farmer in Walhalla, South Carolina.

SANDERS, CLARA A. aged 22 years married to BECKAM, SIMON aged 28 years May 28, 1891 by Rev. Robert Wilson at 77 Drake Street. He a native of Lancaster County, South Carolina and she of Charleston. He a physician.

SANDERS, ELIZA aged 21 years married to SOLGIAN (?), VINCENT aged 28 years January 29, 1880 by Father John P. Twigg at The Cathedral of St. John the Baptist. He a native of Dalmatia, Austria and she of Charleston. He a mariner.

SANDERS, GAINES H. married to BURKE, CATHERINE February 8, 1879 by Father Daniel J. Quigley at The Cathedral of St. John the Baptist. He a native of Alabama and she of Charleston. He a longshoreman.

SANDERS (Mrs.), HARRIET HENRIETTA DANAMORE aged 36 years married to BRAZZEL, RICHARD aged 32 years February 26, 1890 by Father F. J. Shadler at 7 Line Street. He a native of Fairfield County, South Carolina and she of Walterboro, South Carolina. He a laborer.

SANDERS, HENRY married to KNOX, ELIZABETH March 26, 1880 by William B. Yates. She a native of Charleston.

SANDERS, JAMES O'H. aged 33 years married to BAIL, ALICE LOUISA aged 19 years November 4, 1891 by Rev. Robert Wilson at 20 Washington Street. Both natives of Charleston. He a clerk.

SANDERS, JANIE aged 19 years married to DORSEY, PATRICK aged 35 years December 23, 1890 by Rev. Robert Wilson at 4 Wragg Square. Both natives of Charleston. He a laborer.

SANDERS, JOHN P. married to CORDES, MARY R. June 4, 1885 by Rev. William H. Campbell at St. Paul's Church. Both natives of Charleston. He a clerk.

SANDERS, LILY aged 23 years married to WILSON, EDWARD M. aged 30 years July 15, 1880 by Rev. C. C. Pinckney at the residence of Mr. Sanders in Society Street. Both natives of Charleston. He a bookkeeper.

SANDERS, MARY H. aged 28 years married to BARNES, EDWIN L. aged 30 years August 29, 1889 by Rev. Robert Wilson at 77 Drake Street. He a native of Kershaw County, South Carolina and she of Beaufort County, South Carolina. He a teacher in Camden, South Carolina.

SANDERS, R. W. aged 30 years married to BUTLER, HENRIETTA E. aged 17 years September 3, 1888 by P. E. Gleason, Trial Justice. Both natives of Charleston. He works in a factory.

SANDERS, JULIA aged 22 years married to BRASELL, JOHN aged 19 years July 16, 1886 by Rev. J. Walter Dickson at 203 Line Street. He a native of Charleston and she of Sullivans Island, South Carolina.

SANTEELE (?), FANNIEL E. CLARK aged 46 years married to MAHSTEDT, LOUIS D. aged 44 years July 18, 1893 by Rev. Henry M. Grant at the Circular Congregational Church. He a native of Charleston and she of Paris, Maine.

SANTORE, JAMES MADISON aged 24 years married to BROTHERS, MARY JANE aged 17 years November 11, 1891 by Rev. W. A. Betts at 30 Shepherd Street.

SARVIS, JOSEPH M. married to FORBES, (Mrs.) MARTHA E. RUSS January 2, 1879 by Rev. W. S. Bowman. Both natives of Charleston. He a moulder.

SARVIS, MARION C. aged 28 years married to FERRARA, SARAH A. aged 21 years June 7, 1885 by Rev. Robert Wilson at 16 Morris Street.

SASS, GEO HERBERT aged 37 years married to RAVENEL, ANNA ELIZA aged 30 years December 20, 1883 by Rev. Charles S. Vedder at the Huguenot Church. Both natives of Charleston. He a lawyer.

SASSARD, A. D. married to DAVIS, MAMIE March 31, 1890 by Rev. W. A. Betts.

SASSARD, HERBERT W. aged 24 years married to HUTCHMACHER, MARGARET H. aged 20 years July 5, 1883 by Father P. L. Duffy at 183 East Bay Street. He a native of Columbia, South Carolina and she of Charleston. He an engineer.

SASSARD, HERBERT WEBB married to SONTAG, OTTILIE March 20, 1879 by Rev. W. S. Bowman. Both natives of Charleston. He a machinist.

SASSER, CHARLES C. married to THOMPSON, NELLIE January 15, 1891 by Rev. William H. Campbell at St. Paul's Church. He a farmer in Maryland.

SAUER, EMMA MARY aged 19 years married to HEINSOHN, JOHANN H. aged 24 years March 24, 1886 by Rev. Louis Muller at 64 St. Philip's Street. He a native of Germany and she of Charleston. He a grocer.

SAUER, JOHANNA LISETTE aged 20 years married to HEINSOHN, FRANTZ aged 22 years June 5, 1888 by Rev. Louis Muller at the residence of the Bride's father - east side of St. Philip Street. He a native of Charleston and a policeman.

SAULS, DAVID AUSTIN aged 30 years married to VOLMER, JOHANNA WILHELMINA aged 22 years February 5, 1890 by Rev. T. P. Burgess at 422 Meeting Street. He a native of Walterboro, South Carolina and she of Charleston. He a merchant in Walterboro.

SAVASTUNO (?), ANDREW aged 27 years married to SWELGAN (?), AGNES aged 22 years July 30, 1891 by Father Harry P. Northrop at The Cathedral of St. John the Baptist. He a native of Naples, Italy and she of Charleston. He a photographer.

SAVERING, LAURA C. aged 17 years married to BROWN, HENRY aged 30 years March 6, 1887 by Rev. Luther T. Beattie in King Street. He a native of Alabama and she of Virginia. He works for the railroad.

SAWADSKE, JOHN HENRY aged 20 years married to DAVIS, ANNIE ELLEN aged 18 years May 3, 1881 by Rev. John H. Honour at 14 John Street.

SAWRASKEY, ANNIE aged 23 years married to BELDING, J. C. aged 22 years May 1, 1881 by Rev. L. H. Shuck at 29 Nassau Street. He a native of St. Johns, New Brunswick and she of Charleston. He a porter.

SAXTON, JAMES M. aged 24 years married to BROTHERS, MARY JANE aged 17 years November 11, 1891 by Rev. W. A. Betts at 30 Shephard Street. Both natives of Charleston. He a sashmaker.

SCADY, FREDERICK W. H. aged 26 years married to BOWEY, MARGARET A. aged 29 years December 3, 1892 by Rev. N. K. Smith at 511 Meeting Street. He a native of Copenhagen, Denmark and she of New Castle on Tyne, England. He a steward on a boat.

SCARBOROUGH, HENRY aged 53 years married to HERREN, HARRIET A. aged 25 years January 11, 1887 by Rev. Leroy F. Beattie. He a native of South Carolina and she of Charleston. He a planter.

SCARPA, MARY J. aged 17 years married to CISA, BONAVENTURA aged 27 years December 19, 1883 by Father J. J. Woolahan at St. Mary of the Annunciation Roman Catholic Church. He a native of Spain and she of Charleston. He a stevedore.

SCARTHER, ANTONIO aged 33 years married to SHERIDAN, CATHARINE aged 22 years April 3, 1888 by Father F. J. Shadler at St. Joseph's Roman Catholic Church. He a native of Greece and a fruitier.

SCARVEY (?), JAMES FRANCIS aged 25 years married to RICHBOURG, SARAH ELIZABETH May 4, 1890 by Father F. J. Shadler at St. Joseph's Roman Catholic Church. Both natives of Charleston.

SCHACHTE, NANNIE aged 23 years married to HASELL, HARRY Z. aged 25 years February 22, 1893 by Rev. Charles S. Vedder at 149 King Street. He a native of Edgefield County, South Carolina and she of Charleston. He an insurance agent.

SCHAEFER, BERTHA PECK married to TROWER, HAROLD EDWARD June 10, 1890 by Rev. Richard S. Frazier at St. Michael's Church. He a native of England. She a native and resident of Georgia.

SCHALLWIG (?), B. aged 28 years married to AMME, R. C. R. aged 23 years November 2, 1882 by Rev. Louis Muller in Magazine Street. He a native of Austria and a barkeeper.

SCHARDT, BARBARA MAGDALENA aged 20 years married to KULING (?), DAVID JACOB aged 21 years January 3, 1889 by Rev. Johannes Heckel at St. Johannes Lutheran Church. Both natives of Nashville, Tennessee. He a druggist.

SCHARDT, (Mrs.) WILHELMINA ECKART aged 34 years married to HECKEL JOHANNES aged 43 years April 30, 1878 by Rev. W. S. Bowman at the residence of J. C. H. Campsen. He a native of Bavaria and she of Germany. He a minister.

SCHARF, F. W. aged 23 years married to HEINS, C. H. G. aged 23 years November 24, 1882 by Rev. Louis Muller at 169 Coming Street. He a native of Charleston and a mechanic.

SCHARFER, ANNA MARY DOROTHEA aged 21 years married to DOOD, BERHARD JOHANN aged 24 March 28, 1889 by Rev. Louis Muller at the residence of the Bride's father - Spring Street at the corner of Rose Lane. He a native of Prussia and she of Charleston. He a grocer.

SCHARFER, JOHANN HEINRICH aged 22 years married to KOPER, ANNA HELENE aged 22 years January 24, 1889 by Rev. Louis Muller at the residence of the Bride's father in Mt. Pleasant, South Carolina. He a native of Charleston and she of Mt. Pleasant, South Carolina. He a grocer.

SCHARFF, REGINA aged 22 years married to BARWICK, EDWARD S. aged 23 years December 11, 1890 by Rev. T. P. Burgess at 38 Percy Street. Both natives of Charleston. He a machinist.

SCHEIBE, H. A. L. aged 22 years married to THEES, C. H. aged 20 years February 10, 1880 by Rev. Louis Muller at the St. Matthew's Lutheran Church. Both natives of Charleston.

SCHELLETTER, CHARLOTTE aged 24 years married to KOLNDORFF, ERNST aged 28 years September 19, 1878 by Rev. Johannes Heckel. He a native of Germany and she of Prussia. He a baker.

SCHELLETTER, D. aged 17 years married to SCHMIDT, J. J. aged 26 years December 2, 1879 by Rev. Johannes Heckel at 125 Calhoun Street. He a native of Charleston and a baker. She a native of Prussia.

SCHELLETTER, LOUISA married to WILLIAMS ,ARTHUR February 9, 1878 by Rev. R. S. Trapier at 2 Water Street.

SCHELLING, AUGUST aged 28 years married to PUNDT, EDITH FLORA aged 18 years December 17, 1884 by Rev. Robert Wilson at 43 Hanover Street. Both natives of Charleston. He a mechanic.

SCHELLING, C. aged 20 years married to RIDGEWAY, L. M. aged 28 years November 16, 1882 by Rev. E. J. Meynardie at 145 Calhoun Street. He a native of South Carolina and a merchant.

SCHERKE (?), S. HENRY aged 21 years married to FIELTZ, SARAH P. aged 21 years May 9, 1895 by Rev. J. C. Yongue at 14 Hampstead Square. He a native of Charleston and she of Berkeley County, South Carolina. He a painter.

SCHIELMELMAN (?), A. B. aged 26 years married to WILLINGEROD (?), RUDOLPH G. aged 27 years June 3, 1880 by Rev. Louis Muller in King Street. He a native of New York and she of Williamsburg County, South Carolina. He a bookkeeper.

SCHILLETTER, AUGUST aged 24 years married to FINCKEN, LAVINIA ELISE aged 23 years April 25, 1889 by Rev. Louis Muller. He a native of Prussia and she of Charleston. He a baker.

SCHILLING, ALEX M. aged 33 years married to SCHUMACHER, CATHERINE aged 26 years May 4, 1894 by Rev. A. Ernest Cornish at 16 Bee Street. He a native of Washington, D. C. and she of Charleston. He a clerk in Washington.

SCHILLING, ALEXANDER M. aged 26 years married to BODE, HENRIETTA aged 19 years June 17, 1886 by Rev. C. E. Chichester, at 390 Meeting Street. Both natives of Charleston. He works for the railroad.

SCHILMILMAN, A. A. aged 26 years married to WILLEGEROD, RUDOLF G. aged 27 years June 3, 1880 by Rev. Louis Muller. He a native of New York and she of Williamsburg County, South Carolina. He a bookkeeper.

SCHIPMAN, A. C. aged 33 years married to MITCHELL, JOHN F. aged 37 years February 16, 1891 by Rev. M. S. Watkins at 47 Columbus Street. He a native of Jacksonville, Florida and she of Berkeley County, South Carolina. He a painter.

SCHIRMER, CHARLES C. married to BONNELL, ELIZABETH October 2, 1884 by Rev. W. T. Thompson in Church Street.

SCHIRMER, LOUISA JANE aged 21 years married to TOWLES, HENRY A. aged 35 years March 15, 1881 by Rev. Edward T. Horn in Bull Street. He a native of Savannah, Georgia and she of Charleston. He a merchant in Wadmalaw, South Carolina.

SCHIRMER, MARY LOUSIE aged 38 years married to TIEDEMANN, OTTO aged 40 years February 4, 1891 by Rev. Edward T. Horn. Both natives of Charleston. He a merchant.

SCHIRMER, WILLIAM married to GAILLARD, MARY J. August 5, 1891 by Rev. William H. Campbell at St. Paul's Church. He a mechanic.

SCHLEPPEGRELL, F. W. aged 25 years married to GAMBATTI, J. A. aged 23 years August 28, 1882 by Rev. P. J. Wilson in King Street. He a native of Charleston and a clerk.

SCHLEPPEGRELL, JOHANN A. aged 28 years married to VOIGHT, ANNA REBECCA JOSEPHINE aged 20 years August 2, 1887 by Rev. Louis Muller. He a native of Prussia and she of Charleston. He a merchant.

SCHLEY, H. M. aged 33 years married to DRAKE, E. A. aged 24 years February 15, 1882 by Rev. Claudian B. Northrop at 176 Meeting Street. He a native of Germany and she of Pennsylvania. He a planter.

SCHLUETER, DORA H. aged 17 years married to BUNGER, HERMAN H. aged 21 years January 18, 1886 by Rev. Luther K. Probst. He a native of Germany and she of Walhalla, South Carolina. He a merchant.

SCHLUETER, HERMAN aged 27 years married to DORRE (?), ANNIE M. aged 20 years August 6, 1885 by Rev. Luther K. Probst. He a native of Germany and she of Charleston.

SCHLUETER, SOPHIE C. aged 28 years married to LADY, WILLIAM D. aged 30 years January 10, 1892 by Rev. R. C. Holland at 2 Montagu Street.

SCHLUETER, WILLIAM HENRY aged 24 years married to KORNAHRENS, SOPHIE ENGEL aged 23 years October 14, 1884 by Rev. Claudian B. Northrop at 53 Coming Street. He a native of Walhalla, South Carolina and she of Germany. He a saloon keeper in Washington, D. C.

SCHMETZER, LOUIS aged 27 years married to GARRETT, EMMA aged 27 years June 6, 1885 by Rev. John E. Beard at 8 Aiken Street. Both natives of South Carolina.

SCHMIDT, HENRIETTA D. aged 23 years married to GREMIN, JOHANN H. aged 24 years February 18, 1880 by Rev. Louis Muller in King Street. Both natives of Hanover. He a grocer in Savannah, Georgia.

SCHMIDT, J. J. aged 26 years married to SCHELLETTER, D. aged 17 years December 2, 1879 by Rev. Johannes Heckel at 125 Calhoun Street. He a native of Charleston and a baker. She a native of Prussia.

SCHMIDT, WILHELM NICHOLAS aged 24 years married to STENKEN, ANNA META aged 29 years February 11, 1883 by Rev. Louis Muller at the corner of Calhoun and St. Philip Streets. Both natives of Germany. He a grocer.

SCHMIDT, WILHELM NICHOLAS aged 30 years married to BUCK, CATHARINA MARY FREDERICKA aged 23 years September 20, 1888 by Rev. Louis Muller. He a widower.

SCHMONSEES, C. H. aged 25 years married to WITT, MARIE FREDERICKA aged 20 years October 13, 1881 by Rev. Johannes Heckel. Both natives of Hanover. He a saloonkeeper.

SCHMONSEES, HENRY aged 32 years married to SOHL, MARTHA MARIA aged 32 years May 26, 1883 by Rev. Claudian B. Northrop at the corner of Blake and Drake Streets. Both natives of Germany. He a saloonkeeper.

SCHNECK, FRANK M. aged 22 years married to VAN VALKENBURG, JOSIE L. aged 21 years December 12, 1889 by Rev. R. D. Smart.

SCHNEFF, PHILIP aged 25 years married to GAYNOR, BRIDGET February 7, 1878 by Father Harry P. Northrop at St. Patrick's Church. He a native of Philadelphia, Pennsylvania and she of Ireland. He a painter.

SCHNEIDER, E. M. aged 23 years married to MASCHE, E. J. D. aged 35 years September 18, 1879 by Rev. Louis Muller. He a native of Prussia and she of Bavaria. He a shoemaker.

SCHNEPF, PHILIP aged 25 years married to GAYNOR, BRIDGET aged 25 years February 7, 1878 by Father Harry P. Northrop. He a native of Philadelphia, Pennsylvania and she of Ireland. He a painter.

SCHRAGE, JOHN F. aged 20 years married to BOLCHOZ, MAMIE L. aged 18 years December 18, 1895 by Father J. J. Monaghan at 497 Meeting Street. Both natives of Charleston. He a machinist.

SCHRIBERT, EDWARD H. aged 21 years married to FULTZ, SARAH P. aged 21 years May 9, 1895 by Rev. J. C. Yongue at 14 Hampstead Square.

SCHROEDER, ADELINE LOUISE aged 25 years married to STUART, ALEXANDER AUGUSTIN aged 27 years December 23, 1883 by Rev. Louis Muller. He a native of Charleston and she of Germany. He a spinner.

SCHROEDER, CHARLES H. aged 36 years married to DUNCAN, ANNA M. aged 17 years April 14, 1887 by Rev. G. R. Brackett. Both natives of South Carolina. He a physician.

SCHROEDER, DIETRICH aged 30 years married to HACHE, SOPHIE DORETHA MANN aged 30 years February 8, 1891 by Rev. Louis Muller at 96 Radcliffe Street.

SCHROEDER, JULIUS NICHOLAS aged 27 years married to LESSEMANN, EMILIE MARIE aged 25 years November 6, 1888 by Rev. Louis Muller at the residence of the Bride's mother at the northwest corner of Laurens and Wall Streets.

SCHROEDER, J. G. E. C. aged 31 years married to ASCHENBACH, IDA W. B. D. aged 21 years April 28, 1887 by Rev. Louis Muller. Both natives of Germany. He a druggist.

SCHROEDER, MARGARETHE HEDWIG aged 19 years married to WIETERS, JOHN CHRISTOPHER aged 37 years February 28, 1878 by Rev. Louis Muller at the corner of King and Broad Streets. Both natives of Germany. He a grocer.

SCHROEDER, MARY A. aged 28 years married to JOHNSON, JOHN aged 41 years March 24, 1895 by Rev. Charles S. Vedder at 14 Bedens Alley. Both natives of Charleston. He works at the News and Courier newspaper.

SCHROEDER, META CATHARINE aged 22 years married to ZIEGLER, JOHANN H. CONRAD aged 24 years July 7, 1878 by Rev. Louis Muller at 66 Radcliffe Street. He a native of Charleston and she of Germany. He a grocer.

SCHROEDER, WILHELM LUDWIG aged 24 years married to BURGER, JOHANNA MARGARETHA ELISE aged 22 years December 12, 1889 by Rev. Louis Muller at the home of the Bride's uncle in Summerville, South Carolina.

SCHULAMTHER, JOHN D. married to MEYER, MARGARETHA January 26, 1879 by Rev. Louis Muller. Both natives of Prussia.

SCHULLER, AUGUSTINE aged 31 years married to BUTLER, MARY A. aged 28 years September 23, 1888 by Father F. J. Shadler at St. Joseph's Roman Catholic Church. He a native of Holland and she of Charleston. He a merchant.

SCHULTZ, ANNIE aged 19 years married to MAHR, CHARLES December 27, 1877 by Rev. W. S. Bowman. He a merchant.

SCHULTZ, ADELINE M. aged 19 years married to DeANTONIO, JOSEPH aged 29 years April 23, 1889 by Rev. R. C. Holland at the Wentworth Street Lutheran Church. He a merchant.

SCHULTZ, CHRISTIAN HENRY aged 27 years married to MOISSON, JULIA aged 28 years May 29, 1887 by Father F. J. Shadler at St. Joseph's Roman Catholic Church. Both natives of Charleston. He a grocer.

SCHULTZ, (Mrs.) DOROTHY DUNNEMANN aged 33 years married to RENKEN, HEINRICH aged 33 years April 26, 1891 by Rev. Louis Muller at the corner of Morris and Smith Streets. He a native of Hanover and she of Germany. He a grocer.

SCHULTZ, FANNY aged 24 years married to GANNON, M. J. aged 38 years September 4, 1886 by Rev. A. S. Thomas. He a native of New York and she of Atlanta, Georgia. He a mariner in New York.

SCHULTZ, HEINRICH aged 24 years married to DUNNEMANN, JOHANNA DORETHA WILHELMINA aged 26 years July 13, 1884 by Rev. Louis Muller at the corner of Bull and Coming Streets. Both natives of Germany. He a grocer.

SCHULTZ, JEANETTE aged 24 years married to WEST, DAVID T. aged 33 years December 28, 1884 by Rev. Louis Muller in the King Street Road. He a native of New Jersey and she of South Carolina. He a farmer.

SCHULTZ, MARTIN aged 40 years married to WRIEDT, (Mrs.) SUSANNAH POLZ aged 43 years November 25, 1877 by Rev. Louis Muller at the residence of Henry Behrens - King Street near Woolfe Street.

SCHULTZE, JOHN WILLIAM GERHARDT aged 24 years married to MEYER, ANTOINETTE MAGADALENA aged 18 years December 6, 1877 by Rev. Louis Muller at the corner of King and Tradd Streets. Both natives of Charleston. He a clerk at the express company.

SCHULTZE, WILHELMINA SOPHIA aged 23 years married to WEINHEIMER, CARL AUGUST aged 21 years March 8, 1888 by Rev. Louis Muller at the residence of the Bride's father.

SCHUMACHER, CATHERINE aged 26 years married to SCHILLING, ALEX M. aged 33 years May 4, 1894 by Rev. A. Ernest Cornish at 16 Bee Street. He a native of Washington, D. C. and she of Charleston. He a clerk in Washington.

SCHUMACHER, JOHN D. aged 19 years married to MEYER, ANNA MARGARETHA aged 21 years January 26, 1879 by Rev. Louis Muller at the corner of King and Beresford Streets. Both natives of Prussia.

SCHUMACHER, MARGARETHE aged 28 years married to NONTA, WILLIAM A. aged 49 years June 29, 1890 by Rev. Johannes Heckel at the residence of John H. Peate in King Street. Both natives of Hanover. He farmer on the King Street Road.

SCHUMACHER, OTTO H. aged 27 years married to MEIBURG, (Mrs.) ANNA. M. S. aged 30 years April 29, 1884 by Rev. Louis Muller at the corner of St. Philip and George Streets. He a native of Germany and she of Charleston. He a grocer.

SCHUMACHER, SOPHIA aged 20 years married to JUTZELER, CHRISTIAN F. aged 24 years October 21, 1886 by Rev. Louis Muller at 128 Wentworth Street. Both natives of Germany. He a cooper.

SCHUMHOFF, H. H. aged 26 years married to LUNSING, C. N. aged 40 years June 25, 1882. He a native of South Carolina and she of Georgia. He a planter.

SCHURFER, GESINE CATHERINE M. aged 20 years married to PINCKNEY, AUGUST W. aged 27 years May 6, 1886 by Rev. Louis Muller in Mt. Pleasant, South Carolina.

SCHURMANN, ADELINE aged 16 years married to WESSEL, ALBERT CHRISTIAN aged 33 years June 6, 1883 by Rev. Louis Muller at 66 Radcliffe Street.

SCHUTTE, AUGUSTA W. H. aged 21 years married to BOETTE, CARL aged 24 years October 2, 1891 by Rev. Louis Muller at the corner of Pitt and Montagu Streets. Both natives of Prussia. He a grocer.

SCHUTTE (?), HENRY married to ORTON, GERTRUDE November 8, 1877 by Rev. R. S. Trapier in King Street.

SCHUTTE, H. M. C. aged 24 years married to MEYER, H. R. aged 24 years November 25, 1885 by Rev. Louis Muller at 66 Radcliffe Street. Both natives of Germany. He a grocer.

SCHWACKE, ANNIE aged 19 years married to ENTER, JACOB aged 24 years January 2, 1893 by Rev. K. Boldt at the corner of Washington and Laurens Streets.

SCHWACKE, CARL L. aged 31 years married to RADEMANN, META aged 20 years February 21, 1886 by Rev. Louis Muller. Both natives of Germany. He a merchant.

SCHWACKE, SARAH ELLA aged 29 years married to HARTZ, WILLIAM aged 43 years August 6, 1891 by Rev. R. C. Holland at 426 King Street. Both natives of Charleston. He a merchant.

SCHWETMANN, SOPHIE H. C. aged 23 years married to MEYER, ROBERT W. aged 29 years October 28, 1891 by Rev. Louis Muller at 106 Broad Street. Both natives of Summerville, South Carolina. He a machinist.

SCOFIELD, JAMES aged 41 years married to NELSON, SUSAN aged 49 years April 14, 1895 by Rev. J. C. Yongue at 9 Blake Street. He a native of New York and she of Union, South Carolina. He a painter.

SCOFIELD, WILLIAM R. aged 31 years married to RILEY, KATE M. aged 26 years March 22, 1887 by Rev. Luther T. Beattie at 231 Coming Street. He a native of New Jersey and she of Charleston. He a mechanic.

SCOTT, ALEXANDER CARLAN aged 25 years married to BUTTERFIELD, (Mrs.) FLORENCE SPEIN aged 21 years February 8, 1888 by Rev. G. R. Brackett. He a native of Scotland and she of London, England. He a carpenter.

SCOTT, (Mrs.) EMMA HUGER LOWNDES aged 30 years married to STEWART, SIMON V. aged 30 years November 26, 1885 by Rev. John Johnson at St. Philip's Church. He a native of South Carolina and she of Charleston. He an insurance agent.

SCOTT, F. G. aged 30 years married to GOODIN, ELOISE aged 20 years September 21, 1880 by Rev. John Johnson in Eutawville, South Carolina. He a native of Virginia and she of St. Johns, Berkeley County, Couth Carolina. He a minister. Both reside in Eutawville.

SCOTT, ISABELLA M. married to SISSON, M. H. aged 39 years January 13, 1884 by Rev. D. A. Blackburn.

SCOTT, JAMES F. married to MILLER, SALLIE December 7, 1890 by Rev. W. A. Betts.

SCOTT, MARY aged 27 years married to MITCHUM, THOMAS B. aged 49 years November 19, 1891 by Rev. W. A. Betts. He a native of Williamsburg County, South Carolina and she of Augusta, Georgia. He a cooper.

SCOTT, MARY A. aged 28 years married to BOLGER, JOHN aged 40 years January 12, 1891 by Rev. W. S. Watkins at 20 Stone Court. He a native of Edinborough, Scotland and she of Augusta, Georgia. He works in the cotton mill.

SCOTT, R. aged 15 years married to CONLEY, H. W. aged 20 years February 23, 1891 by Rev. W. S. Watkins at 24 Blake Street. He a native of Barnwell County, South Carolina and she of Williamsburg County, South Carolina. He works for the railroad.

SCOTT, WILLIAM F. aged 21 years married to BARRY, BRIDGET aged 21 years September 24, 1889 by Father Daniel J. Quigley at St. Patrick's Roman Catholic Church. Both natives of Charleston. He a boilermaker.

SCOWCROFT, JOHN COOPER aged 29 years married to DOYLE, ELIZABETH December 25, 1878 by Father Claudian B. Northrop. He a native of England and she of Charleston. He a clerk.

SCREVEN, CHARLES RUFUS aged 24 years married to LILLY, LAURA ANNIE aged 24 years December 2, 1883 by Rev. J. H. Tillinghast at 3 Cooper Street. Both natives of Charleston. He works for the railroad.

SCREVEN, JOHN J. aged 21 years married to EHRLICH, REBECCA aged 21 years September 8, 1887 by Rev. Robert Wilson at 4 Wragg Square. Both natives of Charleston. He a driver.

SCREVEN, LILLA aged 21 years married to McCAFFER, CHARLES W. aged 28 years January 28, 1885 by Rev. Robert Wilson at 17 Woolfe Street.

SCULLY, BRIDGET aged 40 years married to SHANNAHAN, MICHAEL aged 45 years January 19, 1879 by Father Daniel J. Quigley at The Cathedral of St. John the Baptist. Both natives of Ireland.

SEABROOK, ANNIE SARAH aged 19 years married to LEGARE, THOMAS aged 23 years February 28, 1878 by Rev. George W. Stickney at Johns Island, South Carolina. He a native of Charleston and she of Beaufort, South Carolina. He a planter.

SEABROOK, CATO A. aged 52 years married to BECKETT, EMMA J. aged 43 years November 3, 1892 by Rev. G. R. Brackett at the Enston Homes. He a native of Edisto Island, South Carolina and she of Johns Island, South Carolina. He a teacher in Columbia, South Carolina.

SEABROOK, E. E. aged 20 years married to RUDD, T. H. aged 29 years August 17, 1882 by Father Daniel J. Quigley in Meeting Street. Both natives of Charleston. He a mechanic.

SEABROOK, FRANKLIN aged 24 years married to SEABROOK, LYDIA aged 24 years February 5, 1880 by Rev. J. E. Jackson in Drake Street. He a native of James Island, South Carolina and she of Bluffton, South Carolina. He a farmer on James Island.

SEABROOK, H. H. aged 22 years married to BLANCHARD, WILLIAM R. aged 30 years November 3, 1880 by Rev. John Johnson at St. Philip's Church. Both natives of Columbus, Georgia. He a merchant.

SEABROOK, H. H. aged 19 years married to BLANCHARD, JEFFERSON aged 24 years January 13, 1881 by Rev. Sidi H. Browne at the residence of Rev. S. S. Blanchard in Meeting Street.

SEABROOK, JOSEPHINE married to WHALEY, EDWARD M. July 15, 1890 by Rev. R. S. Trapier at St. Michael's Church.

SEABROOK, J. married to CASSIDY, DENNIS October 25, 1880 by William B. Yates, Chaplain. He a native of Charleston.

SEABROOK, LYDIA aged 24 years married to SEABROOK, FRANKLIN aged 24 years February 5, 1880 by Rev. J. E. Jackson in Drake Street. He a native of James Island, South Carolina and she of Bluffton, South Carolina. He a farmer on James Island.

SEABROOK. PETER G. aged 58 years married to RUDD, CHRISTINA ANNIE aged 44 years March 25, 1891 by Rev. W. A. Betts at 14 Hampstead Square. He a native of St. John's Parish, South Carolina and she of Charleston. He a gardener on Enston's Farm.

SEABROOK, R. aged 23 years married to MIMS, M. S. aged 18 years August 19, 1882 by Rev. J. V. Welsh at 68 Line Street. He a native of South Carolina and a laborer.

SEALEY, THOMAS J. aged 32 years married to LAW, JOHANNA H. aged 20 years September 17, 1891 by Rev. R. C. Holland at 186 St. Philip Street. He a native of Augusta, Georgia and she of Charleston. He a carpet layer.

SEARLE, REGINALD F. aged 32 years married to HEACOX (?), EFFIE HUBBARD aged 35 years by Rev. H. B. Browne at 78 Drake Street. He a native of Burke County, Georgia and she of Charleston. He a carpenter.

SEASE, GEORGE D. aged 37 years married to KENNEDY, MINNIE aged 20 years February 6, 1887 by Rev. H. B. Brown at 78 Drake Street. He a native of Burke County, Georgia and she of Charleston. He a carpenter.

SEAVY (?), LUCY R. RUSSELL aged 29 years married to TURNER, MICHAEL P. aged 36 years October 21, 1893 by Father Joseph D. Budds at The Cathedral of St. John the Baptist.

SEEBER, CAROLINE aged 25 years married to KLATTE, JOHN aged 35 years February 5, 1884 by Rev. Luther K. Probst at the Wentworth Street Lutheran Church.

SEDRICK, MAGGIE aged 25 years married to NELLIGAN, JAMES M. aged 28 years June 23, 1884 by Father Daniel J. Quigley at 94 St. Philip Street. He a native of Green Brier, Virginia and she of Charleston.

SEEBECH, JOHANN F. aged 20 years married to LILIENTHAL, MATILDA aged 18 years January 18, 1885 by Rev. Claudian B. Northrop at 24 Beaufain Street. Both natives of Germany. He a grocer.

SEEL, FRANCIS J. aged 19 years married to PALMER, LILLIE LUCY aged 18 years April 18, 1895 by Rev. J. L. Stokes at 231 Coming Street. Both natives of Charleston. He a clerk.

SEEL, LILLIE H. aged 17 years married to HEITMAN, FREDERICK aged 24 years July 17, 1895 by Rev. Edward T. Horn at 587 King Street. Both natives of Charleston. He an engineer.

SEEL, LOUIS aged 30 years married to SIGWALD, ROSA A. aged 18 years November 14, 1884 by Rev. Luther K. Probst. He a native of South Carolina and she of Charleston. He a butcher.

SEGALLES, N. aged 27 years married to FERRIS, S. aged 23 years April 7, 1881 by Rev. L. H. Shuck. He a native of Greece and she of South Carolina. He a fruitier.

SEIGLING, FREDERICK C. aged 50 years married to KLEIN, E. E. C. aged 45 years December 9, 1880 by Rev. Louis Muller at the northeast corner of Wentworth and Lynch Streets. Both natives of Germany. He a grocer.

SEIGLING, MARY P. aged 20 years married to LANNEAU, WILLIAM S. aged 22 years June 30, 1892 by Rev. Edward T. Horn at St. Johannes Lutheran Church. Both natives of Charleston. He a clerk.

SEIGNIOUS, EVA A. aged 21 years married to MURRAY, VANDERHORST aged 21 years December 12, 1895 by Rev. John Kershaw at 155 Wentworth Street.

SEIMERS, FREDERICK aged 28 years married to DOSCHER, IDA aged 22 years March 28, 1879 by Rev. Johannes Heckel at the residence of Mr. Oetjen. He a native of Hanover and she of Hamburg, Germany. He a merchant.

SEIMSEN, CLAUS MATHIAS aged 21 years married to BEHRENS, JUSTINE W. F. aged 35 years October 26, 1878 by Rev. Louis Muller at 31 Nassau Street. He a native of Schleswig-Holstein and she of Hanover. He a farmer.

SELBY, ANNA LAURA aged 22 years married to GLEASON, MATTHEW B. aged 25 years September 22, 1889 by Rev. J. E. Carlisle at 231 Coming Street. He a native of Charleston and she of Ohio. He a lightman.

SELBY, (Mrs.) LILLIE ANN TAYLOR aged 23 years married to BRANIGAN, EDWARD G. aged 30 years February 15, 1885 by Rev. John O. Wilson at 82 Wentworth Street. He a native of Pennsylvania and she of Zanesville, Ohio. He works in the cotton mill.

SELBY, MARY ELIZABETH aged 22 years married to BRYANT, FRANK E. aged 25 years December 30, 1883 by Rev. John E. Beard at 2 Hampden Court. He a native of Chester County, South Carolina, and she of Maryland.

SELDON, JOSEPH married to BENNETT, JULIA January 8, 1880 by Rev. A. Toomer Porter. She a native of Charleston. He a resident of Georgia.

SELIGMAN, ELLA married to BACOT, LEWIS November 3, 1885 by Rev. William H. Campbell at the residence of Edward Locke. He a clerk.

SELLMANN, HERMAN aged 27 years married to KLINGENBERG, LINA CAROLINE A. aged 22 years November 23, 1886 by Rev. Louis Muller at 14 Wentworth Street. Both natives of Germany. He a brewer.

SENEKEN, HELENE W. aged 24 years married to ROUSE, WILHELM C. D. aged 25 years February 24, 1892 by Rev. Louis Muller at 23 Aiken Street.

SENSENEY, HARVEY G. aged 27 years married to HALLENBECK, SARAH aged 20 years January 23, 1895 by Rev. J. L. Stokes at 201 Spring Street. He a native of Lexington County, South Carolina and she of New York. He an engineer.

SERELLE (?), N. H. aged 39 years married to TESKEY, I. aged 32 years November 25, 1882 by Rev. Luther K. Probst at the Wentworth Street Lutheran Church. He a native of Charleston and a mechanic.

SERES, (Mrs.) EMMA R. DIERS aged 24 years married to HEUSEN, HENRY F. aged 24 years May 25, 1887 by Rev. Luther K. Probst at the Wentworth Street Lutheran Church. He a native of Germany and she of Charleston. He a laborer.

SERES, PETER A. aged 22 years married to DIERS, EMMA R. aged 20 years December 9, 1883 by Rev. Luther K. Probst. Both natives of Charleston.

SERES, ROSA married to STONEBRIDGE, RICHARD August 29, 1885 by Father F. J. Shadler at St. Joseph's Roman Catholic Church. She a native of Charleston.

SEXTON, A. M. aged 60 years married to BOWICK, (Mrs.) M. B. WARNOCK aged 60 years July 23, 1879 by Rev. H. F. Chreitzberg at 63 America Street. He a native of Colleton County, South Carolina and she of Spartanburg, South Carolina. He a watchmaker.

SEXTON, EVA A. aged 17 years married to PRINCE, L. H. aged 23 years October 2, 1879 by Rev. J. V. Welsh at 64 Radcliffe Street. Both natives of Charleston. He a clerk
SEY, ELIZA aged 22 years married to PRINCE, THOMAS L. aged 38 years June 8, 1884 by Rev. John E. Beard. He a native of London, England and she of South Carolina. He a mechanic.

SEYLE, CORNELIA BENNETT aged 23 years married to ALLEN, ROBERT EMMETT aged 23 years October 4, 1881 by Rev. A. Coke Smith at 100 St. Philip Street. He a native of Due West, South Carolina and she of Charleston. He a merchant.

SEYLE, LORENA E. aged 20 years married to KECKLEY, ARTHUR C. aged 23 years November 21, 1888 by Rev. J. E. Carlisle at the Spring Street Church. He a native of Charleston and a railroad worker.

SEYLE, WILLIAM E. aged 23 years married to FASH, JULIA aged 18 years August 15, 1886 by Rev. Robert Wilson at 44 Spring Street. Both natives of Charleston. He a mechanic.

SEYLE, W. J. aged 35 years married to MILLER, M. F. aged 33 years December 16, 1879 by Rev. W. S. Bowman at 122 St. Philip Street. He a native of Charleston and she of Georgia. He works for the railroad.

SEYMOUR, ELLEN REBECCA aged 21 years married to THOMAS, GEORGE aged 34 years November 24, 1878 by Rev. W. S. Bowman at the corner of Amherst and Nassau Streets. He a native of Darmstadt, Germany and she of Charleston. He a baker.

SEYMOUR, MARY E. aged 32 years married to LONG, RICHARD F. aged 43 years April 19, 1883 by Rev. C. C. Pinckney at Grace Church. He a native of Germany and she of Charleston. He a merchant.

SEYMOUR, ROSA aged 22 years married to STANSELL, C. B. aged 24 years February 1, 1888 by Rev. R. W. Lide at 168 Queen Street. He a native of Elka, South Carolina and she of Charleston. He a farmer in Elka.

SHACKLEFORD, HENRY DUBOIS aged 23 years married to BEVIN, LILA IDA aged 19 years June 10, 1879 by Rev. R. N. Wells. Both natives of Charleston. He a clerk.

SHACKLEFORD, JANE aged 24 years married to McCRADY, L. aged 30 years October 24, 1882 by Rev. John Johnson at 16 Church Street. He a native of Charleston and an lawyer.

SHACKLEFORD, LEE married to PORTER, HATTIE H. SIMONS May 29, 1888 by Rev. Richard S. Trapier.

SHAFER, ROBERT E. L. aged 23 years married to BOWICK, EMMA S. aged 15 years January 12, 1888 by Rev. H. B. Browne.

SHANAHAN, CHARLES F. aged 22 years married to BRELAND, MARY VICTORIA aged 19 years October 7, 1888 by Rev. R. D. Smart at Bethel Church. He a native of Charleston and she of Berkeley County, South Carolina. He a railroad engineer.

SHANNAHAN, MICHAEL aged 45 years married to SCULLY, BRIDGET aged 40 years January 19, 1879 by Father Daniel J. Quigley at The Cathedral of St. John the Baptist. Both natives of Ireland.

SHARKEY, MAGGIE aged 20 years married to MURRAY, PETER aged 29 years January 31, 1884 by Father J. J. Woolahan at St. Mary of the Annunciation Roman Catholic Church. Both natives of Charleston. He an engineer.

SHAROGO (?), G. W. aged 34 years married to MURPHY, E. T. aged 34 years February 19, 1882 by Father J. J. Monaghan. He a native of Ohio and she of Ireland. He a painter.

SHARP, ALBERT A. aged 25 years married to PUNDT, MARIANNE aged 20 years November 30, 1895 by Rev. J. C. Yongue at 14 Hampstead Square. He a native of Orangeburg, South Carolina and she of Charleston. He works for the railroad in Jamison, South Carolina.

SHAW, CHARLES C. aged 21 years married to WHEELOCK, CARRIE N. aged 21 years April 20, 1880 by Rev. E. C. L. Browne at Woodland Plantation. He a native of Woburn, Massachusetts and she of Clinton, Massachusetts. He a merchant.

SHEERS, ANNIE aged 26 years married to SLANSON, WILLIAM aged 27 years October 11, 1884 by Rev. Charles S. Vedder. He a native of South Carolina and she of Germany. He a pilot.

SHEPHARD, JOHN J. aged 36 years married to EVANS, (Mrs.) SARAH REYNOLDS aged 41 years June 8, 1884 by Rev. John E. Beard. He a native of Onslow County, North Carolina and she of Brunswick, North Carolina. He an engineer.

SHEPHARD, WILLIAM S. aged 36 years married to McINVAILLE, SARAH B. aged 23 years February 3, 1895 by Rev. Edmund Wells. He a native of Onslow, North Carolina and she of Darlington, South Carolina. He a clerk in Hartsville, South Carolina.

SHERIDAN, ANN E. aged 27 years married to SHOKES, G. M. aged 32 years October 10, 1880 by Father Harry P. Northrop. Both natives of Charleston. He an engineer.

SHERIDAN, CATHARINE aged 22 years married to SCARTHER, ANTONIO aged 33 years April 3, 1888 by Father F. J. Shadler at St. Joseph's Roman Catholic Church. He a native of Greece and a fruitier.

331

SHERIDAN, ELIZA aged 20 years married to STOLZE, CHARLES LOUIS aged 23 years February 17, 1878 by Father Daniel J. Quigley. Both natives of Charleston. He a printer.

SHERIDAN, ELIZA aged 20 years married to STOLZ, CHARLES LOUIS aged 23 years February 17, 1878 by Father Daniel J. Quigley at 72 King Street. Both natives of Charleston. He a printer.

SHERIDAN, ELIZABETH aged 19 years married to QUINLAN, JAMES W. aged 24 years May 2, 1893 by Father Joseph D. Budds at St. Mary of the Annunciation Roman Catholic Church. Both natives of Charleston. He a merchant.

SHERIDAN, MARY aged 20 years married to SIGWALD, THOMAS April 7, 1878 by Father Daniel J. Quigley at 72 King Street. Both natives of Charleston. He a mechanic.

SHERIDAN, MATTHEW P. aged 23 years married to RICKLES, ELIZABETH M. aged 18 years April 27, 1884 by Rev. P. L. Duffy. Both natives of Charleston. He a bookbinder.

SHERLOCK, ALEXANDER aged 24 years married to VALENTINE, JOSEPHINE aged 20 years February 6, 1893 by Father J. J. Monaghan at 4 Hanover Street. He a native of Scotland and she of Charleston. He a longshoreman.

SHEVATH, (Mrs.) MARY DONNELLY aged 38 years married to JOHNSON, FRANK aged 44 years November 18, 1895 by Rev. J. L. Stokes. He a native of Sweden and she of Charleston. He a watchman.

SHIEDER, THOMAS B. aged 21 years married to EASTERLIN, ELLA LEE aged 17 years August 5, 1888 by Rev. J. W. Ford.

SHIER, ALICE M. M. aged 25 years married to GREEN, THOMAS DAVIDSON aged 26 years July 8, 1878 by Rev. W. S. Bowman in Meeting Street opposite Citadel Green. He a native of Baltimore, Maryland and she of Charleston. He a confectioner.

SHINGLER, ELLA aged 22 years married to RIGGS, WALTER aged 25 years January 12, 1881 by Rev. L. H. Shuck at 5 South Bay Street.

SHINGLER, IDA IMOGEN aged 23 years married to SHINGLER, WILLIAM HENRY aged 23 years October 18, 1883 by Rev. G. R. Brackett at 10 Alexander Street. Both natives of Charleston. He a wharfinger.

SHINGLER, LILLY aged 22 years married to HUGHES, DWIGHT aged 29 years February 15, 1882 by Rev. L. H. Shuck at the corner of Wentworth and St. Philip Streets. He a native of Summerville, South Carolina and a clerk.

SHINGLER, WILLIAM HENRY aged 23 years married to SHINGLER, IDA IMOGEN aged 23 years October 18, 1883 by Rev. G. R. Brackett at 10 Alexander Street. Both natives of Charleston. He a wharfinger.

SHIPE, MARTIN aged 32 years married to PIERSON, SUSANNA SPARKMAN aged 34 years December 25, 1886 by Rev. H. B. Browne at 78 Drake Street.

SHIRER, J. H. aged 22 years married to THOMAS, A. E. aged 40 years August 30, 1882 by Rev. C. Shokes at 24 Bee Street. He a native of South Carolina and a farmer.

SHIRER, MARY JANE aged 23 years married to SMITH, HERBERT A. aged 24 years October 21, 1884 by Rev. Luther K. Probst. Both natives of Charleston. He a bookkeeper.

SHIVER, I. B. aged 31 years married to SYSAN (?), ELLA aged 30 years October 10, 1886 by Rev. Robert Wilson at 4 Wragg Square. Both natives of Charleston. He a patternmaker.

SHIVER, NANNIE married to BYERS, WILLIAM J. January 29, 1885 by Rev. C. E. Chichester at 55 Meeting Street. He a native of Charleston.

SHOFT, MAGGIE aged 19 years married to WILFORS, BRAXTON B. aged 23 years April 14, 1887 by Rev. John O. Wilson. He a native of Texas and she of North Carolina. He a clerk.

SHOKES, ALEX W. aged 35 years married to DuBOSE, ANNIE aged 28 years December 14, 1884 by Rev. John E. Beard in Line Street. Both natives of Charleston. He a carpenter.

SHOKES, CHARLES C. aged 20 years married to TURNER, ANN aged 37 years April 7, 1890 by Rev. Robert Wilson at 4 Wragg Square. He a native of Charleston and she of Columbia, South Carolina.

SHOKES, EMMA A. aged 24 years married to CLARK, DANIEL J. aged 30 years August 13, 1887 by Rev. T. P. Burgess. Both natives of Charleston. He works in the iron foundry.

SHOKES, FLORENCE aged 20 years married to SALVO, VINCENT Y. aged 22 years September 25, 1890 by Rev. John Johnson at 31 Hanover Street. Both natives of Charleston. He a carpenter.

SHOKES, G. M. aged 32 years married to SHERIDAN, ANN E. aged 27 years October 10, 1880 by Father Harry P. Northrop. Both natives of Charleston. He an engineer.

SHOKES, HARRIET LENORA aged 28 years married to BUNCH, SILAS SYLVESTER aged 34 years August 25, 1881 by Rev. A. Coke Smith at 217 Coming Street. Both natives of Charleston. He a painter.

SHOKES, MARIAH aged 38 years married to GALLOT, ROBERT B. aged 40 years December 10, 1884 by Rev. J. V. Welsh at 13 Aiken Street. He a native of Brooklyn, New York and she of Charleston. He a porter on a steamship.

SHOKES, MARTHA LOUIS aged 15 years married to KNOX, LEWIS CHAFFEE aged 15 years March 5, 1883 by Rev. E. J. Meynardie at 12 Norman Street. Both natives of Charleston. He a laborer.

SHOKES, MARY ELIZABETH aged 18 years married to BAHR, WILLIAM N. aged 23 years June 14, 1878 by Rev. W. S. Bowman at 8 Aiken Street. Both natives of Charleston. He a policeman.

SHOKES, WILLIAM J. aged 25 years married to FERRELL, ALICE F. aged 21 years April 5, 1883 by Rev. J. V. Welsh at 24 Bee Street.

SHOKES, WILLIAM H. aged 23 years married to ISSEAR (?), CELIA aged 22 years June 30, 1890 by John Ahrens at 643 King Street.

SHOMA, (Mrs.) EMMA C. BLAXMAN aged 23 years married to BOND, JAMES P. aged 22 years April 27, 1887 by Rev. John O. Wilson. He a native of South Carolina and she of Chicago, Illinois. He a physician.

SHRINER, L. J. aged 21 years married to TOWLES, H. A. aged 35 years March 15, 1881 by Rev. Edward T. Horn. He a native of Savannah, Georgia and she of Charleston. He a merchant and farmer.

SHRIVER, ALBERTINE aged 16 years married to BENKE, CLAUS R. aged 27 years August 10, 1893 by Rev. J. L. Shokes at 231 Coming Street. Both natives of Charleston. He a laborer.

SHUCK, LEWIS aged 30 years married to BURK, ADDIE D. aged 24 years November 15, 1887 by Rev. Charles Stackley at 12 Water Street. He a native of Warrenton, North Carolina and she of Charleston. He a clerk.

SHULER, HENRY F. aged 24 years married to BAGNOLL, CARRIE J. aged 23 years July 15, 1893 by Rev. J. L. Stokes at 603 King Street. He a native of South Carolina and she of North Carolina. He a bookkeeper.

SHULKEN, JOHN aged 24 years married to FERREL, MELISSA aged 23 years January 25, 1880 by Rev. Edward T. Horn in Savage Street. He a native of Germany and a grocer. She a native of Ridgeville, South Carolina.

SHUMAKER, JOHN aged 21 years married to THOMPSON, (Mrs.) S. M. JACKSON aged 22 years March 20, 1892 by Rev. J. H. Smith at 2 Stone Court. He a native of New Orleans, Louisiana and she of Berkeley County, South Carolina. He works in the cotton mill.

SIEBERT, THEODORE CONRAD aged 23 years married to GRADICK, M. EMMA aged 17 years November 24, 1880 by Rev. W. L. Bowman at the home of the Bride - 7 Aiken Street. He a baker.

SIEGLER, ALBERT aged 24 years married to DURKINS, ELISE G. aged 24 years April 27, 1884 by Rev. William Lonergan. He a native of Edgefield, South Carolina and she of Maryland. He a weaver.

SIELCKEN (?), FREDERICKE DORETHA aged 39 years married to SPEKETER, CLAUS aged 54 years November 14, 1886 by Rev. Louis Muller at the St. Matthew's Lutheran Church. Both natives of Germany. He a miller.

SIGALLES, NICHOLAS aged 27 years married to FERRIS, SARAH aged 23 years April 7, 1881 by Rev. L. H. Shuck in Meeting Street near Hibernian Hall.

SIGWALD, ADELE L. aged 20 years married to SALVO, JOSEPH H. aged 25 years March 26, 1885 at 22 Columbus Street. Both natives of Charleston. He a carpenter.

SIGWALD, ALICE G. aged 23 years married to PORTER, JOSEPH J. aged 21 years April 8, 1891 by Rev. J. Thomas Pate at 106 Columbus Street. He a native of Orangeburg, South Carolina. He a machinist.

SIGWALD, A. L. aged 19 years October 21, 1880 married to COLLINS, H. W. aged 19 years October 21, 1880 by Rev. H. F. Chreitzberg at 22 Columbus Street. He a native of Summerville, South Carolina and she of Charleston. He a salesman.

SIGWALD, BOWMAN aged 23 years married to HOLLER, LOUISE aged 14 years December 25, 1889 by Rev. R. C. Holland at 47 Nassau Street. Both natives of Charleston. He a scroll driver.

SIGWALD, CORNELIA B. aged 16 years married to MEYERS, STEDTMAN aged 28 years March 19, 1888 by Rev. J. W. Fuller at 11 Mount Street. Both natives of Charleston. He a grocer.

SIGWALD, E. M. aged 28 years married to BELL, A. W. aged 29 years December 9, 1880 by Rev. W. S. Bowman at 55 Spring Street. He a native of Colleton County, South Carolina and she of Charleston. He a railroad conductor in Orangeburg, South Carolina.

SIGWALD, HENRY W. aged 63 years married to KECKLEY, (Mrs.) MARY DAGGETT aged 38 years October 23, 1887 by Rev. Robert Wilson at 311 East Bay Street. Both natives of Charleston. He an engineer.

SIGWALD, JULIA aged 23 years married to SALVO, JAMES R. aged 21 years October 26, 1886 by Rev. J. Walter Dickson at 106 Columbus Street. He a native of South Carolina and she of Charleston. He a salesman.

SIGWALD, LAWRENCE F. aged 22 years married to McINTOSH, LIZZIE aged 25 years April 5, 1892 by Rev. J. L. Stokes at 106 Columbus Street. Both natives of Charleston. He a horseshoer.

SIGWALD, LILA M. aged 22 years married to BEATTIE, JULIAN B. aged 23 years December 7, 1884 by Father F. A. Schmetz at 269 Meeting Street. Both natives of Charleston. He works for the railroad.

SIGWALD, LOUISA LOCKWOOD aged 23 years married to REED, JAMES POWELL aged 37 years December 10, 1885 by Rev. Luther K. Probst at the Wentworth Street Lutheran Church. He a native of Wilmington, Delaware and she of Charleston. He a car builder.

SIGWALD, LENORA A. aged 23 years married to VIDAL, JAMES H. aged 38 years April 27, 1887 by Rev. Luther K. Probst. Both natives of South Carolina. He a merchant.

SIGWALD, PATRICK O. married to COCHRAN, KATE May 1, 1878 by William B. Yates, Chaplain.

SIGWALD, ROSA A. aged 18 years married to SEEL, LOUIS aged 30 years November 14, 1884 by Rev. Luther K. Probst. He a native of South Carolina and she of Charleston. He a butcher.

SIGWALD, THOMAS married to SHERIDAN, MARY aged 20 years April 7, 1878 by Father Daniel J. Quigley at 72 King Street.

SILCOX, DANIEL S. aged 22 years married to WARE, IDA AMELIA aged 20 years January 5, 1886 by Rev. Charles S. Vedder. He a native of South Carolina and she of New York. He a clerk.

SILES, EVA E. aged 17 years married to SMITH, GEORGE aged 22 years October 6, 1887 by Rev. Robert Wilson at 44 Spring Street. Both natives of Charleston. He a resident of Savannah, Georgia.

SIMBERG, A. aged 45 years married to FROHOLM, J. S. aged 37 years June 15, 1882 by Rev. Luther K. Probst at the Sailors Home. He a native of Sweden and a sailor.

SIMKIN, ELSWORTH aged 21 years married to BARTH, CATHERINE aged 20 years November 8, 1885 by Rev. J. V. Welsh at 24 Bee Street. He a native of Pennsylvania and she of Charleston. He a machinist.

SIMKINS, KATIE aged 21 years married to MARTIN, OSCAR F. aged 30 years January 18, 1887 by Rev. Johannes Heckel at 4 Short Street. He a native of Illinois and she of Charleston. He a gas fitter.

SIMMER, HARRY E. aged 27 years married to O'DELL, KATIE BRONSON aged 25 years March 3, 1885 by Rev. John O. Wilson at 6 Montagu Street. He a native of England and she of New York. He the manager of the Singer Sewing Machine Company.

SIMMONS, ANNA L. aged 23 years married to ROGERS, JOHN E. aged 24 years October 3, 1888 by Father J. J. Monaghan at 493 Meeting Street. He a native of New York and she of Charleston. He a paperhanger.

SIMMONS, ANNIE H. aged 25 years married to LYONS, ROBERT B. aged 28 years July 11, 1878 by Rev. C. C. Pinckney at grace Church. He a native of Union County, South Carolina and she of Charleston. He a farmer.

SIMMONS, ARCHIBALD B. aged 22 years married to MISHAW, ADRIANNA V. aged 18 years August 30, 1893 by Rev. J. C. Yongue at 43 Blake Street. He a native of Long Island, South Carolina and she of Georgetown, South Carolina. He works in the bagging factory.

SIMMONS, EDWARD L. aged 23 years married to STEVENSON, CATHERINE A. aged 23 years June 24, 1889 by Father F. J. Shadler at St. Joseph's Roman Catholic Church. Both natives of Charleston. He a sashmaker.

SIMMONS, ELIZA aged 17 years married to HERIOT, JULIAN W. aged 27 years June 11, 1889 by Rev. C. C. Pinckney at Grace Church. He a native of Richland County, South Carolina and she of Colleton County, South Carolina. He a clerk.

SIMMONS, GERTRUDE E. aged 20 years married to COMAR, JAMES B. aged 20 years April 13, 1879 by Rev. Daniel J. Quigley at The Cathedral of St. John the Baptist.

SIMMONS, JOHN W. aged 42 years married to ALTMAN, CAROLINE FRANCIS aged 36 years December 23, 1888 by Rev. H. B. Browne at 78 Drake Street.

SIMMONS, JULIA married to REEDER, OSWALD June 26, 1883 by Rev. William H. Campbell.

SIMMONS, MARY E. aged 28 years married to EDWARDS, JAMES A. aged 24 years November 22, 1891 by Rev. W. A. Betts at 20 Hampstead Square. He a native of Berkeley County, South Carolina and she of Colleton County, South Carolina. He works at the electric light company.

SIMMONS, MATILDA married to SIMMONS, SEDGWICK aged 25 years April 15, 1880 by Rev. A. Toomer Porter at the Church of the Holy Communion. He a native of Charleston and a clerk.

SIMMONS, SEDGWICK aged 25 years married to SIMMONS, MATILDA April 15, 1880 by Rev. A. Toomer Porter at the Church of the Holy Communion. He a native of Charleston and a clerk.

SIMMS, ADDY E. aged 18 years married to CAMPBELL, JAMES A. aged 28 years April 12, 1887 by Rev. J. V. Welsh. Both natives of Charleston. He a clerk.

SIMMS, MARY married to KINLOCH, JOHN M. March 24, 1881 by Rev. William H. Campbell at St. Paul's Church.

SIMON, S. LEWIS aged 28 years married to MAYRANT, KATE D. aged 25 years November 16, 1887 by Rev. C. C. Pinckney at Grace Church. He a native of Charleston and she of Sumter County, South Carolina. He a civil engineer.

SIMONDS, LOUIS D. married to RHETT, MARY B. December 11, 1894 by Rev. William H. Campbell at St. Paul's Church. He a bank officer.

SIMONIN, GEORGE ANTHONY aged 30 years married to FLATLEY, MARY FRANCES aged 18 years February 24, 1884 by Rev. P. L. Duffy at The Cathedral of St. John the Baptist. Both natives of Charleston. He a printer.

SIMONS, ARTHUR ST. J aged 33 years married to INGLESBY, CAROLINE aged 24 years December 27, 1894 by Rev. C. C. Pinckney at Grace Church.

SIMONS, ANNIE H. aged 25 years married to LYONS, ROBERT B. aged 28 years July 11, 1878 by Rev. C. C. Pinckney at Grace Church.

SIMONS, A. EDWARD married to SIMONS, SARAH January 9, 1890 by Rev. Richard S. Trapier in South Battery.

SIMONS, CHARLES L. married to DURKIN, M. W. August 6, 1885 by Rev. William H. Campbell at the residence of Mrs. Durkin. Both natives of Charleston. He a clerk.

SIMONS, CHARLOTTE married to LAURENS, HENRY R. October 22, 1884 by Rev. William H. Campbell.

SIMONS, HARLESTON REID married to OGIER, HARRIET RUTLEDGE January 15, 1878 by Rev. Richard S. Trapier at the residence of Dr. Ogier.

SIMONS, HARRIET married to PRINGLE, ROBERT A. November 10, 1886 by Rev. William H. Campbell at St. Paul's Church. He a merchant.

SIMONS, HATTIE aged 21 years married to PORTER, JAMES aged 26 years December 20, 1877 by Rev. A. Toomer Porter at St. Paul's Church. Both natives of Charleston. He a lawyer.

SIMONS, JAMES S. aged 23 years married to PICKENS, MARY R. aged 23 years October 27, 1892 by Rev. C. C. Pinckney at 34 Smith Street. Both natives of Charleston. He a weaver in the cotton mill.

SIMONS, JEANNIE R. married to RICHARDSON, DAVISON December 30, 1891 by Rev. William H. Campbell. He a planter in Sumter, South Carolina.

SIMONS, LOTTIE A. aged 19 years married to WOLFE, LAWRENCE S. aged 29 years November 5, 1885 by Rev. Thomas M. Galphin at 47 Rutledge Avenue. Both natives of South Carolina. He a dentist in Orangeburg, South Carolina.

SIMONS, MARY A. married to TUCKER, WILLIAM H. October 12, 1893 by Rev. William H. Campbell at St. Paul's Church.

SIMONS, MATILDA married to SIMONS, SEDGEWICK aged 25 years April 15, 1880 by Rev. A. Toomer Porter at the Church of the Holy Communion. Both natives of Charleston. He a clerk.

SIMONS, ROBERT A. aged 23 years married to FOLLIN, ANNIE L. aged 20 years December 20, 1881 by Rev. C. C. Pinckney at Grace Church.

SIMONS, SARAH married to SIMONS, A. EDWARD January 9, 1890 by Rev. Richard S. Trapier in South Battery.

SIMONS, WILLIAM W. married to CALDER, MARY April 16, 1895 by Rev. William H. Campbell at St. Paul's Church. He an insurance agent.

SIMPSON, SAM aged 32 years married to ZIMMERMANN, ELLA aged 36 years May 21, 1895 by Rev. Charles S. Vedder. He a native of Bordeaux, France and she of Orangeburg, South Carolina He a mariner.

SIMS, (Mrs.) ALICE R. O'BRIEN aged 33 years married to BARTH, WILLIAM H. aged 35 years July 8, 1893 by Rev. J. C. Yongue at 14 Hampstead Square.

SIMS, ALICE R. aged 23 years married to SIMS, B. W. aged 19 years October 21, 1880 by Rev. H. F. Chreitzberg at the residence of B. W. Sims - the corner of Reid and Meeting Streets. Both natives of Charleston. He works for the railroad.

SIMS, B. W. aged 19 years married to SIMS, ALICE R. aged 23 years October 21, 1880 by Rev. H. F. Chreitzberg at the residence of B. W. Sims - the corner of Reid and Meeting Streets. Both natives of Charleston. He works for the railroad.

SIMS, ISABELLE aged 36 years married to McBRIDE, ANDREW aged 50 years September 6, 1881 by Rev. A. Coke Smith at 123 St. Philip Street. He a native of Charleston and a cotton manufacturer.

SIMS, MARY married to KINLOCH, JOHN M. March 24, 1881 by Rev. William H. Campbell at St. Paul's Church. He a native of Charleston and a laborer.

SINDORT (?), C. H. F. W. aged 34 years married to LINSIBRINK (?), E. N. H. aged 18 years July 20, 1880 by Rev. Louis Muller at the residence of the Bride's mother - King Street near Broad. He a native of Hanover and she of Charleston. He a merchant.

SINGLETARY, GEORGE O. aged 24 years married to HUDSON, MARY JANE aged 27 years May 5, 1889 by Rev. R. W. Lide at the residence of A. Hudson - 623 King Street. He a native of Summerville, South Carolina and she of Colleton County, South Carolina. He a carpenter.

SINGLETARY, MARY J. married to BEATY, JAMES H. October 5, 1890 by Rev. W. A. Betts.

SINGLETARY, WILLIAM T. aged 22 years married to HANCOCK, MAGGIE A. aged 16 years December 13, 1894 by Rev. J. C. Yongue at 24 Blake Street. Both natives of Berkeley County, South Carolina. He a farmer in Berkeley County.

SINKLER, ANNE S. aged 19 years married to WALKER, WILSON aged 21 years November 18, 1889 by Rev. John Johnson at St. Philip's Church. Both natives of Charleston. He an engineer in Milledgeville, Georgia.

SINKLER, CLARE L. aged 25 years married to PRIOLEAU, ELIAS aged 31 years June 1, 1893 by Rev. Charles S. Vedder at the Huguenot Church. He a native of Cordesville, South Carolina and she of Charleston. He a cotton shipper.

SINKLER, HELEN aged 21 years married to WARLEY, WILLIAM H. aged 26 years November 9, 1893 by Rev. John Johnson at St. Philip's Church. Both natives of South Carolina. He a bank officer.

SINKLER, THOMAS S. aged 26 years married to FINLEY, CAROLINE aged 24 years October 20, 1887 by Rev. E. C. L. Browne at the Unitarian Church. Both natives of Charleston. He a clerk.

SIRES, A. aged 29 years married to FERGUSON, C. B. aged 23 years December 28, 1880 by Rev. Luther K. Probst at 38 Reid Street. Both natives of Charleston. He an engineer.

SIRES, (Mrs.) CLARA B. FERGUSON aged 36 years married to BYNUM, CLARENCE W. aged 38 years December 20, 1894 by Rev. J. C. Yongue at the corner of Reid and Nassau Streets. He a native of Richland County, South Carolina and she of Charleston. He a planter in Richland County.

SIRES, EDMUND C. aged 34 years married to DURR, ANN ELIZA aged 30 years February 12, 1879 by Rev. J. E. Johnson at 308 Meeting Street. Both natives of Charleston. He an engineer.

SIRES, M. J. aged 17 years married to DEA, J. M. aged 24 years May 26, 1882 by Rev. Luther K. Probst at 81 Queen Street. He a native of South Carolina and a pilot.

SIRES, OSCAR D. aged 25 years married to ALEXANDER, BLANCHE L. aged 21 years March 12, 1895 by Rev. J. L. Stokes at 145 St. Philip Street. She a native of England. He a baker.

SIRES, W. J. married to LEA, J. W. May 26, 1882 by Rev. Luther K. Probst. Both natives of South Carolina.

SISSON, M. H. aged 39 years married to SCOTT, ISABELLA M. January 13, 1894 by Rev. D. A. Blackburn.

SKINNER, MARGARET MODD aged 22 years married to WILLIAMS, EUGENE HAMILTON aged 24 years November 3, 1881 by Rev. H. F. Chreitzberg at 375 King Street. He a native of Round O, Colleton County, South Carolina. He a physician in Round O.

SKINNER, OLIN D. aged 24 years married to GIBSON, AGNES R. aged 21 years October 30, 1888 by Rev. J. E. Carlisle at 33 Radcliffe Street. He a native of Colleton County, South Carolina and she of Charleston. He a machinist in Cheraw, South Carolina.

SKINNER, WILLIAM J. aged 21 years married to O'BRIEN, LULA T. aged 18 years October 10, 1888 by Rev. J. E. Carlisle at 50 Hanover Street. He a native of Colleton County, South Carolina and she of Charleston. He a clerk.

SKIVINGTON, FANNIE R. aged 19 years married to BRADLEY, WILLIAM A. aged 23 years April 3, 1883 by Rev. Luther K. Probst. He a native of Huntingdon County, Pennsylvania and she of Bloomfield, Tennessee. He a manufacturer.

SLANESON (?), W. M. aged 24 years married to HAM, ALICE R. aged 17 years June 27, 1880 by Rev. R. N. Wells at 15 Church Street. He a native of Clarendon County, South Carolina and she of Charleston.

SLANSON, WILLIAM aged 27 years married to SHEERS, ANNIE aged 26 years October 11, 1884 by Rev. Charles S. Vedder. He a native of South Carolina and she of Germany. He a pilot.

SLATTERY, JOHN P. aged 32 years married to COLLINS, MARY F. aged 22 years January 16, 1889 by Father Daniel J. Quigley at St. Patrick's Roman Catholic Church. He a native of Hoboken, New Jersey and she of Charleston. He a planter in Colleton County, South Carolina.

SLAVICK, M. E. married to TRUAL, EUGENIA aged 19 years August 18, 1879 by William B. Yates, Chaplain. Both natives of Charleston.

SLAWSON, MARIAN married to QUINCY, WILLIAM F. November 25, 1891 by Rev. William H. Campbell. He an express company messenger.

SLOAN, EARL married to WITT, ALICE R. October 11, 1894 by Rev. William H. Campbell at the residence of C. O. WITT. Both natives of Charleston. He works in the phosphate mill.

SMALL, HELEN R. McINNES aged 40 years married to CUNNINGHAM, GEORGE J. aged 46 years November 17, 1881 by Rev. Edward T. Horn at 3 George Street. He a native of Tennessee and she of Charleston. He a butcher.

SMALL, JOSEPHINE aged 19 years married to FALCONETTE, THOMAS aged 31 years July 18, 1883 by Father Harry P. Northrop. He a native of Austria and she of Charleston. He a mariner.

SMALL, MARY CAROLINE T. aged 22 years married to DRESSEL, JOHANN GEORGE aged 24 years May 18, 1881 by Rev. Edward T. Horn at 4 Bull Street.

SMALL, M. C. F. aged 22 years married to DRESSEL, J. G. aged 24 years May 18, 1881 by Rev. Louis Muller at 4 Bull Street.

SMALLS, JAMES H. married to WHALEY, CHARLOTTE CORDES June 12, 1877 by Rev. Richard S. Trapier at St. Michael's Church.

SMART, ALICE aged 19 years married to KELLY, ROBERT aged 22 years June 4, 1878 by Rev. J. V. Welsh. He a native of St. Bartholomew's Parish, South Carolina and she of Charleston. He a laborer.

SMART, ELLA married to DAVIS, WILLIAM July 19, 1878 by William B. Yates, Chaplain.

SMIDORF, C. H. F. W. aged 34 years married to LINSIBRUIK (?), E. M. H. aged 18 years July 20, 1880 by Rev. Louis Muller at the residence of the Bride's mother in King Street near Broad Street. He a native of Hanover and she of Charleston. He a merchant.

SMITH, ALEXANDER aged 29 years married to BECKETT, ADELA M. aged 24 years August 3, 1892 by Rev. R. A. Webb at Westminster Presbyterian Church.   He a native of England and she of Florida. He a civil engineer.

SMITH, ALGERNON S. aged 32 years married to HAYDEN, ANNIE B. April 21, 1889 by Rev. John Johnson. Both natives of South Carolina. He a factor.

SMITH, ANGUS aged 23 years married to MORGAN, ELIZABETH aged 17 years November 15, 1885 by Rev. Luther K. Probst at Summerville, South Carolina. He a native of Charleston and she of Florida. He an engineer.

SMITH, ANNA married to PINCKNEY, LAWRENCE M. May 9, 1893 by Rev. William H. Campbell at St. Paul's Church.

SMITH, ANNE CLELAND aged 27 years married to REED, BENJAMIN HUGER aged 27 years December 9, 1884 by Rev. John Johnson at 18 Meeting Street.

SMITH, AUGUST W. aged 22 years married to RICKELS, DORIS REBECCA aged 17 years January 8, 1884 by Rev. Johannes Heckel at 55 Smith Street. He a native of Augusta, Georgia and she of South Carolina. He a blacksmith.

SMITH, CHARLES K. aged 25 years married to BEHLING, HILMER aged 26 years September 9, 1894 by Rev. J. L. Stokes at 17 Laurel Street.

SMITH, C. A. aged 26 years married to BOSWICK, C. O. aged 16 years August 15, 1882 by Rev. J. V. Welsh at 12 Bogard Street. He a native of Charleston and a fireman.

SMITH, EDITH aged 21 years married to MARSHALL, WILLIAM F. aged 27 years April 3, 1883 by Rev. C. C. Pinckney in Smith Street. He a native of South Carolina and she of Charleston. He a clerk.

SMITH, EMILY aged 27 years married to GRUBER, P. NORMAN aged 37 years March 16, 1890 by Rev. J. Thomas Pate. Both natives of Charleston. He a finishers and bookbinder.

SMITH, GEORGE aged 22 years married to SILES, EVA E. aged 17 years October 6, 1887 by Rev. Robert Wilson at 44 Spring Street. Both natives of Charleston. He a resident of Savannah, Georgia.

SMITH, G. E. aged 20 years married to REILS, W. F. aged 22 years December 30, 1880 by Rev. Johannes Heckel at 125 Calhoun Street. Both natives of Charleston. He a blacksmith.

SMITH, HARRIET KINLOCH married to MANIGAULT, ARTHUR March 30, 1891 by Rev. Richard S. Trapier in Meeting Street. He a native of South Carolina and she of Charleston. He a planter in Santee, South Carolina.

SMITH, HENRY aged 28 years married to CARROLL, MARY aged 18 years June 5, 1881 by Father F. J. Shadler at the residence of the Bride. He a native of Norwich, England and she of Charleston. He works in the gas house.

SMITH, HENRY A. M. married to RUTLEDGE, EMMA B. June 24, 1879 by Rev. R. Trapier in Legare Street.

SMITH, HERBERT A. aged 24 years married to SHIRER, MARY JANE aged 23 years October 21, 1884 by Rev. Luther K. Probst. Both natives of Charleston. He a bookkeeper.

SMITH, HERBERT L. aged 27 years married to GREEN, REBECCA W. aged 27 years April 19, 1888 by Rev. G. R. Brackett. He a native of Georgetown, South Carolina.

SMITH, JABEZ aged 21 years married to BESSINGER, JANE aged 19 years July 22, 1883 by Rev. J. E. Beard at 14 Blake Street. He a native of Barnwell, South Carolina and she of Bamberg, South Carolina. He works in a factory.

SMITH, JAMES M. aged 27 years married to EHRLICH, JULIA aged 29 years February 14, 1894 by John Ahrens, Trial Justice. He a native of Pickens, South Carolina and she of Charleston. He a blacksmith.

SMITH, JOHN aged 26 years married to JONES, (Mrs.) ELMIRA SMITH aged 32 years January 23, 1887 by Rev. H. B. Browne at 98 America Street. He a native of England and she of Charleston. He a miller.

SMITH, JOHN DILL aged 26 years married to RUNCKEN, BERTHA MARGARETHA aged 17 years May 10, 1885 by Rev. Louis Muller at the southwest corner of East Bay and Laurens Streets. He a native of Beaufort, North Carolina and she of Charleston. He a mariner.

SMITH, JOHN D. aged 21 years married to HUTTO, ELLENDER L. aged 22 years December 3, 1893 by Rev. J. L. Stokes at 37 Cooper Street. He a native of Greenville, South Carolina and she of Augusta, Georgia. He a carriage trimmer.

SMITH, JOHN H. aged 32 years married to DUNNING, MELVINA C. aged 34 years December 1, 1881 by Rev. Luther K. Probst in Mt. Pleasant, South Carolina. He a native of Albany, New York and she of Charleston. He a planter.

SMITH, JOHN T. aged 21 years married to WESTENDORFF, CORNELIA aged 20 years April 25, 1881 by Rev. John Johnson at 72 Anson Street. He a native of England and she of Charleston. He a merchant in Brooklyn, New York.

SMITH, JOHN GRAY aged 29 years married to KNAPP, ELIZA J. aged 24 years January 1, 1878 by Rev. John Johnson at 110 Tradd Street. Both natives of Charleston. He a mariner.

SMITH, JULIA W. aged 22 years married to WIER, JOHN BENSON aged 29 years October 2, 1884 by Rev. G. R. Brackett. He a native of Anderson, South Carolina and she of Charleston. He a drummer in Greenville, South Carolina.

SMITH, JULIUS EUGENE A. aged 24 years married to PACORSKI, VERONICA JOSEPHINE aged 19 years November 17, 1889 by Father J. J. Monaghan at 66 Drake Street. He a native of Aiken, South Carolina and she of Charleston. He a plumber.

SMITH, JULIUS E. aged 18 years married to PETERSON, EMMA CHARLOTTE aged 20 years February 3, 1884 by Rev. Luther K. Probst.

SMITH, J. EDWARD aged 27 years married to HUGUENIN, MARIA A. aged 24 years November 29, 1877 by Rev. C. C. Pinckney at Grace Church.

SMITH, J. HENRY aged 29 years married to EHRLICH, SARAH aged 39 years January 23, 1887 by Rev. H. B. Browne at 98 America Street. He a native of South Carolina and she of Charleston. He a miller.

SMITH, J. L. aged 21 years married to MONGIN, KATIE aged 31 years August 29, 1880 by Rev. R. N. Wells at 88 Church Street. Both natives of Charleston and residents of Savannah, Georgia. He a merchant.

SMITH, MARGARET married to WEKING, – January 18, 1881 by William B. Yates, Chaplain.

SMITH, MARIAN aged 17 years married to PITTS, JESSE W. aged 21 years August 6, 1893 by Rev. J. L. Stokes at 239 Coming Street.

SMITH, MARY aged 23 years married to COX, SAMUEL aged 27 years December 14, 1890 by Rev. W. S. Walkins at 47 Columbus Street. He a native of Charleston and she of Greenville, South Carolina. He a moulder.

SMITH, MARY A. aged 23 years married to FORTUNE, DANIEL EL F. aged 22 years February 6, 1883 by Father P. L. Duffy at The Cathedral of St. John the Baptist. Both natives of Charleston. He a stevedore.

SMITH, MARY HAMILTON aged 34 years married to MATTHEWS, J. E. aged 60 years September 18, 1890 by Rev. T. P. Burgess at 15 Limehouse Street. He a native of Charleston and she of Grahamville, South Carolina.

SMITH, MARY JANE aged 37 years married to WALKER, WILLIAM E. aged 36 years April 18, 1886 by Rev. C. E. Chichester at the Planter's Hotel. He a native of Massachusetts and she of South Carolina. He a mariner.

SMITH, MARY J. aged 16 years married to DUC, CHARLES A. aged 33 years November 10, 1883 by Rev. J. A. Cliffton at 189 Coming Street. Both natives of Charleston. He a tinsmith.

SMITH, MATTIE married to JOHNSON, ROBERT March 13, 1879 by Rev. R. N. Wells. He a native of New York and she of Columbia, South Carolina. He a mechanic.

SMITH, MAUDE aged 27 years married to CAMPBELL, MOSES G. aged 28 years February 20, 1890 by Rev. Edwin C. Dargan at 36 Charlotte Street. He a native of Tuskegee, Alabama and she of Greenville, South Carolina. He a bookkeeper in Tuskegee.

SMITH, ROBERT PRINGLE aged 25 years married to LESENSE, HARRIET LOUISE aged 27 years November 30, 1882 by Rev. John Johnson in King Street. He a native of Charleston and she of Charleston. He a merchant in Savannah, Georgia.

SMITH, ROSA aged 16 years married to BROWNING, A. THOMAS aged 21 years August 15, 1888 by Rev. H. B. Browne at 471 Meeting Street. Both natives of Charleston. He a railroad brakeman.

SMITH, ROSS A married to WHITNEY, MARY June 1, 1881 by Rev. A. Coke Smith at 69 Broad Street. He the compiler of city and state directories in Lynchburg, Virginia.

SMITH, R. A. aged 30 years married to CAPERS, M. E. aged 24 years December 19, 1882 by Rev. E. C. L. Browne. He a native of Charleston and a dentist.

SMITH, SAMUEL aged 21 years married to WALTER, ANETTA aged 16 years August 29, 1891 by Rev. R. D. Smart at 207 Calhoun Street. He a native of England and she of Charleston. He a printer.

SMITH, SARAH R. aged 31 years married to BOHLEN, FREDERICK C. aged 39 years January 1, 1893 by Rev. J. C. Yongue at 44 Aiken Street. He a native of Bremen, Germany and she of Berkeley County, South Carolina. He a clerk.

SMITH, THEODORE aged 23 years married to BRICKMAN, MARY ELIZA aged 16 years June 10, 1884 by Rev. J. H. Tillinghast at 223 Meeting Street. He a native of Charleston and she of Augusta, Georgia. He a plumber.

SMITH, THOMAS aged 27 years married to GERKEN, ANNE aged 30 years September 11, 1892 by Rev. John Johnson at 53 Church Street. He a native of Liverpool, England and she of Germany. He a watchman.

SMITH, WILHELMINA aged 19 years married to FERGUSON, GEORGE MOUZON aged 24 years December 8, 1881 by Rev. A. Coke Smith. Both natives of Charleston. He a mechanic.

SMITH, WILLIAM H. aged 55 years married to OWENS, ROSALIE aged 38 years January 19, 1892 by Rev. Edward T. Horn at 108 Tradd Street. Both natives of Charleston. He the Assistant Chief in the Fire Department.

SMITH, W. S. aged 21 years married to JORDAN, L. C. aged 25 years April 11, 1882 by Rev. C. C. Pinckney in Queen Street. He a native of Charleston and a wharfinger.

SMYTHE, MARY F. aged 22 years married to REYNOLDS, THOMAS H. aged 26 years April 29, 1880 by Father P. L. Duffy at The Cathedral of St. John the Baptist. He a native of New York and she of Charleston. He a stonemason.

SMYTHE, LOUISA CHEVES aged 22 years married to STONEY, SAMUEL GAILLARD aged 37 years October 22, 1890 by Rev. G. R. Brackett at the 2nd Presbyterian Church. He a native of South Carolina and she of Charleston. He a merchant.

SNOWDEN, ROBERT LEE aged 28 years married to WARLEY, PAULINE aged 26 years April 27, 1886 by Rev. John Johnson at the residence of the Bride - 171 Broad Street. Both natives of South Carolina. He works in the Naval Stores.

SOHL, ANNA M. aged 21 years married to STRAMM, HERMAN A. aged 25 years April 18, 1895 by Rev. Alfred Freyschmidt. He a native of Germany and she of Charleston.

SOHL, ANNA aged 40 years married to NEUMAN, J. F. aged 27 years December 7, 1879 by Rev. Johannes Heckel at 125 Heckel at 125 Calhoun Street. He a native of Charleston and she of Hanover. He a baker.

SOHL, HENRY aged 24 years married to MEYER, REBECCA MARIA aged 26 years May 15, 1881 by Rev. Louis Muller at the southwest corner of Coming and Bull Streets.

SOHL, MARTHA MARIA aged 32 years married to SCHMONSEES, HENRY aged 32 years May 26, 1883 by Rev. Claudian B. Northrop at the corner of Blake and Drake Streets.

SOHREN, VERONICA aged 32 years married to BREDEMAN, AUGUST W. aged 30 years January 3, 1895 by Father Daniel J. Quigley at St. Patrick's Roman Catholic Church. He a native of Charleston and she of Germany. He a salesman.

SOLGIAN, (?) VINCENT aged 28 years married to SANDERS, ELIZA aged 21 years January 29, 1880 by Father John P. Twigg at The Cathedral of St. John the Baptist. He a native of Dalmatia, Austria and she of Charleston. He a mariner.

SOLOMON, H. aged 26 years married to COHEN, L. S. aged 26 years May 26, 1882 by Rabbi David Levy at 3 Orange Street. He a native of Georgia and a merchant.

SOLOMON, JANIE R. aged 22 years married to FALK, J. M. aged 22 years December 22, 1880 by Rabbi David Levy. Both natives of Charleston. He a merchant.

SOLTAIRE, AMELIA aged 19 years married to JONES, DAVID aged 30 years October 18, 1893 by Rev. Robert Wilson at 4 Wragg Square. He a native of Kershaw County, South Carolina and she of Charleston. He a carpenter.

SOLTAIRE, LORENA aged 16 years married to JOSEPHS, CHARLES aged 22 years May 10, 1885 by Rev. R. A. Rapsly at 2 Cooper Street. He a native of Augusta, Georgia and she of Charleston. He a carpenter.

SOLTZE, CHARLES LOUIS aged 23 years married to SHERIDAN, ELIZA aged 20 years February 17, 1878 by Father Daniel J. Quigley. Both natives of Charleston. He a printer.

SONNICHSEN, BOYD aged 26 years married to BONDS, (Mrs.) JOHANNA ADELINE MARGARET LILIENTHAL aged 17 years May 16, 1887 by Rev. Louis Muller at 96 Radcliffe Street. He a native of Germany and she of Charleston. He a farmer.

SONNICHSEN, HELEN SOPHIE aged 23 years married to SAHLMANN, JOHN CHRISTOPHER aged 28 years March 21, 1878 by Rev. Louis Muller. He a native of Charleston and she of Prussia. He a grocer.

SONTAG, CAROLINE H. aged 25 years married to GUTEKUNST (?), GEORGE G. aged 23 years April 19, 1883 by Rev. Luther K. Probst. He a native of Georgia and she of Chicago, Illinois. He a brewer in Walhalla, South Carolina.

SONTAG, OTILLIE married to SASSARD, H. W. March 20, 1879 by Rev. W. S. Bowman. Both natives of Charleston. He a machinist.

SONTAG, THERESA A. aged 20 years married to HEIDEWICH (?), BERNARD aged 26 years January 10, 1886 by Rev. Luther K. Probst. Both natives of Charleston. He a merchant.

SORG, LUDWIG HUGO aged 30 years married to PLESSMAN, LOUISA FREDERICKA aged 32 years July 14, 1887 by Rev. Louis Muller at 96 Radcliffe Street.

SORIA, MANUEL aged 28 years married to LOGAN, ELIZABETH L. aged 18 years March 21, 1886 by Rev. Luther K. Probst at the Wentworth Street Lutheran Church. He a native of Cadiz, Spain and she of Charleston. He a laborer.

SOSNOSKI, JOSEPH S. aged 23 years married to EDDINGS, JOSIE aged 24 years September 1, 1894 by Rev. A. Ernest Cornish at 300 Meeting Street. Both natives of Edisto Island, South Carolina. He an engineering apprentice.

SOUBEYROUX, HONORE T. aged 23 years married to DuFORT, PAULINE C. aged 21 years October 15, 1885 by Father J. J. Woolahan at St. Mary of the Annunciation Roman Catholic Church. Both natives of Charleston. He an accountant.

SOUBEYROUX, LOUIS L. aged 28 years married to CORMIER, VICTORIA ANGELIQUE AGATHA aged 18 years January 11, 1881 by Father Claudian B. Northrop at St. Mary of the Annunciation Roman Catholic Church. Both natives of Charleston. He a clerk.

SOUTHALL, ANNIE aged 14 years married to MEREE, THOMAS D. aged 22 years October 16, 1887 by Rev. S. S. Blanchard at 73 America Street. Both natives of Charleston. He a railroad hand.

SOUTHALL, (Mrs.) MARY MITCHELL aged 26 years married to JUDGE, MICHAEL aged 47 years November 16, 1881 by Rev. J. Mercier Green at St. Stephen's Church. He a native of Ireland and she of South Carolina. He a laborer.

SPADY, MARION P. aged 30 years married to CROSBY, IRVIN C. aged 30 years February 3, 1886 by Rev. C. C. Pinckney at 88 Society Street. Both natives of Savannah, Georgia. He a druggist.

SPAIN, CORNELIUS aged 50 years married to MORRISSEY, BRIDGET aged 40 years November 17, 1878 by Father C. J. Croghan at St. Joseph's Roman Catholic Church. Both natives of Ireland. He a watchman.

SPAIN, MARY aged 23 years married to BARRETT, PATRICK aged 30 years September 2, 1888 by Father Daniel J. Quigley at St. Patrick's Roman Catholic Church. He a native of Ireland and she of Charleston.

SPAIN, WILLIAM J. aged 25 years married to DIVINE, KATE J. aged 25 years July 25, 1888 by Father John J. Wedenfeller at St. Joseph's Roman Catholic Church. He a native of Augusta, Georgia and she of Charleston. He a clerk.

SPARKMAN, EDWARD H. aged 33 years married to KIRK, E. AUGUSTA December 19, 1878 by Rev. Richard S. Trapier at St. Michael's Church.

SPEAR, HORACE P. aged 38 years married to KLECKLEY, ANNA M. aged 24 years August 20, 1887 by Rev. John O. Wilson. Both natives of Georgia. He a broker.

SPEISSENGER (?), ANNA J. aged 25 years married to EASON, R. H. aged 32 years October 15, 1880 by Rev. R. N. Wells. Both natives of Charleston. He a clerk.

SPEISSENGER (?), JOHN W. aged 21 years married to CANTY, MAGGIE aged 24 years December 19, 1886 by Rev. J. V. Welsh at 40 Bee Street. Both natives of Charleston. He a mechanic.

SPEKETER, CLAUS aged 54 years married to SIELCKEN (?), FREDERICKE DORETHA aged 39 years November 14, 1886 by Rev. Louis Muller at the St. Matthew's Lutheran Church. Both natives of Germany. He a miller.

SPELL, ANNIE aged 22 years married to POPE, CLAUS JOHANN aged 22 years April 5, 1886 by Rev. Louis Muller at 93 Queen Street. He a native of Germany and she of Charleston. He a clerk in Coosaw, South Carolina.

SPELL, ELLA married to HEMMINGWAY, ARTHUR January 20, 1891 by Rev. W. A. Betts.

SPELL, VICTORIA aged 22 years married to LARSON, JOHN aged 28 years May 18, 1884 by Rev. Luther K. Probst. He a native of Norway and she of South Carolina. He a carpenter.

SPELLMAN, DANIEL married to CARROLL, ADELLA June 9, 1889 by Rev. H. L. P. Bolger at 63.5 Broad Street. He a merchant in Yemassee, South Carolina.

SPENCE, LEON C. aged 25 years married to CRAMER, MARY J. aged 30 years August 28, 1892 by John Ahrens, Trial Justice. He a native of Carol County, Georia and she of Canada. He a doctor at the Waverly House.

SPIKES, ORRIE aged 18 years married to PALMER, BOLLER aged 21 years July 28, 1889 by Rev. J. E. Carlisle at 603 King Street. He a native of Richmond County, Georgia and she of Graniteville, South Carolina. He a sashmaker in Savannah, Georgia.

SPINCKEN (?), (Mrs.) HELENE J. aged 42 years married to STEENCKEN, CHRISTIAN E. aged 28 years November 29, 1891 by Rev. Louis Muller. Both natives of Prussia. He works in a restaurant.

SPINK, ALONZO S. aged 45 years married to SPINK, (Mrs.) SARAH BUSHEE aged 41 years October 7, 1883 by Rev. S. A. Walker at 315 East Bay Street. He a native of Boston, Massachusetts and she of Providence, Rhode Island. He a clerk.

SPINK, KATE married to INGLAN, JAMES December 1, 1878 by William B. Yates, Chaplain.

SPINK, (Mrs.) SARAH BUSHEE aged 41 years married to SPINK, ALONZO S. aged 45 years October 7, 1883 by Rev. S. A. Walker at 315 East Bay Street. He a native of Boston, Massachusetts and she of Providence, Rhode Island. He a clerk.

SPIRES, MATTIE aged 20 years married to TAYLOR, PETER C. aged 30 years November 9, 1887 by Rev. John O. Wilson at 51 Columbus Street. He a native of Berkeley County, South Carolina and she of Lincoln County, Georgia. He works in the phosphate mill.

SPRAGUE, FRANK W. aged 35 years married to JENKINS, FRANCIS aged 23 years March 5, 1885 by Rev. Thomas A. Grove at 5 Nassau Street. He a native of New York and she of Sullivans Island, South Carolina. He a laborer.

SPRAGUE, MARY E. aged 17 years married to DUNLAP, ALEX aged 20 years April 5, 1893 by Rev. J. C. Yongue. Both natives of Charleston. He a blacksmith.

SPRECKEN, MARY ANN aged 24 years married to KASSENS, DIETRICH aged 23 years August 10, 1892 by Father J. J. Monaghan at St. Patrick's Roman Catholic Church. He a native of Germany and she of South Carolina. He a bank officer.

SQUIRES (?), JOHN HENRY aged 25 years married to CONLEY, MARY aged 26 years June 8, 1890 by Father J. J. Monaghan at 136 St. Philip Street. He a native of New York and she of Ireland. He a painter.

ST. AMAND, BEULAH aged 23 years married to STEIMEYER, GEORGE aged 25 years January 19, 1878 by Rev. Charles S. Vedder.

ST. AMAND, CLARENCE W. aged 27 years married to TOBIAS, ISABEL aged 26 years February 15, 1884 by Father Daniel J. Quigley at 6 Rutledge Avenue.

ST. AMAND, FLORENCE E. aged 22 years married to BARBOT, CHARLES JULIUS aged 25 years October 13, 1890 by Father Claudian P. Northrop at The Cathedral of St. John the Baptist. Both natives of Charleston. He a clerk in Wilmington, North Carolina.

ST. CLAIR, KATIE aged 21 years married to McDONALD, WILLIAM O. aged 23 years July 1, 1891 by Rev. R. C. Holland. He a native of Charleston and she of Marion County, South Carolina. He a clerk.

STAKELEY, IDA F. aged 17 years married to ALMERS, AUGUSTINE aged 17 years March 17, 1884 by Rev. J. E. Beard at 64 Nassau Street. Both natives of Charleston. He a laborer.

STALEY, WELLINGTON A. aged 22 years married to BUILDT, ANNIE T. aged 22 years December 12, 1886 by Rev. Luther K. Probst at the Wentworth Street Lutheran Church. Both natives of South Carolina. He works for the railroad.

STALL, JOHN R. aged 35 years married to KENNEDY, ELIZA aged 26 years May 15, 1889 by Rev. H. B. Browne at 89 America Street.

STALLINGS, S. ALFRED aged 23 years married to KING, LOUISA HATTIE aged 19 years April 26, 1890 by Rev. T. P. Burgess at 6 Hampstead Court.

STALVEY, CATHARINE MANSFIELD aged 19 years married to GIESEA (?), AMOS LEONARD aged 33 years January 6, 1884 by Rev. John Willson at the corner of Church and Queen Streets, room 39, The Calder House. He a native of Germany and she of South Carolina. He an engineer.

STANSELL, C. B. aged 24 years married to SEYMOUR, ROSA aged 22 years February 1, 1888 by Rev. R. W. Lide at 168 Queen Street. He a native of Elka, South Carolina and she of Charleston. He a farmer in Elka.

STANDELL, LIZZIE L. aged 24 years married to LANNEAU, BASIL R. aged 22 years November 7, 1894 by Rev. David M. Ramsey at 53 Laurens Street.

STANTON, CATHERINE aged 26 years married to WALSH, JOHN aged 30 years November 10, 1890 by Father F. J. Shadler at St. Joseph's Roman Catholic Church. Both natives of Ireland. He a laborer.

STANTON, FRANKLIN L. aged 24 years married to LEGARE, EMILY W. aged 27 years August 12, 1881 by Rev. L. H. Shuck at 27 Church Street.

STAUBER, ADAM aged 29 years married to BLACK, MAMIE aged 20 years September 15, 1895 by Rev. Alfred Freyschmidt at 45 State Street. He a native of Germany and she of Savannah, Georgia. He a baker.

STAUNTON, BRIDGET aged 22 years married to LINSKEY, PATRICK aged 25 years October 13, 1878 by Father Daniel J. Quigley at The Cathedral of St. John the Baptist. Both natives of Ireland. He a clerk.

STAWOVICH (?), MAMIE A. aged 19 years married to ORTMANN, R. J. aged 21 years April 30, 1891 by Father Daniel J. Quigley at St. Patrick's Roman Catholic Church.

STEADMAN, ARTHUR A. aged 27 years married to BANCROFT, MATILDA aged 23 years November 27, 1881 by Rev. C. C. Pinckney at 4 Thomas Street. Both natives of Charleston. He a clerk.

STEENCKEN, CHRISTIAN E. aged 42 years married to SPINCKEN, HELENE J. aged 28 years November 29, 1891 by Rev. Louis Muller. Both natives of Prussia. He works in a restaurant.

STEENCKEN, JOHANN H. aged 24 years married to BUCK, ANNA MARIA SOPHIA aged 23 years March 4, 1886 by Rev. Louis Muller at 140 Cannon Street. Both natives of Charleston. He a wheelwright.

STEHMEYER, ANNA MARIA aged 21 years married to KOSTER, JOHANN aged 37 years November 10, 1887 by Rev. Louis Muller at the corner of Meeting and Hasell Streets. He a native of Prussia and she of Bremen, Germany. He a grocer.

STEHMEYER, DIETRICH aged 24 years married to STURCKEN, MARIE ELIZABETH aged 22 years November 25, 1888 by Rev. Louis Muller at the St. Matthew's Lutheran Church.

STEINBRECKER, WILHELM aged 28 years married to BRUNS, ADELINE MARGARETHE aged 26 years February 11, 1886 by Rev. Louis Muller at the northwest corner of Calhoun and Alexander Streets. Both natives of Germany. He a saloonkeeper.

STEINCKE, EMILIE FREIDA LOUISE aged 18 years married to POPE, DIETRICH aged 24 years February 5, 1878 by Rev. Louis Muller in Market Street between King and Meeting Streets. He a native of Hanover and she of Charleston. He a grocer.

STEINMEYER, GEORGE E. aged 25 years married to ST. AMAND, BEULAH aged 23 years January 19, 1878 by Rev. Charles S. Vedder at 7 Friend Street.

STEINMEYER, L. aged 25 years married to JAMES, R. aged 31 years October 12, 1882 by Rev. D. J. Sims. Both natives of Charleston. He a mechanic.

STEITZ, ANNA AMELIA aged 18 years married to STENDER, FREDERICK W. aged 42 years June 9, 1885 by Rev. Johannes Heckel in Hasell Street. Both natives of Charleston. He a merchant.

STELLING, CLAUS aged 24 years married to DUHRELS, META DORETHA aged 24 years October 11, 1891 by Rev. Louis Muller at 96 Radcliffe Street. Both natives of Prussia. He a clerk.

STELLING, EIBE FREDERICK aged 20 years married to FREITAS, MARY EUGENI9A aged 21 years December 13, 1877 by Father Harry P. Northrop at St. Patrick's Roman Catholic Church. Both natives of Charleston. He a salesman.

STELLING, EIBE FREDERICK aged 19 years married to FREITAS, MARY EUGENIA aged 18 years December 13, 1877 by Father Harry P. Northrop at 17 America Street.

STELLING, HEINRICH aged 23 years married to RODEMANN, ANNA CATHARINE aged 24 years October 31, 1886 by Rev. Louis Muller at the corner of King Street and Rogers Alley. Both natives of Germany. He a grocer.

STELLJES, HENRIETTA ADELAIDE SOPHIE aged 19 years married to MULLER, HERMAN HEINRICH aged 28 years March 1, 1883 by Rev. Louis Muller at the northeast corner of King and Wentworth Streets. He a native of Georgia and she of Columbia, South Carolina. He a saloon keeper.

STELLJES, HENRIETTA F. M. aged 23 years married to JESSEN, HEINRICH LUDWIG aged 26 years December 1, 1881 by Rev. Louis Muller.

STELLJES, HERMAN DIETRICH aged 28 years married to KOSTER, WILHELMINA SOPHIE HENRIETTA aged 23 years March 26, 1878 by Rev. Louis Muller at the corner of Smith and Cannon Streets. He a native of Germany and she of Charleston. He a grocer.

STELLJES, J. D. F. aged 29 years married to FINCK, META R. S. aged 19 years October 22, 1885 by Rev. Claudian B. Northrop at the corner of Smith and Vanderhorst Streets. Both natives of Charleston. He a grocer.

STELLJES, R. M. MOLLENAUER aged 49 years married to MUNTER, F. E. R. A. aged 35 years February 7, 1884 by Rev. Louis Muller. Both natives of Germany. He a druggist.

STELLO, HERMANN aged 28 years married to REID, ANNA CATHERINE aged 24 years September 12, 1878 by Rev. W. S. Bowman in Spring Street near King Street. He a native of Germany and she of Charleston. He a laborer.

STELLO, KARL CHRISTIAN aged 26 years married to BLOCK, JOHANNA MARIA SOPHIA aged 24 years January 30, 1883 by Rev. Louis Muller at 76 Spring Street. He a native of Prussia and she of Charleston. He a grocer.

STELLO, KARL CHRISTIAN aged 30 years married to BUSE, ELIZA MARIA aged 25 years September 28, 1886 by Rev. Johannes Heckel at 520 King Street. He a native of Germany and she of Charleston. He a merchant.

STENDER, ANNA aged 17 years married to PUCKHABER, JOHANN HEINRICH aged 27 years March 4, 1883 by Rev. Louis Muller at 390 King Street. He a native of Charleston and she of Germany. He a baker.

STENDER, FREDERICK W. aged 42 years married to STEITZ, ANNA AMELIA aged 18 years June 9, 1885 by Rev. Johannes Heckel in Hasell Street. Both natives of Charleston. He a merchant.

STENDER, HENRIETTA JOHANNA aged 19 years married to PUCKHABER, GEORGE LUDWIG aged 21 years November 19, 1889 by Rev. Louis Muller at the residence of the Groom's mother in 466 King Street above Ann Street. He a native of Charleston and she of Prussia. He a baker.

STENDER, M. aged 18 years married to J. F. E. MEYER aged 32 years November 16, 1879 by Rev. G. R. Brackett at the residence of H. Stender - in King Street. He a native of York County, South Carolina. She of Charleston. He a farmer.

STENHOUSE, JANET FULTON married to CUNNINGHAM, THOMAS H. March 12, 1879 by Rev. W. F. Junkin. He a native of Anderson, South Carolina and she of Charleston.

STENKEN, ANNA META aged 29 years married to SCHMIDT, WILHELM NICHOLAS aged 24 years February 11, 1883 by Rev. Louis Muller at the corner of Calhoun and St. Philip Streets. Both natives of Germany. He a grocer.

STENKEN, HELEN aged 24 years married to PRAUSE, WILHELM C. D. aged 25 years February 26, 1892 by Rev. Louis Muller at 23 Aiken Street. Both natives of Charleston. He a clerk.

STENMEYER, MARY ELIZA aged 20 years married to PLOWDEN, WALLACE McINNIS aged 28 years April 19, 1881 by Rev. Charles S. Vedder. He a native of South Carolina and she of Charleston. He a farmer.

STEPHENS, CHARLES aged 40 years married to TRUALL, (?) (Mrs.) L. TOOMER aged 46 years November 24, 1887 by Father F. J. Shadler in King Street. She a native of Port Royal, South Carolina. He a native of Hamburg, Germany. He a pilot in Beaufort, South Carolina.

STEPHENS, DELLA VICTORIA aged 19 years married to ROSIS, ISIDORE aged 23 years August 9, 1878 by Father J. J. Woolahan at St. Patrick's Roman Catholic Church. Both natives of Charleston. He a cigarmaker.

STEPHENS, JAMES aged 25 years married to RUDD, J. MARGARET aged 18 years December 27, 1889 by Rev. J. Thomas Pate at 231 Coming Street. Both natives of Colleton County, South Carolina. He a laborer in Summerville, South Carolina.

STEPHENSON, JANE aged 17 years married to GAILLARD, EDWARD T. aged 23 years July 12, 1887 by Rev. G. R. Pinckney at Grace Church. He a native of South Carolina and she of Georgia. He a clerk.

STEVENS, ANN ELIZA aged 23 years married to MARSHALL, FRANCIS H. aged 26 years April 8, 1886 by Rev. Luther K. Probst. He a native of Savannah, Georgia and she of Charleston. He a clerk in Savannah.

STEVENS, ANNIE ELIZA aged 18 years married to HORTON, BENJAMIN F. aged 23 years October 12, 1890 by Rev. R. D. Smart. at 81 Line Street. He a native of South Carolina and she of Charleston. He a fireman.

STEVENS, H. W. L. aged 21 years married to BURSE, CAROLINE S. aged 18 years September 28, 1880 by Rev. John H. Honour at 14 John Street. He a native of Bluffton, South Carolina and a grocer. She a native of Walhalla, South Carolina.

STEVENS, JENNIE aged 22 years married to WESTCOTT, THOMAS aged 30 years February 17, 1890 by Rev. Robert Wilson at 4 Wragg Square. He a native of Edisto Island, South Carolina and she of Charleston. He a painter.

STEVENS, WILLIAM S. aged 28 years married to PATRICK, NINA aged 25 years November 16, 1892 by Rev. Edward T. Horn. He a native of Augusta, Georgia and she of Charleston. He a clerk.

STEVENSON, CATHERINE A. aged 23 years married to SIMMONS, EDWARD L. aged 23 years June 24, 1889 by Father F. J. Shadler at St. Joseph's Roman Catholic Church. Both natives of Charleston. He a sashmaker.

STEWART, AUGUSTINE C. aged 32 years married to PATRICK, ALICE SHEPHERD aged 29 years November 6, 1892 by Rev. J. L. Stokes at 231 Coming Street. Both natives of Charleston. He a painter in Savannah, Georgia.

STEWART, MAUD L. aged 15 years married to PLAYER, PETER aged 21 years October 29, 1893 by Rev. J. C. Yongue. He a native of Berkeley County, South Carolina and he works in the cotton mill.

STEWART, SARAH ANNE aged 21 years married to JOHNSON, WILLIAM aged 26 years July 7, 1885 by Father Thomas E. McCORMACK at St. Patrick's Roman Catholic Church.

STEWART, SIMON V. aged 30 years married to SCOTT, (Mrs.) EMMA HUGER LOWNDES aged 30 years November 26, 1885 by Rev. John Johnson at St. Philip's Church. He a native of South Carolina and she of Charleston. He an insurance agent.

STEWART, WILLIAM aged 33 years married to RANTIN, ISADORA aged 27 years July 9, 1889 by Rev. J. E. Carlisle in Addison's Court. He a native of Philadelphia, Pennsylvania and she of Charleston. He works for the railroad.

STINGLUFF, HARRY L married to YATES, JENNIE November 8, 1893 by Rev. William H. Campbell at the residence of Mrs. Yates. Both natives of Charleston. He a collector.

STODDARD, FRANKLIN A. aged 38 years married to ICARD, ELIZABETH W. aged 36 years July 6, 1884 by Rev. Robert Wilson at 3 Marsh Street. He a native of Boston, Massachusetts and she of New York. He operates a steamboat.

STODDARD, LAURA B. aged 28 years married to JARVIS, WILLIAM NELSON aged 38 years July 9, 1888 by Rev. E. C. L. Browne at the Unitarian Church. He a native of Newark, New Jersey and she of Charleston. He a sea captain in Philadelphia, Pennsylvania.

STODDARD, LAWRENCE E. aged 28 years married to COUNTS, IRENE T. aged 18 years October 2, 1889 by Rev. Edwin C. Dargan at Citadel Square Baptist Church. He a native of Charleston and she of Savannah, Georgia. He a baggagemaster.

STOHOFFER, MARIE aged 27 years married to LIRMAN, JEAN NICOLAS aged 30 years July 19, 1888 by Father John O. Schachte at 3 New Street. Both natives of France. He an architect.

STOLL, LENA aged 29 years married to MELCHERS, ALEXNADER aged 52 years October 30, 1883 by Father F. J. Shadler at 381 King Street. Both natives of Charleston. He a baker.

STOLL, MARY ELIZABETH aged 21 years married to MUSTARD, ALLEN CALVITT aged 28 years October 19, 1881 by Rev. J. C. Stoll in King Street.

STOLL, WILLIAM aged 24 years married to HALL, DORA C. aged 18 years April 6, 1879 by Rev. J. V. Welsh in Radcliffe Street.

STOLZ, CHARLES LOUIS aged 23 years married to SHERIDAN, ELIA aged 20 years February 17, 1878 by Father Daniel J. Quigley at 72 King Street.

STOLZE, ANNIE AMELIA aged 27 years married to DROZE, EDWIN MARION aged 26 years September 11, 1884 by Rev. Luther K. Probst. Both natives of Charleston. He a tinsmith.

STONEBRIDGE, RICHARD married to SERES, ROSA August 29, 1885 by Father F. J. Shadler at St. Joseph's Roman Catholic Church. She a native of Charleston.

STONEY, ROSA M. married to BRYAN, ISAAC M. April 30, 1878 by Rev. Ellison Capers at St. Michael's Church.

STONEY, SAMUEL GAILLARD aged 37 years married to SMYTHE, LOUISA CHEVES aged 22 years October 22, 1890 by Rev. G. R. Brackett at the 2nd Presbyterian Church. He a native of South Carolina and she of Charleston. He a merchant.

STOPFEL, PHILIPINA aged 29 years married to KENNEDY, AUSTIN J. aged 26 years November 3, 1885 by Father F. J. Shadler at St. Joseph's Roman Catholic Church. Both natives of Charleston.

STOPPELBEIN, JOSEPH aged 20 years married to BRUNNING, MARY aged 16 years February 14, 1884 by Father John P. Twigg.

STOPPELBEIN, L. B. aged 26 years married to TORLAY, CAROLINE F. aged 25 years December 16, 1885 by Rev. John Johnson at St. Philip's Church. Both natives of Charleston. He a merchant.

STOPPELBEIN, MILTON S. married to MILLER, REBECCA V. October 3, 1878 by William B. Yates, Chaplain.

STORM, WALTON aged 23 years married to JONES, LULA S. aged 19 years November 15, 1883 by Rev. C. C. Pinckney at Grace Church. He a native of New York and she of Charleston. He a lawyer.

STOUDEMIRE, MARTIN aged 55 years married to ARNOLD, JANE aged 47 years July 23, 1884 by Rev. W. P. Mouzon at 189 Coming Street. He a native of Goose Creek, South Carolina and she of Lexington County, South Carolina. He a carpenter.

STRAMM, AUGUSTA aged 21 years married to CLAUSS, ANDREW THEODORE aged 25 years September 9, 1886 by Rev. Johannes Heckel at 16 Wentworth Street. He a native of Charleston and she of Georgia. He a clerk.

STRAMM, HERMAN A. aged 25 years married to SOHL, ANNA M. aged 21 years April 18, 1895 by Rev. Alfred Freyschmidt. He a native of Germany and she of Charleston.

STRANGHAN, HENRY aged 24 years married to RIVERS, LELA aged 15 years September 29, 1890 by Rev. R. J. Smart at 207 Calhoun Street. He a native of Charleston and she of Bullock County, Georgia. He in the turpentine business.

STRATTON, JOHN PAUL aged 25 years married to DOWELL, HARRIET MARY aged 27 years January 24, 1883 by Rev. P. L. Duffy at 1 Trumbo Court. Both natives of Charleston. He a clerk.

STRAUSS, C. W. aged 25 years married to WEBER, CHARLES aged 26 years October 12, 1879 by Rev. W. S. Bowman at 7 Minority Street. He a native of Charleston and she of Walhalla, South Carolina. He a clerk.

STRAUSS, HENRY aged 25 years married to KORNAHRENS, ANNA MARIA WILHELMINA aged 21 years November 16, 1884 by Father Claudian B. Northrop at 56 Hasell Street. He a native of Walhalla, South Carolina and she of Charleston. He a merchant

STRAUSS, LEOPOLD aged 30 years married to ISEMAN, LIZETTE aged 19 years May 21, 1878 by Rabbi David Levy at 412 King Street. He a native of Germany and she of Darlington County, South Carolina. He a merchant in Bennettsville, South Carolina.

STRECKFUSS, CATHARINE aged 18 years married to DOSCHER, ERNST H. aged 28 years October 12, 1887 by Rev. Louis Muller at the corner of Line and King Streets. Both natives of Prussia. He a grocer.

STRECKFUSS, CHARLES F. aged 27 years married to JEFFORDS, FANNIE GEORGIANA aged 21 years November 10, 1878 by Rev. W. S. Bowman at 587 King Street. Both natives of Charleston. He a farmer in Georgia.

STRECKFUSS, (Mrs.) CHRISTINE MEYER aged 54 years married to REHKOPF, FREDERICK G. aged 55 years February 7, 1884 by Rev. Louis Muller at 66 Radcliffe Street. Both natives of Germany. He an undertaker.

STROBLE, ALICE U. aged 17 years married to O'NEALE, GEORGE E. aged 22 years October 25, 1883 by Rev. J. V. Welsh at the corner of Fishburne Street and Rutledge Avenue. Both natives of Charleston. He a carpenter.

STROBLE, CHARLES WILLIAM aged 22 years married to JOHNSON, MARY H. aged 14 years March 2, 1884 by Rev. J. E. Beard at the corner of Nassau and Shepard Streets. He a native of Charleston and she of South Carolina. He a laborer.

STROBLE, HENRY aged 19 years married to CAMMER, MAMIE ELIZABETH aged 21 years May 6, 1892 by Rev. J. A. Clifton at 207 Calhoun Street. Both natives of Charleston. He a farmer.

STROBLE, R. aged 23 years married to RELGEA, M. A. aged 16 years December 26, 1882 by Rev. J. V. Welsh at 2 Fishburne Street. He a native of Charleston and a laborer.

STROBLE, T. PRESTON aged 20 years married to GAUSE, SALLY aged 22 years February 9, 1890 by Rev. J. Thomas Pate at the residence of the Bride's mother. He a native of Charleston and she of Germany. He works for the railroad.

STROBONZE, JOHN aged 29 years married to MOORE, ELEANOR aged 16 years December 18, 1890 by Rev. C. E. Chicester. He a native of Austria and she of England. He a longshoreman.

STROHECKER, AMANDA married to BLACKWELL, SAMUEL aged 46 years December 15, 1881 by Rev. Edward T. Horn at St. Johannes Church. He a native of Darlington County, South Carolina and she of Charleston. He a physician in Darlington.

STROMAN, JACOB P. aged 22 years married to McGILLVRAY CAROLINE aged 21 years December 15, 1885 by Rev. John Johnson at 10 Atlantic Street. He a native of South Carolina and she of Charleston. He a physician in Orangeburg, South Carolina.

STRONG, LOUIS CHARLES aged 23 years married to OLIVER, LUCY B. aged 27 years November 1, 1895 by Rev. Charles S. Vedder at 116 Church Street. He a native of Vermont and she of Boston, Massachusetts. He in the mercantile business in Boston.

STRONG, (Mrs.) MARGARET DARCEY aged 30 years married to CARTOMIL, JOHN aged 34 years November 3, 1878 by Father C. J. Croghan at St. Joseph's Roman Catholic Church. Both natives of Ireland. He a farmer.

STROTHER, LOUISE A. aged 26 years married to PETSCH, ALEXANDER H. aged 27 years January 3, 1883 by Rev. E. C. L. Browne at the Unitarian Church. Both natives of Charleston. He a clerk.

STROTHER, LOUISA VIRGINIA aged 22 years married to JOHNSON, NATHANIEL McCALL aged 24 years February 23, 1881 by Rev. E. L. Browne at the Unitarian Church. He a native of Marlboro County, South Carolina and she of Charleston. He a planter.

STUART, ALEXANDER AUGUSTIN aged 27 years married to SCHROEDER, ADELINE LOUISE aged 25 years December 23, 1883 by Rev. Louis Muller. He a native of Charleston and she of Germany. He a spinner.

STUART, EMMA aged 21 years married to BRECKENRIDGE, M. JAMES aged 28 years February 26, 1890 by Rev. Edwin C. Dargan at 36 George Street. He a native of Walhalla, South Carolina and she of Kingstree, South Carolina. He a printer.

STUART, WILLIAM C. aged 26 years married to RHETT, MARIE ALICE aged 25 years October 15, 1892 by Rev. Albert R. Stuart. He a native of Richland County, South Carolina and she of Charleston. He a lawyer in Newport News, Virginia.

STUBBS, RUSSELL A. aged 24 years married to PARKER, LILLY aged 23 years October 15, 1895 by Rev. J. C. Yongue at 51 Wentworth Street. He a native of Alabama and she of Edisto Island, South Carolina. He a merchant.

STUCKE, CHARLES HENRY aged 20 years married to HAHN, ANNIE C. aged 17 years May 29, 1881 by Rev. Johannes Heckel. He a native of Walhalla, South Carolina and she of Charleston. He a baker.

STUCKENBROK, F. I. aged 25 years married to HALPIN, A. J. aged 22 years January 8, 1880 by Rev. Louis Muller at 66 Radcliffe Street. He a native of Hanover and she of Prussia. Both residents of Summerville, South Carolina. He a grocer.

STURCKEN, ANNIE H. aged 20 years married to MURRELL, JAMES J. aged 21 years June 9, 1895 by Rev. J. L. Stokes at 32 Bogard Street.

STURCKEN, ELISE D. aged 20 years married to MENDERNIAN (?), J. H. aged 26 years October 23, 1881 by Rev. Louis Muller at 8 Line Street. He a native of Hanover and she of Charleston. He a grocer.

STURCKEN, HENRIETTA E. aged 18 years married to HEINS, CARSTEN HEINRICH aged 26 years February 21, 1878 by Rev. Louis Muller at the corner of Meeting and Mary Streets.

STURCKEN, JOHN F. aged 27 years married to DeCAMPS, HELENA CATHARINE aged 22 years November 19, 1890 by Father J. J. Monaghan at St. Patrick's Roman Catholic Church. Both natives of Charleston. He a shipping clerk.

STURCKEN, JOHN H. R. aged 28 years married to WILSON, ZILLA H. SMITH aged 40 years June 15, 1892 by Rev. J. H. Smith at the 2nd Adventist Church. He a native of Charleston and she of South Carolina. He works in the cotton mill.

STURCKEN, MARIE ELIZABETH aged 22 years married to STEHMEYER, DIETRICH aged 24 years November 25, 1888 by Rev. Louis Muller at the St. Matthew's Lutheran Church.

STURCKEN, WILLIAM HERMAN aged 44 years married to BARFIELD, FLORENCE aged 23 years May 24, 1891 by Rev. G. R. Brackett at 2 Allway Street. He a native of Charleston and she of Richmond, Virginia. He a cigarmaker.

STURGEON, CHARLES aged 21 years married to MORASKA, MAGGIE aged 19 years March 3, 1889 by Father Daniel J. Quigley at St. Patrick's Roman Catholic Church. He a native of Orangeburg, South Carolina and she of Poland. He a baker.

STURKIE, ROSE aged 15 years married to HELLER, GUSTAV, H. aged 32 years January 17, 1887 by Rev. Johannes Heckel at 524 King Street. He a native of Germany and she of South Carolina. He a carpenter.

STURM, H. W. L. aged 21 years married to BURSE, CAROLINE S. aged 18 years September 28, 1880 by Rev. John H. Honour at the Wentworth Street Lutheran Church. He a native of Bluffton, South Carolina and she of Walhalla, South Carolina. He a grocer.

SUDARSKY, SARA aged 22 years married to BEHRMAN, SELIG aged 27 years May 8, 1891 by Rabbi David Levy at the Hasell Street Synagogue.

SUDER, ELVIRA ARMSTRONG aged 37 years married to YOUNGINER, GEORGE WASHINGTON aged 38 years December 20, 1877 by Rev. G. R. Brackett at the Second Presbyterian Church. He a native of Lexington County, South Carolina and she of Charleston. He a farmer in Oak Hill, Lexington County, South Carolina.

SUGGS, W. CHARLES aged 20 years married to ELLIS, CARRIE S. aged 16 years February 29, 1888 by Rev. H. B. Browne at 97 Drake Street. He a native of Darlington County, South Carolina and she of New York. He a mill operator.

SUHRSTEDT, CATHARINA A. aged 26 years married to POMMER, MAX L. aged 23 years May 23, 1892 by Rev. Louis Muller in King Street.

SUHRSTEDT, JOHANN F. C. aged 27 years married to HUSTEDT, CATHARINA W. aged 20 years October 14, 1891 by Rev. Louis Muller at King Street near Shephard Street. He a native of Charleston and she of Germany. He a fireman.

SULLIVAN, (Mrs.) ABBIE M. WEBBER aged 36 years married to MAGRATH, CHARLES aged 29 years May 24, 1890 by Rev. C. S. Vedder at 120 Meeting. He a native of Prussia and she of Walhalla, South Carolina. He a mariner.

SULLIVAN, CATHARINE aged 23 years married to COSTELLO, JAMES EREVIN aged 20 years March 20, 1884 by Rev. R. A. Lapsley at 76 America Street. He a native of Augusta, Georgia and she of Aiken, South Carolina.

SULLIVAN, ELLA E. aged 26 years married to RILEY, ALEX A. aged 26 years December 26, 1892 by Father J. J. Monaghan at St. Patrick's Roman Catholic Church. Both natives of Charleston. He a blacksmith.

SULLIVAN, JERRIE aged 21 years married to CARROLL, DELIA aged 23 years September 4, 1881 by Rev. J. E. Chapins at the corner of St. Philip and Radcliffe Streets. He a native of Charleston and a farmer.

SULLIVAN, JULIA A. aged 21 years married to LYNCH, THOMAS P. aged 26 years October 26, 1885 by Rev. J. E. Beard at 64 Nassau Street. Both natives of Charleston.

SULLIVAN, M. A. aged 23 years married to McSWEENEY, W. aged 23 years October 3, 1882 by Father J. J. Monaghan at St. Patrick's Roman Catholic Church. He a native of Charleston and a laborer.

SULLIVAN, T. aged 21 years married to CAVERT, D. aged 23 years September 4, 1881 by Father J. E. Chapins at the corner of St. Philip and Radcliffe Street. He a native of Charleston.

SULLIVAN, WILLIAM FRANCIS married to PALMER, MARY aged 22 years February 6, 1889 by Rev. John J. Wedenfuller at St. Joseph's Roman Catholic Church. Both natives of Charleston.

SULLIVAN, WILLIAM PATRICK aged 23 years married to McDONALD, MARY ELLEN aged 35 years April 20, 1884 by Father Daniel J. Quigley.

SUMEN, SALIA married to ALTMAN, ISAIAH October 11, 1881 by Jacob Mills. He a native of North Carolina and she of Adams Run, South Carolina. He a laborer.

SUMMERALL, RICHARD A. aged 23 years married to LUZE, LILLIE aged 19 years February 12, 1893 at 13 Judith Street.

SURAU, CHARLES E. aged 32 years married to PETERMANN, JOHANNA aged 30 years February 13, 1881 by Rev. Luther K. Probst at 3 Ann Street.

SUREN, PAUL aged 27 years married to LEMKINS, CARRIE aged 22 years September 10, 1884 by Rev. F. A. Stemitz at St. Patrick's Roman Catholic Church. He a native of Germany and she of Charleston. He a baker.

SUTLET, EMILY aged 19 years married to BROWN, HENRY aged 30 years July 16, 1884 by Rev. R. A. Lapsley at 1 Bischoff's Square. He a native of South Carolina and she of Georgia. He a carpenter.

SUTTON, EMMA LEE aged 19 years married to BRANNON, JOHN aged 25 years July 17, 1884 by Rev. W. P. Mouzon. He a native of Ireland and she of Augusta, Georgia. He a painter.

SWAN, GEORGE H. aged 21 years married to DAVENPORT, JULIA M. aged 16 years January 7, 1878 by Rev. J. Mercier Green at St. Johannes Chapel. He a native of Jersey City, New Jersey and she of Charleston. He a pilot.

SWARTZ, C. married to ROWE, AUGUST September 9, 1879 by William B. Yates, Chaplain.

SWARTZBERG, MOSES aged 30 years married to MANN, HANNAH G. aged 33 years March 30, 1886 by Rev. P. H. Diamondstein at 110 Coming Street. Both natives of Germany. He a merchant.

SWEAT, BARNEY B. aged 23 years married to ADAMS, M. SUSAN aged 17 years February 12, 1889 by Rev. H. B. Browne at 75 Columbus Street. Both natives of Colleton County, South Carolina. He works in the cotton mill.

SWEATMAN, ANNETTE aged 16 years married to BARRINEAU, JOHN A. aged 25 years July 28, 1889 by Rev. J. V. Welsh at 40 Bee Street. He a native of Williamsburg County, South Carolina and she of Summerville, South Carolina. He a farmer.

SWEENEY, EVELYN C. aged 20 years married to JOHNSON, GEORGE W. aged 25 years January 22, 1884 by Rev. Charles A. Stakely. He a native of Charleston and she of South Carolina. He a merchant.

SWEENEY, JOHN married to O'BRIEN, LIZZIE November 29, 1881 by Father Daniel J. Quigley at The Cathedral of St. John the Baptist. He a native of Ireland and she of Charleston. He a railroad conductor.

SWEENEY, JOHN JAMES aged 24 years married to McKENNA, MARY aged 24 years January 21, 1883 by Father John P. Twigg. Both natives of Charleston. He a policeman.

SWEENEY, MARY JANE aged 29 years married to PATRUZO, FRANCIS F. aged 27 years November 28, 1883 by Father John P. Twigg at St. Patrick's Roman Catholic Church. Both natives of Charleston. He a clerk.

SWELGAN (?), AGNES aged 22 years married to SAVASTUNO (?), ANDREW aged 27 years July 30, 1891 by Father Harry P. Northrop at The Cathedral of St. John the Baptist. He a native of Naples, Italy and she of Charleston. He a photographer.

SWEN, GEORGE N. aged 21 years married to DAVENPORT, JULIA MARCELLA aged 16 years January 7, 1878 by Rev. J. Mercier Green at 114 King Street.

SYKES, G. C. M. aged 20 years married to GALLAGHAN, DAVID aged 27 years May 6, 1886 by Rev. Louis Muller. Both natives of Charleston. He a grocer in Mt. Pleasant, South Carolina.

SYMMES, ELEANOR married to DAVIS, JAMES B. June 9, 1887 by Rev. William H. Campbell. He works in the phosphate factory.

SYSAN (?), ELLA aged 30 years married to SHIVER, I. B. aged 31 years October 10, 1886 by Rev. Robert Wilson at 4 Wragg Square. Both natives of Charleston. He a patternmaker.

TAFT, WILLIAM NELSON aged 33 years married to BOWEN, (Mrs.) MARY RICHARDSON MOSES aged 23 years August 2, 1881 by Rev. C. C. Pinckney at Grace Church. She a native of Sumter, South Carolina. He a postmaster.

TANDER, HEINRICH aged 37 years married to HENRICKSEN, (Mrs.) BRIDGET JEREKING aged 28 years December 16, 1885 by Rev. Edward T. Horn in State Street. He a native of Norway and she of Wales. He a ship builder.

TANWELL, E. married to TRUMAN, R. November 21, 1879 by William B. Yates, Chaplain.

TARKA (?), ANDREW aged 30 years married to KAISER, MARY aged 21 years July 1, 1888 by Father P. J. McManus at St. Patrick's Roman Catholic Church. He a native of Germany and a shoemaker.

TARRIS, ROWENA G. aged 27 years married to OGREW, JOHN A. aged 25 years September 13, 1887 by Rev. Robert O. Wilson at 4 Wragg Square. Both natives of Charleston. He a mechanic.

TAVAST, DANIEL aged 23 years married to COOK, ADDIE aged 20 years March 13, 1888 by Rev. C. E. Chichester at 4 State Street. He a native of Finland and she of Charleston. He a mariner.

TAVEL, ELIZABETH aged 25 years married to BELL, STEPHEN R. aged 27 years June 16, 1890 by Rev. Richard S. Trapier at St. Philip's Church. Both natives of Charleston. He a clerk.

TAVEL, E. KNOX aged 26 years married to FISHER, E. V. aged 25 years December 21, 1880 by Rev. E. C. L. Browne. Both natives of Charleston. He in the mercantile business.

TAVEL, MARY ANN aged 20 years married to CAMMER, JULIAN F. aged 18 years March 10, 1892 by Rev. J. L. Stokes at 231 Coming Street. Both natives of Charleston. He works in the barrel factory.

TAYLOR, EDWARD aged 31 years married to WADFORD, ANNA aged 19 years March 11, 1888 by Rev. H. B. Browne at 20 Cooper Street. He a native of Richmond County, Georgia and she of South Carolina. He a millhand.

TAYLOR, GEORGE married to KEPPARD, E. November 19, 1880 by William B. Yates, Chaplain.

TAYLOR, HARRIET aged 21 years married to ARMSTRONG, D. G. aged 23 years July 8, 1891 by Rev. W. T. Thompson at 47 Rutledge Avenue.

TAYLOR, JOHN THOMAS aged 42 years married to JACKSON, (Mrs. ROSANNA NIXON aged 30 years June 17, 1891 by Rev. W. A. Betts at 14 Hampstead Square. He a native of Charleston and she of Berkeley County, South Carolina.

TAYLOR, JOSEPH A. aged 20 years married to JARROTT, EUGENIA aged 19 years March 11, 1891 by Rev. J. Thomas Pate. He a native of Charleston and she of Spartanburg, South Carolina. He a moulder.

TAYLOR, PETER C. aged 30 years married to SPIRES, MATTIE aged 20 years November 9, 1887 by Rev. John O. Wilson at 51 Columbus Street. He a native of Berkeley

County, South Carolina and she of Lincoln County, Georgia. He works in the phosphate mill.

TAYLOR, WILLIAM aged 33 years married to LEE, MARIE aged 18 years January 7, 1885 by Father F. A. Schmetz at St. Patrick's Roman Catholic Church. He a native of New York and she of Charleston. He a mariner.

TAYLOR, WILLIAM OSCAR aged 23 years married to VERONEE, LEONTINE INEZ aged 22 years July 12, 1885 by Rev. G. R. Brackett. Both natives of Charleston. He a patternmaker.

TAYLOR, W. J. married to VAN DELKEN, A. J. April 4, 1880 by William B. Yates, Chaplain.

TEAGUE, WILLIAM FRANCIS married to ROBERTSON, MARY ANN April 1, 1883 by Father P. L. Duffy at The Cathedral of St. John the Baptist. Both natives of Charleston. He a lighthouse keeper.

TEAGUE, WILHELMINA DORIS aged 25 years married to KUHLAND, WILHELM CHRISTOPHER aged 34 years December 1, 1889 by Rev. Louis Muller at the corner of Chapel and Alexander Streets.

TEAUX, M .J. married to KEITH, P. S. February 21, 1882 by Rev. T. E. Chapins at The Cathedral of St. John the Baptist. Both natives of Charleston. He a bookkeeper.

TECKLENBURG, ANNA MARIA aged 26 years married to WAGNER, CARL B. aged 30 years February 8, 1888 by Rev. Louis Muller at the southeast corner of Wentworth and St. Philip Streets.

TELMANOTEE,–married to DUNCAN, MARY May 9, 1878 by William B. Yates, Chaplain.

TEMPLE, CHARLES S. W. aged 36 years married to HIGGINS, ELIZABETH aged 25 years April 12, 1879 by Rev. J. V. Welsh at 62 Radcliffe Street.

TENNELL, ONETA married to DESTINO, SPERO February 27, 1879 by Rev. L. H. Shuck. He a native of Greece and she of Beaufort, South Carolina. He a merchant.

TENTON, W. J. aged 56 years married to NEWMAN, (Mrs.) SARAH J. FORSYTH aged 53 years September 4, 1892 by Rev. A. M. Chreitzberg at 75 Spring Street. He a native of North Carolina and she of South Carolina. He a carpenter in Denmark, South Carolina.

TERRELL, ALBERT E. aged 25 years married to LEE, ETTA MILES aged 23 years January 1, 1879 by Rev. William C. Power at Bethel Church.

TERRELL, ALBERT W. married to LEE, ELLA M. January 1, 1879 by Rev. William C. Power at Bethel Church. He a native of St. Thomas Parish, South Carolina and she of Darlington, South Carolina. He an engineer.

TERRELL, MATTIE aged 24 years married to MARTIN, WILLIAM H. aged 28 years February 24, 1887 by Rev. H. Browne. He a native of North Carolina and she of South Carolina. He a tinner.

TERRELL, THOMAS aged 22 years married to McMILLAN, CHARLOTTE WOODWARD aged 21 years April 25, 1879 by Rev. R. N. Wells. Both natives of Charleston. He a mechanic.

TERRY, ADA aged 19 years married to MORELLI, SESTILIO aged 24 years March 8, 1893 by Rev. John Johnson at 49 King Street. He a native of Italy and she of Elberton County, Georgia. He a shoemaker.

TERRY, OSCAR MORRIS married to NEIMAN, ROSA SOPHIA ELIZABETH January 10, 1878 by William B. Yates, Chaplain.

TESKEY, I. aged 32 years married to SERELLE (?), N. H. aged 39 years November 25, 1882 by Rev. Luther K. Probst at the Wentworth Street Lutheran Church. He a native of Charleston and a mechanic.

TEXWARD (?), S. aged 24 years married to HARVEN, G. C. aged 55 years February 13, 1882 by Rev. J. V. Welsh at 56 Spring Street. He a native of South Carolina and a laborer.

THACKERY, ROBERT aged 27 years married to CUMBIE, SARAH aged 18 years May 2, 1887 by Leroy F. Beaty at 231 Coming Street. He a native of England and she of South Carolina. He a bricklayer.

THAMES, HENRY L. aged 22 years married to BENSON, MAMIE aged 20 years February 8, 1893 by Rev. G. L. Stokes at 476 Meeting Street. He a native of Columbus, Georgia and she of North Carolina. He a weaver in the cotton mill.

THAMES, L. M. aged 24 years married to WITHERS, ANDREW aged 31 years November 3, 1880 by Rev. W. S. Bowman at the Wentworth Street Lutheran Church. He a native of York, South Carolina and she of Charleston. He a lawyer in York.

THARIN, VIRGINIA E. R. married to McLEISH, ARCHIBALD July 19, 1878 by William B. Yates, Chaplain, at 10 Church Street.

THATCHER, JOHN QUINCY aged 31 years married to JOHNSON, CONSTANCE EUGENIA aged 21 years October 4, 1881 by Rev. Charles S. Vedder. He a native of Wilmington, Delaware and she of Charleston. He an engineer.

THAYER, JAMES H. aged 26 years married to AXSON, SALLIE B. aged 25 years June 23, 1881 by Rev. L. H. Shuck at 17 Meeting Street. He a native of Charleston and a resident of Augusta, Georgia. He a clerk.

THAYER, JAMES HENRY aged 34 years married to AXSON, LOUISE COURTNEY aged 26 years July 12, 1889 by Rev. P. W. Lide at the residence of Mrs. J. W. Axson - 69 Cannon Street. He a native of Charleston and she of Greenville, South Carolina. He a bank teller.

THEES, C. H. aged 20 years married to SCHEIBE, H. A. L. aged 22 years February 10, 1880 by Rev. Louis Muller. Both natives of Charleston. Both natives of Charleston. He a clerk.

THEILE, ADDINA MARIA aged 28 years married to THEILE, HENRY aged 32 years April 28, 1892 by Rev. W. A. C. Muller in King Street. He a native of Georgia and she of Charleston. He a grocer.

THEILE, ANNA META MARGARETHE aged 21 years married to THEILE, JOHANN DIETRICH aged 31 years March 27, 1883 by Rev. Louis Muller at the southeast corner of King and Sheppard Streets. He a native of Germany and she of Charleston. He a grocer.

THEILE, HENRY aged 32 years married to THEILE, ADDINA MARIA aged 28 years April 28, 1892 by Rev. W. A. C. Muller in King Street. He a native of Georgia and she of Charleston. He a grocer.

THEILE, JOHANN HEINRICH DIETRICH aged 31 years married to THEILE, ANNA META MARGARETHE aged 21 years March 27, 1883 by Rev. Louis Muller at the southeast corner of King and Sheppard Streets. He a native of Germany and she of Charleston. He a grocer.

THEILING, ANNA F. aged 19 years married to LILIENTHAL, JOHN A. aged 24 years July 30, 1885 by Rev. Louis Muller at 66 Radcliffe Street.

THEILING, FRITZ CHRISTIAN aged 27 years married to BUSCH, HENRIETTA WILHELMINA aged 26 years August 8, 1886 by Rev. Louis Muller at the southwest corner of Ann and Elizabeth Streets. He a native of Charleston and she of Walhalla, South Carolina. He a baker.

THEILING, JOHN H. aged 21 years married to THEILING, (Mrs.) MARY A. HIMMELREICH. aged 26 years August 2, 1883 by Rev. Luther K. Probst. He a native of Charleston and she of Germany. He a carpenter.

THEVEATT, MARTHA M. aged 25 years married to COTTEN, JOSEPH W. aged 27 years July 10, 1895 by Father J. J. Monaghan at 38 Mary Street. He a native of North Carolina and she of South Carolina. He a railroad conductor.

THIELE, P. aged 45 years married to ZIEGLER, M. C. aged 26 years November 9, 1882 by Rev. Louis Muller at the corner of Market and Church Streets. He a native of Charleston and a cabinetmaker.

THIEME, ALBERT aged 26 years married to MICHLKE, BERTHA HELENE CATHARINE aged 20 years April 16, 1888 by Rev. Louis Muller.

THOMAS, A. E. aged 40 years married to SHIRER, J. H. aged 22 years August 30, 1882 by Rev. C. Shokes at 24 Bee Street. He a native of South Carolina and a farmer.

THOMAS, CATHERINE aged 30 years married to LOVETT, CHARLES HENRY aged 40 years March 3, 1884 by Father P. L. Duffy at The Cathedral of St. John the Baptist. Both natives of Charleston. He a machinist.

THOMAS, GEORGE aged 34 years married to SEYMOUR, ELLEN REBECCA aged 21 years November 24, 1878 by Rev. W. S. Bowman at the corner of Amherst and Nassau Streets. He a native of Darmstadt, Germany and she of Charleston. He a baker.

THOMAS, JAMES WHITFIELD aged 25 years married to EGAN, MARIE ANTOINETTE aged 28 years October 2, 1888 by Rev. R. J. Smart.

THOMAS, JOSEPH M. aged 24 years married to DENLE, LIZZIE M. aged 18 years June 17, 1880 by Rev. R. N. Wells at 72 Tradd Street. Both natives of Charleston. He a merchant. Both natives of Charleston. He a merchant.

THOMAS, LEWIS aged 35 years married to HOOTS, SARAH aged 20 years February 28, 1880 by Rev. H. F. Chreitzberg in Cannon Street. Both natives of Colleton County, South Carolina. He a laborer.

THOMAS, L. M. aged 24 years married to WITHERS, ANDREW aged 31 years November 3, 1880 by Rev. W. S. Bowman at the Wentworth Street Lutheran Church. He a native of York, South Carolina and she of Charleston. He a lawyer in York.

THOMAS, MARY aged 18 years married to DAVIS, ARTHUR L. aged 21 years March 11, 1888 by Rev. H. B. Browne in America Street. Both natives of Columbia, South Carolina. He a railroad brakeman.

THOMAS, M. L. married to EASTERBY, F. C. June 1, 1882 by Rev. Luther K. Probst at the Wentworth Street Lutheran Church. He a native of Charleston and a merchant.

THOMASON, JANE ELIZABETH aged 20 years married to JONES, RICHARD WILLIAM aged 29 years April 13, 1879 by Rev. Charles S. Vedder at 92 Church Street.

THOMLINSON, ALVIN R. aged 32 years married to BAILEY, CONSTANTIA C. aged 24 years April 15, 1885 by Rev. C. C. Pinckney at Grace Church. Both natives of Charleston. He a merchant.

THOMPSON, ALMA aged 22 years married to LAMB, JAMES J. aged 30 years December 25, 1895 by Rev. G. R. Brackett at 23 Cannon Street.

THOMPSON, CAROLINE E. married to KNIGHT, S. W. January 9, 1878 by William B. Yates, Chaplain.

THOMPSON, CAROLINE aged 17 years married to FUNT, VINCENT aged 23 years August 30, 1885 by Rev. John O. Wilson at 82 Wentworth Street. He a native of Spain and she of South Carolina. He a mariner.

THOMPSON, CHARLES aged 27 years married to BENNETT, MATTIE L. aged 23 years May 30, 1892 by Rev. John Johnson at 83 Church Street. He a native of New Jersey and she of Adams Run, South Carolina. He a ship carpenter.

THOMPSON, CHARLES AUGUSTUS aged 26 years married to LEITCH, MARY aged 25 years March 3, 1878 by Father Claudian B. Northrop. He a native of Charleston and she of London, England. He a tinner.

THOMPSON, CHARLES H. aged 25 years married to BATCHELDOR, FRANCES E. aged 30 years September 11, 1892 by Rev. John Johnson at 53 Church Street.

THOMPSON, ELIZABETH aged 23 years married to PLATT, THOMAS D. aged 41 years April 30, 1893 by Rev. J. L. Stokes at 231 Coming Street. He a native of Summerville, South Carolina and she of Charleston. He a carpenter.

THOMPSON ELLA R. aged 32 years married to WOODWARD, JULIUS aged 35 years February 6, 1894 by Rev. J. L. Stokes at 231 Coming Street. He a native of Barnwell County, South Carolina and she of Walterboro, South Carolina. He works in the cotton mill.

THOMPSON, EMMA married to KING, FRANCIS March 6, 1878 by William B. Yates, Chaplain.

THOMPSON, GEORGE W. aged 55 years married to BENKER, LOUISA GERTRUDE aged 25 years September 28, 1886 by Rev. H. B. Browne at 78 Drake Street. He a native of South Carolina and she of Charleston. He a farmer.

THOMPSON, GEORGIANA aged 29 years married to GILBERT, JOHN W. aged 27 years February 12, 1885 by Rev. John Johnson at 5 Franklin Street. Both natives of Charleston. He works in a factory.

THOMPSON, IDA E. aged 18 years married to JONES, IRVING L. aged 32 years August 27, 1890 by Rev. John Johnson at 20 Laurens Street. She a native of Charleston. He a boilermaker.

THOMPSON, J. D. aged 20 years married to KNOWLES, SYNTHIA D. aged 20 years September 13, 1891 by Rev. Edmund Wells at 22 Aiken Street. Both natives of Charleston. He the Superintendent at the spinning factory.

THOMPSON, J. E. aged 26 years married to HUDSON, ANNIE aged 18 years October 12, 1887 by Rev. H. B. Browne. He a native of Screven County, Georgia, and she of Augusta, Georgia. He an engineer.

THOMPSON, JACOB M. married to KARSEN, ANNIE E. August 19, 1888 by Rev. William H. Campbell. He a machinist in Florence, South Carolina.

THOMPSON, JENNIE M. aged 22 years married to FEDDERWITZ, JOHN H. H. aged 24 years February 1, 1888 by Rev. John Johnson in Reid Street. He a native of Georgia and she of New York. He a clerk.

THOMPSON, JOHANNA aged 18 years married to DAVIS, MOSES aged 21 years February 4, 1883 by Rev. John H. Tillinghast at 88 America Street. Both natives of Charleston. He a painter.

THOMPSON LOUIS NAPOLEON aged 21 years married to ROUSELEY, SALLIE ELIZABETH aged 16 years November 16, 1884 by Rev. R. A. Lapsley at the corner of Nassau and Sheppard Streets. He a native of Augusta, Georgia, and she of Charleston. He works in the cotton factory.

THOMPSON, MINNIE S. aged 18 years married to JONES, BEVERLIE C. aged 29 years April 14, 1895 by Rev. G. R. Brackett at 23 Cannon Street. Both natives of Charleston. He an engineer.

THOMPSON, M. J. married to SALTERS, T. November 29, 1882 by Father John P. Twigg at St. Patrick's Roman Catholic Church. He a native of Charleston and a laborer.

THOMPSON, NELLIE married to SASSER, CHARLES C. January 15, 1891 by Rev. William H. Campbell at St. Paul's Chapel. He a farmer in Maryland.

THOMPSON, REBECCA aged 23 years married to MURRELL, JAMES J. aged 46 years October 12, 1890 by Rev. John Johnson at 53 Church Street. Both natives of Charleston. He works for the railroad.

THOMPSON, (Mrs.) S. M. JACKSON aged 22 years married to SHUMAKER, JOHN aged 21 years March 20, 1892 by Rev. J. H. Smith at 2 Stone Court. He a native of New Orleans, Louisiana and she of Berkeley County, South Carolina. He works in the cotton mill.

THOMPSON, S. W. S. married to LARISEY, H. M. July 9, 1879 by Rev. G. R. Brackett.

THOMPSON, U. CLAUDIA aged 25 years married to KNOPF, JOSEPH aged 21 years May 8, 1887 by Rev. Louis Muller at the St. Matthew's Lutheran Church. He a native of Blackville, South Carolina and she of Marion, South Carolina. He a clerk in Blackville.

THOMPSON, WILLIAM R. aged 24 years married to HAMETT, GERTRUDE H. aged 23 years December 5, 1888 by Rev. H. B. Browne at 95 Columbus Street. He a native of Pennsylvania and she of Charleston. He an insurance agent.

THOMPSON, W. LOUIS aged 22 years married to ANTONIO, MARY ANN aged 23 years June 3, 1889 by Rev. H. B. Browne at 78 Drake Street. He a native of New York and she of Winnsboro, South Carolina. He a plumber.

THOMSON, ANNA S. aged 17 years married to JONES, JOHN aged 18 years February 14, 1884 by Rev. J. E. Beard at 13 Columbus Street. He a native of Spartanburg, South Carolina and she of New York. He a weaver in the cotton mill.

THOMSON, CHARLES W. M. aged 28 years married to JEFFORDS, LILLA A. aged 28 years December 26, 1894 by Rev. C. C. Pinckney.

THOMSON, ISABEL aged 17 years married to BARBER, JESSEY aged 19 years February 18, 1881 by Rev. J. V. Welch at 5 park Street. He a native of Summerville, South Carolina and a laborer.

THOMSON, MARY aged 25 years married to ALDRICH, W. C. aged 30 years February 8, 1880 by Rev. John Johnson in Broad Street. Both natives of Charleston. He a machinist.

THOMSON, SAMUEL married to GLADDEN, MARY ELIZABETH February 12, 1878 by William B. Yates, Chaplain.

THOMSON, THOMASINA WOODSON married to GALLUCHAT, MINOR CLINTON aged 21 years January 31, 1878 at the Huguenot Church. He resides in Manning, South Carolina.

THORNAL, JULIA A. aged 17 years married to LAMKIN, OCTAVIAN E. aged 22 years May 7, 1893 by Father J. J. Monaghan at 136 St. Philip Street. He a native of Charleston and she of St. Stephen's Parish, South Carolina. He a tinner in Savannah, Georgia.

THORNAL, ROSA B. aged 23 years married to POWELL, JOHN A. aged 22 years September 30, 1894 by Rev. J. C. Yongue at 96 America Street. He a native of Massachusetts and she of Quebec. He a mariner.

THORNHILL, JAMES aged 21 years married to HOLLEMAN, ALICE aged 20 years December 28, 1887 by Rev. H. B. Browne. He a native of Sumter County, South Carolina and she of Darlington County, South Carolina. He works in the cotton mill.

THORNHILL, J. T. EDWIN aged 30 years married to WILBUR, LULA MARGARET aged 25 years November 4, 1886 by Rev. A. J. S. Thomas at the corner of Pitt and Vanderhorst Streets. He a native of Virginia and she of Charleston. He a merchant in Augusta, Georgia.

THORNLEY, JAMES WILLIAM aged 25 years married to MARSH, MARY HARRIET aged 18 years September 27, 1883 by A. Coke Smith at 700 King Street. He a native of Moncks Corner, South Carolina and she of Charleston. He a merchant.

THORNLEY, M. N. aged 22 years married to FRANK, ROSA aged 22 years August 4, 1895 by G. W. Rouse, Trial Justice. He a native of Berkeley County, South Carolina and she of Louisville, Kentucky.

TIBBES, SARAH T. aged 27 years married to COFFEY, THOMAS E. aged 38 years October 16, 1884 by Father Daniel J. Quigley.

TIEDEMANN, GERTRUDE aged 23 years married to KLENKE, JOHN aged 27 years December 7, 1886 by Rev. Johannes Heckel at St. Johannes Lutheran Church.

TIEDEMANN, HELEN H. aged 20 years married to ROBSON, JOHN W. aged 30 years June 15, 1893 by Rev. Edward T. Horn at 152 Broad Street. He a native of Spartanburg, South Carolina and she of Charleston. He a merchant.

TIEDEMANN, JOHANNA CATHERINE A. aged 24 years married to LANGE, GUSTAV L. aged 30 years December 17, 1877 by Rev. Louis Muller at the St. Matthew's Lutheran Church. Both natives of Charleston. He a miller.

TIEDEMANN, KATHERINE aged 21 years married to BARGAMANN, WILLIAM aged 24 years November 23, 1881 by Rev. Johannes Heckel in King Street. He a native of Oldenburg, Germany and she of Hanover. He a baker.

TIEDEMANN, OTTO aged 40 years married to SCHIRMER, MARY LOUISE aged 38 years February 4, 1891 by Rev. Edward T. Horn. Both natives of Charleston. He a merchant.

TIEDEMANN, SOPHIA W. C. aged 23 years married to SALMANN, FRITZ aged 28 years September 15, 1880 by Rev. Louis Muller at the residence of Mrs. Tiedemann - Judith Street. Both natives of Charleston. He a miller.

TIERNEY, FRANCIS C. aged 19 years married to O'ROURKE, JENNIE PHILOMENA aged 20 years May 5, 1890 by Father J. J. Monaghan. He a native of Columbia, South Carolina and she of Charleston. He a laborer.

TIGHE, (Mrs.), ANNIE MURPHY aged 35 years married to OSTENDORFF, JOHN H. aged 23 years November 15, 1891 by Father J. J. Monaghan at St. Patrick's Roman Catholic Church. He a native of Charleston and she of Ireland. He a merchant.

TIGHE, BERNARD J. married to DONOHUE, ANNE March 12, 1879 by Father C. J. Croghan. He a native of Ireland and she of Charleston. He a clerk.

TIGHE, MARY ANN aged 30 years married to CULLETON, EDWARD M. aged 31 years April 29, 1891 by Father J. J. Monaghan at St. Patrick's Roman Catholic Church.Both natives of Charleston. He a bricklayer.

TIGHE, MARY ANN aged 20 years married to ELLSWORTH, J. S. K. aged 22 years August 28, 1881 by Father Harry P. Northrop at St. Patrick's Roman Catholic Church. He a native of Charleston and a moulder.

TILGHAM, CHARLES C. married to EAGAN, SUSIE E. July 12, 1894 by Rev. D. A. Blackburn. He works for the railroad.

TILLISON, ANTONE aged 27 years married to MAHONEY, MARY A. aged 37 years January 30, 1887 by Rev. John Johnson at 53 Church Street. He a native of Norway and she of Ireland. He a mechanic.

TIMMONS, ELMIRA aged 18 years married to COHEN, JOSEPH aged 19 years September 16, 1883 by Rev. E. J. Meynardie at 145 Calhoun Street. He a native of Columbia, South Carolina and she of Cincinnati, Ohio. He a weaver in the cotton mill.

TIMMONS, M. O. aged 29 years married to HEYOTT, ANNIE J. aged 22 years November 25, 1886 by Rev. H. B. Browne. Both natives

TIPPETT, CAROLINE aged 24 years married to FLUDD, JOHN OSCAR aged 22 years February 10, 1889 by Rev. T. P. Burgess at 10 Amherst Street. He a native of Concord, North Carolina and she of Charleston. He a carpenter.

TIPPETT, MICKY aged 19 years married to FAGAN, JOHN T. aged 21 years June 7, 1885 by Rev. J. E. Beard at 64 Nassau Street. He a native of South Carolina.

TISDALE, EMMA aged 21 years married to HODGE, ERNEST aged 21 years May 3, 1892 by Rev. A. Chreitzberg.

TISDALE, J. G. aged 33 years married to WHITE, H. A. aged 25 years January 15, 1880 by Rev. W. P. Mouzon at 85 Queen Street. He a native of Sumter, South Carolina and she of Georgetown, South Carolina. He a farmer in Sumter.

TITJEN, MARGARETHA ANNA aged 21 years married to RUGHEIMER, AUGUST RUDOLPH aged 23 years April 3, 1889 by Rev. Louis Muller in King Street.

TOALE, GEORGE E. aged 29 years married to JOHNSON, IDA ELLEN aged 29 years November 18, 1891 by Rev. R. A. Webb at 25 George Street. He a native of Connecticut and she of Charleston. He a merchant.

TOBIAS, ISABEL aged 26 years married to ST. AMAND, CLARENCE W. aged 27 years February 15, 1884 by Father Daniel J. Quigley at 6 Rutledge Avenue.

TOBIN, EDMUND J. aged 30 years married to LANGAN, MARY aged 23 years October 23, 1890 by Bishop Harry P. Northrop at The Cathedral of St. John the Baptist. Both natives of Charleston. He a laborer.

TOBIN, MARGARET TERESA aged 17 years married to BUERO, ANGELO aged 23 years December 26, 1883 by Father J. J. Woolahan at St. Mary of the Annunciation Roman Catholic Church.

TOBIN, MARY aged 15 years married to CORKLE, CHARLES aged 23 years May 13, 1878 by Father John P. Twigg at The Cathedral of St. John the Baptist. Both natives of Charleston. He a stonecutter.

TODD, ALICE E. aged 17 years married to MANN, THEODORE aged 25 years April 2, 1889 by Rev. H. B. Browne at 142 St. Philip Street. He a native of North Carolina and she of Charleston. He a farmer.

TODD, EDWARD W. aged 23 years married to ROYA, MARY L. aged 19 years February 4, 1895 by Rev. J. C. Yongue at 23 America Street. Both natives of Charleston. He works for the railroad.

TODD, MAMIE aged 16 years married to WHITE, THOMAS aged 21 years February 17, 1889 by Rev. H. B. Browne at 8 Williams Court. He a native of Columbia, South Carolina and she of Charleston. He works for the railroad.

TOLLE, EMMA aged 24 years married to WESTERVELT, THEODORE G. aged 26 years February 21, 1887 by Rev. J. Mercier Green. He a native of South Carolina and she of Charleston. He an electric worker.

TOLLISON, MARTIN aged 33 years married to HENDRICKS, MAGGIE A. CASSIDY aged 26 years March 29, 1892 by Rev. E. C. Chichester at 120 King Street.

TOLLNER, HELENA M. aged 18 years married to OETJEN, HENRY W. M. aged 23 years February 17, 1885 by Rev. Johannes Heckel at 7 Wall Street. He a native of Charleston and she of Germany. He an oil salesman.

TOMB, SARAH A. aged 55 years married to TOMB, W. H. aged 42 years July 3, 1879 by Rev. W. S. Bowman at 14 Bee Street. He a native of New Jersey and she of Washington, D. C. He an engineer.

TOMB, W. H. aged 42 years married to TOMB, SARAH A. aged 55 years July 3, 1879 by Rev. W. S. Bowman at 14 Bee Street. He a native of New Jersey and she of Washington, D. C. He an engineer.

TOOMER, HARRIET R. married to DOAR, STEPHEN D. April 15, 1885. Both natives of South Carolina. He a physician.

TOOMER, MAURICE S. aged 25 years married to ALBRECHT, PAULINE F. aged 22 years January 31, 1886 by Rev. Luther K. Probst. Both natives of Charleston. He a painter.

TOOMER, VIRGINIA W. aged 22 years married to TWYFORD (?), HENRY H. aged 26 years April 11, 1893 by Rev. C. C. Pinckney in Lynch Street.

TORBERT, JOHN E. married to LUCAS, HELEN T. January 8, 1890 by Rev. William H. Campbell at St. Paul's Church.

TORCK, MADELINE E. aged 25 years married to DOSCHER, HENRY L. aged 30 years January 12, 1892 by Rev. R. C. Holland at the Wentworth Street Lutheran Church. He a native of Charleston and a packer.

TORCK, EIBE HEINRICH aged 27 years married to ALBRECHT, EMMA ADELAIDE aged 27 years May 22, 1881 by Rev. Louis Muller in King Street above Spring Street. He a native of Charleston and she of New York. He a clerk.

TORLAY, CAROLINE F. aged 25 years married to STOPPELBEIN, L. B. aged 26 years December 16, 1885 by Rev. John Johnson at St. Philip's Church. Both natives of Charleston. He a merchant.

TOUHEY, DAVID JOSEPH aged 26 years married to FURLONG, MARY FRANCKS aged 23 years January 1, 1879 by Father Claudian B. Northrop at St. Mary of the Annunciation Roman Catholic Church. Both natives of Charleston. He a bookkeeper.

TOURNES, JOHN A. aged 24 years married to MEYERS, SUSAN aged 15 years July 4, 1880 by Rev. J. V. Welsh at 64 Radcliffe Street. Both natives of Charleston.

TOVEY, MARY aged 25 years married to OSWALD, HENRY C. aged 25 years November 18, 1885 by Rev. Edward T. Horn at St. Johannes Lutheran Church. He a native of Georgia and she of Charleston. He a bookkeeper.

TOWELL, CHARLES W. aged 19 years married to QUICK, MARY J. aged 16 years March 19, 1885 by Rev. J. V. Welsh at 6 Spring Street. Both natives of Charleston. He a laborer.

TOWLES, HENRY A. aged 35 years married to SCHIRMER, LOUISA JANE aged 21 years March 15, 1881 by Rev. Edward T. Horn in Bull Street. He a native of Savannah, Georgia and she of Charleston. He a merchant in Wadmalaw, South Carolina.

TOWLES, MARTHA W. aged 20 years married to LASSITER, ROBERT B. aged 26 years November 5, 1895 by Rev. David M. Ramsey.

TOWNSEND, JOHN F. married to WINTHROP, ANNA EVELINA February 24, 1891 by Rev. Richard S. Trapier at 126 Tradd Street. He a native of Edisto Island, South Carolina and she of Charleston. He a planter on Edisto Island.

TOYE, E. aged 28 years married to O'KIEFE, L. aged 22 years May 16, 1882 by Rev. J. M. Green. He a native of Charleston and a boilermaker.

TOYE, JOHN H. aged 31 years married to GLEASON, SARAH AGNES aged 21 years January 25, 1881 by Father T. Edward Chapins at 63 America Street. Both natives of Charleston.

TOYE, MARY aged 17 years married to CRAFT, JAMES aged 20 years July 13, 1887 by Father P. J. McManus. He a native of Charleston and she of South Carolina. He works in a factory.

TOYE, ROSA aged 20 years married to MURPHY, MAURICE J. aged 25 years June 19, 1895 by Father J. J. Monaghan at St. Patrick's Roman Catholic Church. Both natives of Charleston. He a railroad switchman.

TRAF (?), CHARLOTTE BUKERMANN aged 50 years married to LEHMAN, GEORGE aged 53 years October 20, 1884 by Rev. Johannes Heckel at 55 Smith Street.

TRAPIER, HANNAH HEYWARD aged 21 years married to JERVEY, ARTHUR POSTELL aged 25 years February 12, 1878 by Rev. W. B. Howe at St. Philip's Church. Both natives of Charleston. He a clerk.

TRAPIER, SHUBRICK married to HAYWOOD, GERTRUDE September 4, 1879 by Rev. Richard S. Trapier at St. Michael's Church.

TRAUTWEIN, CARL A. aged 25 years married to LAWES, LUCIE MILLER aged 31 years July 15, 1891 by Rev. Louis Muller at 96 Radcliffe Street. He a native of Germany and she of Charleston. He a painter.

TRAUTWEIN (?), MARIE CATHERINE aged 20 years married to VOIGT, RUDOLPH CARL aged 25 years January 10, 1889 by Rev. Louis Muller at the residence of the Groom's father in Liberty Street near St. Philip's Street. He a native of Charleston and she of Orangeburg, South Carolina.

TRAYNOR, CHARLES E. married to PURCELL, LIZZIE A. aged 16 years August 24, 1885 by Father F. J. Shadler at St. Joseph's Roman Catholic Church. He a native of Ireland and she of Charleston. He a policeman.

TRENHOLM, CHARLES L. aged 22 years married to GRICE, HELEN aged 24 years April 5, 1893 by Rev. Edward T. Horn at the residence of George D. Grice.

TRENHOLM, EDWARD G. aged 23 years married to RHETT, ELIZABETH W. aged 19 years December 17, 1889 by Rev. John Johnson at St. Philip's Church. He a native of Buncombe County, North Carolina and she of South Carolina. He a merchant.

TRENHOLM, ELOISE aged 30 years married to CALDWELL, RICHARD aged 50 years April 16, 1895 by Bishop Ellison Capers in south Church Street.

TRENHOLM, GEORGE M. married to BISSELL, CLAUDIA A. November 17, 1881 by Rev. William H. Campbell. He a lawyer.

TREVIATHAM, JOHN D. aged 36 years married to FLUDGER, FLORENCE aged 33 years December 17, 1890 by Rev. J. Thomas Pate at 116 Calhoun Street. He a native of North Carolina and she of South Carolina. He a baggagemaster in Florence, South Carolina.

TRIEST, FANNIE aged 20 years married to GOLDSMITH, ISAAC A. aged 23 years September 24, 1889 by Rabbi David Levy.

TRISLEY (?), SAMUEL D. aged 30 years married to OWENS, MARIA aged 21 years November 7, 1888 by Rev. J. E. Carlisle. He a native of Charleston and she of Berkeley County, South Carolina. He works for the railroad.

TROTT, MAGGIE H. married to WINCEK (?), JOHN H. November 6, 1884 by Rev. W. T. THOMPSON at the residence of the Bride's mother.

TORCK, MARIE LILIA aged 21 years married to BARRAGAN, WILLIAM FRANCIS aged 22 years January 29, 1879 by Father Claudian B. Northrop at St. Mary of the Annunciation Roman Catholic Church. Both natives of Charleston. He a salesman.

TROUCHE, PAUL E. aged 27 years married to FLEMING, MAGGIE V. aged 23 years October 10, 1894 by Father J. J. Monaghan at St. Patrick's Roman Catholic Church. Both natives of Charleston. He a stationer.

TROWER, HAROLD EDWARD married to SCHAEFER, BERTHA PECK June 10, 1890 by Rev. Richard S. Frazier at St. Michael's Church. He a native of England. She a native and resident of Georgia.

TRUAL, EUGENIA aged 19 years married to SLAVICK, M. E. August 18, 1879 by William B. Yates, Chaplain. Both natives of Charleston.

TRUALL (?), (Mrs.) L. TOOMER aged 46 years married to STEPHENS, CHARLES aged 40 years November 24, 1887 by Father F. J. Shadler in King Street. She a native of Port Royal, South Carolina. He a native of Hamburg, Germany. He a pilot in Beaufort, South Carolina.

TRUMAN, R. married to TANWELL, E. November 21, 1879 by William B. Yates, Chaplain.

TRUMBO, SALLIE HARVEY aged 28 years married to HOWARD, WILLIAM H. aged 40 years July 10, 1883 by Father P. L. Duffy at The Cathedral of St. John the Baptist.

TUCKER, MARTHA married to MAZYCK, EDWARD K. April 29, 1886 by Rev. William H. Campbell at the residence of William H. Tucker. He a clerk.

TUCKER, MARY POST married to PRIOLEAU, THOMAS G. January 31, 1885 by Rev. William H. Campbell at St. Paul's Church. Both natives of Charleston. He a clerk.

TUCKER, MATILDA aged 20 years married to BARR, JAMES aged 24 years December 27, 1881 by Rev. H. F. Chreitzberg at 13 America Street. Both natives of Sumter, South Carolina. He a mechinist.

TUCKER, R. aged 19 years married to CHICHESTER, JAMES G. aged 20 years
May 4, 1882 by Rev. J. V. Welsh at 24 Bee Street. He a native of Charleston and a
butcher.

TUCKER, THEODORA married to HERBERST, JAMES C. June 17, 1879 by William
B. Yates, Chaplain.

TUCKER, WILLIAM H. married to SIMONS, MARY A. October 12, 1893 by Rev.
William H. Campbell at St. Paul's Church.

TUCKER, WILLIAM HYME married to SIMONS, MARY A. April 19, 1883 by Rev.
William H. Campbell at St. Paul's Church.

TUPPER, FLORENCE aged 22 years married to CAPERS, CHARLES B. aged 24 years
June 15, 1880 by Rev. L. H. Shuck. He a native of Beaufort, South Carolina and she of
Charleston. He a clerk.

TUPPER, FREDERICK aged 45 years married to GATEWOOD, VIRGINIA A. aged 32
years June 9, 1881 by Rev. John Johnson at 24 South Bay Street. He a native of
Charleston and an insurance salesman.

TUPPER, HENRY married to BELLINGER, MARY R. February 3, 1891 by Rev. Richard
S. Trapier at St. Michael's Church. Both natives of Charleston.

TUPPER, JAMES married to ROBINSON, MARY GERVAIS February 5, 1883 by Rev.
Richard S. Trapier at St. Michael's Church.

TUPPER, JEANNIE DAVIS aged 25 years married to CALDWELL, RICHARD aged 28
years October 17, 1878 by Rev. L. H. Shuck at the corner of Meeting and Ann Streets.
Both natives of Charleston. He a clerk.

TUPPER, SAMUEL Y. aged 25 years married to GELDINGS, DEAS F. aged 20 years
April 6, 1880 by Rev. John Johnson at St. Philip's Church. Both natives of Charleston. He
an accountant.

TURLEY, A. aged 26 years married to KENNY, M. aged 24 years September 24, 1882 by
Father J. J. Monaghan at St. Patrick's Roman Catholic Church. He a native of Ireland and
a laborer.

TURNER, ALICE ESTELLE aged 22 years married to HESS, THOMAS JESSIE aged
35 years October 21, 1883 by Rev. John H. Tillinghast.

TURNER, ALICE L. aged 34 years married to HEFFRON, JAMES aged 37 years
February 21, 1891 by Father F. J. Shadler. Both natives of Charleston. He a blacksmith.

TURNER, ANN aged 37 years married to SHOKES, CHARLES C. aged 20 years
April 7, 1890 by Rev. Robert Wilson at 4 Wragg Square. He a native of Charleston and
she of Columbia, South Carolina.

TURNER, CARL W. aged 25 years married to EHLERS, ANNA aged 28 years June 19,
1894 by Rev. Alfred Freyschmidt. Both natives of Germany. He a butcher.

TURNER, CHRISTOPHER J. aged 24 years married to CARMODY, CATHERINE M.
aged 22 years June 4, 1888 by Father Daniel J. Quigley at St. Patrick's Roman Catholic
Church.

TURNER, ELIZABETH aged 29 years married to KENNEDY, NOAH LANEY aged 28 years March 21, 1878 by Rev. John Johnson. Both natives of Charleston. He a streetcar conductor.

TURNER, KATIE ETHEL aged 18 years married to EARL, THOMAS aged 30 years March 24, 1885 by Rev. J. E. Beard. He a native of Canada and she of New York. He a newspaper correspondent in New York.

TURNER, LOUIS W. aged 22 years married to BOYCE, ELIZABETH L. aged 20 years November 29, 1892 by Rev. J. L. Stokes at 22 Bogard Street. Both natives of Charleston. He a machinist.

TURNER, MICHAEL P. aged 36 years married to SEAVY (?), LUCY R. RUSSELL aged 29 years October 21, 1893 by Father Joseph D. Budds at The Cathedral of St. John the Baptist.

TURNER, RICHARD H. aged 27 years married to MARE, AUGUSTA L. aged 18 years January 27, 1885 by Rev. G. R. Brackett in Aiken Row. He a native of Bryan County, Georgia and she of St. Mary's, Georgia. He a clerk in Savannah, Georgia.

TURNER, WILLIAM S. married to RHOADES, LOTTIE April 14, 1891 by Rev. William H. Campbell. He resides in Greenville, South Carolina.

TWEITMANN (?), HEINRICH W. aged 23 years married to RONNER, ANNA REBECCA CATHERINE aged 22 years September 8, 1887 by Rev. Louis Muller in King Street near Line Street. He a native of Charleston and she of Prussia. He a merchant.

TWYFORD (?), HENRY H. aged 26 years married to TOOMER, VIRGINIA W. aged 22 years April 11, 1893 by Rev. C. C. Pinckney in Lynch Street.

TYLEE, EDWIN A. aged 21 years married to PATRICK, JULIA E. aged 21 years January 22, 1893 by Rev. Edmund Wells at 95 Nassau Street. Both natives of Charleston. He a clerk in Summerville, South Carolina.

TYRRELL, ADDIE L. aged 26 years married to CORBY, JOHN T. aged 38 years June 12, 1889 by Rev. C. E. Chichester at 40 Spring Street. Both natives of Charleston. He a machinist.

UFFERHAUS (?), ANNA MARIA aged 17 years married to HARKEN, JOHANN HEINRICH aged 24 years October 23, 1887 by Rev. Louis Muller in Rutledge Avenue above Shepherd Street. Both natives of Charleston. He a grocer.

ULMER, BENJAMIN F. aged 20 years married to WOODRUFF, VIRGINIA H. aged 17 years July 7, 1895 by Rev. Charles S. Vedder in Broad Street. Both natives of Savannah, Georgia. He works in the Naval Stores in Savannah.

ULMO, HENRY WALTER aged 24 years married to LONEGAN, LIZZIE EMMELINE aged 20 years April 7, 1881 by Rev. E. J. Meynardie. Both natives of Charleston. He a machinist in Savannah, Georgia.

ULMO, MARY L. aged 20 years married to FARR, RICHARD W. aged 25 years April 27, 1892 by Rev. Edwin C. Dargan at 128 Calhoun Street.

VACH, BARBARA ELIZABETH aged 27 years married to RIEPER, NICHOLAS W. aged 27 years February 14, 1888 by Rev. Johannes Heckel at the residence of C. N.

Doscher at the corner of Meeting and Hasell Streets. He a native of Hanover and she of Nassau. He a merchant.

VACH, H. C. E. aged 22 years married to GOODWIN, H. P. aged 30 years March 23, 1887 by Rev. Louis Muller. He a native of England and she of Germany. He a tailor.

VADEN, CARRY P. aged 18 years married to WILLIAMS, HARRY CLIFFORD aged 26 years December 24, 1888 by Rev. R. C. Holland at 39 Chapel Street. He a native of Richmond, Virginia and she of Charleston. He a merchant in Richmond.

VALDEZ, FRANCISCO A. aged 38 years married to McMANUS, CATHERINE ANN CORKLE aged 40 years December 12, 1887 by Rev. John O. Wilson at 58 Hasell Street. He a native of Havana, Cuba and she of Charleston. He a cigar packer.

VALENTINE, (Mrs.) AGNES JACKSON aged 36 years married to GOODWIN, JESSE R. aged 21 years March 27, 1889 by Rev. H. B. Browne at 22.5 Sheppard Street. He a native of Lexington, South Carolina and she of Berkeley County, South Carolina. He works in a mill.

VALENTINE, CATHERINE E. HYOTT aged 35 years married to DAVIS, JEREMIAH A. aged 53 years April 11, 1886 by Rev. C. E. Chichester at the Mariner's Chapel in Market Street. He a native of Providence, Rhode Island and she of South Carolina. He a sailmaker.

VALENTINE, JOSEPHINE aged 20 years married to SHERLOCK, ALEXANDER aged 24 years February 6, 1893 by Father J. J. Monaghan at 4 Hanover Street. He a native of Scotland and she of Charleston. He a longshoreman.

VALENTINE, (Mrs.) SARAH AUGUSTINE PARKINS aged 28 years married to WHITE, WILLIAM CHARLES aged 29 years October 16, 1878 by Rev. R. N. Wells. He a native of Charleston and she of Springfield, Massachusetts. He a mariner.

VALZY, ANNIE aged 16 years married to FLATMAN, CHARLES M. aged 20 years January 10, 1892 by Rev. Edmund Wells at 28 Cooper Street. He a native of St. James Parish, South Carolina and she of Orangeburg, South Carolina. He a laborer.

VANASDALAW, L. married to DEAGNESLARD, M. October 16, 1879 by William B. Yates, Chaplain.

VAN DELKEN, H. aged 22 years married to CAHILL, S. T. aged 20 years January 17, 1882 by Father T. E. Chapins at St. Patrick's Roman Catholic Church. He a native of South Carolina and a railroad worker.

VAN DELKEN, HENRY aged 32 years married to FURLONG, MARGARET aged 25 years February 7, 1893 by Father J. J. Monaghan at St. Patrick's Roman Catholic Church. Both natives of Charleston. He a railroad conductor.

VAN DOLKEN, A. J. married to TAYLOR, W. J. April 4, 1880 by William B. Yates, Chaplain.

VANHORN, GEORGE M. aged 20 years married to BARRINEAU, SARAH E. aged 17 years December 23, 1894 by Rev. J. C. Yongue at 108 America Street. He a native of North Carolina and she of South Carolina. He works in a factory in Sumter, South Carolina.

VAN VALKENBURG, JOSIE L. aged 21 years married to SCHNECK, FRANK M. aged 22 years December 12, 1889 by Rev. R. D. Smart.

VARDELL, JAMES C. married to GADSDEN, REBECCA H. May 11, 1892 by Rev. William H. Campbell at St. Paul's Church.

VARDELL, W. aged 24 years married to BAYNARD, E. J. aged 24 years January 19, 1882 by Rev. C. C. Pinckney at Grace Church. He a native of Charleston and a clerk.

VARNER, LUCINDA LONG aged 30 years married to GRIFFIN, BENJAMIN aged 22 years June 26, 1894 by Rev. Thomas A. Grove. He a native of North Carolina and she of South Carolina. He works in the cotton mill.

VARNIE, E. married to SACK, W. H. August 10, 1882 by Rev. J. V. Welch at 24 Bee Street. He a native of South Carolina and a laborer.

VAUGHN, JAMES E. aged 35 years married to FALK, CAROLINE V. aged 25 years September 22, 1881 by Rev. L. H. Shuck at 27 Church Street. He a native VARNER, Dublin, Ireland and she of Orangeburg, South Carolina. Both residentss of Orangeburg, South Carolina. He a mariner

VAUGHN, JAMES H. aged 36 years married to DONAHOE, (Mrs.) MARY T. NOLAN aged 36 years February 7, 1894 by Rev. J. Murray at St. Peter's Church. Both natives of Charleston. He a laborer.

VAUGHN, JOHN J. aged 25 years married to BLAKE, MARGARET S. aged 19 years January 26, 1887 by Father Daniel J. Quigley at St. Patrick's Roman Catholic Church. Both natives of Charleston. He a grocer.

VAZY, DELIA aged 25 years married to GARBIN, JOHN aged 26 years September 8, 1878 by Father John P. Twigg. Both natives of Ireland. He works for the railroad.

VENNING, LILLIE BELLE aged 22 years married to HENDRICKS, EDGAR LEE aged 24 years January 9, 1884 by Rev. G. R. Brackett. He a native of Fayetteville, South Carolina and she of South Carolina. He a clerk.

VENNING, SOPHIA aged 21 years married to HARLESTON, R. M. aged 33 years July 14, 1880 by Rev. A. Toomer Porter. Both natives of Charleston. He a resident of Ashepoo, South Carolina and a planter. She a resident of Mt. Pleasant, South Carolina

VERDERY, GEORGE W. aged 27 years married to ADDISON, BEULAH aged 18 years September 27, 1884 by Rev. Luther K. Probst. He a native of Augusta, Georgia and she of Charleston. He works for the railroad.

VERDI, ROSA aged 21 years married to MAURO, CHARLES aged 27 years December 30, 1895 by Father J. J. Monaghan at St. Patrick's Roman Catholic Church.

VERONEE, ALICE PAULINE aged 18 years married to CANNON, DANIEL W. aged 24 years April 15, 1881 by Rev. R. W. Memminger in Meeting Street. He a native of Charleston and she of Grahamville, South Carolina. He works for the railroad.

VERONEE, ADDIE aged 20 years married to GILBERT, LAMBERT C. aged 26 years May 20, 1880 by Rev. G. R. Brackett. He a native of Charleston and she of Blackwell, South Carolina. He a painter.

VERONEE, ALBERTINE married to PIEPER, WILLIAM H. F. August 6, 1890 by Rev. W. A. Betts.

VERONEE, EDWARD D. aged 26 years married to BOYLE, MARGARET JULIA aged 26 years December 9, 1885 by Rev. G. R. Brackett. Both natives of Charleston. He a mechanic.

VERONEE, IDA MAY aged 16 years married to KING, JAMES PATRICK aged 23 years March 27, 1883 by Rev. J. H. Tellinghast. He a native of Augusta, Georgia and she of Charleston. He a mechanic.

VERONEE, JOHN S. aged 29 years married to AXSON, EVA EVANGELINE aged 18 years May 19, 1887 by Rev. John O. Wilson at 114 Nassau Street. Both natives of Charleston. He a street car driver.

VERONEE, JOHN S. aged 38 years married to WILLIAMS, HELEN H. aged 18 years December 25, 1895 by Rev. A. Ernest Cornish at 120 Columbus Street. Both natives of Charleston. He a car driver.

VERONEE, KATE C. aged 24 years married to HERREN, SAMUEL J. aged 32 years May 10, 1888 by Rev. J. E. Carlisle at the Spring Street Church. He a native of Lancaster County, South Carolina and she of Charleston. He works for the railroad in Marion, South Carolina.

VERONEE, LEONTINE INEZ aged 22 years married to TAYLOR, WILLIAM OSCAR aged 23 years July 12, 1885 by Rev. G. R. Brackett. Both natives of Charleston. He a patternmaker.

VERONEE, S. J. B. aged 56 years married to McCANTS, (Mrs.) MARY FOULTZ aged 41 years March 30, 1890 by Rev. J. Thomas Pate at 100 Columbus Street. He a native of Charleston and she of Berkeley County, South Carolina.

VERONEE, WILLIAM C. aged 51 years married to RIVERS, LUCIA B. aged 24 years November 1, 1885 by Rev. J. V. Welsh at 24 Bee Street. He a native of Beaufort, South Carolina and she of Charleston. He a policeman.

VERONEE, WILLIE COLSON aged 18 years married to ALDERSON, ROBERT LEE aged 26 years November 23, 1881 by Rev. E. J. Meynardie at Bethel Church. He a native of Charleston and she of South Carolina. He a mechanic.

VICEDOMINI, A. W. S. married to Baker, ANN April 18, 1884 by Rev. W. T. Thompson at 161 King Street.

VICEDOMINI, E. aged 27 years married to RUGIERO, M. aged 28 years November 26, 1882 by Father P. L. Duffy at The Cathedral of St. John the Baptist. He a native of Charleston and a mariner.

VIDAL, JAMES H. aged 38 years married to SIGWALD, LENORA A. aged 23 years April 27, 1887 by Rev. Luther K. Probst. Both natives of South Carolina. He a merchant.

VIERLING, F. E. L. aged 22 years married to WOLF, L. G. aged 17 years April 2, 1882 by Rev. Louis Muller at 4 Calhoun Street. He a native of Germany and she of Maryland. He a baker.

VINCENT, WILLIAM J. aged 50 years married to WILSON, SOPHIA F. aged 30 years July 26, 1881 by Rev. J. V. Welsh at 47 Radcliffe Street. He a native of Charleston and a clerk.

VISANSKA (?), JULIUS M. aged 29 years married to BUTECHNER (?), SARAH F. aged 24 years March 12, 1895 by Rabbi I. P. Mender at 2 Bull Street. He a native of Richmond, Virginia and she of Charleston. He a merchant.

VOIGHT, ANNA REBECCA JOSEPHINE aged 20 years married to SCHLEPPEGRELL, JOHANN A. aged 28 years August 2, 1887 by Rev. Louis Muller. He a native of Prussia and she of Charleston. He a merchant.

VOIGT, RUDOLPH CARL aged 25 years married to TRAUTWEIN (?), MARIE CATHARINE aged 20 years January 10, 1889 by Rev. Louis Muller at the residence of the Groom's father in Liberty Street near St. Philip's Street. He a native of Charleston and she of Orangeburg, South Carolina.

VOLMER, JOHANNA WILHELMINA aged 22 years married to SAULS, DAVID AUSTIN aged 30 years February 5, 1890 by Rev. T. P. Burgess at 422 Meeting Street. He a native of Walterboro, South Carolina and she of Charleston. He a merchant in Walterboro.

VON EITZEN, HENRIETTA aged 24 years married to WETTLAUFER, J. aged 23 years December 8, 1885 by Rev. Johannes Heckel at 109 East Bay Street. He a native of Germany and she of Charleston. He works in a restaurant.

VON EITZEN, MARIA aged 23 years married to FELGENTRAGER, GUSTAV aged 32 years December 15, 1887 by Rev. Johannes Heckel at 109 East Bay Street. He a native of Prussia and she of Charleston. He a carpenter.

VON GLAHN, HEINRICH aged 22 years married to HEUER, ELISE A. aged 20 years April 12, 1888 by Rev. Louis Muller.

VON GLAHN, MINNA J. C. aged 25 years married to BUTT, JOHANN M. aged 35 years March 30, 1892 by Rev. Louis Muller at the corner of Warren and St. Philip Streets. He a native of Prussia and she of Charleston. He a grocer.

VON HARTEN, ANNIE M. aged 32 years married to COKLE, EDWARD T. aged 28 years February 18, 1887 by Rev. Luther K. Probst. He a native of South Carolina and she of Georgia. He a merchant.

VON HOLLAND, JOHN aged 22 years married to DUDLEY, JESSIE McLEE aged 22 years September 16, 1894 by Rev. Edmund Wells at 32 Line Street. Both natives of Charleston. He a stonecutter.

VON KOLNITZ, ELLA JULIA aged 23 years married to MITCHELL, JOHN McGILL aged 24 years November 1, 1877 by Rev. W. S. Bowman. Both natives of Charleston. He a farmer in Mt. Pleasant, South Carolina.

VON KOLNITZ, LEONORA aged 19 years married to HOLMES, WILLIAM H. aged 31 years April 26, 1893 by Rev. Edward T. Horn at St. Johannes Church. Both natives of Charleston. He a farmer in Georgetown, South Carolina.

VON KOLNITZ, MINNIE E. married to FITCH, WILLIAM. aged 30 years November 7, 1893 by Rev. Edward T. Horn at the corner of Smith and Vanderhorst Streets. He a native of Columbia, South Carolina and she of Charleston.

VON OLSEN, HENRY aged 19 years married to MONDELL, CAROLINE aged 19 years February 8, 1880 by Rev. W. S. Bowman at 14 Bee Street. He a native of Germany and she of Fairfield, South Carolina. He a baker.

VON OWEN, ARNOLDE CORNELIA aged 24 years married to JATHO, GEORGE WILHELM aged 24 years April 6, 1881 by Rev. Louis Muller.

VON SANTEN, ANNE ISABELLA aged 21 years married to ESTEE, CHARLES A. aged 22 years September 10, 1884 by Rev. Luther K. Probst. He a native of Washington, D. C., and she of Anderson, South Carolina. He a railroad clerk.

VON SPRECKELSEN (?), ANNA M. aged 22 years married to McNEILL, GEORGE R. aged 24 years June 26, 1892 by Rev. G. R. Bracket at 113 St. Philip Street. He a native of Charleston and she of Augusta, Georgia. He a car driver.

VONDERLEITH, THEODORE R. aged 37 years married to COBLE, ALICE C. aged 20 years December 21, 1893 by Rev. Edmund Wells at the Cannon Street Baptist Church. He a native of Athens, Georgia and she of Mecklenburg, North Carolina. He a clerk.

WACHTER, MARY G. aged 36 years married to ZERBST, F. HENRY aged 65 years February 3, 1895 by Father J. J. Monaghan at 8 Bogard Street. He a native of Oldenburg, Germany and she of New York City. He a "gentleman."

WADE, CLAUDIUS L. aged 21 years married to HARMON, JULIA J. aged 16 years December 6, 1891 by Rev. T. P. Burgess at 25 Cooper Street. He a native of Jefferson County, Mississippi and she of Summerville, South Carolina. He a car driver.

WADFORD, ANNA aged 19 years married to TAYLOR, EDWARD aged 31 years March 11, 1888 by Rev. H. B. Browne at 20 Cooper Street. He a native of Richmond County, Georgia and she of South Carolina. He a millhand.

WAGENER, ALETHA aged 21 years married to REEVES, EDWIN T. aged 32 years October 29, 1891 by Rev. Edward T. Horn at Sullivans Island, South Carolina. Both natives of Charleston. He works for the railroad.

WAGENER, MATTIE E. aged 20 years married to HYER, WILLIAM C. aged 23 years October 6, 1891 by Rev. J. T. Pate at 418 Meeting Street. Both natives of Charleston. He a plumber in Greenville, South Carolina.

WAGNER, CARL B. aged 30 years married to TECKLENBURG, ANNA MARIA aged 26 years February 8, 1888 by Rev. Louis Muller at the southeast corner of Wentworth and St. Philip Streets.

WAGNER, THEODORA W. married to WOODS, EDWARD O. February 19, 1889 by Rev. Richard S. Trapier.

WALDEN, KATE aged 24 years married to BOWICK, TRAVIS aged 18 years May 23, 1886 by Rev. J. W. Dickson at 20 Blake Street. He a native of Charleston and she of South Carolina. He a laborer.

WALDEN, RUDOLPH aged 26 years married to BERGEMAN, JUSTINE aged 22 years January 30, 1878 by Father Harry P. Northrop at 94 St. Philip Street. He a native of Germany and she of Charleston. He a baker.

WALJEN, ERNST C. aged 45 years married to BUSE, DORA MARIA M. aged 31 years February 21, 1886 by Rev. Louis Muller at 526 King Street. Both natives of Germany. He a merchant.

WALKER, ANNA E. aged 17 years married to HODGES, JOHN T. aged 20 years February 11,1878 by Rev. J. V. Welsh at the residence of Mr. and Mrs. Williams. Both natives of Charleston. He a barber.

WALKER, EMILY aged 20 years married to CRAVEN, EMANUEL WILLIAM aged 22 years December 27, 1877 by Father S. Redington at St. Patrick's Roman Catholic Church. He a native of Ireland and she of Charleston. He a merchant.

WALKER, HARRIET H. aged 21 years married to BUTLER, C. J. aged 32 years March 3, 1885 by Rev. C. C. Pinckney in Wentworth Street. Both natives of Charleston. He a turpentine manufacturer in Orangeburg, South Carolina.

WALKER, HARRIET A. aged 17 years married to CROUCH, EDWARD P. aged 35 years April 12, 1889 by Rev. Charles A. Stakely. Both natives of South Carolina. He a contractor.

WALKER, HARRY CALEB aged 22 years married to COATES, EMILY ISABEL aged 16 years September 1, 1884 by Rev. W. P. Mouzon at 6 President Street. Both natives of Charleston. He a blacksmith.

WALKER, JANE married to HUGHES, ROBERT June 19, 1879 by William B. Yates, Chaplain.

WALKER, JULIUS aged 40 years married to LOWNDES, MARGARET W. aged 24 years November 3, 1892 by Rev. C. C. Pinckney at St. Philip's Church. He a native of Columbia, South Carolina and she of Charleston. He a barber in Columbia, South Carolina.

WALKER, ROBERT MURDOCH aged 25 years married to RAVENEL, EMILY CHARDON aged 21 years February 18, 1890 by Rev. Charles S. Vedder at the Huguenot Church. He a native of Columbia, South Carolina and she of South Carolina

WALKER, ROSA ELLA married to WILLIAMS, H. DeTREVILLE April 8, 1890 by Rev. J. Marion Boyd at 212 Calhoun Street.

WALKER, SUE HOWARD aged 25 years married to HARDY, GASTON aged 26 years April 16, 1884 by Rev. John Johnson at 5 Church Street. He a native of Virginia and she of Charleston. He works for the railroad.

WALKER, WILLIAM E. aged 36 years married to SMITH, MARY JANE aged 37 years April 18, 1886 by Rev. C. E. Chichester at the Planter's Hotel. He a native of Massachusetts and she of South Carolina. He a mariner.

WALKER, WILSON aged 21 years married to SINKLER, ANNE S. aged 19 years November 18, 1889 by Rev. John Johnson at St. Philip's Church. Both natives of Charleston. He an engineer in Milledgeville, Georgia.

WALL, MARGARET aged 21 years married to FOGERTY, SIMON aged 37 years November 29, 1878 by Father Harry P. Northrop at St. Patrick's Roman Catholic Church. He a native of Ireland and she of Charleston. He a merchant.

WALLACE, EDWARD B. aged 20 years married to BOWEN, FRANCES E. aged 20 years December 28, 1890 by Rev. G. R. Brackett at 40 Mary Street. He a native of Darlington County, South Carolina and she of Charleston. He a clerk in Savannah, Georgia.

WALLACE, ELENORA aged 24 years married to KUHL, CHARLES G. aged 25 years May 15, 1887 by Rev. John Johnson at 53 Church Street. He a native of Virginia and she of Charleston. He a slater.

WALLACE, GEORGIA married to AZON, MARVIN October 29, 1886 by Rev. Richard S. Trapier at St. Michael's Church.

WALLACE, JAMES W. aged 23 years married to O'BRIEN, ELLA F. aged 22 years May 5, 1885 by Father F. J. Shadler at St. Joseph's Roman Catholic Church. Both natives of Charleston. He a clerk.

WALLEN, C. married to FRIEND, JOHN September 6, 1879 by William B. Yates, Chaplain.

WALLING, C. E. aged 20 years married to CONANT, E. I. aged 24 years December 11, 1879 at the residence of the Bride - the corner of Line Street and Sires Alley.

WALPOLE, JOHN B. married to BURDEN, ISABELLA E. December 12, 1895 by Rev. William H. Campbell. He a farmer on Johns Island, South Carolina.

WALSH, ANDREW M. aged 28 years married to RYAN, MARY ANN aged 27 years November 25, 1883 by Father P. L. Duffy at The Cathedral of St. John the Baptist. He a native of Charleston and she of Brooklyn, New York. He a drayman.

WALSH, (Mrs.) ANNIE CATHARINE MAUDE JONES aged 35 years married to HILL, HERMAN aged 39 years February 5, 1888 by Rev. H. B. Browne at 78 Drake Street. He a native of Darmstadt, Germany and she of Sumter County, South Carolina. He a stiller in Jacksonville, Florida.

WALSH, BARTON aged 25 years married to LEBBY, BESSIE WILLIAMS aged 23 years February 9, 1887 by Rev. G. R. Brackett. Both natives of South Carolina. He a bookkeeper.

WALSH, JAMES F. aged 29 years married to GERAGHTY, M. E. aged 16 years July 28, 1880 by Father Claudian B. Northrop at St. Mary of the Annunciation Roman Catholic Church. Both natives of Charleston. He a merchant.

WALSH, JOHN aged 32 years married to CAULFIELD, ANNA aged 19 years August 21, 1879 by Father C. J. Croghan at St. Joseph's Roman Catholic Church. He a native of Ireland and she of Charleston. He a furniture dealer in Newark, New Jersey.

WALSH, JOHN aged 30 years married to STANTON, CATHERINE aged 26 years November 10, 1890 by Father F. J. Shadler at St. Joseph's Roman Catholic Church. Both natives of Ireland. He a laborer.

WALSH, MARGARET M. aged 28 years married to HESLIN, WILLIAM F. aged 28 years July 29, 1891 by Father J. J. Monaghan at St. Patrick's Roman Catholic Church. He a native of Brooklyn, New York and she of Charleston.

WALSH, MARY ANN aged 33 years married to MAGUIRE, MORRIS aged 41 years April 24, 1889 by Father Daniel J. Quigley at St. Patrick's Roman Catholic Church. He a native of Ireland and she of Charleston. He an engineer.

WALSH, MARY J. aged 23 years married to HAGAN, JAMES aged 23 years February 17, 1885 by Father F. J. Shadler at St. Joseph's Roman Catholic Church. He a native of Charleston and a gas worker.

WALSH, NORAH C. aged 27 years married to O'SULLIVAN, JOHN J. aged 27 years November 29, 1883 by Father J. J. Woolahan at St. Mary of the Annunciation Roman Catholic Church. He a native of Boston, Massachusetts and she of Charleston. He a bookkeeper.

WALSH, SARAH aged 26 years married to FULCHER, ROBERT B. aged 27 years November 19, 1883 by Father J. J. Monaghan. He a native of North Carolina and she of Charleston. He a painter.

WALSH, WILLIAM aged 24 years married to MORRISSEY, MARY aged 23 years April 23, 1888 by Father F. J. Shadler at St. Joseph's Roman Catholic Church. He a native of Ireland and she of Charleston. He works at the gas house.

WALTER, ANETTA aged 16 years married to SMITH, SAMUEL aged 21 years August 29, 1891 by Rev. R. D. Smart at 207 Calhoun Street. He a native of England and she of Charleston. He a printer.

WALTER, EUNICE aged 18 years married to GREEN, FREDERICK L. aged 28 years July 8, 1884 by Rev. L. F. Guerry at St. Philip's Church. He a native of South Carolina and she of Charleston. He a bank officer.

WALTER, M. aged 27 married to HEMMERMAN, C. aged 22 years April 16, 1882 by Rev. Louis Muller. He a native of Germany and a painter.

WALTERS, ANNIE MARGARET aged 21 years married to PATTERSON, ULYSSES McP. aged 24 years November 12, 1883 by Rev. R. A. Lapsley at 94 Calhoun Street. He a native of Charleston and she of Bremen, Germany. He works in the phosphate factory.

WALTERS, MARY ANNA aged 26 years married to McGUIRE, WILLIAM H. aged 25 years August 16, 1892 by Rev. Thomas B. Wright at Summerville, South Carolina.

WALTON, E. aged 20 years married to LEQUEX, O. aged 19 years December 4, 1882 by Father Daniel J. Quigley. He a native of Charleston and a railroad worker.

WALTON, SIMEON O. aged 26 years married to McCULLOUGH, JOSEPHINE aged 20 years May 19, 1889 by Rev. H. B. Browne He a native of Prussia and she of Charleston.

WARD, ANNA CATHERINE aged 22 years married to MACKEY, JOHN R. aged 25 years February 8, 1881 by Rev. H. F. Chreitzberg. He a native of New Orleans, Louisiana and she of Charleston. He a mechanic.

WARD, ELIZA B. aged 25 years married to SALVO, EMON C. aged 26 years June 3, 1884 by Rev. W. P. Mouzon. He a native of Colleton County, South Carolina and she of Charleston. He a farmer in Colleton County.

WARD, E. H. aged 19 years married to KERRISON, E. L. aged 37 years July 15, 1882 by Rev. C. C. Pinckney at Grace Church.

WARD, L. V. L. married to DeLAND, AGNES October 16, 1879 by William B. Yates, Chaplain.

WARE, IDA AMELIA aged 20 years married to SILCOX, DANIEL S. aged 22 years January 5, 1886 by Rev. Charles S. Vedder. He a native of South Carolina and she of New York. He a clerk.

WARE, T. FOLLETE aged 39 years married to WILSON, MARY E. aged 35 years April 19, 1883 by Rev. C. C. Pinckney at 15 Logan Street. He a native of Baltimore, Maryland and she of Rhode Island. He a merchant.

WARING, J. B. aged 27 years married to HARLESTON, M. S. aged 30 years November 6, 1879 by Rev. J. C. Jackson in Columbus Street. He a native of Charleston and she of South Carolina. He a stationer.

WARING, SARAH EMILY aged 20 years married to DeCARADENC, ST. JULIAN PAUL aged 20 years April 16, 1879 by Father Claudian B. Northrop in Radcliffe Street.

WARING, THOMAS R. married to WITT, LAURA C. November 23, 1878 by Rev. William H. Campbell at St. Paul's Church.

WARKEN, P. K. aged 34 years married to JENKINS, J. E. aged 38 years February 3, 1882 by Rev. T. A. Grove at 6 Nassau Street. He a native of South Carolina and a laborer.

WARLEY, PAULINE aged 26 years married to SNOWDEN, ROBERT LEE aged 28 years April 27, 1886 by Rev. John Johnson at the residence of the Bride - 171 Broad Street. Both natives of South Carolina. He works in the Naval Stores.

WARLEY, WILLIAM H. aged 26 years married to SINKLER, HELEN aged 21 years November 9, 1893 by Rev. John Johnson at St. Philip's Church. Both natives of South Carolina. He a bank officer.

WAULHAME (?), DIETRICH H. O. married to KATHMANN, SUSAN ETTA April 11, 1878 by William B. Yates, Chaplain.

WARNER, EUDORA aged 18 years married to CHARLON, JOHN T. aged 35 years June 19, 1879 by Rev. J. Mercier Green at the corner of King Street Road and Lowndes Avenue. He a native of Charleston and she of Ridgeville, South Carolina. He a farmer.

WARREN, ELIZA NORRIS aged 24 years married to KING, CHRISTOPHER WALTER aged 22 years February 21, 1884 by Rev. W. F. Junkin. He a native of Colleton County, South Carolina and she of Walterboro, South Carolina. He a merchant in Adams Run, South Carolina.

WARREN, FREDERICK B. married to LALOR, E. MARY December 25, 1889 by Rev. William H. Campbell at 64 President Street. He a clerk in Jacksonville, Florida.

WARREN, KATIE aged 24 years married to CONLEY, WILLIAM J. aged 23 years February 20, 1884 by Father F. A. Schmetz at St. Patrick's Roman Catholic Church. He a native of Prince Edward Island, Canada and she of Charleston. He a barber.

WARREN, MARY IDA aged 19 years married to WILKINSON, EDWARD aged 24 years November 13, 1878 by Rev. C. C. Pinckney in Tradd Street.

WATERMAN, M. F. married to WATSON, WILLIAM J. April 29, 1879 by William B. Yates, Chaplain.

WATERMANN, RUDOLPH BERNHARDT aged 33 years married to MARTIN, CHRISTINA LISSETTE aged 19 years February 20, 1881 by Rev. Luther K. Probst at 35 Market Street. He a native of Germany and she of Charleston. He a grocer.

WATERS, B. married to WILLIAMS, W. November 1, 1879 by William B. Yates, Chaplain.

WATERS, FRANCIS aged 28 years married to McBRIDE, ELIZABETH aged 23 years April 19, 1883 by Rev. G. R. Brackett. Both natives of Charleston. He a painter.

WATERS, B. married to WILLIAMS, W. November 1, 1879 by William B. Yates, Chaplain.

WATSON, F. D. aged 28 years married to LAMBERT, J. B. aged 29 years December 28, 1880 by Rev. L. H. Shuck. He a native of Columbus, Georgia and she of Augusta, Georgia. He a merchant.

WATSON, HANNAN V. aged 16 years married to MADDEN, JAMES E. aged 21 years October 19, 1890 by Father F. J. Shadler at St. Joseph's Roman Catholic Church. Both natives of Charleston. He a boilermaker.

WATSON, H. P. aged 36 years married to MAND, BARBARA E. aged 22 years March 18, 1890 by Rev. Johannes Heckel at 123 Smith Street. He a native of Alabama and she of Germany. He the manager of a sewing machine company.

WATSON, L. married to JONES, T. V. November 30, 1879 by William B. Yates, Chaplain.

WATSON, MARY aged 20 years married to CROGHAN, PATRICK WASHINGTON aged 28 years January 23, 1881 by Father P. L. Duffy at The Cathedral of St. John the Baptist. Both natives of Charleston. He a stonecutter.

WATSON, MARY aged 30 years married to GODSON, EDWARD aged 37 years December 10, 1883 by Rev. J. C. Butler at 96 Tradd Street.

WATSON, MARY J. aged 20 years married to CROGHAN, PATRICK WASHINGTON aged 28 years January 23, 1881 by Father P. L. Duffy at The Cathedral of St. John the Baptist. Both natives of Charleston. He a stonecutter.

WATSON, M. F. aged 23 years married to FALKNER, H. J. aged 34 years April 13, 1882 by Rev. John Johnson at 45 George Street. He a native of New York and a farmer. He a resident of Oak Hill, Florida.

WATSON, THOMAS aged 42 years married to HOGARTH, FRANCES V. aged 40 years June 15, 1886 by Rev. John Johnson at St. Philip's Church. Both natives of Charleston. He a machinist.

WATSON, WILLIAM J. married to WATERMAN, M. F. April 29, 1879 by William B. Yates, Chaplain.

WATT, DANIEL aged 46 years married to CAMERON, ELIZABETH M. aged 22 years May 20, 1891 by Rev. G. R. Brackett at 10 Mile Hill. He a native of Scotland and she of Walhalla, South Carolina.

WATTS, JOHN W. married to CHURCHILL, JULIA May 13, 1890 by John Ahrens, Trial Justice, at 157 Nassau Street.

WATTS, JOHN N. aged 58 years married to BRANFORD, EDWARDINA aged 51 years August 21, 1890 by Rev. R. M. Lide at 62 Line Street. He a native of Manchester, Virginia and she of Charleston. He a blacksmith.

WATTS, KATIE aged 20 years married to HODGES, ERNEST aged 21 years January 5, 1891 by Rev. J. Thomas Pate. He a native of Charleston and she of Georgia. He a barrelmaker.

WAULHANAME (?), DIETRICH H. C. married to KATHMANA, SUSAN ELLA April 11, 1878 by William B. Yates.

WAY, EMMA A. aged 18 years married to HYAMS, M. D. aged 28 years April 7, 1887 by Rev. Leroy F. Beattie. Both natives of Charleston. He a mechanic.

WAY, GEORGE aged 22 years married to PRIESTER, SALLIE A. aged 17 years January 20, 1887 by Rev. H. B. Browne at 499 Meeting Street. Both natives of South Carolina. He a druggist in Ridgeville, South Carolina.

WAY, OLIVIA M. married to CUMMINGS, GEORGE W. December 28, 1890 by Rev. W. A. Betts at Cumberland Church.

WAY, WILLIAM B. aged 34 years married to CANALE, SUSIE M. aged 25 years October 5, 1887 by Rev. H. B. Browne at 35 Society Street. He a native of Colleton County, South Carolina and she of Charleston. He a physician in Ridgeland, South Carolina.

WAYNE, FLORENCE AMANDA aged 21 years married to MUIRHEAD, J. MURRAY aged 37 years November 10, 1880 by Rev. W. S. Bowman at the. He a native of Edisto Island, South Carolina and she of Charleston. He a planter.

WAYNE, WILLIAM O. aged 34 years married to ALLSTON, ESTHER SIMMONS aged 25 years July 1, 1891 by Rev. John Johnson at St. Philip's Church. He a native of Charleston and she of St. Stephen's Parish, South Carolina. He works in the phosphate mill.

WEATHERFORD, WILLIAM aged 21 years married to RANTIN, MAGGIE ELIZA aged 18 years April 4, 1894 by Rev. J. C. Yongue at 14 Hampstead Square. He a native of South Carolina and she of Savannah, Georgia. He a wood turner and machinist.

WEAVER, LUCINDA aged 20 years married to GAMBATTI, ALEXANDER aged 27 years February 18, 1879 by Father Harry P. Northrop. He a native of Charleston and she of Aiken, South Carolina. He a jeweler.

WEBB, AGNES MARY aged 27 years married to KIMBELL, WILLIAM R. aged 28 years September 10, 1893 by Father J. J. Monaghan at St. Patrick's Roman Catholic Church. He a native of South Carolina and she of Charleston. He a fireman in Savannah, Georgia.

WEBB, ANNIE VIRGINIA aged 23 years married to RYAN, WALTER BRAY aged 32 years March 19, 1891 by Rev. G. R. Brackett at 12 Friend Street. Both natives of Charleston. He a shipping clerk.

WEBB, EMMA C. aged 20 years married to EAGAN, EDWARD aged 25 years July 20, 1884 by Rev. R. A. Lapsley at 8 Cooper Street. He a native of Charleston and she of Georgia. He a sashmaker.

WEBB, EMMA SLATER aged 22 years married to PITTMAN, JAMES B. aged 24 years January 6, 1887 by Rev. John O. Wilson at 94 Wentworth Street. He a native of Columbia, South Carolina and she of Virginia. He a slater.

WEBB, E. M. aged 19 years married to INGLESBY, J. aged 24 years June 27, 1882 by Rev. Richard Webb at 25 Church Street. He a native of South Carolina and she of Georgia. He a broker.

WEBB, JOHN aged 23 years married to CAMPSEN, FRANCES MARIE META aged 20 years November 7, 1888 by Rev. Louis Muller at the residence of the Bride's mother in Hasell Street, 2 doors from Anson Street.

WEBB, KATE CECELIA aged 17 years married to DUNNING, WILLIAM HENRY aged 21 years September 21, 1884 by Father Daniel J. Quigley. Both natives of Charleston. He an engineer.

WEBB, MARY ANN aged 48 years married to GRAY, JOHN aged 49 years September 24, 1890 by Rev. John Johnson at 46 King Street. He a native of Scotland and she of New York City. He an upholsterer.

WEBB, MARY E. aged 24 years married to BLACKMAN, JOHN M. aged 24 years December 19, 1894 by Rev. G. R. Brackett at 12 Friend Street. He a native of New York and she of Charleston. He a clerk.

WEBB, MARY WINTHROP aged 28 years married to GIBBON, GEORGE EDWARD aged 32 years August 25, 1885 by Rev. E. C. L. Brown. Both natives of Charleston. He works in the phosphate mill.

WEBB, MARY E. aged 44 years married to HILL, WILLIAM B. aged 42 years March 1, 1888 by Rev. E. C. L. Browne. He a native of James Island, South Carolina and she of Charleston. He a clerk.

WEBB, RICHARD aged 37 years married to JENKINS, (Mrs.) ELIZABETH WALTERS aged 38 years July 30, 1891 by Rev. Robert Wilson at 4 Wragg Square. He a native of Charleston and she of Orangeburg, South Carolina.

WEBB, R. aged 24 years married to FLUDD, MARY JANE aged 21 years April 10, 1879 by Rev. J. Mercier Green at the corner of Line and Meeting Streets.

WEBB, THOMAS R. aged 32 years married to LOCKWOOD, ANNA aged 22 years January 25, 1883 by Rev. C. C. Pinckney at the residence of Mrs. Webb in Wentworth Street. He a native of Colleton County, South Carolina and she of Charleston. He a clerk.

WEBBER, ADAM aged 42 years married to CUMBEE, MILDRED L. aged 16 years January 20, 1895 by Rev. J. C. Yongue at 14 Hampstead Square. He a native of Wisconsin and she of Berkeley County, South Carolina. He a barber.

WEBBER, GEORGE aged 21 years married to KRAMER, IDA E. aged 16 years April 13, 1880 by Rev. J. V. Welsh at 64 Radcliffe Street. Both natives of Charleston. He a moulder.

WEBER, ADAM aged 25 years married to DUNBY, BRIDGET aged 22 years January 21, 1879 by Rev. Louis Muller at 1 Duncan Street. He a native of Nova Scotia and she of London, England.

WEBER, CHARLES aged 26 years married to STRAUSS, C. W. aged 25 years October 12, 1879 by Rev. W. S. Bowman at 7 Minority Street. He a native of Charleston and she of Walhalla, South Carolina. He a clerk.

WEBER, FREDERICKE JOHANNA aged 22 years married to LUDEN, MARTIN WILHELM aged 25 years February 26, 1885 by Rev. Louis Muller at the corner of King and Woolfe Streets. He a native of Germany and a grocer.

WEBER, HEINRICH F. W. aged 24 years married to MARTSCHINK, META D. aged 23 years April 26, 1891 by Rev. Louis Muller at the corner of Tradd and Legare Streets. Both natives of Prussia. He a grocer.

WEBER, WILLIAM aged 23 years married to PASSMORE, EMMA aged 23 years February 25, 1885 by Rev. John O. Wilson at 82 Wentworth Street. He a native of Cincinnati, Ohio and she of Preston, Ohio. He a canvasser in Preston, Ohio.

WEDE, J. T. aged 20 years married to ABRAMS, R. aged 20 years February 21, 1882 by Rev. J. M. Green at 20 Amherst Street. He a native of Georgia and she of South Carolina. He a blacksmith.

WEDEMEYER, ANNA LOUISE aged 30 years married to HENRICKS, JOHANN CHRISTOPHER aged 42 years May 12, 1889 by Rev. Louis Muller at the residence of the Groom - East Bay Street near Tradd Street.

WEEKLEY, ANNIE aged 22 years married to WHITE, JOHN B. aged 21 years October 18, 1893 by Rev. David M. Ramsey at Citadel Square Baptist Church. He a native of Charleston and she of South Carolina. He a law clerk.

WEEKS, THOMAS J. aged 22 years married to BROTHERS, ANNIE E. aged 15 years June 28, 1893 by Rev. J. C. Yongue. He a native of Washington County, North Carolina and she of Georgia. He works for the railroad.

WEICKING, HERMAN R. aged 36 years married to ENGELHARDT, LOUISA M. aged 30 years January 13, 1878 by Rev. W. S. Bowman. He a native of Hanover and she of Strasbourg, Germany. He a merchant.

WEITZ, (Mrs.) SUSAN married to MITCHELL, WILLIAM H. March 18, 1880 at 47 Spring Street.

WEIKERT, WILLIAM G. aged 27 years married to MICHEL, LIZZIE L. aged 19 years January 23, 1889 by Father Daniel J. Quigley at St. Patrick's Roman Catholic Church. He a native of Spartanburg, South Carolina and she of Charleston. He a railroad conductor.

WEILE, FRANTZ L. aged 27 years married to RICHTER, HENRIETTA R. D. C. aged 25 years March 24, 1885 by Rev. Louis Muller at 16 Archdale Street. Both natives of Charleston. He a baker.

WEINBERGER, SARAH aged 24 years married to LEWINTHAL, PHILIP aged 39 years July 20, 1881 by Rabbi David Levy at 82 King Street. He a native of Georgia and she of Charleston. He a merchant in Darlington County, South Carolina.

WEINHEIMER, ANNA HELENE aged 33 years married to GERARD, FRIEDRICH GUSTAV aged 41 years June 6, 1888 by Rev. Louis Muller at the corner of King and Tradd Streets. He a widower.

WEINHEIMER, CARL AUGUST aged 21 years married to SCHULTZE, WILHELMINA SOPHIA aged 23 years March 8, 1888 by Rev. Louis Muller at the residence of the Bride's father.

WEINHOLTZ, ANNIE J. aged 25 years married to BURKE, JOHN aged 29 years June 2, 1878 by Father Daniel J. Quigley at The Cathedral of St. John the Baptist. Both natives of Charleston. He a salesman.

WEINHOLTZ, RUDOLPH aged 27 years married to HADRE, MARIE B. aged 19 years April 27, 1893 by Rev. Edward T. Horn. Both natives of Charleston. He a clerk.

WEINKEN, C. H. aged 21 years married to GEHLKEN, F. J. aged 22 years February 26, 1882 by Rev. Luther K. Probst at 24 Montagu Street. He a native of Florida and she of South Carolina. He a grocer.

WEISKOFF, – aged 18 years married to MARKENS, GEORGE aged 22 years October 16, 1878 by Rabbi David Levy at 325 King Street. He a native of Richmond, Virginia and she of Charleston. He a merchant in Jacksonville, Florida.

WEISKOPF, S. aged 25 years married to LEVY, A. aged 22 years December 6, 1882 by Rabbi David Levy at 7 Franklin Street. Both natives of Charleston and a merchant.

WEITERS, JOHN C. aged 37 years married to SCHROEDER, MAGARETHA H. aged 19 years February 28, 1878 by Rev. Louis Muller. Both natives of Germany. He a grocer.

WELBORN, H. EBIE aged 23 years married to HERNANDEZ, VIOLA aged 21 years April 24, 1890 by Rev. E. S. Dargan at 33 Nassau Street. He a native of Williamston, South Carolina and she of Charleston. He a farmer.

WELBROCK, JOHANN H. aged 31 years married to MENSING, JENNIE N. aged 24 years February 25, 1892 by Rev. Louis Muller in Guignard Street. He a native of Hanover and she of Charleston. He a merchant.

WELCH, S. L. aged 22 years married to MAZYCK, ROSA F. aged 20 years March 22, 1887 by Rev. L. F. Beattie. He a native of South Carolina and she of Charleston. He an electric worker.

WELCH, STEPHEN L. aged 27 years married to PURSE, CARRIE W. aged 23 years April 14, 1892 by Rev. Edwin C. Dargan at 29 Nassau Street. He a native of Orangeburg, South Carolina and she of Charleston. He a merchant.

WELLING, ARTHUR aged 22 years married to BEE, MARY aged 27 years September 24, 1880 by Rev. R. N. Wells in King Street near Morris Street. Both natives of Charleston. He a mechanic in Moultrieville, South Carolina.

WELLING, ELIZA R. aged 24 years married to OWENS, WILLIAM H. aged 26 years January 16, 1894 by Rev. A. Ernest Cornish at 91 America Street. He a native of Lincolnville, North Carolina and she of Charleston. He works in a factory.

WELLING, LAWRENCE L. aged 21 years married to MELCHERS, AGNES WILHELMINA ADELA aged 19 years April 12, 1883 by Rev. Louis Muller in Drake Street near Blake Street. He a native of Charleston and she of Walhalla, South Carolina. He a merchant.

WELLS, OLIVET aged 17 years married to McBRIDE, LAWRENCE B. aged 19 years August 27, 1894 by Rev. J. L. Stokes at 231 Coming Street. He a native of Charleston and she of Winchester, Virginia. He a drug clerk.

WELLS, ELLA R. aged 21 years married to GROTE, JOHN S. aged 24 years October 22, 1895 by Rev. J. C. Yongue at 14 Hampstead Square. He a native of Germany and she of Charleston. He serves on a United States revenue cutter.

WELSH, J. married to KENNEDY, JOHN October 31, 1882 by Rev. John Johnson at 94 St. Philip Street. He a native of Ireland and a farmer.

WELSH, EDWARD ANDREW aged 33 years married to POWERS, KATIE NOBLE aged 25 years January 28, 1891 by Father J. J. Monaghan at St. Patrick's Roman Catholic Church. He a native of Mt. Pleasant, South Carolina and she of Ireland. He a sashmaker.

WELSH, E. JANIE married to MURPHY, J. D. November 6, 1877 by William B. Yates, Chaplain.

WELSMAN, CAROLINE NAPIER aged 24 years married to JENKINS, EDWARD E. aged 48 years June 13, 1878 by Rev. John Johnson. He a native of South Carolina and she of Charleston. He a physician.

WENNHOLZ, ANNIE J. aged 25 years married to BURKE, JOHN aged 29 years June 2, 1878 by Father Daniel J. Quigley at The Cathedral of St. John the Baptist.

WERKING,— married to SMITH, MARGARET January 18, 1881 by William B. Yates, Chaplain.

WERNER, ANNIE W. S. aged 23 years married to LESENSE, AUGUST aged 25 years January 11, 1891 by Rev. L. R. Nichols at 24 South Battery. Both natives of Charleston. He a merchant.

WERNER, ISABEL G. aged 26 years married to DURBECK, LOUIS S. aged 39 years November 9, 1885 by Rev. Luther K. Probst. He a native of South Carolina and she of Charleston. He a printer.

WERNER, JULIANE W. M. aged 25 years married to KRACKE, FREDERICK D. C. aged 33 years October 2, 1883 by Rev. Louis Muller at 29 Rutledge Avenue. Both natives of Charleston. He a merchant.

WERNER, ANNA MATHILDE aged 27 years married to DRESSEL, GEORGE PHILIP aged 27 years November 10, 1886 by Rev. Louis Muller at 89 Smith Street. He a native of Georgia and she of Charleston. He a merchant.

WERNER, ANNA WILHELMINA S. aged 23 years married to LESEMANN, AUGUSTUS H. D. aged 25 years February 18, 1891 by Rev. Louis Muller in Smith Street near Calhoun Street.

WESSEL, ALBERT CHRISTIAN aged 33 years married to SCHUNEMANN, ADELINE aged 16 years June 6, 1883 by Rev. Louis Muller at 66 Radcliffe Street. Both natives of Germany. He a grocer.

WESSEL, FREDERICKA J. H. aged 21 years married to MAYES, WILLIAM aged 25 years February 14, 1891 by Rev. S. P. H. Elwell. He a native of Nashville, Tennessee and she of Germany.

WESSEN, FREDERICK HEINRICH aged 33 years married to RAUL, AUGUSTE HENRIETTA CAROLINE aged 25 years July 3, 1884 by Rev. Louis Muller in Nassau Street near Jackson Street. Both natives of Germany. He a carpenter.

WEST, DAVID T. aged 33 years married to SCHULTZ, JEANETTE aged 24 years December 28, 1884 by Rev. Louis Muller in the King Street Road. He a native of New Jersey and she of South Carolina. He a farmer.

WEST, EDWIN F. aged 28 years married to GOWERS, JANE F. aged 22 years July 2, 1879 by Rev. Charles S. Vedder at the Huguenot Church. He a native of Johns Island, South Carolina and she of Charleston. He a drayman.

WEST, JAMES H. aged 26 years married to BLACK, P. aged 26 years July 6, 1880 by Rev. J. V. Welsh at 64 Radcliffe Street. He a native of Philadelphia, Pennsylvania and she of Charleston. He a clerk.

WEST, JAMIE D. aged 26 years married to HUDSON, LADSON M. aged 22 years July 28, 1889 by Rev. J. E. Carlisle. He a native of Colleton County, South Carolina and she of Berkeley County, South Carolina. He a collector.

WEST, JOSEPH L. aged 34 years married to JOHNSON, HENRIETTA R. aged 24 years August 5, 1891 by Rev. R. D. Smart at 165 Spring Street. He a native of Princeton, New Jersey and she of Charleston. He a farmer.

WEST, WILLIAM ANDERSON aged 24 years married to RODGERS, AMELIA ELIZABETH aged 22 years June 17, 1879 by Rev. H. F. Chreitzberg at the Spring Street Methodist Episcopal Church.

WESTBERRY, JOHN W. aged 22 years married to LANIGAN, ANNIE E. aged 22 years December 11, 1892 by Father J. J. Monaghan at St. Patrick's Roman Catholic Church. He a native of South Carolina and she of Charleston. He a merchant.

WESTCOTT, CHARLES B. aged 24 years married to HUNTER, ROSA L. aged 22 years November 1, 1881 by Rev. Luther K. Probst. He a native of Savannah, Georgia and she of Charleston. He a merchant.

WESTCOTT, C. THOMAS aged 30 years married to STEVENS, JENNIE aged 22 years February 17, 1890 by Rev. Robert Wilson at 4 Wragg Street. He a native of Edisto Island, South Carolina and she of Charleston. He a painter.

WESTENDORF, CHARLES H. married to WURTHMAN, SUSAN November 20, 1890 by Rev. W. A. Betts at 2 Short Street. He a native of Williamsburg County, South Carolina and she of Clarendon County, South Carolina. He works in the cotton mill.

WESTENDORF, CHARLES H. aged 40 years married to BRICKMAN, (Mrs.) MARY Meynardie aged 46 years August 4, 1887 by Rev. H. B. Browne. Both natives of Charleston. He a policeman.

WESTENDORF, CORNELIA aged 20 years married to SMITH, JOHN T. aged 21 years April 25, 1881 by Rev. John Johnson at 72 Anson Street. He a native of England and she of Charleston. He a merchant in Brooklyn, New York.

WESTENDORF, EMMA VIRGINIA aged 31 years married to POWELL, JAMES ABNEY aged 23 years December 27, 1887 by Rev. G. R. Brackett.

WESTERLIND, IDA A. aged 28 years married to JENSSEN, INGERMAR aged 27 years December 15, 1891 by Rev. R. C. Holland. Both natives of Sweden. He the captain of a boat.

WESTERLIND, JAMES C. aged 27 years married to DUNCAN, CATHERINE A. aged 17 years February 10, 1881 by Rev. G. R. Brackett. He a native of Charleston and a railroad worker.

WESTERLIND, MARIA aged 40 years married to NELSON, CHRISTEN aged 32 years February 2, 1888 by Rev. C. E. Chicester at 119 King Street. He a native of Arendal, Norway and she of Lilla Edil, Sweden. He a carpenter.

WESTERLIND, OTTO aged 26 years married to DEKSON, GENA A. C. aged 26 years July 18, 1884 by Rev. Luther K. Probst. He a native of Sweden and she of Denmark. He a carpenter.

WESTERLY, CATHARINE married to JORDAN, JAMES April 13, 1880 by William B. Yates, Chaplain.

WESTERVELT, THEODORE G. aged 26 years married to TOLLE, EMMA aged 24 years February 21, 1887 by Rev. J. Mercier Green. He a native of South Carolina and she of Charleston. He an electric worker.

WESTMORELAND, JESSE M. aged 60 years married to KINLOCH, MATILDA aged 40 years November 9, 1887 by Rev. John Johnson at St. Philip's Church. He a native of Greenwood, South Carolina and she of Charleston. He a wholesale druggist.

WETHERBY, CATHERINE married to JORDAN, JAMES April 13, 1880 by William B. Yates, Chaplain.

WETTLAUFER, J. aged 23 years married to VON EITZEN, HENRIETTA aged 24 years December 8, 1885 by Rev. Johannes Heckel at 109 East Bay Street. He a native of Germany and she of Charleston. He works in a restaurant.

WETZEL, ELOISE P. aged 23 years married to MEYER, WILLIAM H. aged 22 years October 28, 1885 by Rev. Louis Muller at St. Matthew's Lutheran Church. Both natives of Charleston. He a bookkeeper.

WHALEY, CHARLOTTE CORDES married to SMALLS, JAMES H. June 12, 1877 by Rev. Richard S. Trapier at St. Michael's Church.

WHALEY, FRANK J. aged 33 years married to DAWES, JOSEPHINE aged 22 years June 1, 1893 by Rev. N. Keff Smith at 15 Ann Street. He a native of Winnsboro, South Carolina and she of Charleston. He a machinist.

WHALEY, JOSEPH B. aged 22 years married to QUICK, ELIZABETH March 31, 1884 by Rev. J. E. Beard at 5 Johnson Court. Both natives of Charleston. He a laborer.

WHALEY, EDWARD M. married to SEABROOK, JOSEPHINE July 15, 1890 by Rev. Richard S. Trapier at St. Michael's Church.

WHALEY, HELEN SMITH aged 20 years married to RHETT, R. GOODWYN aged 27 years November 15, 1888 by Rev. C. C. Pinckney at Grace Church. He a native of Columbia, South Carolina and she of Charleston. He a lawyer.

WHALEY, HENRY C. aged 22 years married to GODFREY, MARY L. aged 18 years July 2, 1890 by Rev. T. P. Burgess at 18 Amherst Street.

WHALEY, THOMAS P. aged 25 years married to ROBERTSON, HENRIETTA R. aged 24 years November 7, 1895 by Rev. G. R. Brackett at 166 Broad Street. He a native of Pendleton, South Carolina and she of Charleston. He a physician.

WHARTON, LIBERTY C. married to HARPER, JOHN H. June 22, 1882 by Rev. Richard S. Trapier.

WHARTON, THOMAS J. aged 60 years married to WILBURN, (Mrs.) LAURA O. SCHROEDER aged 40 years April 30, 1891 by Rev. Edwin C. Dargan at 186 Coming Street. He a native of Augusta, Georgia and she of Charleston. He a lumber merchant.

WHEELER, JAMES HENRY aged 39 years married to AUBINOE, ISABELLA aged 22 years August 29, 1878 by Rev. R. N. Wells at 6 Calhoun Street. He a native of Washington, Texas and she of Alexandria, Virginia. He a clerk.

WHEELER, JAMES HENRY aged 23 years married to HUCHET, MARY THEODOSIA aged 23 years August 29, 1878 by Rev. R. N. Wells. He a native of Washington, Texas and she of Alexandria, Virginia. He a clerk.

WHEELER, JOHN W. aged 29 years married to CLARK, ROSIE E. aged 24 years October 30, 1893 by Rev. David M. Ramsey at 6 Court House Square.

WHEELOCK, CARRIE N. aged 21 years married to SHAW, CHARLES C. aged 21 years April 20, 1880 by Rev. E. C. L. Browne at Woodland Plantation. He a native of Woburn, Massachusetts and she of Clinton, Massachusetts. He a merchant.

WHELAN, JAMES aged 29 years married to COLE, ANNA aged 28 years May 3, 1883 by Father J. J. Woolahan at St. Mary of the Annunciation Roman Catholic Church. Both natives of Ireland. He a laborer.

WHETSTONE, (Mrs.) CELIA MORRELL aged 29 years married to FLUCK, ELI aged 28 years July 11, 1886 by Rev. H. B. Browne at 78 Drake Street. He a native of Montgomery County, Pennsylvania and she of Savannah, Georgia. He a clerk in Savannah.

WHILDEN, ELLA A. aged 22 years married to LOCKWOOD, ROBERT H. aged 23 years November 26, 1885 by Rev. W. T. Junkin at the residence of W. W. Whilden in Rutledge Avenue. He a native of Charleston and she of South Carolina. He the captain of a tugboat.

WHILDEN, F. F. aged 27 years married to EASON, M. aged 25 years March 30, 1882 by Rev. G. R. Brackett in Drake Street. He a native of Charleston and a clerk.

WHILDEN, HATTIE J. aged 23 years married to BRIGGS, ABRAM J. aged 31 years November 30, 1887 by Rev. G. R. Brackett. He a native of Summerton, South Carolina and she of Sumter, South Carolina. He a physician in Summerton.

WHILDEN, MARY L. aged 31 years married to MILLINGS, C. J. aged 39 years April 27, 1892 by Rev. G. R. Brackett at 35 Bull Street. He a native of Darlington County.

WHILDEN, SARAH aged 21 years married to O'BRIEN, JOHN S. aged 24 years September 3, 1891 by Rev. J. Thomas Pate at 231 Coming Street. Both natives of Charleston. He an engineer on board the USS Wistana.

WHITE, ANN E. HOUCK married to MARTIN, THEODORE L. April 15, 1881 by Rev. A. Misseldine. He a native of Charlotte, North Carolina and she of Charleston. He a physician.

WHITE, ANNIE E. aged 20 years married to CURTIS, LAWRENCE E. aged 23 years May 20, 1894 by Father J. J. Monaghan at St. Patrick's Roman Catholic Church. Both natives of Charleston. He a tinner.

WHITE, ELLEN aged 25 years married to KEILAN, JOHN aged 26 years March 1, 1881 by Father Harry P. Northrop at St. Patrick's Roman Catholic Church. Both natives of Ireland. He a policeman.

WHITE, GEORGE M. aged 32 years married to REEDER, ANNIE A. aged 29 years April 29, 1895 by Father J. J. Monaghan at 260 Coming Street. He a native of Oconee, County, Georgia and she of Montreal, Canada. He a farmer in Walhalla, South Carolina.

WHITE, H. A. aged 25 years married to TISDALE, J. G. aged 33 years January 15, 1880 by Rev. W. P. Mouzon at 85 Queen Street. He a native of Sumter, South Carolina and she of Georgetown, South Carolina. He a farmer in Sumter.

WHITE, IVAN PATRICK aged 29 years married to SANDERS, CATHARINE MARY ELIZABETH aged 31 years January 15, 1888 by Father John O. Schachte at The Cathedral of St. John the Baptist. He a native of Oconee, County, Georgia and she of Montreal, Canada. He a farmer in Walhalla, South Carolina.

WHITE, JAMES T. aged 23 years married to GREGORIE, EMMA aged 17 years September 8, 1887 by Rev .H. B. Browne at 31 Columbus Street. He a native of Manning, South Carolina and she of Edgefield, South Carolina. He works in the cotton mill.

WHITE, JOHN B. aged 21 years married to WEEKLEY, ANNIE aged 22 years October 18, 1893 by Rev. David M. Ramsey at Citadel Square Baptist Church. He a native of Charleston and she of South Carolina. He a law clerk.

WHITE, JOHN ALFRED aged 23 years married to GREEN, CLARA E. aged 20 years November 27, 1886 by Father P. J. Wilson at St. Mary of the Annunciation Roman Catholic Church. Both natives of Charleston. He a bookkeeper.

WHITE, JULIA aged 25 years married to WILSON, JAMES M. aged 29 years November 12, 1895 by Rev. Robert Wilson at St. Luke's Church.

WHITE, MARY TERESA aged 18 years married to BENNETT, JACKSON aged 21 years January 19, 1886 by Rev. H. B. Browne at 104 Nassau Street. Both natives of Charleston. He a machinist.

WHITE, THOMAS aged 21 years married to TODD, MAMIE aged 16 years February 17, 1889 by Rev. H. B. Browne at 8 Williams Court. He a native of Columbia, South Carolina and she of Charleston. He works for the railroad.

WHITE, WILLIAM CHARLES aged 29 years married to VALENTINE, (Mrs.) SARAH A. PARKINS aged 28 years October 16, 1878 by Rev. R. N. Wells. He a native of Charleston and she of Springfield, Massachusetts.

WHITE, WILLIAM E. aged 38 years married to HASELTON, EUGENIA E. aged 26 years January 26, 1888 by Rev. J. E. Carlisle at 68 America Street. He a native of Grand Rapids, Michigan and she of Charleston. He a mechanic.

WHITE, WILLIAM J. aged 27 years married to LYONS, SARAH J. aged 21 years July 14, 1880 by Father P. L. Duffy at The Cathedral of St. John the Baptist. He a native of New York and she of Charleston. He a plasterer.

WHITE, W. E. aged 19 years married to COUTURIER, J. E. aged 40 years July 11, 1882 by Rev. E. J. Meynardie at 145 Calhoun Street. He a native of Germany and she of South Carolina. He a merchant.

WHITEHEAD, AMOS P. aged 37 years married to GAILLARD, ANNIE aged 21 years December 5, 1888 by Rev. C. C. Pinckney at Grace Church. He a native of Atlanta, Georgia and she of Charleston County. He operates a cotton press.

WHITEHEAD, (Mrs.) FRANCES GILL aged 22 years married to MONROE, WILLIAM E. aged 21 years December 18, 1884 by Rev. J. E. Beard at the corner of Aiken and Blake Streets. He a native of South Carolina and she of Maryland. He a cooper.

WHITEMAN, MARY P. aged 23 years married to DIBBLE, T. O. SOMERS aged 25 years January 23, 1884 by Rev. John Johnson in Queen Street. Both natives of Charleston. He a merchant in Orangeburg, South Carolina.

WHITESIDES, SARAH aged 20 years married to MASON, MOSES aged 24 years June 5, 1883 by Father Daniel J. Quigley at The Cathedral of St. John the Baptist. Both natives of Charleston. He a mariner.

WHITNEY, ELLA T. married to CADIZ, FRANK A. September 28, 1881 by Rev. Richard S. Trapier.

WHITNEY, MARY married to SMITH, ROSS A. June 1, 1881 by Rev. A. Coke Smith at 69 Broad Street. He the compiler of city and state directories in Lynchburg, Virginia.

WHITNEY, ELLA T. married to CADIZ, FRANK A. September 28, 1881 by Rev. Richard S. Trapier.

WHITSON, MARTIN W. aged 23 years married to MOSIMANN, MARY F. aged 18 years November 22, 1888 by Rev. J. E. Carlisle at 530 Meeting Street. He a native of Pittsburg County, North Carolina and she of Charleston. He a plasterer and brickmason in Chester County, South Carolina.

WHITTAKER, CATHERINE S. aged 50 years married to McKINNON, NEILL C. aged 55 years February 27, 1878 by Rev. G. R. Brackett at 118 St. Philip Street. He a native of Richmond, North Carolina and she of Charleston. He a farmer in Chesterfield County, South Carolina.

WHITTIG, JOHN aged 42 years married to GRIFFTH, (Mrs.), MARY KEEGAN aged 34 years April 2, 1884 by Father P. L. Duffy at The Cathedral of St. John the Baptist. He a native of Germany and she of Charleston. He a loom fixer at the cotton mill.

WICHMAN, A. aged 36 years married to HUTCHMER, L. U. aged 21 years February 15, 1882 by Father Harry P. Northrop at 74 Wentworth Street. He a native of Germany and she of South Carolina. He a tailor.

WICKHAM, HELENE aged 36 years married to PERCY, HAROLD aged 55 years January 12, 1892 by Rev. T. P. Burgess at 6 Wragg Square.

WIDNER, MINNIE aged 22 years married to HOLLMAN, HIRAM aged 26 years November 16, 1891 by Rev. J. H. Smith. He a native of Darlington County, South and she of North Carolina. He a car driver.

WIECKING, HERMANN R. aged 36 years married to ENGELHARDT, LOUISA M. aged 30 years January 13, 1878 by Rev. W. S. Bowman. Both natives of Germany. He a merchant.

WIECKING, JOHN aged 45 years married to LINSMANN, EVANGELINE REBECCA aged 30 years July 2, 1889 by Rev. Johannes Heckel at the residence of Mr. Jurgenson - 38 Calhoun Street. He a native of Hanover and she of Germany. He in the lighthouse service.

WIENGES, DANIEL M. aged 21 years married to DENNIS, CATHARINE aged 17 years September 25, 1888 by Rev. J. E. Carlisle at 19 Blake Street.

WIENGES, FRANCIS M. aged 22 years married to HUTSON, JOSEPHINE R. aged 16 years May 3, 1892 by Rev. A. M. Chreitzberg. Both natives of Charleston. He works in the bagging factory.

WIER, JOHN BENSON aged 29 years married to SMITH, JULIA W. aged 22 years October 2, 1884 by Rev. G. R. Brackett. He a native of Anderson, South Carolina and she of Charleston. He a drummer in Greenville, South Carolina.

WIESSE, PAUL aged 25 years married to BARGAMANN, META CATHARINE aged 22 years October 31, 1886 by Rev. Louis Muller at the corner of King and Calhoun Streets. Both natives of Germany. He a baker.

WIESER, J. H. aged 25 years married to HEGER, E. C. aged 19 years October 14, 1879 by Rev. Louis Muller at 180 Coming Street. He a native of Austria and she of Charleston. He a photographer.

WIETERS, JOHN CHRISTOPHER aged 37 years married to SCHROEDER, MARGARETHE HEDWIG aged 19 years February 28, 1878 by Rev. Louis Muller at the corner of King and Broad Streets. Both natives of Germany. He a grocer.

WIGGINS, WILLIAM T. aged 21 years married to RODGERS, JENNIE LEGARE aged 18 years November 19, 1893 by Rev. J. L. Stokes at 231 Coming Street. He a native of Beaufort, South Carolina and she of Charleston. He a stevedore in Berkeley County, South Carolina.

WIGHTMAN, HARRIET CAROLINE aged 20 years married to GRIMES, JAMES THOMAS aged 21 years April 18, 1883 by Rev. John Johnson in Queen Street. He a native of Branchville, South Carolina and she of Charleston. He works for the railroad.

WIGHTMAN, MARTHA V. aged 20 years married to PEAKE, HENRY M. aged 27 years December 16, 1885 by Rev. John Johnson in Queen Street. He a native of Charleston and she of South Carolina. He works for the railroad.

WIGHTMAN, WILLIAM EDWARD married to PEAKE, MARY HARDEE July 30, 1889 by Rev. William H. Campbell at the residence of R. C. Barclay at 5 Rutledge Avenue. He an engineer.

WILBUR, LULA MARGARET aged 25 years married to THORNHILL, J. T. EDWIN aged 30 years November 4, 1886 by Rev. A. J. S. Thomas at the corner of Pitt and

Vanderhorst Streets. He a native of Virginia and she of Charleston. He a merchant in Augusta, Georgia.

WILBUR, HERBERT aged 26 years married to BULWINKLE, HENRIETTA aged 26 years April 8, 1891 by Rev. Edwin C. Dargan at 23 Montagu Street. He a native of Columbia, South Carolina and she of Charleston. He a clerk.

WILBURN (Mrs.), LAURA O. SCHROEDER aged 40 years married to WHARTON, THOMAS J. aged 60 years April 30, 1891 by Rev. Edwin C. Dargan at 186 Coming Street. He a native of Augusta, Georgia and she of Charleston. He a lumber merchant.

WILDER, ELLEN L. aged 22 years married to BRODIE, WILLIAM M. aged 23 years November 6, 1887 by Rev. John O. Wilson at the corner of Rutledge Avenue and Beaufain Street. Both natives and residents of Augusta, Georgia. He a spring builder.

WILDREN, MATILDA aged 40 years married to REMION, LOUIS aged 47 years July 27, 1885 by Father Daniel J. Quigley at St. Patrick's Roman Catholic Church. Both natives of France. He a merchant.

WILEY, HENRIETTA married to RAYMOND, THOMAS August 13, 1879 by William B. Yates, Chaplain. Both natives of Charleston.

WILFORS, BRAXTON B. aged 23 years married to SHOFT, MAGGIE aged 19 years April 14, 1887 by Rev. John O. Wilson. He a native of Texas and she of North Carolina. He a clerk.

WILKEN, HERMAN aged 23 years married to FALLS, ZORADA, aged 20 years October 26, 1892 by Rev. William T. Thompson. He a native of Germany and she of South Carolina. He a bookkeeper.

WILKERSON, EDWARD S. aged 25 years married to HORLBECK (?), VIRGINIA aged 19 years August 12, 1888 by Rev. H. B. Browne at 73 America Street. He a native of Charleston and she of Petersburg, Virginia. He an engineer.

WILKERSON, HELEN aged 36 years married to PACY, HAROLD aged 55 years January 12, 1892 by Rev. T. P. Burgess at 6 Wragg Square. She a native of New York. He a clerk.

WILKERSON, JAMES M. married to ARTHUR, FRANCES S. January 1, 1879 by Rev. William C. Power. He a native of St. James Parish, Goose Creek, South Carolina and she of Oglethorpe, Georgia. He an engineer.

WILKIN, EDWARD H. aged 22 years married to NORDEN, META ELIZA aged 25 years March 26, 1887 by Rev. Charles S. Vedder at the Huguenot Church. He a native of England and she of Charleston. He a carpenter.

WILKINS, FREDERICK A. aged 41 years married to GLENN, EMMA LAURA aged 25 years December 9, 1886 by Rev. A. H. Misseldine at 43 Anson Street. He a native of England and she of Charleston. He a baker.

WILKINS, WILLIAM G. aged 24 years married to EDWARDS, ELIZA aged 17 years November 9, 1884 by Rev. Johannes Heckel at the corner of Anson and Market Street. He a native of Germany and she of South Carolina. He a miller.

WILKINSON, CLAUDE H. aged 29 years married to LaROCHE, E. D. aged 28 years June 30, 1891 by Rev. Charles S. Vedder. He a native of Edisto Island, South Carolina and she of Colleton County, South Carolina.

WILKINSON, EDWARD aged 24 years married to WARREN, MARY aged 19 years November 13, 1878 by Rev. C. C. Pinckney. Both natives of Colleton County, South Carolina. He a farmer.

WILKINSON, ELLEN M. aged 26 years married to FOGERTY, DANIEL aged 37 years August 11, 1893 by Father Joseph D. Budds at 134 Market Street. He a native of Charleston and she of New York.

WILKINSON, JAMES MORTON aged 26 years married to ARTHUR, FRANCES SUSAN aged 22 years January 1, 1879 by Rev. William C. Power in Woolfe Street. He a native of St. James, Goose Creek, South Carolina and she of Oglethorpe, Georgia. He an engineer.

WILKINSON, WILLIAM M. married to HUGER, CAROLINE W. April 30, 1877 by Rev. Richard S. Trapier at St. Michael's Church.

WILLE, MARY A. aged 17 years married to EILER, WILLIAM H. aged 29 years February 7, 1884 by Rev. Luther K. Probst. He a native of Reading, Pennsylvania and she of Charleston. He a moulder.

WILLEGEROD (?), RUDOLF G. aged 27 years married to SCHILMILMAN, A. A. aged 26 years June 3, 1880 by Rev. Louis Muller. He a native of New York and she of Williamsburg, South Carolina. He a bookkeeper.

WILLIAMS, AMANDA T. aged 20 years married to JENKINS, EDWARD N. aged 24 years February 12, 1885 by Father F. J. Shadler at St. Joseph's Roman Catholic Church. Both natives of Charleston. He a sashmaker.

WILLIAMS, ANNIE aged 23 years married to ELLIS, JOSEPH F. aged 24 years November 3, 1895 by Rev. A. Ernest Cornish at 104 America Street. He a native of Charleston and she of Barnwell County, South Carolina. He a laborer.

WILLIAMS, ARTHUR married to SCHILLETTER, LOUISA February 9, 1878 by Rev. Richard S. Trapier at 2 Water Street.

WILLIAMS, BENJAMIN M. aged 24 years married to LAIN, MARY ELLEN aged 16 years May 14, 1894 by Rev. Edmund Wells at 579 King Street. He a native of Colleton County, South Carolina and she of Hampton County, South Carolina. He a weaver in the cotton mill.

WILLIAMS, BERTHA V. aged 20 years married to ROSENBERGER, S. M. aged 30 years June 16, 1885 by Rabbi David Levy at 95 St. Philip Street. He a native of New York and she of Charleston. He a merchant in Camden, South Carolina.

WILLIAMS, CAMPSON aged 21 years married to MURRAY, JENNIE aged 18 years October 25, 1889 by Rev. T. P. Burgess at 2 Hampstead Square. Both natives of Colleton County, South Carolina. He a laborer.

WILLIAMS, CATHARINE aged 24 years married to KELLY, THOMAS J. aged 27 years January 5, 1886 by Father F. J. Shadler at St. Joseph's Roman Catholic Church. Both natives of Charleston. He a postal worker.

WILLIAMS, ELLEN aged 35 years married to BECKMAN, J. F. aged 45 years August 14, 1890 by Rev. J. Marion Boyce at 21 Montagu Street. He a native of Kentucky and she of Charleston. He a jeweller.

WILLIAMS, EMMA aged 17 years married to COOPER, CHARLES W. aged 19 years November 5, 1886 by Rev. H. B. Browne at 16 Stone Court. Both natives of Charleston. He a moulder.

WILLIAMS, EUGENE HAMILTON aged 24 years married to SKINNER, MARGARET MOOD aged 22 years November 3, 1881 by Rev. H. F. Chreitzberg at 375 King Street. He a native of Round O, Colleton County, South Carolina. He a physician in Round O.

WILLIAMS, S. G. aged 22 years married to HUDSON, M. T. aged 18 years May 4, 1882 by Rev. L. H. Shucks at 27 Church. He a native of North Carolina and she of Georgia. He an engineer

WILLIAMS, FLORENCE E. aged 20 years married to ROGANS, THOMAS J. aged 29 years November 29, 1891 by Rev. R. C. Holland. He a native of England and she of Charleston. He a traveling salesman.

WILLIAMS, FLORENCE E. aged 35 years married to HARRISON, JOHN T. S. aged 45 years May 6, 1888 by Rev. G. R. Brackett. Both natives of Charleston. He a musician.

WILLIAMS, FREDERICK L. aged 28 years married to BLAKE, MARY G. aged 26 years September 25, 1889 by Father W. J. Quigley at St. Patrick's Roman Catholic Church. He a native of Canada and she of Charleston. He an electrician.

WILLIAMS, HARRY CLIFFORD aged 26 years married to VADEN, CARRY P. aged 18 years December 24, 1888 by Rev. R. C. Holland at 39 Chapel Street. He a native of Richmond, Virginia and she of Charleston. He a merchant in Richmond.

WILLIAMS, HELEN H. aged 18 years married to VERONEE, JOHN S. aged 38 years December 25, 1895 by Rev. A. Ernest Cornish at 120 Columbus Street. Both natives of Charleston. He a car driver.

WILLIAMS, H. DeTREVILLE married to WALKER, ROSA ELLA April 8, 1890 by Rev. J. Marion Boyd at 212 Calhoun Street.

WILLIAMS, JANE E. married to LONG, WALTER C. March 11, 1894 by Rev. William H. Campbell at the residence of the Bride's mother. He a painter.

WILLIAMS, JOHN H. aged 29 years married to DAVIS, MARY H. aged 19 years September 11, 1889 by Rev. R. D. Smart at 104 Rutledge Avenue. He a native of Richmond County, Georgia and she of Charleston. He works for the railroad.

WILLIAMS, MINNIE B. aged 16 years married to PASSAILAIGUE, JOHN C. aged 19 years February 28, 1894 by Rev. J. L. Stokes at 231 Coming Street. Both natives of Charleston. He works for the railroad.

WILLIAMS, N. T. M. aged 45 years married to ----- aged 32 years December 31, 1882 by Rev. Luther K. Probst. He a native of Charleston and a moulder.

WILLIAMS, RUBY aged 21 years married to BARNETT, CHARLES D. aged 23 years November 12, 1890 by Father P. L. Duffy. He a native of Flat Rock, South Carolina and she of Augusta, Georgia. He a mechanic in Asheville, South Carolina.

WILLIAMS, SALLIE ROSE married to CHISOLM, LOUIS H. December 16, 1884 by Rev. Richard S. Trapier at St. Michael's Church.

WILLIAMS, THOMAS J. aged 24 years married to JENKINS, G. A. aged 22 years July 4, 1880 by Father P. L. Duffy at The Cathedral of St. John the Baptist. He a native of Sullivans Island, South Carolina and she of Charleston. He a tinner.

WILLIAMS, W. married to WATERS, B. November 1, 1879 by William B. Yates, Chaplain.

WILLIAMSON, WINFIELD aged 40 years married to HUNT, ELLEN aged 30 years April 21, 1892 by Rev. Robert Wilson at 4 Wragg Square. He a native of North Carolina and she of Columbia, South Carolina. He resides in Lincolnton County, North Carolina.

WILLIE, ANNA S. aged 19 years married to DUFFIE, WILLIAM P. aged 31 years September 8, 1885 by Rev. J. V. Welch at 47 Line Street. Both natives of Charleston. He a policeman.

WILLIE, JOSEPHINE aged 26 years married to CHURCHILL, JOHN aged 34 years September 6, 1883 by Rev. Louis Muller at 80 America Street. He a native of Georgia and she of Charleston. He an engineer.

WILLIFORD, LIZZIE M. aged 20 years married to BURK, WILLIAM H. aged 36 years January 23, 1894 by Rev. Lucius Cuthbert. He a native of Charleston and she of Sumter County, South Carolina. He a pilot.

WILLIFORD, LEON E. aged 21 years married to DuBOSE, MARTHA A. aged 18 years February 24, 1895 by Rev. Edmund Wells at 20 Cooper Street. He a native of Morrisville, North Carolina and she of Berkeley County, South Carolina. He a manufacturer.

WILLINGEROD (?), RUDOLPH G. aged 27 years married to SCHIELMELMAN (?), A. B. aged 26 years June 3, 1880 by Rev. Louis Muller in King Street. He a native of New York and she of Williamsburg County, South Carolina. He a bookkeeper.

WILLIS, J. JOHN aged 21 years married to HENNS, W. MAGGIE aged 16 years April 9, 1890 by Rev. Edwin C. Dargan at Citadel Square Baptist Church.

WILLIS, JACOB T. aged 26 years married to CULLINANE, MARY V. aged 20 years November 23, 1884 by Father F. A. Schmetz at St. Patrick's Roman Catholic Church. He a native of North Carolina and she of Charleston. He a blacksmith.

WILLIS, (Mrs.) SARAH E. MIDDLETON aged 44 years married to BORINER, WILSON B. aged 49 years March 18, 1891 by Rev. R. C. Holland at 59 Tradd Street. Both natives of Charleston. He a builder.

WILSON, ARTHUR EDWIN aged 26 years married to TRENHOLM, CATHERINE DORA aged 22 years February 6, 1881 by Rev. Louis Muller at the northeast corner of Spring and Norman Streets

WILSON, CHARLES married to FICKLING, L. J. April 19, 1892 by Rev. John Gass. He a native of Barnwell, South Carolina and she of Charleston. He a railroad conductor.

WILSON, EDMUND M. aged 30 years married to SANDERS, LILY aged 23 years July 15, 1880 by Rev. Thomas Sanders. Both natives of Charleston. He a bookkeeper.

WILSON, EDWARD M. aged 30 years married to SANDERS, LILY aged 23 years July 15, 1880 by Rev. C. C. Pinckney at the residence of Mr. Sanders in Society Street. Both natives of Charleston. He a bookkeeper.

WILSON, ELLA aged 22 years married to HUGHES, J. aged 26 years November 16, 1891 by Rev. J. H. Smith.

WILSON, E. M. aged 27 years married to RAMSEY, M. G. December 30, 1879 by Rev. Edward T. Horn at St. Johannes Lutheran Church. He a native of Savannah, Georgia and she of Charleston. He a clerk.

WILSON, JAMES M. aged 29 years married to WHITE, JULIA aged 25 years November 12, 1895 by Rev. Robert Wilson at St. Luke's Church.

WILSON, JOHN E. aged 23 years married to JOHNSON, SALLIE E. aged 22 years March 5, 1893 by Rev. J. C. Yongue at 47 Columbus Street. He a native of Augusta, Georgia and she of Edgefield, South Carolina. He works in the cotton mill.

WILSON, JOHN J. aged 21 years married to HENNE, MAGGIE aged 16 years April 9, 1890 by Rev. Edwin C. Dargan at the Citadel Square Baptist Church. Both natives of Charleston. He a laborer.

WILSON, JOHN W. aged 39 years married to FOURES, MAGGIE A. aged 32 years July 3, 1886 by Rev. Charles A. Stakely at 8 Wragg Square. He a native of Hartford, Connecticut and she of Orangeburg, South Carolina. He an engineer.

WILSON, MARGARET E. aged 26 years married to FITZGERALD, WILLIAM T. aged 25 years June 6, 1886 by Father Daniel J. Quigley at St. Patrick's Roman Catholic Church. Both natives of Charleston. He works for the railroad.

WILSON, MARY ANN aged 18 years married to FILIBESTI, MICHAEL aged 20 years December 7, 1891 by Rev. W. A. Betts at 21 Hanover Street. He a blacksmith.

WILSON, MARY E. aged 35 years married to WARE, T. FOLLETE aged 39 years April 19, 1883 by Rev. C. C. Pinckney at 15 Logan Street. He a native of Baltimore, Maryland and she of Rhode Island. He a merchant.

WILSON, MARY HOWE aged 28 years married to BALL, ELIAS aged 41 years April 2, 1891 by Rev. Robert Wilson at St. Luke's Church. He a native of Berkeley County, South Carolina and she of Columbia, South Carolina. He a planter in Berkeley County.

WILSON, PAUL J. aged 18 years married to ROUMILLAT, LELA T. aged 19 years March 17, 1881 by Father F. J. Shadler at St .Joseph's Church.

WILSON, SAMUEL W. aged 27 years married to GREEN, MARY JANE aged 26 years January 23, 1878 by Rev. W. C. Dana. He resides in Sumter County, South Carolina.

WILSON, SOPHIA F. aged 30 years married to VINCENT, WILLIAM J. aged 50 years July 26, 1881 by Rev. J. V. Welsh at 47 Radcliffe Street. He a native of Charleston and a clerk.

WILSON, WILLIAM M. aged 25 years married to DuBOSE, THEODOSIA A. aged 25 years June 19, 1892 by Rev. A. M. Chreitzberg. He a native of Georgetown, South Carolina and she of Williamsburg County, South Carolina. He a printer in Augusta, Georgia.

WILSON, ZILLA H. SMITH aged 40 years married to SENKEN, JOHN H. R. aged 28 years June 15, 1892 by Rev. J. H. Smith at the 2nd Adventist Church. He a native of Charleston and she of South Carolina. He works in the cotton mill.

WINCEK (?), JOHN H. married to TROTT, MAGGIE H. November 6, 1884 by Rev. W. T. THOMPSON at the residence of the Bride's mother.

WINGARD, CHARLES N. aged 24 years married to HICKS, MARGARET MATILDA aged 25 years September 23, 1883 by Rev. J. E. Beard at 2 Cooper Street. He a native of Lexington, South Carolina and she of Sumter, South Carolina.

WINGATE, MARY aged 19 years married to EVANS, JOHN WILLIAM aged 30 years November 14, 1886 by Rev. H. B. Browne. Both natives of Charleston. He works for the railroad.

WINGATE, T. E. aged 45 years married to CALDER, (Mrs.) S. F. PRINCE aged 39 years September 28, 1879 by Rev. E. A. Wingard at 570 King Street. Both natives of Charleston. He a bootmaker.

WINKLER, LUCIA aged 20 years married to CARROLL, GEORGE aged 23 years July 24, 1892 by Father A. Hirshmeyer at The Cathedral of St. John the Baptist. Both natives of Charleston. He a printer.

WINKLER, MAMIE aged 23 years married to RYAN, WILLIAM aged 23 years October 10, 1889 by Father Daniel J. Quigley at St. Patrick's Roman Catholic Church. Both natives of Charleston. He a physician.

WINNINGHAM, HENRY H. aged 29 years married to KING, ANNA C. aged 21 years February 5, 1879 by Rev. Charles S. Vedder at 92 Church Street. Both natives of Charleston. He a fireman.

WINSTOCK, REBECCA aged 23 years married to ROSENBERG, ABRAM aged 24 years May 27, 1885 by Rabbi David Levy in St. Philip Street near Wentworth Street.

WINTER, B. G. aged 22 years married to BURKE, M. H. D. aged 23 years November 14, 1882 by Rev. Louis Muller at 24 America Street. He a native of Charleston and a clerk.

WINTER, HEINRICH ALBERT FREDERICK aged 27 years married to BURKE, SOPHIE A. WILHELMINA aged 21 years November 6, 1884 by Rev. Louis Muller at 40 America Street. Both natives of Charleston. He a saloon keeper.

WINTERLEICH, E. W. aged 25 years married to GALLNITZ (?), R. V. aged 31 years November 16, 1880 by Rev. Louis Muller at 66 Radcliffe Street. Both natives of Saxony. He a watchmaker.

WINTHROP, ANNA EVELINA married to TOWNSEND, JOHN F. February 24, 1891 by Rev. Richard S. Trapier at 126 Tradd Street. He a native of Edisto Island, South Carolina and she of Charleston. He a planter on Edisto Island.

WINTHROP, MARY R. married to JOHNSTON, WILLIAM April 18, 1883 by Rev. Richard S. Trapier at St. Michael's Church.

WIRTH, V. E. L. aged 29 years married to McINTYRE, GEORGE F. aged 33 years August 20, 1879 by Rev. E. A. Wingard at 14 Bee Street. Both natives of Charleston. He a merchant.

WISE, AGNES aged 17 years married to RAGON, HARVEY F. aged 22 years August 29, 1895 by Father J. J. Monaghan at St. Patrick's Roman Catholic Church. He a native of Chattanooga, Tennessee and she of Charleston. He a basketmaker.

WISE, CATHARINE aged 22 years married to KENNY, JOHN H. aged 38 years November 17, 1887 by Father F. J. Shadler at St. Joseph's Roman Catholic Church. He a native of Charleston and she of Bennettsville, South Carolina. He a builder.

WISE, C. A. married to OLIVER, J. H. October 16, 1879 by William B. Yates, Chaplain.

WISE, JULIA EVELINE aged 20 years married to KECKLEY, HENRY J. aged 21 years October 29, 1893 by Rev. Edmund Wells in Cramer Court. Both natives of Charleston. He a bricklayer.

WISE, LILLIE aged 24 years married to KENT, JONATHAN S. aged 28 years February 6, 1881 by Rev. Luther K. Probst. He a native of Charleston and an engineer.

WITHAM (?), WILLIAM S. aged 31 years married to COCHRAN, JEAN aged 20 years February 10, 1885 by Rev. John O. Wilson at 16 Ashley Avenue.

WITHERHORN, HANNAH aged 20 years married to LINK, SAMUEL aged 26 years September 7, 1890 by Rabbi David Levy at the corner of Green and College Streets. He a native of Augusta, Georgia and she of Charleston. He a merchant in Orangeburg, South Carolina.

WITHERS, ANDREW aged 31 years married to THOMAS, L. M. aged 24 years November 3, 1880 by Rev. W. S. Bowman. He a native of Yorkville, South Carolina and she of Charleston. He a lawyer in Yorkville.

WITHERS, ANNIE J. aged 42 years married to HAMETT, A. C. aged 49 years January 10, 1890 by Rev. R. A. Webb at 17 Ann Street. Both natives of Charleston. He a clerk.

WITHERSPOON, JOHN aged 70 years married to GEDDINGS, ANNA L. aged 25 years October 2, 1888 by Rev. John Johnson in Broad Street. He a native of Society Hill, South Carolina and she of Charleston. He a planter in Society Hill.

WITHINGTON, EUGENE married to MEYERS, ANNIE E. November 25, 1886 by Rev. Luther K. Probst. Both natives of Charleston. He a printer.

WITHINGTON, H. P. aged 24 years married to BEE, M. E. aged 19 years September 2, 1879 by Rev. J. M. Greene in Cannon Street. Both natives of Charleston. He a mechanic.

WITHINGTON, WALTER T. aged 27 years married to BROWN, FLORENCE E. aged 25 years October 7, 1886 by Rev. Robert Wilson at 26 Hanover Street. Both natives of Charleston. He a carpenter.

WITT, ALICE R. married to SLOAN, EARL October 11, 1884 by Rev. William H. Campbell at the residence of C. O. Witt. Both natives of Charleston. He works in the phosphate mill.

WITT, BELLE married to MITCHELL, JULIAN May 14, 1895 by Rev. William H. Campbell at St. Paul's Church. He a lawyer.

WITT, HEINRICH aged 25 years married to GRAVER, (Mrs.) ANNA CATHERINE FUNKE aged 32 years December 28, 1882 by Rev. Louis Muller German at the corner of King and Reid Streets. He a native of Germany and she of Charleston. He a grocer.

WITT, LAURA C. married to WARING, THOMAS R. November 23, 1878 by Rev. William H. Campbell at St. Paul's Church.

WITT, LOUIS aged 25 years married to MOCHSING, META aged 26 years October 13, 1881 by Rev. Johannes Heckel at the Freundschaftsbund Hall. Both natives of Hanover. He a grocer.

WITT, MARIE FREDERICKA aged 20 years married to SCHMONSEES, C. H. aged 25 years October 13, 1881 by Rev. Claudian B. Northrop. Both natives of Hanover. He a saloonkeeper.

WITTINGTON, MAMIE E. aged 24 years married to NOLAN, ARTHUR C. aged 25 years December 25, 1891 by Rev. A. M. Chreitzberg at the corner of Meeting and Mary Streets. She a native of Macon, Georgia. He works in the cotton mill.

WITTKE (?), CAROLINE aged 20 years married to MILLER, WILLIAM T. aged 40 years May 22, 1894 by Rev. John Johnson. He a native of Charleston and she of Rock hIll, South Carolina. He a sailmaker.

WITTSCHEN, ALBERT aged 22 years married to BUSCH, HANNAH aged 18 years August 31, 1884 by Rev. J. E. Beard. Both natives of Charleston. He a laborer.

WITTSCHEN, E. C. ELIZABETH aged 24 years married to KOPER, CLAUS aged 21 years October 1, 1891 by Rev. R. C. Holland in Mt. Pleasant, South Carolina. He a native of Mt. Pleasant, South Carolina and she of Charleston. He a farmer in Mt. Pleasant.

WITTSCHEN, LENA CATHARINE aged 24 years married to KANGETER, HEINRICH aged 30 years November 25, 1883 by Rev. Louis Muller.

WITTSHIRE, TRUMAN G. aged 35 years married to LEOPOLD, (Mrs.) EMILY GODFREY aged 35 years June 25, 1891 by Rev. Robert Wilson at 47 Cannon Street. He a native of England and she of Berkeley County, South Carolina. He a weaver in the cotton mill.

WITZEL, CATHARINE LOUISA aged 19 years married to MAPPUS, HENRY aged 23 years February 24, 1884 by Rev. Claudian B. Northrop at 4 Hampden Court. He a native of Germany and she of Charleston. He a grocer.

WOHLERS, BERNARD aged 43 years married to REINDHARDT, MARIA M. F. aged 28 years February 23, 1891 by Rev. Louis Muller at the residence of Mr. Rugheimer at 154 King Street. Both natives of Germany. He a merchant.

WOHLERS, HEINRICH aged 62 years married to LITJEN (?), ELISE B. aged 48 years April 7, 1892 by Rev. Louis Muller at 3 Mile House. He a native of Prussia and she of Oldenburg, Germany.

WOHLERS, H. C. aged 24 years married to KLEINKE, H. L. aged 21 years October 27, 1887 by Rev. Johannes Heckel. Both natives of Charleston. He a mechanic.

WOHLERS, SOPHY aged 16 years married to NORD, EDWARD aged 21 years July 3, 1889 by Rev. J. H. Wheeler at the residence of H. T. McGee - 20 Rutledge Avenue. He a native of Omaha, Nebraska and she of Charleston. He a watchmaker.

WOHLMER, MARIE ELLA A. aged 27 years married to MEYER, AUGUSTUS W. aged 34 years March 25, 1883 by Rev. Luther K. Probst at the corner of Cooper and Aiken Streets. Both natives of Charleston. He a mechanic.

WOHLTMANN, JOHN aged 22 years married to HOFSTETTER, OTTILE ANGELICA CAROLINE aged 22 years May 13, 1886 by Rev. Luther K. Probst. He a native of South Carolina and she of Charleston. He a merchant.

WOLD, HELLE JUEL (?) aged 50 years married to CLARK, (Mrs.) SARAH COWLES RUSSELL aged 48 years November 5, 1880 by Rev. C. E. Chichester, at the Sailors' Home in Market Street. He a native of Norway and she of Virginia. He a clerk.

WOLD, AGNES CHRISTINA aged 23 years married to LARSEN, PETER JOHN aged 23 years October 31, 1890 by Rev. C. E. Chichester at 223 Cumberland Street. He a native of Denmark and she of Arendal, Norway. He a driver.

WOLF, L. G. aged 17 years married to VIERLING, F. E. L. aged 22 years April 2, 1882 by Rev. Louis Muller at 4 Calhoun Street. He a native of Germany and she of Maryland. He a baker.

WOLFE, GEORGIA D. married to FABIAN, ANDREW F. March 16, 1879 by William B. Yates, Chaplain.

WOLFE, JOHN B. aged 32 years married to ZIMMERMAN, NECADA aged 20 years October 19, 1893 by Rev. J. C. Yongue at 11 D Street. He a native of Orangeburg, South Carolina and she of Colleton County, South Carolina. He a fireman.

WOLFE, JOHN FREDERICK aged 25 years married to PRINCE, EUGENIA EVELINE aged 17 years April 29, 1879 by Rev. W. S. Bowman at 231 Meeting Street. He a native of Baltimore, Maryland and she of Charleston. He a baker.

WOLFE, LAWRENCE S. aged 29 years married to SIMONS, LOTTIE A. aged 19 years November 5, 1885 by Rev. Thomas M. Galphin at 47 Rutledge Avenue. Both natives of South Carolina. He a dentist in Orangeburg, South Carolina.

WOLFE, WILLIAM J. D. aged 23 years married to BIEL, MARY H. aged 19 years November 26, 1888 by Rev. T. P. Burgess at 7 Lee Street. Both natives of Charleston. He works for the railroad.

WOLFE, WILLIAM J. aged 24 years married to KORNAHRENS, HELENA aged 21 years September 14, 1890 by Rev. R. C. Holland at the Wentworth Street Lutheran Church. He a native of Orangeburg, South Carolina and she of Germany. He a merchant in Orangeburg.

WOOD, AMY C. aged 22 years married to DORN, JOHN L. aged 19 years April 16, 1895 by Rev. J. C. Yongue at 27 Blake Street. He a native of Edgefield County, South Carolina and she of Rhode Island. He works in the cotton mill.

WOOD, CHARLES F. aged 22 years married to IVERSON, ESSIE aged 16 years March 22, 1893 by Rev. N. K. Smith at 12 Drake Street. He a native of Rhode Island and she of Walhalla, South Carolina. He works in the cotton mill.

WOOD, LAURA A. aged 22 years married to HARLOW, PATRICK J. aged 27 years April 12, 1883 by Father J. S. Kelly. He a native of Elizabeth City, New Jersey. She a native of Charleston.

WOOD, NELSON aged 29 years married to DUVAL, GERTRUDE aged 24 years January 9, 1895 by Father Daniel J. Quigley at 30 Pitt Street. He a native of Indiana and she of Charleston. He a horse dealer in Indiana.

WOOD, SUSAN JANE married to O'CONNOR, PETER December 25, 1878 by Rev. William C. Power.

WOODHALL, M. S. married to JONES, (Mrs.) M. S. DAVIS aged 62 years November 12, 1885 by Rev. W. T. Jenkins at the northwest corner of Wentworth Street and Rutledge Avenue. Both natives of New York. He a mariner on Long Island, New York.

WOODRUFF, VIRGINIA H. aged 17 years married to ULMER, BENJAMIN F. aged 20 years July 7, 1895 by Rev. Charles S. Vedder in Broad Street. Both natives of Savannah, Georgia. He works in the Naval Stores in Savannah.

WOODS, EDWARD O. married to WAGNER, THEODORA W. February 19, 1889 by Rev. Richard S. Trapier.

WOODWARD, JULIUS aged 35 years married to THOMPSON, ELLA R. aged 32 years February 6, 1894 by Rev. J. L. Stokes at 231 Coming Street. He a native of Barnwell County, South Carolina and she of Walterboro, South Carolina. He works in the cotton mill.

WOODWARD, SARAH M. aged 22 years married to NAUGHTON, PATRICK aged 21 years April 11, 1887 by Father F. J. Shadler at St. Joseph's Roman Catholic Church. He a native of South Carolina and she of Georgia. He a saloon keeper.

WOODWORTH, M. J. aged 29 years married to PALMER, J. P. aged 28 years December 8, 1882 by Rev. Charles S. Vedder at the Planters Hotel. He a native of South Carolina and a plumber.

WOTTON, CHARLES aged 20 years married to BOYD, AMELIA aged 16 years October 24, 1878 by Rev. J. L. Chambliss at the residence of the Bride's mother. Both natives of Charleston. He a farmer in Hamburg, South Carolina.

WRAGG, A. M. aged 23 years married to LANIER, JOHN FRANKLIN aged 35 years April 5, 1887 by Rev. T. P. Burgess. He a native of North Carolina and she of South Carolina. He a mechanic.

WRAGG, HENRY HARMON aged 24 years married to Dickson, CARRIE A. aged 19 years December 25, 1881 by Rev. R. A. Mickle in America Street. He a native of Charleston and a carpenter.

WRAGG, JOHN F. aged 33 years married to RANDALL, MARY R. October 15, 1891 by Rev. Edwin C. Dargan at 20 Shephard Street. He a native of Charleston and she of Columbus, Georgia. He a millwinger.

WRAGG, MARY married to HEYWARD, WILLIAM M. July 12, 1892 by Rev. William H. Campbell at Grace Church.

WRAGG, SEPTIMA married to MURE (?), WILLIAM July 8, 1884 by Rev. William H. Campbell at St. Paul's Church. Both natives of Charleston. He a clerk.

WRAGG, WILLIAM WIGG aged 26 years married to DAWSON, MARY A. aged 21 years January 3, 1894 by Rev. John Johnson at the residence of C. Dawson. Both natives of Charleston. He a stationer.

WREDE, KATHERINE M. aged 16 years married to JAEGER, CARL F. aged 24 years September 30, 1894 by Rev. Edward T. Horn.

WREDE, (Mrs.) MARY V. AHRENS aged 37 years married to COOK, HENRY A. aged 46 years March 10, 1892. He a native of Germany and she of Charleston. He a baker.

WRIEDT, (Mrs.) SUSANNAH POLZ aged 43 years married to SCHULTZ, MARTIN aged 40 years November 25, 1877 by Rev. Louis Muller at the residence of Henry Behrens - King Street near Woolfe Street.

WRIGHT, CAROLINE F. aged 22 years married to LUCAS, WILLIAM H. aged 32 years November 9, 1886 by Rev. John Johnson. Both natives of Charleston. He a stationer.

WRIGHT, E. M. aged 23 years married to LEE, ALLISON aged 25 years June 28, 1887 by Rev. John Johnson. He a native of Alabama and she of South Carolina. He a salesman.

WRIGHT, JOHN WILSON aged 23 years married to ADDISON, ELIZABETH CRAMER aged 20 years November 28, 1883 by Rev. G. R. Brackett. He a native of Anderson, South Carolina and she of Sumter, South Carolina. He a telegraph operator in Manning, South Carolina.

WRIGHT, ROSA A. aged 28 years married to DONOHUE, JOHN T. aged 30 years November 24, 1892 by Father J. J. Monaghan at St. Patrick's Roman Catholic Church. He a native of Wilmington, North Carolina and she of Charleston. He a moulder.

WRIGHT, WILLIAM HENRY married to DICKINSON, ELLA July 22, 1878 by William B. Yates, Chaplain.

WULBURN, JOHN H. aged 22 years married to McINTOSH, BELLE aged 19 years November 5, 1891 by Rev. W. T. Thompson at 69 Wentworth Street. Both natives of Charleston. He a clerk.

WULBURY, HENRY W. aged 24 years married to KLATTE, DORETHA H. aged 24 years November 7, 1894 by Rev. Edward T. Horn.

WURTHEM, DIETRICH H. C. married to KATHMANN, SUSAN E. April 11, 1878 by William B. Yates, Chaplain.

WURTHMAN, SUSAN married to WESTENDORF, CHARLES H. November 20, 1890 by Rev. W. A. Betts at 2 Short Street. He a native of Williamsburg County, South Carolina and she of Clarendon County, South Carolina. He works in the cotton mill.

WYLDE, EDWARD C. aged 23 years married to GUTHKE, LAURA L. aged 20 years November 9, 1898 by Rev. L. H. Baldwin at the corner of Meeting and Woolfe Streets. Both natives of Charleston.

WYLLY, FREDERICK COURTNEY aged 28 years married to DAWSON, EMMA LUCIA aged 22 years October 12, 1881 by Rev. G. R. Brackett. Both natives of Charleston. He a merchant.

WYNNE, MARY A. aged 40 years married to CAREE, SAMUEL C. aged 50 years February 14, 1893 by Father Daniel J. Quigley at 35 Mary Street. He a native of Wilmington, North Carolina and a railroad conductor.

WYSONG, RUFUS C. aged 27 years married to GILL, MARY E. aged 23 years June 29, 1887 by Rev. Robert Wilson. Both natives of Charleston. He an engineer.

YATES, ANNIE married to FROST, EDWARD December 4, 1888 by Rev. Richard S. Trapier.

YATES, BELLE SUMTER married to ROBERTS, DAVID June 13, 1881 by Rev. Richard S. Trapier.

YATES, CAROLINE S. married to CUTHBERT, FRANCIS P. April 20, 1893 by Rev. William H. Campbell at St. Paul's Church. He works in the phosphate mill.

YATES, CORNELIUS HARRINGTON aged 25 years married to JONES, ROSA LILLIAN aged 24 years November 8, 1888 by Rev. E. C. L. Browne at the Unitarian Church. He a native of Cheraw, South Carolina and she of Williamston, South Carolina. He a clerk.

YATES, FLORENCE married to RALPH R. October 8, 1894 at St. Michael's Church.

YATES, JENNIE married to STINGLUFF, HARRY L. November 8, 1883 by Rev. William H. Campbell at the residence of Mrs. Yates. Both natives of Charleston. He a collector.

YOE, FANNIE K. aged 17 years married to HARD, WILLIAM D. aged 37 years June 16, 1887 by Rev. John O. Wilson at Trinity Church. Both natives of South Carolina. He a hospital superintendent.

YOUNG, JOHN ALEX aged 19 years married to CONNOR, WINNIE aged 19 years July 31, 1888 by Rev. John J. Wedenfeller at St. Joseph's Roman Catholic Church. Both natives of Charleston.

YOUNGER, F. W. aged 34 years married to DORKEWITZ (?), A. C. aged 21 years May 16, 1882 by Rev. Louis Muller in King Street. He a native of Germany and an engineer. She a native of Charleston.

YOUNGINER, GEORGE WASHINGTON aged 38 years married to SUDER, ELVIRA ARMSTRONG aged 37 years December 20, 1877 by Rev. G. R. Brackett at 23 Cumberland Street. He a native of Lexington, South Carolina and she of Charleston.

ZAERIUS (?), FANNY married to HALL, THOMAS F. December 7, 1878 by William B. Yates, Chaplain.

ZELLER, (Mrs.) HANNAH SILVERSTEIN aged 22 years married to BOWMAN, SAUL aged 24 years November 4, 1888 by Rabbi David Levy at 77 Wentworth Street. Both natives of Charleston. He a merchant.

ZEPRADEL,— married to OSTENBURG, A. September 21, 1879 by William B. Yates, Chaplain.

ZERBST, F. HENRY aged 65 years married to WACHTER, MARY G. aged 36 years February 3, 1895 by Father J. J. Monaghan at 8 Bogard Street. He a native of Oldenburg, Germany and she of New York City. He a "gentleman."

ZERBST, J. aged 22 years married to MEHRTENS, — aged 28 years December 21, 1879 by Rev. Louis Muller at the corner of Pitt and Duncan Streets. He a native of Charleston and a grocer. She a native of Hanover.

ZIEGLER, GEORGIANA married to REEVES, EDWARD LEROY April 14, 1879 by William B. Yates, Chaplain.

ZIEGLER, JOHANN H. CONRAD aged 24 years SCHROEDER, META CATHARINE aged 22 years July 7, 1878 by Rev. Louis Muller at 66 Radcliffe Street. He a native of Charleston and she of Germany. He a grocer.

ZIEGLER, M. C. aged 26 years married to THIELE, P. aged 45 years November 9, 1882 by Rev. Louis Muller. Both natives of Charleston. He a cabinetmaker.

ZIEGLER, ROBERT A. aged 19 years married to GONZALEZ, ELIZABETH aged 21 years January 16, 1889 by Father J. J. Monaghan at St. Patrick's Roman Catholic Church. Both natives of Charleston. He works for the railroad.

ZIMMERMANN, ELLA aged 36 years married to SIMPSON, SAM aged 32 years May 21, 1895 by Rev. Charles S. Vedder. He a native of Bordeaux, France and she of Orangeburg, South Carolina He a mariner.

ZIMMERMAN, NECODA aged 20 years married to WOLFE, JOHN B. aged 32 years October 19, 1893 by Rev. J. C. Yongue at 11 D Street. He a native of Orangeburg, South Carolina and she of Colleton County, South Carolina. He a fireman.

ZOBEL, FREDERICK aged 26 years married to BETANCOURT, MARY aged 24 years January 10, 1892 by Rev. Edward T. Horn in Smith Street.

ZWINGMANN, ANNIE AUGUSTA aged 18 years married to GLADDEN, GEORGE aged 30 years September 19, 1880 by Rev. R. N. Wells. Both natives of Charleston. He a shoemaker.

ZWINGMANN (?), C. M. aged 23 years married to LYNCH, PETER F. aged 26 years November 22, 1887 by Father John W. Schachte at The Cathedral of St. John the Baptist. Both natives of Charleston. He a storekeeper.

ZWINGMANN, HENRIETTA aged 22 years married to RUNEY, JOHN aged 24 years January 16, 1889 by Father F. J. Shadler at St. Joseph's Roman Catholic Church. Both natives of Charleston. He a clerk.

Heritage Books by Brent H. Holcomb:

Bute County, North Carolina Land Grant Plats and Land Entries

*CD: Early Records of Fishing Creek Presbyterian Church,
Chester County, South Carolina, 1799–1859*

CD: Kershaw County, South Carolina Minutes of the County Court, 1791–1799

CD: Marriage and Death Notices from The Charleston [S.C.] Observer, *1827–1845*

CD: South Carolina, Volume 1

*CD: Winton (Barnwell) County, South Carolina Minutes of
County Court and Will Book 1, 1785–1791*

*Early Records of Fishing Creek Presbyterian Church, Chester County,
South Carolina, 1799–1859, with Appendices of the Visitation List of
Rev. John Simpson, 1774–1776 and the Cemetery Roster, 1762–1979*
Brent H. Holcomb and Elmer O. Parker

Kershaw County, South Carolina Minutes of the County Court, 1791–1799

*Marriage and Death Notices from Columbia, South Carolina Newspapers, 1838–1860;
Including Legal Notices from Burnt Counties*

Marriage and Death Notices from The Charleston Observer, *1827–1845*

*Winton (Barnwell) County, South Carolina Minutes of
County Court and Will Book 1, 1785–1791*

www.ingramcontent.com/pod-product-compliance
Lightning Source LLC
Chambersburg PA
CBHW070715280326
41926CB00087B/2134